KV-383-090

INDUSTRY AND TRADE

A study of industrial technique and business organization; and of their influences on the conditions of various classes and nations

BY

ALFRED MARSHALL

The many in the one, the one in the many

MACMILLAN AND CO. LIMITED
ST MARTIN'S STREET, LONDON
1921

First Edition, August 1919
Second Edition, December 1919
Third Edition, August 1920
Reprinted 1921

PREFACE

THE present volume is a study of industry and trade; with special reference to the technical evolution of industry, and its influences on the conditions of man's life and work. It is designed to be followed by a companion volume, which is to be occupied with influences on those conditions exerted by the resources available for employment; by money and credit; by international trade; and by social endeavour.

Its motto is:—*The many in the one, the one in the many.* Many tendencies have gone to the making of each industry and each economic institution: therefore a thorough realistic study of any part of the economic field, calls for some reference to the interaction of many diverse tendencies, and gives occasion for some care in analysis. And, conversely, almost every important tendency is so far modified by the conditions under which it operates, that an exhaustive study of it may need to range over many fields of work. This motto supplements the motto of my *Principles* which is:—*Natura non facit saltum: i.e.* economic evolution is gradual and continuous on each of its numberless routes.

My aim has been to present as accurate a picture as I can of a part of the field of economics, and not to advocate any particular conclusions. A politician is compelled to seek his allies among those who desire the same ends as his; and therefore political influences on economic studies are not always wholesome. But a student's natural allies are those, whose aims and methods of work are akin to his own. It is of no concern to him whether a particular argument makes for or against his own ultimate conclusion: in either case he is equally grateful for any solid new suggestion that is contained in it; and equally repelled by any that seems to be based on inadequate data, or to reason inconsequently on those data. My own experience has been, for instance, that, the more I knew of the work of Sir W. J. Ashley and the late Professor Schmoller, the warmer became my regard for them; in spite of the opposition between the main drifts of their work and of my own. Similarly, looking back on the years, in which I was much occupied in arguing that the net advantages of bimetallism are less than those of monometallism, I found that the person from whom I had learnt most on the matter, and whom I should have most welcomed as a colleague in that connection, was a leading bimetallist, Sir David Barbour.

The volume has no claim whatever to be a contribution to economic history: but an endeavour has been made to turn a few hints derived from the past to account in explaining the present: these will be found chiefly in Chapters III to VIII of the first Book, and in Appendices B to G. The table of Contents, which brings together the Section headings, indicates the general drift of the volume; and may incidentally suggest to a reader what parts of it he may with advantage shun. Analytical subtleties have been avoided as far as possible. But broad reasonings, essential for the argument, have been set out briefly; even when they have been more fully studied in my *Principles*.

For many years after the publication in 1890 of the first volume of my proposed complete *Principles of Economics*, I continued to work at its second volume: part of the type for that was set up in 1904 and is now used at last—I am told that this long waiting of type for its ultimate appearance is unique. Shortly afterwards I decided to bring out separately a more or less independent volume, devoted to Industry and Trade. Later on two volumes appeared to be necessary for the purpose: and at last it seemed best to round off the present volume in such manner that it would be an independent unit.

I may perhaps be forgiven for adding that my progress has been delayed, not only by weak health and constitutional unfitness for rapid work; but also by heavy professional duties till 1908; by preparing evidence and memoranda for various Royal Commissions on currency and other matters: and by service on the Royal Commission on Labour, 1891—5; during which I received from working men and other witnesses, and from members of the Commission, the most valuable education of my life.

Nearly half a century has passed since I set myself to obtain some insight into industrial problems by obtaining leave to visit one or more representative works in each chief industry. I tried to get such a knowledge of mechanical technique (chemical technique was beyond my range) as would enable me to understand the resources and the mode of operation of all elementary plant in general use: I sought also to study the relations between technique and the conditions of employment for men and for women.

In pursuit of the latter aim I made it a practice to ask what pay was being earned by each class of operatives, whom I passed. Afterwards I asked to be allowed to guess in every case. If my guess was right within a shilling or two a week, I passed on. If not, I asked for explanation; and I almost always found that the reason lay in a cause, sometimes technical, sometimes relating to special conditions of the workers in question, which I did not know. The result was a conviction that inequalities of pay were less arbitrary than was often asserted, and were more directly under the influence of broad "natural" causes.

But I believed that the causes of these causes were not wholly beyond human control; and that they might probably be so modified as to bring about a nearer approach to equality of conditions, and a better use of the products of human effort for the benefit of humanity. I developed a tendency to socialism; which was fortified later on by Mill's essays in the *Fortnightly Review* in 1879. Thus for more than a decade, I remained under the conviction that the suggestions, which are associated with the word "socialism," were the most important subject of study, if not in the world, yet at all events for me. But the writings of socialists generally repelled me, almost as much as they attracted me; because they seemed far out of touch with realities: and, partly for that reason, I decided to say little on the matter, till I had thought much longer.

Now, when old age indicates that my time for thought and

speech is nearly ended, I see on all sides marvellous developments of working-class faculty: and, partly in consequence, a broader and firmer foundation for socialistic schemes than existed when Mill wrote. But no socialistic scheme, yet advanced, seems to make adequate provision for the maintenance of high enterprise, and individual strength of character; nor to promise a sufficiently rapid increase in the business plant and other material implements of production, to enable the real incomes of the manual labour classes to continue to increase as fast as they have done in the recent past, even if the total income of the country be shared equally by all. The average level of human nature in the western world has risen rapidly during the last fifty years. But it has seemed to me that those have made most real progress towards the distant goal of ideally perfect social organization, who have concentrated their energies on some particular difficulties in the way, and not spent strength on endeavouring to rush past them.

Accordingly the present volume is in the main occupied with the influences which still make for sectional and class selfishness: with the limited tendencies of self-interest to direct each individual's action on those lines, in which it will be most beneficial to others; and with the still surviving tendencies of associated action by capitalists and other business men, as well as by employees, to regulate output, and action generally, by a desire for sectional rather than national advantage. The hopes and the fears of humanity in these matters underlie a great part of Book III, to which Books I and II are introductory: but of course the desire of the mere student for knowledge for its own sake, and without special reference to any purpose to which it can be applied, may be detected throughout.

Some matters considered in the final chapter of the volume have been affected by events and discussions, so recent that adequate place for their study could not be carved out of the text: and consequently much of Appendix P, and especially its last two sections, may be regarded as properly belonging to that chapter, to which indeed the Appendix is attached.

A little must be said about the use of terms. I have followed the practice, that prevails on the other side of the Atlantic, of shortening "United States of America" to "America," where no confusion could be caused thereby: there is no adjective corresponding to "United States." "British" trade is commonly taken to mean that of the United Kingdom; while the substantive "Great Britain" refers only to a part of the Kingdom. I have ventured to use "Britain" as the substantive corresponding to "British" in its broader use.

Of this volume as of my *Principles*, but even more than of that, I may say that my wife has aided and advised me at every stage; and that everywhere much of whatever is good is owing to her suggestions, her care and her judgment: the index is entirely her work. Mr A. W. Flux also helped me greatly in regard to a considerable part of an early draft. Dr Clapham has kindly safeguarded my ventures on historical ground in Book I and the early Appendices; and my nephew, Mr C. W. Guillebaud, was reading my proofs, when the war called him to more important work at Whitehall.

BALLIOL CROFT,
CAMBRIDGE.
16 *June*, 1919.

P.S. A demand for a second issue of this volume affords opportunity for the restoration of the present pp. 657–672 to their proper place in the text: thus repairing the error, just noted, of under-estimating the space that would be required for the final chapters, which had caused those pages to be relegated to Appendix P (841–857). In consequence the numbering of the former pages 657–840 has been increased by sixteen. In addition a few small corrections have been made, chiefly on the suggestion of friends. I have been under no temptation to controversy, the sterile consumer of time and energy.

14 *November*, 1919.

P.P.S. The present issue is almost identical with the third: which differed from the second only in a few small details, chiefly verbal corrections.

January, 1921.

CONTENTS

BOOK I

SOME ORIGINS OF PRESENT PROBLEMS OF INDUSTRY AND TRADE

BOOK II

DOMINANT TENDENCIES OF BUSINESS ORGANIZATION

BOOK III

MONOPOLISTIC TENDENCIES: THEIR RELATIONS TO PUBLIC WELL-BEING

BOOK I

SOME ORIGINS OF PRESENT PROBLEMS OF INDUSTRY AND TRADE

CHAPTER I

INTRODUCTORY OBSERVATIONS

1. *The present urgency of the allied problems of industry and trade.* I, I, 1.

As indicated on the title page, the present work is designed to make a small contribution to the study of the progress of industrial technique, and of business organization; as well as of the distribution of the benefits thence arising among various sections of the people and various nations.

No previous age has had such large opportunities as the present for applying material resources in the elevation of human life. The forces of Nature are being turned back upon her to compel her to render ever larger returns to man's efforts in every branch of industry; any resistance that she may offer to the agriculturist and the miner being quickly reduced by the incessant development of fresh sources of rich supply, and by easy and rapid communication between distant places. New countries are quickly falling into line with old. Some of them are making greater advances in economic organization and industrial technique in a decade, than Europe as a whole has made in any century except the last: and, though this progress is continually depriving old countries of favourable markets for familiar wares; yet the very causes, to which it is due, are meanwhile opening up larger and more various

I, I, I. markets in the same countries, or in others. Thus material wealth has rolled in on the populations of old countries with unprecedented rapidity, and on new countries faster still.

Moreover there still hangs above all countries, old and new alike, the shadow of war. A time may indeed come when the combative instincts, implanted in man's nature by countless centuries of fierce struggle for existence, may be stilled by a *Pax Cosmopolitana*, enforced by an international police: and some small countries are even now partially protected by the desire of their more powerful neighbours to preserve a "balance of power." But so long as wars are imminent, no rate of material progress will enable the industries that prepare for war to dispense with sustained and severe labour. A single modern armoured cruiser may be more than a match for all the navies of the world fifty years ago: but no increased facilities for building an efficient warship can lessen the compulsory labour of any nation for the purposes of defence on the waters. Improvements in the technique of rowing boats do not lighten the labour, which is required of those who desire to hold a good position in a great race[1].

But Nature's opportunities cannot long retain their present large generosity; for the world is small. Science may indeed enable a fairly vigorous life to be maintained in tropical regions, which have hitherto proved fatal to high energies: but ere very many generations have passed, the limitation of agricultural and mineral resources must press heavily on the population of the world, even though its rate of increase should receive a considerable check.

Let us turn from the cosmopolitan point of view to the national. It is true that those countries, which have abundant resources relatively to their populations, may grow in comfort, if not in luxury, for several generations: but, even if manu-

[1] The above paragraph stands as it was set up in type before the World-war was in sight. The action of Germany has increased the desire of everyone for the establishment of an agreement among nations, to intervene with force against any nation that declares war; except in accordance with a judgment of a supreme international court to which it has appealed. But the experiences of the war indicate also that the force needed to coerce a strong group of nations, who have made large secret preparations for war, may be very great: and they suggest that those, who desire peace, may not venture to neglect the sinews of war.

facturing operations could be conducted by a twentieth part of the labour now required by them, the difficulty of obtaining adequate supplies of food and raw produce would ere long weigh heavily on densely peopled countries.

These matters are of especially urgent concern to Britain. Before the great war she was more prosperous than ever: the real incomes of both her well-to-do and her working classes are higher than those of corresponding classes in any other densely peopled country; and the methods of her industry have advanced at an ever increasing rate. But yet she has in some respects lost leadership. Her best methods are now the common property of the Western World; and recent advances in them have been very largely due to the enterprise and inventive faculties of other countries.

The maintenance of her material well-being above that of other countries of Europe, in spite of some *relative* slackening of the industrial initiative by which she achieved her success, cannot be expected to last for ever. That it should have been maintained till now is marvellous, and calls for study. We need to know on what Britain's industrial leadership was based; and how it may be conserved, and perhaps even enlarged again.

The test of leadership is the doing things, which other countries with similar economic problems will be doing a little later, but are not ready and able to do yet. One of the best indications of the nature and extent of a country's leadership is to be found in the character of the goods which she exports, and of those which she imports. And, while a certain part of her foreign trade is essential to her existence; another, and much larger part, is conducive to her leadership. These are strong reasons for giving a prominent place to foreign trade in a study of the bases of her economic prosperity.

But there is another and a higher reason. Industrial leadership counts for much among national ideals. And if an individual, devoted merely to material ends, is but a poor creature, still more ignoble is a nation that is devoid of national ideals; that is, of ideals which recognize a national life as something more than the aggregate of individual lives. Now as the individual life is made up largely of social intercourse,

I, I, 1. so is the national. A healthy national pride has been associated with industrial leadership, especially as indicated in the clearly written records of international trade: and the mutual knowledge which results from close trade intercourse has done something, and may do much more, towards the development of an ideal comity of nations.

Further, the notion of national trade has been bound up with the notion of solidarity between the various members of a nation. The trade of one individual with another is mainly of private concern: while the causes which enable large quantities of anything to be made for foreign sale at a profit, generally lie deep down in resources and faculties that are not wholly individual, but are in great part the collective property of a nation as a whole. A country's foreign trade is something more than a number of dealings between individuals at home and abroad; it is the outcome of the relations in which the industries that belong to her, that are a part of her life, and embody much of her character, stand to the industries of other countries.

Thus national industries and national trade act and react on one another, but the dominant force is that of industry. The main courses of trade are governed by the relations between the surrounding industries, in the same way as watercourses are governed by the contours of the hills: a map showing the contours of the leading industries of the world would show what must be the main courses of trade, except in so far as they are obstructed by costs of transport or customs duties; very much as a map which shows the contours of the hills shows also what must be the courses of the water. But the water reacts on the hills, and trade reacts on industry: the industrial history of every country would have been different if her opportunities for foreign trade had been different.

Finally in regard to sectional interests. Nearly all of them are changing their character and becoming increasingly plastic: but the chief change is the assimilation of the training, and consequently the capacity, of the working classes generally to those of the well-to-do. The spread of education is rapidly effacing those distinctions of mind and character between different social strata, which have prevailed in nearly all densely peopled countries during several thousand years; but were in large measure the artificial results of the cumulative advantage that a small initial predominance in force gave to the more fortunate sections of each nation.

We are indeed approaching rapidly to conditions which have no close precedent in the past, but are perhaps really more natural than those which they are supplanting:—conditions under which the relations between the various industrial strata of a civilized nation are being based on reason, rather than tradition. No doubt much force still remains in the old contention that when wealth is applied in harnessing Nature in servitude to man, by far the greater part of the aggregate benefit resulting from it, is reaped by those who have themselves accumulated little or nothing. No doubt it is as true, now as ever, that the chief work of progress is done by a relatively small number of men, whose faculty for the work can be tested only by their work: no other means of selecting them rightly has been yet devised. No doubt also those who, if of less initiative, are yet doing important work involving high mental strain, have a reasonable claim to a certain largeness in the conditions of their lives. But, for all that, it is becoming clear that this and every other western country can now afford to make increased sacrifices of material wealth for the purpose of raising the quality of life throughout their whole populations. A time may come when such matters will be treated as of cosmopolitan rather than national obligation: but that time is not in sight. For the practical purposes of the present and the coming generation, each country must, in the main, dispose of her own resources, and bear her own burdens.

2. *Economic conditions are mostly the result of slow and gradual development; and, partly for that reason, they commonly show the One in the Many, the Many in the One. It is necessary to look backwards a little, in order the better to look forwards.*

Economics is concerned mainly with general conditions and tendencies: and these as a rule change but slowly, and by small steps. Occasionally they may receive a strong impetus in one

I, I, 2. direction or another from a political event, such as a revolution; or a change in a country's boundaries or alliances. A great invention, like that of the application of steam power to work that used to be done by men or horses, may enable a single generation to live through twice or thrice as much economic change as had come to its predecessors. But the printing press did not rise to nearly its full power even in a couple of centuries: and the present generation is the first that has seen the whole rise of several great inventions from nothing to dominating positions: thus the maxim that "Nature does not willingly make a jump" (*Natura abhorret saltum*) is specially applicable to economic developments.

Partly in consequence, economic conditions and tendencies show, even more than most others, the One in the Many, the Many in the One: for those, which prevail at any place and time, reflect the habits of action, thought, feeling and aspiration of the whole people, or at least some large part of them. Each reacts on the character of the population: but the roots of all are deep set in the human characteristics of the place and time: thus the One is seen in the Many. And conversely each tendency embodies in some degree almost every influence, that is prominent then and there: insomuch that a full study of it would present incidentally a nearly complete picture of the whole: thus the Many are seen in the One.

The present indeed never reproduces the past: even stagnant peoples gradually modify their habits and their industrial technique. But the past lives on for ages after it has been lost from memory: and the most progressive peoples retain much of the substance of earlier habits of associated action in industry and in trade; even when the forms of those habits have been so changed under new conditions, that they are no longer represented by their old names. Such changes increase the difficulty of so interpreting the past that it may be a guide to the present.

But probability is the only guide of general use in life. There are a few matters, in which mere reasoning avails. There are a good many more, in which the observation of current events is both necessary and sufficient: and, where sufficient, it is superior to other sources of instruction; because records of current events can be supplemented, and witnesses may perhaps be in effect challenged and cross-examined. But observation of the present only shows what is perhaps its rate of movement: some guidance is needed also as to the rate of increase of movement. That can only be got by looking backwards.

All sorts of trustworthy records of the past may gratify a worthy curiosity: but for the purposes of economic study those only are of much service, which are sufficiently ample to suggest their own explanation. For explanation is simply prediction written backwards: and, when fully achieved, it helps towards prediction. A chief purpose of every study of human action should be to suggest the probable outcome of present tendencies; and thus to indicate, tacitly if not expressly, such modifications of those tendencies as might further the well-being of mankind.

It is true that even careful prediction is likely to overlook some influences at present latent, which will in fact greatly affect the result; while only a careless explanation can overlook any influence by which the result has been actually fashioned. But explanation shares with prediction the main difficulty, which is caused by the complex interweaving of the effects of many causes acting in the same field, and mutually influencing one another: every short explanation in economics is likely therefore to be misleading, unless indeed it be almost a truism. Moreover the progress of study opens out new problems to be considered, and thus it broadens the area of conscious ignorance even more than it increases the stock of ascertained knowledge[1].

3. *The scheme of the present work as a whole.*

As the original intention of publishing the two volumes of this work together has been abandoned, something should be said at once of the relations between them. The Table of Contents indicates the arrangement of this Volume: an introduction to Book I will follow in the next section; and similar

[1] This subject is briefly discussed in Appendix A, with special reference to the guidance which economics has derived in the last half century from the experience of the physical sciences: together with a few remarks on the relations between the economic and ethical conditions of well-being, none of which may be ever left out of sight, though the economic conditions are necessarily the more prominent in such a study as the present.

I, I, 3. introductions to Books II and III will be found in their first chapters.

The present Volume as a whole may be regarded as concerned first with the origins of modern industrial technique and business organization; secondly with the parts played by particular nations in developing them; and thirdly with the problems rising out of that development. These problems are considered in Book II, with little or no reference to monopolistic tendencies; which are dealt with in Book III. In Books II and III there is an ever-increasing drift towards consideration of the harmonies and discords of interest among the several sections of a nation, and between each of those sections and the nation as a whole.

The sections to be most considered here are in the main of two kinds. A nation as a whole may be regarded as composed of irregularly shaped *horizontal* strata, arranged in pyramidal form, those most poorly endowed being at its base; and each successive stratum consisting of people better endowed than the last. The endowment may be measured in terms of money or of faculty: and the problem is to bring these two measurements as nearly as may be into accord; while narrowing the lower and broadening the upper strata. The issues arising out of this sectionalism are of the most far-reaching character.

But another set of issues, though of no great importance from a social point of view, is often more prominent in discussions of commercial policy: it arises out of the conflicting interests of particular industries in various matters, and especially in regard to external trade. Employers and employed in any one industry constitute, as it were, a *vertical* compartment, with interests in some measure peculiar to it. The problem here is to reach such an adjustment as will be most to the benefit of the nation as a whole, without pressing hardly on any compartment: and some tentative suggestions as to the relations of the Ideal to the Attainable will be ventured accordingly.

A time may come when even the aggregate interests of a nation may be willingly sacrificed in some measure to larger cosmopolitan interests. But attempts to realize that ideal now are not practicable: though some limited arrangements may be made among groups of nations, such as those that constitute the British Empire; while a yet larger, though looser, grouping is suggested by the active alliances in support of freedom which have been developed during the World-war. In the second Volume these harmonies and discords are to be studied more closely, in connection with the harmonies and discords of interest among different nations.

Changes in the purchasing power of money, though not as important as appears at first sight, put difficulties in the way of agreements between different sections; and they confuse the statistics of international trade, though they do not materially affect its general drift. Therefore it is proposed that the second Volume shall include a short study of money and credit in relation to industry and trade.

4. *Some details as to the arrangement of Book I. Causes of the large use of appendices and footnotes.*

The function of Book I is to indicate broadly some chief origins of the industrial technique and organization, that prevail now in the Western World. England, afterwards incorporated in Britain, was at one time a pupil of other industrial lands; though she always had certain, rather narrow, specialities. In the course of a few centuries she became, first their competitor on even terms; and afterwards their leader in many great industries.

The four or five decades, in which her leadership was chiefly developed, are sometimes described as those of the Industrial Revolution: but in fact what then happened was not a Revolution; it was merely one stage of Evolution which had proceeded almost without interruption for several hundred years. From the early Middle Ages till the present day economic evolution has presented on one side an ever increasing power of capital: and especially of capital applied in considerable quantities by professional business men; as distinguished from the resources of a great estate when applied, however ably, to its own development. On another side this evolution has diminished the strain thrown on human muscles, relatively to that handed over to the subservient energies of animals, of water, of wind, and of coal. On yet a third side

I, I, 4. it has changed the general character of industrial organization in two opposite directions. Modern work is more narrowly specialized, in so far as the number and variety of the operations performed by a modern worker are on the average less than those of the elementary skilled handicraftsman: but it is less narrowly specialized, in the sense that an operative, who has mastered the accurate, delicate and prompt control of machinery of any kind in one industry, can now often pass, without great loss of efficiency, to the control of similar machinery in an industry of a wholly different kind, and perhaps working on different material.

The first of these three sides of the great evolution—that of the increased application of material resources as capital in the production of things for sale—was set on its way in various parts of Europe, while England still lagged behind. But early in the eighteenth century she ran up to the best models of the time; she passed them quickly in that production by powerful machinery, which was another stage of the great evolution; and meanwhile Mercantilism was declining largely under the influences of Dutch, French, and English writers (Chapter III and Appendices B, C, D). As the age of steam came on, she threw off nearly all remaining shackles and became the acknowledged leader of the world in massive industries. Later on she obtained a further advantage through her policy of free trade; and through the troubles which befell her chief rivals, America and Germany, in the third quarter of last century. But by that time she had become over-confident; and every class and condition of her people expected to be able to earn and to spend much more than those in similar conditions in other old countries, while yet taking their work rather easily. But a reaction set in, they learnt that they must meet strong rivals, especially in Germany and America, on equal terms: that in order to continue to lead they must learn as well as teach, and work as hard as the most strenuous of their rivals. This movement was interrupted by the World-war; but the issue of the war has been found to depend, even more than had been anticipated, on the abundance of mechanical appliances; and the movement is likely to be accelerated on the balance by the war (Chapters IV, V and Appendix E).

I, I, 4.

Englishmen, like others, have learnt and are learning much from France; especially in the fine individual perception of form and colour, which belongs to the artist as much as to the manufacturer. Germany is the chief leader in the application of organized "team work" by scientific specialists to the problems of industry. And America surpasses all in the economies derived from intense mechanical specialization, the third chief feature of modern industrial evolution: for she has turned to good account the opportunities which are offered by her large homogeneous home market, by the concentration of her forces of capital, and the ever-welling spring of energy and inventive faculty of a vast population. It includes many who are rich, but not many of those idle rich who have, at various times, damped the energies of many old seats of high industry (Chapters VI, VII, VIII).

From this brief account it will appear that Book I is not in any sense a contribution to economic history: its aim is merely to indicate that the present structures of industry and trade, in so far as they are considered in the present work, are, for the greater part, direct and almost necessary consequences of conditions, which have developed almost continuously from the Middle Ages to the present time. The particular facts, to which attention is directed, have no other claim to precedence over those which are ignored, than that they seem in a special sense responsible for the good and the evil of some of the economic features of the present age.

Finally something must be said as to the reasons which have induced a rather large recourse to the use of appendices and footnotes. The writer, when reading books on subjects which do not fall wholly within his line of study, but yet have important bearings on it, often strives in vain to reach the broader issues, while avoiding the narrower. The division between broad and narrow issues must be in some measure arbitrary: for some matters of chief interest to one person are of secondary interest to another. A busy man of affairs in particular is likely to want to probe thoroughly on their practical side those issues which affect his action, and as to which he has special knowledge and responsibility: while in regard to other matters,

I, I, 4. he may prefer broad statements, the grounds for which he may leave to be judged by others. Business men are those from whose guidance economic students have profited most in recent years, and may hope to profit increasingly in the future: and efforts have been made, by Section-headings and otherwise, to facilitate appropriate selection.

There is however one group of appendices which was not deliberately planned; and for the length of which apology must be made. Present policies of international trade have developed from roots in the later Middle Ages in courses sufficiently regular to offer occasion for drawing inferences from past history in relation to present conduct: and therefore considerable space was given in Book I to the rise and decay of Mercantile policy and some kindred matters. But it has been found impossible to bring out the second Volume, containing a study of international trade, at the same time as the first; and these matters have little relevance to the subjects now in hand. After some hesitation, it has been decided to retain them in proximity with the observations on concurrent changes in industrial technique and structure: but to relegate them to the end of the Volume, in spite of the great addition which they make to appendices already rather long.

CHAPTER II

SOME GENERAL RELATIONS BETWEEN INDUSTRY AND TRADE

1. *The trade of a place is likely to be increased by an advance of her stronger industries, but to be lessened by an advance of her weaker industries.* I, II, 1.

The present chapter is in some respects more closely akin to the studies of international trade, which will come later, than to the present Book. But there will be some advantage in having a few broad results at hand immediately; for they bear in various ways on the subjects of this Book; and, though less closely, on those of Books II and III.

The only full statistics of trade are those which are collected by customs house officials at the frontiers of countries; and therefore imports and exports always suggest the notion of goods passing between different countries. But the elementary principles, with which we are concerned in this chapter, have no reference to nationality: they are almost as applicable to the trade between two neighbouring parts of the same country as they are to international trade. Therefore the illustrations will be generally taken from that particular kind of trade, the statistics of which are accessible and familiar: but the argument will be understood to apply also in a great measure to the external trade of any province or county, such as Normandy or Lancashire, or of any industrial city, such as Leeds or Chemnitz. If the local spirit of any place ran high: if those born in it would much rather stay there than migrate to another place: if most of the capital employed in the industries of the place were accumulated from those industries, and nearly all the income enjoyed in it were

I, II, 1. derived from its own resources:—if all these conditions were satisfied, then the people of such a place would be a nation within a nation in a degree sufficient to render propositions, which relate to international trade, applicable to their case from an abstract point of view; though in the absence of any statistics of the imports and exports of the place, they would to some extent still lack reality. This observation of course does not apply to a residentiary town such as Bournemouth, or Newport in Rhode Island.

Industrial leadership has generally been accompanied by a large foreign trade: and, partly for that reason, there is a widespread notion that the volume of her foreign trade is a fairly good measure of a country's prosperity. Let us inquire broadly how much truth there is in this notion.

Much of the mystery which hangs about the trade of a nation may be dispelled by the reflection that the trade between two nations is the aggregate of the trade between their individual members, (the commercial transactions of Governments being left out of account): and that therefore it is likely to present many of the same features as theirs, though in a disguised form.

It is obvious that the trade of an individual is not a fairly good measure of his prosperity, unless he be a merchant or shopkeeper: that is, unless he have adopted trade as his industry. The volume of the trade of a merchant is no doubt a *prima facie*, though not conclusive, proof of his business efficiency and prosperity. But if a man's main business is to produce, the test is most untrustworthy: because a little energy given to some branches of production leads to a larger trade than much energy given to others.

Take, for instance, a woollen manufacturer, who has been in the habit of spinning his own yarn. Suppose him forced to give up his factory, his land being perhaps needed for a new railway. When building on a fresh site, he decides to buy his yarn, and to erect weaving sheds twice as large as his old ones. Henceforward he uses about the same capital, and buys about the same amount of coal and labour as before: but his outlay on yarn for his large weaving shed is much greater than his outlay on wool for the small one used to be; and his output of cloth is about doubled. His trade is greatly increased. Does the change reflect increased prosperity? Is it to his credit?

We cannot say. The cause of the change of plan may have been that his weaving sheds were more successful than those of his competitors: but it may have been that his spinning mills were less successful than theirs. Mere volume of trade shows nothing. To find even an approximate answer we must go behind the facts given, and ascertain their causes. This is obviously true of private trade, and it is equally true of national trade.

For a country like an individual may increase her trade as a consequence of a decrease in facilities for producing something which she imports. For instance, a bad harvest at home is likely to increase England's trade. She must import more grain, and export more manufactures to pay for it. On the other hand her trade might be lessened by the discovery of high grade iron ores, which would enable her to dispense with those that she now imports from Spain; or again by an energetic development of dairy and poultry farming, which would enable her to dispense with much of her imports from Denmark. Again improvements in her methods of building motor cars tended to lessen her trade, until her cars were as much sought for as those of France, which she at one time imported largely: and further improvements seem likely to augment her exports of them and increase her trade; at all events in directions in which the consummate mastery of their massive production, recently acquired by America, is not paramount. To speak more generally:—

A country's foreign trade is likely to be increased by a rapid advance in those of her industries which are already ahead of similar industries in other countries: because such an advance increases her power of exporting at a profit. But her foreign trade is likely to be lessened, or at all events its growth is likely to be checked, by an advance in those industries in which she is relatively weak; because such an advance will tend to diminish her need of imports.

It is, however, true that a general advance of a country's methods and resources of production, affecting equally those in

I, II, 2. which she has been at a relative advantage and those in which she has been at a relative disadvantage, will put all her affairs on a larger scale: and her trade will increase with the rest of her affairs. Further, and this is perhaps more important, her exporting industries are likely to owe their success over foreign competitors in a great measure to an unusually high average of constructive ability and initiative among employers, and of sustained energy and fidelity of work amongst employees. These qualities engender and attract men of great industrial strength. And, when a country is growing in strength, a disproportionately large share of it is likely to belong to her exporting industries, and therefore to increase her trade: industrial leadership is thus reflected in foreign trade.

This rule is however not universal. It sometimes happens that a sleepy industry is invaded by a few active and enterprising men from outside, or migrates from a stagnant district to one that is progressive: its advance may then oust a large class of foreign imports from the home market; with the net result of lessening the country's foreign trade.

On the whole, and in the absence of all knowledge as to the causes at work, it is reasonable to suppose that an ascertained increase in a country's foreign trade reflects an increase in her general prosperity. But we may never assume that a rise or fall in that trade indicates a *proportionate* increase or diminution in her prosperity: we may not measure her prosperity by her foreign trade. We must go behind the returns, and judge each item of imports and exports by itself. On investigation, some will indicate strength in natural resources and others weakness: some will indicate industrial progress, and others will indicate industrial decadence, not perhaps positively, but relatively to other countries.

2. *The direct gain that a town, a province, or a country derives from its external trade is the excess of the real value to it of its imports over that of the things, which it could have produced for itself by the labour and capital needed for producing its exports and working the trade.*

As an ordinary rule, when anyone voluntarily exchanges one thing for another, he expects the latter to be of greater service to him than the former; perhaps for his own use, perhaps for trading away. His gain by the exchange is the superior value to him of what he receives over what he gives up. If he made the first thing himself, and will use the second himself, this gain may be stated as the excess of the services which the second thing will yield him, over the effort which it cost him to make the first; or—which is sometimes nearly the same thing—over the services which he could have got by making for himself other things with an expenditure of effort and resources equal to that needed for making the first[1].

What is true of trade between individuals is true of trade between towns, or provinces, or countries. But there are seldom any statistics showing the imports and exports of any locality, which is not either a country, or an isolated province belonging to a country; and it will be best to speak here only of countries. The *prima facie* gain, which a country derives from her foreign trade, consists in the excess of the value to her of the things which she imports, over the value to her of the things which she could have made for herself in their place; *i.e.* with the amounts of capital and labour devoted to producing the things, which she exported in exchange for them (the costs of working the trade being of course reckoned in).

But our statistics do not, and cannot, afford a direct means for estimating this excess. And consequently it is necessary to use them indirectly on a plan, which suggests more definite ideas: it is not strictly correct, but it serves fairly well for some purposes. On this plan, it is tacitly assumed that the country would make for herself those things which she imports, if she could not get them by trade: and accordingly her gains from her trade are taken to be the excess of the cost to which she would be put if she made her imports herself, over that to which she is put by making other things and exporting them in

[1] It will be noted that this statement differs fundamentally from one that is substituted for it in popular discussions: the statement, namely, that in a free exchange each person gives up what is of less real value to him than to the receiver. When a peasant who lives chiefly on polenta and cabbages sells his fowls to buy clothes, he receives the power of purchasing things of more value to him than the fowls. But if the purchaser of the fowls is a rich man, their possession cannot afford him as much real benefit as it might have done to the seller.

I, II, 3. exchange for her imports. This result is of course very far from the truth in regard to such things as Britain's imports of tropical foods: for she could not produce any great quantities of these herself; and she would for the greater part go without them, if she could not import them. If her imports of French and other woollens were arrested, she would indeed make up the greater part of the deficiency by her own products, which would be pushed into uses for which imported products are now preferred; her exporting industries being of course subject to an equivalent check. But if her imports of wheat and other staple grains were arrested, she would be forced to make up the deficiency by her own production, even though that would require poor crops to be wrung by great labour from unsuitable soils, and climates.

This is however only the *prima facie* gain; her trade exerts many other influences on her well-being, some good, and some evil. It may, for instance, educate her finer industries and those which make most for leadership: or it may tend to stifle them. It may increase or diminish the steadiness of employment of her working classes; and so on. And there are other issues, to be reckoned with later on. Account will need to be taken, for instance, of exports which she sends out when lending capital to other countries, and for which she receives no corresponding imports at the time. Again allowance will need to be made for the influences of different kinds of trade in stimulating industrial energy, in ministering to the wants of the needier classes of the population and in affecting the amount and security of their employment.

3. *Countries, whose advantages are distributed in unequal proportions among different industries, may generally carry on a trade profitable to both, even though one of them is absolutely the stronger all round.*

Trade between two individuals is the result of relative differences in the ease with which they can make different things. One man may conceivably be able to do everything easier than the other: but if he has a great advantage in doing some things, and only a small advantage in doing others, then it may probably be worth his while to give all his energy to doing those things in which he had a *relative* advantage; and to escape doing those for which he is at a relative disadvantage, though at a positive advantage.

For instance a business man could often do the work of his assistant, or his foreman, or one of his workmen, better and more easily than it is done by the man whom he pays to do it. But he would be foolish to do it himself, if that involved, as it probably would, the neglect of other work that is peculiarly his. Again, a medical man may possess more strength and more knowledge of horticulture than the gardener whom he hires; and be able to do the gardener's work better and with less effort: and, if the gardener could not obtain it otherwise, he may well spend a day's wages on medical advice, given in a few minutes, which rescues him from many days' pain and loss of wages; though it costs little to the physician. In such cases each man does work for which he has a differential advantage, though he may be at an absolute disadvantage.

Again, the owner of cold wet land may habitually supply oats to his neighbour, whose land has a southern exposure and a deep loamy well-drained soil. To grow a quarter of oats may have cost him much more labour and other outlay than it would have cost his more fortunate neighbour: so that in raising the oats he is at a great *absolute* disadvantage. But his land though ill suited for oats is even more unsuited for wheat: and, because his absolute disadvantage in the production of wheat is greater than in the production of oats, it is to his advantage to "export" oats to his neighbour and to "import" wheat: he has a *relative* advantage in the production of oats. The existence of the trade is not to his credit or to his discredit: but it is a sign of the poverty of his resources. If by drainage, improved rotations, etc. he managed to grow a good deal of wheat without inordinate labour and outlay, he would lose this trade: and that would be to his credit[1].

Now it will be found that somewhat similar cases occur in the trade between two countries, whose peoples cling to their several native lands, whether from inertness, or for the sake of patriotic ideals. In such a case the nation that is the less well

[1] This group of illustrations is on similar lines to those of Ricardo's celebrated chapter on Foreign Trade.

I, II, 3. endowed with natural resources, or the faculty for industrial organization, must act like one of the less fortunate individuals just described. It must turn to the best account those resources and faculties, which are less markedly inferior than others to similar resources and faculties in the possession of its neighbours. Its fortune will remain inferior to theirs: but it will not lag behind them as much as it would, if it were compelled to provide for itself those things, for the production of which its relative advantages were very low.

But the case of trade between two districts of a modern western country is different. For if the industries of one of them were so much richer than the other in natural and acquired resources and in organizing faculty, that a man of given natural ability and energy could earn nearly the full wages of the more fortunate district shortly after migrating into it; then migration would have set in long ago so strongly as to change the location of those industries which required high faculties. The backward district might continue with low wages; but that would be because its social conditions and general influences were not adapted to bring out the best energies of its inhabitants; and, possibly, because it had become a sort of sink, towards which people who could not obtain employment in the more energetic and enterprising district gravitated. After a time however it might awake from its torpor, assimilate the processes and the energy of the more advanced district and thus earn equal wages with it. Capital would follow the effective demand for it from one district to another very rapidly.

Trade between such districts shows little to correspond either to trade resulting from the faculties of the business man or the medical man, which are fixed in the individual and not capable of being transferred to his foreman or gardener; or again to properties of the rich warm land that are fixed in it. International trade on the other hand shows much to correspond with them: for the migration of labour and capital from one country to another, is still slow, though not so slow as it was formerly. No doubt lethargy and other obstacles prevent the inhabitants of some backward districts even of western countries from migrating to neighbouring districts, where they might soon learn to turn their latent strength to good account: while, on the other hand, alert people migrate from one country to another without great difficulty, at all events where no change in languages is involved.

This class of considerations will need to be pursued further in connection with the problems of international trade. But before passing away from the general principle which is indicated in this section, there may be some advantage in pointing to a few more results which flow from it, and have influenced the evolution of national industry and trade throughout the world a good deal more than might seem probable at first sight.

It is true that if a country were twice as well endowed as her neighbour with *all* natural resources, with *all* industrial aptitudes, and with capital; then there could be no trade between them. It would be twice as heavy a task to produce a quarter of wheat in the second country as in the first: but so it would be to produce a bale of cloth or a piece of machinery. All commodities would exchange for one another at the same rates in one country as in the other: and a merchant would gain nothing for his pains if he took the goods of one country to sell them in exchange for goods of the other. But in fact every industry is full of specialities, some large and some small. Britain and Germany are on nearly the same level in industrial capacity generally: and each is wont to buy from the other considerable quantities of textile, and engineering, and other products.

The greater part of such trade would indeed have been impossible without those modern facilities for transport and communication, which enable a very slight differential advantage to effect interchange, even in the face of moderate import duties. But if the richer country could produce double as much as the other could with equal effort in some industries, and only half as much again as the other in the remaining industries, then there would be so great a profit to each in exporting those things in which she was at a relative advantage and importing those in which she was at a relative disadvantage as to overbear even a heavy cost of transport.

The trade would be profitable: and that is all we are concerned with just now. But even here it is worth while

I, II, 3. to insist that the best business is not necessarily that which brings in the highest profits immediately: for other business may be doing more to strengthen the basis on which all rests. Thus the lad who carries parcels often earns higher wages than he would while learning a skilled trade: but in the long run it would have paid him better to earn less at first. Similarly, a country may rightly ask whether her foreign trade is such as to promote the education of her industries. The answer varies curiously with circumstances. For instance, when Japan first welcomed foreign traders, she sent to England fine metal work, which could have been produced there with less effort than in Japan: for some parts, though not all, could have been made by machinery. In return she imported things made wholly by machinery with a quickness and accuracy which were beyond the competition of hand work. Japan was at an absolute disadvantage in both kinds of production. But she was at a greater disadvantage where machinery could do all the work, than where it could do only a part. And some would have said—let her tax heavily imports of western manufacturers, so that her people may learn western methods. But (partly under the influence of treaty obligations) Japan on the whole welcomed foreign manufactures, meanwhile studying western methods; and she now uses machinery freely where it is appropriate. Thus both absolute and relative national disadvantages are quickly altered in this era of rapid change. And indeed each part of every country's trade is coming increasingly under the influence of causes, which affect in the first instance countries other than those with which that trade is carried on: the international element is becoming increasingly prominent in the history of all trade.

For instance, when any change in England's trade with Italy occurs, the Englishman is likely to have already in his mind the changes in English conditions which bear on it. And therefore, before forming any opinion on the change, he should make some study of recent events in Italy: he should look for changes in the relative efficiency of different Italian industries; and again for changes in Italian demand for the products of other countries, whether of such a nature as to compete directly with English products or not. And especially he should take account of any change in the costs of transport between Italy and other countries and also in the development of Italy's internal traffic: for such changes often have a greater effect on England's trade than others, which fill a much larger place in the mind of the Englishman.

In all economic history, and especially in recent economic history, and most of all in the recent history of trade, the international point of view is essential. It is easy to remember that one's own country is ever growing and changing: but it sometimes requires effort to consider how many of the changes near at hand are partly due to the expansion of life far away.

4. *A small country often has a relatively large foreign trade: for she can seldom supply nearly all her own wants as regards raw materials and other things; and her frontier is generally long relatively to her population and industry. But some causes tend in the opposite direction.*

When the foreign trades of two countries of unequal size are compared, with the purpose of finding a rough measure of their relative economic activities, it is obvious that account must be taken of their relative population: the great excess of the trade of China over that of New Zealand does not suggest any lack of energy on the part of the islanders. But if, avoiding this danger one compares the amount of trade per head of the population of two countries of very unequal size, one falls into an almost equal error in the opposite direction. This danger is more subtle than the first: and there is no simple rule which will guard against it. But it will be found that if the populations of two countries are equally vigorous and alert, and equally well supplied with capital; then the trade per head will generally be the larger in the smaller country: for, in all probability, she will have less varied resources; and, partly as a consequence, her industries will be less capable of supplying her various needs. An additional reason is that she is likely to have relatively long frontiers, adjacent to those of other countries. A comprehension of these facts is so important as an aid to reading between the lines of a sketch of the evolution of national trade and industry,

I, II, 4. that there may be an advantage in looking at a great many illustrations of the way in which it works out.

A place which produces but few things must necessarily depend largely on external markets. To take an extreme case, a village, given up to fishing, trades away nearly the whole of its produce; and the neighbouring farming villages trade away by far the greater part of theirs. But the country which contains these villages and some towns, with simple manufactures, will be more nearly self-sufficing; and its external trade will be less in proportion to population than that of the farming villages, and much less than that of the fishing village.

Again, rich mines of precious metals and stones have been found in arid districts where agriculture is difficult and the conditions of life are not attractive to an industrial population. Consequently industry in those districts has been highly specialized: they export practically the whole of what they produce, and import practically the whole of what they consume.

Again, each State of the American Union must import from elsewhere many things, which the United States as a whole can supply for herself: and therefore if statistics were kept of the aggregate external trade of each State, the total would be many times as great as the total of the foreign trade of the United States. Ireland's trade with England and Scotland has always been greater than her trade with the rest of the world; and the aggregate foreign trade of the United Kingdom was therefore less than that of Great Britain[1].

[1] This was put in evidence in 1825 when Great Britain's trade with Ireland ceased to be classed as foreign, and her foreign trade shrunk; though Ireland's trade with other countries was added to hers. In recent years approximate statistics of Ireland's external trade have been collected, and they show it to be about half as great again per head of the population as that of England and Scotland. The external trade of Greater London is probably greater than the aggregate of that of the United Kingdom.

The foreign trade per head of the Australians was lessened by more than a third when the Colonies were united into one Commonwealth. The change would probably have been much greater if Australia had offered more facilities for intercolonial trade: for the great desert in her centre sends much even of her local trade round by sea, though a good deal passes between Melbourne and the Western district of New South Wales. Further, more than a third of her population is concentrated in four sea-ports, whose cosmopolitan tendencies and opportunities prevent them from having the bias, that more restful districts have, towards local rather than foreign trade.

Again, when natural and artificial causes were combining to give the West Indies nearly a monopoly of the production of sugar, some of these islands imported not only all their clothing and other manufactures, but also nearly all their food. On the other hand India had at the time but little foreign trade, in spite of her vast population, and the high value which Europe placed upon many of her products. For she had little need of European products: she could herself supply most of the things which she desired to have; and Europeans could not then get access to more than a narrow fringe of the large and rich land. Consequently while the foreign trade of the West Indies was for a time one of the largest in the world, that of the whole Continent of India remained small.

Again, so long as England's exports of cloth were made chiefly of her own wool and other home-made material, each thousand pounds' worth of them carried nearly a thousand pounds' worth of the services of her own capital and labour: but now that her cloth is largely made of imported material, that is no longer the case. Further her imports of raw wool, etc. are reckoned as part of her foreign trade: therefore the increase in her foreign trade due to her exports of cloth appears greater than it is.

Similarly the recent growth of Germany's foreign trade has been partly due to the fact that her population, which is larger than that of this country and is growing much faster, is beginning to work up imported raw material on a great scale for home consumption and for export. An additional reason is that railways have given her great new facilities for trade with the seven countries, whose frontiers march with hers. This brings us to consider the two geometrical facts, that a small country has a larger frontier in proportion to her area than a larger country of the same shape; and that the average distance of her people from the nearest foreign markets is likely to be less[1].

[1] The areas of similar figures necessarily stand to one another in the proportion of the squares of their several linear dimensions. Thus, if a country with an area of ten thousand square miles has a frontier of six hundred miles; then another country of similar shape, but a hundred times as large, will have a frontier of only six thousand miles. The smaller country will have ten times as long a frontier in proportion to its area, and therefore probably in proportion to its inhabitants and its industries, as the larger; and in so far as the frontier is a

I, II, 4. Thus Belgium has excellent access to all the world by sea, and a frontier which marches with those of France, Germany and Holland. And, though Switzerland has no access to the sea, her frontiers march with those of four great countries; and her northern, western and southern industrial districts have closer economic relations in some matters with parts of Germany, France and Italy, respectively, than they have with one another; even though they are now united by tunnels through the Alps. These conditions increase their foreign trades.

And yet a large country has her own advantages. Her large area gives greater facilities for the development of those great industrial districts in which, as we shall see presently, concentrated specialization is now carried to its highest extent: and such districts have generally a better approach to her own large markets than the industrial districts of a small country can have to foreign markets, even if their frontiers are not beset by import duties. These broad causes will be found to be among those which have tended to move industrial leadership from cities and from small to large countries; bravely as some small countries are still striving.

Again, industrial leadership—that is the power of doing now what others will presently be doing, or at all events trying to do—enables a country to cater for a great variety of wants which she feels; and which others in like conditions feel, or at least will feel when tempted by the offer of the things that fit those wants. She offers variety: she does not glut the foreign markets with things with which they are already well stocked. She sends those things which have a certain distinction, as being new in substance or in quality, or as attaining familiar ends by easier and simpler means. Whether her population is large or small, it is sure to contain a high proportion of rich people, who can afford to spend freely on imported luxuries and choice goods of all kinds. She is likely to have good means of communication, so that her exports and her imports alike can easily reach their destination. And lastly; since foreign trade

sea line, it will probably supply harbours suitable for the cheapest form of transport. In so far as it is a land line, there will probably be large openings for foreign trade with people close at hand; and with whom traffic will be easy, familiar, and cheap, unless indeed it is obstructed by high tarifs.

itself is an industry, her industrial ability is likely to show itself in conducting that trade with energy and efficiency.

5. *An increase in the distance which goods can be carried at a given cost, is likely to increase the trade in those goods in a greater ratio. Spheres of influence of different centres of trade.*

We have now seen how the unequal distribution of (differential) advantages in different places tends to cause trade to grow up between them. But of course the merchant has difficulties to overcome, risks to run, and expenses to pay: and it will not be worth his while to push the trade unless the differences in value of the things, which he buys and sells in the two places, give a sufficient margin to remunerate him for overcoming all these obstacles.

As a rule, the chief obstacle is the cost of transport; at all events if we take it broadly so as to include insurance, commission expenses and locking up of capital till the returns are brought home: and this cost increases, though irregularly, with the distance. But the area of a circle varies as the square of its radius. Therefore improvements in the mechanism or the organization of transport, which increase the distance over which trade in certain goods can be carried at a given expense, are *prima facie* likely to increase in the square of that ratio the area over which the trade can be conducted profitably. This rule may be called *Lardner's Law of Squares in transport and trade,* for convenience of reference[1].

The facilities for transport from any place in various directions frequently differ widely in character; and so do the markets to be reached. Thus the cheap sea routes at the command of a maritime port may lose much of their value if the population along the neighbouring coasts is sparse, and inland transport from the coast is difficult: and therefore the district, over which trade is profitable, is likely to be of irregular shape. Nay more, the advantage of cheap sea routes

[1] It was made prominent for the first time in Lardner's epoch-making *Railway Economy,* 1850; though its general bearing was probably recognized earlier. Its geometrical method is greatly developed in Alfred Weber's *Standort der Industrien,* Part I, 1909, especially the third chapter and the appendix.

I, II, 5. may vary from one class of goods to another; the expenses of land traffic being a greater obstacle to the movement of bulky goods of low value than of light and costly goods.

But the rule applies fairly well to a trading port in close touch with an archipelago or river delta studded with rich markets. Such a port is indeed likely to derive moral advantages, as well as commercial, from its commanding position. And, in this sense it is true, that the law of squares has had much to do with the brilliant careers of Athens, Alexandria, Byzantium, Marseilles, and Venice; of the Hanseatic League, and of Holland[1].

Causes that delayed England's rise to leadership were that her industries were neither concentrated, nor united by good communications; while she was not specially well placed for availing herself of the economies indicated in the law of squares in external trade. But afterwards transoceanic traffic became more important than that of inland seas and rivers; and the law of squares aided her more than it did any other country, especially during the early days of railways. In recent years, on the other hand, large inland countries have been helped by an ever extending net of railways to reap more benefit from that law than she has.

Of course many hindrances to communication are of a personal rather than a mechanical nature: and they are much under the influence of sentiment, and still act more strongly against international than against domestic trade. Improved education and extended travel are indeed slightly diminishing those which arise from differences of language, of business usage, of commercial law and jurisdiction, and so on. But national sentiment is not always moderated by international intercourse.

It is obvious however that even a great economy of transport will not enable a place to send its goods into the sphere of influence of an equally strong rival centre of production. For example, if a district well adapted for wheat be surrounded by a belt of pasture land, then a fall in the cost

[1] Some of the above considerations are further developed below, in connection with recent changes in the conditions of marketing in various classes of large cities. (See II, VI, 5; and Appendix J, 6.)

of sending out wheat and bringing back cattle will extend the trade: but, however low that cost, the wheat cannot be sent across the pasture land into other wheat territory. Similarly the export of coal or heavy iron goods from a great producing centre will extend rapidly under the influence of lowered transport charges, until it approaches the sphere of influence of a rival centre. Five-thousand-ton barges on the Rhine, and increased railway facilities, have sent English coal into South Germany and Switzerland: but the neighbourhood of the Westphalian mines has always been closed to it.

When two centres of trade are competing for any neutral territory, an improvement which lowers equally the costs of the communication of both of them with that territory, will increase the trade of both in about equal proportions. But if the improvement benefits one more than the other, the second may lose trade by the change. Thus the Panama Canal, which facilitates trade between England and Peru, may yet lessen that trade; because it facilitates even more the trade between many parts of North America and Peru.

This points to the general observation that new economies of transport between two places exercise their *full* influence on trade between them, only in so far as they are *differential*, that is in excess of new economies in competing trades. For instance, a general fall in the costs of transport induces a country to buy many things from abroad which she would otherwise have produced for herself, or else foregone. But it is likely to diminish the advantages that her immediate neighbours have for selling to her things for the production of which they are not so well equipped as some more distant competitors. It is indeed true that the costs of handling, or—to use a railway phrase—"the terminal charges" are nearly the same for long distances and for short; and that therefore increased economies in the building and working of ships affect the total costs of long distance trade in a less proportion than those of short distance trade. But yet the total lowering of costs is much greater for very long distances than for short: and in consequence European countries now buy many things from other Continents which they used to buy not very long ago from neighbours.

I, II, 6. 6. *Some consequences of the facts that the costs of traffic over long distances have fallen more than those over short distances; and that both have fallen unequally.*

In early times the discomforts and risks of a long journey or voyage were often very great; and were magnified by prejudice and imagination. Even to-day, if one hires an ordinary villager, with or without a cart, to carry luggage twenty miles, one must commonly pay more than twice as much as for ten miles: because if he goes twenty miles he must sleep away from home.

But, on the other hand, the international money market, the post, and latterly the telegraph have lowered those costs of trade which are not directly connected with the handling of the goods. And on the whole it is probably not far from the truth to assume that the total costs of maritime trade have been lowered about in proportion to the economies in transport, which have been effected by the discovery of the art of tacking, by improvements in the construction of ships, which give them greater carrying power for a given gross tonnage, by the substitution of steam ships for sailing ships, of steel ships for wooden ships, of high pressure boilers for low and so on. And any consequent lowering of freights (even after allowance has been made for the maintenance of *some* of the costs of handling in ports at a relatively high rate) has generally caused the water area which can be profitably covered by any kind of heavy traffic to increase in the square of the ratio in which they have been lowered. The progress of land transport has been less uniform and more spasmodic. For the art and habit of making good roads have risen and decayed more than once; and the whole conditions of transport in any district are revolutionized when a railway system appears in it.

It often happens that goods can start on an easy route, but must break away from it to the right or left in order to reach their destination: and in such a case the area which can be profitably covered by any class of trade has the shape of an elongated oval or diamond.

Suppose for instance a town were placed on a river running (very slowly) due north and south, along which heavy goods could be carried profitably about one hundred miles in either direction; while the cost for each mile by land was ten times as great. Then, assuming the purchasers everywhere to be ready to pay the same price for the same goods, and neglecting the expenses of transhipment, we find that the town's market for those goods would have the shape of a long diamond, twenty miles from East to West, and two hundred miles from North to South; its area being about two thousand square miles. Meanwhile light perishable goods, which could not endure a slow journey by water, but could afford to be carried a hundred miles by land, would have a market of rather more than thirty thousand square miles.

The case is substantially similar when traffic starts by sea, or by railroad, and has to be carried by road for a part of the journey. For that part, though short in distance, may easily be the costlier of the two. We shall see presently how much, that seems obscure in the history of the prices of wheat in England during the nineteenth century, finds its explanation in the fact that the prohibitory costs of transport for the first hundred miles from many districts ceased as soon as they had been connected by good roads or railroads with tidal water.

A simple illustration of this principle may be found in the building of Alpine chalets. When one has to be built very far from any road, logs are roughly hewn into the requisite shape by the adze and hand-saw at a very heavy cost of labour and wood. But if the chalet is to be built near a valley, which has a rough road and a simple saw-mill; then the logs are brought down the road over snow in winter, and are sawn into boards, which are carried along the road, to a point just below the chalet. The builder, however, must still apply the hand-saw, the adze and the plane to do a great deal of work which is done with a tenth or a hundredth part of the labour by large wood working mills with expensive plant, such as can pay their way only in broad valleys with ample road or railroad communications. In such a microcosm we see increased supplies of capital, and improved means of communication, gradually extending the economies of massive production to one district after another, and one class of commodities after another. The broad history of trade is little more than the continued application of similar principles to provincial, national and cosmopolitan problems.

CHAPTER III

FOUNDATIONS OF ENGLAND'S INDUSTRIAL LEADERSHIP. HER DRIFT TOWARDS MASSIVE PRODUCTION

I, III, 1. 1. *Introductory. England's forerunners in the industrial leadership of Western Europe. The spirit of economic nationality.*

The purpose of the present chapter is to sketch England's preparation for leadership in modern methods of massive production. The energies of her people showed themselves early in war and in maritime trade and adventure: and the characteristics of her later industrial qualities were foreshadowed by the uses to which she put water power in the inception of massive textile work. But "massive industry" in that full sense of the term, in which scope is offered for the complex and multifarious resources of modern technique, calls for a very much larger aggregate use of power than could be supplied by all the streams of England. This introductory chapter therefore passes quickly over the advance of England's industries through Mediaeval and Mercantile conditions to that in which considerable masses of workers were aggregated, for good and for evil, in districts that provided water power adequate for relatively large and highly organized textile manufactures.

The forerunners of modern "national trade" are not to be found in any empire of olden time, however firmly it was held together by political and military influences. But they may be found in great industrial cities in the Early, and especially in the Middle Ages: since in these, direct communication by word of mouth sufficed for nearly all the purposes of the modern printing press, post and telegraph: therefore they developed as patriotic a pride in their work as in their military strength.

And, as List says, that which is now called the spirit of economic nationality, is really the spirit of Bruges or Antwerp; of Venice, Florence or Milan, spread over a whole country. It first permeated to Holland, a land of cities intimately united by an all pervading network of waterways. There were jealousies among her cities: but they worked on the whole harmoniously for the common purposes of trade; and a national trade was created under these conditions before the time was ripe for a large national industry. But a chief advantage, which Holland ultimately obtained over her rivals in trade, was by her adoption of standardized shapes for her ships and other vessels. Each of several cities undertook the supply of a particular group of interchangeable parts; and thus the methods applied, during the World-war, by several countries to the production of munitions (and notably by Germany to that of submarines) were anticipated by Holland, long before engineers had even contemplated the delicate accuracy of work attained by modern semi-automatic machinery. Englishmen fought eagerly with Holland, and gained little thereby: but their debts as pupils to her are immense.

One keynote of the contrast between the early economic history of England and Holland is incidentally struck in Petty's illustrations of his great rule that "Each country flourisheth in the manufacture of its own native commodities." He continues, "viz. England for woollen manufacture, France for paper, Luicland (Liège) for iron-ware, Portugal for confectures, Italy for silks. Upon which principle it follows that Holland and Zealand must flourish most in the trade of shipping, and so become carriers and factors of the whole world of trade[1]."

He was arguing that England had a better "native commodity" for shipping than appeared: but he did not venture to claim that it was very great. For the Netherlands and Venetia are lowlands watered by great streams: England is an island of which the main watercourses flow away from one another; and the seas connecting them break turbulently round long promontories. Her harbours were not specially well placed for the trade of early times, her inland waters did relatively little

[1] *Political Arithmetic*, A.D. 1676, p. 16. See Appendix B for an outline sketch of the debts of modern industry and trade to the City States and to Holland.

I, III, 1. towards concentrating her industry, and in the early Middle Ages her people cared little for the sea. But yet the sources of her strength and of her ultimate wealth lay in her geographical position, and in the climate attendant on it. Her position had attracted the boldest venturers from both sides of the North Sea and the Baltic; and Professor Schmoller, an able, if somewhat severe critic of English history, says of them:—"there arose from the intermarriage of these invaders a sportive variety of men of rare bodily vigour, strong of will, calm in deliberation, and bold in action[1]."

There are indications of a tendency to regard the industrial qualities, which have been prominent in England during recent times, as accidental successors of the earlier strenuousness of Englishmen under arms:—accidental in the same way as it was a matter of accident that the Yorkshire hills, whose water power attracted woollen industries in the eighteenth century, owed their later industrial prominence to their coal, of which the earlier woollen manufacturers had taken little or no account. It is therefore worth while to insist that the energies of Englishmen have always had the same fundamental character: but the brief historical sketch which occupies the remainder of this chapter will be superfluous to many readers; and may be omitted.

[1] *Die englische Handels Politik des* 17 *und* 18 *Jahrhunderts*, published in his *Jahrbuch*, vol. XXIII. List, another critic of England, equally able and almost equally severe, while remarking that the influence of blood may be overrated, and that there was less freedom in England under the Tudors than in the German and Italian cities, attributes much of England's wealth to "the people's innate love of liberty and of justice." *National System of Political Economy*, ch. VI. pp. 49 and 50. And elsewhere he observes that "of all the industrial pursuits, navigation most demands energy, personal courage, enterprise, and endurance; qualifications that can only flourish in an atmosphere of freedom" (*ib.* ch. X. p. 108). Roscher points out (*Handels Politik*, § 6) that vicissitudes of commercial enterprise, and the resolute independent bearing that was fostered among the people by a seafaring life, combined to weaken class distinctions in trading cities, even when their political constitution was oligarchic: and thus there was a constant spring of fresh energetic blood upwards in them. Petty argues that trade does not always flourish best under popular Governments; but he gives some curious instances of his rule that "Trade is most vigorously carried on in every State and Government by the heterodox part of the same, and such as profess opinions different from what are publicly established." (*Political Arithmetic*, p. 25.)

2. *The qualities, which gave leadership to Englishmen in industry and trade in the nineteenth century, had their roots in early times.* I, III, 2.

From 1066 down to the present time England's history has been that of the same people, never disturbed for long by any sort of grievous violence, never forcibly moulded by a series of imperious personalities, never under a dominating influence from outside. They brought with them the characteristics of firm will, self-determination, thoroughness, fidelity and love of freedom—strong qualities, which they have never lost; but also some deficiency in graciousness and delicacy of manner—pleasant qualities, which they have never completely gained. They have learnt greatly from others: but they have pursued their own course so independently and steadily, that their political and economic institutions have grown side by side in harmony; and they stand out now as the leading type of continuous development. Their methods in industry and trade were for long ages far behind the highest level that had been reached; but at last they threw their own special characteristics into business affairs with such energy, and such quickness of adaptation to the ever increasing massiveness of the economic problems of the Western World, that they became its chief pioneers of progress and trade.

In fact the qualities of body and character, which ultimately gave to Englishmen a certain leadership in industry and trade, had their origin in early times; and persisted throughout some six centuries, in which they found much scope in deeds of courage and endurance on land and sea, and in popular games: the English archer was the progenitor of the English artisan. Continuity can be traced also in England's political history. The "growing pains" of the Tudor age were in part an indication of the fusion of England, or at all events of all England except her northern counties, into an economic unity. Local restrictions and other regulations faded away: and their place was gradually taken by laws and royal ordinances, which applied generally to the kingdom as a whole: this was in part cause, and in part consequence, of the beginnings of a consciousness of economic nationality. The new order was to be based on the old: but with greater breadth of action came somewhat greater

I, III, 2. breadth of thought, and also some slight softening of temper: the new order of administration was associated with a new order of trade; and internal trade became generally more open, while external trade was still regulated, though not on mediaeval lines.

England's foreign trade was for a long while in the hands of foreigners, whose conduct was mitigated by the Staple; and for some time more largely in the hands of "Regulated Companies," that is, companies which had an exclusive privilege and a small common purse, while each member traded on his own account: but afterwards privileged joint stock companies came to the front. Thus the joint stock principle was applied for some time almost exclusively to trade with distant lands, and the settlement of plantations; but it began comparatively early to attack the development of the mineral resources of the country itself. This might have been anticipated: for the land was the chief wealth and the chief source of new wealth; and the owners of land were at their ease in work connected with it. Capitalistic resources flowing from the land (either to its owner or as tribute to the sovereign) had indeed been applied directly, with very little intervention from professional commerce or industry, to most of the great constructive undertakings from the building of the pyramids down to the end of the seventeenth century. Important exceptions have to be made for the chief works constructed by the great trading Cities, but not for many others; unless the funds which Roman and other armies dug out with the sword should be entered under a separate head. The land yielded its wealth directly to the building of cathedrals, churches and monasteries: of castles, palaces and great mansions: and many of the passing glimpses which we get of the manner in which the tasks of assembling great quantities of materials from afar, and organizing the work of large numbers of artisans and labourers, were conducted in early times, are afforded by the records of cathedrals and monasteries[1].

[1] These matters are considered further in Appendix C, where something is said as to the steps by which Englishmen, starting late in the industrial race, learnt from others, and gradually rose to positions of rivalry with their teachers: and as to the slow spread of relatively free and democratic methods of life and action over a large part of the land; feudal order giving way in some measure to institutions more akin to the temper of the artisans of a great industrial city. A little is also said in the third Section of that Appendix as to

I, III, 3.

3. *The progress of England's internal and external trade during the Mercantile Age.*

The trade of the Mercantile Age impressed the imagination of those who recorded it; and some writers of our own times imply that it was large. But it was not. At the time of the Restoration England's foreign trade was less than a hundredth part of her present foreign trade in money value, and less than a two-hundredth part in volume. And though it increased fivefold during the next hundred years; yet in 1760, when the establishment of England's supremacy at sea told that the main work of the great trading companies was accomplished, it had not attained to a sixtieth part of its present bulk.

One cause of the slowness of the growth of foreign trade was that the new markets beyond the seas were really very narrow. It is true that more than half the coast lines of the new continents had been "discovered": but the countries behind those lines were still almost inaccessible. The sea-ports which were open to western traders gave them access to small islands of trade, rather than to large territories: they could not always venture very far out of hearing of the sea waves. Their goods might indeed be distributed by native merchants: but only the munitions of war, and luxuries for the rich, would generally bear carriage far into the interior. And further, in the highly civilized parts of the East they met textile and metal goods made by as subtle a skill as their own. They could sell a few trinkets in some ports in exchange for precious metals, furs, ivory, etc. given by ignorant people on terms extravagantly favourable to the European traders. But the quantities of such goods, which were on offer, were small: the aggregate volume of that particular trade was trivial when judged by a modern standard. The profits to be earned in the more solid trade for spices, tea and other vegetable products were at a constantly falling rate per cent., though in constantly increasing aggregate volume.

the influence which foreign trade exerted in developing the organized association of capitals for large purposes: for though joint stock companies, with and without monopolistic privilege, were set up early in mining and other industries, their scope was far narrower than that of companies concerned at first mainly with European affairs, and afterwards with those of Asia and America.

I, III, 3. Later on the Plantations were growing; and there was an increasing demand by Englishmen beyond the sea for those simple, strong, serviceable goods which they were accustomed to use. But it was still only cloth and other light goods that would bear the expenses of the long journey, for ships did not yet carry very large cargoes; and, if there was any journey to be made at all at the further end, it was difficult unless it could be made by river. No doubt this exception is important; as very few centres of population were far from tidal water: and even such things as bricks could go out as ballast in tobacco ships[1].

[1] Thus Mun (about 1622), partially anticipating the notion of "invisible exports" of shipping services (which will be examined in Volume II), says:—"If we send one hundred thousand pounds into the East Indies to buy pepper there and bring it hither, and hence send it to Italy or Turkey, it must yield seven hundred thousand pounds at least in those places, in regard of the excessive charge which the merchant disburseth in those long voyages in shipping, wages, victuals, insurance, interest, custom imposts, and the like; all which notwithstanding the King and the Kingdom gets": he reckons the costs of the double trade as six times that of the original exports. He says also that the cost of carriage of wheat to Italy about doubles its value, and he takes, as probable prices of pepper, 3*d.* in the East Indies, 1*s.* 8*d.* in Amsterdam and 2*s.* in London. (See pp. 22, 12, 14 of the 1755 Reprint of *Treasure by Foreign Trade.*)

Even in 1701 the Commissioners of Customs reported that England had 3280 ships with an aggregate tonnage of but 261,000; *i.e.* about 80 tons on the average. They did not hold nearly as much cargo as sailing ships of the same nominal tonnage in the nineteenth century; and they travelled slowly. They could not have carried among them as much cargo on long voyages in a year as can be carried now by a single large steamship.

The estimates of the volume of trade made by earlier writers, though somewhat better founded than their estimates of national wealth and income, are widely divergent: and no trust can be given to them. It seems probable that the cautious Petty exaggerated a little, when he put the exports of England at £m.10, under which he includes shipping services of the value of £m.1·5, the greater part of the trade being of course with neighbouring countries: while he puts the exports of "the whole commercial world" at £m.45. (*Political Arithmetic*, A.D. 1676, pp. 82—4.)

The following figures are taken from Chalmers' *Estimate of the strength of the British Isles*, A.D. 1812, p. 315, which appear to have been prepared with great care. They relate to England only, the first three lines represent averages.

	Tonnage of ships cleared outwards.	Value of cargoes exported.
A.D. 1663—1669	143,000	£2,043,000
1726—8	456,000	£7,892,000
1749—51	661,000	£12,599,000
1764	742,000	£16,202,000.
To these may be added recent figures for the United Kingdom,		
1913	67,820,000	£523,461,000.

Moreover the obstacles to the transport in bad weather of heavy goods in many parts of England, including some busy hives of industry, were very great. In fact nearly all journeys had to be made on foot, on horseback, or by water. And this retarded the expansion and consolidation of the higher constructive forms of English industry more than might seem probable at first sight. For frequent long journeys involved such delays, fatigues, and exposure to bad weather, as to restrict the freedom of action of the middle-aged and elderly men; in whose hands the main control of enterprise was firmly grasped in that age of discipline. For these and other reasons, the prices charged for imported goods long remained very high.

I, III, 3.

The demand for good roads came rather from the general quickening of agriculture and of urban industry, than from concentrated manufacture for export. Fairly good level roads were made for the use of heavy waggons; and a splendid system of arterial roads carried passengers and news at a rate not dreamt of before. The abundance of "stage-coaches, machines, flys, and post-chaises" was held to be a chief cause of the sudden unification of manners and of social life which startled the middle of the eighteenth century[1].

Good roads came late, and canals came later still. But when

Chalmers' table is made out to show that England's trade progressed in times of peace and generally retrograded during war: all the years selected above are years of peace. Much of what he describes as "exports" went to Ireland; and the external trade of Great Britain and Ireland was certainly less than that of England alone (see above, p. 24). On the other hand allowance must be made for the smugglers' trade, which does not appear in the records.

The difficulties of internal communication caused many London traders to be in closer touch with the neighbouring ports of the Continent than with the more distant parts of England. A detailed inventory of London's trade and its routes is given in *Atlas Maritimus et Commercialis* (1728), p. 110. London bought from abroad many things, which were to be had at a lower price in some parts of England, not very remote. Foreigners were apt to judge England by London; and hence chroniclers and writers of romance have represented the use of foreign goods as much more common in England than it really was. This anonymous book is avowedly in the main a compilation, and probably made some use of the first edition (1723) of Savary's *Dictionnaire Universel de Commerce*: it is a vast store of information.

[1] See a quotation from a pamphlet of 1761 in Lecky, *Eighteenth Century*, ed. I. vol. VI. p. 169. Compare also Smiles, *Lives of Metcalfe and Telford*, and the history of roads in Walford's *Famines of the World*. The difficulties of the royal troops in meeting the invasion of the Highlanders in 1745 gave a great impetus to the making of roads.

I, III, 3. at last they were taken in hand they were pushed forward vigorously. They united the head-waters of England's chief rivers and formed a network round her manufacturing districts. Together they built up in England a larger and more active home market for commodities, that conformed to the law of Increasing Return, than had ever been known before. And the home demand, enforced by the foreign and colonial demand for similar products, acted upon industries which had now at last attained a force of unity and concentration, nearly as intensive as that of her great teacher Holland, and more extensive[1].

Defoe had said, "It is a kind of proverb attending the character of Englishmen that they are better to improve than to invent, better to advance upon the designs and plans which other people had laid down, than to form schemes and designs of their own....The wool indeed was English, but the wit was all Flemish." But he went on to show in detail how we outdid our teachers; how "we have turned the scale of trade, and send our goods to be sold in those very countries, from which we derived the knowledge and art of making them[2]."

England's first great undertaking, that of drainage on a large scale, was carried out for her by Dutchmen; Dutch engineers superintended Dutch workmen, and paid them from funds

[1] Yarranton's *England's improvement by sea and land* (1677) is much occupied with "the advantage of making the great rivers of England navigable." His numerous charts and his arguments have the cogency of a modern pamphlet. He contends that, when once the chief rivers had been rendered navigable as far as possible, the whole country could be consolidated by a few good roads made to join their head-waters; and that they could be kept in repair easily, because they would be on "good hilly sound dry land." Nowadays transport is cheap, and transhipment—except in a few cases where mechanical aid reaches very far—is relatively expensive. But in his time transhipment was thought of lightly; and it was reasonable to hold that his plan would have brought industries, which dealt with heavy goods, nearly up to as high a level of concentrated efficiency as was already being reached by the woollen industries, whose trains of pack horses could go everywhere. This may be illustrated by a statement made in 1724 (in opposition to the claims of some exclusive traders) that the wools of Worcester, Salop and Stafford were used partly in Gloucester, Devon, Kent, and Hampshire. The case was more complex in regard to those of Lincoln, Northampton, Rutland, Leicester, Warwick, Oxon. and Bucks.: for one sort of them went to the Northern Counties; another sort to Norfolk and Devonshire. Some Norfolk wools were sent to North Wales and "there draped into cloth," and ultimately sold in London, and so on. (Unwin, *Industrial organization in the sixteenth and seventeenth centuries*, pp. 188—9.)

[2] *A plan of the English Commerce*, 1728, pp. 299—301.

supplied by Dutch capitalists. To make a good harbour or quay; to erect an efficient windmill, watermill, fulling-mill, or large pump, Dutch aid had been required. The first English iron cannons had been cast in Sussex by a Frenchman: and lessons from French and Italians, Dutch and Flemings, Germans and Swedes had been required to equip Englishmen as workers in cloth and silk, pottery and paper, as miners and metallurgists[1].

But victory over difficulties gave courage for victory over new difficulties. Each victory tended to increase the area over which the goods could be marketed, and therefore the scale of production; and therefore in many industries at least the economy of production; and therefore again, the area over which the goods could be marketed: and so on in ever widening circles. And with each expansion there grew up increased spirit for new ventures, and increased recompense for the risk and expense of working out new inventions, and reducing them to a practical shape.

4. *England's Mercantile policy was adapted to conditions which were passing away, as the increasing mobility of industry promoted the concentration of textile industries in the neighbourhood of water power.*

The spirit of Mercantilism was consistent with a national organization of *external* trade, even before England had made much progress towards internal unity in industry. It adapted itself especially to the pioneering work done by the great monopolist Trading Companies; and to the introduction, by a far-sighted monarch, of skilled foreign artisans for the inception of new industries. But Colbert's resolute attempt to organize French industries by despotic rule in the second half of the seventeenth century obtained only a partial and transient success: and Englishmen were even at that time more capable of taking care of themselves, and more restive under regulation than the French. A century later they had become so much more mobile and masterful that they could organize themselves

[1] Tucker, who was a severe critic of his countrymen, writes in 1750, "England's manufacturers have ever been in high repute for their skill and ingenuity." But his instances come from the minor industries, and do not imply the larger inventiveness.

 in a widespread industrial structure; and had neither the need nor the inclination to be regimented.

In the Middle Ages the monarch and the compact ruling class were often vastly superior to the masses of the people in education, in breadth of outlook and in knowledge of the world, as well as in wealth and military strength. With some exceptions for the great commercial cities, Government alone was in a position to take the initiative in large economic affairs. Custom was the main defence of the weak against the strong; and the action of Government itself in small affairs was often most blessed, when it did little more than enforce custom. The fourteenth century saw indeed the beginning of a general assertion of the spirit of individual liberty; and that was the necessary condition for the spread among the people of habits of independent thought as to the methods of their industry and trade. From that time onward they made more rapid progress in mental capacity and moral strength than their rulers did: and, by the middle of the eighteenth century, they had moved perhaps about halfway upwards from the semi-serf-like condition of earlier centuries to that of the present day; when they are not very far inferior in shrewdness, and constructive ability to the ruling classes.

Every step of that progress increased the importance of the advantage which the common people derived from the more intimate knowledge possessed by each of his own circumstances, and the technical problems of his own work, than could be possessed by Government officials. It thus increased the probability that industry and trade would develop on the most advantageous lines, if left free to take their own courses: and it diminished in some directions, as much as it increased in others, the power of Government to control the courses of industry and trade in the public interests. The *possible* functions of Government expanded almost obtrusively in many directions: but meanwhile there was so great an increase in the complexity of the problems of industry, and so small an increase in the mental capacity of Government for dealing with them, that its *appropriate* functions in the matter did not expand in like manner, for the time at least.

There was however meanwhile a slow increase in the power of

the people to govern the Government that governed them: and this power was destined to become so large and far-reaching, that many tasks may now reasonably be intrusted to Government in the twentieth century which would have been grossly mismanaged in the first half of the nineteenth, and would have been hot-beds of corruption in the eighteenth: thus a certain new tendency to a widening of the appropriate functions of Government gradually set in.

Here it is to be considered that policies, such as those of the Mercantilists, necessarily reacted on the moral character of those who administered them. It increased their temptations to use public authority for purposes of private gain. It developed the strong and the enterprising elements in human nature: but it also gave great scope to those who were selfish and cruel.

Moral developments are nearly always the complex results of many causes; and a student of any one side of human life must be on his guard against a bias to attribute them mainly to those particular causes which loom largest in his eyes. But history seems to show that wherever Mercantile policy has been active, those persons, whose private interests have been closely touched by it, have tried with some success to bend that policy for their own benefit. Occasionally a strong upright personality, like that of Colbert, might stay the evil for a time. But corruption seems generally to have increased when there has been much money to be gained by political influence. The monopolies and other special privileges granted by the Tudors and the Stuarts, were permeated by evil uses of money. And on the larger stage of the eighteenth century, a more highly organized corruption was effected by the riches which the Trading Companies and the individual "Nabobs" had drawn from the East and the West under a policy framed on Mercantile principles[1].

[1] Lecky's *England in the Eighteenth Century* has much information on these subjects. The demoralizing influence exerted by the Mercantile slave trade on the population of the great western ports of England, which were chiefly concerned in it, is well known. Silver and sugar seldom came to Europe without a stain of blood. We have been too quick to forget the horrors which caused Samuel Johnson to give his famous toast: "Here's to the next insurrection of the negroes in the West Indies" (Goldwin Smith, *The United Kingdom*, vol. II.

I, III, 4. Corruption, thus initiated in one part of public life, must have had some tendency to spread. The particular threads of connection between immoral bargainings for commercial favours, and a low moral tone in public affairs generally, are not easy to be traced, especially in regard to distant times. But it is to be noted that the protests against Mercantilist policy, which came with increasing force during the eighteenth century, till they culminated in Adam Smith's denunciation, were based on moral as much as on economic grounds.

Accordingly it is argued in Appendix D that the interferences by Governments with the free courses of industry and trade which the Mercantile Age inherited from the Mediaeval, are not to be brought under any sweeping measure, either of eulogy on account of the patriotic motives by which they were generally induced, or of blame on account of their failure to apprehend the vast difficulties of many of the tasks which they undertook.

For indeed the further we are looking backwards the greater is generally the allowance to be made for changes in the prevalent standards of public and private morality. A statesman may have fallen below the level that is customary in England and several other countries to-day, and yet merit our respect for having risen above the ordinary level of his own age. And he may possibly have been right in constraining the industrial energies of the people to move in certain limited directions: because there was but little independent enterprise in the land; while that little could not be brought up to high intensity, unless concentrated on a narrow area. From this point of view Adam Smith's criticisms on the Mercantilists of his own age may seem harsh. But it is to be remembered that he knew the weaknesses and the corruption of those who

p. 407). The profits on the slave trade would have been enormous if any large part of the victims had survived the voyage (Craik, *History of Commerce*, vol. III. p. 113).

Forces, making for the degradation of morals, interact and mutually strengthen one another. The general laxity of Court life, corrupt practices in politics, the influence of the slave trade, and extreme drunkenness among the highest and the lowest classes, were part cause and part consequence, each of the others. In 1743 it was stated in evidence before a Committee of the House of Commons that the annual consumption of spirits was 19,000,000 gallons, of which 4,000,000 were illicit. The total population was a little over six millions.

were posing as masters of economic statecraft. His condemnation of officious meddling by such men in the affairs of industry and trade is indeed not limited to the conditions of his own time. But he had no means of anticipating the vast increase in the resources of Government, and in the honesty of public officials which began in the nineteenth century. He could look backwards only: and, though the growth of a sturdy upright middle class had given much strength to the country's political structure, experience gave little reason to anticipate that the leading statesmen of the country would cease to regard public affairs as a source of private booty. He did not suppose that private interest always leads traders and producers on those paths which are most conducive to the public weal: for indeed he continually pointed out cases in which it led them in other directions. But he did show that the *general* tendency of their conduct in pursuit of gain was to hunt out methods by which their energies might yield goods or services of increased value to the public. He did this work so thoroughly that later generations have made no great addition to it; though they have introduced many qualifications into it, and given it scientific cohesion.

They have however made a vital change in its general character, when regarded from a social point of view. For they have laid great and ever increasing stress on a point, which had not become prominent when he wrote. It is that his general argument is valid only when "value" is expressed in terms of money.

If a capable builder sets up houses all of a rental of £200 a year on a certain piece of land, his own interest will lead him to adapt them to the requirements of his future customers. But suppose he is to build two classes of houses, one of which will accommodate twenty people to the acre, while the other will accommodate two hundred to the acre; and that one part of his ground is healthy, while the other is unhealthy: then his private interest will lead him to put the denser population on the unhealthy ground. For well-to-do people will generally pay a higher percentage of increase in rental or purchasing price on account of a favourable soil than working classes will. But, from a social point of view, the health of two hundred of the

I, III, 5. working classes is of more value than that of twenty of the well-to-do persons; unless indeed some of them happen to be of exceptional mental quality. Adam Smith's *Wealth of Nations*, interpreted by his *Theory of Moral Sentiments*, supplies a sound basis for the introduction of such considerations. And, in fact, nearly all the far reaching movements which his disciples are starting in the modern world, for increasing the constructive activity of the State in social matters, can be brought within the scope of his policy by paying adequate attention to the difference between money value and social value. This consideration is not always prominently expressed: but it will be found to underlie nearly all the most serious modern economic studies.

5. *The new structure of the textile industries, which was set on foot in the latter half of the eighteenth century, indicates the gradual transition from the methods of the Mercantile Age to those of the nineteenth century.*

The movement towards capitalistic and massive production, which has proceeded in England with ever increasing rapidity and volume during the last century and a half, has two sides; both of which became prominent in the textile industries, earlier than in any others of like importance. On the one side was the growth of free capital, as distinguished from that which was directly associated with ownership or use of land: and on the other was the diffusion of habits of thought and action among the various strata of the population in which tradition and habit counted for less than in early times: movement became larger and more general; and increasing attention was given to new opportunities and new methods of turning old opportunities to account.

Distrust of changes in the methods of work and pay died out slowly. Old traditions of the villein's duty to his lord, and his lord's reciprocal obligations lingered for good, as well as evil, long after villeinage had ceased to be formally recognized. The old solidarity of the village left odours, some sour and some sweet, in the largeness of the open commons on which lean animals lingered out a meagre life. The enclosure of commons, excellent as it was from a broad national view, was opposed with some justice, as a plunder of the very poor, for the benefit of the well-to-do; and it increased the hardship which was inherent in rigorous, if futile, edicts against wanderers from the place of their settlement. Mobility increased: but it was often ill-directed; and the consequent rapid increase in the numbers of the most unfit became a great evil early in the nineteenth century, as we shall see presently.

Large new opportunities were developed by the increasing rate of growth of England's material wealth, which was largely due to the continued freedom of her island territory from devastating wars. This freedom gave to her manufacturers and her agriculturists alike, security for reaping the rewards of effort invested in improvements that would bear fruit slowly. The choicest horses and cattle were left to breed in peace, being beyond the reach of foraging bands of soldiery: and the buildings, the machinery and the stocks of trade and industry, were undisturbed. This cause had equipped England with the sinews of industrial competition before she showed signs of industrial leadership; and during the eighteenth century it contributed much to her rise to the position of undisputed supremacy in the world's market for capital.

The abundance of capital gave scope for men with marketing ability of a constructive order. This is to be clearly distinguished from a laborious astuteness in bargaining, on which people with small capitals, and especially agriculturists, in all countries often lay stress: priding themselves on their skill in buying a thing for less than it is worth, and selling a thing for more than it is worth. That miserable ingenuity is no doubt barren: it is the one side of trade, which is amenable to the old sweeping charge against all trade: viz. that in it no one can gain save at the expense of another; and that the more energy is diverted to it, the poorer the country will become.

The constructive trader, on the other hand, aims high, and sees far: he is constantly forecasting future developments of demand, and endeavouring so to turn to account the rising force of new methods of production as to supply something which can be produced in large quantities at a low cost, and force its way into general consumption. It is to force its way, because it is sold for less than people had previously thought it to be worth; while yet it has cost him, and is in a sense worth to him, much less than what he sells it for. For this task elasticity of mind and delight in hard work are needed: and these qualities are not often found among those who have inherited wealth: but they were found in high degree among the undertakers, most of whom had risen from the ranks.

Such an undertaker sought out "homely" producers who had the skill and aptitude for making certain classes of things economically and well; instructed them as to the precise character of the thing which he wanted; supplied generally the material and sometimes the requisite plant: and by ever widening experience learnt how better to enlarge and economize the processes of marketing. He himself needed the power of going to the centre of each practical problem as it arose; concentrating the forces of his mind on it; working out connections between it and outlying considerations; developing practical conclusions with a just sense of proportion; and pursuing resolutely the line of policy thus indicated, but with a mind always alert for new ideas, especially such as were demanded by the changing circumstances and conditions of his problem. These are faculties which have been conspicuous in the Jewish race longer than in any other: but they were also such as could be, and were, quickly and strongly developed in that sturdy English character, of which the foundation had been laid by the sea-rovers.

On the other hand, the undertaker of the work and risks of organizing supply so as to meet and stimulate demand, was drawn on continually to become increasingly in some sense the employer of the homely producers whose work he controlled. The process by which he was developed into a capitalist manufacturer was gradual and continuous; and, when it was completed, his functions as a "master of men" rose to an equal level with his functions as an organizer of production and marketing. For this he needed qualities of mind and character somewhat similar to those of a capable captain of a ship trading on long voyages far from home: and these also were natural to the English and had been developed by their work in the world. Similar combinations of faculties were to be found in all the countries of Western Europe, and were afterwards to be conspicuous in North America. But Englishmen seem to have had a fuller and stronger supply of them than any other nation. I, III, 5.

Under the new conditions, all risks of marketing were borne by the capitalist trader, while the implements of production were supplied in some cases by the trader, and in others by the workers. When the trader supplied workshop or factory with its equipment, the industrial side of his services became more prominent, if not more difficult than the marketing side. He was therefore commonly and appropriately described as a manufacturer, rather than a merchant. This change in organization is commonly described as a transition from the "domestic" phase of industry to the "capitalistic." But a great deal of production, which is entirely under capitalistic control, is domestic; in the sense that the work is done by operatives in their own homes. The so-called "sweated" industries of the present time belong to this class; and it is well known that they give as large opportunity to the abuses of the power of capital as any others. It seems therefore best to avoid the use of the term "domestic"; and to contrast the man of means, knowledge and resources with the "homely" producer: that is, the man whose resources are so small, and *whose outlook is so narrow,* that he cannot obtain good access to general markets.

The primitive homely manufacturing producer corresponds to the peasant, who produces only for his own use and for sale to neighbours; while he can, at the same time, be fairly certain that such things as he needs will be brought within his reach by traders, without requiring him to have knowledge or contact with distant markets. He may himself be a small employer, providing for his assistants all the requisites of their work: but, as his capital is small, the capitalistic basis of his control over them is commonly ignored.

A great part of the homely industries of the country, at a later stage, were financed by capitalist traders to this extent at least that they undertook in advance to buy specified products at certain prices: that is to say the producer carried no considerable risks in regard to any particular contract, when once he had attained a fair security as to the prices he would pay for material and for such labour as he might require.

Arrangements of this kind existed early in the South of

I, III, 5. England cloth industry: and they became common elsewhere in the eighteenth century, when changes in the fashion and texture of goods and in the technique of industry were bewildering those who loved to tread in ancient paths: and they were giving great scope for new energetic men, well supplied with capital; who were also alert and fertile of suggestions for new patterns for home consumption, and for adjusting the new English resources to the tastes of foreign consumers, especially in the Levant and in Asia. Such arrangements were very suitable to transitional conditions; and are often regarded as peculiar to them. But in fact they are common at the present time. For instance, a capitalist builder often contracts to erect a house in accordance with definite specifications, at a certain price: the purchaser may intend to occupy the house, or he may be a merchant, sometimes inappropriately called a "speculator," who buys with the intention of letting or selling.

An almost equally familiar case is that of the textile manufacturer who contracts to deliver a quantity of some fabric, of quality and design selected by a merchant, at a certain price: though he often fortifies himself by buying in advance the materials which he will need. This method enables the merchant to turn to the fullest account his powers of contriving improved models, patterns, etc., of the goods of which he has attained a special knowledge; and also of anticipating the future course of demand, with reference to coming changes of fashion and taste, and to fluctuations of general economic prosperity. The producer on the other hand (who may be a man of rather narrower outlook, if not of homely disposition) gains by freedom to escape from a task for which he is not peculiarly fitted, and to give nearly his whole energies to the administration and technical work of making[1].

[1] Prof. Unwin, in reference to Prof. Westerfield's *Middlemen in English business, particularly between* 1660 *and* 1760, says:—"Simultaneity of integration and differentiation is to be found in the sixteenth century, and even in the Middle Ages, in all the more developed branches of industry and commerce. The fact is that where a series of independent capitals are employed in close contact with each other, any expansion of capital in one of the allied functions tends to an overflow into the neighbouring functions, and thus to one form or other of integration. The capital of the Hanseatic, Italian, or native exporter of cloth in the fifteenth century tended constantly to flow over into the *entrepreneur* functions; whilst, on the other hand, the prosperous clothier was always striving to become an exporting merchant" (*Economic Journal*, Dec. 1915).

It is of course to be understood that the changes now discussed moved gradually and irregularly. The rising sea seldom encroaches on the sand with uniform progress, even when the wind is nearly still: and in stormy weather the retrogression of a great wave may uncover the whole ground that belongs to the rise of the mean level of the sea during an hour. The economic atmosphere is never quite still, and it is often greatly perturbed: therefore progress is seldom uninterrupted.

6. *The financial structure of English agriculture and its influence on progress.*

For a long while agriculture and mining had been the only industries, except those connected with shipping, in which large capitals had been employed. In both of them nearly the whole of the capital needed had been drawn from the revenues of the territorial magnates, to whom the soil and the mineral strata below it alike belonged: and though, as has already been noted, mining took very early to joint stock finance, agriculture moved persistently on its old lines. The direct economies to be got by the aggregation of large areas of land under a single *management* were small and doubtful. But the *ownership* of a large area of land gave social prestige; and (especially in the hundred years ending with the Reform Bill of 1832) it gave political power and access to well paid posts under Government. It therefore attracted rich men, more particularly those who wished to buy their way into good society: and thus the aggregation of ownership tended to provide the land with an abundant supply of capital needed for the expensive improvements towards which agriculture was steadily making its way. "Farmer George" promoted the tendency to think that superfluous wealth might give a high return in the pleasure of owning a large property well developed, just as easily as in that of owning a castellated mansion. And though no outlay was approved by those whose opinion was most worth having, unless it aimed at a financial success, sufficient to lead other agriculturists in the same direction; yet men were willing to risk capital freely in experiments which might yield no good return, except in showing the way to others better conceived and more fruitful of gain.

I, III, 7. Some of these ventures must be tried in the first instance on "the home farm." But those which added to the value of the land and its buildings, and not merely to the current flow of stock or crop, could be safely made wholesale by the landowner for his tenants: the English system under which the tenant looks to the landlord for the provision of buildings and of capital to be sunk in the land was peculiarly appropriate to the transitional stage in which agriculture then was. Except in drainage, water supply and road making, it might be true that an additional £10,000 applied in the improvement of 1000 acres would not give better returns than £500 applied with equal skill and intelligence in the improvement of 50 acres: but, as things were, the £10,000 were more likely to be forthcoming for the large property than the £500 for the small; and on the whole they were likely to be applied with a broader intelligence, though perhaps not with as much care and knowledge as to details[1].

7. *The merging of England in Britain.*

Henceforward it will be best to speak not of England but of "Britain," as short for the "United Kingdom of England, Scotland and Ireland."

It is indeed true that the main trend of the industrial development of the eighteenth century and a considerable part of the nineteenth was the result of work done south of the Tweed. The great French war however fused England

[1] Of course this arrangement has its difficulties; as is shown by the agitations, which have recurred at intervals during more than a century on the part of tenant farmers, for increased security against the appropriation of the land: but on the whole there seems good reason to think that it will hold its own, when properly guarded, against all others, at all events on British soil.

As to the growth of the demand for large capitals on agriculture reference may be made to Mr R. E. Prothero's *English Farming*. He quotes (p. 206) from Arthur Young:—"Where is the little farmer to be found who will cover his whole farm with marl at the rate of 100 or 150 tons per acre? who will drain all his land at the expense of £2 or £3 an acre? who will pay a heavy price for the manure of towns, and convey it thirty miles by land carriage? who will float his meadows at the expense of £5 an acre? who, to improve the breed of his sheep, will give 1000 guineas for the use of a single ram for a single season? who will send across the kingdom to distant provinces for new implements, and for men to use them? who will employ and pay men for residing in provinces where practices are found which they want to introduce into their farms?"

and Scotland into a single country in sentiment and in action. I, III, 7.
The trade of Ireland was regarded in some measure as on a different footing from that of England, even after the goods sent from one to the other had ceased to be reckoned officially as "exported": but from the beginning of the nineteenth century England and Scotland had become, in fact as well as in name, a single country with one national spirit in regard to economic problems generally, and especially those which related to trade with the rest of the world. The chief agencies in this unification were roads, railroads, and common work in financial and colonial enterprise.

Late in the eighteenth century good roads began to connect the Lowlands of Scotland on the one hand with her own Highlands, and on the other with the Northern counties of England. The more potent influence of her railroads did not become effective till the middle of the nineteenth century: but meanwhile her banking had established its preeminence as a safe and efficient means for enabling a country with only a very little free capital, so to economize its use, that those, who were endowed with good business faculties, could generally obtain control of the means needed for giving them effect. The English system of banking was very inefficient in this direction; and Lancashire industries were largely financed by their own Bills of Exchange with but little aid from the banks. But the Bank of England was already the centre of stable international finance: and the Scotch system owed its combination of economy with efficiency to being able to lean on English support in international trade. This fact made for the commercial unity of the two countries more powerfully than appears on the surface: it went together with the security at home and on the seas, which both derived from the strength of the British navy and army.

But perhaps the strongest force making for unity was the leadership which the special bent of the Scotch genius, aided by a superb system of national education, achieved in pioneering the expansion of the British Empire. Scotchmen have had a much larger share, in proportion to their numbers, than Englishmen proper, in discovering what parts of the world offered the best field for western enterprise. They had com-

I, III, 7. paratively little share in the foundation of the early "Plantations": but they knew how to rise to difficulties, and how to make their way up from the ground till they stood at the top of great ventures; which, though often risky, have yielded very high returns. So they have grown rapidly in wealth: they hold high places in almost every part of "Greater Britain": and their influence in finance generally is more prominent than that of any other group of people of similar size, except the Jews of Western Europe, whose mental aptitudes are indeed in some respects similar to theirs. They are preeminently leaders in agriculture; where their widely diffused intelligence has long worked on lines similar to those on which Danish agriculture is being developed. Their manufacturing industries hold a high rank; while the ship-building on the Clyde, and that of the Scottish colony at Belfast, are unsurpassed. England and Scotland are now one.

Ireland, other than North Eastern Ulster, has suffered grievous wrongs; and has done not a little wrong herself. When England's tardy atonement for her wrong-doing has borne full fruit, Ireland may become, what she has never been yet, truly united to her: but the large economic developments, which may be hoped from that unity, lie beyond our present range. The fact, that she has already developed the economies of cooperative dairying in advance of most other countries, is one of many that are of good augury for her future.

CHAPTER IV

BRITAIN'S INDUSTRIAL LEADERSHIP: ITS LONG FREEDOM FROM CHALLENGE

1. *Characteristics of modern manufacturing processes.*

I, IV, 1.

The present chapter aims at setting out the essential difference between Britain's industrial leadership and those which preceded it; and at indicating the combination of causes which enabled it to endure long without effective challenge.

Let us look backwards a little, and forwards a little. The general features of the new industries were governed partly by technical causes, partly by the special circumstances of the time, and partly by the peculiar character of Englishmen. These three diverse influences made for the same result; viz. the massive production of things so uniform in substance and in shape as to give large scope for play of the economies, which the specialization of manual tasks had been developing for several centuries with ever increasing intensity throughout Western Europe. England lagged long behind; but she came up with her rivals in the seventeenth century, and was to pass them in the eighteenth.

When a cyclist is learning to ride, each adjustment needed to save him from falling demands the whole attention of his mind: and yet practice enables him to make such an adjustment, while thinking of other things and wholly unconscious of the unevenness in the road or the puff of side-wind which has demanded it. Again, as Prof. Bücher's *Arbeit und Rhythmus* has shown, musical rhythm has been called in to the aid of elementary industrial work by almost all races: and the Englishman, even when not specially musical, has ever been prone to an exact regularity of movement, a firm coordination of eye and hand, that have in them something of the rhythm as well as the regularity of machinery. The cross-bow was a nearer approach to a machine than the bow of an English archer: but the ceaseless flight of English arrows, each straight to its aim, was in some measure the mediaeval counterpart of the quick uniform flow of bullets from a modern machine gun.

In early times an Englishman's sturdy joy in the feeling that whatever his hand found to do, he did with all his might, had been mingled with, and marred by, a proud and dull contempt for whatever his hand had not as yet taken to: and he had been a slow learner from foreign artisans. In the eighteenth century he had not freed himself wholly from a dull sense of superiority: but he was much readier to learn than before: the Revocation of the Edict of Nantes in 1685 was a chief incident in a sustained policy of Continental autocrats, which rid them of sturdy subjects. More than half a million of the ablest of them came to England, bringing with them that knowledge of technique, which was most needed by her just at that time. In particular the Huguenots taught her to make many light glass and metal wares, in which French genius excelled: and in a very short time such wares, made by the coal which was then coming to England's aid, were being sent to France and sold at a good profit. She was then well on her way to "outrun her teachers," as Defoe said: she outpaced them in energy, and she outpaced them even more conspicuously in invention.

But England's chief strength lay in heavier industries, and the eighteenth century hardly sufficed to make ready for her chief work in her most appropriate material. For even at the end of the eighteenth century, the reduction of iron to standardized primary forms, suitable for further processes of standardized production, could not be effected easily, nor on a large scale.

The particular route on which English industrial tendencies found development was determined by the fact that textile materials are delivered by nature in standardized primary forms, well suited for massive change into standardized finished products. Cotton, wool and other fibres are fine homogeneous cylinders of different shapes. Cotton is flat, wool is round; but both lend themselves to be laid out in orderly array by machinery, and thus to be spun into yarn. Yarn is a homogeneous cylinder of uniform diameter and unlimited length, perfectly standardized: it is ready to be at once further worked up into standardized cloth by standardized machinery, which can be driven by the blind force of nature, being dependent on the guidance of intelligent fingers only in its minor details. This is the fundamental cause of the series of quick leaps, by which machine-made textiles bounded beyond the reach of the competition of more primitive forms of industry; and thus set the type of that method which spread first over nearly all England's industries, and in the course of time over those of other western countries.

The essence of the method was to watch the action of the human hand in fingering the wool and in twisting, and drawing out the yarn; or in throwing the shuttle, and making the weft lie compact; or in hammering or drilling iron; or in any other operation that needed to be performed many times in the same way. Next the work was divided into two parts, that which was absolutely monotonous, and that which had an element of variety. That which was various was left provisionally on one side to be still done by hand: that which was monotonous was further studied, broken up into parts each of which was a simple movement of the finger, or the hand. It was known that all work of that kind could be done by a wooden or steel finger or crank of some sort; the only question was whether the trouble of isolating one or more of those tasks and making a separate machine for them would be adequately remunerated.

But that was a vast undertaking, not to be fully grasped at once: its difficulties will indeed never cease. In the early nineteenth century it had not made very great way: the automatic agencies, which play a great part now in spinning mills and weaving sheds, had not been developed: there was still a great deal of purely mechanical work to be done, which demanded no strength, no discretion, and not even a very high degree of promptitude. Thus there were opened out, as the aggregate output increased, a disproportionally large number of opportunities for the work of young children; and as the new demand appeared in the first instance chiefly in places where the settled population was scanty, this demand had very disastrous results[1].

Mechanical standardization spread from one process to another in the same industry, and from one industry to another. And gradually it was found that the machines, adjusted to standardized work, helped one another; because the uniformity of the product, when it left one machine, suited it for being operated by the next. So progress went on cumulatively. Each step forward made the next simpler; and by slow steps were evolved the root notions of those semi-automatic machines of the present day, each of which performs a great many operations one after another on the material fed into it. Thus the links which had to be filled in by hand work became constantly fewer and shorter, till in some branches of industry there was

[1] In Book II attention will be drawn to modern developments of mechanical technique, which turn on the power of a machine to use many hands instead of two, and to perform operations beyond the reach of human hands. Wool was the material to which the chief inventions were first applied. Even as late as 1783, cotton cost 16*d.* a pound, and yet the value of the woollen (including worsted) products of England was then nearly twenty times as great as that of her cottons. The export of her cottons surpasses that of her woollens early in the nineteenth century: but the total value of her cotton products did not pass that of her woollens. (For further facts see Ellison, *Cotton Trade of Great Britain*, ch. x.) The influence of early improvements in textile manufacture was therefore most conspicuous in regard to wool.

The history of textile inventions and their results is in brief as follows: Kay's Fly Shuttle and Paul's spinning by rollers began in 1738 a series of inventions as to spinning; which was continued by Hargreave's spinning jenny, Arkwright's improvements in detail, and Crompton's spinning mule (1779). These together gradually increased the facilities for spinning so much that yarn was superabundant; for indeed "one spinner in 1812 could produce as much in a given time as 200 could have produced before the invention of Cartwright's jenny." (Ellison, *l.c.* p. 56.) Consequently weavers' skill rose for a time to a relatively high value: and a vast number of them invested their capital in hand looms and in attaining a skilful mastery of them. But in 1785 Cartwright's power loom initiated a reversal of this process. The hand loom held its own for a long while: partly because the power loom was slow to learn how to coax the weft to lie compactly on the warp: but the hand loom weavers saw their employment gradually leave them, till in 1840 few but old or obstinate men remained in the industry. The loss of employment by the hand spinners had not been very seriously felt: because they had little specialized skill, and many of them had some alternative employment: but the fate of the hand loom weavers was very tragical. Meanwhile the power loom, added to the hand loom, had been able to absorb all the vast output of yarn—except such as was exported—turned out by the steam spinning mills: and that caused a disproportionate demand for children's labour, which was to become a national calamity of the first order.

little for the human hand to do, except to act as a kind of overseer over the machines that were its servants. Traces of the method can indeed be found in nearly all mechanical work, almost from the dawn of civilization: but England applied it so systematically, with so much resource, and to tasks of such magnitude as to make it her own.

The demands of foreign armies, not excluding the French, for strong solid cloth of standardized pattern, gave a great stimulus to the massive production of her woollen factories. And the vast consumption of large and small arms, and their ammunition, added much to the value of mechanical appliances for the wholesale manufacturer of metal products, each of standardized form and fitting accurately with others[1].

Thus production became ever more massive; till at last a single business required so extensive a plant, so large an operative staff and so plentiful resources as to be beyond the range of any but a powerful capitalist (or a union of small capitalists in joint stock or "cooperation").

This last stage developed slowly. British water power came generally in such small driblets as not to facilitate the erection of very large factories even in the textile industries. Massive production in the full sense of the word was a creation of steam power: and, as we are to see shortly, the total steam power used in manufactures (the mining and smelting industries being left out of account) did not become very important till the second quarter of the nineteenth century. By that time railways had become no mean competitors with factories in the consumption of coal: and were beginning to become the chief factor of those conveniences of marketing, without which massive production (in the full sense of the term) could not have been developed[2].

[1] Sombart's *Krieg und Kapitalismus* develops this and other relations between war and capitalistic concentration.

[2] The textile industries in 1839 used steam engines of 74,000 h.p. and water wheels, etc., of 23,000 h.p.: in 1907 they used engines mainly based on steam power, of 2,000,000 h.p., and this was but a quarter of the total h.p. in industrial uses, other than mining. The conclusion that in 1839, the textile industries were the chief users (mining again being left out) of steam machinery is suggested by the fact that even in 1851 they owned three-fourths of all the factories which employed more than 350 persons. See *Census Report* for 1851, vol. I. pp. cclxxvi—cclxxix.

I, IV, 2. 2. *The massive results at which English inventions were aimed, called for simplicity in method and machinery: but that could seldom be reached without working patiently through complexity. Nearly all of them were associated with uses of coal and iron in making and driving the new appliances.*

Although coal and iron were not the original causes of England's leadership, yet all that makes that leadership unique in the world's history was partly dependent on them. Without them she could at best have attained a prominence like that of Holland, and on a rather larger scale. With their mighty aid, she has pioneered so strongly, that the leading ideas of those mechanical industries which are transforming the world to-day are fundamentally hers. But iron, the material of all these industries, was largely used in England because she had large uses for it; though she had not a plentiful supply of it.

Iron is the great saver of time, and the chief engine of thorough solid work; as well as the chief material of those subtle and powerful engines and instruments, in which modern invention has found its scope. Its strength, efficiency, and perhaps its hardness, were appropriate to that sturdy resolute Norse character; which, having been revived by Puritanism, was working under the surface, even when the higher ranks of society were dissolute. So the English insisted on having iron at all cost. To make it, they burned down their own oak forests and those of Ireland, till their supply of new ships was imperilled: and then they bought it from abroad, in spite of its high price, so insistently that they consumed seven times as much per head as the rest of Europe[1].

[1] In 1740 it was fifteen pounds against two annually on the Continent. See Sir J. Guest's evidence before the Committee on Import Duties in 1840. Thanks to her Norman conquerors, English smiths had early been famous. But in the Middle Ages her lack of metallurgical skill caused iron to be nearly as costly as brass and tin; so that its use could hardly be afforded in farm implements and carts. Blast furnaces were introduced early in the fifteenth century, and England soon did a large export trade in iron cannon. Late in the seventeenth century her supply of oak for smelting ran short; and in 1740 her output of iron was but 17,000 tons. Iron was smelted by coal on a small scale by the German Sturtevant in 1612; and by the English Dudley in 1621. Darby developed it a century later. Roebuck's improved blast came in 1760; Cort's rolling mills and puddling process about 1783.

It was not till the middle of the eighteenth century that some old inventions for smelting iron by coal bore much practical fruit. But from that time onward English agriculture and manufacture have had practically unlimited supplies of the main implement needed in economizing human labour, and in applying the force of waterfalls and steam power to the heaviest and to many of the most delicate tasks of industry.

A special bent of the English genius had shown itself in the multitude of operations to which water power, often supplemented by horse power, had been turned. But the steam engine, before Watt's improvements, was too wasteful and awkward to be applied except for pumping and similar work. And so great was the leakage of steam from imperfect cylinders, that his inventions by themselves would have failed to make steam power very cheap; if Boulton had not trained up a generation of mechanics, and of master mechanics, who could make cylinders and pistons true. The work of Boulton and Watt belongs wholly to the age of iron; it would have found no place in the age of wood[1].

Wood had indeed been the chief material by which Holland had worked her way; and wood was till recently the material of the ships that bore England's commerce. But her complete emancipation from tutelage coincided with and was largely caused by her mastery of iron. Her exports of iron products have never approached in value her exports of textile goods; and yet it was in iron industries, and not in textile that the force of her character was most fully shown. And indeed the later and more complex, though not the earlier and simpler, stages of her progress in the textile industries depended on the mastery of iron, and have been thought out largely by workers in iron.

The leading characteristic of English inventions has not

[1] Arthur Young in his *Tour through the North of England*, 1770 (vol. III. p. 14), tells us about the Crawley works at Newcastle "supposed to be the greatest manufactory of the kind in Europe," where they made anchors weighing 70 cwt.: and there were to be seen "copper rollers for squeezing bars into hoops, scissors for cutting bars of iron, turning cranes for moving anchors into and out of the fire, and the beating hammer lifted by the cogs of a wheel." These were "all moved by water."

I, IV, 2. been their ingenuity. For indeed the mechanical clocks and other automata of Byzantium and of Germany and France showed an ingenuity, increasing through several centuries up to the eighteenth; which has not been surpassed, if it has been equalled, in England. But each was a separate work of a master mechanic. Even late in the eighteenth century, the resources of mechanical engineering did not reach out to the making of complex machinery on a large scale, which could be depended on to do its part without fail, quickly, and at the right time; and thus create new master-pieces with little aid from the human hand[1].

Another special bent of English genius showed itself in the resolution with which inventors sought simplicity: their ingenuity had not completed its task until it had effaced nearly all traces of itself, and left behind no detail that was not apparently simple. Such complexity as remains is chiefly in the organization of the factory itself as a whole, and in the adaptation of each part to others with which it needed to cooperate.

Massiveness of work has some drawbacks from the social point of view. But it made England powerful: it carried her through the great French war, and enabled her to subsidize nations with greater natural resources than her own. And incidentally it gave her for a long time almost a monopoly of industrial invention. She moved forwards, the rest of the world followed.

The English inventor was at an advantage in being able to make a long series of working models of each invention; and to improve and simplify them, till they were bound to conquer in competition with hand work: but the German or the Frenchman could not. The Englishman could afford to sink capital in experiments more easily than they could. For he had access to a great variety of highly skilled artisans, with a growing stock of engines capable of work more exact than the work of the

[1] Nevertheless it seems probable that as much hard thought went into the chronometer of the Englishman, John Harrison, in the middle of the eighteenth century, as into many huge toy clocks. The list of England's early debts to foreign inventors, especially in regard to mining, has been somewhat enlarged by W. H. Price's *English patents of monopoly*. An instructive account of England's economic development during this period of the mechanical inventions is given by Dr Clapham in *The Cambridge Modern History*, vol. x

human hand: thus every experiment cost him less; and it was executed more quickly, and far more truly, than it could have been anywhere else. When at last success had been fully achieved, the new contrivance could be manufactured more cheaply; and could be applied in production on a scale far greater, than in any other country.

The methods of industry changed so fast that the son of a wealthy manufacturer, who had not exceptional energy and adaptability, soon found himself undersold by rugged but powerful men; whom the banks were ever ready to furnish with the capital needed for a quick rise from the artisans' bench to a post of command.

Such men, in spite of their conspicuous limitations, were admirably qualified to deal with simple direct problems of organization, and adaptation of mechanical means to ends; and the high incomes, which they commonly earned, were but a low price for their services to production. They retained their old simple habits, sometimes even eating the plainest food out of a common bowl with their operatives; and they often added nearly the whole of their net incomes to their capital. The manufacturing industry of England was thus favoured for a long time, and on a great scale, by a large supply of high class ability, which was exactly adapted to its needs; while it was to be had for a relatively low price because it had no access to any other opening for its ambitions except mere business.

The industrial energies of Englishmen were not indeed entirely given to the organization of their own work in control of the forces of nature. They achieved a striking success in pottery under the guidance of Wedgwood, without the aid of any important new mechanical device; but rather by that delicacy of perception which had become conspicuous at various times in their wood-carving and other decorative industries, as well as in their literature.

And, with all, agriculture remained their chief industry; their gentry threw equal energy into the chase of the fox and of improved methods of farming. In agriculture, as in manufacture, they aimed at large measures, by which Nature might be induced to use her forces on a great scale in their behalf. This was shown by Bakewell and others, who realized that a relatively small amount of labour directed to improving the fountain-heads of a great breed of stock, would yield an abundantly increasing return. And it was shown by Coke and others, who organized improved rotations; and—what was no less important—turned horse power to account in altering the character of the land, and making clay soils porous and strengthening sandy soils; and again in drawing horse hoes to clean crops that had been sown with mechanical precision. For good and evil they were apt to disdain the Continental peasant's hand work, and his patient care for petty details: the ruinous tendency of the farmer's wife to withdraw herself from the work of the dairy and other light labour had not then become prominent[1].

3. ***The great war retarded Britain's economic progress: but it threw other European countries back, and so strengthened her leadership.***

Recent developments of Britain's foreign trade will be considered in the second Volume: but a little must be said here as to the external influences which were acting on her industry towards the end of the eighteenth century and in the first quarter of the nineteenth.

Her ever growing mastery of the forces of nature and of technique did not make wholly for the increase of her foreign trade. In so far as it promoted her efficiency in those industries in which she was already leading, it did indeed enable her to put more of her goods on foreign markets at a profit to herself: and thus it increased her trade. But in so far as it lessened her relative disadvantage in the production of those things which she had been accustomed to import, it checked her imports, and therefore her exports; and her trade increased less fast than it otherwise would have done[2].

[1] As late as 1850, 92,000 out of a total of 225,000 farmers in England and Wales (*i.e.* 41 per cent.) employed no hired labour: 8000 employed ten or more; while 5000 employed 20 or more. (See the *Census Report*, 1851, vol. I p. lxxix.)

[2] For instance, the application of improved pumping and lifting machinery to England's salt mines brought her salt industry from its backward place. She no longer depended on the evaporation of sea water by the sun; and her lack of the powerful sun of the Mediterranean Coast no longer gave her an import trade in salt: later on, she obtained a relative advantage and began to export it. Huguenot immigrants, having taught her to make many light textile, glass

Again the growing richness of her home markets lowered the cost of production of those of her exports which conformed to the law of Increasing Return, and therefore enabled her to sell more of them abroad. But it acted in the opposite way with regard to wheat: and her exports of that dwindled away in the later years of the eighteenth century. As soon as her population had once outgrown her small territory, and had become dependent on imported food, every further increase in its numbers increased her foreign trade in wheat; except in so far as it was counteracted either by restrictions on importation, or by improvements in her own arts of cultivation. The one raised the cost of imported wheat and impoverished her people; the other lowered the cost of home grown wheat and enriched her people: but the two affected her foreign trade in much the same way.

By the end of the eighteenth century the process of weeding out her imports of those things, which she had learnt to produce for herself, was nearly complete. Henceforward her industrial advances were almost exclusively in industries in which she was already leading: and, therefore, except when they were checked by heavy import or export duties at home or abroad, they added more to her foreign trade than to her general prosperity: that is, they increased the percentage of her home products which she exported.

And further her growing exports of her cotton, and other goods made of imported material, increased her foreign trade much more than in proportion to the value of the work she incorporated in them: because the value of that raw material, as to which she was only middleman, entered into her trade twice, first as an import and afterwards as an export; whereas the values of her exports of wool and iron, which were wholly products of her industry, entered only once.

The period of the great French war is very instructive as regards monetary policy, but not as regards trade. For, indeed, the course of trade was governed largely by military exigencies,

and metal goods which she had previously bought from the French, her trade in some of these goods was almost suspended for a time: but later on, when she was sending these goods to France, her growing skill in small metal work increased her trade. These facts, and several which follow, illustrate general principles discussed above, I, II, 1.

I, IV, 3. and by the success with which smugglers and others could evade customs officers and Napoleon's cruisers. Partly for this reason it varied violently and irregularly: while the import and export statistics cannot be trusted, and cannot even be interpreted accurately. It seems, however, clear that England's total exports expanded more slowly during the war than before it; and that they consisted to an increasing extent of re-exports of tropical produce, in which England's command of the seas gave her almost a monopoly. The economic value of this monopoly was indeed overrated at the time, and has been overrated since, in spite of Pitt's protest[1].

The war impoverished the Continent, even more than England, and therefore did not lessen the *relative* advantage, which she had obtained before the war, in those manufacturing industries which required a large stock of capital. Whatever of lasting economic effect it produced, was perhaps mainly through its indirect influence in arresting her social and political development, and even causing some reaction.

English manufacturers had counted on finding eager foreign markets after the peace, but they were disappointed. The countries, which had been the scenes of the war, turned their energies to repairing its devastation: but, as iron was then very little used for structural purposes, England's exports were not in demand for them. There was a slightly increased demand for ordinary metal and textile goods: but that did little more than compensate for the cessation of the demand for clothing and other necessaries by armies in the field. Thus English manufacturers were really poorer than they had expected to be; and the fall in general prices, which followed the destructive war, made them seem poorer than they were. But the springs of prosperity were growing fast during those years when people were most sad, and largely because they were sad. Twice indeed they let their hopes get the better of their judgment. They

[1] He computed that in 1798 England's foreign commerce yielded to the merchants and others engaged in it a gross income of £12,000,000, and a net income of £3,000,000. (Lowe, *State of England*, ed. of 1822, pp. 24—28 and Appendix 4—8.) It may be noted that Oddy (*Analysis of European Commerce*, 1805, VII. ii) says that before the war "the French had greatly more of the West India trade than we, and could undersell us on the Continent."

boldly exported goods to the Continent in 1815, and to South America in 1824—5. But in neither case could the goods be marketed profitably. The crises of 1816 and 1826 however sobered the impetuous, and strengthened the resolute. Men worked hard, and lived sparely: so capital grew apace[1].

I, IV, 3.

Capital was needed in ever increasing quantity by the new developments of industry. For, though the stream of inventions involving fundamentally new ideas had somewhat slackened, yet improvements in detail flowed in at an ever increasing rate. And the old inventions as well as the new made incessant demands for fresh capital: partly because, as a rule, about a generation passed after the fundamental idea of a new invention had been grasped, before it was ready for general use. Very often indeed another generation elapsed before the details had been so far perfected, and the general organization of the manufacture had been so far adapted to its powers and requirements, that it could take its proper place in industry. Thus the demand for capital in manufacturing and other industries increased constantly throughout the nineteenth century; partly because the constructive ideas of one, two, or even more previous generations, were simultaneously growing more powerful, more economical, more adapted to large production and more hungry for fresh resources[2].

[1] The great French economist, Say, made a tour in England at the close of the war; and he was filled with wonder, almost with horror, at the intense, restless industry of all classes of Englishmen. "Everybody runs, absorbed in his own affairs. Those who allow themselves the smallest relaxation from their labours are promptly overtaken by ruin" (p. 12 of the English edition of his *Notes*). He finds the explanation of this hardness of life in his estimate that "the Government had consumed one-half of the produce of the soil, the capital, and the industry of the English people," *ibid.* p. 21.

[2] Thus in spinning, the fundamental idea of spinning by rollers came in 1730, but was not made efficient for nearly forty years. By 1780 the spinning mule was in operation; and the great fall in the cost of spinning a pound of yarn came some time after 1784. Deduction being made of the price of the raw cotton, this cost fell from nine shillings to one (for medium counts) between 1784 and 1812. The power loom had been invented at the beginning of this period, but was not made efficient till the end of it: and during the same interval the scarcity of raw cotton had been gradually relieved by the growth of a new source of supply in the Southern States of America. Consequently the cotton industry increased more than five-fold during the next generation; and by the middle of the century it had absorbed not much less than a hundred millions of capital.

I, IV, 4. And gradually a change in the nature of the investment of capital showed itself. It is well known that in early times the chief forms of immovable capital were improvements in land and houses; and the chief forms of movable capital were farm stock and merchants' stores and ships. The water-driven textile and other machinery of the eighteenth century absorbed an amount of capital which went beyond previous experience, but was yet very small relatively to the demands of the nineteenth century.

In the second quarter of the nineteenth century the value of the implements of production which were chiefly made of iron, began to outrun that of the current stocks of materials to which they were applied. The value of factories and other business premises began to rival that of houses. Coal-mining took a place in the front rank of industries, and the building of railways absorbed more new capital than any other industry[1].

4. *In the second quarter of the nineteenth century the growth of railways helped to consolidate England's industries, and to expand her trade.*

In 1825, when Stephenson's locomotive had not won its great triumph on the Stockton and Darlington Railway, a Committee of the House of Commons published a Report setting forth the nature of England's industrial leadership, and its chief causes; and among these it already found a high place for railways; though they were then worked by horses, or in a few cases by stationary engines[2].

[1] The only definite statistics available as to the distribution of capital expenditure relate to joint stock companies: of course manufacture was almost entirely in the hands of individuals and private firms. But it is interesting to note that the new joint stock capital of the expansive years 1834—6 amounted to a hundred and thirty-five millions, of which seventy were for railways, seven for mines, eight for canals and navigation, and the rest chiefly for finance and miscellaneous. See Levi's *History*, p. 220.

[2] The subject of the Report is the advisability of removing the restrictions on the exportation of tools and machinery. It owns that all well-known kinds of machinery can be produced abroad without great difficulty; and that to prohibit or put difficulties in the way of their exportation is in effect to give an educative bounty to the growing manufactures of machinery of our rivals. And on the other hand the price, which such manufacturers are willing to pay for drawings or specimens of new contrivances, was so high as to much more than cover the premium which insurance companies charged for guaranteeing its safe exportation in spite of prohibition. The Report proceeds to argue, that in

But from 1825 onwards a new impetus to England's economic freedom, mobility, and energy was given by the opening of a railway on which coal and other goods were to be hauled by a locomotive; though passengers were to ride in single coaches drawn by horses.

The steps, by which Stephenson had made the engine a practical success, were characteristically English; and so were the uses to which it was put. Steam railways suited the English temper; and the configuration of England was specially suited for their early work. There was no place in the world where they could get at once so heavy and remunerative a traffic as between her various industrial districts, and from them to London. So small are the distances between the chief centres of industry that the six thousand miles of railways that were open in 1850 connected nearly all the chief towns and industrial districts of England and Scotland. They carried goods and passengers at charges which were much lower than those demanded by other means of fairly rapid transport, though they were high when measured by modern standards. They enabled perishable goods to travel far; and thus raised the price of many things to the producer, while lowering them to the consumer.

They saved time and fatigue in travel. They enabled the head of a large business, even if pressed for time and weighted by years, to keep its outlying connections firmly in hand. They

spite of the fact that it is impossible to prevent foreigners from using our best machinery, yet it can always be a little ahead of theirs; and we can hold our own. "Our minerals have a neighbourhood, whence, from the proximity of railroads, canals, and rivers, they may be conveyed with great facility to all parts of the kingdom, either for home manufacture or exportation. Almost all our great manufacturing towns, and establishments for the construction of machines, enjoy similar facilities; and thus, with the continual improvement of machinery, enable us to keep down the cost of production....The freedom, which under our government every man has, to use his capital, his labour, and his talents, in the manner most conducive to his interests, are inestimable advantages; canals are cut, and railroads constructed, by the voluntary association of persons whose local knowledge enables them to place them in the most desirable situations, and these great advantages cannot exist under less free governments. These circumstances, when taken together, give such a decided superiority to our people, that no injurious rivalry either in the construction of machinery or the manufacture of commodities can reasonably be anticipated" (pp. 12, 16 of the Report).

The history of British railways and canals is considered in Book III in connection with the relations of monopolies to national advantage.

I, IV, 4. were aided by parallel developments of the banking system, the newspaper, the telegraph, and the postal service, in all of which England was ahead of her Continental rivals: and they gave her for a time a preeminence in the concentrated force of her internal trade and industry, and therefore of her external trade, to which nothing in the history of the world had been comparable except the force which Holland derived from her waterways. They strengthened her industry in just those respects in which it already had differential advantages, and thus increased her foreign trade even more than in proportion[1].

In the second quarter of the nineteenth century the Continent of Europe was no longer devastated by wars. Industry was increasingly secure and free. English manufacturing methods were introduced by English artisans, working machinery that had been bought in England, or made on English models; and in many cases, capital, managing capacity, and operatives were supplied from England. For enterprise was still timid, especially in regard to railway and other industries which were still unfamiliar. Thus at last England repaid to the Continent services which Holland had rendered to her, when her low-lying lands were drained by Dutch capital, Dutch engineers, and Dutch workmen. The Continental demand for railway material, however financed, opened out a good vent for England's (or, rather, Britain's) iron products; though by this time her iron-masters found some strong rivals in Belgium and elsewhere. These new railways facilitated her foreign trade generally, in spite of the pressure of high duties on almost every frontier.

Her trade, and therefore also her industries, were promoted also by great further improvements in the art of ship-building. But here the initiative came from America: and the history of Britain's shipping was not altogether creditable to her. The volume of her tonnage reached a maximum at the end

[1] Other causes aided. The telegraph began to be a considerable force about 1840; just when the penny postage had been forced on a reluctant Government by the energy of Rowland Hill. The first electric cable to France was laid in 1850. The newspaper stamp was reduced from 4*d.* to 1*d.* a sheet in 1836; and it remained at a penny till 1855. The advertisement duty was reduced from 3*s.* 6*d.* to 1*s.* 6*d.* in 1833, but was not abolished till 1853. The tax on paper was reduced in 1835 and 1839, but not abolished till 1861

of the great war, when she had a real monopoly of much maritime traffic: though her monopoly of trade was less complete than is often supposed, and of course a large part of her shipping was engaged in the service of the war. That level was not reached again till 1840. For indeed the Navigation Acts, which professed to foster the growth of British shipping, had been counteracted by considerable duties on Colonial timber; and by heavy duties on foreign timber, which in the absence of preference would have been much cheaper. The world's stock of shipping was indeed increasing; so that Britain's trade was promoted by low freights. But she herself built very little more tonnage annually than her Colonies did; and the shipping of the United States grew rapidly till it passed hers about 1850, just as the last vestiges of the Navigation Laws were repealed and the almost prohibitory duties on foreign timber were reduced to a moderate level[1].

5. *The growth of factories made prominent the evils inherent in crude capitalistic control, but was not largely responsible for them.*

The "Industrial Revolution" in that special use of the term, in which it is limited to the end of the eighteenth century and the first third of the nineteenth, is sometimes associated with the supersession of the merchant undertaker by the capitalist manufacturer: and the large factory is apt to be taken as the centre of that capitalistic exploitation of labour which Karl Marx denounced as characteristic of the modern age. But the ground taken by Marx himself is broader than that: for he says: "Capitalistic production only then begins, when each individual capital employs simultaneously a comparatively large number of labourers[2]."

[1] The Navigation Acts incidentally forbade American produce to be brought to Britain save in British ships: and, as America copied these Acts, both British and American ships had as a rule to cross the ocean one way empty. But the treaty of 1815 secured equal freedom to the ships of the two countries in each other's ports. The operation of the Acts in their later stages was complex, and raised some specially intricate questions in regard to reciprocity. At the end, as at the beginning, much thought was given to their bearing on the supply of men for the Navy. See Dr Clapham in *The English Historical Review*, 1910.

[2] He adds: "The labourer can sell no more than what he has—*i.e.* his indi-

I, IV, 5. We saw in Chapter III how the ever increasing distance of the operative producer both from the sources of supply of his material, and from the ultimate purchasers of his product, rendered him increasingly dependent on capitalist merchants for employment. The dependence was direct and obvious when he worked up his own material in his own cottage. It was less direct and obvious when he worked for a small employer, whose resources were so small and whose outlook was so narrow, that he could not afford to carry much stock and could not obtain good direct access to general markets: but it was not much less thorough; for if the merchants could not, or would not, accept the product on terms which enabled the small masters of a neighbourhood to pay the current rates of wages, the operatives would commonly be forced either to submit to a reduction, or to go short of employment.

Moreover a small master was generally in a position to know the necessities of each worker; and he was often tempted to take advantage of that knowledge. In fact the system of work for such masters, themselves under the control of capitalist merchants, is familiarly described now as the "sweating" sys-

vidual isolated labour power....The capitalist buys the labour power of 100 men, and enters into separate contracts with 100 unconnected men instead of with one....He pays them the value of 100 independent labour powers, but he does not pay for the combined labour power of the hundred" (*Capital*, vol. I. pp. 311 and 323 of Engel's English edition, 1883; pp. 285 and 297 of the sixth German edition). We must not stay now to consider all the implications of this argument. As is well known, he suggests that the capitalist employer obtains a "Surplus Value," consisting of all excess of production of 100 men working "cooperatively" with all the economy and efficiency of subtle organization, over a hundred times the production of an isolated workman. He is not troubled by the fact that in some industries the "cooperative" efficiency of the hundred is more than twenty times their efficiency when working in isolation: and that in such cases the employer would, on Marx's showing, receive in profits about twenty times as much as he pays in wages; whereas, in many such industries, the net profits are in fact not a tenth of the wages bill.

It will be argued in the second Volume that so long as there is active competition among employers, each will be forced to pay as wages the equivalent of the net value that the hundred men, working cooperatively, add to the product: *net*, that is after deducting all other expenses incurred in the production, together with profits on the whole at a rate which, on the average, diminishes slowly from generation to generation. Thus the main benefits of the efficiency of "cooperative" production accrue to the consumers: that is, to the working classes, *in so far as the industry is occupied either directly or indirectly in producing commodities or services which are consumed by them.*

tem; because it is commonly believed that a crude employer with small capital, suffering under pressure from above, will resort without remorse to measures more harsh and petty than any for which the large employer has, as a rule, either the inclination or the opportunity. Recent investigations have however proved that this common opinion goes too far: it does injustice to a class of men, many of whom work hard for low gains, and are by no means lacking in human sympathies. The employment of children at an excessively early age was common under the domestic system: and, though they were for the greater part under the protection of their parents, yet on the whole the evidence seems to show that they were often treated by their parents more cruelly than the great majority of the children in factories were. It is important to remember that workmen, who were paid (directly or indirectly) by the piece, often handled their young assistants barbarously[1].

[1] Defoe was envious of the Flemish because their manufactures had kept the people so busy that hardly a child above five years old, but could do something to earn its bread: he says that Henry VII when in exile (*i.e.* before 1485) had been set by this on considering the great injury that could be done to them by stinting the supply of English wool (*Plan of English Commerce*, p. 126). And in 1671 Chamberlayne reported that in Norwich children from six to ten years of age have earned £12,000 more than they spend, chiefly by knitting fine stockings. See Hull's footnote to p. 308 of his edition of Petty's *Works*.

The elder W. Cooke Taylor (*Tour in the Manufacturing Districts of Lancashire*, 1842, p. 145) reports how a very old man told him that in the days when spinning was yet done by hand, and yarn was scarce, and "the spinners were the masters of the weavers...were really the days of infant slavery," adding: "the creatures were set to work as soon as they could crawl, and their parents were the hardest of task masters." The old man with characteristic lack of reason "was indignant at the clamour which had been raised for infant protection" which led up to Lord Ashley's great Act of 1844; and contrasted his own hard life with "the light toil and positive comfort of the factory children." See also Hutchins and Harrison, *History of Factory Legislation*, ch. I. Popular history underrates the hardships of the people before the age of factories.

The chief collection of material bearing on the subject is in the great *Report on the Employment of Children in Factories*, 1832—4, by a Commission under the presidency of Tooke, the great economist. It lays bare the grievous sufferings and waste of life caused by very long hours, and the cruel discipline which was thought necessary to induce the weary children to continue on the move; and the Commissioners and Sub-Commissioners are agreed in calling for vigorous State intervention. But stress is laid on the fact that in many kinds of hand labour "manufacturers" (the word being used in its original sense) "work hard from twelve to fifteen hours a day to earn a bare subsistence; and this frequently from a very early age, and in a state of confinement which may be truly called injurious to health" (*Second Report*, p. 6). The evidence also shows

I, IV, 5. It appears clear therefore that other causes must have cooperated with the extension of the factory system to make the fate of manufacturing workers generally, and of children in particular, as hard as it certainly was during the two generations in which the system was taking its present shape: there were in fact many causes acting powerfully in that direction. The first of these causes was a continued increase in the rate of the growth of population: it was itself partly the result of the constantly increasing separation of the labourer from the land; and it widened that separation still further. For a time harsh Settlement regulations put hindrance in the way of marriage; but they could not be maintained effectively, and the population of England nearly doubled between 1801 and 1841. The deep significance of this increase at a time when modern provisions for the comfort of large densely populated lands was unknown, is indicated by the fact that, if its rate had been maintained for four centuries, the population would have multiplied a thousand-fold in that time: and a million-fold in eight centuries.

Other causes of distress were the growing changefulness and instability of employment: these were mainly attributable to war; and to the violent fluctuation of prices, especially of wheat, which resulted from it: to the growing separation of the producer from the ultimate market for his wares: to that increase of speculative trading, often on a relatively small foundation of capital, which collapsed in an exceptionally rapid succession of disastrous commercial crises; and lastly to the increasing dependence of the cotton and other industries on sales in countries so distant that news from them was several months on its way.

This drift towards unsteadiness of employment did not affect uniformly all industries, nor even all parts of the same

that the worst cruelties were confined to a relatively small number of factories: though frequently practised by overlookers, by far the greater part of them were wrought by ordinary workmen on their assistants; *e.g.* by cotton spinners on piecers and scavengers (*First Report*, p. 45). Mr Tufnell states that the expensive setting up of machines for carrying off dust from the card-rooms and scutching-rooms, and ventilating by fans, and substituting a direct supply of steam for the old plan of raising the whole rooms to an unhealthy temperature by huge fires, had been effected in representative *large* factories, *though not then prescribed by law* (*Supplementary Report*, Part I. p. 227).

industry. It has already been noticed that there was a time, at which hand loom weavers were ever pressing spinners for more yarn; another, at which the spinning mills, driven by water power, could furnish more yarn than those weavers could use; and a third, at which hand-weavers were left almost without any remunerative work. And further, as Rogers observed, the transition from farm work to factory work made the employment of women more steady, without raising their wages when employed. But it made the employment of men less steady, even in those industries in which they were not largely ousted by women and children. Hired men have always been wont to spend their harvest wages unwisely; though the peasant owner has seldom thrown aside his traditionary caution. The employee of a manufacturer who works for an uncertain market, is apt to have frequent harvest-like orgies of work and high pay, followed by long intervals of low-paid work or idleness: and, if it happens that his wife and children are in relatively steady work, he is likely to squander his high wages. Thus families in the manufacturing districts, whose aggregate earnings were twice as high as those of families at work on farms, often lived in greater squalor.

This brings us to the darkest spot in the dark field of the struggle of the factory system with a crude and immature mechanical technique. The centre of the evil lay in the fact that much of the work done on the new methods was within the range of even young children. Later on the machinery became more massive, and adult males won back from both women and children many of the operations, that had taken the place of the old male artisan labour; and thus technical changes facilitated the good work of factory laws. But there is much pathos in the story of the older artisans, who lost the capital value of all the skill invested in them, and did not live long enough to see that later stage[1].

[1] The simplicity of the first machines adapted for spinning, and their small size, fitted them for being tended by children. The mills were by the side of small streams, and had but little local supply of labour: and in the early period of mill labour, apprentices from six to twelve years of age were prominent among the workers. Gradually a local population grew up, and apprentices gave place to the children of neighbouring cottages. Later on, steam power drew the factories into the broad valleys and the towns. The machines for spinning

I, IV, 5. The technical conditions of the early textile factories; the war; the high price of bread; the rough manners of the crude, vigorous, keen-witted men, risen from the ranks, who had outpaced and superseded the older race of employers; and, last but not least, the ineptitude of the governing classes in legislation and in administration: all these causes combined to bring misery and degradation to men, women and children. The cruel enforcement of English ideas as to land tenure on the Irish population had largely peopled Lancashire with miserable immigrants, who tended to bring other workers down to their own low level. A blundering poor-law had made it possible for pauper children to be collected from the workhouses of town and country throughout the land and sent to the factory districts in waggon loads, there to be herded without care from father or mother[1].

There were indeed large and ever increasing groups of highly paid artisans; strong in self-respect and sense of duty, and rejoicing in a family life which for cleanliness, comfort and sobriety compared favourably with any that could be found in other countries, or had existed previously in England. But the incursion of the offscourings of low-paid labour, largely agricultural, from the South of England and Ireland into the best hives of high-class industry, brought with it a degradation

became more bulky, and required greater skill and exertion for producing fine counts. But children still remained in the majority: though they were not strong enough for the heavier work, which these required, till a somewhat later age. (This statement is quoted substantially from Gaskell, *Artisans and Machinery*, pp. 137—142, 1836.) An overlooker had the boldness to tell the Committee of 1832 that small children were preferable to those over the age of 14; because they had to stoop less to the low frames: and, on its being suggested that the frames might be raised, replied that even then the older children could only be paid as much as the younger (Q. 3076—9).

[1] In 1836 there were 120,000 persons, chiefly Irish, living in cellars in Manchester alone, in fearful filth, often accompanied by a pig; poor, wasteful, and dissolute (Gaskell, *l.c.* pp. 82—3). Many more details are given by him; also by "Alfred" (Samuel Kydd) in his thoughtful and well-balanced *History of the Factory Movement*, 1847; and in other histories. It was rightly argued in the debate in 1815 on the elder Sir Robert Peel's Factory Bill that there was need for stopping a system which could be so abused that a London parish stipulated with a Lancashire manufacturer that "with every twenty sound children, one idiot should be taken." Peel confessed that his own house at one time employed nearly a thousand "parish children supplied from London, Birmingham, and other populous districts."

of the quality of life, from which the chief manufacturing district of England has not wholly freed itself. There are still to be seen there relics of the old time, when parish children, brought to Lancashire mills to earn money for which they were responsible to no one, started a habit among children, even of respectable families, of "setting up on their own," as soon as their earnings were sufficient. It was not easy to exaggerate the evils of many of the new factories: but they were exaggerated; and, in return, partisan advocates exaggerated the great real difficulties which were involved in an efficient remedy[1].

The factories which were chiefly concerned in this conflict of interests, had no special favours to demand from Parliament: they worked largely for export, and had little fear of competitive imports. But it was strenuously argued on their behalf that, if the Protective duties on wheat were removed, operatives would be able to buy more food with less money: and therefore their real wages would rise; and yet the manufacturers might get their labour at a lower money cost than before. Some economists supported this suggestion, and were often supposed to be hostile to the Factory Acts; but they were friendly to the Acts[2].

6. *Influences of war and fiscal policy on England's industry and trade in the first half of the nineteenth century.*

We now pass to consider the influences which the war, and the financial policy associated with it, exerted on the life of the people; and especially of those classes, who were least able to

[1] For instance, the advocates of stringent factory regulation were apt to put forward exceptional cases of wrong-doing as representative of the general conditions of factory work: its opponents brought forward as representative the experiences of people, living in places in which there was a large low-grade population, who could honestly say that the children, employed in some neighbouring well-conducted factories, were the healthiest and most moral whom they saw. Again some expert evidence was given to the effect that England's lead in the cotton industry was so strong that, if the hours during which the machinery was at work were reduced, she could obtain for her diminished exports a remunerative price; while other expert evidence contended that even a small increase in the costliness of her cotton goods would close many foreign markets to her.

[2] See Appendix E, 5.

I, IV, 6. maintain themselves in the face of adverse circumstances. The dark shadow of the French Revolution had enlisted the fears of the well-to-do classes on the side of their human sympathies, in arranging a system of poor-relief, which inverted the law of nature: for it made life least uncomfortable for those of the labouring classes who were least deserving: and it caused those, who had the least nobility of character, to marry early and to leave the largest number of descendants; and they in many cases lived to become degraded helots in manufacturing districts.

Further, the capital required by war could not have been obtained entirely by taxation without extreme measures, and in fact a very large part of it was obtained by loans. The loans could not be taken up abroad, so they came from the existing stock of capital: thus making capital scarce for industrial purposes, and securing high rates of interest and profits to capitalists and employers. Meanwhile the rents of landlords were raised by the high price of wheat. Thus the incomes of the well-to-do classes were raised relatively to those of their fellow-countrymen by the war: and, when it was over, they were left with a mortgage on the revenue of the country. Under the circumstances, the revenue ought to have been raised by taxes which fell lightly upon the working classes: but in fact they were so levied as still further to raise the income of the landlords; and, if the attempt which they made in 1815 to fix the price of wheat at 80*s.* a quarter had been successful, it would have compelled a great number of labourers' families to live on an aggregate weekly income about equal to the price of a single bushel of wheat. According to Charles Booth's well-known estimate, at the end of the nineteenth century, those Londoners were to be accounted as "poor," (that is, "as living under a struggle to obtain the necessaries of life,") who had a "regular income of 18*s.* to 21*s.* a week for a moderate family," and 18*s.* to 21*s.* was fully the price of *six* bushels of wheat[1].

[1] The complaint that the system of war loans mortgaged industry to protect property is voiced by Disraeli in *Sybil.* Newmarch, in a memorable defence of Pitt's loans, suggests that loans may come from "the overflowings" of capital that would otherwise have been "wasted," and that in such a case they do not materially encroach on the resources of industry (*Statistical Journal* for 1855, p. 138). In Pitt's time capital was scarce, even in England: but, as the war lasted long, more than half its expense was paid out of taxation; though in no

These evils, grave as they were, affected England's leadership less than might have been expected. In their most intense form they affected only a small part of the population. The production per head was very much greater in England than anywhere else; and though many employers were amassing great wealth, that was because they were reaping the profits of very large concerns: there was no other country in which the working man was allowed to retain for himself anything like as large a share of the value, which he produced when aided by a given capital. This fact is sufficient by itself to raise doubts as to the correctness of a statement, which has frequently been made, that the substitution of work in large factories for work in cottages and small workshops increased greatly the power of the capitalist to exploit the people. I, IV, 6.

Nearly every sort of fiscal policy works some good and some evil. Whether the good or the evil preponderates depends much on the adaptation of policy to the conditions of industry and trade in the country affected; and on the foresight, breadth of vision and ability with which it is developed. British statesmanship was not deficient in these qualities at the beginning of last century: but many a well-navigated vessel has missed her best course in a cyclone.

The early excesses of the French Revolution had excited beyond the boundaries of calm reason, not only the despotic rulers of the Continent and the privileged classes which made common cause with them; but also many lovers of freedom, as may be seen by comparing Burke's earlier utterances with the frenzy of his later years. On the other hand the general declaration of war against France caused all Frenchmen, however deeply they abhorred those excesses, to regard war to the end without compromise as their first duty. And, while men's motives were thus mixed, the results to the world were almost exclusively evil. Britain indeed suffered in some ways less

single year was a contribution made from that source which absorbed nearly as large a share of the national income as that levied in the later years of the present World-war. Disraeli's jibe was, however, in some measure justified by an abuse of the power of the landowners after the war; for they levied taxes which increased their own incomes, and threw more than the whole burden of the war on the industrial classes, and especially the poorer classes of workers. Similar, though much milder, tendencies can be observed now.

I, IV, 6. from the war than many other countries: but her fiscal policy was set on evil courses.

Pitt, the pupil of Adam Smith, and of the French advocates of Free trade, began his career with attempts to make the British tarif more simple and less restrictive; and he pressed for a commercial treaty with France, which would have gone very far towards breaking down the tarif frontier between the two countries. But his project was thwarted: and the events which began with the French Revolution made him ultimately responsible for a tarif which was grievously complex and oppressive. He seems indeed never to have formally abandoned the hope of returning to his early projects, when the stress of the war should be over: but meanwhile he was impelled to seek revenue by paths of least resistance.

He laboured throughout under exceptional difficulties. For he found himself compelled to impose, or at all events to acquiesce in imposing, heavy charges not always well considered on all classes of the population. A great increase of local rates was partly caused by bad methods of poor-relief: but the rise of wheat to famine prices, chiefly under the influence of war and bad harvests, would in any case have demanded a large local outlay, to be defrayed by the well-to-do for the benefit of the needy. The expenses of the war called for a renewal of the income tax, which reached at one time two shillings in the pound. These causes lessened Pitt's power to withstand, and perhaps even his eagerness to withstand, the pressure put on him by landlords and manufacturers to give them some sort of compensation by the imposition of duties on products that competed with theirs, even when the taxes were such as would yield but little to the revenue. He was compelled to levy many excise duties which he knew to be very unpopular. And, far-seeing man though he was, he did not care to look very far ahead when arranging a new import duty; for the independence of England was at stake; and, if that could be rescued, his emergency measures might be repealed before they had done lasting harm.

Pitt, killed by Austerlitz, left a heavy task to successors less strong than himself; and it would have needed men of exceptional strength, either during the war or immediately on its close, to work upwards along the steep and narrow path that led back to the ideals which he had left behind. So England was afflicted by an exceptionally ill-conceived protective tariff for many years. It was so complex that, if its origin in the crisis of the war were forgotten, it would appear to have been the work of self-confident men; and its details were generally so full of needless vexations and hindrances to industry and trade, and so ill-adapted to the ends at which they aimed, that it would have appeared to be the work of dull men.

I, IV, 6.

This fact had a great influence on history. For Englishmen were averse to abstract discussions. They did not care to inquire whether a system of Protection could be devised which would be free from the meddlesomeness and the waste, the corruption and the cruelty of that system which they knew. And as soon as the public could be induced to overcome their repugnance to the idea of change, the reformers found no serried ranks of firm reasoning to oppose them. The course of the battle might have been nearly the same, but its after-effects would have been widely different, if the task to be accomplished had been one for hard thinkers rather than expert orators.

The task indeed was not quickly accomplished. For violent change was uncongenial to the English temper: and some of those statesmen, who did most for free trade, had to conquer themselves before they began their struggle with others. This was especially the case with Peel. And yet the twenty years which elapsed between his great reforms and those of Huskisson, had broken down much of the crust of traditional opinions; and, by aid of the extension of the franchise in 1832, they had so much lessened the force of vested interests, that Peel, though less venturesome than Huskisson, was able to venture far more boldly than he had done[1].

[1] Huskisson, 1823—7, abolished most prohibitions and many duties which were in operation. But many Protective duties appealed strongly to vested interests, and he did not venture to do more than lower them. Even in 1839, after his work had been carried a good deal further, there were left nine hundred separate articles on the Customs list. The taxes on many of these were in effect prohibitive. (The details are set forth in an instructive appendix to the great Report on Import Duties of 1840.) The excess of aggregate receipts over drawbacks on six hundred of them was less than £3000. Speaking in 1825, Huskisson said (*Speeches*, vol. II. p. 343) that any one who walks along the beach from Brighton to Hastings can find at almost every village "persons who will engage to deliver him, within ten days or a fortnight, any prohibited

I, IV, 6. It is doubtful whether Pitt's early movement for tarif reform would have had sufficient driving force, even if it had not been cut short by the great war. But in Peel's time motive power was supplied by the increasing strength of vocal manufacturing interests; and by the irritation resulting from the confidence with which the landlords assumed that the well-being of agriculture was the supreme interest of the country, and by the relentless import duties and prohibitions which they consequently imposed on grain. Without that driving power the subtle arguments of Ricardo and other thorough thinkers could not have been effectively rendered into the language of the market-place, even by interpreters as lucid as Cobden and as eloquent as Bright. But the wishes of the townsfolk helped them to thread their way through difficult reasonings: enthusiasm grew, and spread to the country folk; and at last it became possible to convince agricultural labourers that their real wages would be raised by the free admission of products that competed with those of the fields which they ploughed. Their money wages might conceivably fall a little; and so might even the wages of those who worked at other pursuits: but the prices of their food would fall much more; and their worst miseries would be over[1].

In Peel's time the centre of the conflict was the Sliding Scale of duties on corn. That showed Protectionist ingenuity at its worst. At the beginning of the controversy the majority of Englishmen probably believed, what they were told on authority, that it would steady the price of wheat. At the end of the controversy there was scarcely any thoughtful Englishman who was not convinced that it increased fluctuations in the

article of manufacture, which he can name, upon an advance of £30 per cent. beyond the prime cost in Paris."

[1] This broad statement must be left for the present: a study of the complex issues involved in it belongs to a later stage of our study. The general belief that money wages would fall a little does not seem to have been based on any careful or exact reasoning: but it was probably correct. For up to that time wages had seldom been governed directly by economic forces. Employers nearly always had the upper hand in bargaining. Farmers especially raised or lowered wages by agreement among themselves, at such levels that labourers' families could just live in moderate health and moderate strength, provided the whole of their income was spent for strength-giving ends: and similar influences operated in manv industries, though with less force.

price of wheat; that it made the trade of farming precarious, and intensified agricultural depressions; but that meanwhile it so discouraged importation as to keep the average price high to the consumers, without conferring any proportionate benefit on the landlords, still less on the Exchequer or on the farmers. The Sliding Scale was not an essential part of the Protectionists' policy. But they defended it, and thus it served as a measure of their economic insight; and when the plain man was convinced that its claims could not be defended, he was inclined to give willing ear to criticisms of their other claims. Thus the great bulk of popular opinion swung round with irresistible force.

The defenders of the old system were, with few exceptions, ill-informed and weak in argument: they were discredited by the personal interest which most of them had in maintaining a high price in corn; as well as by the old-fashioned way in which they assumed that the welfare of the country depended on the prosperity of those who had a stake in it, and especially the owners of land; and they were worsted in almost every encounter on Royal Commissions, in Parliament, and on the platform. Their case was weakened before the Reform Bill of 1832 had transferred political power from the owners of land and decayed boroughs to the commercial and industrial classes: and after that the old Protection of agriculture could not long survive[1].

Disraeli had assailed Peel's action bitterly; but on becoming Chancellor of the Exchequer in 1852 he frankly said that a return to Protection was impossible. The subsequent vigorous reform of the British Parliament gave a free course to experiments in production and traffic; which it might not have been worth while to make if each step had needed to be defended and explained

[1] Reference may be made to Appendix E for some account of the causes of the failure of sliding scales: and for an argument that the movements of the price of wheat after 1849, though not what was expected by those who advocated the repeal of the duty, was just that which they might have anticipated if (1) they had known the peculiarly narrow conditions of the world's supply of wheat, so long as land transport was dear, and even sea transport not very cheap: (2) they could have foreseen the influx of gold beginning in 1850; also the war with the country from which England expected her chief supplies of wheat; also the disturbed conditions of the world till 1871; and lastly the building of railroads to American wheat fields, sometimes at the rate of nearly 10,000 miles a year; and so on.

I, IV, 6. to Customs and Excise officers, with the risk of being prohibited by them after some delay and when already half taken. At last every harbour on the coast line became a free port for the importation and housing of all goods except tobacco, alcoholic and stimulating drinks, and sugar; and for the exportation of all goods whatever. And the country became a free factory for the production of all goods except alcoholic liquors.

The freedom to adopt whatever trade one would, and manufacture whatever one would (*laisser faire* in its original sense), together with the freedom to send goods whithersoever one would, and to fetch them whencesoever one would (*laisser aller*), made England the *entrepôt* of the world. They gave her not only unprecedented trade, but also unprecedented advantages for developing every new idea of her own, before it reached other nations; and for learning any new foreign idea that could be adapted to her use.

But a difficult investigation always loses something from contact with the market-place. Nature is not simple, but complex. The immediate effects of any system of taxation are likely to differ from their ultimate effects: and both immediate and ultimate effects may vary much with the varying conditions of different countries. And, as the case against Protection in England (and Scotland) was far stronger than that against Protection in any other country, it was not to be expected that the reformers should confuse their English hearers by taking account of the conditions of other countries, unless they were compelled to do so: and from that they were saved by the low intellectual character of the opposition with which they had to contend. So they based sweeping general propositions on English facts and English conditions.

This gave to their argument much apparent lucidity and simplicity, which hastened their victory. And their victory was twofold. For it was followed by so great an increase of England's prosperity, that other nations began to open their ports in imitation of her; and this doubled the benefits which Free trade conferred on England.

But in the long run it might have been better both for England and for Free trade, if they had been compelled to make prominent those cumbrous qualifications which they omitted.

For then other nations would have been warned beforehand that the removal of Protective duties could not be expected to confer the same unmixed benefits on their best industries as it had done on those of England. As things were, they had to learn it in the hard school of experience: and they are now further removed from a calm inquiry as to whether the benefits of Protection outweigh its evils even to them, than they might have been if the English reformers had gone to work in a more scientific way[1].

[1] The above statements are developed in Appendix E, 4.

CHAPTER V

BRITAIN'S INDUSTRIAL LEADERSHIP UNDER STRONG CHALLENGE

I, v, 1. 1. *A rare consilience of favourable influences promoted the expansion of Britain's industry and trade after she had thrown her markets open to the world.*

The main purpose of this chapter is to indicate the new conditions of industrial leadership, which call for at least as high and sustained energy as Britain showed when she first outpaced her rivals.

The events of the second half of the nineteenth century belong to a survey of contemporary conditions. The few remarks made on them in the present chapter, are designed to do little more than indicate the way in which Englishmen have settled down to work out and develop, in cooperation with other nations, those methods of large, highly organized industry and trade in which they received but little aid from others up till about 1850. We have first to consider the causes which accelerated their advance in the third quarter of the eighteenth century, and those which led them generally to overrate that advance: secondly, the causes which brought about a well-founded, but exaggerated suspicion that all was not well with them. Thus we shall be brought to the present time, and come in touch with problems which will occupy the remainder of this work.

Looking back again, we see that a combination of causes, which is unprecedented in the history of the world, had developed England's industrial leadership from 1750 onwards. She had indeed been struck by several great misfortunes, especially her quarrel with her chief colony, her war with France, her poor laws and her corn taxes. But these evils were nothing in comparison with those which had afflicted her rivals on the Continent; while in America both capital and industrial skill were still scarce. After 1850 England had rid herself of her corn law; and of other restrictions, which were less injurious practically, though perhaps not better conceived: and she then had an equally unprecedented combination of advantages enabling business men to make money, even when they were not throwing themselves with energy into that creative work by which industrial leadership is made and maintained.

It has often been remarked that a man's energies are at their best when he is emerging from poverty and distress into the command of great opportunities. He rejoices in a little comfort; but he does not care to spend too much money or time on luxury. He is happy and proud in conquering difficulties. The fear of distress is still so fresh in his mind, that he subordinates, naturally and without effort, the allurements of the present to making secure provision for the future: he works hard without pain, and he accumulates capital greatly. That was the position even as late as 1850 of a large number, perhaps nearly half, of the older captains of industry: they had grown up in cottages, in which bread was often so scarce that the mother was forced to stay the children from eating before they had had enough. Such men sometimes indulged in bouts of gross indulgence: but they did not care for, and did not even know how to manage, those forms of elegant display, which in later years were to consume a large part of the national income[1].

England's relative strength was further heightened by the distresses of war which fell upon her neighbours. The chief of these were the slaughter and enfeeblement of bread winners, and the destruction of capital. Those who are killed, injured, or invalided in war, are mostly young men: the whole expense

[1] Newmarch remarks (*History of Prices*, vol. v. pp. 368—9) that during the five years 1846 to 1850 as many people found employment on the railway works as in the whole of the factories of the United Kingdom; and that nearly the whole of the railway calls, which supplied the means for their employment, were met either by efforts of economy or by increased exertions; and that the consequent distribution of extra wages "mitigated the disastrous effects on the working classes of the commercial and political convulsions of 1847, 1848, and 1849." In 1851 England was ready to open the great Exhibition, at which the whole world learnt suddenly how great were the numbers of those things which could be bought in London better or cheaper than elsewhere; and of those which could not be bought at all elsewhere.

I, v, 1. of their nurture has been borne by the community, and they have as yet repaid but little of it by their industrial work. This is true generally; and especially when nearly the whole nation is in arms.

England of course had her own troubles: especially those of the Crimean War 1854—6 and the Indian Mutiny 1857—8; but her finances were handled with courage; and her debt was very little increased[1]. On the other hand, the American Civil War of 1860—4 destroyed more wealth and industrial energy, and closed more opportunities of producing wealth, than any other war of nearly equal duration up to that time. And from 1859 to 1871 Western Europe was the scene of a series of wars, the last of which was more destructive than any other short war except the American Civil War[2].

During all these wars many nations, which remained neutral, reaped high gains: but none of them reaped gains to be compared to England's. For she had a preeminence, amounting under the special circumstances of the time to a partial monopoly, in the three things that were most urgently needed by those who were preparing for war, or engaged in war, or repairing the wastes of war; viz.: the material of war, including the personal outfit of the soldiers; the services of trading ships; and the loan of capital. These gains were high in substance: and they were higher still in appearance; that is, when expressed in terms of money. For the general tendency towards a rise of prices, as a consequence of the increased supply of gold, was reinforced in regard to many things, not only by increased consumption and destruction of them in connection with the wars; but also by the temporary or permanent removal of many producers from their factories and workshops to the battlefield:—a fact which recent experiences have brought home to the whole Western World.

Further, these wars, while retarding the progress of her

[1] It was as low in 1860 as in 1850. The war did little to hinder any of England's exports: but she was largely dependent on Russia for tallow and kindred products, and to a less degree for wheat. These therefore rose much in price here (though, after a while, considerable supplies found their way to North German ports and thus to England).

[2] France and Sardinia were at war against Austria in 1859; Prussia and Austria against Denmark in 1865; Prussia against Austria in 1866, and against France 1870—1.

rivals, increased the demand for her iron. The implements of war, which were chiefly made of it, grew in volume and in expensiveness. And as in the old times great roads had been made for military purposes; so every successive war strengthened the lessons first taught by the Crimean War, that under modern conditions an efficient railway system is a strategic necessity[1].

By 1870 England had built about two-thirds of her present railways. She had joined every important centre of industry with every other; and there was little room for the making of new lines which would create important additional traffic. But she still found much to be done in providing additional tracks, in increasing the number of quick trains, and in admitting third class passengers to them, not only on a few trunk lines, but on cross lines in every direction. This practice, which was not adopted thoroughly by any other large country, turned the special configuration of England to the best account, and it bound her chief industrial centres into a more compact unity than was to be found on a scale at all comparable with hers anywhere else. Combined with the freedom of her business from the inspection of Excise and Customs officers, and with the efficiency of her banking system, it gave her exceptional facilities for the rapid and elastic adjustments of business.

But there was menace in the fact that railways had, in 1870, rendered a much larger percentage of all the services which they were capable of rendering to England than they had done to any other large country: and that from that time forward the development of railways has done more for the industrial efficiency of her chief rivals than it has done for her[2].

[1] Thus the Northern States built a railway across the American continent, partly because the isolation of the Pacific Slope had been felt as a peril to national unity during the stress of the Civil War. The railway building of Germany for some years before and after her great war with France was mainly directed by strategic considerations; and the German railway *personnel* is organized in peace to be ready as a department of the army in war.

[2] The railway mileage of the United Kingdom was 6,600 in 1850; 15,500 in 1870; and 23,400 in 1912. This mileage of 6,600 in 1850 was nearly twice as great as that of Germany, and nearly four times as great as that of France; but it was passed by that of Germany just after the Franco-German War, and by that of France about twelve years later. The railway mileage of the United States, which was about three times as great as that of the United Kingdom from 1840 to 1870, is now more than ten times as great nominally. But of course in the more thinly peopled districts the lines are very lightly equipped.

I, v, 1. But, though her territory was so small that she was bound to see railways rendering new benefits of the first order to other countries after they had ceased to increase her advantages very greatly, it was otherwise with shipping. The contest between wood and iron as a material for shipbuilding became acute about 1850. The first place, at all events for steam-vessels, was taken by iron a little later; and by 1870 the contest was finished.

In the first half of the nineteenth century it had seemed that England's children beyond the seas would contest with her the primacy in shipping. But iron, which was ultimately to be a chief source of America's strength on the seas as well as on the land, was then needed so urgently for the land as to divert her energies from the seas. It was used chiefly for her railways; and she could invest capital in them to yield her a much higher rate of profits than that for which English capital was compelled to work, and to which therefore American capital would be limited in the general shipping trade. Up to the middle of the century she had derived a great benefit from the material for shipbuilding afforded by the forests of Maine. But wood was yielding place to iron just as the Civil War drove her shipping from the ocean. And when the war was over, her new fleet was built to trade on the great lakes and along the coasts, where native shipping had a monopoly, rather than on the great world routes. England therefore was freed from the chief rivalry with which she had been threatened; and she found in the shipping trade a profitable and ever-growing scope for her iron and for her energies[1].

Also the train traffic per mile is denser in England than in any other large country: and this in spite of the fact that a great deal of internal trade in heavy products, which in most other countries would go by land, goes by sea from one part of England to another. These points are developed in another connection in Book III.

[1] The victory of iron over wood as the material for ships, though not fast, was not so slow as that of steam power over sails; and of course, while England used to import most of the materials for the rigging of ships, she herself provided the engines and the coal for steam-ships: this tended to lessen her foreign trade.

In 1850, thirty-five years after steam propulsion had been proved a success, only about one ship in sixty was driven by steam; though there were in addition a large number of steam-boats. In 1860 about an eleventh of the British tonnage engaged in the foreign trade was driven by steam, and in 1870 about a fifth. In the decade 1860 to 1870 the British iron steamer fleet grew from 454,000 to 1,113,000 tons.

As roads running at right angles to railways fed them and increased their traffic, so railways fed ships. Steam-ships became cheaper to build, and cheaper to work; they carried increased cargoes in proportion to their displacement, and required for a given displacement fewer men and less coal to drive them at a high speed. And exactly as Holland had done before her, England found in the carrying trade a rich field in which to turn to account her large stores of movable capital.

Further, her capital, her trade, and her industries had combined to give her better foreign connections than any other country had by post and telegraph, and by banking and other credit agencies; and London had become the clearing house of the world. These causes mutually strengthened one another: each new means of communication developed her foreign trade; and each extension of her foreign trade made new communications practicable and profitable.

Meanwhile Bessemer's process had much cheapened the cost of making steel of a kind which was shortly to displace iron from most of its uses. The process required ores nearly free from phosphorus: but there was a good, though small, supply of these ready at hand; and one great company, which had access to them, paid a dividend of nearly a hundred per cent. on its capital in an exceptional year.

Lastly, the Free trade policy of England had been largely followed on the Continent; and just those years, in which the industries of her chief rivals were most interrupted by the alarms and the ravages of war, were the years in which they offered not only the most eager demand for her goods, but also the freest entry for them.

These causes combined to increase her external trade rapidly. In fact its money value was twice as high from 1870 to 1874 as it had been before the gold discoveries. The importance of this fact was, however, much exaggerated by popular opinion, which pays more attention to movements of prices, than to movements of real values.

Thus rich old firms could thrive by their mere momentum, even if they had lost the springs of energy and initiative. Men whose childhood had been passed in the hard days before the repeal of the corn laws; who had come to business

I, v, 2. early in the morning, and stayed late in the afternoon; who had been full of enterprise and resource, were not infrequently succeeded by sons who had been brought up to think life easy, and were content to let the main work of the business be carried on by salaried assistants on the lines laid down in a previous generation. But yet so strongly were such men supported by the general inflation of prices, that in most cases they made good profits and were satisfied with themselves. Thus an extraordinary combination of favourable conditions, induced undue self-complacency—the arch enemy of strength.

2. *After 1873 various signs of weakness were perceived; and later on some exaggerated alarms arose. But the national character is again showing itself in a resolute facing of difficulties.*

This over confidence was startled by the crisis, or more strictly the commercial depression, of 1873. But its immediate causes lay chiefly outside of Britain: and indeed the disturbance reached her in two sets of troubled waves, of which the centres were respectively the United States and Austria, in both of which countries the inflation of credit had been reckless. There was nothing in the depression to force on her notice the more permanent underlying dangers of her position[1]: she seemed to many to combine the solidity of mature age with the energy of youth.

But the depression lasted long; and was accentuated by

[1] It may be well to quote a passage from one of the ablest, most broad minded and acute of British economists: but one who used to say that he was the last of those who had learnt from Ricardo direct without the mediation of Mill.

Bagehot, after referring to the little roughnesses, and sharp practices, which were making their appearance in England as the result of the increasingly "democratic structure of commerce," observed that such defects "are compensated by one great excellence. No country of great hereditary trade, was ever so little 'sleepy,' to use the only fit word, as England; no other was ever so prompt at once to seize new advantages. A country dependent mainly on great 'merchant princes' will never be so prompt; their commerce perpetually slips more and more into a commerce of routine....The rough and vulgar structure of English commerce is the secret of its life; for it contains 'the propensity to variation,' which, in the social as in the animal kingdom, is the principle of progress" (*Lombard Street*, 1873, pp. 10, 11). But when such matters are discussed to-day, Germany is seen to have much of the strength both of an old and a new country.

I, v, 2.

monetary troubles. For the yield of the gold mines had been diminishing; while currency changes, which really caused some new demand for gold, and appeared to cause a great new demand for it, accentuated the fall of prices that would in any case have been caused by the collapse of credit. Distress was nearly universal in the western world. France indeed had calmly set herself to solid business as soon as the second siege of Paris was finished, and she was little affected by the general collapse of credit. But Germany had been rendered over-confident by the successes of the war; the influx of the French indemnity had thrown her speculative classes off their balance, and in 1875 she was in even a worse plight than Britain. So Britons nourished for nearly another decade the comfortable notion that they could afford to take things easily and yet expect a better income than anyone else.

But gradually the continued fall in prices caused people to repeat the error which they had made when over-estimating progress during the earlier time of inflated prices. The country's foreign trade was increasing very slowly; and the fall of prices made people suppose that it was shrinking. Thus they now doubly over-estimated the misfortunes of the years of shrinking prices: and many of them were made anxious by observing that in some branches of trade and industry other countries were making progress which, if not greater in amount, was yet at a greater rate than their own. This feeling of disquiet grew; and the able Commission on the Depression of Trade in 1885—6 reported that: "In neutral markets, such as our own colonies and dependencies, and especially in the East, we are beginning to feel the effects of foreign competition in quarters, where our trade formerly enjoyed a practical monopoly. The increasing severity of this competition, both in our home and in neutral markets, is especially noticeable in the case of Germany. In every quarter of the world the perseverance and enterprise of the Germans are making themselves felt. In the actual production of commodities we have now few, if any advantages over them; and in a knowledge of the markets of the world, a desire to accommodate themselves to local tastes and idiosyncrasies, a determination to obtain a footing wherever they can,

I, v, 2. and a tenacity in maintaining it, they appear to be gaining ground on us. We cannot avoid stating here the impression which has been made upon us during the course of our inquiry that in these respects there is some falling off among the trading classes of this country from the more energetic practice of former periods." The information collected by the Commission while tending to "dispel much misapprehension...and to encourage a more hopeful view...of our commercial position ...will also show that if our position is to be maintained it must be by the exercise of the same energy, perseverance, self-restraint, and readiness of resource by which it was originally created[1]."

Things went smoothly during the upward swing of commercial credit which culminated in 1890—1; and troubles of the United States, arising out of a doubt as to the solidity of their currency, kept back for a time the competitor from whose power of initiative there seemed most to fear. But a series of failures of British investments in South America, Australia and elsewhere had undermined confidence nearly as much as those of 1873—5. Labour disputes also became rife, and indeed those of 1892—3 were partly the cause and partly the effect of a deadening of British enterprise, which showed itself in an unparalleled prolongation of a two per cent. Bank rate of discount (the market rate being seldom above one per cent.) for three years 1894—6.

Meanwhile attention had been directed to instances in which Britain's industrial technique had been surpassed by those of Germany and America. The most important case was that of the heavy steel industry. That had received a strong impetus from Bessemer's great invention in 1856. But the small supply

[1] Final Report [C. 4893], §§ 74, 75, 76, and 106. It is noteworthy that this trouble was most conspicuous in parts of the country in which the social distinctions between employers and employed have been greatest. Thus an account of the "Decay of a famous industry" (*Times*, 19. 12. 04), mentions as one among several causes of the weakness of the West of England woollen trade the fact that, while "many mills have been worked by the same family for over a century...some of the manufacturers, who had made large fortunes and acquired large landed estates, retired to these and took a good deal of their capital with them." But in Yorkshire there was more energy; artisans were better paid; and the industry "was not content to go on making the same old cloths with the same old slow-going looms."

of Britain's ores suitable for his treatment speedily ran short. I, v, 3.
Meanwhile America's greatly increased output of steel was matched by an equal increase in her own demand for its structural and other uses; but the markets, to which Britain had access, were assailed by German steel made with consummate technical skill by aid of a new process. It had been invented by an Englishman; but it was specially adapted to the ores of Alsace and Lorraine, and not to those to which Britain has good access. However alert she had been in improving and developing the technique of her heavy steel industry, it must have been outpaced by that of Germany: but the continued use of old-fashioned plant by many of her works caused her output of heavy steel to remain almost stationary while that of Germany increased fast[1].

Britain lagged even more conspicuously behind in many industries that called for high and extended scientific training: the chief of these were devoted to the manufacture of colours, and of medical and explosive products, from coal-tar bases. This was the more striking because Germany, being indifferently supplied with gaseous coal, imported much of her tar from Britain.

3. *The needs of Britain's industries gave additional momentum to a movement, that had long been on the way, for a reform of her educational system*[2].

English business men were slow to recognize a chief cause of decline in their industrial leadership. But about 1904 they began to see clearly that they must follow other nations in promoting industrial efficiency by improved education. The movement, thus initiated, is making way, tardily indeed for the lack

[1] The Metallurgical Committee of the British Iron and Steel Institute as late as 1917, reported with reference to the output of the British basic open-hearth furnaces, that British technique and organization generally compared unfavourably with that of Germany; and that this was the chief cause of their relatively small output. They added that, though the efficiency of the individual British workman was maintained, his short hours of working and high wages stinted the supply of capital needed to bring the plant of the industry up to its highest possible efficiency. It may be added that British production of finished steel products, including ships, remains high; and her exports of them remain very high.

[2] The large matters opened out in this Section and the next are considered here chiefly in relation to Britain's leadership: their broader relations will be studied in the course of Books II and III.

I, v, 3. of hearty support from those who themselves received no good education. But it does make way in school and in college; for the working classes, and for the well-to-do, and even for the relatively sluggish lower middle classes. The nation is beginning to recognize that mere accumulation of knowledge stunts rather than educates the mind; that the mind can be strengthened only by gradually increasing calls on its strength and spontaneity; and that while much general education may be advantageously given to all youth, there is also a need for specialized education adapted to the needs of agriculture, and every other industry, as well as to the learned professions. This matter is of vital importance: and must detain us a little.

There is consolation in the reflections that the poverty of England's educational system has been in large measure due to a strange freak of fortune; and that she still holds a leadership, almost unchallenged except by other English speaking countries, in that education of character which is obtained from individual activities, rather than from instruction whether verbal or in print. The playground had a notable share in the "real" education of her youth: and the paths of the ocean have been the Universities of an exceptional number of her men. During the last two centuries, at all events, they have had a more intimate acquaintance at first hand than any other people with the physical conditions and the habits of the populations of the world at large.

It is to be noted also that the intellectual alertness, which this real education developed, was well adapted to stimulate that sort of invention which was most needed in the second half of the eighteenth century and the first half of the nineteenth. But the present age calls increasingly for a new class of improvements of method, and—in a less degree—for improvements of appliances, which cannot be created by a single alert individual. Many of those, by which man's command over nature has been most enlarged during the last few decades, have been the product of sustained researches by large groups of specially qualified students extending over long periods of time.

It has already been observed[1] that Scotland developed an excellent system of education very early; and that partly in consequence, Scotchmen have taken a large share in the expansion

[1] Above, pp. 53, 54.

of the British Empire: thus the weaknesses which have prevented Britain from taking her proper place in the studies, that lie on the borderland between academic and business work in the present age, belong to England in the narrow sense of the term, more than to Scotland. But subject to this correction it must be confessed that British education has lagged behind that of Germany in some respects by more than a generation[1]. I, v, 3.

The causes of this hindrance to Britain's industrial leadership seem however to be due to unfortunate accidents in political structure, more than to weakness of national purpose. Popular education, which ought to have been accepted two centuries ago as a chief duty of the State, was regarded in England till recently as an incidental duty of the clergy of the Established Church: for they almost alone were possessed of property that had been set aside for purposes higher than the immediate pursuit of material gain. But a large part of the industrial and trading classes had passed into other religious denominations: some of the country clergy shared the prejudice of neighbouring squires against educating the working classes above the mere necessities of manual work; and in new industrial districts the clergy had no funds available for education.

A new ferment appeared late in the nineteenth century: and ere long, in spite of opposition from some of those, whose larger

[1] In 1872 a British deputation visited Germany and Switzerland to study their methods of education. The following notes are abstracted from an account of some of their experiences which has recently been given by one of its chief members:—"In Saxony we found a national system of education, conducted in magnificent school buildings, attended by all, with scholarships admitting clever poor boys from elementary to secondary, and thence to technical schools, or to the Polytechnic or University. Attendance was compulsory till the age of 14. In England at that time there was no national system, no compulsion. Many children did not go to school at all: those who did, attended irregularly. The school buildings were meagre and unsuitable: there were no secondary schools for the masses; and therefore no promotions of able students from below. 'The best educated children in English elementary schools were half-timers from the factories, who attended half-time from 8 to 13. In Germany the boys, who left school at 14, were required to attend evening continuation schools; there were also such schools for girls, with apprentice workshop schools, special classes for those engaged in certain trades, and agricultural schools.' All the Universities and Colleges in England together contained less students 'taking up research and the higher branches of chemistry' than a single German University (that of Munich) which was visited" (*The Real German Rivalry*, by Sir Swire Smith, 1916).

I, v, 3. opportunities should have made them the best friends of the education of the people, the State began to take up its neglected duty. For a time nothing more was attempted than a sound, but strictly elementary education, which began rather late and ended very early. But almost every year brought new evidence that a niggardly policy of education was a mistake even from a purely commercial point of view: and now, Britain has gone a long way towards providing the children even of the poorest classes with opportunities for sound general education, and for semi-technical education in continuation schools and otherwise; together with a series of scholarships, or educational ladders, by which an able child, born even in the lowest ranks, may rise to high work. In the course of a generation the more intelligent artisans and agricultural labourers may be expected to have a better comprehension of the fundamental principles of their work than had been possessed two generations ago by many farmers and manufacturers.

The education of the well-to-do classes in England had not been as much neglected as that of the working classes. But it was held back by mediaeval shackles. For until the middle of last century nearly all the instruction at Oxford and Cambridge was given by men, whose incomes were chiefly derived from College Fellowships. They were compelled to be in Holy Orders; and as they would vacate their Fellowships by marriage, they generally looked forward to spending the second halves of their lives in country rectories, where learning would be of little use and science of no use. Celibacy remained compulsory for some time longer: not till the present century have the majority of the teachers at the chief English Universities regarded the advancement of knowledge as the main business of their lives. Oxford had indeed long ago contrived to use Plato, Aristotle and Thucydides as stalking horses, from behind which to practise demure shooting at problems of the day; and in recent years she has developed considerable scientific schools. The Cambridge school of mathematics has long been unsurpassed in the training of the reasoning faculty, in so far as that can be dissociated from experimental initiative: and her physical and biological laboratories already supply a considerable number of leaders of the world's studies in their several departments.

Meanwhile new Universities have sprung up in several great centres, modelled in some respects on that at Manchester, whose chemical laboratory had been brought into the front rank by Roscoe; and all of them give the chief place to chemistry, engineering, and other studies, which bear directly on industry. Their influence furthers the growing inclination of manufacturers and other business men to profit by German and American experience; and make large use of scientific knowledge and research in their works. A strong impulse in the same direction is now given by the establishment in 1915 of the Committee of the Privy Council for Scientific and Industrial Research; which, aided by a powerful Advisory Council, with appropriate Committees, is bringing a great part of the best scientific ability of the country to bear on the requirements of business; thereby continuing and enlarging earlier efforts, of which the foundation of the National Physical Laboratory in 1900 may be taken as representative.

The new demand for the extended study of science, with special reference to the requirements of industry, might have been in danger of laying too much stress on technical details, to the relative neglect of those fundamental discoveries, which are parents of all scientific technique. But the critical position of the country, arising out of the World-war, has caused the most eminent scientific men among others, to put their services without stint at the disposal of the Government: and it has also gained the public ear for their counsels. Under their guidance, care is being taken that even technical education shall be so used as to develop the faculties; it is not being directed mainly to loading up the minds of the students with facts, and enabling them to feel at home in the workshop.

4. *National funds are rightly given liberally to the advancement of knowledge for its own sake. Research for the attainment of particular ends is receiving some support from open associations of producers or traders, specially interested in their attainment.*

It is now generally recognized that national industry requires three distinct classes of laboratories. The first seeks the extension of knowledge at large: the second aims at knowledge in

I, v, 4. regard to special requirements of a particular branch of industry: the third checks the quality of the output of individual works.

History shows that almost every scientific discovery, which has ultimately revolutionized methods of industry, has been made in the pursuit of knowledge for its own sake, without direct aim at the attainment of any particular practical advantage: Universities are the proper places for such pursuit of "pure" science, and for the establishment of laboratories, etc., devoted to it. But though the eagerness of an academic student should increase with every prospect of establishing a new truth, independently of any practical gain which it may promise; yet his studies will lose nothing, and the world may gain much, from his keeping in touch with some of those industries, whose methods might be improved by increased knowledge of the properties of the products which he is studying. Therefore it is well that laboratories devoted to the advance of pure science should take some account of the work of a second class of laboratories, whose researches are specialized on the attainment of particular practical ends.

In some cases a single giant business which is pioneering new developments of a subtle industry may reasonably set up a great laboratory for the conception and testing of improvements on current usage: and the influences which such laboratories may exert on industrial structure will take prominent places in this and the following two Books, with special reference to German practice. But such a laboratory, if adequate for dealing with any important issue that may arise, is likely to be too costly in original outlay and maintenance for any but very exceptional businesses: and therefore the task is one of those in which the growing tendency to association among businesses in the same branch of industry is to be welcomed. It may be arranged that each member of the association has some duly qualified right to request that a particular investigation should be made in the laboratory: suitable arrangement being made for a special contribution in case its expense should be great, as well as for the ownership of patents in exceptional cases.

Such association, so long as it remains true to its avowed design, is wholly constructive: and has no kinship with "combinations" in the dyslogistic sense of the term; that is, conspiracies to monopolize a particular branch of industry or trade in such ways as would cause the public to pay higher prices than they would if that branch were open without contest to the enterprise of any new comer. But the experience of the ages shows that associations set up for constructive purposes are in danger of being turned to destructive ends: and therefore it may perhaps be to the public interest that some limited contribution should be made from public funds to the support of such associations; partly in order to facilitate the intervention of public authority in case an association should develop anti-social tendencies. The exigencies of the World-war have enabled many men to break away from old habits, old prejudices against neighbours, old delights in the secrecy and autonomous control of their own affairs; and to work with old rivals for the common good of the country: therein lies much public gain. But on the other hand caution is needed lest arrangements should be set up, which depend for their beneficial working on altruistic sentiments, that may fade when the national emergency has passed.

Similar remarks apply to the suggestions that a locality, which is the chief seat of any branch of industry, may properly subsidize an appropriate technical laboratory; with a general understanding that its own rate-payers should have priority in all claims on its services. Public opinion seems to have received a strong and wholesome stimulus in this direction from the full recognition of the fact that many things, which Britain used to buy from Germany, were the products of more extended technical research than could easily be brought to bear by herself.

Technical research laboratories, while in touch with the chief scientific laboratories on the one hand, could on the other lend help to a third class of laboratories which have long been found necessary in the steel and many other industries, whose chief work is mechanical rather than chemical. Such a laboratory does not, as a rule, do any considerable research work: but it enables the business, to which it is attached, to make sure that each of its products from day to day, or even from hour to hour, is chemically or mechanically true to its proper standard[1].

[1] Authoritative studies of this matter by specialized experts may be found in *Science and the Nation*, by Cambridge graduates, 1917; and in *The British coal-tar industry, its origin, development and decline*, edited by Prof.

I, v, 4. Every industrial country obtains some information bearing on industry and trade from its Ambassadors and Consuls. But, with a few brilliant exceptions British Consuls seem to have lagged far behind those of America and Germany in such matters. Great improvements in this direction are contemplated: but the Consular service is not likely to be able to meet all the wishes of producers and traders as to the requirements of each country for particular manufactures, and as to her sources of supply of special materials needed in manufacture. For large questions arise when access is opened out to materials that require treatment somewhat different from those already in use: and a firm, which makes a thorough study of such a problem, is likely to confer at least as great aggregate benefits on other firms as on itself: but, as the cost will be heavy, few will venture on it, unless those will share in the cost, who are likely to share in the reward. The Research Committee of the Privy Council finds an appropriate field in promoting such associations.

Private associations for obtaining facts as to the solvency, etc., of customers in foreign countries have long done good work. This is a delicate matter on which the best opinions seem to differ; but it is probable that, with larger experience, an extension of this plan may enable British firms to sell with advantage more extensively in countries in which purchasers require long credit on small tangible security. This class of trade is chiefly in the hands of Germans, especially in South America, and other countries in which the English language does not carry far: and there seems to be some justification for

W. M. Gardiner, 1915. These works record numerous cases in which members of the small band of British scientific men have made revolutionary discoveries in science; but yet the chief fruits of their work have been reaped by businesses in Germany and other countries, where industry and science have been in close touch with one another. Sometimes a British inventor has set up a manufacture on his own lines, with the best results; but after his death the business has fallen into the hands of men with merely administrative and commercial instincts; and it has then been left behind by foreign rivals, who have continued to work on the lines of the original inventor with patience and system, though not always with much creative genius. An excellent compressed account of the new movement has been begun in the two first *Reports* (1916 and 1917) of the Committee of the Privy Council for Scientific and Industrial research [Cd 8336, 8718]: and their continuation is likely to constitute a good history of Britain's awakening from her too easy contentment with the equipment that sufficed for the middle of last century.

the claim by Germans that their methods of financing business meet some requirements of the new age, to which the methods of "conservative" British houses are not altogether appropriate. But more of this hereafter.

The maxim "know thyself" applies to nations as to individuals. Old and young are alike inclined to think more of their own strengths than of their weaknesses: and it is specially incumbent on Britain to strive against that stiffness of the joints that is almost inevitable in each old industry, and in the general relations of industries and trades in each old country. Above all is an old business in an old country in danger of underrating the advantages of that which is new. Much that passes for heavy conservatism is one of those faults of judgment, from which neither young nor old are free: but such errors are probably more injurious to an old country or industry than to one that is relatively young and therefore alert.

Britain has perhaps suffered as much from the conservatism of her working men as from that of her business men. It seems that where no restrictive traditions interfere, the British skilled artisan gives generally as much good work for a given pay as any other. But often operations, which had been difficult and therefore highly paid, are made easy by improvements in machinery or technique: and then obstacles are apt to be put by the artisans in the industry in the way of their being performed cheaply in an old country. Meanwhile they are relegated to unskilled men, women and boys in countries whose industries have not developed firm traditions: this is a matter of great importance to Britain; but it belongs to the second Volume of this work.

Again, the charge of excessive conservatism is sometimes brought against British banks. No one disputes their unrivalled efficiency in the rather narrow range of tasks which they undertake: but there is a growing feeling that, especially in regard to new ventures abroad, rather more elastic financial enterprise is required than that of the British banking system; even when the great "accepting houses" are reckoned in[1].

[1] See below, pp. 341—349. A German writer claims that Germans lead in every part of the London market, and especially in the great Accepting Houses through whose hands much of the national capital passes But the instances

I, v, 5. 5. *Britain's industrial leadership is in process of being fulfilled and merged in that of the British Federation of Nations; the younger members of which are learning much from the present leadership of her first great Colony.*

Britain surprised the rest of the world, if not herself, by the energy which she has shown in the World-war: and the English-speaking peoples of four continents have proved themselves to be united in spirit and in truth. This chapter may therefore appropriately end with a claim that Britain's industrial leadership is to be measured by the achievements of Britons in their new homes as well as in their old: it is but carrying into larger affairs the familiar truth that parents, who have brought up a goodly array of noble and vigorous children, have done more for the world than is shown by their own achievement, somewhat narrowed as this may have been by their responsibilities.

It was observed long ago that a colony often outstripped her mother-state. For emigrants are on the average bolder, sturdier, and more fertile of initiative than those who stay at home; and their departure leaves the old country poorer in human resources than she would otherwise have been. They may take but little of her capital with them: but much of her capital follows them. Her own people are wealthier individually than they would have been without opportunities of investing their means in the development of rich natural resources in the care of their trusted relations: but she herself is poorer, and is to some extent less able to maintain her leadership, than she would have been if her territory had been large and rich enough to enable all her labour

quoted by him include, as might be expected, names of Jews, long domiciled in this country. The splendid faculties of that race for such work have brought them to the front here, and to an even greater extent in Eastern and Central Europe: and the writer believes that he has found that "though English manufacturers of textile machines supplied practically the whole world,...those who obtained orders for the manufactures of Manchester, Oldham, or Accrington, from Spain, South America, and even France, were commission firms founded by Germans. The Englishman refused to make quotations otherwise than in yards and shillings, and to sell them otherwise than for cash payment." See pp. 24, 25 of an English translation (published under the title *England's Financial supremacy*) of some recent articles in the *Frankfürter Zeitung*, under the heading, "English preponderance in finance (*Finanzvormacht*): England's mistaken calculation: Germany and the inheritance of the City."

and capital to be applied within her own limits, without forcing reluctant nature to yield large returns from a limited area of agricultural land and mineral strata. No doubt improvements in transport by land and sea enable her to obtain food and minerals from her Dominions and elsewhere at relatively low cost, so long as the paths of the ocean are relatively secure under the protection of a strong fleet. No foresight of the dangers to be developed by submarine warfare could have prevented the restraint which it threatens to the easy development of Britain's economic life, and industrial leadership. But the prosperity of her daughters beyond the seas; and the generous and wise assistance, which they have given her when under assault, are indications of rare qualities, which have been at the root of her industrial leadership.

Her daughters will probably be recognized in their turn as industrial leaders in various directions. But the time for that has not yet come: for a young country must win elementary victories over nature. Her free capital is seldom equal to the urgent demands for it, which are made by the industries of agriculture and transport: and therefore, vigorous as her people may be individually, she has little opportunity for pioneering the more complex methods of industry in advance of older countries, which have abundant capital and energy free for such work.

The British Confederation of Nations, to use a fine term suggested by General Smuts, was struck almost to the death by a crude blunder of dull, though well meaning men, out of touch with the spirits of liberty and progress, who drove away Britain's first great colony. She has become a chief leader for all the world; and the supreme leader for those peoples, who are bringing spacious territories under control. England herself has only one acre to each inhabitant, the United Kingdom has only two. But the United States even now has thirty: the Canadian Dominion has three hundred, and Australia has six hundred. Therefore it is natural and right that they should look to the past development and the present experience of their eldest sister for guidance as to their own development: by such means may the Industrial Leadership of Britain attain its broadest and fullest development[1].

[1] A little more is said on the matter below, I, VIII, 6.

I, v, 5. To conclude, we have seen that leadership in industry and trade has been obtained in the past by cities or by nations, which have thrown energy into the use of their own "native commodities," to use Petty's phrase; and that victories in the home market have prepared the way for victories in foreign markets. We have seen that England's leadership was cast in a larger mould than any which went before it: partly because her resources were greater than those of any of her predecessors in leadership; and partly because, when her time came, the sphere of trade had been enlarged by opening up of new continents and improved means of communication: but mainly because she yoked the forces of nature in her service in production on so large a scale and by such powerful methods that her people could with relatively small efforts to themselves produce large quantities of things that were in general demand abroad. By applying the law of Increasing Return to production on a large scale she made the whole world tributary to her wants, so that the English artisan could in many respects fare as sumptuously as the well-to-do classes in some parts even of Western Europe.

As has already been suggested, France affords the chief instance of a leadership based mainly on individual skill; and Germany of a leadership based mainly on trained ability and high organization. But the dominant instance of the economies of massive production is afforded by the United States; though the lessons to be learnt from her are obscured by the fact that the richness and variety of her natural resources render her almost independent of many of those benefits of foreign trade, which are essential to Western Europe. A chief question towards which we have to work our way is this: Will the new "giant" production exercise as far-reaching an influence over the social and industrial structure of each several country and of the world as a whole, as was exercised by large production in the middle of the nineteenth century?

CHAPTER VI

THE INDUSTRIAL LEADERSHIP OF FRANCE. INDIVIDUALITY AND REFINEMENT IN PRODUCTION

1. *The physical features of France have not favoured industrial concentration.* I, vi, 1.

The economic development of France has been more continuous than that of any other great country except England: and yet it has diverged from that of England more widely than has that of any other, which bears equally high marks of constructive genius. And further, her industrial qualities are representative of those of Western Europe generally in a fuller degree than are those of any other country.

There was a time indeed, at which the ascendancy among Latin nations belonged clearly to Italy: and, though crippled during centuries of internal conflict and of oppression by external force, she is throwing out flashes of genius, so reminiscent of the two ages in which she was the centre of the world, that she may ere long be again a chief leader: but the time is not yet. Spain contested for a while the leadership of the Latin nations on at least equal terms with France: but her best industrial qualities were largely due to Saracenic blood; and the Inquisition purged her of individual originality so thoroughly, that her later economic history is almost devoid of interest. Portugal's genius for exploration was brilliant; but passed quickly. Belgium contains many cities, which have made their mark in economic history; and there was (before the World-war) no country of equal size that could compete with her output of agricultural, mineral, and manufactured products. But she has been the battlefield of Europe; and foreign rule has left its marks on her.

I, VI, 1. France is in close touch with all these countries: she has given to them and received much from them; as well as from her eastern neighbours, Germany and Switzerland. She is thus in a sense the epitome of all Western Europe. But on the other hand, she affords the most important instance of a great industrial country, whose people are not inclined to the methods of massive production; and whose chief strength lies in the fine results, which they attain with comparatively little aid from those methods. This is a reason for making some study of her leadership before passing to those of Germany and the United States of America; for their chief industrial achievements have been the development of those methods, in various directions beyond the lines to which England herself has brought them. Among the influences, which have contributed to the special features of French industry, three groups appear to be prominent—geographical, racial and political. The geographical group has of course largely shaped the racial; and both have affected the political.

The soil of France has been the meeting place of the best energy of the North with the best culture of the South. But during the Middle Ages there was no political unity; and the various parts of what are now France were continually at war with one another. Industry made progress in some of the towns: but few of them rivalled those of Italy in population and wealth. And her industrial forces lacked concentration. The influences of Italian and Spanish culture, which were working northwards in the South of France, had a long way to go before they met those coming southwards from the Low Countries. The Seine, the Loire, the Garonne serve for internal communication on a small scale; and nearly all of the chief centres of French industry have clustered along their banks and those of the Rhone; or else at her relatively few sea-ports, or near her frontiers. The industries of the North, the South, and the East have never been intimate with one another[1].

[1] The only French port which has ever attained quite the first rank in world commerce is Marseilles: and that indeed was a considerable centre of trade for an exceptionally long time. It is a good haven, with fair access to other trading ports, and with a great river near at hand. But the mountain barrier,

France had excellent main roads very early. And long before England had any canals, the engineering genius, which distinguishes the French, had provided a splendid system of them. In the eighteenth century the good roads and the canals of England had passed those of France in number and in adaptation to the needs of business. But France set herself to bring both up to a high standard: and in consequence of England's neglect of her canals those of France soon passed far ahead. Their chief work is, however, limited to the great plain between Paris and the Northern coalfields[1].

The geographical distribution of the industrial districts of France has retained its general character with comparatively little change to the present time. Railways have indeed spread over her whole surface. But Paris dominated France; and the railway companies trusted to Government aid more than to local initiative. So the country divided out into a number of basins, each with its apex at Paris and extending to the frontier, and each with its own railway system: so there is very little easy communication between the industrial districts, save through Paris; and in all France there is no dense industrial district nearly as large as can be found in England, Germany, or even Belgium[2].

through which the Rhone cuts its way, is so near to the sea, that its delta is too shifting, its mouth is too shallow, and its main course is too rapid for easy navigation. Had the Rhone been gentler, France might have been reckoned with the Southern rather than the Northern countries of Europe.

[1] Wood was the predecessor of coal as the chief freight on French canals. See Dupin, *Forces productives et commerciales de la France,* 1827, Livre VII. His study of English roads and canals had been translated into English in 1825 and exercised much influence in England. Foville (*La France économique*, p. 94), as evidence of the low viability of France before the days of railways, states that in 1817 wheat sold for 37 fr. the hectolitre in the Côtes du Nord, and for 80 fr. at Colmar; and even in 1847 for 29 fr. in l'Aude, and for 49 fr. in le Bas Rhin. And yet the main roads were so good that the journey from Marseilles to Paris could, Lardner tells us (*Railway Economy*, p. 28), be effected by road in sixty hours. A map, showing on an excellent plan the volume of the traffic on the various French waterways, is reproduced in Colson's *Transports et Tarifs,* and in an English Report [Cd 1636—7].

[2] See the maps in Levasseur, *Population Française*, vol. L; and Diercke's *Schul-Atlas für höhere Lehranstalten*, a most handy book for the student of economics. The great mining and industrial district in the North of France adjoins the still larger Belgian district. The department of Meurthe et Moselle is exceptionally prosperous; but its chief trade is with its old comrades which have been under German rule since 1870. (See Blondel, *La France et le marché*

I, VI, 2. 2. *The political conditions of the seventeenth and eighteenth centuries suppressed the middle class; so that French industry was mainly given to cheap local products, on the one hand; and, on the other, to fine goods, embodying some artistic feeling and individual judgment.*

The obstacles, which geographical and racial causes thus opposed to the growth of concentrated massive production, might have been overborne without much difficulty, if France had contained a strong middle class, and large well-to-do working population such as existed in England: but in this matter the course of her political evolution had been exceptionally unfortunate.

The internal wars, which had desolated France, died out slowly during the sixteenth century: and in the seventeenth the royal power was consolidated by Richelieu and Mazarin. When Louis XIV took the reins into his own hands in 1661 France was prosperous and rich. He strove to make her also glorious and orthodox: but his wars impoverished her; his taxes were fatal to the growth of capital; and, by revoking the Edict of Nantes, he presented to the rivals of France a bounteous gift of an industrial population sufficient to have created a wealthy Kingdom. In fine, the last of the able Kings of France left her partially exhausted[1].

As the eighteenth century drew on, the extravagance of the French Court, and the selfish use which the privileged classes made of their power, pressed heavily on the people. The taxes were paid chiefly by the working classes, who stinted themselves perforce with a wasteful economy. The luxury of the rich and the poverty of the poor combined to make France a bad market for substantial simple goods, which were not choice enough for

du monde, p. 99.) The geographical distribution of industries in 1789 is set out by Levasseur (*Histoire...avant* 1789, Book VII. ch. VI). The development of the vast water power of the Jura, the Alps, and the Pyrenees, may possibly create a new centrifugal force. If the mountains of central France had been rich in water power they might have ultimately linked together the scattered industries: but they are very dry.

[1] See some statistics in the account given by Levasseur of "the decadence of France during the wars of religion" (*Histoire des classes ouvrières avant* 1789, vol. II. pp. 55—56); following on a description of her vigour during the Renaissance.

the rich, nor cheap enough for the common people. But all the more did the market which she offered for high-class tasteful goods excel all others in richness and discernment. More and more did her best artisans specialize themselves on work that called for individual taste and thought as regards form, arrangement and colour: meanwhile English artisans were specializing themselves rather on work that required strength, resolution, judgment, persistence, power to obey and to command, and withal an abundant use of capital. France produced more and more delicate textile and metallic work made by individual care to catch individual choice. England (while attaining brilliant success in some decorative industries and especially in furniture) produced more and more of the implements and the solid comforts, which are needed by a strong well-to-do people, and which make them stronger and more well-to-do.

So far stress has been laid on the influences which demand exercised on supply. Rich and discriminating purchasers evoked the fine and delicate sensitiveness, and the best power of individual initiative from artisans, shopkeepers and merchants: while the absence of a strong middle class and the poverty of the working classes, except in Paris and a few other places, prevented the growth of large and profitable businesses, engaged in producing and marketing common goods by highly organized methods in specialized centres of industry.

This is, however, only one side of the case. The other, which redounds wholly to the credit of France, is that her people like most of her neighbours, but perhaps more than any others, except the Italians, from whom they learnt much, early loved every form of Art. They held artists in high esteem; gloried in architecture, the mother of the arts; and gently persuaded artistic ideas to filter down, through those industries in which a delicate taste is generally required, to those which cater for more common wants[1].

[1] This tendency has been brought into prominence by Levasseur's histories. He generally places "Industry" between "Arts" and "Commerce": and, a long series of chapters stretching from the Middle Ages to the Second Republic, begins by considering the predominant influences, home and foreign, which were at work in the fine arts, with architecture at their head. Through those "producers" who earned their living by sculpture, painting and engraving, he proceeds to the artistic side of high-class furniture, jewellery and enamelling;

I, VI, 2. In short, the more the people of France were oppressed by evil courses which were heading for the Revolution, the more brilliant was her success in many branches of decorative work. But a deep-set national contrast is illustrated by the fact, that in the eighteenth as well as the nineteenth century Paris was surpassed by London in designing masculine costume; which is required to subordinate itself to the free movements of its wearer, and to combine something of grace with solid strength and durability: while French products held the lead in regard to feminine costume[1].

Thus France affords yet another illustration of Petty's great rule that the commodities, in the manufacture and export of which a nation has flourished, have been generally of native material[2]. But they have also been chiefly of such a fashion as to meet a distinctive home demand; thus obtaining the advantages of organized division of skilled labour for the home market before they venture out far into foreign markets: and the fact that the home market of France was highly specialized on fine products, gave her an advantage in making them for export; much of which remained with her after an end had been put by the Revolution to that uneven distribution of wealth in which it took rise. Thus the special features of French industry seem to be attributable mainly to political, military and social causes, and perhaps to some subtle racial influences, which lie outside our present view.

Lord Lauderdale writing in 1806 dwelt on this aspect of French export trade: and held that its basis in mere division

passing thence to "industry," in which a modicum of artistic instinct supplements a large amount of common labour in its application to metal, textiles, etc. In the later periods of French history, science is found associated with art in relation to industry.

Perhaps it is not an accident that the chief centre of artistic industry in France was on the main route from the Mediterranean to Paris. Silk, its material, belongs to the climates of Italy and the South of France: it was the favourite material of Italy; and it lends itself more than any other textile to fine artistic effects.

[1] It may be noted that in 1785 a tide of fashion for English goods of various kinds swept over France: but was repressed by strong decree (although Free trade was just then in favour with the French Court) on the ground that England would not reciprocate (Macpherson's *Annals*, vol. IV. p 82).

[2] See above, p. 33.

of labour was less firm than that of England, which was "derived from dexterity in supplanting and performing labour by capital": or, to use another phrase which he quotes from a French document of 1785, from "the use of machinery in every operation in which it can be employed[1]." I, VI, 3.

3. *The Revolution removed many obstacles to massive production. But the equal division of property made for industrial quietism; and in spite of the exceptional brilliancy of her engineers, France owes relatively little to the aid of mechanical power in manufacture.*

One of Colbert's chief ambitions was to endow his favourite manufactures with the strength that may be derived from capitalistic production on a large scale. Accordingly he set up, directly or indirectly, many considerable factories, which had some sort of royal privilege, and which were called "Royal." The Gobelins and a few others belonged to the King and were managed on his account: the majority had merely a more or less extensive monopoly granted to them; supplemented often by some grant of money, or at least some exemption from taxation. But the seed was sown in uncongenial soil. Royal protection barely defended them against the hostility of the Métiers, or brotherhoods of the masters of crafts. A new era began with the Revolution, though it inherited very much from the old[2].

[1] Basing himself on the same document, he shows that the finer qualities of woollen, silk, linen, and glass-ware were better and cheaper in France than in England; while the coarser kinds were better and cheaper in England. France excelled in china, England in earthenware; France in gold and silver work, England in hardware. Similar contrasts had been made earlier. Thus *Britannia Languens*, 1680, lamenting that "the English have never attained to near so universal a manufacture as the French," is full of comparisons of the flimsy, but tasteful French goods, with the strong, serviceable English: and so are the *Dialogue between Content and Complaint*, 1677; and Fortrey's *England's Interest and Improvement*, 1673. Defoe says that "As the Englishman gives more strength of sinews to his strokes in the loom, his work is firmer and faster and carries a greater substance with it" than foreign goods do.

In Marlborough's wars the French armies dispensed with English woollens, and so they went in rags (*Atlas Maritimus*, A.D. 1728, p. 109). Napoleon therefore connived at the clothing of his soldiers in English stuffs, even while straining every nerve to exclude English goods in general from the Continent.

[2] These observations may be taken in conjunction with the general discussion of Colbert's economic policy in Appendix D, 6. A study of the struggles of "la grande industrie" will be found in Levasseur's *Histoire...avant* 1789, especially Book VI. ch. III. See also pp. 762—7; and 952—4.

I, VI, 3. The troublous period 1793—1815 saw France deprived of many of the bravest, strongest, and best of her sons. But those, who remained, derived a new spirit from that partial freedom which they had won; and, the Taille being removed, even the poorer peasants were no longer pressed down by extreme want. So fresh energies were given to the arts of peace. But those arts were cultivated in the main on old lines. There was still a lack of the capital required for the general adoption of English machinery; and the people were still, for good and evil, somewhat disinclined towards English conditions of work.

The restrictive regulations of the State and of the Métiers before the Revolution had checked the spirit of enterprise: and the universal application throughout France of the law of equal inheritance (which had been only local before) is said to have materially lessened the inclination of a manufacturer to get together an expensive plant; since it was almost sure to be broken up at his death[1].

Again, this law of equal inheritance increased the number of artisans whose minds were partly given to their little plots of land; and who, while willing to work at convenient times for low pay in or near their own homes, were not willing to abandon their land except for very high wages. These causes strengthened the individuality of the French work.

There is a sense in which solidarity is characteristic of the French temper. It is an integral part of French idealism. It dominates those great waves of sentiment which from time to time sweep over the nation. It gives an intense fervour to their patriotism. It promotes, and is promoted by, their tendency to lean upon the Government for aid in difficulty; and to approve an amount of regulation and authoritative interference in their affairs which would be burdensome to Englishmen. Pushed to extremes it becomes hostile to independence and self-reliance[2].

[1] See Poinsard, *Libre-échange et protection*, pp. 479—485, 489—490, and 522—523. The gradual growth of joint stock companies for manufacture slightly diminishes the force of these considerations, since shares in a company could be divided without disturbing the business.

[2] Compare M. Demolins' discussion of the different conceptions of solidarity held by the Frenchman and the Anglo-saxon, *À quoi tient la supériorité des Anglo-saxons*, III. 4.

But on the other hand the great economic solidarity of the French family, especially in the country and small towns, fosters a certain aloofness, a certain disinclination to the organization of self-help, as well as to the steady and unyielding routine of the factory. M. Blondel says:—"It is because the spirit of association has remained very superficial with us, that people have been able to say with good reason that, what we want to learn is not so much how to produce, as how to combine the elements that constitute an industrial operation, and how to turn our own inventions to account and derive benefit from them[1]."

In all this time France was held back by the scarcity of her capital; by some lack of initiative among her business men, as distinguished from her professional classes; and not least by the meagre food of her working classes. For machinery had already increased greatly the volume and weight of the work, for which each operative was responsible: but had not attained to anything like its present facility in taking the main brunt of all heavy work on its own shoulders[2].

Here seems to lie the chief explanation of the fact that even when English methods of massive production were introduced into France, they seldom attracted the best workers. Cotton factories grew up under the shelter of Protection: but their work went heavily, and they did little credit to French energy. To the same cause it was due that England was able to export considerable quantities of plain silk stuffs to neutral markets in the face of French competition, and a little even to France herself.

[1] *La France et le marché du monde*, p. 109. The considerable success of the cooperative movement in France may be quoted on the other side. But its most brilliant example at Guise has been marked by the dominance of an individual will.

[2] Arthur Young (*Travels in France*, 1787—9) tells of the great state which could be kept up in France on a moderate income, partly because servants were contented with low wages and cheap food. It is well known that when Thomas Brassey was building railways in France, the native navvies could do but little work in comparison with the English standard, until he had got them on to English diet: after which they did not lag very much behind. But, as might have been expected, a similar experiment in regard to French textile operatives did not yield equally good results (*Report of Committee on Factories*, 1832, Q. 6441). Much information on wages and food in France and elsewhere is to be found in Symons' *Arts and Artisans at home and abroad*, 1839.

I, vi, 3. The finer silk manufactures called out all the best French qualities. The French climate favoured the production of raw silk and its manufacture. And, what was much more important, the French understood the importance of taste, variety and novelty in design, which the English did not. They had schools for designers; they granted copyright to new designs. In France a single manufacturer would have several designers at work on his premises, while in England a single designer would work for several manufacturers. And in the more delicate and intricate patterns, the economy of machine power counted for little: a rather proud retiring worker in his own cottage would do the best work, caring for the design and sometimes improving on it[1].

This organized team work in design anticipated organized team work in the technical applications of science. As far back as 1833 French manufacturers had anticipated the modern practice of Germany and other countries in applying chemical skill to "beautiful improvements in calico printing....There is not a printing ground there without its laboratory, or without its working chemist, whose business it is to carry on experiments with a view to improve the processes[2]."

The case was similar as to machinery. A few men of exceptional ability and aptitude organized excellent machine factories, the products of which were unsurpassed. But in general French machine factories were behind those of Belgium, and not in advance of those of Switzerland[3].

[1] There is much evidence on this subject in the *Report on Import Duties*, 1840, and Leaf (Q. 3260) gives as one reason for the superior taste of the French artisans, that "provisions being cheaper, they are not compelled to work such long hours for their maintenance, and they are able to take more pleasure, and to cultivate taste more than the workpeople do here."

The Select Committee on Arts and their connection with Manufactures 1835—6 also were much occupied with the influence of foreign importations in rousing the British manufacturer to a sense of his deficiencies in design and in technique: when the excellence is in quality, and not in cheapness, the "foreign goods are found to be French in nearly all cases." The present writer has seen a man weaving, in a cottage not far from Lyons, a fabric which was to be sold for 130 francs a metre: he scorned power looms, partly because a single spot of grease would cost more than a week's earnings.

[2] Evidence of a Lancashire cotton printer before the Committee on Manufactures, etc., 1833, Q. 3577—3587.

[3] See the evidence of the famous Maudslay and of Galloway before the Committee on the Export of Tools and Machinery of 1825: also that of Withers,

In the latter half of the nineteenth century the increase of wealth in France became very rapid, in spite of her great military expenditure in peace and in war. For the Frenchman works well, though he is averse to being driven; and though fond of amusements, especially in the towns, he takes them in inexpensive ways. His income is generally smaller than that of the Englishman; but his wife is an economical manager, and turns inexpensive food to good account. So expenditure is generally kept down below income; and France is in the first rank of capitalist countries[1].

It is however a noteworthy, and not altogether healthy sign, that she appears to devote no very large share of her wealth to new industrial and commercial enterprises at home or abroad. The growth of her factories hardly keeps pace with that in several neighbouring countries. And her very large holdings of foreign securities are said to consist mainly of Government bonds, with a relatively small addition in the shares of industrial undertakings: in so far as this is true, its cause may perhaps be sought partly in the fact that her people do not travel much. And yet Frenchmen are specially fitted for certain large enterprises by their talent for engineering. From early times French cathedrals and fortifications, French roads and canals have borne evidence to high creative faculty. Since the Revolution the engineering profession has been held in special honour in France: there is perhaps no other country in which the ablest lads are so generally inclined towards it. The excellent technique of her railways testifies to a high level of engineering ability; and the success of the Suez Canal and other great undertakings indicates largeness of conception on the part of her leading men.

an English engineer established in Belgium, before the Corresponding Committee of 1841.

[1] It is said that, where there are only one or two children, French parents are apt to work less and to save less than where there are many children for whom portions have to be provided. In so far as this is true, we may not count as a cause of the high average wealth of the French the fact that they have spent less on rearing their families than more prolific races. But of course the aggregate wealth of France, and her importance in the world would have been much greater if they had been more prolific. On the general subject of the influence of a low birth-rate on the growth of wealth see Levasseur, *Population Française*, vol. III; and Leroy Beaulieu, *Économie Politique*, Part VII. ch. II.

I, VI, 4. Another side of the same faculties is shown in such manufactures as those of the bicycle, motor car, submarine, and aeroplane; where French inventors have led, and a few French operative mechanics displayed a skill, a judgment and a resource which are nowhere surpassed. As these new delicate industries have reached the stage of massive production, the faculty of disciplined steadfast work becomes more important: the motor car, the submarine and the aeroplane tend to find their chief homes in other countries, as the bicycle did long ago. But there is no sign that her engineers will cease to devise, or that her small but noble army of first-class mechanics will cease to execute, new constructions in the van of progress.

4. *Individuality in production contends under ever increasing difficulties against the forces of massive organization. Illustration from industries connected with fashion.*

This same tendency is shown even more conspicuously in those industries in which the leadership of France has been long established. The individuality of her designers and her best operatives still shows itself most fully in that mastery of form and colour which calls into being an endless variety of products, each of which is individual in character and each of which is a harmonious whole. Thus new Parisian goods are sold at very high prices to the richest customers in all countries. In the next stage copies of them, made chiefly by local hand labour, are sold at rather high prices to the moderately rich. The last stage is the adoption of the new fashion for general use: and, for that purpose, people in commercial countries, endowed with a high faculty for organization, study the imported French model, catch the keynotes of its ideas: they translate these ideas as far as possible into mechanical language, and produce passable imitations for the middle and working classes[1].

To meet such competition France is driven to make a little

[1] Going further, American and other dealers in various textile fabrics of changeful fashions will get independent ideas as to some new fabric or pattern, by studying the general trend of textile products and costumes in Paris. But these ideas need to be translated into the language of highly specialized machinery before they can be commercially successful. So they have been taken to some appropriate centre, perhaps Saxony, where they are put into practical shape.

use of massive methods herself, even in industries to which they are not wholly appropriate. But the tendency of the age is to require the producer to show his goods to the purchaser. The purchaser does not, as a rule, now go to the producer unless he is in quest of goods of a very special kind: therefore, when the French goods have reached the stage of semi-mechanical imitation, the untiring push and bold energy of the travellers for German and other firms have had an advantage over their French rivals. Meanwhile, however, Paris may have made one or more new models, which can be sold at scarcity prices to those who are tired of the last model, partly because it has become somewhat vulgarized. Thus French creative faculty is the source of a constant stream of wealth: but the breadth of this stream does not increase as fast as does the number of people in the two hemispheres who follow the lead of France.

Her special faculties are of more force in the clothing than in the textile industries. But the texture and patterns of some of her woollens as well as her silks, and the patterns even of her cottons enable her to sell at prices that yield good wages to her operatives. The fine and delicate perception shown in her wines and other food products is as marked, though not as unique, as that shown in her ornamental fabrics.

To maintain her position France needs a continual supply of fresh inventive minds; and here the predominance of Paris may possibly prove a source of danger: even Lyons is said to depend increasingly on Paris designers. Every great capital city attracts the brightest and strongest minds from the whole country: but in France this attraction is more powerful than elsewhere. Comparatively little of the intellectual and artistic vigour of Paris is to be seen in provincial towns, and still less among the agricultural population. The sterling qualities of resolution, family affection, and thrift, which prevail among the peasants, give strength and stability to France in an hour of peril. But they do little towards filling the gaps in the ranks of brilliant inventors and designers, which are caused by the exhausting nervous strain of Paris, as of every huge city. Worth himself was not a Frenchman. The strong designs of Morris and some other Englishmen for wall paper, and other decorations have made way even in Paris. And such work as that of Liberty

I, VI, 4. has shown Paris how Englishmen have profited by the supreme lessons of Indian art.

England must herself look forward to a time when her natural resources will have become scanty, while the arts and resources of routine mechanical manufacture will be the common property of all the four quarters of the globe. The experience of France in the past must raise for England some hopes and some anxieties. These are likely to be heightened and deepened as the twentieth century draws on: and Englishmen will learn in the future, as in the past, some of their most instructive lessons from across the Channel.

In conclusion it may be remarked that those French industries, which have received most aid from Government by bounties, and by Protective duties against competitive imports, are not those which have flourished most. Chief among them are her shipping industries, her heavy steel industries, and her manufactures of common textile stuffs. None of these indeed are specially congenial to the temper of her people: but their progress has been sufficiently slow to give some support to the notion that Governmental aid to old industries tends to check enterprise; unless indeed those, who receive it, are exceptionally full of energy and encouraged by openings for great work. Government has given little or no special aid to those industries whose products confer distinction on France on account of their fineness and delicacy; and cause them to be preferred to all others in neutral markets, and therefore to sell at higher prices than are to be had for similar products of other countries.

CHAPTER VII

THE INDUSTRIAL LEADERSHIP OF GERMANY: SCIENCE IN THE SERVICE OF INDUSTRY[1]

1. *The economic unity of Germany was achieved tardily, and in spite of many hindrances: but the movement was working under the surface for some time before it succeeded with apparent suddenness.* I, VII, 1.

At various times in her history France has disputed the leadership of the Continent of Europe with Spain and Austria. But Spain has declined; and Austria is no longer the chief leader of the German people. In fact her richest province is Bohemia, which is Slav rather than German; and less than a quarter of the population of Austria-Hungary is German. Therefore the "German Empire" of to-day stands out as the chief heir of the great traditions of the German race.

We have seen that England and France have passed each through alternating periods of rapid progress and relative retrogression: but that their history has been in the main one of continuous increase in unity and strength. In marked contrast has been the history of the German people. During a great part of the Middle Ages and for some time afterwards, it was full of glory. For several centuries internal discords and hostile invasions forced Germany into the background; but

[1] This chapter was written before the World-war, and the use of the present tense in it may be taken to refer generally to the years 1910—13. As little change as possible has been made in revising it during 1917: though many of those, who have owed much to Germany in the past, have felt that German character has changed, since the whole youth of the nation in their most susceptible years were brought under the influence of a militarism, whose spirit and ethics were those of Frederick II.

 in the last half century she has moved rapidly and steadily forwards to a place in the first rank of the pioneers of political and economic progress. In this sense she is a new country; and we shall see presently how she shares with America and other countries, which are commonly regarded as "new," some of the advantages of youth. But her present strength is not fully to be understood without some reference to her inheritance of germs of great qualities from the distant past. Atavistic influences need to be noted in regard to races, in the same way as in regard to individual families.

History shows the German as affectionate to those near him; but as rather narrow in his sympathies, and as inclined to "particularism"; that is, to undue insistence on the separate interests of the particular social, economic or political group in which he finds himself; and yet finding pleasure in fighting in the pay of strangers. The present German inclination towards Cartels has something reminiscent of the Hanseatic and other Leagues of German cities in the Middle Ages.

The land, that is now Germany, contained in the Middle Ages more cities that could claim leadership in trade and industry than any other except Italy. They joined together in Leagues, generally of an informal character, and with ever-shifting boundaries: though with enough consistency to perform the almost national task of clearing the northern seas of piracy. This shifting of boundaries was due partly to the dominant note of German character, partly to the fact that changing conditions favoured affinities, first in one direction, and then in another over the wide land.

Gradually most of the cities lost prominence and sank back into the surrounding dominion, from which indeed they had never been wholly emancipated. Then came the Provincial stage, in which German Principalities, great and small, grew and declined: they combined and recombined under the influence of the same causes as had operated before, together with the alliances and the intermarriages of princely families.

The Roman Empire, though by this time regarded increasingly as a German Empire, was not a very effective bond of union: partly because its chief seat was in remote Vienna and it looked eastwards as well as westwards and northwards.

Even the rise of Prussia seemed rather to accentuate than to allay German discord: for Prussia was suspected of some want of consideration for the interests of others.

Misfortune followed Germany till about 1850. A few of her industries, especially in Saxony and the Rhineland, attained some success; but speaking generally she remained poor relatively to France as well as England, and backward relatively to both of them as well as to Belgium and Switzerland. But when one looks below the surface, one can see that the true German spirit was merely overlaid by incessant strife. It never died: its revival was largely due to a revolt against the slaughter of Germans by Germans under Frederick II and under Napoleon. Driven in on themselves by political failures their thoughts founded "an empire in the air," that is, an empire in philosophy, literature, and music. This empire in the air was not Prussian. It was German. And the ideal empire was the foundation of the material[1].

In the first half of the nineteenth century the Universities were common meeting places of men from all parts of Germany. Passing from one to another, teachers and students alike propagated a German, as distinct from a Provincial, movement in philosophy and learning, in literature and music. This intellectual unity had made great progress before much attention was paid to economic problems. But gradually the inconveniences of the commercial subdivision (*Zersplitterung*) of Germany became prominent: so that some, who cared but little for mere material considerations, took advantage of the irritation caused by these inconveniences; and pressed for commercial unity, partly for its own sake, and partly as a means to larger ends. The movement took the form of the Zollverein, or Fiscal-league. In 1852 the League encircled practically the whole of Germany by a single customs frontier, within which goods moved freely:

[1] When Frederick II died, the following incomparable groups were alive: Haydn, Mozart and Beethoven; Kant, Fichte and Hegel; Lessing, Goethe and Schiller. But Macpherson, *Annals of Commerce*, under date 1762, quotes, as proof that Prussia would not become industrial, a proclamation by a Prussian Governor of Saxon Freiburg, who was less liberal than his master:—"It is an indecency not to be suffered for burghers to presume to talk of state affairs, in which such pitiful creatures can do neither good nor harm."

I, VII, 1. the taxes collected at the frontier being paid into a common purse[1].

The League finally removed those hindrances to internal commerce, which in List's words "lame internal traffic, and have much the same effect as if every limb of the human body were bound by tight ligatures, so that the blood could not flow from one to another." Its benefits were unalloyed by any considerable drawback from the point of view either of the enlightened Free-trader Nebenius or the enlightened Protectionist List. This was mainly because it introduced a free circulation into a territory which nature had made compact, and which man's quarrels and jealousies alone had separated. Of course the success of the Zollverein affords no good argument in favour of a commercial union, imposed on countries to which nature has assigned separate frontiers, widely removed from one another. For that would introduce much friction: and, if it involved the imposition of complex differential duties on things which now pass British frontiers freely, it would perhaps reproduce on a larger scale many of the evils from which Prussia suffered, when her territory consisted of some seventy fragments scattered over Germany. The success which has followed the founding of the German Zollverein, so far from affording a strong argument in favour of such a union, tends rather to suggest that it should not be undertaken lightly[2], though a closer union in spirit of the various members of the British Confederation of States would be worth more than much economic gain.

[1] The need for it is best comprehended by a glance at maps, showing the tarif frontiers which it removed. In this connection see the map in the *Encyclopaedia Britannica*, s.v. Germany; also map 107 in the Atlas of the *Cambridge Modern History*. The present subdivision of Thuringia corresponds rather closely to those which were common throughout Germany not long ago: but import duties are not levied at the frontiers of the several Principalities now. The human element in the formation of industrial Germany is well shown in Dawson's masterly study of the *Evolution of Modern Germany*, especially chs. III, V, VI.

[2] We must return to these subjects at a much later stage; meanwhile reference may be made to the further account given of the Zollverein in Appendix F. Sombart, *Die Deutsche Volkswirthschaft*, I. II. lays stress on the hindrances which the minute subdivision of her territory put in the way of specialized production for sale at a distance. They are partly responsible for the fact that simple homely "domestic" work held as prominent a position in many parts of Germany a hundred years ago, as it did in England some two hundred years ago.

2. *The facilities for traffic, begun by the Zollverein, were developed by railways, and have helped to build up much the largest industrial district in Europe.*

The Rhine, deepened at critical points, now bears a large number of barges of 5000 tons each, which carry coal and other heavy products at relatively low freights, nearly up to the Swiss frontier. Other rivers have been improved in like manner though to a less extent: while an admirable system of canals connecting the chief river basins of Germany is already doing much, and is expected ere long to do a great deal more, for the general cheapening of heavy traffic throughout the northern half of the country[1].

Her first railways came chiefly to those districts, which were already best supplied with water communications; and were the richest, partly for that reason. Even in 1850 Westphalia, Rhineland and neighbouring parts of Germany formed an "extensive basin of population, commerce and industry, subordinate and tributary to which the other systems of railways of the Germanic states may be considered[2]." In this, as in other cases, strength has been the source of strength.

Railways have made the lower Rhineland and Westphalia into much the strongest compact economic unit which exists, or which seems to be in progress of growth, anywhere on the Continent of Europe. And it is connected by close networks of railways on the south with the iron-mines of Luxemburg and Alsace, and the industrial districts of the upper Rhine; while on the east a similar band stretches out through Saxony to

[1] By aid of canals goods can be sent from the Rhine into Switzerland and the South of France; and Berlin, in a level district, has been connected without difficulty with Hamburg, Stettin and Breslau; and so on. Much of the inland water traffic is indeed liable to be suspended in winter by ice; and summer drought often obstructs traffic in the higher reaches of most rivers. But in spite of this compulsory idleness of the plant during a considerable part of the year, the inland freights by water are generally about a third of those by rail; though they themselves are low in comparison with the English rates. More is said on these matters below, III.

[2] Lardner, *Railway Economy*, p. 460. Railways came late to Germany: in 1840 she had only 400 miles of them; and she had imported from England and Belgium most of their plant. Now she has a larger mileage of them than any other country in Europe: their density of traffic is much less than that of English railways, but it grows rapidly.

I, VII, 2. Silesia. These two broad bands produce about half of the iron and steel products of the Continent of Europe[1].

To the advantages of a central position, and the absence of any considerable range of mountains, except in Southern Bavaria, Germany adds those of a very large expanse of land, nearly the whole of which repays diligent and wise cultivation. Her soil is not indeed as rich, nor her climate as favourable, as that of France; nor has she much land that is as good as (say) the best fourth part of that of Britain. But she has no hopeless waste lands to compare in the aggregate with the cold rain-sodden moors and low mountains of Scotland, Ireland, Wales and England: and her hot summers are better suited for wheat, sugar-beet and some other crops, than those of Britain are. On the whole she could probably supply food to a larger population in proportion to her area than Britain could, though less than France could, with an equal application of labour and mechanical appliances per acre. But in fact her population is less dense than that of Britain and much denser than that of France[2].

Further she has half of the known coal deposits of Europe; and her potash deposits are without any rival. But her supplies

[1] There are rather thin places in these two bands, especially near the Middle Rhine and in the stretch between Westphalia and Saxony. The extension of the band running eastwards beyond Saxony is narrow. But the two bands together are quite beyond the rivalry of the two national districts on the Continent next in industrial importance, which cluster round the old seats of mediaeval industry in Italy and the Low Countries. A general map of Europe shows an area of dense population made up of most of Belgium, together with the neighbouring parts of France; and this is so compact as to be comparable with Rhineland plus Westphalia, to which it is next in rank.

[2] The percentages of the occupied population, male and female, in the three great divisions (1) agriculture, forestry, and fishing; (2) manufacture and mining; (3) trade and transport respectively, are: in the United Kingdom, 13·0; 45·8; 16·3: in Germany, 35·2; 40·0; 12·4: in France, 41·8; 35·5; 9·5. (The figures for Germany relate to 1907; the rest to 1901.) Forty-five per cent. of those Germans whose occupation is mainly in agriculture, etc., are women: but this fact is partly accounted for by the considerations that, (1) many men whose main occupation is different, work in the fields a good deal; and (2) agriculturists in military service are not reckoned in these figures; nor are Poles and others who work in Eastern Germany in the summer and return home for the winter. The families connected with the first group in Germany number in all only 17·7 million, while the corresponding figure for the second group is 26·4 million: though the numbers of those employed are not very different.

of iron ore came chiefly from Alsace and France before the World-war.

It is a notable, though not altogether accidental, fact that the richest, or nearly richest, provinces of all the seven countries by which Germany is surrounded, are contiguous to her frontiers; and find traffic for her railways. Part of this is transit or "through" traffic. But much greater importance attaches to trade which is conducted in through trucks between every part of Germany and the countries by which she is surrounded.

British exports and imports must generally be moved at some expense, and often with some extra risk, from truck to ship and from ship to truck. But, in suitable cases, truck loads can be sent straight from the producer into the warehouse of the consumer alike in Germany's import and in her export trade. She does not send as much as three per cent. of her exports to any country whose frontiers do not march with hers, except only the United States and the United Kingdom.

The markets of Europe are at present richer in the aggregate than those of any other quarter of the world. Germany is in the heart of them, and railways have made Europe like a steppe which a caravan can traverse in any direction; while the cost of carriage by the modern caravan is but a very small fraction of that by the old. Were it not for the heavy tarifs which she and her neighbours levy at their frontiers, it is probable that the economy of transport which railways within and beyond her territory are providing, would have widened the European markets accessible to her manufacturers nearly in proportion to the square of that increase in economy: and, even as it is, they have widened the markets very greatly[1].

Thus the geographical features which have always adapted her for unity, have been turned to full account. During the long years of her subdivision, she had singularly little opportunity for massive production: suddenly she obtained exceptional advantages for it. She has developed these advantages on lines peculiarly her own. On one side they represent the

[1] As to the Law of Squares in transport and trade, see above, p. 27. As to the advantages which Germany derives from her configuration and position, see Gruber, *Wirtschaftsgeographie*, Division I.

I, VII, 2. strict discipline which men of iron (Frederick II, Bismarck and others) have developed for good and evil in Prussia, and in a less degree in the rest of Germany. On the other side they represent that zeal for education, which was associated with the rise of the national spirit. These two motive forces, acting on Germany's great geographical advantages, have naturally, if not necessarily, made her the leader in the applications of science to massive production.

In fine, from the geographical and material points of view France and Germany are in some respects similar to one another, but from the human point of view the contrasts are more marked than the resemblances. For two hundred years, during which France was united by a strong national feeling, Germans were largely occupied in fighting one another: and yet individualism is a French rather than a German characteristic.

Thus the products of the workshops of France make their way through their excellence and in spite of their high price: and, when they yield ground to products of her factories, the cause is often that her high grade individual work can no longer hold its own in competition with cheaper machine-made productions: for these are ever approaching nearer to the delicacy and variety of that work, in which the sensitive hand does more, and the machine does less, than in the large factory. But in Germany the case is the reverse. Where artistic sensibility is required, the best handiwork of Germany is seldom either as individual or as fine as that of France; and it does not always reach the highest standard of England in products, that demand absolute exactness and delicacy of finish. As a rule the products of her workshop and domestic industries rank rather below than above the products of her factories, and make their way by a cheapness which reflects long hours of labour and low earnings. A displacement of such exports by factory-made goods generally indicates a diminished use of ineffective methods of production, and an increased use of methods in which her faculty for organization, her habits of order and her methodical training are turned to good account[1].

[1] The growth of large businesses in some parts of Germany has been very rapid; but not in all. The last industrial census, that of 1907, showed as many persons employed in small businesses (1—5 employees) as in large concerns

3. *Germany's zeal for solid education lays the foundation of her industrial progress.* I, VII, 3.

Germany holds a leading place in scientific studies; and she is without a rival in the organized applications of science to practical problems. In 1828 Liebig set up a chemical laboratory at the University of Giessen; and a great part of the subsequent rapid advance in the chemical technique of production is due to his pupils, and to others taught by them in Germany and elsewhere. France indeed, the true mother of chemistry, has continued to work mainly on her own lines. But America's scientific studies came early under German influence; and Britain followed gradually.

A chief strength of German education lies in its order and system. Discipline is indeed a foe to spontaneity; while spontaneity is the chief creator of original work, and especially of that which makes epochs in thought. This danger has not been overlooked: and organized efforts for the increase of spontaneity have a place in Germany's educational as well as in her military system: but after all spontaneity is the only effective inspirer of spontaneity, and its only trusty guide. The disciplined life of the German schoolboy is indeed a good preparation for subordinate work in factory or counting-house. But it attains only a partial success in the education of self-reliance; of the ability to forbear as well as to bear; and of quick intuitive sympathy. The education which boys receive from boys is the chief source of that political faculty, which in spite of some blemishes, has held together the British Federation of Nations in bonds of sympathy and affection; and history seems to show that the German people are somewhat deficient in it.

Not the least of the benefits which railways have conferred on the industries of Germany, lies in their quickening of the intercourse of her Universities. Though German Schools have a severer discipline than the English, yet in German Universities both students and teachers have great freedom; while the constant migration of teachers as well as students from one Uni-

(51 or more). Medium concerns (6—50 employees) showed only two-thirds as many as each of the other groups. An excellent compressed account of *Industrial Germany* by Mr W. H. Dawson throws much light on the subjects of this and of some later chapters

I, VII, 3. versity to another brings a national opinion to bear on each one: and thus, in spite of the freedom, which is generally allowed to each Professor to choose his subject and his method of dealing with it, German Universities combine order and efficiency in a remarkable degree.

Thus all the world has had much to learn from German methods of education. But the lesson must be itself criticized, and made the starting point for further progress. In particular it seems doubtful whether the discipline of German school life is a good preparation for making use of the unlimited opportunities for spontaneity which are offered at the University. Moreover a wayward teacher sometimes turns his liberty to bad account by directing his pupils' attention to secondary issues before they have mastered leading principles. In the result it appears that though German original work is of prodigious volume, it often is somewhat lacking in penetrative power. The matter is one on which an Englishman will speak with diffidence. But there are some reasons for doubting whether the average student at a German University is as well taught, or takes his studies as seriously as the average student at English Universities, in spite of the undue predominance of games in them. But most of the vast number of German University students (some 65,000) get so far in touch with scientific studies, that in after life they are inclined to take seriously any scientific issue that impinges on their business; and they then find some five thousand trained chemists ready to respond to invitations to earn their livelihood by special skill[1].

Again, the military drill, which is imposed on all citizens of full physical strength, gives some firmness to very weak characters, and helps to prevent the growth of a class of professional paupers. But perhaps it does some injury to many fine and sensitive characters, and even checks the development of the subtler forms of manual skill; as well as of the highest genius that might find vent in literature, art, and science.

These qualifications are important, but it remains true that the amount of intellectual activity in Germany is greater than

[1] Some trenchant opinions on these matters, supported by statistics of which use has been made in the text, will be found in *Modern Germany* by J. Ellis Barker, 1912, chs. XX and XXV.

in any other country; and that the broad enlightenment, which most high officials and heads of large businesses have acquired at the Universities, enables Germany to apply science to industry with a breadth and system which establish a claim to industrial leadership of a special kind[1].

Availing herself of the economies of massive production in education, Germany can afford to offer it at charges which are within the reach of the lower middle class, and even of artisans; and therefore the supply of scientific routine-services rises faster than the demand for them does: though that grows very fast, as a consequence of the rapid increase in Germany's exports of goods in the production of which those services can be turned to account. Consequently the great benefits of a large system of education are accompanied by some evil, which is sometimes described as the growth of a "scientific proletariat." The clerk who can merely write and do simple arithmetic has found at last his proper place and the routine experimenter must find his only a little higher up: but, when that has been done, he will become a source of strength to his country from the social point of view, as he is already in an eminent degree from the economic point of view. He contributes increasingly to the success in foreign markets of many of those industries from which Germany derives a chief claim to leadership[2].

In Germany—and the same may perhaps be said of Scandinavia and Switzerland—education gives sobriety and strength to the conduct of the citizen in every-day life: it develops civic virtues; and it inclines the German of to-day to adhere to the habits of low living and high thinking which he has inherited from a generation of forced economy. He is better

[1] The trade schools, which Saxony started in the eighteenth century, were doubtless a chief cause of her early success in manufacture: and German trade schools of all kinds, but especially her "continuation schools," have raised and partly solved questions of ever increasing importance. It is noticeable that some of the most suggestive experiments in this direction have been made in parts of Germany which are not inclined to the extreme stringency of Prussian discipline.

[2] Similarly, the thoroughness and universality of the musical training of her people have given her piano-manufacturers a large choice of designers, and workers apt to judge tones with a true and fine instinct: several of the English, French, and American firms, which have attained the highest success in the industry, were founded by Germans.

I, VII, 4. fed than his father was: the care for his health is directed by more knowledge, and his food, though still simple and not always cooked with French skill, serves its purpose well; because it is chosen and prepared in accordance with the popularized results of chemical and physiological research.

Sixty years ago, perhaps even forty years ago, the German on the average did no more in three hours than the Englishman in two. But while the Englishman has possibly been a little spoilt by prosperity, the German in most trades works harder than he used to do. He does not very much less work in an hour than the Englishman, and he works for longer hours: now, where double shifts are not in vogue, a man who will keep expensive plant working two hours longer than another, may be the cheaper to the employer even at higher wages in proportion to an output per hour, which is only slightly less. Again, the German woman, though well educated, is in no way emancipated from the old ideals of patient devotion to family cares. And the intense interest, which parents take in the schoolwork of their children, is in the first rank among the sources of German progress.

4. *Germany's leadership is mainly in industries, in which academic training and laboratory work can be turned to good account; and these are growing in relative importance.*

In the early stages of modern manufacture scientific training was of relatively small importance. The Germans accordingly, recognizing their own weakness in practical instinct and organizing faculty, took the part of pupils, whose purpose it was to outrun their teachers. They began by the direct copying of English machinery and methods: and they next set themselves to get employment in English firms; and to offer steady, intelligent services in return for a low pay in money, and a silent instruction in the inner workings of the business[1].

The practical knowledge and faculty thus obtained served as

[1] The Committees on Import Duties and on the Exportation of Machinery of 1840, 1841, already referred to, were told that in Prussia "every man is intelligent, and every man thinks." In spite of the prohibition of exportation, every new English machine was bought at Government expense and sent to the Gewerbe Institut at Berlin. It was there tried; and, if successful, a working model was made of it for preservation in the Museum; while the machine itself was given to some progressive manufacturer.

the basis on which to build a large superstructure of business efficiency. This ran out into all branches of industry and trade; but especially into those, in which the systematic training of school and university and technical institute could be of most avail. And all the while Germany has been quick to grasp the practical significance of any master discovery that is made in other countries, and to turn it to account.

Her hopes of an enlarged industrial leadership would however be less than they are, if progress were likely to depend in the future mainly on that mechanical adaptation of means to ends, in which a ready wit and sound judgment are more important than elaborate mental training. But science has had a considerable share in the brilliant mechanical advances made by the present generation; and the greater part of the increased command over nature which man is obtaining, may be traced to the aid of chemical, electrical and biological sciences. Here there is a vast field which has as yet been little cultivated, and for which the resources of the twentieth century are beyond all comparison greater than those of the age of the early mechanical inventions—a field therefore which may, for many generations to come, yield Increasing Returns to effort. In this field motherwit counts for much, but only on condition that it is equipped with thorough training and with high-class laboratories; just as in a naval battle mother-wit and courage are needed for victory to-day as much as ever, but yet are of little avail unless aided by modern equipments.

It is moreover a matter of common knowledge that applications of chemistry and other sciences dominate nearly all the chief recent advances of agriculture: of the industries connected with all but the simplest forms of food, solid and liquid; with new textile materials and dyes; with subtle forms of glass; with compounds of steel and other metals, which render possible far more intense applications of pressure, explosive power, heat, and other forms of physical force, than seemed attainable even a short time ago. In all this Germany has played a conspicuous part. Two or three countries are perhaps fully on a level with her in scientific conceptions of that rare kind, characteristic of the highest genius, which makes epochs in thought and lays the foundations of epochs in industrial practice in the same

I, VII, 5. or a later generation. But none can compare as yet with her in the organized work of detail, by which the epoch-making thought is brought to bear on practice in such a way as to make an epoch in industry.

It has already been noticed that France led the way in the employment of chemists as officials of particular factories. The Germans have led the way in dividing up a scientific problem —whether mainly of the academic sort, or concerned with the attainment of a particular result of commercial value—between a group, or class, or "team" of workers of inferior rank, and generally rather young. The main responsibility for the work lies with a chief, who sets to each man his task: very often the whole group is put to the same, or nearly the same, experiment and other investigation, applied to various products. The German temperament is specially adapted for this work; and the practical applications of science, in which Germany leads, give very large scope for it. Other countries, and especially England and America, seem inclined to move, for good and for evil, on the same lines of massive production of knowledge by methods that are partially mechanical. But Germany holds an unquestioned lead in those fine chemical (including glass) industries which offer large scope for the application of science to practical work. She has larger and more numerous laboratories than any other country both of the first and the second order—that is both such as are devoted to the advancement of science as an end in itself, and those which pursue various technical ends[1].

5. *Germany's industry and trade have some advantages which attach to youth; their strength and its limitations.*

It is noteworthy that in the steel and some other industries, a greater proportion of German works than of English are on that large scale which recent experience has proved to be the most economical: they are equipped with the best semi-automatic plant, and turn their waste heat and gas and other by-products to the fullest account. This by itself proves nothing,

[1] As to relations between the various orders of laboratories see above, pp. 101—2. More is said below (pp. 203—5) as to the need of supplementing the creative work of men of genius by teams of well-disciplined association.

for the English works are older on the average than the German; and it is asserted that a comparison between new English works and new German works is not to the disadvantage of English: but it must be admitted that a large share of the improved scientific methods has come from Germany[1].

A couple of generations ago the inexperienced firm was everywhere grievously handicapped by its lack of trained instinct and experience, and perhaps by its ignorance of important trade secrets. But now the application of scientific principles is constantly ousting established practice; and the new firm can generally buy from a pioneer maker a more efficient and economical plant than the average of that of his older rivals, even if they are quick to throw away all that is obsolete. Again, so fast do the methods of industry change, that employees frequently lose, rather than gain, in efficiency as they approach middle age: and thus what used to be one of the chief advantages of an old-established firm, is now of little service; and indeed it sometimes becomes a hindrance. In this and other ways German industries have advantages over British in being free from the trammels of traditional organization.

She can bring to bear the powers of large concentrated capital and labour on great tasks, in which she can profit by the experience of others, assimilating and improving on their best methods, machinery and organization. Her employers and her workmen in the growing industry are generally younger, have more elasticity and are more free from the fetters of trade custom and usage than they would have been; had not the new age broken suddenly with the traditions of the old, especially in regard to those branches of industry, trade, and transport, in which massive operations have the fullest scope.

Again, a German, when wanting to get a foothold in a market in which English or French traders are established, will take a small order to meet some special or local need; though it requires him to make new patterns or other plant, and to take trouble, for which the order gives no adequate return. But an

[1] Reference has already been made (p. 95) to the curious fortune which aided Germany's steel industries in rising to the first rank by means of an invention, made by an Englishman, but exclusively applicable to phosphoric ores of which Germany could procure large supplies from Luxemburg and Lorraine.

I, VII, 5. old-established firm may be as wise in refusing *some* of these orders as the new firm is in taking them[1].

The Germans excel in the sedulous adaptation of their manufactures to local needs, high and low. They are quick to take account of differences in climate, of taste and custom, and even superstition. They make cheap things for people of impulsive temperament; who prefer a brilliant gala dress, to one made of solid durable material. And with equal patience they get to know enough of the business affairs of individual traders to be able to sell with relatively small risk on long credit, where Englishmen sometimes demand prompt payment: in all this they are much aided by their industry in acquiring the languages of Eastern Europe, Asia and South America. Even in markets in which English is spoken they push their way by taking trouble in small things to which the Englishman will not always bend himself.

On the other hand Germany is in a weak position, in so far as a considerable part of her exports to Eastern Europe, and elsewhere, still consists of simple textile and other goods for sale to homely consumers with limited means, to whom low prices are especially attractive. For countries that started a little behind her in the industrial race are already learning to make such things for themselves; and the causes which have tended to exclude the commoner and cheaper forms of English and French goods from Germany's markets may possibly affect her export trade in the future somewhat prejudicially. Moreover some of those parts of Europe, which are economically within her sphere of influence, are already adopting her own methods of fostering by Protective duties those simpler forms of massive production, in which almost unskilled labour can get fairly satisfactory results by working new machinery bought from western countries or made on western models. She may therefore be forced to turn her export industries, as France and

[1] British manufacturers and merchants complain that some disparagements of their methods, in official reports and elsewhere, ignore considerations such as this. That may be granted: but when all just deductions have been made, the reports of travellers and Consuls leave no room for doubting that Britain has something to learn from Germany in these matters. A similar conflict of opinion exists as to the aid given by German banks to old and new German businesses in foreign countries.

England have done, towards making those finer goods, which half-developed countries cannot make for themselves at all; but which the wealthier consumers in all parts of the world may be willing to buy almost without regard to their price. There are already signs that she is setting herself to this task, with her wonted resolution and energy.

She is also setting herself with much originality and resource to emulate the individual taste and fancy of French goods. And she is bringing her great organizing faculty to bear on work belonging to the border between mechanical and manual production, which is partly industrial and partly artistic. As has already been indicated, France is moving almost against her will somewhat in this direction; and many other countries and especially the United States are moving in it not unwillingly[1].

Again Germany obtains supplies of strong physical workers for her iron industries, for building and for agriculture, from nearly the same Slav and Latin races from which America draws similar supplies. Their standards of life are not high: they are often willing to labour hard for low wages; and they are serviceable not only for unskilled manual work, but also for the management of semi-automatic machines. In this respect Germany and America have an advantage over England, similar to that which, more than a century ago, the new centres of textile industry in England had over its old homes: for in the new centres everyone was willing to do work that was new to him by new methods; while the spirit, if not the formal regulations, of the old gilds offered a more or less open opposition to the introduction of new methods, that tended to lower the value of the knowledge and skill obtained by long training. This advantage will diminish in time. But for the present American manufacturers, who have travelled in England and in Germany, appear to be unanimous in their opinion that a modern American machine is less likely to be worked grudgingly and to less than its full capacity in Germany than in England[1].

[1] Germany will soon become old in some respects, relatively to her Eastern neighbours. In 1891, when the present writer visited some large engineering works in Bohemia, the manager said: "Look at that lad. A few months ago he was working in the country for *5s.* a week. I now pay him *12s.*, and he is

I, VII, 5. There is another side to the progress which the German makes in foreign markets by his alertness, his readiness to take trouble about small details, his familiarity with foreign languages and so on: but that side may be best presented in the words of a German. "In those industries where cartels and syndicates have not yet been formed, too great a rôle is played by dubious practices of many kinds, by infringement of payment stipulations, by unjustifiable deductions, etc.: while on the other hand the cartels are often too ruthless in their action. In this field we have much to learn from the English business man. Long commercial tradition and international business experiences have taught him long ago that broad-mindedness is the best business principle....Tolerance, another quality, which the German lacks, has been of great practical advantage to the Englishman[1]."

There are several matters, closely connected with those just discussed, on which it might have been proper to say something here; but, as they will need to be studied on broad lines later on, it seems best to pass them by. Such are the growth of cartels and other forms of associated action in production and trade, with or without monopolistic tendency: the parts played by German banks in promoting and controlling industrial enterprises; and recent developments of Germany's fiscal policy.

It is obvious that an industry which offers large scope for the economies of massive production stands to gain much from Protective duties, if they can be so arranged as to insure it the almost undisturbed possession of the home market, while keeping open for it opportunities for large sales abroad: its sales at home, and its sales abroad, alike increase its command over economies that help it to undersell rivals in neutral markets. German and American thought has been much occupied with

looking after three semi-automatic machines. In your country none but skilled engineers are allowed to work those machines, though no skill is needed for it: and each engineer is compelled to confine his attention to one machine." Shortly afterwards more liberal methods were adopted in England, partly as the result of the great lock-out of 1893: and in this matter England is now at a less disadvantage than she was relatively to her young competitors.

[1] From the chapter on "Germany and the inheritance of the City" [of London], in *England's Financial Supremacy*, from which the opposite side of the case was quoted above (p. 104 fn.).

this class of considerations; and has made out a strong *primâ facie* case for the conclusion, that national policies in regard to international trade need to rest on a basis somewhat different from that which was appropriate to them before the modern economies of massive production had come into view. We shall, however, find reason for thinking that the *primâ facie* suggestions thus made are inadequate. To begin with, they do not take account of the fact that the economies of massive production are of many different kinds: some are cosmopolitan property, some are national, some are local, and some belong to individual firms: each of these different kinds has its own method of affecting both the national and social issues in question. Further, the new point of view will be found to give reason for attaching not less, but greater, cogency to the old argument that many of the advantages which a single industry derives from a Protective duty in its favour, involve loss and hindrance to other industries; and that, even if it be thought fit to select the whole class of massive production industries for special favour, the ultimate result may be of little service to that class; and may perhaps injure the nation at large. Problems of this kind have not the highest claim on the attention of the economist: but they are closely associated with those which have that claim, as will gradually be made clear. Meanwhile reference may be made to some short remarks on the varying trends of German tarif policy since the complete setting up of the Zollverein, which will be found in Appendix H.

It may be added that erroneous conclusions are sometimes suggested, especially in partisan writings, by comparisons of Germany's industry and trade with those of Britain, without taking account of differences in their industrial ages, their populations or their areas. German industry and trade being younger than British, naturally grew faster: a young boy grows very fast. And since Germany's population is more than a third greater than Britain's, and her area more than a half greater, her industry and trade will not have attained equal distinction, till they exceed those of Britain by at least a third.

CHAPTER VIII

THE INDUSTRIAL LEADERSHIP OF THE UNITED STATES: MULTIFORM STANDARDIZATION

I, VIII, 1.

1. *Introductory.*

Germany's contributions to industrial leadership belong to the modern age; and they will doubtless spread widely and be developed in coming generations: but the range of industries which have been much affected by them up to the present time is not very large, and there seems to be no immediate prospect of its being very greatly extended. On the other hand those tendencies to industrial evolution, in which the United States of America is the chief leader, are likely to influence in various degrees a very large part of the field of manufacture. They are not indeed new: some of them may be traced back to primitive forms of the loom, or to an early printing press; and they have long dominated nearly all textile manufactures, together with a large part of the lighter metal industries. Thus the provinces of French and American methods are on the opposite sides of the broad field of industry. French instincts enable the hand and eye to make subtle discriminations, and ceaseless variations in form and colour; and thus to gratify the fancy and the artistic taste, at prices which are generally beyond the reach of the masses of the people. American methods on the other hand make for the production of business plant and of products for immediate consumption in an almost infinite variety of standardized forms. They analyse the ultimate product into simple parts; and provide a sufficient number of semi-automatic machines with the adjustments necessary for fashioning each part; and, if possible, for finishing it. In some cases a single model of the product will meet fairly well the wants of all purchasers. But, if not, careful study is given to the question how much increase of sales will result from any proposed increase in the number of models made, and how much extra custom it will yield. If the answer is favourable the number of varieties is increased; and the standardization becomes "multiform."

Standardization is of several different kinds, corresponding to differences of the materials used, and the purposes for which the product is needed. It varies also with the structure of the individual businesses which make use of it, and with the marketing and general organization of the industry to which they belong. But such matters must stand over for Book II, where they will occupy a considerable space: our present concern is only with its general characteristics and with the striking consilience of causes, which have given to America the leadership in it. The causes will be considered under the following heads:—her maintenance of the spirit of youth, when already strong among the strongest: the homogeneity of the methods of living of her vast population, in spite of racial differences: her large supplies on the one hand of strong immigrant labour, devoid of special skill, but able to work semi-automatic machines; and on the other hand of keen, resolute, native Americans ready to plan and control: the inevitable preference given by great railways to large consignments travelling long distances, by which a giant business, even if far off, is at an advantage in competition with a smaller business near at hand: and, lastly, the tendencies, partly caused by these conditions, for large masses of capital to be accumulated in the hands of a few strong men, who retain its control in their own masterful hands.

2. *The United States has remained young very long, partly because the geographical distribution of her resources has been such as to tempt men of strong character to move to new scenes, in which their enterprise has been further stimulated.*

A "new country" is commonly taken to be one which has newly come under effective control of an advanced western people: so that, though her aboriginal population may still linger on, it no longer exerts any great influence on the destiny of the

I, VIII, 2. land; and the new inhabitants develop her resources in their own way. In some countries, on the other hand, the new inhabitants are in a small minority; and, even while they direct the work of the older population, they are compelled to acquiesce to a great extent in the survival of primitive forms of industry. It is, however, obvious that these two classes of countries range into one another: there is no broad, clearly marked, dividing line between them.

Again, a country, which has been regarded as old, may become in fact new almost suddenly: for the great body of its people may awake to the attractions of modern industrial methods; and apply them energetically to rich natural resources, which have hitherto lain almost dormant. Japan has become new in this sense during the present generation: India, China, Siberia and even Brazil, with much larger natural resources, may become new ere the present century has passed. All such countries have much to learn from the United States of America, which more than any other, has pioneered the path of new countries; though only those of them, whose resources are comparable with hers in volume and variety, can profit fully by all her experiences. With these facts in view, it seems advisable to enlarge the triangle, of which the three corners are in England, France, and Germany, into a quadrilateral, of which the fourth corner is in the United States. That quadrilateral reaches very far: for deep set physical conditions have combined with various incidents in her history to cause the United States to retain her youth long after she had become a leader in industry.

Colonies established by strong European races in a temperate and stimulating climate, such as that of North America, almost always flourish, in spite of the hardships which they must endure at first. Meat and wood and dairy produce are sure to abound; rude houses are easily built; and a little grain is won from select patches of favourable soil: so the people and their children are well fed, and sturdy. As Adam Smith said, the most important wealth which they bring from their old homes is a "knowledge of the arts of agriculture,...the habit of subordination and some notion of regular government[1]." They

[1] *Wealth of Nations*, Book IV. ch. VII. Part II.

bring also habits of forethought and the willingness to incur present exertion in the expectation of a remote benefit. The splendid material resources of America slumbered until a capital stock of "moral wealth," which is the heir of the ages, arrived from Europe.

The immigrants developed the physical riches of America: and, in return, the new hope, freedom, and changefulness of their lives developed in them germs of high spirit and initiative: these are indeed latent in most people and especially in those who seek new lands, even though they have been driven forth by oppression, rather than allured by the promise of larger opportunities.

The stability and quiet of settled life affect character for evil as well as for good. Few men are prophets in their own land: neighbours and relations are generally the last to pardon the faults, and to recognize the merits, of men who differ from themselves by being less docile and more enterprising. It is doubtless chiefly for this reason that in almost every part of England a disproportionately large share of the best energy and enterprise is to be found among those who were born elsewhere; while, by converse with others who come from different places and have different customs, travellers learn to put on its trial many a habit of thought and action, which otherwise they would have always acquiesced in as though it were a law of nature. The fact that colonists generally have keener and more elastic minds than the majority of those whom they left at home, is a special instance of the rule that change of environment is likely to be caused by activity of mind, and to stimulate that activity. But this assumes that the conditions of the environment are favourable: and that has not always been the case throughout the early years of a new country.

In fact life in secluded villages of a new country, before the age of railways and telegraphs, often became more rigidly set than even in the villages of the mother country. Thus, even Anglo-saxon colonies, when isolated, have aged rapidly: the colonies of Holland are older than Holland, and parts of the province of Quebec are older than France. Some English in North America were touched by this somnolence: but the opening up of the Mississippi Valley shook them out of it: and in some

I, VIII, 2. respects the United States is younger now than at the beginning of last century. For, indeed, the people of the United States differ from other European colonists of the New World in that their nervous energies have been stimulated not only by one great migration across the ocean, but by an exceptional persistence of migration within their own large country. This habit rose rather slowly; but has been in full strength for the last sixty years, and it has been supplemented recently by new strains of immigrants of excitable temperament.

The chief causes of these internal migrations have lain in the facts that the richest parts of the Continent were not accessible to the earlier immigrants: and that the qualities of the best land in the centre of North America made it specially attractive to those new immigrants, and to those descendants of the earlier settlers, who had the greatest vigour, and enterprise. The focus of the economic strength of the United States has therefore not remained by the Atlantic, but has moved into the heart of the Continent. This fact is obviously of primary importance from the political point of view: those, whose sturdy determination prevented the disruption of the nation half a century ago, came in great part from the "Middle West": but its significance is equally vital, though not equally conspicuous, from the economic point of view. Let us look into this.

The soil of the Atlantic Coast, especially in the north, was relatively poor. The best soil of the great Mississippi Valley was so tender that "a walking stick could be pushed into it up to the handle": and the greater part of it was so stored with plant food that it would yield many successive stocks of grain without being manured. In its Northern half, soil and climate specially favour wheat; while further South, maize is the standard crop. The power of dispensing with manure for several years attracted strong men whose resources did not suffice for setting up the appliances of a "mixed" farm, and stocking it with cattle; and this advantage, combined with the general richness of the land, caused "the West," as the Mississippi Valley was long called, to attract those whose sturdy, independent characters fitted them to become the backbone of a great nation[1].

[1] More is said on these matters in Appendix G, 1.

The westward movement in the South, especially before the Civil War,

I, VIII, 2.

The selection of the stronger agriculturists for the work of the far west was reinforced by a similar selection of the most alert, though not the most technically skilled artisans. "As a people," said Horace Greeley, in 1870, "we may be viewed as on the march from the East to the West; the active, aspiring mechanic, who was born in Maine or New Hampshire, migrates to New York or some other Middle State soon after attaining his majority, reaches Illinois or Missouri two or three years later; and will often be found traversing Montana or California before he is thirty[1]."

The movements of the miner are governed by natural causes even more absolutely than those of the farmer: and the two have much in common. Both make heavy freight for railways: and the two largely control the course of railway building: while the geographical distribution of other industries follows rather than directs that course. Water power may indeed attract manufactures to itself in some countries. But it happens that the main cause of the infertility of the mountainous band, which extends from about the hundredth to the hundred and twentieth parallel of longitude, is its want of water: and any railway net, which may spread over it and unite the Pacific Coast to the Mississippi Valley, must depend for local custom largely upon mining centres, together with some basins of land that are naturally rich; and some mountain

was of a different character from that in the North. The cultivation of cotton had been adopted for slaves, because it did not require or even offer much opportunity for the use of expensive appliances; and because it gave nearly continuous occupation throughout the year and therefore required no versatility. Food for workers was grown on the spot: but in the main cotton was a sole crop, and therefore an exhausting crop, and cotton moved westwards because, as Jefferson said, one could "buy an acre of new land cheaper than one could manure an old one."

[1] Greeley was one of the ablest of American journalists, and very great influence was exercised by the articles which he ultimately compressed into "*Essays designed to elucidate the science of Political Economy, while serving to explain and defend the policy of Protection to Home Industry, as a system of National Cooperation for the elevation of labour.*" The passage quoted (p. 286) is part of a characteristic argument that the American working-man "is unlikely to trouble himself with aught to which stability is so essential as it is to cooperators" on the Rochdale model: its "petty and paltry problems" are worthy of "the assembled wisdom of the humble weavers of Toad Lane." His life is cast in a larger mould: nothing less than "National cooperation" is worthy of his efforts.

I, VIII, 3. slopes that offer facilities for irrigation. The richest coal beds at present known are on the western slopes of the Alleghanies, and the richest iron mines are near Lake Superior. The materials needed by the ironmaster can be assembled at nearly equal cost over a great part of the States which lie between the Alleghanies and the Rockies: and these States are among the strongest alike in agriculture, in the production of steel and in general manufacture.

In fact as soon as the slight obstacles which the Alleghanïes offered to intercourse between the Atlantic Coast and the Mississippi Valley had been overcome, the United States possessed an unbroken continuity of large and various resources, to which no rival has yet been developed; and to which no rival seems probable in the near future.

3. ***The various races of which the population is composed are homogeneous in matters of consumption; but they are diverse and mutually supplementary in industrial aptitudes. The homogeneity of demand creates an unrivalled market for standardized products: while the diversity of aptitude leads some to invent and others contentedly to use semi-automatic machinery for making them.***

"The American has a constantly expanding home demand, urging him to extensions and justifying costly improvements and the adoption of new processes. He has also a Continent under one Government....The best places are selected for assembling materials, raw, or partially prepared, for their final forms. In short, it is free, unrestricted trade in everything under the same conditions, same laws, same flag, and free markets everywhere[1]." This perfect fluidity has made many branches of American production marvellously efficient. But, at the same time, it has tended to separate the producer widely from the consumer, and to suppress those methods of production which depend for their strength largely upon the adaptation of products to the special requirements or tastes of the purchaser.

An even stronger force in the same direction is being exerted by the homogeneity of the American demand for

[1] Carnegie, *Rectorial Address at St Andrew's*, 1902, pp. 31—2.

manufactured goods. Even those race differences, which have become almost a dominant factor in American life, lessen this homogeneity but very little. Widely as the Scandinavians are separated from the Italians, and the native Americans from the Poles, in sentiment, in modes of life, and even in occupations, they are yet purchasers of nearly the same goods. Allowance being of course made for differences of climate, they buy similar clothes, furniture, and implements. Some negroes and a few others may cling to old habits and methods, and prefer implements to which they are accustomed to those which are the most effective and economical. But speaking generally all the various races in the country, widely as they differ from one another in character and aptitude, are yet alike in yielding to the dominant spirit of the strong mixed race among whom they have settled. Only in a few cases, chiefly in large cities, are the new comers in sufficient numbers to make a market for goods of kinds peculiar to their old homes. Lastly, they are more quick than any but the most alert inhabitants of the Old World in taking to every improved implement or material which comes to their notice.

Even the farmer is quick in this matter. Much of his clothing and furniture comes to him ready made; and a good deal of his food is prepared for him and put into tins a thousand or more miles away. His implements must be of almost the newest pattern: they can seldom be made in a neighbouring town, and he often buys them direct from a distant factory. In case of accident to any part of a machine, he writes or telegraphs for a numbered facsimile of the broken part. And, when once it is clear that goods must be ordered by post and sent by rail, the extra cost and loss of time involved in sending them a hundred miles instead of twenty is often very small; so that producers and store-keepers in large centres, who can offer a great variety of shape and pattern with low prices, are driving others out of the field.

Next it is to be considered that the population, while homogeneous in demand, supply a unique combination of the faculties and aptitudes needed, on the one hand for inventing the machinery suitable for standardized production; and on the

I, VIII, 3. other for working that machinery with adequate intelligence in return for relatively low wages. Those English, Scotch, and German immigrants, who did not become farmers, generally did somewhat skilled work in the towns or in the mines. From their ranks have come the greater part of the foremen in most trades that require a long training: the full-blooded American, when found in factories at all, is apt to be either in the higher ranks of management; or else engaged in tending machines which called for exceptional alertness rather than slowly acquired manual skill.

In spite of the ever increasing fineness and delicacy of American manufacture, the demand for high manual skill, and especially for men who have served long apprenticeships to a craft, has increased but slowly. It has even diminished in some trades, while in others it has been partially met by men born of European parents in America; and on the whole the inducements offered to the European artisan with a narrow range of high manual skill to emigrate to America are less than formerly. For these and other reasons emigration from England, Scotland, and Germany to America has very much slackened. And that from Ireland, though still considerable, has slackened also; partly indeed because her population is no longer too large for her resources, and her land system is more generous than it was.

Meanwhile the newly awakened though still very poor populations of Italy and of the central east of Europe have learnt to look for a refuge in America; and the facilities for emigration offered to them have been greatly increased. The same economic progress which is keeping English and Germans at home is sending ever increasing numbers of relatively poor and backward peoples across the ocean. Some of them are of high quality: for instance, the rapid progress of California in the art of growing fine fruit is largely due to the inherited skill of Italian immigrants. But more of them take to hard manual work in building, in railway construction, in mining, in heavy steelworks, etc. Some of these indeed rise: for instance, particular departments of some steelworks are so fully manned by Slavs, that they are beginning efficiently to take the places of Irish and others who have hitherto acted as foremen: while very large numbers of them are to be found in relatively light, but monotonous work in large cities. They may lack the resolute will and self-control which put many British, German, and Scandinavian immigrants on terms of equality with native Americans. But they are quick withal, versatile; and, as a rule, easily moulded; they take readily to the use of machinery; and they have no traditions that could prevent them from doing their best in using semi-automatic machines, which are simple of handling, while doing complex work. Thus America has suddenly obtained a plentiful supply of people who are able and willing to do the routine work of a large factory for relatively low wages, and whose aptitudes supplement those of the stronger races that constitute the great bulk of the white population[1].

Even in the Old World progressive industrial districts gain much from the immigration of workers to whom all methods of manufacture are new; and who readily betake themselves to the newest processes, and work these to the best of their power. But none rivals, none but Germany approaches near to the power which America derives from this advantage, in combination with an almost unlimited supply of alert workers in the higher grades: for it affords her an unprecedented scope for Babbage's great principle of economical production, according to which every worker is set to the most difficult and important tasks of which he is capable, and only to those.

The position is indeed not without its difficulties and dangers, some of which are pertinent to our present subject. To begin with, all migration tends to foster isolated action and individualistic aims: separated from old associates, each one is

[1] In the years between 1900 and 1910 America received 8·5 million immigrants. Of these, 6·1 million came from southern and eastern Europe, and only 1·8 from north-western: whereas three-fourths of all the immigrants in the years between 1830 and 1870 came from the United Kingdom and Germany. Statistics of immigration into America appear to be vitiated, though less than those of emigration from Europe, by evasions of the laws prescribing universal military service. There is therefore some interest attaching to the following figures showing the percentages of the total foreign born population, in 1860 and 1910 respectively, which were recorded as born in the following countries: England, 10·4 (for 1860); 6·5 (for 1910): Ireland, 38·5; 15·6: Scotland, 2·6; 1·0: Germany, 30·5; 18·5: Italy, 0·3; 9·9: Austria, 0·6; 8·7: Russia, 0·1; 6·2. See *Abstract of Thirteenth Census*, pp. 190—1. The occupations of immigrants from different countries are analysed in vol. XI of the *Twelfth Census Report*. See also *Report of the Industrial Commission*, vol. XV.

I, VIII, 4. apt to care mainly for his own interests, and those of any friends and relatives who may be with him. And this tendency has been increased by the variety of races and languages among the recent immigrants. It fosters the eager, absorbing pursuit of material success, partly for its own sake; but perhaps even more as an indication of power and as a trophy of satisfied ambition. It contributes to that alertness, that restless energy, that impatience of any occupation which does not enable a man to take out his whole day's income of strength in his day's work, which are characteristic of the United States now. In these respects, again, American conditions resemble those of the industrial districts of England a century ago; when they were crowded with immigrants from agricultural districts, to whom the new methods of manufacture offered wages far above those which their fathers had earned[1].

4. *The drift of America's industries towards massive multiform standardization is further associated, both as cause and as effect, with their widespread geographical distribution, and also with the special features of her great railway service.*

It is a general rule that specialized branches of production are apt to rise in places which offer suitable raw material (including in some cases pure water, and in others water power or coal); which have a favourable climate and access to good markets for the sale of the products. But these conditions being satisfied, the development of a specialized industry in any place was until recently nearly always a gradual process. Sometimes it was fostered by a far-seeing ruler, but it was incapable of sudden creation even by him.

In America the growth of localized industries has always been rather rapid, partly because many of her artisans have been immigrants: a smaller inducement is generally needed to incline a man, who is already on the move, towards a rising centre of industry, than is needed to attract him there from his home; and therefore immigrants with specialized skill drift easily to places where that skill will be highly valued. This cause of

[1] The subject of this Section is studied more closely in the chapters on "Some technical influences on the size of the business unit," below, II, III and IV.

localization was indeed much weakened as soon as automatic machines and other expensive plant, together with high organizing faculty, became a more important factor than manual skill in production. But the advantages offered by large towns with good and cheap railway connections have acted as a continual inducement to the capitalist undertaker and to the workingman to keep to the towns and the thickly peopled districts of the Eastern and Middle States[1].

Nearly all large cities have competitive railway services: and this is, even now, more likely to result in favourable terms for their traffic in America than elsewhere. They offer to the immigrant, who does not speak English, a good chance of finding work under foremen and with comrades who speak his own language, and of being able to follow the religious worship of his fathers. These advantages, together with those which large centres of industry always offer to manufactures, have until recently tended to collect immigrants increasingly in very large cities. But in the last two decades the lower charges, at which dwellings and sites for factories can be obtained in cities of a middle size, have turned the drift towards them in America, as in England: and some factories, sufficiently powerful to be able to buy and sell in large quantities on favourable terms, and to make special arrangements with the railways, have gone into the country and practically founded cities of their own. All these cities offer nearly as high attractions to most classes of immigrants as the giant cities do: and the medium sized cities can market a larger part of their products at moderate distances than a giant city can. Consequently, although the increases of population of very large cities are due in great measure to extensions of boundaries, as they are in England; yet the rate of increase of those with more than half a million inhabitants is less than that of all urban districts, and considerably less than that of medium cities having between fifty thousand and a quarter of a million[2].

[1] In a masterly study of the causes of localization given in vol. VII of the *Twelfth Census Report* it is pointed out (p. ccxiii), that six of the fifteen industries which were mostly highly localized in 1900, had made scarcely any use of machinery till after 1870.

[2] And yet New York city has a greater net manufacturing output than any State except its own and Pennsylvania, and there are twenty other cities each

I, VIII, 4. The Rocky Mountains, the Pacific Coast and some smaller districts are not very densely peopled. But, subject to this exception, it may be said that the population of more than a hundred million has been distributed by constant migrations of industries fairly evenly over her total area of about three million square miles. The transport of agricultural produce to the Atlantic and the Mexican Gulf on the way to Europe accounted for much of the railway traffic in past times: but now by far the greater part even of the large consignments, that are carried long distances, consists of internal commerce.

This vast goods traffic is in some measure a cause, and in some measure a result, of the direction which has been taken by America's industrial leadership. Because her railways were chiefly concerned with carrying large consignments long distances, therefore they developed that traffic with special energy: because their charges for long distance large consignments were very low relatively to their charges for traffic of the kind that (except in regard to coal) predominates in Britain; therefore giant businesses, which sent large consignments to distant middlemen, obtained nearly the full advantage of their special economies of massive standardized production in many varieties.

We are not concerned at present to inquire how far the multiplication of semi-automatic machines, in the control of which a man is not required to use any high faculty, is a real benefit to the world. It undoubtedly increases material comforts; and any harm, that it may tend to do to man's nature, is not conspicuous in America in her present phase, because those who are chiefly affected by it came mostly from narrow

of which has a greater net manufacturing output than any of the sixteen States which stand lowest on the list. (Net output is reckoned after deduction of outlay for material, etc., but not for depreciation, etc.)

In 1910 the largest percentage of urban population was found in New England: but the largest percentage of population in cities with more than 100,000 inhabitants was found in the "Middle Atlantic States" (*i.e.* New York and Pennsylvania): and next in the Pacific States, where population flocks to the great harbour cities, as it does in Australia. Urban districts account for nearly 80 per cent. of the total foreign born population; but for less than 40 per cent. of that in the States between the Mississippi and the Pacific watershed. (The data for the above statements are to be found in Tables 19—27 of Ch. 1, Table 12 of Ch. 5, and Tables 5—7 of Ch. 15 of the *Abstract of the Thirteenth Census.*)

surroundings: their outlook is larger than it would have been, if they had stayed at home[1].

5. *America's movable capital has grown very fast in recent years. Its ownership is widely distributed; but natural selection of singular efficiency has brought to the front a relatively small number of men with high business genius, and has given them control of a great part of it.*

That massive organization of manufacture, in which a few alert minds direct, while the greater part of the work is done by semi-automatic machinery, requires not only large armies of workers with mutually supplementary aptitudes; but also a concentration of a large volume of movable capital in the hands of powerful and enterprising owners.

The material resources of the United States increased rapidly from the time when railways began to bring the Mississippi Valley into close union with the Atlantic border and with the markets of the Old World. But the making of railways, roads, etc. in the new region, the building of farm-houses and development of the farms, absorbed most of her surplus of income over expenditure, large as that was. Even in 1860, the value of farms and farm property was nearly half the whole wealth of the country; and the railways accounted for a good deal more, though it is true that they were largely built with capital borrowed from Europe. There was a vast destruction of capital in the war: rapidly increasing opportunities for investment in land and railways followed it; and these conditions, combined with the supersession of wood as the material of ships, tended to make her withdraw her resources from work in which she would have to compete on equal terms with rich countries, whose opportunities for the investment of capital at home were narrower than hers. But about 1875 a new era set in. The preceding inflation of credit and prices had been checked by a collapse of credit: work was resumed with energy; and the excess of income over expenditure commenced to grow rapidly[2].

[1] Some further results of these conditions are noted below, II, VII, 5.

[2] The money value of farm property kept about even pace with the growth of population between 1860 and 1900; but it has increased much faster since that time; mainly because many people here suddenly awakened to the fact

I, VIII, 5. Most of the new wealth has been distributed among a large part of the population, as holders of real property, or of shares or bonds of those railway and other companies which have long had a solid position. But investments in risky undertakings—such as those connected with the development of petroleum, copper, and other mineral properties—often yield nearly as much loss as gain to the ordinary investor: and yet they may be handled by people with large capital, and exceptional means of information and organizing faculty, so as to yield them large gains. This cause is one among many, which, as will be seen more clearly at a later stage, are increasing the wealth of those who are already rich: it acts in America even more strongly than in other countries. Another cause is that such businesses as mechanical engineering, grain dealing and milling, cattle

that the scarcity-element, which has long been present in the value of land in old countries, is beginning to appear in America. Probably the statistics of farm values in the following table are not liable to the very large errors that are to be feared in those relating to total wealth and to capital in manufactures. It is to be remembered that the figures for 1870 are reckoned in paper currency, which was worth about four-fifths of its gold value; while gold prices were then exceptionally high in world markets. The Census Returns show:—

Census Year	Population	Millions of dollars		
		Total wealth	Value of farm property	Capital in manufactures
1850	23,191,000	7,136	3,967	533
1860	31,443,000	16,160	7,980	1,009
1870	38,558,000	30,068	8,945	2,118
1880	50,155,000	42,642	12,180	2,790
1890	62,622,000	65,037	16,082	6,525
1900	77,256,000	94,300	20,440	9,874
1910	93,401,000		40,991	18,490

The revised figures for total wealth, given in the *Statistical Abstract* 1917, are (in millions of dollars) 107,104 for 1904; and 187,739 for 1912. A part of this enormous increase in recent years is due to a rise in the value of agricultural land caused by the absorption of unoccupied land, and an increase in the home-consumption of agricultural produce so great as to obviate the necessity of selling it at very low prices for exportation.

For some purposes it is better to study rates of growth of wealth per head, than those of aggregate wealth. But the growth of wealth per head would give a very inadequate measure of the economic progress of a country whose population is growing at an exceptional rate. For the additions to the population, whether native born or immigrant, do not bring their share of wealth with them.

The increase in the size of businesses is considered below, III, VII and VIII, and Appendix N.

dealing and meat canning, and even retail dealing, have offered larger scope than anywhere else. Thus strong and persistent men accumulate into their own hands the profits of agglomerated business, which not long ago were distributed among many smaller undertakings. And all such causes work upon the basis of an exceptionally large aggregate of new income in the hands of the commercial classes.

For profits in ordinary business are very high in America, because the growth of capital, rapid as it has been, has not sufficed to fill up nearly all the openings which Nature is still lavishly offering to those who have the faculty to read her hints and to act on them: and therefore a man who obtains profits at a rate that is normal in America, on a very large business over many years, will accumulate a vast fortune. Both the opportunities and the special energies, by which they are turned to account, are as unrivalled as were those of England, when she brought a large use of coal and iron into her service a generation ahead of the rest of the world.

The American problems of the present age are on a vastly larger scale than were the British problems of the earlier age: but the means available for handling them have developed in at least equal proportion. For, while such things as the telegraph and telephone, and facilities for rapid travel under restful conditions, are accessible to all; powerful capitalists are able to set select staffs of shrewd and skilled assistants at high salaries, on the detailed study of one problem after another in constructive business, in speculation, or in the two combined.

Education has always been taken seriously in America; but it has never been regarded as reaching far, by itself, towards making men efficient in business. It has never given the same prestige as can be obtained by the evidence of keen mother wit, which is afforded by a new contrivance, or a new scheme of organization which is effective for its purpose. Thus it has come about that the American genius for inventing, organizing, and arranging is the finest in the world. To concede this is not to attribute to Americans more than their fair share of natural ability. It is but to note that the able young American is almost as sure to become an inventor or an organizer or both, as the able barbarian was to become a leader in battle, or as

I, VIII, 5. the able Florentine in the Middle ages was to seek distinction in art or politics. For young ambition naturally flows to whatever vocation offers the most prominent difficulties to be overcome and the highest distinction for overcoming them. A powerful process of natural selection has thus called out the leaders of American industry from the many millions of lads who were born to the last generation from alert parents of many races; and who entered on life with the resolve that they would prove themselves to be abler and greater than their fellows by becoming rich: and of this effectiveness the money test is on the whole a safer test than any other which the common man can apply[1].

There are in America a great number of men who have become very rich while still in the prime of life and full of enterprise. Some of them have little inclination towards social amusements or culture: they are conscious of being but second-rate powers in the lighter affairs of life; and are happiest when at their places of business, engaged in yet enlarging the fortunes, which they value chiefly as evidence of their organizing genius. As arts and sciences flourish best where their followers work for the approval of brethren of the craft, and not for the sake of money: so business flourishes most where the aim of the business man is not to shine in elegant society, but to be held in respect by those who are the best judges of his special form of strength. This exclusive devotion to one pursuit involves some loss to the life of the individual; but the constructive economic force which it gives to America at this phase of her development is unique.

Meanwhile the thoroughness and alert sense of proportion, which have been developed in business, run over into congenial studies. American work in applied economics has already taken

[1] See a representative discussion in Carnegie's *Empire of Business*, pp. 106—113. He gives a list of many of the "best known industrial establishments in each department....Every one of these works was founded by mechanics.... If we were to include those which were founded by men who entered life as office boys or clerks we should embrace almost every famous manufacturing concern in the country": Wanamaker, Claflin, Jordan, Lord, Field, Barr, Phelps, Dodge; the Stanfords, Rockefellers, Goulds, Sages, Fields, Dillons, Seligmans, Wilsons, Huntingtons; and most of the chief bankers have been clerks, or have come from a still lower grade in the ranks. More is said on this matter below, pp. 358—9.

the first place in the world: and in such studies as those which relate to the respective provinces of competition, cooperation and monopoly, and to the functions of the State in regard to them, American studies appear to be the most real, thorough and penetrating; as will be suggested in Book III of this work.

Looking back on these exceptional conditions of the present industrial leadership of the United States we see that many of them are in a transitional stage.

Her agriculture is rapidly leaving the extensive methods, which are distinctive of the New World; and passing to intensive methods, in which an ever increasing element of Old World practice is embodied. But they will never be simply Old World methods: they will always be in part descended from the typical American agriculture, in which nothing was done by heavy manual labour, if ingenuity could contrive either to do it by machinery, or to evade doing it altogether.

The changes in the character of America's manufactures, combined with the exhaustion of her supply of land stocked by Nature with food for ten or twenty years successive crops, have given to her policy in regard to international trade a character very different from, and in some respects the opposite to, that which prevailed when Protection to nascent manufactures first came under discussion. The keynote then was that she suffered from a lack of the inherited industrial skill of the Old World: a little later the keynote was that the large capitals, which European and especially British manufacturers commanded, enabled them to make use of appliances beyond the reach of the poorer American; and also to ruin him by selling goods at less than cost price (in modern phrase "dumping" them), when he was already in financial straits. But now those American industries, which can exercise the greatest influence on the Legislature and are in general most favoured by it, are among those in which the power of aggregated American capital is greater than that of any other country. This change gives much room for thought: but the questions raised by it are beyond our reach at present[1].

[1] Something is said as to the relations between early phases of American industry and fiscal policy in Appendix G.

I, VIII, 5. The time is not yet in sight when any other country is likely to outstrip her in opportunities and incitements to large enterprises; and therefore her share in industrial leadership is likely long to remain of an exceptionally large mould. In fact no leadership quite like hers is to be expected from any country, which cannot rival both the largeness of her national resources, and the alertness of her vast population.

The world contains undeveloped resources many times as large as hers: and, though her success owes less to her resources than to the exceptional force of character of the people who have come to her shores, and to the stimulus which those energies derived from exceptional opportunities for bold and rich enterprise; yet it is to be noted that the best strains of her population are not growing in numbers very fast. On the other hand the practical applications of social science to the betterment of human life are being developed by her with great ability and zeal. The new strains of her population may probably have not yet shown their strongest sides: and they may contribute important elements which, on the whole, will raise rather than lower the wealth of character that was brought to her shores in earlier years by the forcible but perhaps somewhat too individualistic immigrants from Northern Europe.

To conclude:—the life of North America was for several centuries in the main a continuation of the lives of several countries of Western Europe. But Holland, Spain and France gradually yielded place to England: and from 1760 to about 1850 the life of North America was dominantly British. After that, immigrants from Germany and Scandinavia became prominent; to be followed later on by Italy and by countries of Eastern Europe. Now, nearly the whole of Europe lives again in North America, Britain holding the lead.

And Britain leads elsewhere. Australia and New Zealand are British colonies in the fullest sense of the word; South Africa is predominantly British, but largely also Dutch and partly cosmopolitan. This cosmopolitan element in South Africa seems to foreshadow, more distinctly even than the cosmopolitan element in the United States, the beginning of a new era; in which the influences exerted by relatively old countries on those whose resources are not yet developed, will depend less on consanguinity and racial inheritance, than on similarities of opportunity and of need: or, to use a more general term, "of circumstance." In so far as this view holds ground, it may be expected that the United States will be in some sense the parent of all others of whatever races they may be peopled, which begin to develop large physical resources with new born energy and alertness.

6. *Some slight speculations as to future homes of industrial leadership.*

Those ideas which make for industrial progress have not been the exclusive property of powerful industrial countries. Many of them have come from the smaller countries of Europe: Italy and Scandinavia have been important contributors. But, so long as the main conditions of economic development remain nearly as they are now, the chief initiative seems likely to lie with countries whose great size, rich natural resources, and accumulated capital enable them to concentrate large and highly organized mental and material appliances on the translation into practice of the architectonic ideas of the scientific student and the inventor. The difficulty of forecasting the future in this matter is increased by the growth of these ideas, more than it is diminished by the accumulation of exact knowledge as to the resources of the world, and as to the people who inhabit it.

For instance, the growth of mechanical technique, especially on the American model, increases generally the advantage which a large, but unified and compact, country has in massive production. But Australia and Canada, though well-endowed with natural riches and inhabited by alert populations, suffer from lack of compactness; and their prospects of leadership may be materially affected by inventions that lessen the hindrance arising from this defect. Not long ago communications through the air by telegraphic instrument, telephone and aircraft were not in sight; but even the last is now regarded as a possible aid to ordinary intercourse. If each decade of the next two hundred years should be merely as prolific of inventions as each of the last two decades has been—and that is a low estimate—the conditions which now in some measure limit the scope of industrial leadership to compact countries may have passed away. But though

I, VIII, 6. we cannot look forward far, we may look a little way, and venture on guesses, which may at all events suggest some reflections as to the present: though their value as prediction is of the slightest.

Canada is to some extent a partner with the States in leadership. There is a constant interchange of methods between the two: "American" discussions relating to railways, monopolistic combinations and similar matters, cross the frontier into Canada with little sense of change of atmosphere, such as is palpable when they range to any other country. Her main route from Montreal to her Far-west lay not long ago to the south of the Lakes, through Chicago: but railways are at last penetrating the poor land to the north of the Lakes; and the unification of her East with her West is likely to move the faster, the further it goes. This is indeed partly because the stock of free good land in the States has been exhausted: and it has been found that the rigours of the long winter in the Canadian North-West are less hostile to wheat farming and even to mixed farming than had been supposed. Thus the tide has turned back, and Canada is receiving again her own with increase: for the farmers, who throng into her new wheat lands from the States are men of many races, but are alike in having trained faculties and aptitudes for their work, and in being already supplied with adequate capital. The severity of her climate, which hindered her progress at first, is now selecting for her benefit those individuals who are most able and willing to encounter physical difficulties and hardships; and a vigorous future seems to lie before her.

South Africa has shown great energy under difficulties. Her gold and diamond mines bring wealth, though they do not greatly develop industrial leadership of a western type: but the solid strength of the British and Dutch population, now happily united, may pioneer new and more successful methods of intimate cooperation between white and black races. Her distances are great, and her means of communication still slender: but her resources are vast: *Ex Africâ semper aliquid novi.*

Australia is leading the way bravely in the great endeavour to bring the labouring population as a whole up to a high level of culture and physical enjoyment. It appears indeed that her procedure involves certain forms of restriction which might prove fatal to a country whose natural resources are on less generous a scale than hers; and the rate of increase of her population is somewhat slow. This retardation, partly due to the predominance of urban conditions, has been caused in great measure by her geographical peculiarities.

I, VIII, 6.

For there is a large almost vacant space in her centre: some of the land in it seems indeed to be of good quality: but its rainfall is small and uncertain, and it has not attracted a solid agricultural population. In the neighbourhood of the sea, much of the land was allowed to fall into the hands of large capitalist sheep-farmers and bore but a slender population. This evil is being remedied: but the preferential advantages possessed by Melbourne, Sydney, and other great harbours have attracted to them the greater part of the strength of the people. Most of her communications have been by sea: but a considerable network of railways is growing up in the neighbourhoods of Sydney and Melbourne: and the splendid energies of her people may be trusted to develop the natural resources of their great country in spite of difficulties. New Zealand is on a smaller scale: but her racial and physical conditions are highly favourable for the evolution of the best British tendencies.

Passing away from European races, we find in Japan a bold claimant for leadership of the East on lines that are mainly Western. Her insular position, contiguous to a great Continent, is almost as well adapted for the development of industry and trade as that of Britain. She has learnt so much during the last thirty years, that she can hardly fail to become a teacher ere long. It seems indeed that stronger food than they now have will be required to enable her people to sustain continuous, severe, physical strain: but the singular power of self-abnegation, which they combine with high enterprise, may enable them to attain great ends by shorter and simpler routes than those, which are pursued where many superfluous comforts and luxuries have long been regarded as conventionally necessary. Their quick rise to power supports the suggestion, made by the history of past times, that some touch of idealism, religious, patriotic, or artistic, can generally be detected at the root of any great outburst of practical energy.

I, VIII, 6. India, though less agile, is developing renewed vigour and independence in industry as in thought. She is the home of some of the greatest thoughts that have ever come to the world; and the originator of many of the subtlest and most artistic manual industries. She has suffered in the past from lack of unity, and a scarcity of power for manufactures and transport. But she may yet be found to have considerable stores of coal: and some of her regions may be enriched by electrical energy derived from water power. The rapid recent rise of her larger industries is a source of just pride to her, and of gladness to Britain.

Great futures may also await Russia and China. Each is large, continuous and self-contained: each has enormous resources, which could not be developed so long as good access to ocean highways was a necessary condition for great achievement. Their populations differ in temperament; the persistence of the Chinese being complementary to the quick sensibility of the Russian: each has inherited great powers of endurance from many generations of ancestors who have suffered much. But recent events obscure the outlook.

Up to the present time a tropical climate has been fatal to the best energies of races, however vigorous. It has not indeed extinguished either the subtlety of their thinkers or the physical strength which their workers can exert for short periods; but it has been hostile to the power of undergoing severe continuous strain of mind and body. The tropics contain however much rich land and mineral resources. These are indeed of little avail except where a good supply of water can be obtained. It is needed, not only for domestic uses, but also (in default of any other means) to enable the energy contained in the sun's heat to be converted by aid of various cooling processes into mechanical power. This is another direction in which the progress of technique may possibly alter the conditions of industrial leadership. But for the present it may be concluded that there is no sure ground for thinking that industrial leadership will remain always with the same races, or in the same climates, as in recent times; nor even that its general character will remain unaltered.

CHAPTER IX

TRANSITION TO PRESENT PROBLEMS OF INDUSTRY AND TRADE

1. *The foundations of modern business in general confidence and credit.* I, IX, 1.

The present chapter is designed to afford a link between Book I and Book II by applying some indications, furnished by observation of past phases of industry and trade, as part of the basis for a study of business under present conditions.

A chief feature of economic evolution has been the gradual emergence of the notion of a "business point of view" in regard to the affairs of life. That phrase could not have been understood in a primitive society: and there is a sense in which it may be argued that business operations are merely one drift of a tendency to adapt means to ends, which is universal throughout all forms of life. Biology is indeed discovering numerous ways in which inheritance and natural selection—supplemented by the imitation of the successful actions of parents and other older individuals, and by other post-natal influences—have enabled even low grade animals so to adjust their structure and their operations to their environment, that they may be able to utilize it for their own benefit with ever increasing ease, efficiency and certainty[1].

[1] This remark does not assume that acquired faculties are inherited from parents by children at their birth: it is sufficient for the argument that children automatically imitate the actions of those by whom they are surrounded, and are especially sensitive to suggestions from the examples of mother and father: while acquired skill and faculty in small matters, as well as in large, pass from parents to children by definite instruction. But a protest may be permissible against the pretensions of some exponents of Mendelian doctrine that arithmetical averages of observation of inheritance by mice and vegetables afford

I, IX, 1. Most of these adjustments are in regard to the functions of individual members of a species separately: but one large part of them has to do with the military organization of the various members of a group, and another and yet larger part with their business organization. It is probable that anthills and beehives have been highly organized business concerns during very many more centuries, than those which have seen human business organizations of equal complexity and efficiency: but, so far as we know, the organization of ants and bees has been automatic and unconscious, without direction by foresight and deliberate contrivance. On the other hand there has been some element of conscious adaptation of means to ends in nearly every organization of human business. And, though the automatic elements preponderated greatly over the conscious and deliberate elements in early phases of economic growth, yet changing conditions were gradually met by quiet adjustments. Elementary, partial division of labour grew up between individual members of the same family, between families, and between neighbouring villages, or clans. Here were the origins of business trust and confidence, which were indeed enforced within each group by the social penalty of ostracism: an offender against his neighbours became an outcast, often without refuge.

As small communities merged and increased in size, an offender could more easily move from the scene of his transgression. The extension of neighbourliness lowered its intensity; and in consequence the trust between neighbours became less habitual and instinctive. In other words life became in some degree "business-like"; and ere long the transactions between neighbours began to be governed by arithmetical comparisons

conclusive proof that the characters which children bring into the world with them, are incapable of being affected by the past mode of life of their parents. Mendelians do not claim to know what causes originate differences between elementary germs: it seems to be certain that changes in the mental and moral habits of a human being are reflected in his face: and Mendelian arithmetic has little direct bearing on the question whether the nutrition supplied to germs in the body of a person excessively addicted to drink or other sensual indulgences may not result in the birth of a child with less firm character than it would have had, if the parent had lived soberly and chastely. Some Mendelians concede that it does: and the gradual development of trustworthy statistics of inherited mental and moral characters may ultimately lead to further admissions in the same direction.

between the value of that which was given, and that which was received in exchange.

The traders who bought goods in one locality and sold them in another were distinctively business men. But the greater number even of them seldom needed to look long ahead or very far afield: partly because they were in personal touch with those from whom they bought, and to whom they sold; and were thus directly cognisant of nearly all changes (except those arising out of war, famine and plague) which were likely to upset their calculations in the short time over which each such transaction generally ran. On the other hand a broad confidence in the steadfastness and efficiency of large and various markets is a necessary condition of the highly complex modern division of labour among producers, and between producers and middlemen: for indeed almost every considerable operation of business involves some speculation based on well-informed confidence. The whole mechanism of society rests on confidence: it permeates all life, like the air we breathe: and its services are apt to be taken for granted and ignored, like those of fresh air, until attention is forcibly attracted by their failure. When confidence is shaken by a rumour of war or of civil commotion, or of disturbing financial legislation, or of extensive frauds or rash trading by important firms, then business life is stifled; and men yearn for the wholesome atmosphere that is associated with the general re-establishment of confidence[1].

This trust contains a personal element: but it contains much more. For most of those on whose actions anyone relies are personally unknown to him. It is sometimes called "commercial credit." But that term seems not to cover the whole of it: we may call it "*social credit.*" It is analogous to personal credit. But it is also, and for the larger part, trust in

[1] The methods of business in the remoter districts of New England a century ago throw much light on those of Mediaeval England: the light is all the brighter, because high intelligence and cultured thought were being brought to bear on crude material conditions. Professor Sherwood (*Quarterly Journal of Economics*, VIII. p. 157) tells how his grandfather used to dress flax for the ropes and grain bags needed on his farm, and to make his own shoes; but slowly gave up the habit, as the growth of markets around him gave him a double confidence that he could advantageously dispose of his grain to one set of people, and obtain his ropes and shoes from another.

I, IX, 1. the character of society; in the stability of public order, in freedom from disturbance at home and from foreign attack; in the gradual and harmonious development of economic conditions; in the probity and reasonableness of people generally, and especially business men and legislators; and—to lay special stress on one important detail—in the solidity and good working of that currency which acts as a medium of exchange and a standard measure for gauging economic obligations and transactions of all kinds. The breadth, persistency, and fluidity of modern markets enable the producer to make things on the "speculative" chance of selling them, with a reasonable confidence that he knows beforehand approximately the price at which he will be able to sell them; whether they be finished or half-finished commodities, or raw materials, or implements that have no value except to people engaged in other industries —people whom he has perhaps never seen, but with whom the wide ramifications of business keep him in constant, if unconscious contact.

The modern producer throws all his energies into one particular group of operations, trusting that the same market organization, which secures for him in advance approximately known prices for his sales, will enable him to buy at approximately known prices such things as he may want; whether they be small supplies of personal necessaries and luxuries drawn from distant regions of the earth, or relatively large supplies of just those highly specialized kinds of raw material and implements which are used in his work.

The merchant, the broker, and the financier are those who are most directly concerned with the machinery of modern marketing, and with the stability of the social credit; just as fire insurance companies are most directly concerned in provision against fire. But a general reduction in the risks of fire, which would be an unmixed gain to the general public, would bring loss as well as profit to the insurance companies: and those who have profited most in the aggregate by the growing efficiency and stability of social credit, and market organization are the producing class rather than the trading class; and the general public has gained most of all.

2. *A preliminary review of changes, which sometimes render a very large manufacturing or mining business in a measure independent of other industries in its neighbourhood. A note on the meaning of the word "productive."*

Economic progress has at last undermined some of the foundations of Petty's great rule that "Each country flourisheth in the manufacture of its own native commodities." But yet most of them remain, though changed in form; and they are now, as formerly, intermingled with, and sometimes confused with, the advantages which an industry derives from a large home market. In Petty's time, and very much later, people worked of course much for themselves in their own houses on whatever materials Nature supplied liberally to their hands: and, when a specialized industry began to take the work over, it found a large home demand ready to encourage its development. Abundant raw material, and a large market for the finished products, developed ever more highly specialized skill in the main industry, and ever stronger subsidiary industries to supply its incidental requirements, and to work up its waste products. Each single business was on a small scale; and though it had access to many of the economies of production on a large scale, these were *external* to it, and common to the whole district.

For long ages industrial leadership depended mainly on the number and extent of centres of specialized skill in which these external economies abounded: a relatively small importance attached to those *internal* economies which any single business could attain by the elaboration of its own plant, and to the subtle division of labour between its own employees. But with the growth of capital, the development of machinery, and the improvement of the means of communication, the importance of internal economies has increased steadily and fast; while some of the old external economies have declined in importance; and many of those which have risen in their place are national, or even cosmopolitan, rather than local.

Associated with this change there has been some shifting in the relative importance of different orders of industrial capacity relatively to one another and to capital. The supply of skilled labour has increased: but, partly under American

I, IX, 2. influence, machinery has covered so large a range of work that a comparatively short training enables a youth, who is naturally alert, to control a manufacturing process that not long ago would have required the work of a great number of artisans.

Skilled labour is indeed better remunerated than ever before. But while the earlier stages of machine production tended to raise the wages of skilled labour even faster than those of unskilled; the later stages have tended to diminish, relatively at least, the volume of the demand for that sort of highly developed manual skill, which requires special training from boyhood upwards. There are a few industries in which a considerable supply of skill of this kind is as imperatively necessary as ever: and an attempt to start such an industry in a new home has great difficulties and risks. But the chief need of the large majority of modern industries is for alert intelligence, good judgment, promptness and trustworthiness in conduct on the part of the more responsible employees. Where this need has been met, resolute and capable men and women can generally be found who will quickly acquire adequate familiarity with the materials, the plant, and the operations of the industry. Such an industry can be started by a powerful firm; if it imports a considerable staff of leading men into a district, the population of which is energetic and has a fair share of alert intelligence. Modern facilities of communication by railway, and motor traffic; by post, telegraph and telephone facilitate this independence of local aid: and a powerful firm can sometimes set up a railway siding of its own.

Another disruptive influence, which helps a strong business in able hands to be independent of its surroundings, is the certainty with which business success attracts capital. It is often more difficult for a small business to borrow a thousand pounds than for one, which is ten times as large, to borrow fifty thousand: and there is practically no limit to the amount of capital that the public is ready to place at the command of a joint-stock company, which has already done great things, and is believed to be in strong hands. For indeed the stock of capital has grown so much faster even than the scope for its use in industry, that capital is always at the command of those who have both the mental faculty and the moral character needed for turning it to good account.

The keynote of this change was struck by the American Francis Walker, who said as early as 1876 that the man who has the faculties required "to shape and direct production, and to organize and control the industrial machinery...rises to be master of the situation. It is no longer true that a man becomes an employer because he is a capitalist. Men command capital because they have the qualifications to profitably employ labour. To these captains of industry...capital and labour resort for opportunity to perform their several functions[1]."

The drift of capital and labour to the control of the best business faculty within a country is gaining force, and is being accompanied by a similar drift from one country to another. The great business energy of Germany attracts to her industrial districts labour from countries in Europe equally well endowed by Nature. The great business energy of the United States has caused her population to increase very rapidly, even after her best natural resources have passed into private ownership, and the new comer might be able to obtain elsewhere better opportunities of becoming the owner of rich land with but little outlay. It is true that these countries have not recently borrowed very much external capital for public and private investment to match the increase of this population; but the reason is that indigenous capital has been growing very fast in Germany, and at a stupendous rate in the United States.

And again a new keynote is struck:—"A few managing Britons or Americans can now readily be obtained to establish manufactures in any part of the world, and educate nations to become satisfactory workers....The seat of manufacturing is now, and will continue to be more and more, simply a question where the requisite materials are found under suitable conditions. Capital and labour have lost the power they once had to attract raw materials; these now attract labour and capital[2]." This keynote may perhaps have been struck a little too sharply. But it is certainly true that manufactures on a large scale can

[1] *The Wages Question*, ch. XIV.

[2] Carnegie, *Rectorial Address at St Andrew's*, 1902, pp 7, 8.

I, IX, 2. be created, wherever the resources of nature are favourable, much more quickly than was possible before the recent developments of mechanical processes of production. It is no longer necessary that several generations of workers should successively be trained to a gradually higher pitch of specialized skill. And, what is in many cases almost as important, a new industry is not as dependent as formerly on the parallel development of subsidiary industries in its neighbourhood, which may supply its minor wants and turn its by-products to account. Machinery and other implements can now be brought from almost any distance in standardized shapes; and the other services, many of which used to be rendered by subsidiary industries, can now be performed in subsidiary workshops, erected for the purpose by a single vast factory.

The great business, which is set up far from cognate industries, has to trust very much to its own resources not only on its "productive" side, but also in regard to marketing; that is in regard to buying what it needs and selling what it produces. This points to the facts, which will receive much attention later on, that an increasing part of the activity of a manufacturing firm is now given to marketing; and that indeed the line of division between production and marketing is increasingly blurred.

According to popular usage agriculture, fishing, mining and manufacture are productive, because they produce new goods *into the field of business*: while transport and commerce merely change the positions and the ownership of goods which are already in that field. But man does not make coal, he merely transports it from its bed to the surface; and thus makes it potentially useful; its usefulness is nearly complete when delivered by carrier and merchant into a private cellar; and is quite complete when delivered by a domestic servant to the fireplace. Thus the common distinction between "productive" industries and others rests on no scientific basis. But it corresponds to a division, which plays a considerable part in economic studies; the objections to coining a new term to take its place are very great; and for the present at least we must be content to use it[1].

[1] The student of science whose discoveries promote the advance of manu-

3. *General causes which have given to the leaders of productive industry much of the prominence and responsibility, that formerly belonged almost exclusively to great merchants.* I, IX, 3.

The chief beginnings of bold capitalistic speculation were in the long distance trade, and especially in that between different countries. As has already been noted, it was relatively small in volume, being confined mainly to a few fine and costly manufactures; and to things, which could be obtained only by special favour of Nature in particular places: but, slight as it was, this trade was the chief training ground for those faculties which distinguish the master minds in business at the present day. In it alone was there large scope for economic initiative and far-reaching foresight; for the power of controlling great numbers of subordinates of all ranks, from the unskilled porter to the highly responsible officer who was often at once captain of a ship and chief administrator of a large moving storehouse of valuable goods. During long ages the land and the authority of Government were indeed the chief sources of great accumulations of wealth: but gradually even powerful rulers began to lean for financial support on the shoulders of those who had reaped the harvests of large mercantile business[1].

facture has as good a right in the abstract to be called productive, as the commanding officer has to be called a soldier, though he may not handle any weapon.

[1] Of course every great empire of early as well as of recent times has afforded a training ground for the faculties of organization and administration in regard to the affairs of Government in peace and war; and, in the hands of a man possessing business genius and aptitude, the work sometimes reached a high standard of technical excellence. But the proceedings were based on force rather than on free bargaining: arbitrary decisions governed incomings and outgoings alike; and those who amassed large fortunes from handling the public revenues, from selling privileges, and even from the ownership of large tracts of land, were not always endowed with high constructive faculty. The resemblance of the fortunes of Richelieu, Mazarin and Fouquet to those of predatory Roman Proconsuls has been made familiar by Dumas. The large share of the fortunes of eminent merchants, which was derived from the necessities of King and State on the Continent generally, is indicated by Ehrenberg, *Das Zeitalter der Fugger*. M. d'Avenel (in *Les riches depuis sept cent ans*; and the suggestive chapter "De quoi se composaient les anciennes fortunes," of his *Découvertes d'histoire sociale*) discusses the importance of ransoms as a source of wealth; and observes (p. 260) that a prisoner served as a sort of negotiable bill of exchange, according to his ransom, with which a debt might be paid.

I, IX, 3. Merchants were the "Venturers" or "Adventurers" from whom modern enterprise descended. They had a large part in the coordination and the finance of localized manufacture, as soon as it began to outgrow the capacity of the small master working with two or three assistants. The clothiers and other merchants, who let out wool to be spun and woven to their orders on the Yorkshire streams at the end of the eighteenth century, were men of a larger scope than the "manufacturers": and Liverpool Merchants looked down upon the Manchester cotton spinners, even after a hundred years of mechanical inventions had raised the capitalist manufacturer up to the level of leading merchants in regard to the magnitude of his operations, and had entrusted to him a greater responsibility than theirs as a leader of men. It may possibly be true that no industrial leader of recent times has excelled Watt and Stephenson in creative faculty, or Boulton in administrative: for they were forced to rely mainly on their own strength; whereas only a small percentage of those ideas, which are turned to account in any existing business, were created in that business. But yet the work of some great manufacturing and other productive businesses in the present age has demanded a combination of faculties almost as rare as those of Watt and Boulton; together with other acquirements and resources which were not in demand, and were not forthcoming, in the earlier age.

This development is the result of many causes: most of which are connected with the magnitude and complexity of modern industrial operations, and their intricate relations to and dependence on one another. The stage has been passed at which a great idea is almost self-sufficing: it has to be elaborated in connection with others already in possession of the same or neighbouring parts of the industrial field; and its application is therefore not an act, but a long process, needing patience and large resources of mind and perhaps of capital. For instance, when a new mechanical idea has been created, its translation into a smoothly-working business machine generally involves a long series of experimental stages: the constant increase in the size and complexity of the machine-unit often causes such an experimental stage to need the consideration of many more side issues than formerly; and perhaps to cost hundreds or thousands of pounds, where tens or hundreds would have sufficed for the simpler and smaller appliances of a few generations ago. There is therefore a large class of improvements, of which prominent examples may be found in the heavy steel industry and again in the manufacture of monster printing presses or other machines, which are beyond the range of anyone who does not unite the command of a great business concern, with the possession of high faculty for appreciating new inventions, if not for creating them. Again, most of the so-called "chemical" industries, together with others in some of those connected with metals, glass, oil, explosives and other things, which are not commonly regarded as chemical, offer exceptional opportunities for those great business men in Germany and elsewhere, whose genius is partly scientific, and who have founded laboratories within their own works. So far as these considerations are concerned, the growth of large industrial capitals tends to promote technical progress: the inclination of the great manufacturer to take a direct interest in engineering chemical and other studies works wholly for good in raising the prestige of industry.

Again, a progressive business must sometimes rouse an interest in its improved and new-fashioned products: and if they are very expensive, as for instance electrical power plants are, the marketing side of the business must be very strong and enterprising and courageous: he who can discharge these functions adequately must include among his qualities and aptitudes those of a great merchant.

Lastly the administrative head of a giant business must hold together several thousands of employees of various grades in an order which, while harmonious and disciplined, yet elicits their individual and spontaneous enterprise: and for this he must have some of the chief qualities that are required of the commander of an army. He is not a "captain" of industry; he is a "general" in control of several regiments.

Thus it appears that the term a "large business" has become ambiguous. Not very long ago a business was almost always concentrated in one place: it might have agencies and branch offices elsewhere; but they were under the control of the central bureau. Now, however, a single company frequently owns

I, IX, 4. several large establishments engaged in the same or allied branches of a great industry; each of them being self-contained as regards plant, material and executive, though all are under the same supreme financial control. So far as technical efficiency is concerned, each of these establishments is a separate business. But the central control can bring the experience of each part to bear in guiding the whole: and can defray the costs of large experiments, the benefit of which will be available to the whole. Again, each may have some advantage in being secure either of a good market for its products, or of a good supply of its own requirements in half-finished products, from some of its sister establishments acting under orders from the directors of the one financial business that includes them all. Further the technique of each establishment may be indirectly strengthened by the opportunity afforded to it of keeping expensive specialized plant in nearly continuous activity on a relatively small range of work; while other parts of orders, coming to the central bureau, are told off to different establishments, which also work intensively within a narrow range. In so far as this can be done the technical efficiency of the business as a whole appears to correspond rather to its aggregate capital than to that which is invested in any one of its establishments.

In fact, however, the question is much more complex than this. "No one is so wise as all the world"; and no single business is as powerful as the whole industry to which it belongs. A large open market effects an automatic distribution of tasks to those establishments which are severally best fitted for them. The domination of a few large businesses may impair the efficiency of the open market; and the aggregate technical efficiency of the country may be less than if each large establishment had been less independent[1].

4. *Some observations on the assumption that social and economic tendencies, which are general and seem natural, are to be accepted as inevitable and beneficial.*

Increasingly throughout our coming study we shall be concerned to inquire how far industrial progress is dependent on

[1] The subjects of this Section are considered more fully in Book II; and reference is made to some of them in the last chapter of the volume.

individual and how far on collective action: how far it depends on ceaseless initiative; and how far on broad ideas and knowledge, which when once acquired pass speedily into common ownership; and become part of the collective wealth, in the first instance of the countries to which the industries specially affected belong, and ultimately of the whole world. We must consider how the embodiment of a new knowledge or a new idea in a new or improved industrial implement or method is likely to require the control of a large capital. We must examine the limitation which this condition imposes on the utilization of the world's stores of creative faculty in the development of the material sources of well-being. We must inquire how far the gains, which accrue to a giant business as the apparent results of its fine initiative and its prudent courage in taking financial risks, are really its own; how far such gains are increasing the dominance of large capitals; and lastly how far the tendencies thus resulting are desirable, and how far they are inevitable.

Even thoughtful men are still often in some measure under the dominion of the old notions that those changes, which are general, are probably irresistible; and that to resist them is flying in the face of nature. But subordination to natural tendencies, when pushed to its extreme logical issue, is blind fatalism. It is true that capitalistic aggregations, approximating to the mechanical routine of a socialistic bureaucracy, have so far been most prominent where economic progress has been most rapid; but so also have the pallid faces caused by a scarcity of fresh air and sunlight. Sources of individual or social decay are sometimes most dangerous, when they are associated with great achievements, and rich benefits.

Darwin's "law of the survival of the fittest" is often misunderstood; Nature being supposed to secure, through competition, that those shall survive who are fittest to benefit the world. But the law really is that those races are most likely to survive, who are best fitted to thrive in their environment: that is, to turn to their own account those opportunities which the world offers to them. A race of wolves that has well organized plans for hunting in packs is likely to survive and spread; because those plans enable it to catch its prey, not because they confer a benefit on the world.

I, IX, 4. The common opinion is, however, not as wholly false in substance as it is in form. For almost every increase in power, which any race of men has acquired, can be traced to some social qualities which have enabled that race to overcome the difficulties that lie in the way of obtaining the necessaries and comforts of life; or to overcome its human enemies, or both. Success in war may indeed be partly due to ferocity of character. But, though it could perhaps not have been predicted *à priori*, the social qualities, habits and institutions of a conquering race have in the past generally been of a stronger fibre than those of the conquered. The temper which enables wolves to maintain the discipline of the pack, has in it something that is noble; and the world has in fact gained a good deal from those qualities which have enabled the dog, a domesticated wolf, to take a high rank among living creatures. But man is not bound to follow the slow steps by which the race of wolves has passed through disciplined ferocity to higher things.

Again, by aid of "natural selection" certain insects, and flowers from which they gather honey, mutually modify one another, till the insects ensure themselves an abundance of food by the untiring efficiency with which they fertilize the flowers. And in like manner, while it is true that those institutions tend to survive which have the greatest faculty for utilizing the environment in developing their own strength; it is also true that, in so far as they in return benefit the environment, they strengthen the foundations of their own strength, and thereby increase their chance of surviving and prospering. On this account then we may admit that the mere existence of broad tendencies towards the dominance of the joint-stock form of administration and towards combinations of semi-monopolistic scope, affords some reason for thinking that these tendencies make for the public good. But it is only a *primâ facie* reason, and not a very strong one.

The earlier socialists, neglecting the teachings of history, constructed ideal societies, which probably would have been unstable even in a world consisting solely of people, whose unselfish love of humanity was as eager and unalloyed as their own. Marx and his followers resolved to be practical, and argued that history showed a steadily hastening growth of large businesses

I, IX, 4.

and of mechanical administration by vast joint-stock companies: and they deduced the fatalistic conclusion that this tendency is irresistible; and must fulfil its destiny by making the whole State into one large joint-stock company, in which everyone would be a shareholder. But no one would have much scope for independent initiative, and a glib tongue would be likely to give a man more prominence and influence than could often be attained by originality and energy: while those, who just escaped discipline as sluggards, might often have an unduly easy existence.

BOOK II

DOMINANT TENDENCIES OF BUSINESS ORGANIZATION

CHAPTER I

THE ADJUSTMENT OF PRODUCTION TO DEMAND IN AN OPEN MARKET

II, I, 1. 1. *Some introductory observations.*

The general relations of Books II and III to Book I have already been indicated: the growth of massive production, and the ever increasing size of the representative business unit in almost every branch of industry and trade, which have moved with ever increasing speed during recent centuries, are now to be studied in their present forms, and with some regard to their probable future tendencies. It remains to add a few words here as to the relations between the methods of business in open markets, with which alone Book II is concerned; and those in markets in some degree under monopolistic control, which are the subject of Book III.

The line of division between the two classes is indeed indistinct: they shade into one another by imperceptible degrees. And, further, "competition" and "monopoly" do not cover the whole field of industry and trade. Some good work is done and more might with great advantage be done by associations which aim at the joint performance of special tasks. Some of this "cooperative work," in the original use of the term, has long been done by several Institutes of Engineers and others, whose interests are partly of a professional and partly of a business character. II, I, 1.

In this respect British business men may profit by a study of the constructive part of the work of German cartels: for that can be separated from their control of marketing, and in some cases of production, in the pursuance of monopolistic ends. Such associated efforts need not encroach on the freedom of each business to manage its own affairs in its own way: they are entirely in accordance with the frank and generous character of the British race; and they have been developed rapidly in several directions, with the patriotic purpose of facilitating the provision of munitions and other requirements of the country during the World-war.

No doubt such cooperation is not in harmony with that of aggressive competition, which was frequently to be observed among the crude, though energetic men, who mastered English industry in the first half of last century. They were, no doubt, often inclined to regard business as a species of warfare, in which every man's hand must be against his neighbour: and they sometimes found more pleasure in the empty defeat of competitors than in an increase of solid prosperity, which was shared by all. And some prominent writers have disparaged the spirit of economic freedom by the assumption that it involves that old bitter contentiousness. But in fact there is no necessary connection between the two. The representative British business man of the present century has a broader mind and a more generous character than such an argument assumes: his progress in mind and character towards higher things during recent generations is one of the most notable changes on record.

It is however true that the complacency, which was generated by too easy success in the third quarter of last century, has not yet wholly disappeared from all branches of British industry[1]. Many opportunities and occasions for cooperative effort, especially in relation to the scientific problems of industry, have been neglected; and the World-war found so much to be desired in this respect, that the active intervention of Government became more urgent than might otherwise have been the case. But so hearty has been the response in nearly every industry to the

[1] See I, v, 1, 2.

II, I, 1. suggestions of the Committee of the Privy Council on Scientific and Industrial Research; so numerous and energetic have been the leaders in science and industry who have freely given their aid in the work; that cooperative Research Associations are springing into activity in nearly every considerable industry, which offers an opening for such study. It is however true that there are a few subjects, such as that of Fuel Research, which are of direct value to so many industries, that the simplest form of cooperation for their study is that of the nation as a whole: and public opinion has concurred in national expenditure on their account.

In Books II and III, open and controlled markets are studied from the economic and not the ethical point of view. Human nature is assumed to be much the same in both: and an attempt is made to discover how far each method of organization tends to promote general well-being on that assumption. Obviously there are several industries in which monopoly must predominate: it is indeed the only practicable method in such a case as the supply of water to a town from a distant source. On the other hand the most malignant features of unscrupulous competition, which recent research has brought to light, have been seen in the pursuit and maintenance of monopolistic control in industries which might retain an open market. The main cause of this is not to be found in any exceptional ferocity of those who are striving to obtain or maintain a monopoly: for such men's minds are generally of too large a mould to be inclined to do evil without adequate motive. The main cause is that they stand to gain large profits from the destruction of a competitor; together with high prestige for business ability, which they may perhaps value even more: while in a really open market no one has very much to gain by destroying any one of his rivals.

The present chapter is a compressed account of the relations among production, consumption, and value; or—to use an alternative phrase—among supply, demand, and price. It contains nothing of importance that is not well understood by experienced men of affairs; while its form is on lines familiar to economic students. But it is of course arranged with a view to the purposes immediately at hand; and a few considerations are therefore extended rather far. Some readers will probably elect to omit it: and partly, in order to aid decision on this point, a few of the chief matters discussed in it are indicated by the following statements:—

Production and marketing are parts of the single process of adjustment of supply to demand. The division between them is on lines which are seldom sharply defined: the lines vary from one class of business to another, and each is liable to modification by any large change in the resources of production, transport, or the communication of intelligence.

The term "cost of production," as used in business and in economic literature, generally includes tacitly some portion of the costs of marketing, the extent of which is to be inferred from the context. It can seldom be definitely interpreted without reference (1) to the market for which the production is undertaken; and (2) to a "representative" producing business.

The responsiveness of demand to changes in price (which is sometimes called its "*elasticity*") is a gradual process: and, partly for this reason, the diminution in the costs of manufacture, which corresponds to an enlarged scale of operations, is a gradual, and sometimes an uncertain process.

The cost of producing a single thing can seldom be isolated: for its production is nearly always part of a process, which is concerned with many other things of the same class.

The cost of production of almost every class as a whole is associated with (though it is not strictly speaking a "joint" cost with) that of producing other classes. The "prime," or immediate, costs of producing a thing can often be isolated. But its proper share of the "general" expenses of the business by which it is made, cannot be determined according to any fixed rules.

Thus the tendency of market prices towards cost of production (including normal profits) by a representative firm is much obscured, though not annulled, by the almost ceaseless operation of various disturbing causes.

II, I, 2. 2. *Ambiguities of the terms Market, and Cost of production.*

The term *market* is used in many different connections; and in scarcely any two has it exactly the same significance. This difficulty has its origin in the ordinary discourse of life; where the context, or a special explanation, indicates the particular use of the term intended: and economists are compelled to conform, in this as in many similar cases, to general usage. But a short account of the chief groups of these various uses will be proper to our present purpose[1].

In all its various significations, a "market" refers to a group or groups of people, some of whom desire to obtain certain things, and some of whom are in a position to supply what the others want. A market may consist of all the inhabitants of a town, or of the whole country: or it may consist in effect only of those of them who have a special interest in something, as for instance zinc or leather. In some cases, dealings over the whole Western World may be worked out in such constant unison as to justify the phrase "world-market." Everyone buys, and nearly every producer sells, to some extent in a "*general*" market, in which he is on about the same footing with others around him. But nearly everyone has also some "*particular*" markets; that is, some people or groups of people with whom he is in somewhat close touch: mutual knowledge and trust lead him to approach them, and them to approach him, in preference to strangers. A producer, a wholesale dealer, or a shopkeeper, who has built up a strong connection among purchasers of his goods, has a valuable property. He does not generally expect to get better prices from his clients than from others. But he expects to sell easily to them because they know and trust him; and he does not sell at low prices in order to call attention to his business, as he often does in a market where he is little known.

The demand and the supply of a modern market are not definite stocks on hand at any time, but streams flowing at various rates during a year or some other appropriate period. There are a few exceptions. For instance, in a market for fish

[1] See the concluding remarks of Appendix A.

on a hot day, with no access to cool storage, the supply is merely the stock in hand; and the demand is a short sharp movement on the part of a compact group of people. But as a rule supply is a gradual process, liable to be influenced at every stage by varying facilities for production, and varying expectations of the terms on which the product can be marketed.

The term *cost of production* is commonly used in two very different senses. Where the affairs of a particular business are under discussion, it always means *money cost*; that is, the aggregate of the outlays in money, that are incurred directly or indirectly in the production of a certain thing. Among these are commonly included a reasonable rate of profit, together with insurance against risks: remuneration of the work of the owner of the business does not appear as a separate item in the accounts; but goes with interest on capital under the head of profits.

But in the discussion of social problems, it is often necessary to inquire whether certain businesses, which may or may not be adequately remunerative to the persons concerned, are worth what they cost to the country or the world: and in this connection the term cost of production refers to real cost. The *real cost of production* of a thing is the aggregate of efforts and sacrifices which are incurred in its production. Thus the work of very young children in factories, even though paid for in money at the full market rate, is seldom worth its real cost: the satisfactions, which are derived from its contributions to production, are not worth the social cost of child life spent in grievous and depressing toil, and without an adequate education to prepare for the duties of after life[1].

A little care in wording will avoid all confusion between real and money costs of production. But there is another difficulty about the term "*cost of production for a market*" which is apt to be overlooked, and calls for careful attention. The manufacturer, or other producer, adjusts his production to his market so as to obtain for himself the greatest net excess of receipts over

[1] The degree of correspondence between the price paid for any particular industrial work and its real cost, though a matter of vital importance from the social point of view, is not very closely connected with the subject of this Book. The relations of risks to costs are considered in II, VI.

II, I, 2. his "expenses" or "money cost" of production; with due allowance for his own trouble and risk, and for the use of his capital.

Until goods are marketed their production is seldom of much avail in the modern world: and there is no uniformity of practice on the part of manufacturers and other producers as to the extent to which they themselves incur labour and expense on behalf of the marketing of their goods. A manufacturer may sell to wholesale dealers who, after inspecting his goods on his premises, take their own measures for bringing them, together with other goods, to the notice of retailers: but even he must incur trouble and expense in attracting the attention of the merchants: and remuneration for this has to be included in the price received by him; for otherwise he would not earn profits adequate to his outlay. Heavier costs for marketing are incurred by a manufacturer, if he sends round incessant streams of expensively equipped travellers to dealers of various sorts: and much heavier still, if he also advertises largely in order that the general public may demand goods bearing his name or trade-mark from the dealers.

Considerations of this kind will be found to underlie the general reasonings of economists as to the relations between demand, supply, and value; but perhaps they have not been made sufficiently prominent. The rule is simple. When considering the operations of demand and supply in governing price in any general market, we must aggregate the expenses up to one and the same point in regard to every transaction; and take the demand price at that point. The customs of each particular branch of industry and trade indicate the most convenient point for this purpose: it is generally the point of delivery to a wholesale dealer, and less frequently to the retailer. In a few cases, such as that of bread, it is commonly the point of delivery to the ultimate consumer, either at his own house or when fetched by him—a difference in detail of some practical importance[1].

[1] A manufacturer sometimes sells in his own shops to the ultimate consumer goods such as are generally sold to a middleman; and then his point of delivery may be reduced back close to the customary (manufacturer's) point by deducting the expenses, direct and indirect, of his shops together with allowance for his own trouble and risk in regard to them, from the total expenses of his business; and at the same time deducting the *gross* profits of the middle-

3. *Increased supply, demand being constant, lowers price both immediately and ultimately; though in various degrees for different things. Increased demand for a manufactured product generally sets up forces tending to lower cost, and therefore price, except when increased supplies of raw material can be obtained only at greater cost: but its immediate effect is always to raise price.*

So far little account has been taken of the time required for the development of the full results of changed conditions, whether on the side of demand or supply. Economic doctrines, when expressed in short and handy form, generally neglect this element of time: they imply that certain results will follow on certain causes, leaving the common sense of the reader to supply the qualification—"provided no great change, working in a different direction, set in before the effects of these causes have time for full development." This qualification being ignored, the doctrines are taken to be unconditional; and thus trouble arises: for, though the causes perhaps begin to produce the effects assigned to them, they have not gone far before their influence is modified or even overborne by other causes with different tendencies. This shows that economic doctrines cannot be stated correctly in a few words.

The growth of demand is in fact gradual. People take some time to learn the uses of a thing which they had regarded as beyond their means. When the price comes within their reach, the more alert may begin to use it, and others in their own class may gradually follow. But there may be hindrances in the way: the thing itself may be of little service without subsidiary appliances that are not yet provided for general use. Thus a fall in the price of gas cannot produce its full effects on consumption till people have had time to experiment with gas-engines

men, through whose hands similar goods generally pass, from the price which he receives. The results thus reached will correspond to those suggested by an observation of the relations between wholesale demand, supply, and price. They may be faulty in particular instances: but if the profits of manufacturers who retail their own goods were habitually much greater than is indicated on this plan, the practice of the market would change: middlemen would be eliminated; and the point of delivery at which expenses and price would alike be reckoned, would be the ultimate consumer. All this, however, must be taken broadly; and subject to the reflection which will shortly be developed that the production of goods and the marketing of goods are not acts, but processes.

II, I, 3. and gas-cooking stoves for unaccustomed uses; and perhaps not even till a gradually increasing demand has improved and standardized, and thus cheapened the gas-engines and stoves: and this growing familiarity may of course be checked by a further development of, say, electrical appliances. Again, a fall in the fares charged on a tram line or suburban railway will not have exhausted its effect on increasing the traffic, till new houses have been built near one end to accommodate people whose work lies near the other end.

In this connection it will be well to introduce an academic term, that will be much needed later on. If a given fall in the price at which a thing is offered causes a great increase in the amount demanded, the *elasticity* or *responsiveness of demand* is said to be great; and, if it causes only a small increase, the elasticity is said to be small[1].

It is a general rule that a lowering of the price, at which a thing is offered, increases demand. The increase will be great or small according as the demand is elastic or inelastic: and either a long or short time may be required for developing the extended uses of the commodity, which are rendered possible by the fall in price. But (at all events if exceptional cases, in which a thing is driven out of fashion by a fall in its price, be neglected) the influence of price on demand is similar in character for all commodities. And, further, those demands which show high elasticity in the long run, generally show a high elasticity almost at once: so that it is reasonable to speak of the demand for a commodity as being of high or low elasticity without specifying how far we are looking ahead.

But while the response of demand to increased supply acts on price always in one direction, though with varying degrees of intensity; the response of supply to increased demand acts on costs, and therefore on price, in different directions according to circumstances. Its immediate tendency is to raise price: its later effect, in the case of manufactured and some other goods, is gradually to lower costs and therefore price.

It is, of course, true that an increase in the scale of produc-

[1] If the increase in amount for each small fall of price is proportionately equal to the fall, the elasticity is said to be one; if twice as great, it is said to be two; if only three-quarters as great, it is said to be three-quarters; and so on.

tion of each manufacturing (or other "Increasing Return") industry opens out to it almost invariably opportunities for a gradual increase of the internal economies to be derived from fit coordination of more extensive varieties of specialized ability, skill and plant; as well as for the standardization of products, and for dealing in the most favourable markets. Again an increase in the scale of production of the industry as a whole, or even in that of the industries which supply its needs, tends to open to each business in the industry, whether large or small, access to improved plant, improved methods, and a variety of other "external" economies. But all these tendencies are *gradual*: some move fast; others require several years, and others again several decades for their full development.

Even stronger cases can be found of the importance of the element of time in regard to the economies of manufacture on a large scale. A large, standing, order for rifles or cartridges of a particular pattern can be filled more cheaply than a small one; because the large order will enable the cost of adapting plant specially to that pattern to be spread very thin over a large surface. In fact, this position is somewhat similar to that of the printing trade, which will take an order for fifty thousand copies of a book at a much lower rate than for five thousand, and at a very much lower rate than for five hundred; because the same expense of setting up type has to be incurred in all three cases. And yet a sudden and unexpected order for a million rifles, *to be delivered promptly*, could not be filled at as low a rate as one for a hundred thousand. For the larger order would require more plant: and much labour skilled and unskilled, not specially adapted to the work, might need to be forced into it. Thus, the tendency to a rise of the price at which increased quantities of anything can be obtained (or their "supply-price") dominates as a rule all industries in regard to short periods. It is therefore even more necessary to make explicit reference to the period of time which is allowed for the adjustment of supply-price to changed conditions of demand, than it is to make reference to the period required for the adjustment of demand-price (that is the price at which any given amount will find purchasers) to changed conditions of supply[1].

[1] With regard to short periods, and especially to the transactions of a

II, I, 3. It is to be further observed that the effects of a steady increase in demand for a commodity on the economies at the command of the industry, which makes it, cannot be properly studied without some reference to the conditions of industries, which supply it with plant and other things. If its increased demand for their products enables it to fill its requirements at lower costs than before, then an increase in the demand for its products will enable it to lower their price more than would have been possible otherwise: and therefore yet further to increase its sales, and therefore to obtain yet further economies of production on a large scale and so on. That is to say, the economies of production on a large scale can seldom be allocated exactly to any one industry: they are in great measure attached to groups, often large groups, of correlated industries.

It is not necessary to pursue this matter further here, because so long as competition works freely throughout the industries concerned, the share which each industry in such a group obtains of the aggregate economies and gains resulting from the increased demand, is governed by broad causes; a comparatively small place being left for commercial strategy. But if any of the industries in the group are under some degree of monopolistic control, the matter becomes important, as will be seen in Book III.

So far no account has been taken of the dependence of manufacture on supplies of raw material coming from the two "extractive" industries, agriculture and mining. They are commonly classed as "Diminishing Return industries," because in them Nature's resistance to a greatly increased demand generally overbears in the long run the force derived from those resources which man provides: but in fact the constraints which she exerts in the two cases differ fundamentally.

dealer's market there is an "elasticity of supply" which corresponds closely to elasticity of demand: that is, a given rise in price will cause a great or a small increase in the offers which sellers accept, according as they have large or small reserves in the background, and as they have formed low or high estimates of the level of prices at the next market. But in the more fundamental problems of supply our primary concern is with the costs at which a given amount of the commodity can be produced on good notice; and therefore amount cannot here conveniently be regarded as a function of price.

Good cultivation will enable a field to yield the same amount of produce decade after decade in return for the same amount of labour as before: but, no improvement in the arts of cultivation being assumed, it will not, as a rule, enable an increased produce to be raised without the application of labour and capital increased more than in proportion. In other words, what is called "Diminishing Return" in regard to agriculture relates to the difficulty of increasing the *annual* flow of produce, not of maintaining that flow. But what is often called by the same name in regard to mining relates to the difficulty of getting more produce out of a mine, when its accessible and rich supplies of ore have been lessened by a given *aggregate* amount, with but little reference to the period of time over which the operations have extended.

In agriculture improved knowledge and methods are always contending against Nature's resistance to the demands made on her by an increasing population. And no guess can be made as to whether the ratio, which the agriculturist's produce bears to his efforts, direct or indirect, will increase or diminish; until it is known whether the rate of improvement of his methods and appliances is greater or less than the rate of increase of the demands which he makes on his land[1].

Of course this tendency to Diminishing Return in agriculture is of little practical importance in a sparsely peopled country; but it may press heavily on a country, which has a dense and rapidly growing population, unless large supplies of agricultural produce can be obtained on favourable terms from abroad. The pressure may be relieved a little, but only a little, by better adjustments, as for instance better forms of land tenure, or better education of the farmer[2].

[1] In regard to the action of an individual farmer, this tendency may be expressed in terms of money: but in regard to broad problems it must be expressed in terms of amounts of appliances and of products, in spite of the inconvenience caused by varieties of labour, of farming plant, and of crops. For the price of staple foods tends to rise more than in proportion to any increase of demand relatively to supply: so that the necessity for a greatly increased production from the land is likely to increase the aggregate money receipts of cultivators more than their aggregate outlays. This difficulty is often overlooked.

[2] It is therefore on a wholly different footing from those tendencies to diminishing return which arise when any producer distributes his resources inappropriately; as when a farmer takes either more land or less land than is appropriate to his capital: or when the number of planing machines in a

II, I, 4. 4. *The cost of production which controls value relates to whole processes of production rather than to any particular parcel of products.*

The cost of any one thing—a bale of cloth, a lawn-mower, or an engraving—cannot be definitely isolated from that of similar things made in the same process with it; that is, of things made by the aid, in whole or part, of the same business ability and organization, the same labour, and the same machinery and other plant. In other words, the cost of production, which exercises a dominant influence on value, is the cost of a whole process. This elementary but important principle (or chief head) of the doctrine of value has already been to some extent implied in the statement that the immediate influence exerted on cost, and therefore on price, by a great increase in the demand for a manufactured product is generally in the opposite direction to its ultimate effect.

We must go far from the facts of life to get a case, in which the cost of production of a single thing can be exactly deduced from the total cost of the business in which it is made: we must imagine a steady demand without fluctuations for the products of a business, all of which are of the same kind and made under the same conditions. If a hundred things are made by it annually,

locomotive factory is either so large that several of them are habitually idle, or so small that work is frequently held up to wait for the planing machine. Such troubles are not very frequent: they are transitional: they do not enter as a primary factor into the conditions of human progress: and some little confusion seems to have been caused by speaking of the permanent tendency to Diminishing Return as though it were merely a particular instance of numerous passing incidents. For they do not, as it does, materially affect the rise and decline of nations; or threaten to offer, ere many centuries have passed, a stern opposition to a further considerable increase of the population of the world.

This is not of great importance in relation to the structure of business; which is the chief matter now in hand. For indeed the reasonings, by which a farmer decides whether his capital will reach out to the profitable cultivation of an additional piece of land that happens to be available for hire, are of the same character as those by which he decides whether it will be better to buy his own steam cultivator, or to hire one on occasion. And again the reasons by which a manufacturer decides whether to put an additional floor on one of his buildings or to take a new piece of land and put a low building on it are similar to those by which he decides whether to instal an electric supply of his own or not. But, from the social point of view, land in an old country is in a class by itself: for however it changes hands from one owner to another, the country's stock of it is fixed: and this is a matter of the first importance in regard to the incidence of taxation and other large issues.

then the cost of each is a hundredth part of the total annual cost of the business: or, in other words, it is the special cost of that thing together with a hundredth part of the general costs of the business for a year. This imaginary case is commonly taken as the starting-point in discussions of value. But it is not representative; and its suggestions are misleading. It is true that the *prime cost* of a particular thing can frequently be isolated: but its full cost cannot. We must here go a little into detail as to this familiar distinction. Its prime cost, in the narrow use of the term that is common in many industries, consists of those direct expenses for wages, coal, material, wear and tear of plant, etc., which are incurred by making it, and which would have been avoided if the process of production had stopped short of making it. But its full cost includes an appropriate share of the *general charges* of the business.

Thus the taking of an additional order is likely to involve an increase of the wages bill to nearly the full amount of the wages paid to the artisans and labourers who work on it: but foremen and other trusted artisans are seldom dismissed even in slack times; and therefore parts at least of their wages are not prime costs in the strictest use of the term. Again, it is customary not to include any part of the office charges in prime costs; because the salaries paid at any time are but little affected by the amount of work that happens to be in hand at the time. But there are exceptions to this general rule also; for, when work is slack a vacancy in the office may be left unfilled for the time; or occasion may be taken to dismiss someone whose services are no longer desired.

The general charges include interest on capital employed; depreciation of buildings, machinery, etc., otherwise than by actual wear and tear; salaries of officials and others who cannot conveniently be discharged at short notice; and the whole cost of building up the organization of the business both internally and in relation to its customers. And, over all, allowance must be made for the earnings (*i.e.* excess of profits over interest on capital, and insurance) of the heads of the business.

The distinction between special (or prime) and general costs has always the same character: but it differs in detail according to circumstances. In particular a great part of those costs

II, I, 5. which are properly regarded as "general" when a passing transaction is in view, must be regarded as "special" when reference is made to one which extends over a long period. This consideration is very important in connection with the division of costs between two classes of things, in the production or marketing of which some use is made of the same plant, or the same business organization. If the period in view is short, it will often be impossible to assign approximately to each its proper share of the costs which are common to both; though such an assignment can be made fairly well with reference to a long period of time. The full significance of this contrast between short and long period results is apt to be overlooked: and it will appear to hold the key to many difficulties which we shall encounter later on; especially in connection with problems of marketing in the present Book, and the next. See also Appendix J.

5. *The distribution of the general costs of a business between the various products, to which its resources are devoted: whether they are "joint" in the sense of being practically inseparable, or are produced "in common" for any other reason.*

This class of consideration is reinforced if we look at cases of a group of "*joint products*" in that narrow sense of the term in which it is not practicable, or at all events not convenient, to produce any one member of the group without at the same time producing the others. Instances of such groups are the meat, skin, and wool of a sheep; or again wheat and its straw. If the relative proportions of each of these were fixed absolutely by Nature, the cost of each group would need to be set as a single thing against the aggregate of the prices which could be got in the market for the several members of the groups. Cost of production would have no part in determining their relative prices: that would lie wholly in the hands of demand.

In practice, however, there are few, if any, cases of joint products the cost of production of both of which together is exactly the same as that of them alone. So long as any product of a business has a market value, it is almost sure to have devoted to it some special care and expense. If straw were valueless, farmers would exert themselves more than they do to make the ear bear as large a proportion as possible to the stalk. Again, the importation of foreign wool has caused English sheep to be adapted by judicious crossing and selection so as to develop heavy weights of good meat at an early age, even at the expense of some deterioration of their wool. It is only when one of two things produced by the same process is valueless, unsaleable, and yet does not involve any expense for its removal, that there is no inducement to attempt to alter its amount. And it is only in these exceptional cases that we have no means of assigning the separate supply price of each of the joint products. When it is possible to modify the proportions of these products, we can ascertain what part of the whole expense of the process of production would be saved, by so modifying these proportions as slightly to diminish the amount of one of them, without affecting the amounts of the others: and the expense of production of that part of this particular product which would not have been produced, if there had been a lower expectation of demand for it, may in some sense be taken as indicating its cost of production. At all events, it may be said that there is some tendency so to adjust the proportions of the several members of a group even of "joint products" in the narrow use of the term, that the excess of receipts over outlay on the whole group shall be greater than it would have been if Nature had been left to adjust those proportions in her own way. To that limited extent there is some correlation between cost and value even in regard to such products.

When two things, say locomotives and stationary engines, are made in the same works, and in a great measure by the same labour and plant, it is often said that their costs are "joint"; but, this term has a special historical association with groups of things, such as wheat and straw, which cannot be produced separately; and it seems better to speak of such groups as having "common" or "allied" costs.

In cases of such common or allied production, each thing is charged with a share of those expenses which are incurred on account of the general work of the business; it is next charged with a considerably larger share of those expenses for plant, for superintendence, for advertising, etc., which more specially

II, I, 6. belonged to the particular department by which it is made, in addition to the prime costs incurred directly and specially for it. Simple arithmetic in this case needs to be supplemented by careful analysis and thoughtful study of each problem as a whole: and, as we shall see later on, much systematic and organized effort has been given by accountants and others to the task.

Let us push this a little further. Suppose a manufacturer to be doubting whether to set up some expensive plant, or some addition to the office staff, or some new selling agency, which could not pay its way by the work it did for any one class of his products, but would save a little on each of three classes. If he decided that the aggregate of these savings would make the proposed outlay remunerative, he would adopt it, and regard its cost as part of the costs of those three classes. There would be no direct means of dividing out the cost among them: but he might divide it out roughly in proportion to the savings he made on them. This distribution would have no strict logical basis. But it would be nearly that which competition would have compelled; if each of the three classes had had to meet similar products made by manufacturers, who specialized on them, and found full employment for a machine, or other appliance similar to that which he was contemplating.

6. *General conclusions as to limitations of the tendency towards such an adjustment of supply to demand, as would cause market price to cover expenses of production with normal profits.*

This account of the adjustment of supply to demand has aimed only at indicating broad tendencies, which conduce towards the attainment of an equilibrium position; though incessant changes in the conditions, which must be satisfied by a position of equilibrium, prevent them from reaching it. To revert to a familiar illustration, the gravitation, which effects a smooth surface on a pond when the air is still, is making always for an equally restful result on the surface of the ocean: but there the winds build up mighty waves; while tides alternately raise and lower the general surface by amounts, which vary with the positions of the moon and sun: and the explanation of these movements, and their partial prediction are based on a study of elementary physical laws. In like manner business enterprise tends to increase the supply of anything, when the price at which it can be marketed will return its expenses of production with fairly good profits: and this tendency is working at any moment towards an imaginary position of equilibrium, which would be promptly reached if the general conditions then prevailing were rigidly fixed. But in fact it is not reached; any more than is that imaginary position of equilibrium of the sea, which would be reached if the relative positions of the earth, sun and moon were fixed, and the winds were stilled.

Almost every one of the expenses of maintaining any process of production is liable to incessant change. At one time additional machines may have to be bought when the market for them is exceptionally favourable to the seller: while another set may be bought at a time when machine makers were willing to accept a price, which did not go very far beyond covering the mere prime cost of production. The same shop under one manager will turn out more and better work at the same expense than under another. The same manufacturer, using his best energies without stint, will at one time put out a commodity which the market absorbs quickly at a price much beyond its full expenses of production; but at another he will have missed his aim, and be compelled to force his product on the market at a heavy loss. In these and innumerable other ways the return to a whole process of production may be kept for a considerable time a good deal above, or below, the level which might return its whole expenses with normal profits. But yet the tendency to keep expenses and price in close relation to one another is strong and persistent in an open market in regard to whole processes of production; the deviations from normal equilibrium, though ceaseless, are seldom very wide. Thus far-reaching are the various uncertainties of demand on the one side and of supply on the other.

But indeed a perfect adjustment is inconceivable. Perhaps even it is undesirable. For after all man is the end of production; and perfectly stable business would be likely to produce men who were little better than machines.

II, I, 6. The general position is, then:—Every manufacturer, or other business man, has a plant, an organization, and a business connection, which put him in a position of advantage for his special work. He has no sort of permanent monopoly, because others can easily equip themselves in like manner. But for the time being he and other owners of factories of his class are in possession of a partial monopoly. The prices of the stock, which they put on the market, will be governed by the demand of that market relatively to that stock, nearly in the same way as if they had a true monopoly. Nearly in the same, but not quite: for in the case of a permanent monopoly consumers will seldom gain much by waiting for lower prices; whereas, if prices rise above cost of production in an open trade, those consumers, who can do so conveniently, will wait for the effect of competition in bringing down prices. Combinations for regulating prices aim at consolidating provisionally this partial monopoly, and at putting it in good working order: and this fact goes far towards explaining their gradual, and in some cases almost unconscious, drift towards monopoly in the full sense of the term. So important indeed are these considerations, that the greater part of Book III will be occupied with the complex issues which are raised, on the one hand by monopolistic tendencies in markets, that are in the main open; and on the other by competitive influences on monopolistic policy.

CHAPTER II

DEBTS OF INDUSTRIAL TECHNIQUE TO SYSTEMATIC RECORD AND TO STANDARDIZATION

1. ***In early times the cumulative progress of industrial technique was in the main dependent on the informal records of customary usage: and this primitive method was until quite recently the chief resource of agriculture in sparsely peopled districts.*** II, II, 1.

If custom had been absolutely rigid, it would have been an almost unmixed evil. But the resistance which it offered to the bold reformer resembled that presented by a glacier to anyone who might try to change its shape: custom and the glacier are plastic, but both refuse to be hurried in their adjustments. Custom has discouraged any attempt at improvement which involved a sudden breach with tradition: but, except in some ceremonial matters, it has been tolerant of modifications in substance, form and method which did not obtrude themselves. On the one hand, stagnant social conditions do not crush out of everyone the desire to humour his own fancy, or his love of novelty, or his inclination to save trouble by a rather better adjustment of implements to the work done: and, on the other hand, the solidity of custom has rendered the supreme service of perpetuating any such change as found general approval.

Had each put his individual fancies into practice without restraint, few would have followed his erratic movements: there would have been no *corpus*, or body of general thought, in which they could have been merged; and, in the absence of written record, they might probably have perished without leaving direct successors. But custom supplied a permanent body of general design, on which each fresh mind might try to make some variation for the sake of economy of effort, of in-

II, II, 1. creased utility, or more pleasing effect. And custom under favourable conditions was able to make utility, economy and artistic delicacy work harmoniously together in improving the *standard* commodity of common life.

Modern conditions have given some solid foundation for the common statement that utility and beauty are hostile to one another. For when a thing is marked out for description as useful, it is almost sure to be a device for attaining some utility, old or new, by a new method; that is to say, it has not had time to be gently moulded by innumerable light touches of successive makers, who have tried to bring it more into harmony with their sense of fitness. But in the ages of patient custom time was abundant. Perhaps not one in twenty of the tentative mouldings was well conceived: but those which were bad, passed away; while those which the people approved, were almost unconsciously incorporated in hallowed usage; and they became material for further moulding by the delicate breathings of the spirit of the race. Thus it comes that the carpet, the axe, and above all the sword, have been gradually standardized in different places, and often on quite different lines; but always so gently as to combine grace with efficiency in high degrees. So far as we can tell, men had then generally less quick, subtle, and fine instincts than now; and if each generation had moulded its own implements with little guidance from the past, the effects might probably have been crude; but, working on the plastic standard received from the past, each made its own step towards the Ideal[1].

[1] In like manner melodies and ballads, which have been standardized by unwritten tradition, have offered opportunity and incentive to every bard in each successive generation, to make slight variations in his recital. Some would not please even himself; and few would meet with enduring favour. But whenever a man of genius arose, he would leave ballads or melodies a little altered for the good: and thus the finest ballads, especially those which have come down to us with the name of Homer, and the most delicate traditional music have some charms that are beyond the reach of individual poets or musicians.

It is not indeed to be denied that a few ceremonial costumes which have come down from early times are ugly as well as inconvenient; and indeed some of them seem to have been developed as a means of proclaiming a superiority to manual work. The surviving vestiges of ancient costumes in the Alps include some, which are not admirable from any point of view; but they are cherished as indications of hereditary rank and of loyalty to the village or valley,

Even in a primitive civilization, changes in appliances, in methods, and in the purposes for which they are to be used, are mutually dependent on one another: and this cause alone would greatly limit the practical influence of isolated new ideas. Here however the institution of slavery sometimes came to the aid of progress, by forcibly breaking down prescriptions of custom: for it enabled a new idea, which had taken hold of a few strong men, to be realized in practice more quickly than if the manual workers had been free, but comatose and unintelligent. It has often been observed that progress has owed much to the subordination of the masses of the population to the will of a dominant race, whose minds have not been occupied with petty cares. But mankind will not have achieved their destiny till the masses can pioneer for themselves.

Even where custom opposes no great resistance to change, progress cannot be very fast unless a man's best thoughts are recorded in some way, so that others may profit by them. For large inventions and other advancements are seldom completed by a single man; and not always by a single generation. In fact, they are often named after those who have planted the flags of conquest on the crests of the battlements; while those who led the way, but did not live to partake in the ultimate victory, are forgotten. For the highest constructive instincts are apt to die with him who has developed them: their offspring may live in those, whom he has influenced personally; but otherwise they bear little fruit except in so far as he has embodied them in a form which is generally accessible.

During the greater part of the life of the world most of the people have spent nearly the whole of their time in the fields: compact centres of life and thought were rare: and, before the days of printing, a scattered population had little opportunity for the stimulus and suggestion, which one man can derive from the thoughts and experiences of another. Tradition ruled; and particular experiences seldom developed into successive steps of cumulative progress. These facts go far to account for the

whose flag they in effect are: and this loyalty may have tended to some accentuation of local peculiarities. It seems that with comparatively few exceptions those parts of the local costume, which are worn in every-day life, are convenient and in good taste.

II, II, 1. slow progress of technique till recent times. It may be true that the native brain power of the individual has not greatly increased with the ages; and it is certainly true that emergency and opportunity have frequently proved agricultural populations to be strong in resource as well as in resolution. But yet the conditions of agricultural life have not been such as to bring to the front those men, who had the faculty requisite for making great occasions for themselves: one reason for this being that the ownership of land has come by inheritance in a somewhat greater degree than the ownership of considerable industrial resources. Further, every agricultural problem has peculiarities of its own: and some sides of it can be mastered by shrewd, experienced, alert, instinctive judgment, better than by systematic reasoning based on ordered knowledge. Therefore the agriculturist has never been apt to search for the general in the particular, and the particular in the general. His instinct and insight have for the greater part died with him. The progress of his art remained for the greater part empirical, until men trained in industry, or commerce, or in scientific schools came to his aid[1].

[1] Even now we read that in Britain, though many of the big farms are excellently managed, "all depends on man's instinct and memory." It is true that agricultural methods are being improved in some places by agriculturists themselves; but this progress is for the greater part confined to districts in which agriculturists have learnt the importance of a good education, by which is meant "not so much further knowledge of a technical sort, as the more flexible habit of mind that comes with reading, the susceptibility of ideas, that is acquired from acquaintance with a different atmosphere than the one in which a man ordinarily lives." The work of a tenant farmer on a holding of 150 to 500 acres is often of high quality, both technically and in regard to business methods. But men mostly "learn by example, by looking over the hedge"; and the bad farming one sees so often in England alongside the best, is not due to any lack of knowledge, but to the low mental calibre of many of the men occupying the land. (The above statements are reproduced from the concluding article of a notable record of "A Pilgrimage of British Farming," *The Times*, 6 Jan. 1913.)

Mr R. E. Prothero (*English Farming, Past and Present*) shows that the work of agricultural pioneering did not begin to combine "science with practice," and proceed steadily by one firm stepping-stone of recorded advance to another, till about 1812. The great work of Townshend, Bakewell, Coke and other early guides was mainly based by empirical methods on practical experience. Attention has already been called to the use which some monasteries made, even before the "Revival of Learning," of Latin literature on behalf of the agricultural arts.

2. *Various uses of the term Standard. Influences on technique exerted by clear and exact registration of the results of progressive experiments, such that each can be used as a stepping-stone to later endeavour.* II, II, 2.

Custom standardizes unconsciously and crudely processes and products alike. The modern science of industrial technique deliberately standardizes some products and many processes; and deliberately leaves many products and some processes open to varying tastes and humours, to fluctuating needs, and to the caprices of fashion. But deliberate standardization is used as a means to the attainment of some definite aim: and it is in turn deliberately modified, or even set aside, as soon as that aim either loses importance, or is found to be accessible by a better route which requires different standards. A standard may be *Particular* to an individual producer, or it may be *General* to the greater part of an industry or even the whole western world[1].

General standardization for industrial purposes is sometimes set up at a stroke by authority of Government, or of a convention of leaders in the industries most directly concerned. Thus, for instance, the present electrical standards, Watt, Ohm, Ampère, etc. were fixed by an international convention: and every Government appoints, and changes from time to time, the exact measurements and other specifications of rifle cartridges, whether made in its own or in private workshops. No one would assert that the general adoption of standards, differing by a little from any of these, would be much less useful: but there is a vast advantage in the existence of definite standards, adhesion to which within less than a thousandth part may be required in certain cases. This kind of standardization, as well as the Particular standardization of the individual parts of a typewriter, or a reaping and binding machine, etc. by an individual maker, will be considered shortly. But just now we are concerned rather with that General standardization which is evolved gradually and embodies the progressive evolution of improved technique.

[1] Mediaeval regulations as to standardization provided a somewhat futile occupation to the Aulnager; and they flourished in a form, partly mediaeval and partly modern, under Colbert.

II, II, 2. For instance, every decade has seen the standard shape and proportions of racing yachts moulded by the thought and experience of numerous capable experts in several countries. Each designer is ever striking out some more or less important deviation from ordinary practice: if his venture seems to him good, he embodies it in his own practice, and it becomes part of his Particular standardization. If it meets with approval by others, it is soon embodied (with perhaps some modification) in the General standard shape as has been the case with racing yachts. But the best shape for a racing yacht depends a good deal on the conditions under which it is to be sailed, and a little also on the personality of its captain; and similar personal considerations affect, in various degrees, the choice of business methods. When the athlete strikes out a particularly successful way of taking hurdles, his Particular standardization is not at all sure to become General, until experience has shown to what extent his success with it is due to his idiosyncrasy.

A similar cause retards even more the general adoption of a modification in the method of conducting a certain class of business operations which has proved successful in a particular case. But technique is less dependent on personal peculiarities; and an experiment bearing on the technique of an industry may be trusted, as a rule, to give the same results in the hands of any two competent investigators. Specialized students generally have access to exact printed records of the course of every set of experiments; which form the basis of the prevailing standard method of attaining any end in which they are interested; and a comparatively short description of anyone's work generally enables others to know what he has tried, where he has failed, and where he has succeeded. If therefore the suggestions embodied in his work are accepted, and become the basis of the General standard method, others are able to start for further investigations from the point which he has reached, and with nearly the same advantage as if they had made the original experiments themselves. Let us then pass to consider the methods of work of the modern inventor, who turns to account the best results of scientific research that bear on his purpose; and adds to them.

3. *Distribution of the studies, that make for progress, among men of various kinds and degrees of ability.*

We now revert to subjects touched in Book I: they will occupy us a good deal[1].

An improvement in business method is generally initiated by a man of affairs, who sets himself to attain a particular practical end by the best route. The same is generally true of advances in industrial technique, in so far as they are made in the course of business: but the greater part of the work, which lies at the bases of those advances, is made by other men with different motives and different methods. It is made by mere students: that is, by men who labour, not with reference to the attainment of any particular practical end, but in search of knowledge for its own sake. They group together for investigation phenomena which are fundamentally akin, so that the study of many particular relations between them may set thought on the track of general rules or "laws" of causation, tendency, or coexistence: imagination creates movement; caution checks reason by working out parallel but independent trains of thought: and, wherever possible, each general rule is tested by application to particular instances, in which it may be confirmed or discredited by experiments or observations of specific facts. Some of these architectonic workers, but not many, have the power and the will to embody their ideas in specific practical inventions of commercial value: and occasionally a man will be found, who combines the faculties and aptitudes required for high scientific research with those of a great business administrator[2].

The pursuit of knowledge by the pure student for its own sake is generally a richer source of new knowledge, than is the

[1] See especially pp. 99—103; and 132—134.

[2] This interdependence of the work of the professional student and the man of practical ways and means is being worked out in several ways. Thus the electric incandescent lamp must not contain more air than would fill a millionth part of its volume at ordinary pressure: and the way for this perfection "was prepared by an army of men, whose main object was the advancement of knowledge; and who could scarcely have imagined that the processes, which they had elaborated, would soon be in use on a commercial scale, and entrusted to the hands of ordinary workmen....The requirements of practice react in the most healthy way upon scientific electricity." (Lord Rayleigh, quoted in Iles, *Inventors at Work*, ch. XIX.)

II, II, 3. pursuit by the business man of that particular knowledge which bears directly on a specified practical aim: for an idea, which generates new ideas, will be pursued to its consequences by the student; while the practical man will be inclined to drop even the most fertile idea as soon as he has extracted from it the help, if any, which it can give him in attaining his practical purpose. But nevertheless the methods of the two, if both are able investigators, will have much in common. Each of them concentrates his attention for a time on some particular subject, learns nearly all that is already known about it; analyses it; selects for his main study, or at least his first study, some part of it; extends his observation in regard to that part; exerts his constructive imagination; devises developments which offer some promise of leading to new knowledge or to improvements in technique; makes systematic experiment in regard to those developments; makes provisional record of their results, and studies those results. Perhaps he makes further observations, further analyses, further imaginations, and further experiments; until at last he has attained a result which he believes to be of value. He will estimate its value with reference chiefly to the services it may render to the world, or to the prestige or the reward which he will reap from it, according to the bent of his character and mind.

Whether he communicates his results to a learned society, and leaves others to earn money by them, or applies them in practice himself (with or without the protection of a patent), they become in effect the property of the world almost at once. Even if he uses them in a "secret process," enough information about them often leaks out to set others soon on a track near to his own.

Sometimes an investigator is dealing with irregular phenomena, the causes of which are not likely even to be conjectured till much further progress has been made in the high borderland of molecular physics and chemistry; and then his only plan is to make vast numbers of experiments on material chosen almost at random, with a watchful eye for any that tend in the desired direction. He must examine the more palpable qualities of the materials that please him, and seek out others that have any of these qualities in a higher degree; thus reaching his end by sedulous, disciplined imagination, even though he has no access to fundamental laws of causation. Investigations of this kind often need more time than is at the command of any one: they must be done by a "team" of workers under the direction of a master mind. But, when he has before him a particular mechanical aim (as for instance in connection with the phonograph, the telephone, the cinematograph, etc.), his imagination can work straight on along definite processes of reasoning in subordination to general fundamental principles. In both cases he makes use of methods and reasoning, which had been brought up to high standards by the collective efforts of innumerable workers at various times and in various lands: and in return almost every stage of his original methods, in so far as published, contributes to the world's wealth of knowledge[1].

Team work, if somewhat mechanical and lacking in romantic interest, is of very great power in chemistry and some other sciences, as well as in business technique. Its steady expansion is partly cause and partly result of growing tendencies on the part of scientific students and leaders of industry to develop common interests, and work together as allies for the invasion of the borderland between science and technique. In numerous directions the chief leaders of industry are making assiduous use of organized and provisionally standardized general principles: and, aided in very various degrees by the Governments of different countries, they are working for extensions of knowledge which shall be at once technical and general; at once serviceable in their own particular operations, and fertile sources of larger and more exact science in time to come[2].

[1] See Dyer and Martin, *The life of Edison*, ch. XXIV. Edison's laborious research for rare earths that might serve as material for incandescent lamps has lost some of its interest in consequence of the new methods by which wire, a thousandth of an inch in diameter, can be drawn from tungsten and other suitable metals.

[2] Some of the work is done by young men, of rather narrow mental vision. Each of them is contented to plod under instructions at a minute part of a small question; he studies whatever has been printed about it in various scientific memoirs; and works on that material till he has made some advance that can be combined by a stronger mind, with other results obtained by similar plodding. Thus overlapping work is cut down: students of varying aptitudes and abilities are occupied, each with work that is just within his range. The strength even of weak men is turned to account for high work; and that of strong men is given almost wholly to work that is worthy of it: while every step gained

II, II, 4. 4. *Influences on industrial technique exerted by the cumulative power of carefully made machines to create others, that are capable of work even more exactly standardized than their own.*

So far we have considered the influence of recorded and standardized knowledge in regard to method and powers; each new knowledge being the offspring of others that went before, and the parent of many that follow. A simple form of such knowledge, which has contributed greatly to the progress of technique, is embodied in improved constructions of material objects—house, furniture, clothing, implements, etc. But early in last century some ideas, which had been for some time in the make, developed into the great architectonic principle that a well driven machine tool could become the parent of new machine work more exact than itself, which could become in its turn the parent of yet more exact machines; and so on. This idea has so developed, that at last each successive generation, and even each successive decade, has seen results accomplished, which appeared almost impossible till lately. The work has been done chiefly by engineers, who have often loved their workshops, as academic students have loved their laboratories. Chemistry is becoming the mistress of a rapidly increasing number of workers: but engineering has special claims to be regarded as the leading representative of modern industries, at all events from the point of view of an inquiry into the general course of economic progress. For all other large industries are dependent on it for most of their appliances; which are growing rapidly in exactness and efficiency, while falling rapidly in cost. The technique of some of the textile and other industrial groups owes as much to the invention and initiative of mechanical engineers as to their own: and the economist is under exceptional obligations to the semi-technical literature of engineering[1].

is registered, under discriminating judgment, for the benefit of the world. This method seems likely to dominate many branches of study: but of course it can seldom lead directly to epoch-making discovery.

[1] A prominent place must here be given to the Engineering Supplement of the *Times* and to articles in the *Manchester Guardian* and other newspapers, as well as to the *Engineering Magazine* and similar periodicals.

The attention of the progressive engineer is concentrated on some branch of production, which has been neglected, or of which the methods appear to be needlessly cumbrous. It is analysed into its component parts. Each part is again analysed, with the aim of subdividing it into elementary tasks; each of which can be effected by a single procedure, mechanical, chemical or other. Apparatus is devised or adapted for each elementary task. It is tried and amended and tried again. By successive steps larger and more delicate work is thrown upon the apparatus: and it is required, firstly, to adapt itself to ever subtler varieties and nuances of human requirements; secondly, to perform one process after another, that is needed for the ultimate end, with little or no assistance from the hand of man. Thus at last it becomes an "automatic" machine; and it has this much of right to be called a thinking machine, that it changes its mode of action at the right time, acting on hints given from within, which would require the thoughtful care of an attendant, if given from without. Thus complexity of result is attained. But the means need to be simplified: and indeed the subtlest conceptions of the inventor are often given to laboriously simplifying his apparatus, till only the expert can detect the subtlety of his labour.

When all is in order, the machine is nearly self-sufficing. It needs only an alert watcher to attend to any complaint it may utter: but, because it is simple, it seldom complains; and its complaints can sometimes be made to take the form of standing still, till the watcher can attend to it.

The lead in this direction came from the simple strong Boulton. Watt found that much of his steam ran to waste, because Boulton's cylinders and pistons were not true; though they were the best that had been made so far. For indeed the manufacture of machines had not up to that time reached an exactness much more advanced than that to which the Dutch had brought their wooden ship-building many centuries before. So Boulton set himself seriously to improve the common appliances for making machines: and thus struck out the first cardinal idea[1].

[1] His plan, he said, was to "engage and instruct some excellent workmen who (with more excellent tools than it would be worth any man's while to

II, II, 4. Later on attention was more given to the fact that the lathe, "the mother of exact work," was unable to turn her latent power to full use, so long as the movements of its cutting tool had to be governed by the untrustworthy hand of man. Many worked at the difficulty: and at last it was overcome by a simple great man, a fit successor of Boulton and Watt. Maudslay found that every bolt and nut was "a speciality in itself...all bolts and their corresponding nuts had to be specially marked as belonging to one another"; which was specially troublesome "when parts of complex machines had to be taken to pieces for repairs." Accordingly he devised a simple "generating machine," which made fairly accurate screws: and he set one of these to act as Guide screw for the cutting tool; which no longer was moved along according to the judgment of the machine, but automatically moved at a steady rate duly proportioned to the rate of rotation of the material. His "self-acting lathe," governed by fine screws, enabled him to make a machine that would measure easily up to a thousandth part of an inch. He put his best work into appliances with which he made still better work: and thus he went far towards the modern age; in which the most accurate standardization is applied to the master machines, that are responsible for making the most important of those machines, that are responsible for the every-day work of an ordinary engineering shop. But the finest modern engineering work requires gauges true to a ten-thousandth of an inch, which must be read on occasion by a micrometer reading up to a hundred-thousandth part; *i.e.* to a two-hundredth part of the diameter of the human hair. (For some scientific work even greater accuracy is needed; but that is effected by optical instruments making use of diffraction fringes[1].)

procure for one single engine) could execute the invention...with as great a difference of accuracy as there is between the blacksmith and the mathematical instrument maker."

[1] Maudslay devised a measuring machine, "the Lord Chancellor," in which he used his best screws, and also two planes made by an improved method; and originated the saying "Measure up to hundredths of an inch and feel up to thousandths"; that is, press the planes together till their friction offers some resistance to an attempt to shift the bar between them; and then read with a micrometer divisions as finely as you can.

Meanwhile Whitworth, following in Maudslay's steps, had studied the question of the best shapes for screws for various purposes. His Particular standardization of them was approved: and made the basis of an organized General standardization for Britain. In such matters progress is ever eating up her own best results: perhaps it is best that several systems should be tried in various countries; but the movement towards a plastic international standardization, though temporarily checked, may ultimately prevail.

II, II, 4.

The lathe has pioneered not only in exact work, but in complex automatic work. In one of its chief forms sets of tools are placed in "turrets" etc., and these are made to do their work much as did the figures in the great cathedral clocks. The lathe feeds itself; each tool is brought into play in its proper order, and with an appropriate traversing motion. It can make the hub of a cycle wheel, for instance, straight from the bar of steel and without any human interference; and one competent man can be responsible for twelve lathes. Here is a strong case of the rule that "the tendency of all specialized machines is to take the responsibility off the operator and put it on the foreman and his staff of tool makers." This tendency of course diminishes the demand for the skilled artisan, whose eye and hand are in thorough coordination, in those particular works in which such machines are used. But, by their productiveness, they make new openings for him elsewhere: and Sir Benjamin Browne, referring to this social danger, said "many of us remember the great economy which came in when we took to stamping all sorts of small smith work under the steam hammer. Some people thought the days of blacksmiths were numbered; but they have not become fewer, nor are their wages lowered." And yet it seems possible that the continued expansion of the dominion of automatic machines may at last diminish the area of old work in which manual skill is of high account, faster than it opens up new ground in which the hand is again supreme[1].

[1] Exact standardization of particular parts by aid of standardized machinery has enabled cheap watches to be made which will keep good time; and watch screws weighing nine thousand to the ounce, which are seen to be perfect under a microscope, are turned out at a vast rate. Again, in the service of the textile industries, standardization has enabled large sheets of cotton cloth for

II, II, 4. It has already been noted that America is now extending their dominion at a rate far exceeding what seemed probable a few years ago. And the experiences of Britain and other countries during the world-war in manufacturing munitions of war by many millions have made strongly in the same direction.

The changes, of which these instances are representative, have come so gradually that their vast dimensions have only recently been recognized. They all rest in part on the fact that, while the easiest motions of the hand are backwards and forwards, the easiest motions of a machine are rotary. The rate of movement of the hand is limited; and therefore if it is to do much work, it must exert a considerable part of its small strength at each stroke. But, by the aid of gearing and other devices, a machine tool can be made to rotate at any speed, however great, provided it does not generate too much jar or too much heat. These two limitations retarded progress for a long while: but they have now been for the greater part overcome by mechanical and chemical invention; and large turbines now maintain easily 140 revolutions a second, the outside of the wheels running about 900 miles an hour.

Invention enables numerous clear photographs for the cinematograph to be taken in a second; and a single machine to make a quarter of a million matches in an hour. It enables six hours to suffice for casting separately and arranging in line spaced out automatically by wedges the type for 24 large newspaper pages; and for taking a number of stereotypes from them; from each of which long rolls of very wide paper are printed off without hitch at the rate of 20 miles an hour[1].

the envelopes of airships to be made of thickness uniform to within a two hundred and fiftieth part of an inch: and it has so far attracted the interest of working artisans that makers of micrometers reading to a ten-thousandth part of an inch, find it worth while to advertise them largely in the *Journal of the Amalgamated Society of Engineers*. Some other aspects of Particular standardization will be considered later on, see pp. 221—3.

[1] Again, a new steel alloy, which will stand a temperature up to 700° C. without hurt, is able to cut ordinary steel as quickly as ordinary steel can cut wood; but perhaps its most interesting applications are in the substitution of quick movements, each of which treats the material tenderly, for slower movements that must be comparatively rough and harsh. Thus slotting machines are being displaced by drills, which will penetrate a thick steel plate by rapid but comparatively gentle pressure, which leaves no harsh edges. Milling

Thus great are the debts which industrial exactitude owes to machine-made machines, made almost regardless of cost, to be the parents of yet more exact machines; and destined to dominate the massive production of every sort of implement, from the firing apparatus of a monster gun to the motor of an aeroplane. But lest the marvels of such work should get even more gratitude than their due, it may be well to take another instance of fine work in which massive production has no part:—the chemist's balance.

II, II, 4.

The first accurate standardizations of quality were made by the alchemists: each of them worked chiefly for himself; and his standardization was Particular to his own secret pursuits of gold or subtle poisons. Now the standardization of elementary drugs in regard to quality has been authoritatively made General; so that a prescription written out by any physician can be made up accurately by any qualified apothecary. He buys wholesale elementary drugs already standardized, and he compounds them by aid of the chemist's balance, an instrument which remained long without a rival for extreme delicacy and certainty of work. From it have been evolved precision balances which will detect an error of one part in 250,000,000 of a 500 gramme weight. Of course the heat of an observer's body if he were near at hand would disturb the equilibrium: so he stays at a little distance, moves very small weights from one scale to another by mechanical appliance, and watches the balance with a telescope.

Almost as fascinating is the recent suggestion that the elasticity and tenderness of the hand can be rivalled by methods quite different from those of human muscles, which almost alone had been previously imitated. The transmission of pressure by rope and rod, and even by water and electricity, is too uncompromising for much subtle work: but its transmission by air has no such limitations; and it can be arranged cheaply even on a small scale. It is handy and flexible; and

machines are greatly increasing their speed and turning out clean work that needs scarcely any hand finishing. And lastly even fine tools are giving place for delicate work to rapidly rotating emery grinding wheels. For "from being a non-precision method, grinding has become the most perfect device for producing accurate results, measured precisely within thousandths of an inch." (*Encyclopaedia Britannica*, s.v. Tool.)

II, II, 5. it has great advantages for work in mines, for signalling on railways, for riveting in ship-building and in cramped corners in all branches of engineering. The familiar operations of player-pianos by air represent a simple extension of the action of the pneumatic hammer; and a yet higher stage is reached in the marvellous mechanism of the monotype printing machine[1].

5. *The good and evil of machines that supplant fine skilled handiwork.*

Let us return to that increasing tendency of machinery to supplant the skilled hand; which is greatly increasing man's power over nature, and his material wealth, though it is not an unmixed benefit from the social point of view. In fact, if all the world were a single people, with one purpose and that the highest, it might be well to put some check on this rapid supersession of human skill; even at the expense of delaying the increase of material comforts and luxuries. But Britain can exist only by obtaining her necessary supplies of food and raw products in return for the exportation of manufactures: and her hold on external markets can be maintained only by her use of the most effective processes known.

Some mead of sympathy is indeed to be extended to the owners of manufacturing plant, which has been superseded by

[1] But perhaps the subtlest application of the power of air pressure is that which enables it to reproduce the infinitely delicate variations in the pressure exerted by the highly trained hand of the skilled artisan. A shutter is placed over the orifice, through which the compressed air comes to its work, with a slit cut in it of varying width. The shutter moves under the control of the main machine in such a manner that a broad part of the slot is opposite the orifice when the work is at a stage at which much force is wanted; and, when less force is desired, the force is lowered by the opposition of a narrower part of the slot. Such a machine seems perhaps to think for itself more distinctly than almost any other: but its method owes nothing to suggestions by the human hand.

It is interesting to look back from these marvellous achievements to the beginnings of modern machinery, where success in copying the elasticity of the hand was a goal to which inventors aspired, and which the sceptical thought they would never attain. Such was for instance the tardy triumph of machine combing, which originated in Heilmann's observation of his daughter's method of combing out her long hair; and again the success of the power-loom, achieved by making it imitate the small pushes by which the hand-loom weaver packed his work tightly together. Perhaps the first great break with the notion that the movements of the hands should be copied was that of the inventors of the sewing machine; when it occurred to them that a machine can work two needles and threads, though the hands cannot.

recent inventions: but their business ability remains with them; and, if united to brave enterprise, it will enable them soon to be doing well with improved plant, which their good credit will generally enable them to obtain.

The case is more difficult, when the specialized manual dexterity of a skilled artisan is struck by a machine that outdoes it: for if he is no longer young, he can seldom hope to earn high wages by any other kind of purely manual work. His chief defence comes from the facts that improved machinery is likely to increase greatly the volume of the production, for which it is designed: and that his general experience, judgment, and high character may enable him to obtain a position, in which he may direct the unskilled workers who handle the machines that "almost think." This trouble is not easily seen from a distance: but it looms large before the eyes of many skilled workers: and a fair judgment must take account of it, when attention is directed to the cold welcome, which they sometimes give to such machines.

Nevertheless, the stern fact must be boldly faced that the spirit, which induced many hand-loom weavers a century ago to pine in poverty rather than touch the hated power-loom, has not entirely passed away. In so far as it operates it is a grievous handicap to an old industry, when faced by the competition of young industries far away; and during the last few decades it has been a considerable, though an ever diminishing, hindrance to the maintenance of industrial leadership by Britain[1].

[1] Obstacles to the introduction of machinery may be more complex than is here suggested; as can be seen in the following instance. Scissors and blades of knives, forged by hand, have long been among Britain's best products. But latterly German products made of steel shapes, pressed into moulds by powerful machines, have yielded almost as satisfactory results as her hand-forged products; and of course their cost has been low. Sheffield was unwilling to adopt the new method: but having once been fully convinced of its efficiency, is adopting it; and she is striving vigorously to regain the ground lost by her delay. The moulds and machinery for making the pressed blades are too expensive for the independent artisan cutler; and, though he may buy the moulded blocks and finish them himself, his chief vantage ground is lost: thus the industry is passing into the hands of large businesses. They are of course in a better position for developing, and even for imitating, improved technical methods, than the small makers were: but complaints are still heard that, in such matters as the tardy adoption of stainless steel for household cutlery, there is seen something of the preference of old age for things long familiar.

CHAPTER III

SOME TECHNICAL INFLUENCES ON THE SIZE OF THE REPRESENTATIVE BUSINESS UNIT

II, III, 1.

1. *Some introductory observations. Different methods of the expansion of the business unit.*

It has already been indicated that many various causes are tending to increase the size of the representative business unit. Our attention will shortly be directed to developments of marketing, of finance, and of the methods of business administration: but this chapter and the next are concerned exclusively with causes, that are closely connected with the progress of industrial technique. Reference will be made only to such industries as are much under the influence of that progress: they show some technical developments, which make towards an expansion of the business unit in all the industries affected by them; together with others, which tend under some circumstances to aid the large business in overpowering the small; and under yet others to strengthen the small business at least as much as, and sometimes even more than the large.

Unfortunately the use of terms connected with business is not always consistent. A limited store of words is compelled to accommodate itself to the ever-changing needs of the market-place: the context, or verbal explanation supplies the clue to the precise meaning in view at the moment: and, as has been repeatedly observed, the economist must accommodate himself to the practice of the market-place.

Two contiguous factories of the like kind and in the same ownership, but with separate balance sheets, are sometimes classed as separate businesses: while for other purposes dissimilar factories in distant places, with separate management and balance sheets, are classed as a single business, merely because they are in the same ownership. This divergence presents almost insuperable difficulties to officials engaged in a census of manufactures: but it does not greatly incommode the present study, which is concerned with general tendencies rather than specific figures.

On the other hand it is necessary for our purposes to make a clear distinction between two chief forms of business expansion; the vertical and the horizontal. The manufacture of any commodity starts from the basis of the provision of its raw material. This is regarded as a sort of ground floor. The first stage of operations on it constitute, as it were, a "higher" first floor: that is followed by a second, still higher; and that perhaps by a third, and so on; until the finished product is reached.

The product still needs to be marketed: and the producer, unless he is working to order, must be responsible for starting it on its way to "consumers"; that is, those who buy it for use whether in business or in the household. The producing firm may sell at once to wholesale dealers or other middlemen; or it may include the "higher" stages of marketing, and deal direct with consumers: the line of division between making and marketing is, as has already been observed, vague and varying.

Whenever a business expands into a stage higher or lower than that with which it was originally occupied, its expansion is *vertical*. Instances are, when a printing business acquires mills to make its own paper; or, moving in the opposite direction, sets up a binding and a publishing department to enable it to dispose of its products in the finished state: or again, when rolling mills set up blast furnaces, and open iron or coal mines; or, moving in the opposite direction, undertake the manufacture of steel bridges or steel frames for buildings. Works which undertake many different stages are sometimes called *mixed*.

The upper stages of mixed works have little anxiety about their supply of material, for it consists mainly of half-finished products from the lower stages of the same works: and the

II, III, 1. lower stages are generally secure of a vent for their products in the upper stages. But a firm with limited capital can seldom undertake considerable vertical expansions with success; for such expansions are not easily made by gradual steps.

On the other hand, a business may proceed gradually and tentatively when extending its operations *horizontally* in the same stage; as for instance when a book printer increases the size of his plant, without altering its character. Again a manufacturer of locomotives may increase his output, by producing more locomotives of the same type with more intensively specialized plant; or by producing locomotives suitable for greater varieties of traffic at home or abroad; or by adding branches for the production of stationary steam and gas engines. Almost every kind of horizontal extension tends to increase the (internal) economies of production on a large scale which are at his command: but, as a rule, an increase in the variety of his output lessens his gain in this direction; while increasing his facilities for meeting the various wants of customers and for marketing generally. All these general statements will however be found liable to some exceptions.

A large business aggregation may result from the growth of a single unit under exceptionally able and fortunate management; existing departments are enlarged and new departments are added till vast Krupp or Carnegie Steel Works, or Wanamaker stores have grown up from a single root. Or it may result from the "fusion" (or as is sometimes said the "amalgamation") of several businesses in one. The fusion may be vertical; that is it may unite a number of businesses in successive stages of the same large process. Or it may be horizontal; that is it may unite a number of similar businesses.

Horizontal fusions often pass through an intermediate stage of Regulative Federation or Association, or Cartel; the functions of which are to control the prices, the amounts produced, and the methods of marketing of its various members; and in some cases to conduct their marketing for them.

Economies in administration and in production are not easily obtained by a mere federation; they need unified ownership and administration. A halfway house was indeed found in American "Trusts" in the original sense of the word; when a number of businesses in the same industry agreed to assign the control of their general policy to the same body of trustees, who administered the whole in *trust* for all concerned. But, chiefly on account of legal difficulties, this form of organization has disappeared from America; though some European cartels seem to be drifting towards it.

The name Trust is now given commonly to a manufacturing or trading company if its capital and power are sufficient to give it a dominating influence, extending over some branch of industry or trade throughout the whole or a large part of the country to which it belongs[1]. This dominating influence is frequently believed to be monopolistic in character: to involve some menace to public interests; and to call for inquiry, whether the Trust should be subjected to public regulations, in some respects more stringent than those which apply to an ordinary joint-stock company; just as that is subject to some rules which do not apply to a private business.

A trust may be a joint-stock company which owns the whole of the businesses controlled by it. But in many cases it leaves some or all of the businesses, which it controls, nominally in the hands of independent companies with their own directors; and merely secures a majority of the shares of these subordinate companies. Thus it can elect their directors; and, though it must leave them legal freedom to act as they choose during the coming year, yet they well understand that their reelection will depend upon their conforming to the general policy marked out for them: so that there is thorough unity of administration. Local freedom of initiative is indeed commonly encouraged; but it does not go very much further than that which, as already observed, a huge company sometimes concedes to the managers of its branches.

One of the most impressive achievements of modern

[1] Some would confine the name "Trusts" to those large companies which have obtained their dominating position by the fusion of several independent businesses; and not by the expansion of single businesses. The two classes differ in some important respects. But in relation to the most fundamental problems, the practice of the market-place in drawing no distinction between them seems to be right.

 technique is its power to handle masses too great for any force which was at man's command until recently. But, as often happens, that which is most wonderful, is not that which has exercised the greatest influence on the course of evolution. Those industries which need to handle very large single masses must necessarily be concentrated in the hands of a relatively small number of large businesses; but they are not numerous. And a greater influence on the structure of business in general is being exercised by the economies of continuous production, especially in regard to things which can conveniently be made in vast quantities, though they are not handled in large single masses.

Some account of those industries in which the work of transporting materials, or transmitting force plays the chief *rôle*; and require large continuous rights of way, whether in public or private ownership, is transferred to Appendix H; because, though very important, they are governed by exceptional conditions, and are not representative of the general trends of industrial development. Better illustrations for our present purposes are found in the steel and the textile industries. The steel industries dominate many others; and changes in their organization have exercised widespread influences on the organization of industry in general in America and Germany. The textile industries on the other hand offer the best instances of the coexistence of numerous establishments, repeating one another; because the full technical economies of large scale production, though not always of marketing, can be obtained by an establishment of moderate size. The two groups cover nearly the whole ground of industrial organization fairly well: but they do not touch the adaptation of mechanical processes to the varying requirements of particular individuals: and therefore a little is added as to the boot and shoe industry.

2. *Many causes make for the expansion of the business unit in the steel industry, especially in its heavy branches.*

The central task of the heavy steel industries is the handling of great volumes of homogeneous fluid steel, ready to be worked up into an infinite variety of products large and small. There is no other group of industries, in which the forces making for the increase of the business unit are promoted in like degree by the magnitude of the aggregate volume of the homogeneous fluid material which has to be produced, and by the magnitude of the individual masses to be handled. II, III, 2.

Further, there is no other group of industries in which the higher and lower stages work for one another so steadily and on so large a scale; and therefore there is no other group in which large lateral extensions and amalgamations are so likely to be accompanied by large vertical extensions and amalgamations. Iron and coal mines at the "lowest" stage are large users of the rails and the machinery which come from the higher stages: the smelting furnaces receive from the mines at the lowest stage; and pass on their products to the heavy mills: which like all the rest are large consumers of high-class machinery. There is nothing at all analogous to this in any other group of industries: the steel industries are in a class by themselves, just as are railways and water-supply equipments, though for entirely different reasons. Let us consider the operations of the furnaces and the heavy mills.

The size of the most economical furnace is rapidly increasing: and Open-hearth furnace baths already have a capacity of several thousand tons. But a furnace is not amenable to discipline. It will not work economically except at nearly full pressure: it must be laid by for repairs occasionally; and, therefore, complete efficiency is to be obtained only by the presence in a single establishment of a good many blast furnaces that are individually of the modern pattern, in order that a business may be able to adjust total output to varying activities of demand.

In furnaces and in rolling mills alike the individual masses to be handled have mostly become so bulky that every operation must be performed by mechanical force: and thus a new economy arises from increase of size. For it requires no more effort and not much more discretion, to turn a handle that will set in motion a big electric or hydraulic crane than a small one. Supplemented by internal railways, these travelling cranes enable a massive piece of metal to be removed easily, safely and quickly from one department to another of large works, spread over many acres: at each department it finds just those

II, III, 2. appliances and just that specialized skill which are needed for the particular work to be done.

An economy, characteristic of the present age, is inducing owners of blast furnaces to set up rolling mills; and owners of rolling mills to set up blast furnaces, or to amalgamate with existing furnaces. It is that of the heat often to be gained, by passing the molten iron straight from the blast furnace to the converter, and carrying off the blooms from the converter straight to the mills that are to roll them into rails or plates or structural shapes. Again "mixed works" that own mines, furnaces, mills and engine shops can keep each of the four branches at work during many slack times by enlarging and repairing the rails, hoists, machinery, etc. which all the four need in various degrees. Again the waste gases of the furnaces, after heating and pumping air for their own use, have a large surplus energy: this can be turned to account, either directly or through the medium of electricity, in working other branches; and it thus becomes a powerful aid to "mixed" steel businesses in competition with "pure" blast furnaces and with "pure" rolling mills. The influence thus exerted on the structure of the German steel industry will occupy our attention in Book III[1].

No doubt several of these economies have already exercised nearly their full influence on the size of the business unit: because their economic force is now so great that no concern that lacks them can hold its own against well-equipped competitors with equal access to its markets. The United States Steel Corporation has already several sets of mixed works, each of which is possessed of practically every technical economy which size can give. But the cooperation of these various sets of works under a single control is said to give it certain advan-

[1] It should however be added that the importance of this advantage will be diminished if the production of electricity is organized, on a vast scale, as now seems probable. In that case the economy of by-products at the central electrical works will be so great, that a small business may be able to buy its power at less cost than that at which it is obtained now by very large businesses, excepting only those which smelt iron-ores. They will doubtless continue to use the energy contained in their waste gases; though perhaps they will apply a larger part of it in its original form of heat to various uses. As to the services of electricity to the small business generally see Appendix H, 2.

tages in marketing, in obtaining progressive expert guidance, and in economy of transport. It can send each order to be filled up by that set of its works which can handle it best, account being taken of its geographical position; of the quantity of work that it already has on hand; and of any special fitness of its plant for that particular task. Thus, for instance, it can be arranged that each group of works shall keep its sets of rolls almost constantly in operation without being changed; whereas an isolated rolling mill must frequently change its rolls. But this economy can in great measure be obtained by other means: as we are about to see.

3. *Tendencies of Particular standardization to become General.*

The influences exerted by the progress of technique on the structure of business, which have been so far noticed, tend almost without exception to increase the size of the business unit. But the influences exerted by good standardization are not entirely in that direction: and, for this and other reasons, they call for rather close attention.

It was from the first obvious that each railway must have a uniform gauge for the main traffic. But for a long while even the main lines of railways in an advanced country were of various breadths, so that the wagons of one could not run on the lines of another. The inconveniences thus caused compelled General standardization of gauge for all main lines throughout each country; and, with a few exceptions, throughout each Continent.

Meanwhile considerations of its own convenience had caused each railway to seek for Particular standard patterns of rails suitable for the chief varieties of frequent heavy traffic: and after a while it became clear that, if General standards could be agreed on, rolling mills would be able to produce much more freely for stock; and therefore to give more continuous employment to their plant and their staff; and therefore to produce more cheaply. This course, which has been largely adopted, presented no great difficulty: and it was followed by the more difficult and interesting development of standardized shapes for structural steel. The use of iron as the mainstay of building is

II, III, 3. due to the initiative of many men, among whom a chief place must be assigned to Sir Joseph Paxton; steel at a moderate price was not to be had when he planned the exhibition of 1851, and he had to be content with iron. But the subsequent use of structural steel is largely due to a characteristic burst of American initiative.

Mr Carnegie observed that the wooden tressel bridges which were in general use on American railroads, had no longer a *raison d'être.* The English practice of using iron for bridges had been little followed; because iron had been relatively dear, and wood had been cheap. But wood was becoming scarce, and steel was becoming cheap: and the rapidly increasing traffic was worried by wood's constant need of repairs. So he pictured the future in his mind and set himself to prepare for it on American lines. He gradually trained a staff of engineers to plan steel bridges, test them, improve them, and at last reduce them provisionally to standard patterns. Meanwhile he adapted his plant to producing their component parts on a large scale; and prepared to put through a complete bridge much more quickly and cheaply than anyone else. Next, he applied the same notion to steel frames for high buildings, which were just coming into vogue, and which are indeed little more in principle than vast congeries of small bridges.

But there was a difficulty. Though bridges of similar dimensions and designed for similar traffic could well be made of similar pattern, almost every building required individual treatment: and architects, accustomed to other materials, were not always able and willing to make their plans fit in with the technical idiosyncrasies of the manufacture of steel. So the Carnegie Company developed a specialized staff of engineer-architects: and they undertook to design and erect a building which should meet nearly all requirements; and yet be made almost exclusively of units that were already standardized; and therefore far cheaper, than if they had been made to order. The power which the Carnegie Company obtained, partly by this means, enabled it to set the tone of the whole American industry, so far as structural steel was concerned. But the very victory of its method destroyed much of the semi-monopolistic power which it had obtained. And though the average size of the business unit in the heavy steel industry has increased, and is likely to increase; yet, the further standardization goes, and the more care that is given by architects to the choice of standard shapes in their specification, the better will be the outlook of rolling mills of moderate size in regard to structural steel.

The General standardization of rails enables a man to buy a certain quantity of rails of a given kind for delivery at a future time. If an organized market price for such rails is established from time to time, he may make such a purchase without any intention of accepting delivery; and may expect to receive the excess (or to pay the deficiency) of the market price at the time as compared with his contract price: that is, the way is open for general speculation. This development is indeed exceptional. It probably works for good on the whole: but a considerable share of the total price paid by railroads for their rails is intercepted by speculative dealers. The general tendency of their operations is to render prices more steady; and in so far as they do this, their gains are well earned: but there have been occasions on which it has appeared that they have artificially stimulated fluctuations; and in such cases their action has been harmful to consumers and producers, whether they themselves have gained or lost on the balance.

4. *A partial specialization of particular establishments in certain branches of the steel industry has long been in progress, partly under the influence of mutual understandings: and it has received a great impetus from the experiences of the industry under State control during the world-war.*

A spirit of order has long been spreading over British steel rolling mills. Soon it will be true that "the producer can cheapen the cost of production, because he can roll considerable quantities of any given section at one time, and place in stock any surplus with a reasonable prospect of its being required. The buyer can feel sure of obtaining the section that he requires from one firm or another with the least amount of delay and at the least cost[1]."

[1] From Mr Hawkins' Presidential Address to the British Institute of Civil

II, III, 4. Such specialization is not quite as easy in all branches of the steel industry as in that of rolling. But it is even more urgently needed in some branches; and it was making considerable progress, even before the exigencies of the world-war had called for an output of certain classes of munitions in greater volume, and at higher speed than had been reached in any similar case before. The Minister of Munitions became in effect autocratic controller of every business that could take part in the work; and many large establishments were set up for the occasion, chiefly in places where there was abundance both of room, and of the unskilled labour of men, women and children who could perform elementary tasks hour after hour under expert supervision. The method is properly regarded as American, because America has developed it in numerous industries further than any other country has done: and from another point of view it might properly be called British; because it is based on Babbage's famous observation (A.D. 1832) that in a large factory "the manufacturer by dividing the work to be executed into different processes, each requiring different degrees of skill and force, can purchase exactly that precise quantity of both that is necessary for each process." But it has been carried out so thoroughly in the war-munitions industries as to arrest public attention, and give a powerful impetus to a movement which had already made much progress. It will greatly affect the further advance of technique, and the extended organization of business; we may therefore stay a little to consider its peculiarities.

The influence of patriotic sentiment has enabled the employer—in this case ultimately the nation—to carry Babbage's

Engineers, 1901. He continued:—"Our trade and interests being more far-reaching and world-wide than those of any other country, makes the question of standardization more important, but at the same time more difficult for us." The American Society of Civil Engineers had led the way, Germany had followed, and later the four British Societies chiefly concerned agreed to appoint joint committees to take evidence and recommend standard sections for (1) Bridges and general construction, (2) Railway rolling stock underframes, (3) Rails, (4) Ships. He noted that Germany had 67 standard sections and America had 49, whereas Britain used no fewer than 170 different sections. But in the early years of this century great progress had been made in this and similar directions by efforts of the industries themselves; and by those of the National Physical Laboratory, somewhat on the lines of the Physikalisch-technische-Reichsanstalt at Charlottenburg; and by other institutions.

hint further than it has ever been carried before; especially in an old country, where (as was observed at the end of the last chapter) those who have acquired special manual skill are inevitably somewhat jealous of technical improvements that tend to narrow the sphere of their special usefulness. There are in fact very few occupations, in which every operation performed by skilled workers makes demands on their special skill. Sometimes indeed the skilled artisan has an assistant, who learns to move things into their proper places and do like small tasks, without distracting the attention of his chief. But such arrangements are profitable, only when the total aid given by the assistant saves a considerable part of the artisan's time: Babbage's principle is not operative in other cases. When however highly finished and accurate products are required in vast quantities, it may be practicable to pass a great number of them over to an unskilled worker who gives his or her whole time to performing some single operation on each. Under the emergency of war, skilled artisans have concurred in such arrangements, even though contrary to custom.

For instance, the manufacture of shells during the world-war has required millions of wedges to be made, so finely tapered that the wider end of each is only about a thousandth part of an inch broader than the narrower end. But an accurate ring having been made such that the narrower end of a properly made wedge can enter it, while the broader end cannot pass through, the task of testing the wedges, instead of being one of supreme difficulty, is brought within the competence of a careful child. A child might be careless: but the task is well executed by unskilled adults; and similar arrangements for the economy of skilled labour might be extended, wherever the aggregate volume of each such simple task to be performed in any one establishment is sufficient to justify the setting up of special provision for it. That may be effected in the future much more largely than in the past, as a result of the allied tendencies to exact, though plastic, standardization; and to the specialization of considerable establishments on particular tasks in a single large process. Thus a steady demand for vast numbers of similar products has moulded the work of the human hand, somewhat in the same manner as it has that of machines. It

II, III, 4. enables numerous machines, each relatively simple, though semi-automatic, to be set up each adapted to one special task, and each working steadily with but little need for supervision[1].

The centralized control of the munitions' industries has been aided by so much unselfish energy, that it seems to have been but little affected by that comatose slackness which frequently hinders Governmental industries from reaping the full fruits of their advantages of position. And it has focussed increased attention on the economies that may be attained by such co-operative understandings among businesses in the same branch of industry, as would enable each of them to adjust its plant and its arrangements to a single task; or, at least, to a single small group of tasks.

For instance, though ships of any particular character are not needed even by the thousand, the British Government has found it worth while to indicate a few classes of standardized ships, which are suitable to present conditions. This measure is specially adapted to the urgent need for large output in time

[1] The following observations are taken from *The Times Engineering Supplement*, April, 1917: "No shop manager, though possessed of an original and inventive genius, backed up by experience, could have anticipated the profound changes which the demand for munitions has brought about in the designs of machine tools. Less than three years ago nearly all the machine tools in use required experienced men in charge. Yet they were ill-suited for many of the new duties imposed upon them, comprising as they did elements fitting them for purposes of general utility without providing for highly repetitive production.... Some manufacturers have been able to supply very simple single-purpose machines in batches of several hundreds for a single shop. In consequence not only have new works been built, but old firms hitherto engaged in other industries scarcely related to this class of work, in the metal trades, for example, have taken over some sectional portions of munitions from the controlled shops until such time as they could obtain the tools necessary to enable them to carry out more extended tasks. In some instances these firms, by availing themselves of instructions supplied by the builders of the machine tools, were thus enabled to get together a staff of girls or lads, with a few skilled supervisors, soon capable of producing an enormous output of accurately gauged parts. Machinists never realized before how many ways there are of attaining identical results."

For instance, "Machines for producing 18-pounder high explosive shells exclusively have been evolved from the multi-spindle design of automatics. One design deals with the exterior work only, the other with the interior. A pair of machines, each requiring only one attendant, turns out a shell complete in six minutes. The one which deals with the internal operations has eight spindles for holding shells, and a sufficient number of tool spindles in opposition for performing 19 separate functions, comprising drilling, facing, reaming, and threading. The machine which deals with the exterior work has six spindles."

of war: and there is now some general agreement that even in time of peace each shipyard might advantageously concentrate its energies on a limited number of classes of ships; each of which should be standardized as far as was possible, consistently with quick readjustments to meet changes in technique and in the conditions of maritime traffic.

II, III, 4.

But in fact the standardization of component parts is at once more productive of economy and less hostile to progress than that of complex structures. The same standard girders are used with advantage in thousands of different sorts of buildings, and appliances for use on land and sea: while the same standard screws are used for hundreds of thousands of different purposes: and this contrast is of special significance in regard to the contest between giant businesses and those of moderate size. For even the largest business has but a small output as compared with that of an industrial country: and therefore the small producers can often buy particular components, that have been made for open market by aid of larger economies of massive production than are at the command of any single business[1].

Standardization is likely to attain the highest perfection in the case of a product which has been long in use; and of which both the component parts and the general design have been subjected to long and varied trial: for in such a case the experience of the multitude overtops the finest imagination of constructive genius. But, on rare occasions, there may be an imperative need for sudden massive production, which allows no time for protracted experience. An instructive instance of this kind occurred when America had unexpected occasion to provide a large supply of aeroplanes, on models, which the experiences of the war had brought to the front.

Several eminent American engineers "pooled" their faculties in order to devise a general plan for the economical and rapid construction of aeroplane engines by methods specially appropriate to the American genius. They proposed to build the

[1] The North-East Coast Institution of Engineers and Shipbuilders have agreed on a scheme for the standardization of reciprocating triple expansion engines, the principles of which may probably be extended to other types of engines and to many auxiliaries employed on shipboard. It is intended that the specification shall be subject to a revision each year by an expert committee. (*Times Engineering Supplement*, February, 1917.)

II, III, 5. engines in various models, each using the same standard cylinders, pistons, valves, cam shafts, and so on. Thus the parts of wrecked eight-cylinder or twelve-cylinder engines are to be interchangeable, and a new engine could be assembled from the parts of wrecked machines[1].

5. *Recent developments of the means of communication have facilitated the escape of a large business in a heavy industry from the constraint imposed by lack of space for expansion.*

We now pass to a side issue, which has recently become of some importance. It turns on the difference between businesses which, by building high, can employ a large number of operatives on a site of moderate dimensions, and those which cannot expand so as to avail themselves of the full resources of modern technique without access to large space.

The lighter sort of manufactures can generally accommodate a great number of operatives, together with machinery, in high buildings on a relatively small area: and in case of need, sufficient

[1] European aerial engineers assisted in forming the plan: but it was decided not to adopt any European model: because British and French machines, as a rule, are not adapted to American manufacturing methods. They are highly specialized machines, requiring much hand work from mechanics, who are almost artists. Such men are relatively scarce in America: and therefore exact mechanical standardization was applied in American fashion to do as much of the fine work as was possible. But it was found that some finishing work had to be done by the hand at the last in almost every case.

Since however cylinders, pistons, and every other part of the motor had been standardized, they could be produced rapidly and economically by a great many factories operating under Government contracts. They could be as rapidly assembled, either by these plants or at a central assembly plant.

Rapid procedure was indeed rendered possible by previous studies in Britain, France and Italy, as well as in America: for the war-demand for aircraft has been too sudden and intense to be left to private enterprise. For instance, a group of the ablest British experts have served as "The Advisory Committee for Aeronautics," under the presidency of Lord Rayleigh, to study, by aid of experiments at the National Physical Laboratory and the Royal Aircraft Factory, matters relating to aerodynamics, to engines, to materials, to strength of construction and design, etc. Their Report of 1917 speaks of experiments with powerful appliances as to longitudinal and lateral stability in flight; as to various types of magnetic compasses and other instruments; as to the durability of fabrics under various conditions; as to aluminium alloys; as to the location of distant thunderstorms and their progress, etc.

space for extensions can generally be acquired close at hand at a price which is not prohibitive. But heavy industries must do nearly all their work on the ground: their machines are bulky, and most of their movements are effected by small railways, together with overhead gear. Therefore, even when a considerable space for expansions has been provided at starting, a successful heavy business is likely ere long to need more space than is to be had on reasonable terms in a crowded district.

But some classes of operatives used to spend high wages somewhat crudely; and they were not easily attracted into the country: for this and other reasons even heavy industries were slow to move away from densely peopled districts, until pressed by the recent expansion of the business unit, and aided by the telephone and other modern means of communication among businesses at a distance. Meanwhile the working classes have become better educated, less addicted to the coarser enjoyments, and more appreciative of the quiet of a many-roomed house with a garden: also the advantages of working only on a single floor, have extended from the first stages of heavy industries to others for which a firm basis on the earth is not absolutely necessary. It has become increasingly convenient to cover the whole area of work with overhead gear capable of moving along and at right angles to the main line of each building; so that it can take up materials from any part and set them down in any other[1].

6. *Illustrations, drawn from textile and boot industries, of diverse influences which partial standardization and specialization exert on the size of the business unit.*

We have seen how the application of water power to spinning collected that branch of the industry into factories,

[1] A few details may be added. In some cases each building of the works is in addition surrounded by railway lines of normal gauge, and perhaps permeated by narrow gauge lines for special uses: each department of work can have its own province; often so located as to be in contact on one side with that from which it is to receive material, and on the other with that to which it is to deliver. Ample space can be taken for the works at starting; and almost unlimited expansions can be arranged by enlarging the original simple building either longitudinally or laterally or both. Walls are needed only at the outside of a building, which may cover an acre; for the roof, as well as overhead and other gear, can be supported on steel pillars.

II, III, 6. while hand-weaving remained in the cottages: but the power-loom needed factories. At first it was a rough and untrustworthy instrument, likely to deal harshly with the yarn; and the only people who had the technical knowledge and other facilities for the management of textile factories were master spinners. So the growth of machinery seemed at once to crush out the small man, and to bring under one roof the successive processes of a great industry.

But all the while machinery was preparing the way for undoing this vertical consolidation: for improvements in spinning gradually enabled yarn to be made with such absolute certainty and precision to any standard requirement, that the weaver could buy it in open market, or even contract for it in advance, with confidence that he could get what he needed; and the loom became both more powerful and gentler. These improvements have continued by innumerable small stages down to the present day, and now the element of routine preponderates in cotton spinning mills, and in weaving sheds for staple cloths. The size of such factories is not much influenced, at all events directly, by the progress of technique: for that is not increasing materially the expensiveness of the plant required for the best work. But the growing efficiency of the plant is increasing the floor space, the engine power, and the quantity of machinery required to give employment to a given number of workers: and there are larger calls for organizing faculty, and for some ready initiative in throwing out machinery which has been left behind by recent improvements. These branches of the cotton industry are excellently managed by strong, but simple men; and again by joint-stock companies, some of which are largely in the hands of working-men and have something of the character of cooperative societies.

On the other hand, the manufacturer of finished cotton goods of other than the standard patterns must ever be watchful, supple, and quick: for variations in demand for different classes of things in his trade would prevent the work of each one of his departments from being fitted in exactly with that of the others, however steady his aggregate output might be. And, even more than organizing strength, he needs the faculty of reading coming events in a relatively narrow thoroughfare of the world's business, and turning to the best account the flying opportunities which are offered by his changeful relations to men and things[1].

The woollen and worsted industries deal with materials which are very variable in character: and nearly all their products, except such things as blankets, are made for consumers who are under the influence of western fluctuations of fashion. Merinos and other short fibred wools, which are used in "woollen" stuffs in the narrower sense of the term, are often mixed up with shoddy and even wound around cotton yarns: and no manufacturer (*i.e.* maker of stuffs) can be sure of getting exactly the description of such yarn as he wants, except by making it himself. As a rule all the various stages of woollen cloth making (exclusive of dyeing and finishing), are carried on together in rather small factories: for they yield no very great economies of production on a large scale, and individual care and judgment as to details are incessantly required.

The worsted industries, which deal with long staple wools, are organized generally on similar principles to the "woollen" (in the narrower use of the term), except in one important matter. The unravelling and smoothing out of long yarns require an elaborate process; which is, as a rule, that of "combing": the short fibres mingled with the long are taken out and the long are combed out into "tops," for worsted making. This process requires expensive machinery, which was for the greater part invented in England. It is worked by very powerful firms, and the tops are marketed at home and abroad; England thus returning some of the obligations, which she has

[1] There is much of interest on this subject in Chapman's *The Lancashire Cotton Industry*. He observes that the complete command which Lancashire offers to the manufacturer of any sort of yarn that he may need gives scope to even very small men in manufacturing specialities. They "rent buildings and 'turning,' and produce successfully in a small way. Sometimes several firms may be found in one building" (p. 163). Schulze-Gävernitz, *Cotton trade in England and on the Continent*, presented a vivid picture of the advantage which the high organization of his markets gave to the English textile manufacturer over his Continental rivals in 1895: but the organization of their markets has made progress since then; see Landauer, *Handel und Produktion in der Baumwollindustrie*, 1912. *Bulletin* 74 of the Bureau of the Census of the United States 1905 speaks of the hindrances to trade, which arise from the lack of adequate specialization in the American cotton industry.

II, III, 6. incurred, as a consequence of her own inertia, and of Germany's systematic application of chemical science to industry[1].

The arts of dyeing and finishing all kinds of textile materials began to make rapid progress about the time when the power-loom was coming into general use; and, indeed, partly in consequence of the great increase in the volume of the textile industries that resulted from it. It soon became clear that the resources of a cloth factory could not offer nearly as great a variety of refined finish, as could be got by large firms, each of which gave its whole energies to a particular form of finishing. Every such firm, or rather company, is equipped with vast and various special apparatus, and with high technical skill. It can thus bring the appropriate part of extensive technical forces to bear on each task, which it undertakes: the same highly specialized task often needs to be performed at about the same time on a great variety of goods, coming from many customers and designed for many purposes; and thus it is able to obtain many of the advantages of continuous process, even in regard to small transactions[2].

Modern textile industries are in the main the products of British thought and method: the new boot and shoe industries are distinctively American. They have developed with marvellous thoroughness the notion that standardization, adapted to the many various wants of consumers, is an economic force corresponding within its own sphere to the standardization of parts of machinery to meet the varying requirements of particular machines. Not many years ago every well fitting boot or shoe was adjusted in each detail by individual care to the shape of a single foot: but now the call for individual judgment in the industry is almost confined to the economical arrangement of shapes for various portions of boots or shoes of different sorts

[1] The tops are to some extent standardized: but the needs of some manufacturers cannot be met by any judgment less subtle and careful than that of expert buyers in their own employment, who handle and test before accepting. A little more is said on these subjects in Appendix I, 2.

[2] Clapham's *Woollen and worsted industries* is a model study. See also Weld, "Specialization in the woollen and worsted industry," in the *Harvard Journal of Economics*, Nov. 1912. Landauer *l.c.* is specially instructive as to the German finishing industry.

and sizes. So a multitude of steel plates, each corresponding to some part of a boot or shoe of some one of the many sizes and shapes in vogue, are laid on a hide or skin; and adjusted to its irregular shape in such a manner that they cover nearly the whole of it: and the hide or skin is cut up along the boundaries of the plates. Then machines enter the field, and require from their human associates little more than careful feeding.

A passenger in the *Mayflower* founded a boot and shoe industry at Lynn, which spread over Eastern Massachusetts[1]. In 1845 the industry was highly organized, with much standardization and division of labour, but mainly on primitive lines. Then came a long series of brilliant mechanical inventions, which reduced the direct labour cost of a boot to less than a tenth of what it had been; and hand labour practically ceased from the industry. But people's feet vary much, and in order to enable a machine-made boot or shoe to compete with one made to order by hand, the standardization needed to go on the opposite route to that, which it may best follow in making agricultural implements or watches, or other things in which human needs have little variety. In America, though not elsewhere, each factory makes, as a rule, only a single class of boot or shoe,—it may be a high-class boot for girls, or a stout boot for working women—: but, whatever the class is, it makes each quality and pattern in "sizes" and half sizes, and in six or a dozen different widths. The result is that while the work of each operative is very simple, the total output is so subtly organized that the needs and taste of each individual consumer are, save in a few exceptional cases, met almost as delicately and thoroughly as they could be by the careful thought of a skilled artisan.

The machines required for each stage of the manufacture are very numerous and expensive. Many of them are patented, and either sold at very high prices, or hired out at charges apportioned to the number of times they have been used, as indicated by automatic registers. Its high capital charge would prohibit the use by a small manufacturer of a machine, which performs only one short operation, but can do it for a great

[1] See a suggestive study of the boot and shoe industry in *Report of Twelfth Census of the U.S.A.* 1900, vol. VII. p. 754.

II, III, 6. number of boots: the practice of paying in proportion to the work done, puts him on a level in this respect with a more powerful rival. Thus the technical efficiency of the boot machinery organization is of the highest order: but the power, thus obtained, has been turned to harsh uses, by "tying clauses." As we shall see presently, these resemble Deferred Shipping Rebates, in binding a customer who makes any use of the aid of a particular business, to abstain from obtaining aid from any rival business: such action tends to create a harsh monopoly.

The number of businesses that manufacture on a small scale, or devote themselves to subsidiary *processes*, is diminishing generally. But the purchase of ready cut soles, and of some completely manufactured *parts* is on the increase: by this arrangement, manufacturers "get the grade and weight they want, save one operation, and do not have on their hands sole leather that they do not want[1]."

A large manufacturer has however considerable advantage in retailing. He can open many shops in the same city, in each of which a customer's taste and fit can be ascertained; and if he selects a style in which exactly the right fit is not on hand, it can be ordered by telephone and sent to him from a common store in the course of an hour. Thus he procures custom more easily, and at less cost for marketing, than if he kept a full supply of everything likely to be needed in each of two or three giant shops. It is however true that this full standardization enables any retailer, with a considerable stock and near to a large wholesale stock, to market efficiently and cheaply on similar lines[2].

[1] *Report of U.S.A. Census of* 1905, Bulletin 72, p. 12.

[2] Similar remarks apply to other kinds of goods; see Appendix J, 2 and 4. The general trend of this Section is continued in chapters VI and VII of this Book.

CHAPTER IV

FURTHER TECHNICAL INFLUENCES ON THE SIZE OF THE BUSINESS UNIT

1. *The expansion of the business unit in industries which handle continuous streams of homogeneous materials is being promoted by new economies appertaining to uniform and continuous process.* II, IV. 1.

We now pass to a group of industries which handle no large single mass: they have little kinship to the higher stages of the steel industries, but they closely resemble the lower. They turn their material promptly into powder or liquid form, and keep it on the flow through many consecutive processes. During all this time there is very little for the hand to do, except to turn certain handles, etc., at the right time; and not very much for the head to do, except in the organic planning and masterly management of the whole.

Thus paper-mills and flour-mills deal with raw materials already in shapes easily handled. They turn the logs of wood, or the grain, into a homogeneous fluid or powder, by a series of processes, which are automatic; and require little more effort of thought, and not much more effort of hand, to make them available for a vast output than for a small one. A small paper-mill may thrive in such a place as the Black Forest, where a stream of water grinds down logs from the adjacent woods into pulp; mixes it with gluten, etc.; spreads it over rollers; and at last delivers it as made paper, without being touched by a human hand. There is here no waste of labour: but the same wood could have been turned into a better paper, with little further outlay, in a highly organized mill. And the growth of large mills at the expense of small is steady and rapid.

II, IV, 1. Similarly with regard to flour-mills. The farmers in the wheat districts of America, send grain for local consumption to be ground into coarse flour in old-fashioned mills, each of which is commonly worked by its owner unaided. But all over the western world the economy of the large mill in grinding for the market is irresistible.

Modern flour milling is Hungarian in its origin; its later development was characteristic of American resource. But some mills in British sea-ports have overtaken American practice; while they have an advantage in mixing their grains and make the virtues of the various kinds supplement one another. A big ship holding many thousand tons is floated against the walls of a mill; the wheat is made to flow in an endless stream from the ship to the upper floor of the mill. No hand touches it. But after a time all its various impurities, each taken out by a separate process, are delivered to their proper compartments; and flour from any desired mixture of wheats, by a selection of any desired parts of each grain, is delivered at the end after having gone through a score of separate processes[1].

As a uniform powder or liquid can be passed from one

[1] Many other household commodities, such as cocoa, mustard, and soap, are similarly made in vast homogeneous quantities: but the influences which the technique of their production exerts on the size of the business unit is supplemented by, and perhaps even subordinate to, economies of advertising on a large scale.

Cement belongs in part to the same class. But local firms often have special advantages in supplying particular markets with so bulky a product. Moreover its raw materials vary locally: the demand for it is even more irregular than for most other building materials; and the sustained series of perplexing episodes of its history in England, America, and above all in Germany, obstruct any attempt to use it as a basis of generalization.

Another class of difficulties hinders deductions from the histories of the two great groups of chemical industries based on salt and on tar; of the marvellous new developments of the glass industry; and again of the industries connected with high explosives: for they are all to be regarded in some respects as branches of advanced chemical research rather than of mere business. Again geographical causes affect the structure of the industries based on salt. A factory of high explosives requires a certain seclusion, which may be inconvenient to a firm too small to rely mainly on its own resources: an effective guarantee as to the purity and correct admixture of the materials used cannot easily be given except by a large firm: and many diverse advantages are united in such an undertaking as that which Sir Andrew Nobel spread over a large area of waste sandy land in Scotland.

automatic apparatus to another without the aid of the human hand, and emerge at the end of a long course transformed and adapted and transformed again in a score of different operations; so also pieces of steel, set into an automatic complex of machinery, can emerge automatically transformed into a cycle wheel hub, or other complex thing. Here might seem to lie the limit of consecutive automatic machine work.

But the economy of consecutive highly specialized operations can be carried much further, if a series of operations is substituted for a series of machines, and the product to be worked upon passes automatically from one to another in a continuous series. This idea was embodied in the organization of the Chicago meat-packing firms. No two animals are exactly alike: but yet when an ox or a hog, suspended from a rail, passes from one operator to another, each performs one definite operation on the same part of the carcase, with a quickness, a certainty and an efficiency which rivals that of the automatic machine. A minute element of judgment is demanded from the operator; but in the main he is, in his working hours, a most excellent and economical machine, and not much more. This idea has passed over into other industries.

A step, which may prove ultimately to exert a profound influence on the structure of business in some engineering and other industries, was taken when this method of the meat packer was adapted to the needs of setting up the component parts of an intricate mechanism. A striking instance of this is that of the Ford motor works. A standard form and size of chassis having been adopted, all its component parts are made to standard shape by automatic machinery. These appendages, etc. are stored, each in a separate compartment, connected by a slide running down to an appropriate place in a central room. Here is an endless conveyer, which completes a round in about an hour. A frame is put on this: as it reaches each slide, the appropriate part is fixed on it, by men who act as automatically, promptly and easily, as those in meat-packing works: at the end of its round the frame is a complete chassis.

It is claimed that this method enables high-class products to be made at low costs by very highly paid, though not exceptionally skilled workers, moving steadily without strain or hurry: should the claim stand the test of time, the method is likely to put a large part of the industries that are most characteristic of the modern age, almost exclusively under the control of giant businesses. It is however relevant to note that Mr Ford himself began business on a small scale.

Finally, note may be made of a matter of secondary importance. A business which deals with a large homogeneous product is likely to buy large quantities of some things, which are subsidiary to its processes of manufacture or of marketing; and it often sees its way to making them more cheaply or more conveniently than it can buy them. For instance many food and other products can most conveniently be packed for retail sale in small wooden boxes. Some time ago automatic machines were invented for nailing these boxes together: but their full influence on the price charged by box makers was not exerted quickly: and in consequence some very large users of boxes, did a good stroke of business by setting up subsidiary departments equipped with the new machinery, and making boxes for themselves. But this tendency is of doubtful public advantage: for such departments are not, except by accident, under the control of men specially adapted for the work; and they are much less likely to contribute further inventions and improvements to that work than might be expected from independent producers giving their whole faculties to it.

2. *The handling of large masses of homogeneous material is often associated with the utilization of by-products, which further strengthens the tendency to any increase in the size of the business unit.*

There is an intimate connection between the massive manufacture of homogeneous products and the utilization of by-products. For the processes of standardization of the main products tend to segregate by-products: and if any particular element of the original material is cast out by a special process —and this often happens—then a long step has already been made towards the standardization of any by-product, of which that element is the basis. By-product industries are however liable to great vicissitudes. Something which was apparently almost valueless is suddenly made the foundation of an important product, either through a new technical discovery or through the rise of a new demand. For instance, the confident expectations, current not long ago, that electric light would speedily displace gas, took insufficient account of the great rise in the price of coke, which would follow any check to the output of gas: nor did they anticipate the vast field for the consumption of tar, which seems likely to be opened out by its new applications to road surface making.

The advantage of continuity of process is one of several causes that incline large producers to work up their by-products. In old times, when the head of a business was also the master workman, economy and efficiency alike required that the subtle treatment of each by-product should be in the hands of a master of that work; and consequently by-products were generally handed over to subsidiary industries. But in modern times, a great organizer, with abundant capital, can employ experts to travel for him and study the best methods of treatment known at home or abroad, and can set them to put up a large and expensive plant. He has a double set of gains to expect from experiments that tend both to increase the demand for his by-product, and to improve the quality of the goods made out of it: so he will risk larger outlay and be less discouraged by some initial loss than almost anyone else[1].

Some of the by-products of petroleum are subtle and costly chemical compounds, for pharmaceutical and other uses; and they demand the thought and care of highly trained professional analysts. The same is true in regard to several by-products of the "heavy" chemical industries, in which Britain holds a leading place: for she is favoured by her own supplies of coal and salt, and by easy access to sulphur and other necessary materials. In all such industries, new products are frequently

[1] The utilization of horns, as by-products of the slaughter-house, is vividly described by Babbage (*Economy of Manufactures*, A.D. 1832, § 270). So when the Chicago meat-packing firms found a sudden opening for a vast industry with high profits they threw all their force into their main work; and subsidiary industries grew up around them to handle their by-products. But later on some of them applied their overflowing capital and energy to setting this work on a higher plane: and, partly by aid of European methods, they got so much profit from it as to be able to sell their main products at a low price relatively to the cost of the animals. See *Report of the Commission of Corporations on the Beef Industry*, Washington, 1905.

 coming to the front; and a business, which has abundant capital and is controlled by men with scientific interests and large faculty for high enterprise, may constantly introduce into the world not only new methods, but also new things.

But yet the main occupation of these industries is with familiar bulky products: and a great firm may long hold a prominent place in them, if it is managed with discretion and energy, and has an alert apprehension of any improvements in method or product that are on their way. Such industries give scope for bold and wise faculty, ready to sink large capital in organizing scientific studies and experiments: for, though they must in great part be barren of result, they yield splendid rewards on the relatively few routes which lead to success. They may be compared and contrasted with the light chemical industries, which have already been noted as specially characteristic of the German aptitude for organized team work in scientific exploration under capable guidance.

The main basis of those industries is coal tar, which Germany at first procured largely from British gasworks, but afterwards from the coke ovens of steel works, themselves a characteristic product of scientific method. Persistent study has shown that dyes, capable of resisting the effects of strong light, and offering a large variety of pleasant colour effects, can be made, by working on this basis on innumerable routes. Many of the products evolved on the way to the discovery of a new dye, are found to be useful in other combinations for other purposes. Nothing is hastily dropped; every intermediate product and every by-product is tried in various combinations, with the hope of getting some new result of value in some industrial process, or of getting at an old result by a shorter or more economical method. Such work as this can be effectively done only by a business that can afford to work long and patiently at each of a vast number of problems: and anyone who, without adequate scientific apparatus, specialized on the manufacture of a few of the products in most repute, might possibly find himself left stranded, the tide of discovery having swept by him. In fact the complex interactions of new products and by-products show signs of exerting on the light chemical industries an influence different in its nature, but similar in its results, to that which has been exerted on massive mechanical and chemical industries by the ever increasing variety and expensiveness of the plant required by them. An army of high-class experts, such as won the success of the chemical works at Ludwigshafen, or those at Elberfeld, is as much beyond the reach of a man of moderate means as is the plant needed for making armour plates[1].

II, IV, 2.

This case gives much matter for thought: but no general inference can safely be drawn from it. It shows that when an industry is in process of incessant transformation by the creation of new things as well as by the invention of new methods, there is little chance that a general supply of a particular class of by-products will be available, on which a man of moderate means can specialize. But nothing quite similar has ever occurred before: and it is perhaps probable that, when the products, which have been evolved by the colour industries, have been further developed, they will again be handled in some cases

[1] An "economic appreciation of the colour industry," by Dr Kapff, which is at once technical and instructive to the lay reader, will be found in the *Handbuch der Wirtschaftskunde Deutschlands*, 1904, vol. III. ch. 24. He stated that the Ludwigshafen works employed 148 chemists, besides 75 technical, and 305 commercial officials: but that they paid less than four marks a day for their 6300 workpeople, all adults, on the average. See also below, p. 570.

The industry affords an excellent illustration of the intercommunication of various processes:—"A, B, and C, which are intermediate products for making dyes, are also intermediate products for making photographic chemicals. Further treatment of A leads to the production of D, which is a finished photographic chemical and also a very important intermediate body in the manufacture of an important group of dyes. The same treatment of A which produces D also produces E, which is another important halfway house to fresh dyes. The chemical reaction between *a* and *b*, which produces A, also produces B, from which very important photographic chemicals are produced, during the manufacture of which residues are left from which the valuable drug K can be made. It is obvious to anyone that it will only be possible to make A and B economically from *a* plus *b*, if there is an outlet both for the intermediate dye products and for the photographic chemicals....The German manufacturers do not publish manufacturing details of any value in their innumerable text-books. When a process is described with working details one can rest assured that it is because much better processes have rendered it obsolete. Reactions which at the commencement gave yields of 20 to 25 per cent. have been coaxed to give 80 and 90 per cent.: but the achievement of this end has taken, in many cases, years of research in the laboratory and in the works; and the German manufacturer is sufficiently awake to arrange matters so that very few of the staff indeed have a sufficiently intimate knowledge of a wide range of products to be able to give away much that would be valuable to the outsider." (*Manchester Guardian*, 4 Jan. 1915.)

II, IV, 3. most effectively by businesses each of which devotes to one class of work a considerable capital and high ability specialized wholly on it.

3. *The increased dependence of those, who pioneer progress in broad fields of industrial technique, on the aid of large capital.*

The considerations submitted in this and the two preceding chapters seem to point to two conclusions. The first is that future advances of technique on broad lines are likely to need the aid of capital on an ever increasing scale. The second is that much may still be done with moderate means by a resolute man, who is content to concentrate his strength on a narrow field of work so long as his means are but scanty.

The area of science has indeed no boundaries: there is no reason for fearing that new discoveries in it will dwindle into relative insignificance; as those of the explorers of the earth's surface have gradually done, since two new worlds were opened up by the voyages of Columbus and Vasco da Gama. On the contrary, it seems probable that, the further man goes into the unexplored regions of science, the larger will be the scope for new discoveries, which will effect revolutions in the practical arts of industry as in the meditations of the speculative student.

And yet it may be feared that the rapid increase in the power and scope of the arts of production is perhaps preparing the way for a partial retrogression of the social dignity and weight of the productive industries in some directions. The very strength which they derive from science may be a source of lassitude. For, though the creation of new knowledge evokes the highest intellectual energy, yet men's faculties may be somewhat burdened by carrying a great bulk of merely useful scientific knowledge, and turning it to account in business routine. The fact that Aristotle, Newton and Cuvier would have much to learn, if they should meet a mediocre student of modern science on his arrival in Hades, does not tell entirely on the side of the present age. For creative faculties are developed by exercise; and many who might have been fascinated by opportunities of relatively easy creation fifty years ago, now find that very little of the original work, which remains to be done, and yet has the fascination that belongs to bright new ideas, is within the scope of their limited power. This depressing influence, which is already felt in some realms of science, may possibly spread in the realm of business. For the widening range of standardized methods tends generally to increase the dependence of the creative mind on large capitalistic aid in obtaining scope for its activities.

Further, almost every extension of this grasp increases the opportunities and thus raises the prestige of any capitalist; who, though without high creative faculty, is yet shrewd and steadfast, and can organize and adapt to his particular uses the best plant and methods that so far have been devised. The advantage held by the pioneer of improved methods is of course most prominent in new industries; and in those which, though old, are in transitional stages: but it dwindles rapidly when pioneers have overcome the chief difficulties, and their methods are open to all. For instance, when bicycles first came into vogue, every year brought some striking change in their construction and their methods of manufacture: and the products of a firm, which had no initiative, were obsolete almost as soon as they were made. But now a cycle firm with adequate capital, administrative capacity and assiduity, can manufacture at a comparatively low cost for general consumption an ordinary cycle, that is immeasurably superior to those made by the first leaders of the industry; and is but very little inferior to the best that can be made to-day. Thus improvement in the methods and products of a partially standardized industry goes together with a certain decline in the place held in that industry by the high faculties of initiative: they are apt to be overshadowed by the more commonplace faculties of orderly administration and commercial skill; combined with large resources held perhaps in joint-stock ownership.

Again, the aid, thus given to a new industry, increases both the social importance and the monetary value of an invention, which overcomes any difficulty that may be met in regard to the secondary requirements of the industry: for instance the excellence of the aviator-motor engine increases the premium which is offered for textile materials that are, other things

II, IV, 4. being equal, lighter or stronger or more enduring or even cheaper than those yet known. It is indeed true that when a sound new idea is explained to his brother experts by a man, whose only wealth lies in his brains, it will receive due recognition; the rumours of which will in exceptional cases reach the public ear: in this opportunity will be found a chief mitigation of the injury which the increasing dominion of joint-stock companies inflicts upon the spirit of initiative and enterprise; and such matters will occupy us a good deal later on. But yet every expansion in the general scale of an industry is likely to increase in some directions the advantage which an inventor, who is also a capitalist, has over one whose means are narrow[1].

4. *Opportunities of a strong man with moderate means, who concentrates his energies on a speciality.*

It is not to be denied that the increasing economies of specialized machinery and skill are on the side of the powerful capitalist in competition with a weaker rival so long as the tasks on which they are engaged are similar in scope: for large works are at an advantage over small in being able to assign to almost every task a specialized machine, which is perhaps more efficient and certainly cheaper in proportion to its efficiency

[1] Experiments on a laboratory scale or with small mechanical models have as a rule but little commercial value, until they have been fortified by practical proof of their efficiency on a working scale. The sums, needed to be expended on large scale experiments before final success is achieved, sometimes amount to hundreds of thousands of pounds: and there are many industries in which a thousand pounds go no further in this direction than a hundred pounds did a few decades ago. An invention, which cannot be patented, is seldom of much value to anyone who does not already own a considerable business in which it can be used.

It is true that, when an invention is complete, and a patent has been obtained for it, it may be sold, or taken up on some sharing plan, by a capitalist. But he is generally in a position to get the best of such a bargain; for a commercial critic of an invention is seldom inclined to regard its possibilities as very high, relatively to the chance that continued working will bring out latent defects; or perhaps suggest to someone else a superior plan, that is not technically covered by the existing patent. It is to be remembered also that large sums of money are often expended by wealthy inventors on developing and patenting plans that run parallel to their chief plan, in order to delay the advent of rivals on those parallel lines: and, though this practice has been somewhat checked by recent legislation tending to weaken patents which are lying dormant, yet it still tells on the side of the strong capitalist in competition with men of smaller means.

than the general or "omnibus" machines applicable to many uses, on which small works of the old type largely rely[1].

And even if there is little scope for highly specialized plant, the large business will subdivide the work among so many men; and specialize each of them so closely to a particular task, that by constant practice he will be able to perform it better and very much quicker than a skilled artisan, of much higher faculty, who is equally expert at many other tasks. This matter is indeed of somewhat less importance in Britain than in America: as has already been noted, new strains of immigrants have generally but little industrial training, and yet congregate in the towns. This gives an impetus to the desire of the small manufacturer to confine his production to a class of goods so limited that he may be able to specialize his employees as well as his machinery almost as thoroughly and minutely as can be done even in the largest works. A man with moderate means who knows how to turn the economies of partial standardization and complete specialization to his account is not in a bad position.

The task of pioneering the general standardization of structural shapes was indeed heroic in its dimensions; and tasks on a like scale cannot be frequently achieved by a single effort. But smaller and more gradual movements in similar directions are becoming increasingly frequent, and are doing much to bring particular parts of large processes of massive production within the range of a strong man with comparatively small capital.

Such a man may indeed find that the markets in which he looks to buy his material or to sell his products, are controlled to his prejudice by a monopolistic combination in stages of production below his, or above his, as we shall see. But, if the markets are free, standardization relieves him of many troubles of marketing which might weigh him down, and it enables him to give his energies to that work which is specially his.

[1] For some parts of such a machine are almost sure to be idle in each of the many tasks to which it is applied, and their presence is always a source of extra cost, and often of extra work to the machine. Again, each part of it must be made heavy and strong enough to bear the maximum strain imposed in any of its uses; whereas in a specialized machine, every part is kept light except those which will be subject to heavy strain in the constant repetition of its single task.

II, IV, 4. He looks to selling his standardized product without inordinate expenses on advertising, or in building up business connections with individual firms. And, what is often more important, he can enter into any process in which the standardized products are used, with a fair certainty that he will be able to buy them, as he needs them, at a low cost.

This is noticeable in production, the earlier stages of which give large scope for machinery, and require much capital, but not much labour or individual treatment; while the later stages need mainly to be done by hand, and call for the kind of care that is best given by an artisan working on his own account or by a small employer. Thus large steel firms have always supplied small cutlers with their material. Machine-made standardized component parts are built up into good bicycles in many a small workshop. The small milliner, dressmaker, and shoemaker buy many more materials already partly worked up by machinery than is commonly supposed. And the small builder and picture frame maker buy ready made doors, and window frames, or picture frame material from large producers with elaborate plant; while they themselves give their main attention to local needs, to the tastes of particular customers, and to superintending hand work aided by but very little plant. Thus the large business, itself increasingly given to semi-automatic work on standardized products, is often indirectly aiding businesses in which routine has but a secondary place; and in some directions it promotes new openings through which a man of small means but large energy may work his way up to become a leader in industry.

In every industrial country there is a sufficient market for specialities, which can be advantageously produced by a man of moderate means; and he can often turn alert and energetic faculty to the best account by concentrating all his strength on making some one thing, perhaps only of a single size. For then he can afford to provide a machine for every subdivision of his work: and, as it need never be set to more than one task, it can be simple and therefore firm and yet cheap.

The thing at which he works may be a piece of electric apparatus, a portable power-driven hammer or riveter, a new pump or windmill: it may be a complex registering machine, which needs to be revolutionized and again revolutionized; and at last made largely by aid of machines invented for the purpose, before it is ready to take its place as an almost human participant in the clerical work of many kinds of business. In any case he will resolve to have the best plant and the best methods existing for that particular task which he has taken in hand; and he collects around him a staff of men ideally fit for his purpose. They must be alert, and must have every faculty that he needs. But he will not pay for faculties for which he has no great use; and he will not allow skilled men to spend much time on tasks, for which cheaper labour would suffice. When his works are so well equipped, and so highly organized that there seems no great room for further improvement in them, he may probably turn his newly acquired strength to larger fields. Then he will have joined the ranks of the large producers: and is likely to be unconsciously opening avenues through which new small men may work their way up[1].

Thus it comes that, though the small producer is constantly threatened with extinction; though he has in fact been driven from some branches of many industries, and is in process of being driven from others; yet he survives. He is saved by the fact that although machinery may have been applied to what used to be the greater part of a process of production; yet the remainder

[1] A hero of See's characteristically American, and profoundly suggestive, *Chordal's Letters* (1880), illustrates a drift of character which did more than anything else to promote England's leadership, and which is still a chief source of her strength. Sackett, a rising engineer, tells (p. 41) how he looked out a likely, intrusive, troublesome boy. "I set him at work on a three years' apprenticeship. I first set him to chipping castings, and told him he could drop such work forever the moment he could do it well. He seemed to understand my plan and passed through the ordeal quickly. Then I put him on a bolt cutter with the same understanding. He soon graduated, took a rough lathe, then a better lathe, then a vice, then a floor. *He always did the most valuable work of which he was capable.* This was my regular plan in the shop, and secured for every man his proper sphere of action." And this boy later on became a foreman; went to help another employer out of his difficulties; found men spiritless because they had not just the work fit for them; put them to work that brought out what was good in them: and soon his employer "was paying higher wages and getting cheaper work than any one else in his line."

The success of small Jewish masters in the East End of London seems to be partly due to the care with which they select for each man work suited to his latent aptitudes. See "The Jewish Immigrant," by J. A. Dyche, in the *Contemporary Review*, vol. LXXV.

II, IV, 4. is still done in the old way. The money-value of the part done by machinery is likely to shrivel up, and the aggregate demand for labour in it is likely to diminish, though the vent of the product may have been much increased by the fall of its price. But meanwhile the demand for labour in those parts of the work, that still require individual attention, will have grown with the increased output: and the scope for the elasticity, for the initiative, and for the watchful care about details, in which the small producer excels, may have been enlarged in one direction as much as it has contracted in another[1].

Moreover improved mechanical processes are taking over many tasks which each household used to perform for itself. Such industries as dressmaking, baking and washing, once largely domestic, are ever adding to the ranks of small businesses, and creating new steps by which enterprise and initiative can begin their climb upwards.

No doubt some of the forces that are working agianst the small producer are growing cumulatively. We must presently consider how the very inertness of joint-stock companies tempts them to apply some of their large capital in branches of manufacture for which they have no special aptitude, but in which they can turn to account their facilities for borrowing capital at low interest. Meanwhile it may be said, with reference to the present century, that though machinery has ever been extending its domain; yet each conquest has increased the relative importance, from the point of view of the operative, of that ground which it has left open to hand work. It has opened up new ground for general markets: and, there is no cause for wonder at the fact that the number of small businesses is constantly growing; since their products are ever finding new vents in these markets, as well as in the supply of special materials and machines to large businesses.

[1] For instance, if machinery takes over what used to be regarded as three-fourths of a process of manufacture, and after a time performs it at a tenth of the original cost; then, though the real importance of that part remains as great as ever to the consumer, its importance in the statistics of both industry and trade will fall to less than a third of that which used to be three times an important as it. Perhaps the fall in price will have increased the sale of the product five-fold, and, in that case, the employment of labour afforded by what used to be but a fourth of the industry will now give more employment than used to be given by the whole industry.

Thus, so far as the "productive" side of business is concerned, it may be concluded that—though the volume of output required for maximum efficiency in proportion to capital is increasing in almost every industry—yet, at any given time and in any given condition of industrial technique, there is likely to be a point, beyond which any further increase in size gives little further increase in economy and efficiency. And this is well; for small businesses are on the whole the best educators of the initiative and versatility, which are the chief sources of industrial progress.

But this conclusion does not extend to the "marketing" side of business: for we shall find that, on that side, the advantages of large capitals in competition with capitals of smaller size are constantly increasing almost everywhere.

CHAPTER V

CONSTRUCTIVE SPECULATION. ORGANIZED PRODUCE MARKETS

II, v, 1. 1. *Introductory observations.*

A good deal has already been said incidentally as to the ever increasing complexity of marketing, and as to the aids which its operations derive from modern facilities for transport and for the transmission of intelligence. The purpose of the group of three chapters, of which this is the first, is to consider the influences, which these changes are exerting on the costs and methods of marketing in various classes of industries, and on the structure of business in them.

It will appear that the influences, exerted by developments of the means of communication, operate much as do those exerted by changes in the technique of production: on the whole they strengthen the strong producer and dealer relatively to his weaker competitor; but in some directions their aid is of greater service to the weak than to the strong.

Good marketing has always provided or helped in providing; (*a*) a supply, both steady and elastic, of everything for which there is a considerable demand (measured in terms of purchasing power) in any place; and (*b*) a fairly steady supply of employment for the labour, skill, plant and managing faculty required for turning them to effective account. Most of these tasks have been comparatively simple where people have been satisfied with a few products, mostly of local origin; and where, as has often happened, the handicraftsman has been also an agriculturalist, and divided his time between his two occupations so as to meet fairly well the more pressing demands of nature and man: but many of them have gradually become very complex.

The advance of knowledge and wealth has brought so great and ever-changing a variety of goods into ordinary consumption, that if the resources, on which the local dealer could draw, had remained without great change, the stocks needed to meet the impatient demand of the modern western consumer would have been larger in proportion to population than the whole movable wealth of, say, the sixteenth century. And, on the same supposition, the employment found in any place for the highly specialized skill and plant of modern industry would have been so fitful and irregular, that modern knowledge and wealth would scarcely have sufficed to make modern industry commercially possible. But the same causes, that have brought new difficulties, have brought also new methods of overcoming them.

Nearly all western markets are now united by so many various connections, that a need for any common product almost anywhere can be filled in a couple of days, if not in a few hours, from a large reservoir; which can be replenished quickly from still larger reservoirs near or far. In return for these services, which central reservoirs render to local consumption, linked-up local demand provides a fairly steady market in time of peace for nearly all commodities, however highly specialized, the consumption of which is not greatly varied by such widespread influences as changes in the season or in fashion[1].

Thus technical improvements in transport and marketing are ever overcoming old difficulties; but they are also ever stimulating further developments, which open out new difficulties. One of the most prominent of these, the increase in the distances over which food and other goods travel before arriving at their final resting place, has perhaps nearly reached its full force already. For, as backward countries and districts gain on those which had an earlier start in the industrial race, the average distance travelled by ordinary manufactures will diminish. Long distance transport will be increasingly concerned with fine indus-

[1] On this side of its work good marketing may be compared to a fly-wheel, rather than to a reservoir. The engine which drives a single machine, liable to short sudden increase of strain, must have a fairly massive fly-wheel. If it drives a score of such machines it needs a mass perhaps only six times as great: and if it drives five hundred of them, the wheel may be perhaps less than a thirtieth part as massive in proportion to the work done, as if it drove only one.

II, v, 2. trial specialities; and with such crude agricultural and mineral products, as Nature yields in greater relative abundance, or on easier terms, in some parts of the world than in others.

2. *Modern organization tends so to distribute the risks inherent in making and marketing that they fall increasingly on the shoulders best fitted to bear them.*

The intensest risks of early times and of some backward countries even now, have been "consumers' risks" connected with harvest failures. But cheap and speedy transport by land and sea, aided by the telegraph and the specialized activities of dealers in harvest products, have very greatly diminished such risks in the Western World: and there is some tendency to think of "speculation" as a thing, with which no one need be concerned who does not set out to seek it. But in fact the great risks of business have much in common with the many small risks which must be faced by every responsible citizen.

For when a traveller is in doubt which of two roads to take, he speculates. He must ultimately take one risk or the other: he has no choice but to speculate as to their relative advantages and act according to his speculative judgment: and, in the more weighty affairs of ordinary life, everyone is frequently at a crossing of roads. If a man is in a hired house which he much likes, but is not sure how long he will stay in the neighbourhood, he takes a risk, whether he accepts or refuses a long lease of it: and similarly when a man decides for what occupation to prepare his son, and to what school to send him, he must take some of many risks. But the *looking into the future*, which such risks involve, is seldom recognized as speculation: and even business transactions which follow the ordinary routine are not commonly regarded as "speculative": that term being almost confined to dealings in things the future prices of which are eminently uncertain.

The speculative taking of high risks has many varieties. Some are in effect mere reckless gambling. Others are shrewd business ventures, aimed at gains, that must be balanced by losses to traders who are concerned in the same affairs. Others tend to improve the general application of efforts to the attainment of desirable ends: these last alone are entitled to be called "constructive" in the full sense of the term.

Aristotle's doctrine, that neither party to trade can gain except at the expense of the other, is true only of that particular form of trade which is classed as gambling, a class to which many varieties of trade speculation belong. But genuine trade commonly benefits both parties to it: because, though each receives only what the other gives up, what he receives is more desired by him than that which he gives up. In gambling, when conducted fairly and on equal terms, every transaction is an exchange of equal risks[1].

When a man, having superior knowledge as to horses, lays a wager about them on advantageous terms to himself, he effects an immediate increase of his property; but without advantage to the world. On the other hand, when a man has superior knowledge that the supply of anything is likely to run short in any particular country or in the world generally; and buys it either outright or for future delivery; then, on the assumption that his judgment is right, his action is to be regarded as constructive speculation. Such work adds to the world's wealth, just as diverting a stream to work a watermill does, for it tends to increase the supply of things where and when they are likely to be most wanted, and to check the supply of things where and when they are likely to be in less urgent demand. This is its most conspicuous service.

But it also renders another service; which, though less conspicuous, is not much less important: for it often enables a man whose whole energies are needed for the internal work of his business, to insure himself against the risk that the materials which he will need in his business will not need to be purchased at an enhanced price. The risk is governed by broad causes over which he has scarcely any control, and the study of which requires knowledge and faculties other than his own.

[1] This statement is not inconsistent with the fact that if a man stakes half of his fortune of £10,000 on an equal risk, his prospects of material well-being are lowered. For the increase of well-being derived from an addition of say £10 to property or income, is in accordance with fundamental laws of human nature, generally the less, the greater the amount already possessed: and therefore his welfare stands to be diminished by his exchanging a certainty of £10,000 for two equal chances of £15,000 and £5,000. But almost every general rule has its exceptions: and if he could with £15,000 get something that would make him permanently happy, while a loss of half his £10,000 would do him no special injury, the bargain might be wise.

II, v, 2. As a rule the manufacturer who has not contracted to deliver, but works for the general market, desires to be insured against a fall and not against a rise in the price of his material: he stands to lose by such a fall; since purchasers, unless specially pressed for time, will decline to buy his finished product at a price much above that which corresponds to the current price of the material. There is no simple means of insuring against this risk, which corresponds to a contract for delivery of material at a fixed price; but the two sets of risks are in opposite directions, and it is obvious that much economy might be effected by setting these to neutralize one another. In spite of the abuses connected with them, organized markets for dealing in standardized produce, render many services to business men and to the world at large; and perhaps the chief, though not the most prominent of these is their indirect effect in so concentrating risks, that those of them which, like those just considered, are in opposite directions, will tend to extinguish each other.

But, before entering on this matter, it is worth while to note that insurance against a risk may be so important a benefit to anyone whose capital is not large relatively to the risk, that it may be worth his while to pay far more than the actuarial value of it. For instance, suppose that the chance that a building of a certain class worth £10,000 will be destroyed by fire in the course of a year, is one in ten thousand: then the actuarial value of that risk will be £1. And yet, if the destruction of the building would ruin its owner, and the chance that he would be ruined in that way would materially increase the difficulty of his borrowing additional capital, it may be worth his while to pay £10 (or even more if it were not to be had at a lower rate), for a secure insurance against that risk. But an insurance company, with an income from insurance premiums of £1,000,000, would scarcely feel such a loss; and it is therefore able to reckon the risk at its actuarial value. Of course allowance must be made for the company's heavy expenses of administration, for risks of fraud, etc.: but even so it might make good profits by charging only £2 against the risk[1].

[1] The actuarial calculations are of the same kind, but much more intricate in practice: for partial losses by fire, which are very much more frequent than total losses, are commonly included. In consequence much higher rates than

This illustration shows how a bank or any other powerful business might benefit capitalists of smaller means, if a method could be devised by which it could bear their risks, supposed to run all in the same direction: for it would be to their advantage to insure at more than the actuarial value of their risks. But a characteristic of those risks of a business which are governed by causes external to it, is that they turn on price movements which throw about equal risks in the opposite direction on other businesses. If an insurance company could contrive that the risks which it undertook in regard to a particular price movement in the two directions up and down were equal and opposite, the aggregate burden of its risk would be nothing at all: it would need compensation only for its expenses of administration.

A balance of this kind is seldom attempted under the name of insurance. But miscellaneous risks are shared out in various ways, some of which are commonly described as insurance; while many others, not so described, amount in effect to indirect insurance. For instance, bad weather on the day set for a Coronation procession is a risk against which an insurance rate is definitely quoted at Lloyds; and it is of great benefit to caterers for public entertainment whose risks are exceptionally large. Insurance against the danger of fine weather is not of frequent occurrence: but it is notorious that fine weather on a Bank holiday causes indoor entertainments to be deserted for outdoor entertainments and excursions. Now, if it were possible to insure simultaneously indoor entertainments against fine weather and outdoor entertainments (together with railways, etc.) against bad weather, for the same day and to equivalent amounts, the insurers might take many grievous risks off the shoulders of others: they might reap a goodly profit for themselves, and yet bear little net risk themselves: for opposite risks would have partly extinguished one another. We are now to see how a chief function of organized markets is to accomplish what is in effect a double insurance of this kind, though its manner is rather that of wagering than of insurance.

that suggested above are charged: but the general principle by which they are governed is not affected by this.

II, v, 3.

3. *Characteristics of organized markets.*

"An organized market" is one the proceedings of which are formally regulated. As a rule those who deal on it are in effect a corporation: they elect new members and also the executive of their body and appoint the committee by which their own regulations are enforced. In some countries their status is fixed and their actions are superintended by Government. Their regulations generally provide, implicitly or explicitly, for the completion of a contract to buy or sell a quantity of a definite commodity at a certain price, by the utterance of a few words on the one side, and by a brief response, sometimes a mere nod, on the other. They generally prescribe a rather large unit as that to which the contract refers, at all events in the absence of any specific statement to the contrary.

The most highly organized exchanges are the Stock Exchanges of the chief industrial countries. But they can profitably be considered only in connection with the Money Markets to which they belong: and their special problems have but little direct connection with those of the present group of chapters. They may therefore be left on one side for the present.

The chief conditions needed for rendering any class of products suitable to be handled in an organized market are, (1) that it be not quickly perishable; (2) that the quantity of each thing can be expressed by number, weight or measure; (3) that its quality can be determined by tests that yield almost identical results when applied by different officials, assumed to be expert and honest; and (4) that the class is important enough to occupy large bodies of buyers and sellers.

These conditions are sufficient to render organized marketing practicable. But a fifth condition is required to make it attractive: it is that the class of things dealt in should be generally liable to considerable fluctuations in price. For otherwise the dealings would be confined almost exclusively to producers, consumers, and merchants: there would be little scope for those professional dealers who make a living by speculative purchases and sales; and who, as we shall presently see, in some cases render great public services by carrying risks that would otherwise need to be borne by people whose special aptitudes lie in other directions. It is true that this beneficent work is often marred, and sometimes over-borne, by evil practices which intensify fluctuations and mislead honest dealers: but, for the present at least, that evil has to be taken with the good. An organized market generally gives scope for purchases and sales for immediate delivery; and for dealings in "futures," that is in goods to be delivered at specified future times[1].

This fifth condition implies that the things in question are not of such a nature, that their supply can be varied by rapid and extensive changes in the rate of production; so that their price is prevented from fluctuating rapidly, and remains always close to normal cost of production. There are few material things which satisfy all these conditions in very high degree: the chief among them are various grains, especially wheat; and raw cotton. The authorities of each organized produce market define the standard, or standards, in which dealings may be made; and all produce, which comes for delivery in these dealings, is inspected and certified as being truly up to the standard which it claims.

Comparatively few transactions in futures lead to the actual delivery of the produce. In most cases the buyer pays to the seller any amount, by which the official price of the quantity sold may have fallen below that at which the sale was made; or receives from him any amount, by which it may have risen. Either side may insist on completion: but that is generally effected through the organization of the exchange, by bringing together those who wish actually to deliver with those who wish actually to receive; the rest being "rung out." The practical effect of this is that anyone can as a rule buy a future, without being called upon to pay its price either at the time of making the contract, or afterwards. Each party is required to put in a "margin," which will cover a small movement of the price

[1] A contract in relation to a future often takes the form of an "Option" by which the payment of a certain sum secures the right to demand certain things (or to sell them) within a given period at a specified price: these two options may be combined, an option to buy at a stated price being coupled with one to sell at a stated higher price. There are a few cases in which dealings in options are part of legitimate trade. But there appears to be more force in the arguments for prohibiting them by law, than for prohibiting a simple buying or selling of futures; for they are relatively more serviceable to the gambler and the manipulator than to the straightforward dealer.

II, v, 4. against him: and, as soon as the price moves considerably against him, he is likely to be required to make a corresponding addition to his margin.

Thus by far the greater part of the transactions are in substance merely wagers to the effect that the price of produce will rise or fall. Of these wagers some are, as we have seen, careful, deliberate business operations, sometimes classed as "legitimate" speculation: others are the almost random guesses of foolish gamblers; and others again are parts of large manipulative policy, which is in the main evil economically and morally.

4. ***The services rendered by constructive speculation on a Wheat Exchange, illustrated by its efficacy in lightening the burden of risks borne by grain merchants and millers.***

In early times the population bore economic risks, arising out of the uncertainties of the harvests, incomparably more grievous than any that fall on any large class of persons in the present age: and the machinery of modern grain markets cannot be adequately judged without some recognition of the evils from which mankind has been delivered by the gradual development of organized trading in grain: a little is therefore said about them in Appendix I, 1. Milling is now a subtle industry, requiring a highly technical knowledge of machinery and of the many variations of grain. Flour is not now made of any grain that comes first to hand: it is worked to definite standards, for particular districts and classes of consumers, by appropriate blendings of different sorts of wheat; and the miller therefore has more work to do outside of speculation than before. On the other hand, prices in his local market are now so closely bound to those of the world markets, that to form a good opinion about them requires the undivided energy of an able man. The miller is therefore often glad to insure himself against those risks of his business, which arise, not out of the local conditions of which he has special knowledge, but out of world movements.

A produce exchange can best undertake such risks as these, because many minds of first rate ability and many large capitals are occupied there in dealing with just these risks: and because many of the risks are in opposite directions and cancel one another. The broad shoulders of an exchange can carry without effort the intense risk, relatively to his financial strength, which the chance of a rise in price has imposed on one man; and can generally neutralize it by carrying the equal risk, which the chance of a fall in price has imposed on another.

It is of course impossible to recognize officially contracts in every sort of wheat. But a standard sort and quality is set for official dealing: and when actual delivery is being arranged, sorts differing in some specified small degrees are allowed to be substituted for the standard grade, under special adjustments as to price, which are ordered by the officials after inspection[1].

A British miller may bring shiploads of wheat of various descriptions alongside his own elevator, and mix them by automatic flow in various proportions to make different sorts of flour. He often buys direct from far-off farmers or local elevators, through agents on the spot, who know his requirements exactly: but he can, if need be, send special instructions in return to telegraphic reports; basing himself on the last records that have been received in Liverpool, or other centre of the wheat trade, of the prices of standard grades in all the chief markets.

Having ordered the purchase of a certain quantity of what he needs, he "hedges," by selling at once in a central market an equal quantity of standard wheat for delivery at about the time at which he expects that the wheat, which he has just bought,

[1] Grading by American elevator companies, of grain sent to them by farmers, is not always without reproach: though in the main it seems to be fairly correct. Official grading is generally careful though it varies a little from one place to another. A long rod, with a row of small boxes along its whole length, is pushed to the bottom of the truck or other receptacle in which the grain is. The boxes are then opened and filled by a single movement; and old fraudulent methods of making the grain appear better than it is, by concentrating good qualities in those parts of the receptacle from which a sample was most likely to be drawn, are stopped by grading the whole as of the lowest quality shown in any box, where there is any difference. The grading is based chiefly on weight per bushel, colour, condition and cleanliness: the last three elements being decided by individual judgment, which appears to be liable to perceptible though small variations: and it takes little or no direct account of strength in gluten, starch or other matters which are important to the miller. See the *Report of the Industrial Commission*, vol. IV. p. 432. That Commission, appointed in 1898, issued its nineteenth volume in 1902; and is the authority for many statements as to American conditions made in the present work.

II, v, 4. will be in his elevator ready to be made quickly into flour. If wheat falls in the interval, his flour has to compete with that made from cheaper wheat; but, what he loses through that fall, is returned to him almost exactly by his gain on the "future" which he has sold. Conversely, if wheat rises in the interval, he has to pay on the sale of his "future" about as much as he gains from the corresponding upward movement of his flour. By buying a future he does *not* speculate; he throws on the shoulders of the general market the risks and the chances of gain that would otherwise have come to him through general movements external to his own business. The elements of risk, that stay with him, are only the chances of some divergence between the price movement of the standard grade which he has undertaken to sell, and that of flour of the sort which he is preparing to make: and experience shows that that divergence is seldom large. He does not speculate: he insures[1].

Meanwhile many millers have made contracts to deliver flour to bakers and others in specified quantities and at specified times and places: and prefer to buy their grain as they need it. These millers run opposite risks to those of the set just considered: for a rise in the price of wheat might cause them heavy losses. So they insure themselves by buying futures on the Exchange. In so far as the sales of futures by the first set, and the purchases by the second, are for equal amounts and like times, the resulting risks cancel one another: whatever excess of risk there is on the one side or the other remains to be borne by the dealers on the Exchange: and their shoulders are very strong for the work. Of course the miller who buys a future, can demand delivery only in a standard grade: and if he is producing fine qualities he sells his right to that grade, and buys direct those sorts which he wants[2].

[1] Exception must indeed be made for the improbable case in which his sale of a certain grade for future delivery comes at a time, when the price of that grade is being forced up by a campaign on the Exchange to "corner" those who have sold futures.

[2] The general position is set out clearly by Prof. Emery in his work on *Stock and Produce Exchanges*, 1896, and in his paper read to the American Economic Association in 1899. It may be noted that the miller who contracts in advance to deliver flour of a specially fine quality is put in a better position by buying a future on the Exchange than he would probably be by contracting with individual dealers for the delivery to him of the sorts that he expects to

All great wheat Exchanges are in close touch with one another; their movements are now reported at short intervals to the local markets of the districts which they severally dominate; and though passing fluctuations are ignored, a great change from one month to another tends to influence the breadth of sowing and the assiduity of weeding, etc., of any who may be thoughtfully inclined. It is to be remembered that there is no month in the year in which there are not many cultivators in some part of the Northern or Southern Hemisphere, who are making preparation for, or actually sowing, winter or spring wheat.

Long ago English farmers complained that corn-factors arranged to keep down the price of wheat just after harvest when the farmers "had their payments to make," and were compelled to sell; and to raise the price against the public later on[1]. The modern version of that complaint in America is that futures are sold down on the Exchanges immediately after harvest, in order to lower the prices of wheat for immediate delivery; and that the prices are raised afterwards so that the consumer does not gain what the producer loses. And, while farmers' organizations complain that speculation in futures lowers prices, millers' organizations complain that they have the opposite effect: but analysis and statistics seem to show conclusively that neither contention can be sustained[2].

need. Such a contract would be difficult to make, and it would be liable to uncertainty and friction in the execution. While buying a future on the Exchange he puts himself in command of funds apportioned to the prices of the time at which he needs them; he then buys after inspection, and possibly readjusts his combinations of various sorts according to their several conditions and current prices. The British miller, especially on the Mersey, the Clyde, or other chief waterway, has a choice of wheat from a great number of soils and climates in all parts of the world, and has generally at command several alternative combinations of diverse qualities by which he can reach any desired result.

[1] See *e.g.*, evidence of a Sussex farmer before H. of L. Committee on Agriculture, 1836, Q. 34, 25, 6.

[2] The Industrial Commission after a full hearing of the arguments of farmers and others in the opposite direction, concluded (*Report*, vol. VI. p. 223) that "prices prevailing at the time when producers dispose of the greater part of their products are greater in comparison to the rest of the year than they were before the advent of modern speculation."

In regard to German experience, see a chart leading to a similar conclusion in Conrad's *Grundriss der Pol. Oek.* I. p. 220. And Table VII, in Mr Hooker's paper on "the suspension of the Berlin Produce Exchange," *Statistical Journal*, 1900, indicates that the German prices fell below the American exceptionally just after harvest, as a result of the suspension.

II, v, 5. On the whole it seems safe to conclude that, since those, who buy because their investigations lead them to think that the supply is likely to run short, or sell because they are convinced it has been underrated, will gain if they are right and lose if they are wrong; therefore they are in their own interest contributing to the public the best judgment of minds that are generally alert, well-informed and capable. Their influence certainly tends to lessen the amplitude of price variations from place to place and from year to year. But let us turn to look at the evil side of such speculations.

5. *Dealings in organized markets are liable to abuse by unscrupulous men, aided as they often are by the folly of ill-informed speculators: but the power of selling the future command of a thing not yet in possession has important uses.*

Manipulative speculation has many forms and many degrees. Its chief method is to create false opinions as to the general conditions of demand and supply. A clique will lead the market generally to believe that they are working for a fall, when really they are buying quietly and by indirect means much more largely than they are selling; and conversely they will buy openly, when they are really speculating for a fall. To publish definite false news is an extreme measure, bringing so prompt a punishment, that it is generally avoided by shrewd manipulators. But false suggestion is a chief weapon: and it has so many shades, some of which seem trivial, that men of fairly upright character are apt to be drawn on insensibly to condoning and even practising it[1].

When a large command over wheat (or other produce) has been quietly obtained, a clique will sometimes go on buying, till all that can be made available before the time of settlement

[1] A rise in price at (say) Chicago, is often started by ordering the purchase of some millions of bushels in Liverpool on a certain morning; so as to suggest to the Chicago market, when it opens a few hours later, that information in possession of the English wheat trade points to some scarcity in supply relatively to demand. Again, when a powerful speculator wishes to buy, he often makes large sales openly in his own market; and a little later causes to be bought by agents, acting secretly on his account, much larger amounts, partly in distant markets, to which the news of his sales has of course been telegraphed.

is already sold; and then go on buying, till the price has been forced up to an exorbitant level. This process is of course facilitated by the practice, that prevails on American Exchanges, of buying and selling in a sort of auction open to the whole market. The clique, if successful, finally let out every one who has over-sold, at prices varying with his means: for it is against their interest to make people bankrupt. Some of the corners thus made have a considerable place in history. But the very forces of the modern Money-market and modern means of communication, which strengthen the attack, strengthen also and in a greater degree the defence offered by the community. The clique may plot in secret: but their dealings, however disguised, are soon interpreted by operators about as shrewd as themselves. And the larger the plot, the more surely will energy and ability be directed to the inquiry, whether the movement which is on foot is really justified by the general relations of demand and supply in world markets. If that appears not to be the case, a hostile clique well financed will enter the field: and it will be secure of victory, if its calculations are right. For if two teams of nearly equal strength are pulling in opposite directions, that one which is pulling with the slope of the hill must surely prevail[1].

In all such cases a powerful clique reckons on obtaining great, though unwilling assistance, at all events in the earlier stages of its campaign, from the folly of amateur speculators. For such men do not understand that the affairs of a great

[1] Thus Mr Partridge in 1891—2 sold vast quantities of wheat at Chicago, in the belief that the market's estimates of the crop were too low and that the current high price was too high. He was right, so he was able to buy back the wheat at a lower price than he paid for it. The market is not often thus wrong, but it was wrong again in 1897 when Mr Leiter thought that the current estimates of the crop were too high, and the price too low. Having large funds at his back, and aided by others, he bought great quantities, adopting subtle devices for preventing wheat that was not under his control from reaching Chicago; and was thus able to make many of those, who had sold to him, pay very high prices for default of delivery when the time for settlement came. But having won one battle, he attempted another: and, partly because he had ranged strong enmities against him, he failed grievously. His second venture indeed illustrated the general rule that sensational success in great speculation tends to strengthen the nervous, confident temper in which it originated. It engenders rashness in venturing, and an even more dangerous inability to recognize defeat. In fact a great speculator has scarcely ever rested on his victory: he has nearly always persisted till overtaken by disaster.

II, v, 5. speculation require thorough equipment with knowledge that is beyond the reach of the general public: they do not speculate altogether at random; but they act more mischievously and disastrously to themselves than if they did. For when a man decides, without any bias whatever, on which side of an uncertain event he will wager, he will of course lose any charges that may be levied on his wagering, and these will accrue to the members of the Exchange: but he will, as a rule, not lose any more; for, if he acts absolutely at random, he is about as likely to go in the right direction as in the wrong. The fees which he pays help to finance constructive speculation and trade, and contribute a little also towards the expenses of malign strategy.

But ill-informed speculators generally suppose themselves to be basing their action on the most recent news. Now, the latest information accessible to outsiders has nearly always been acted on by well-informed persons, and has exerted the full influence, belonging to it, before it reaches the public. They are therefore likely to buy, when a fall is more probable than a rise, and *vice versâ*; and in the long run they would make losses by which better informed dealers would profit, even if all the news, which comes in their way, were designed to lead them aright. But in fact many of the statements and suggestions, by which they are guided, have been specially prepared with the purpose either of inducing the unwary to buy, because an unscrupulous speculator or clique wishes to unload; or of inducing them to sell for the opposite reason. In other words they are, to their own great loss, a powerful force on the side of evil manipulations of the market[1].

Thus the power of selling the future command of a thing, not yet in possession, is liable to abuse. But, when used by able and honest men, it is beneficial: as is shown by the havoc, caused by epidemics of unorganized speculation in the value of land, such as are not infrequent in new countries. Speculation for a rise in the value of land is always easy: anyone, who has considerable means and believes that the land is being sold

[1] A full explanation of the folly of such men, written many years ago by Crump, *The Theory of Stock Exchange Speculation*, is in the main applicable to present conditions.

under its true value, or turned to uses below those of which it is capable, can move its price upwards by buying, and using his purchases as security for loans with which he buys again. But no one can speculate for a fall in the value of land, except to the extent of selling any that he happens to hold. Those who have knowledge, but no land to sell, are unable to turn it to effect in checking an excessive rise, in the same way as they could if it referred to a thing for which there is an organized market. Of course in all such matters opinion is under influence from a public press, in which wise and honest counsels have the upper hand in ordinary times: but this influence is apt to fail at critical times.

For instance, the land boom of 1887—1890 in Melbourne began in a shrewd anticipation by able men that the business of the city would require a great extension of the areas used for wholesale trade, domestic and foreign; and for general purposes. They bought, and were able to sell at higher prices; for their success hastened a general appreciation of the great possibilities of Melbourne: and they were joined by others, not all of whom were capable business men like themselves. A little later, a large part of the population had bought land to the full extent of their own capital, if not beyond. No effective note was sounded, or could well be sounded, to warn them that the rise in price had far outrun all reasonable expectations; and that when the bubble was pricked, business would be so crippled that the value of land would fall fast and far. Consequently Melbourne passed through a period of grievous distress[1].

[1] While the boom was yet far from its climax, a Melbourne business man told me the price of land in a part which was indeed well suited for commerce and industry, but was adjoined by much neglected land with almost equal natural advantages. The price was in fact higher than in any part of London, except two or three acres near the Royal Exchange. He said that prudent men knew that a terrible catastrophe was near: but having already sold all the land which they controlled, they had no direct means of influencing prices; and their opinions were unheeded. If a great quantity of futures could have been sold by such men, as soon as prices had gone a little beyond their reasonable level, the sellers would have enriched themselves, and conferred on Melbourne as a whole a benefit many times as large as their own gains.

A little is said in Appendix I, 2, about cotton exchanges and trade in some partially standardized crude products.

II, v, 6. 6. *Some marketing risks relating to "ordinary" products can be transferred by forward contracts: but the majority can be delegated only as incidents of the delegation of corresponding functions.*

The methods of transferring risk from the shoulders of one set of men to those of others, more fitted to bear it, which have now been considered, are not applicable to *ordinary* products, that is those for which no highly organized market is available. But something can be done in that direction by other methods; and the increasing complexity of business often inclines the producer to delegate all such responsibilities as he safely can.

When two men are in partnership on equal terms, it is frequently arranged that one gives nearly his whole energies to making, and the other to marketing. Again a very large business, whether in joint stock or not, commonly entrusts to each of several heads of departments responsibility for a group of details, some of which are considerable, relating to the whole affairs of a small business: each of them discharges a share of the functions of the business; but, as a rule, he bears little or no share of its risks. Function can indeed be delegated easily without associated risks: but the class of risks which can be delegated without any corresponding function is narrow. The risks, which can be transferred without function, relate almost exclusively to definite particular transactions; and the chief instance of these has just been considered. The associated functions and risks with which the next chapter is chiefly concerned are incidental to some stage in the journey of various products on the way from manufacturers, or other producers, to ultimate consumers.

We have seen how an organized market enables a producer to secure in advance an adequate supply of certain materials: and how it also enables him to insure against a loss, that might result to him indirectly from a fall in the market value of his material while he is working it up. So far as future supplies of material go, the same security can be had in many classes of work by a contract for future delivery: though it cannot be undone or modified to suit altered circumstances by a compensatory sale, as easily as it could if an organized market offered facilities for a sale of futures. For instance, shipbuilders and other users of half-finished steel products commonly buy their materials in advance as far as possible, when building under contract; in which course they are aided indirectly at least by partially organized markets for some products. Coal, a chief material for many industries, is too various in character to be handled in a highly organized market: otherwise the dealings in such a market might at times surpass all others in volume and excitement[1].

Thus by private contract or otherwise it is sometimes practicable to insure a business against loss by definite changes in recognized prices, as thoroughly as against losses by fire or other specific accident. But it is not possible, it is scarcely even conceivable, that insurance should be effected against the results of slackness in action or errors of judgment. Such risks must remain with those who control the business and appoint its officers. They may delegate some of their functions, and yet bear these risks either in whole or in part: but it is generally impracticable to transfer such risks without transferring the functions to which they are related. A producer can indeed transfer to middlemen some of the risks of marketing, which he must otherwise bear himself: but he can do so only because that transference is incidental to a transference of some functions to them[2].

To this fact and another which is closely allied to it may be traced many of the chief characteristics of modern marketing.

[1] There are many local coal markets in Britain, each having trade terms and usages peculiar to itself: and, though the broad dealings of the London Coal Exchange in almost every variety have introduced some uniformity in the movements of prices, no approach to a satisfactory reduction of all varieties to their equivalents in several standard sorts is yet in sight. Comparatively few consumers make their contracts in advance with mineowners: but the middlemen's dealings in such contracts are so vast as to bear some comparison with those of an organized market. They even occasionally bear the market, in order to obtain favourable terms from coalowners for large contracts for the coming season: but for this purpose they do not sell futures; they merely withhold their customary purchases for a time. (See the account of "the marketing of coal" by Prof. H. Stanley Jevons and Mr David Evans in *Practical Coal Mining*.)

[2] Some "profit and loss sharing" schemes may seem to point in another direction: but the general trend of such schemes does not. The ordinary shareholders of a large joint-stock company bear its chief risks, but delegate nearly the whole of the control.

II, v, 6. The second fact is that though each bargain on an open market, whether an organized cotton market, a cattle market, or a fish market, stands very much by itself; the dealings of a mercantile house with its customers cannot generally be isolated, either as regards their costs or as regards their rewards, as to which more will be said in the next chapter.

CHAPTER VI

SOME BROAD PROBLEMS OF GENERAL MARKETING

1. *The costs and risks of marketing attach to whole processes rather than to particular transactions: many of them are common to a great part, and some even to the whole, of the affairs of a business.*

II, VI, 1.

Let us revert to the notion that "the cost of production, which controls value, relates to whole processes of production, rather than to any particular parcel of products[1]." Let us follow it out on the commercial side of the business of a builder who works only on contract under precise specifications, and contracts in advance for his chief supplies at fixed prices. He has indeed insured himself against all the most prominent risks of marketing; but more risks remain behind than appears at first sight.

Suppose that he has insured against a rise in the standard rate of wages of each chief class of his employees. That will go but a little way, if he does not get hold of at least a fair proportion of able, alert and loyal men, and manage them with tact and firmness: nor is his success likely to be permanent, if he fails to detect and attach to his business those who will in the course of time be fit for promotion to leading places. He cannot insure against the results of errors of judgment in such matters unless by sub-letting contracts; that is, by handing over to middlemen certain functions, with the risks attached to them. Again, as his business increases, he must decide whether an extension of his plant is likely to be turned to sufficient account in future undertakings to be remunerative. He may be doubting whether to enlarge his carpenters' shed, or

[1] See above, p. 190.

II, vi, 1. to buy a steam mortar-grinding machine; or, if he is in a large way of trade, a great derrick gantry. Whichever way he decides any one of these questions, he must run a risk of having cause to regret his decision. Constructive speculation, as was argued at the beginning of the last chapter, is inherent in nearly every business decision: there is generally a choice of risks, but seldom any choice as to whether to take a risk inherent to a function, save by transferring function and risk together.

Now it may appear that, though the productive side of a business involves large decisions as to investments in plant, etc., which will bear fruit slowly and only by means of their services in many various undertakings; yet there is no similar obstacle to the assignment of its particular costs and rewards to each several marketing transaction. But that is not the case. On the contrary there are many marketing problems in which the most advantageous course may be found to lie in making a loss on particular transactions. A great American trader gave instructions that, when a customer, who did not know her own mind, brought back a recent purchase somewhat the worse for its journey, it was to be taken back, and the full money returned, unless there was reason to suppose that she had not acted in good faith: he reckoned that where he thus lost half a dollar in money, he would gain a dollar's worth of good will. The success of his method points to the fundamental principle that the marketing side of the work of a business is an integral process, and not a series of independent transactions.

The marketing reputation and connection of a business may be a larger property (or "capital") in proportion to its earnings, than is the fixed plant of a manufacturer in some industries. Reputation for fairness and generosity in dealing, is a property seldom acquired without special effort and sacrifice, and is a powerful factor of success in all the undertakings of a business. The reputation acquired by large general advertising is easy of attainment, though expensive. It is indeed seldom of much value, unless accompanied by capable and honourable dealing: but, when attained, it extends in varying degrees to all products made or handled by the business: a name or a trade mark which has gained good fame in regard to one product is a great aid to the marketing of others. Again the expenses of advertising by means of a firm's commercial travellers, and the resulting sales, are common to a great part of its business. A single prominent position in a great thoroughfare promotes the sale of many various things: the knowledge that a trader obtains of the character and solvency of his customers, and the opinion, which they form of the soundness of his advice as to the qualities of different sorts of his goods, extend from one part of his business to another.

Some of these considerations will be developed later on. But enough has perhaps been said to support the conclusion that, with a few exceptions, the costs and risks of marketing any one commodity cannot be separated from those of others, which are handled in the same businesses. Each of the trades of the fishmonger, the greengrocer, the grocer, the milliner, etc., has a more or less clearly defined set of costs and risks. But there is seldom a clear line of division between those which belong to particular branches of the same trade. When several trades are combined in the hands of the same Universal Provider, the costs and risks of any one department cannot be stated separately, and only a vague guess can be made as to the part which it has played in making or marring the success of others.

2. *The organization of trade is in the long run as vital to consumers as to producers and traders: but the ever increasing energy, with which sellers push their goods on the notice of buyers, is an inevitable result of modern developments.*

In all this it has been assumed that the necessary arrangements for marketing are, as a rule, the business of the seller; while the buyer remains relatively inactive. Before going further it will be well to consider the causes which make this assumption reasonable and even necessary in the modern world; though it would not always have been reasonable.

Under a system of barter, neither party to a bargain could be called a seller. But as soon as money came into general use, it became obvious that a person who had money and a free range of the market in which to spend it, was in a stronger position than one, who had a stock of goods which he could not

II, VI, 2. turn to account easily except by first exchanging them for money. This superior strength in the position of the buyer was felt strongly in foreign trade; and it contributed much to the Mediaeval and Mercantile preferences against the exportation of the precious metals, and in favour of their importation. As time went on, the cruder arguments in support of these preferences fell into disrepute among thoughtful people: but the fundamental notion that the buyer confers a greater benefit on the seller than he receives in return, governs the policy of many countries at the present time.

Of course the peasant in a backward country, whose supply of food has run short, often has access to only one man from whom he can buy grain, or borrow the means of purchasing: if there are several grain dealers and lenders (for the two functions are commonly combined), they are likely to be acting in combination. The harsh exactions therefore of monopolistic sellers take a much larger place in Mediaeval history, and in the modern history of such countries as India and Russia, than do those of monopolistic buyers. And as we shall presently see, special circumstances in America, and still more in Germany, have put great power into the hands of monopolistic sellers or combinations of sellers. But buyers in England seldom suffer more than a trifling inconvenience from the refusal of a seller to supply them at a fair cost price: for the sources of supply are generally numerous, and they are very rarely combined under one control.

The opinion that buyers have the upper hand has indeed been promoted by the common habit of looking at immediate and transitory rather than ultimate and enduring results; insufficient attention being paid to the distinction between the gain which a seller makes on a particular sale, when the existence of his plant and his business organization is taken for granted; and that which he makes on his sales as a whole, when the cost of setting them up has to be reckoned in.

The advantage of obtaining a broad market is often much exaggerated. It is argued that if a manufacturer is ready to supply a thousand bales of cloth or a thousand mowing machines a week, he may be losing money on an output of five hundred weekly, though they are sold at a price that would give him fair profits on an output of seven hundred, and high profits on an output of a thousand: and it may be suggested that these figures indicate the economies to be gained by production on a large scale. But they do nothing of the sort. They indicate the economy to be gained by adjusting plant and business organization to the demands that will be made on them in normal times, and by preventing as far as may be fluctuations from one season to another. If two cloth manufacturers sell on even terms in the same markets, and have the same percentages of unemployed plant at various times of the year, the fact that one of them can produce ten thousand, and the other only one thousand bales a week, will occasion no great difference in their rates of profit. For the technical economies open to the two will be very nearly the same, and each will have some advantage over the other in administration. And, if the smaller producer has a steadier market, or is in better touch with it, so that he can keep ninety per cent. of his plant at work on the average, while the larger can keep only eighty per cent., then the smaller will make the higher rate of profits.

Thus the statement that the buyer confers a great benefit on the seller assumes that, for some reason or other, the seller's market has fallen short of his power of production, and that the buyer helps to bring it up to that power. A sudden increase in the number of buyers will of course move prices strongly in favour of sellers. But if it lasts only long enough to cause a great deal of new plant to be erected, then it will be a great injury to sellers. For the high profits which they make during the short time of boom, will be much less than the losses of the probably much longer time, that elapses before normal demand has risen so high as to enable them to keep this larger stock of plant running as steadily as before, without selling a large part of the produce at forced prices. This then is the second point to be made clear in interpreting the statement that the buyer stands to gain less from a particular transaction than the seller does: the first point made was that the statement assumes the buyer to have good access to sources of supply other than the seller in question.

To conclude:—in many cases, the buyers would suffer from being *permanently* deprived of part of their needed supply, much

II vi, 3. more than the producers would by being driven to another occupation for their capital and enterprise; and, in the long run, consumers generally stand to lose more from a deficiency of the plant needed to supply their wants, than producers do from a fall of prices which disinclines them to make additions to their plant, and to keep the old plant in a state of thorough efficiency.

But we must get to quite a different point of view to observe *the short run*. For a buyer in the modern world can nearly always get what he wants from other sellers and on about the same terms, if his negotiations with a particular seller fall through. The seller on the other hand looks to a sale, as not only covering the direct, or "prime" costs incurred in producing the thing; but also as contributing something to his remuneration for outlay on plant and other "general" costs of his business: when he has sold a thing on normal terms, he is more than remunerated for the direct or prime costs involved in handling that thing. He has less certainty of selling at current prices whenever he wants to do so, than the buyer has of buying at those prices[1].

3. *The distribution of the general costs of marketing, and especially those connected with the holding of stocks for sale.*

It has already been noticed that producers nearly always bear some considerable costs on account of the marketing of their goods. Those, which the customs and general conditions of any place and time habitually assign to producers, are commonly classed among "costs of production." But if a producer undertakes burdens and tasks which are generally transferred to traders, then it is convenient to regard his costs of production without reference to them: he bears costs of production and some part of the costs of marketing[2].

Formerly most people were content to be supplied with

[1] When a privileged visitor passes through the main door, which separates the buying department of a great linen drapery business from the retailing, he will leave an atmosphere, in which able travellers for manufacturers and wholesale merchants show an assiduous and persuasive courtesy to the employees of the business; and he may enter one, in which employees of similar rank are carefully polite to working women, bent on making their small purchases.

[2] See above, p. 184.

such things as could be conveniently produced near at hand; and, in regard to seasonal products, at such times as Nature afforded them of her own free will. Even the well-to-do were forced to eat but sparingly of fresh meat in winter; and, until quite recently, fresh sea fish was not to be had far from salt water. Fruit seldom travelled far: as a rule every place had to shift with those kinds for which it was suited; and, if the blossoms of one of them were struck by a sharp local frost, the people went almost without it during the coming year. Even the fairly well-to-do had no great variety of clothes or domestic utensils: the great majority of the people had scarcely any imperious demand save for the common necessaries of life, and perhaps a few spices and other slight things.

But all this is changed. In the modern world the necessaries of life absorb an ever diminishing share of the family income. The great body of the people are in a position to pay for a regular and unconditional daily supply of many various kinds of food, all the year round; and the village grocer's and draper's shops contain many scores of different goods made of material brought from all parts of the world. Again, whereas local supplies of wood used to suffice for nearly all purposes; now the most appropriate wood for each purpose of domestic economy is generally supplied, even though it be a product of distant lands.

This imperiousness of demand varies from one kind of goods to another; and, in regard to the same class of goods, from one stratum of society to another. Its effects on marketing costs, and therefore on prices, are most marked in things, which Nature supplies only at particular seasons; and those for which the demand is most uncertain and irregular. If the purchasers of a thing are rich; if its direct cost of production is small; and if several causes combine to increase the difficulty of adjusting supply to demand; then the costs of marketing often double or treble the price received by the producers, before the thing reaches the consumers.

We pass to corresponding changes in the characters and quantities of the stocks needed to be held by producer and trader. The aggregate stocks of grain and other annual products

II, VI, 3. have always borne nearly the same fixed relation to the annual consumption of the people.

The amount, that stands over at harvest time from earlier years, has of course varied with the weather. In spite of the growth of wealth and providence, it has been diminished by the security which cheap and quick transport affords against merely local failures of the crops; and by the arrival of grain from the Southern Hemisphere to eke out Northern stocks, when they dwindle before the next harvest. It is however still true that farmer (or other cultivator), trader, and consumer have to hold among them nearly a whole year's consumption just after harvest, and nearly half a year's consumption on the average. The cheapest housing of the grain has generally been on the land, where it was grown: but, when most of the grain had to be moved to great mills and thence to the consumer, large elevators and other stores grew up; and the trader, who had long "financed" the poorer cultivators by buying their grain shortly after harvest, became responsible for housing it also. Taking the history of the world as a whole, there are no producers' or traders' stocks to compare in importance with those of grain: and the course of their distribution has been followed in great measure by the stocks of other things.

We saw above (I, III, 5) how "homely" producers of woollen and other goods at first used their own wool, or that of their neighbours: how later on they became increasingly dependent on traders for the supply of wool from a distance; and in various degrees were financed and even controlled by them: and how, in the earlier phases of English manufacture by "power" (whether that of falling water or steam), the new men, who rose to the occasion, were dependent for finances on capital which had been accumulated by merchants and others, and was made accessible by banks that then grew up. During that phase the manufacturer kept as little stock as possible; his goods were housed and "carried" financially by merchants and middlemen till they reached the consumer. But gradually many manufacturing firms, and especially manufacturing companies, have come into control of large capital: which has been in some cases mainly inherited from several generations of successful work; in others obtained mainly from the general public through the Stock Exchange.

A powerful modern manufacturing business frequently carries a considerable part of its stocks itself, at all events as far as the retailer. But the extent to which this new tendency reaches, varies greatly from one industry to another. It goes furthest, other things being equal, in industries, the ultimate consumer of whose products is a business firm which has an intimate technical acquaintance with their characters, and each of whose purchases is likely to be of sufficient amount to be considered carefully. Some engineering firms, for instance, generally keep most of their own stocks, and bear most of the responsibility for meeting an effective demand.

But meanwhile there are very many manufacturers, whose capital does not reach much beyond what is required for maintaining and enlarging their plant, and for other purposes of their work. It is therefore still true that traders benefit productive industries and the country generally by taking a considerable part in the carrying of stocks. Such a distribution of burden is all the more reasonable because they can turn over most of their stocks more quickly than formerly. Their turnover increases relatively to the capital needed for it: while, on the other hand, the manufacturer's plant increases in costliness relatively to his net output—that is, to the excess value of his product over that of his material.

Thus in a broad view it may be concluded that, so great has been the increase in the variety of the goods demanded by the people at large, that the aggregate of stocks held by producer and trader would have increased much faster than population, and faster even than aggregate wealth, if very powerful causes had not been acting in the opposite direction. The disadvantages of keeping large stocks are increased, in the case of some kinds of engineering and other plant, by the likelihood that they will be speedily depreciated by new inventions and by changes in technique; while a large stock of goods for consumption may be depreciated even more quickly by changes in fashion and custom. On the other side the advantages to be gained by keeping a large stock are lessened by the rapidity, with which modern methods of production enable a manu-

II, VI, 4. facturer to replenish quickly his stock of anything, for which he has appropriate plant: while the post, the telegraph, the telephone, and the almost omnipresent quick railway service of a compact western country, supplemented by motor traffic, enable every dealer, whether wholesale or retail, to get almost anything that he wants within twenty-four hours, or even less; the way for his easy purchases having been already prepared by trade circulars, catalogues, etc.

For these reasons the stocks held by producers and traders in the western world are an ever diminishing percentage of their turnovers: and thus, although the variety of production and the imperiousness of demand are multiplying rapidly the number of products for which each industry and trade is responsible, there is a general (not universal) fall in that percentage of the retail prices of commodities, which is attributable to the costs of keeping stocks of them.

4. ***Functions of middlemen as links between producer and consumer.***

The chief functions of middlemen generally are however those of studying the wants of consumers, and the resources of producers; and bringing the two into connection: these functions are important even in regard to the minor requisites of business. But they are almost indispensable in regard to household goods, clothing, etc. For such things must commonly be seen before purchase: and they must be delivered in small quantities to innumerable consumers, often on credit.

The ultimate consumer must be reached through a retailer, save in some relatively rare cases. But the retailers in such a country as England are almost as numerous as the whole people of a very small country: and to reach them is a task not lightly to be undertaken by producers, whose main energies must be given to other work. That task falls generally to wholesale dealers, who lay themselves out to study the retail trade. They keep a sufficient variety of goods, coming from many sources, to be able to fill up nearly every order from a retailer promptly from their own stocks. Some of these wholesale traders get their supplies chiefly from a higher stratum of traders; each of whom specializes on a narrow range of goods, but keeps in stock a large variety within that range. In a few cases there is yet a third stratum with still more highly specialized skill and stocks.

A large, strongly capitalized business is often but little dependent on merchants for aid in establishing contact with retailers; for it can organize an effective commercial department of its own. But on the other hand its marketing may extend over a large area; and in that case its commercial department may have enough to do in dealing with merchants and other wholesale traders. Meanwhile the manufacturer of but moderate means often finds his need of aid from wholesale dealers increased by the growing breadth and complexity of trade, about as much as it is lessened by his increased facilities for obtaining direct information from far and near, and for getting into direct touch with consumers. And it remains true generally that the several strata of trade make more thorough studies of the requirements of consumers and of the varieties and qualities of producers' goods than could be effected by any means other than extensive subdivision of labour and specialization of knowledge and skill[1].

It should be added that many goods are commonly supplied on credit by producers to wholesale traders; and by both to

[1] Traders not infrequently aid producers by direct hints as to customers' needs, and even by suggestions as to methods of meeting them: and various arrangements are sometimes made for the division of any gains that may thence arise. Of this more will be said hereafter: but some illustrations may be given at once.

A manufacturer of textile goods designs a number of patterns for the season; and arranges a loom, or other plant for each. He works off samples in various colours; and occasionally in various materials. The merchant, or his agent, inspects the samples; or perhaps visits the factory, where some of them at least are to be seen in the piece. Some of the combinations of colours shown in a pattern may meet with no approval, and never be worked in the piece. The retailer, on the initiative of commercial travellers, receives pattern-books or samples; from which he chooses at once some things for stock, and orders others as occasion arises to meet the selections of particular customers. In other cases a merchant devises a pattern and contracts with a manufacturer to make a cloth or other product to it. Sometimes again a dealer makes suggestions for improvements in details of patterns submitted to him; and this leads to some curious results. Thus a large retail dealer recently boasted that his agents after inspecting patterns of shoes from many makers, select ideas contained in several of them; and he then gives out an order for a considerable make of a pattern in which these ideas are combined. In such a case it is difficult to say to whom the product is properly to be attributed.

II, VI, 4. retailers: and, in so far as this is done, the real taking of risks does not move downwards as fast as it appears to do. This tendency undoubtedly often makes for an undue extension of the number of traders, and especially of retailers: and there is probably some ground for suggestions that there are more traders in many countries than are needed for their work. Such suggestions are strengthened by the observation that advantages of situation or connection sometimes enable a trader, though without any special faculty of artistic or other discrimination, to make very high profits on small sales. And complaints are perhaps made that a particular group of traders secures by combination, prices unreasonably in excess of the producers' prices. Such combinations are, as a rule, distinctly antisocial: but they have existed at all times: and they have often been most mischievous when they have been based on mere implicit understandings, without any explicit and formal agreement.

Thus the relations of traders' policies to public interests are not wholly above question. But yet, in a survey by broad and by long, it appears that traders as a class do not earn much more than adequate remuneration for their work, their capital and their risks. With few exceptions, the field is open; and there is nothing to prevent the influx of new energies where good profits are to be had with abnormal ease.

It is however true that producers often see the prices, which they receive for their goods, increased beyond reason in the charges made to the consumer; and form associations for influencing, and even completely undertaking, the marketing of their goods, at all events as far as the retailer. This task has been done by many German cartels in regard to many standardized goods, especially half-finished products, which serve as materials for further production: we shall see presently that though the direct effects of such action have generally been beneficial to those who take it; its indirect effects on other branches of industry, and on the public at large, are often evil[1].

[1] These matters occupy a considerable space in Book III. The beneficial effects of movements by producers and dealers making for the standardization of fruit and other agricultural produce are noted in Appendix J, 4.

5. *Costs of marketing may be increased by difficulties of meeting demands for a constant supply of goods of uniform quality, and for supplies varying greatly from one season to another.* II, VI, 5.

The chief place among goods that can be marketed easily and at little expense, belongs to staple products which are not perishable nor dependent on seasons. A steady demand for a thing of uniform pattern and quality enables expensive plant to be set up for its making; to be kept constantly running on an even routine; and to require little contrivance, when once its technical details have been brought nearly to perfection. Under similar conditions we find relatively low expenses for holding and housing stocks, with little waste through depreciation, and without any great tax on forethought or contrivance. Marketing costs are rather low, in regard to things, for which the demand is large and uniform, even though it is concentrated on particular seasons of the year; such as very heavy or very light curtains or underclothing, suitable for winter or summer respectively: the same staff, shop front, and store room will generally serve for both sets.

Manufactured goods of textile materials, leather, metals, wood, etc., not being perishable, can often be maintained in constant supply at no very great cost; especially if they are not bulky; are not in uncertain demand, through changes of fashion or otherwise; and are so far standardized, at all events relatively to the needs of the locality, that the demand for them is not greatly affected by varieties of individual need or taste. Under this head come the common sorts of food and apparel, staple household utensils, the tools of the artisan, the gardener and the farmer; and many other things, which are judged by most purchasers from nearly the same point of view. One will elect the cheaper and another the dearer: but there is a tolerably general, though not a close, agreement as to which would be the more eligible at equal prices. Nevertheless a considerable variety of each of such things must be held by the wholesale dealer, and even by the retail dealer. The retailer's choice is narrowed by local conditions; and the wholesaler follows his lead. For instance, a wholesale dealer's traveller visiting a working class district, will put forward samples or illustrated catalogues,

II, VI, 5. representing things likely to suit the technical work and domestic habits of the place: and the shopkeeper, or his assistant, will know in advance or will quickly divine, the particular sub-class of goods which are likely to attract a particular customer.

On the other hand the highest trade in fine specialities remains, and may long remain, in the hands of men and women who are in a sense artists, and in some cases antiquarians also. Those who supply rare vases and prints to connoisseurs, and the most expensive dresses to the leaders of fashion, must spend much thought over each of their sales; and they seldom care to engage in branches of trade which offer scope for large semi-mechanical organization. A subtler and more delicate, though perhaps not always a higher, form of organization is needed for almost all branches of trade which cater for individual idiosyncrasies, and not merely for the staple requirements of various classes and sub-classes of customers. In some of its branches an alert knowledge of mankind and command of a moderate capital will suffice; but in others some high faculty is needed. In many directions the dominance of large capitals is on the increase, even in these trades.

Electricity cannot be stored conveniently; and, partly for that reason, it is supplied more cheaply for uses chiefly in the daytime, than for lighting, the demand for which reaches high peaks on winter afternoons. In similar case is the imperious demand for accommodation at bracing summer resorts during August, when weather and school arrangements make it specially desirable: and no one complains that the charges at hotels and lodging houses are exceptionally high during that month. But it is not generally recognized that the same reasoning affords a partial justification for the practice of some shopkeepers at such places, who sell more cheaply to residents than to visitors[1].

[1] This practice though equitable is not always expedient. On Swiss railways it would be reasonable, but not expedient, to charge higher fares to those whose demands require specially costly provision for a short summer season. But the difficulty is partially evaded by issuing cheap tickets on various plans, of which advantage can be taken easily by permanent residents, though not by tourists.

The class of questions opened in this Section is further discussed in Appendix J.

6. *Heavy industries seek access to their materials. Light industries, and especially the highest and the lowest of them, seek large cities and their environment. Causes of the enduring hold which an alert centre of industry, handling light products, keeps on its markets.*

See remarked in 1880 that goods of few varieties, which can be sold by portable samples, should always seek the cheapest locality for production; but that factories for those things which are massive and individual should be easily accessible to a multitude of buyers[1]. The buyers whom he had in view were partly middlemen; partly ultimate consumers for business purposes, and especially manufacturers in search of plant. It is important to bear in mind that such purchasers will often go far in order to obtain the things best suited for their purposes: price is never neglected; but it is seldom the primary consideration in regard to plant, which is a main factor in efficient production.

Until well on in the eighteenth century, English iron industries sought the neighbourhood of oak forests, where they used up miscellaneous shallow veins of iron ore: their total iron product was very small[2]. Later on they sought to be near to coal, the heaviest of their materials; and to rich veins of ore, even though lying very deep. But quite recently successive economies in the consumption of coal have lowered the importance of near access to coal mines, relatively to those of easy access to iron ore and to markets for their products. As a result the heavy British steel industries are moving to the sea-coast, or the lower reaches of deep rivers. For there they obtain easily imported ore; and can put much of their product on board ship for exportation, or even into the frame of the ship itself, which is ever more greedy of steel[3].

[1] *Chordal's Letters*, ch. XIV. [2] See above, p. 60.

[3] The American demand for steel products grows so fast, that advantageous sites for steel works can be developed easily. The excellent coke of West Pennsylvania holds them on a long rope, and the Atlantic coast has had little attraction for them; so they have tended towards the Great Lakes. Before the world-war the Lakes carried the chief weight of the American shipping; and they give good access to the ores of Lake Superior. The dependence of Britain on foreign supplies of copper has moved her copper industries to the coast of South Wales.

II, vi, 6. This movement towards the sea is easened by the largeness of the capitals which are invested in a massive industry; for a giant steel firm can set up subsidiary establishments to supply some of its needs. But an industry which does not use massive material, and needs skill that cannot be quickly acquired, remains as of yore loth to quit a good market for its labour. Sheffield and Solingen have acquired industrial "atmospheres" of their own; which yield gratis to the manufacturers of cutlery great advantages, that are not easily to be had elsewhere: and an atmosphere cannot be moved[1].

As we have seen, the high value of land in large cities tends to drive away those branches of production which have been taken over by massive machinery, and especially those which must be accommodated in low wide spreading sheds; though large cities retain some hold of work in which each of many floors of a high building can afford space for a multitude of workers, each tending a machine that does light work. Thus many of them are chief centres of printing, especially for newspapers: and of course they are the chief centres of commerce and finance.

But their industrial specialities are mainly of two kinds. They do nearly the whole of the finest manual work, and especially such as has an artistic element; while of course they use subtle mechanical appliances, where these are serviceable. They also make goods of all kinds, and especially clothes to orders of rich customers, that are conveyed to the producers through a special class of shopkeepers: who themselves do much constructive work in designing; pay very highly for the work they put out; and at the same time make extraordinarily high profits on the turnover.

The other industrial speciality of large cities has been in the past, and is still to some extent, the employment of vast numbers of workers who have inherited weakness of body, mind and character from several generations, that have lived unwholesome lives and overstrained their nerves. The large supplies of labour of this class which the conditions of cities have produced together with those which their great facilities for buying the

[1] In this connection may be compared two instructive monographs:—*The cutlery trades*, by G. I. H. Lloyd; and *The tin-plate industry*, by J. H. Jones.

materials and selling the products that appertain to such industries have attracted, have been a blot on almost every old civilization, and not least that of the modern western world. But better knowledge, especially in regard to sanitary matters; a higher sense of social responsibility; and increasing facilities for cheap traffic even over the whole area of such a city as London (which surpasses in population many considerable States) are tending to lighten the dark shade of this blot, if not to remove it altogether.

In short, personal contact is most needed (1) in trade between allied branches of production, at all events in regard to things which have not yet been brought completely under the dominion of either General or Particular standardization; and (2) in all dealings, especially retail, connected with dress, ornaments and other goods, which need to be adapted to individual requirements and idiosyncrasies. The largest industries, and especially those that need massive plant, are located increasingly in industrial districts; the central cities of which are giving themselves more and more to work directly or indirectly connected with marketing. But the advantages to be derived from personal contact between customer, trader and producer have caused capital cities to become the homes of miscellaneous industries of all grades and especially of high grades; and to offer unrivalled opportunities to middlemen, who procure from working artisans and small masters the making of high-class goods to the order of wealthy customers.

Almost every industrial district has been focussed in one or more large towns. Each such large town, or city, has been at first the leader in the technique of industry, as well as in trade: and the greater part of its inhabitants have been artisans. After a time factories, requiring more space than was easily to be had where ground values were high, tended to the outskirts of the city; and new factories grew up increasingly in surrounding rural districts and small towns. Meanwhile the trading functions of the city developed. Warehouses for the products of the district took the place of factories: shops for the accommodation of the district were enlarged; and banks and mercantile houses of all kinds became prominent. Clerks

II, vi, 6. and travellers on behalf of manufacturers and wholesale dealers multiplied; and artisans ceased to completely dominate the town as of yore.

But later still there has been developed in Lancashire, and to a less extent in other great homes of textile industry, a tendency to take advantage of modern means of locomotion; and to use the central city as the starting point, from which visits can be made to factories suitable for the purposes of a particular buyer, even though they may be somewhat remote from the centre. Thus Manchester is now increasingly sought by representatives of merchants and large dealers of various kinds, who are not content with the conveniences offered even by the great warehouses of the city. They prefer to make rounds over an area of some two hundred square miles, visiting many factories, where they can see displayed in "the piece" varieties of some particular classes of fabric in which they have a special interest; and where they can discuss with the manufacturer himself any suggestions which may occur to them for modifications in detail, to suit their individual judgments, or to meet the special tastes or requirements of localities with which they are connected. Appointments can be made by telephone: and a great distance can be covered in a day by motor car, or even by the almost ubiquitous tramways and railways[1].

We are thus brought back to the suggestion made above that heavy steel industries move readily from one place to

[1] The unrivalled growth of the trade, thus centred in Manchester, owes much to foreign merchants. "The English traveller found it difficult to get in touch with demand; and he could not gauge it as the local merchant could. Consequently, a complete reversal of arrangements took place as regards much of the trade. Foreign houses established offices in Manchester. Every important country, and many unimportant ones, in this way affixed commercial tentacles to the metropolis of the Lancashire cotton industry...and it is now commonly agreed that without the foreign houses in Manchester our foreign trade in cotton textiles could not have grown as it has. The late and uncertain advice received from travellers abroad was infinitely inferior to the instantaneous transmission of foreign demand through Manchester foreign houses with ramified connections in the countries to which they related." Of course there is another side to this and "commercial outposts have been thrown out by English houses all the world over." From an account of the Lancashire cotton industry in *The Times*, 27. 6. 1913.

A little is said below (Appendix J, 5) on peculiar features of the industrial conditions of some capital cities.

another, in order to get better access to their materials; but that an atmosphere is not so lightly to be treated.

The leadership in a special industry, which a district derives from an industrial atmosphere, such as that of Sheffield or Solingen, has shown more vitality than might have seemed probable in view of the incessant changes of technique. The explanation is perhaps to be found in the fact that an established centre of specialized skill, unless dominated by a gild or trade-union of an exceptionally obstructive character, is generally in a position to turn to account quickly any new departure affecting its work; and if the change comes gradually, there is no particular time at which strong incitement is offered to open up the industry elsewhere. It is to be remembered that a man can generally pass easily from one machine to another; but that the manual handling of a material often requires a fine skill that is not easily acquired in middle age: for that is characteristic of a special industrial atmosphere. Thus, although even a little obstinacy or inertia may ruin an old home of industry whose conditions are changing; and although the opening out of new sources of supply or new markets for sale may quickly overbear the strength which old districts have inherited from past conditions: yet history shows that a strong centre of specialized industry often attracts much new shrewd energy to supplement that of native origin, and is thus able to expand and maintain its lead. Even the changeful conditions of America show a surprising permanence of many localized industries, which have sprung up almost by accident, and have been maintained in this way[1].

[1] It has already been noticed (I, VIII, 4) that in spite of the constant westward movement of the population of the United States, the influence of inherited manual skill in sustaining a local industry is shown by the fact that six of the fifteen industries which were highly localized in 1900 were very late in making use of machinery.

It may be added that accidents, such as the arrival in times far back of energetic artisan immigrants, have founded industries, which have maintained their preeminence till now, under conditions just described: all these industries handle light and valuable products which will bear carriage easily, and have little occasion for expensive plant. Thus, according to the Census for 1900 Gloversville and its neighbourhood, which produce half the leather gloves of the country, owe their skill to some Scotch glovers who settled there in 1760: Troy had a practical monopoly of detached collars; as the result of the enterprise of a working woman about 1830. Similar, though less extreme cases are those

II, VI, 6. A certain limitation is however imposed on a narrowly localized industry which sends its products for sale over a large territory. For they must be either such as are in general use and not very changeful in character; or such as can be efficiently represented by illustrated catalogues, or in the large packages sent out to wholesale and retail dealers through travelling agents. This resource is indeed well within the grasp of a powerful firm: for that can advantageously supply for itself many things, which smaller firms buy from subsidiary local industries: but when once an industry has fallen for the greater part into the hands of producers on a very large scale, there is on the balance a tendency to a loosening of the ties that bound it to its old home.

of hosiery at Cohoes; of cheap jewelry at Attleboro; of fur hats at Danbury and Bethel.

CHAPTER VII

PROBLEMS OF GENERAL MARKETING CONTINUED: MASSIVE RETAIL TRADE

1. *Massive retail trade is commonly associated with eager forms of competition. But some of its methods were pioneered by workmen's cooperative societies, in which the spirit of brotherhood strengthened the policy of economy.* II, VII, 1

Modern massive retailing is in some respects a counterpart to massive production. But it was pioneered by cooperative trading: which owes relatively little to massive production; and scarcely anything to the faculties of trained men of business of the new world, or even of the old. It is almost exclusively the work of British working-men: it has perhaps narrower limitations than are recognized by its more ardent adherents; but it will be found to have led the way, in a larger degree than appears at first sight, to much that distinguishes present modes of retail marketing from those that prevailed until quite recently.

The founder of cooperation was Owen: he was, on the one side, a brilliant practical business genius; and, on the other, a passionate enthusiast for the improvement of human character as an end in itself, and as the means to an increase of well-being. Numerous small cooperative societies were formed under his inspiration; chiefly as experiments that made for communistic production, with common ownership of the land as the pivotal idea: the cooperative congresses of 1831—2 were rich in social ideals, though lacking in sense of proportion.

But a little later some Rochdale weavers realized that the most wasteful and ill-managed business of the country was that of marketing goods to the working classes: and that, if those

II, VII, 1. classes perceived the bearing of social ideals on that particular piece of bad business, they would have the remedy in their own hands: their social faith could hold them together in business, and their business would give material strength to their faith. Their fundamental notions were to club together small sums—£5 each as a minimum—on which they might begin business: to charge the average retail prices of a working-class district, which were high; and to use the excess of receipts over costs as the basis of further strength. The earlier cooperative societies had desired that all funds subscribed should at once become common property: but the Rochdale weavers recognized that human nature was not ready for that; so, after paying interest on capital, and making a liberal contribution to a social and general education fund, the surplus was used as a Dividend. That is, their surplus was divided among the members in proportion to their purchases. It was a clever contrivance for the reduction of retail prices to reasonably low levels, without running the risk of failure, which might have been brought about if they had started with prices so low as to leave no margin for unfortunate accident. The plan seemed small and even petty from the standpoint of the rich trader: but its combination of idealism and common sense has led the way to large improvements in marketing, some of which have indeed been reached by other routes: but it appears as a whole to stand without a rival in the history of trade.

The Rochdale weavers and their immediate followers gathered men and women into their fold, partly by urging that cooperative stores sold only genuine goods; and sold these at wholesale prices, after deducting (when Dividend was reckoned in) little more than the actual costs of handling them by simple people, whose time was charged at about an average artisan wage rate. But the great force, which drew the faithful to come past many brilliant shops to a humble store, was the faith that competition should give way to cooperation: and, though much of the rude eloquence, in which this doctrine was set out, would hardly bear the test of exact scientific analysis, it had a solid kernel: for it meant that the movement was one by the weak to help the weak: that a new comer was to be welcomed, because he wanted help; and not, according to the joint stock company rule, in proportion to the capital which he contributed. By this ethical incitement, even more than by their good business, cooperators were able to attain at once, though on a very small scale, the chief advantages of the twentieth century Universal Provider: their sales were large relatively to their stocks: their turnovers were rapid, and they had no bad debts. This "Rochdale" method was generally adopted, and has long been regarded as the "British" method of cooperative retailing[1].

But as time went on their very success brought to light a weak point in their system. They had organized a particular class of retail trade on the side of selling: but not on the side of buying. So long as their rivals, the shopkeepers, charged the old exorbitant additions to wholesale prices, the stores could make good business without buying well. But a new race of

[1] "The ideals of the earlier Cooperative congresses" and the rules of the Rochdale Pioneer Society, supplied by representatives of the Cooperative movement to the Labour Commission 1894, were printed in the *Appendix to the Evidence before the Commission as a Whole.* The exceptionally strong international literature of Cooperation is indicated at the end of C. R. Fay's *Cooperation at home and abroad*; which is itself a clear and well-balanced account of principles and practice alike.

A few more details may be added here. As soon as it was practicable, the Stores reduced the contribution necessary for membership to £1: and some of them now allow a new member to start with a first payment of half-a-crown, making up the remainder out of the Dividend. Though the ordinary procedure of a cooperative store is generally known, it may be well to say that the policy of charging the full current market price and then returning part of it as a share of the profits at the end of the year was adopted, with the purpose, which has been accomplished, of attaining several ends. The policy moderated, though it did not quench, the opposition of local shopkeepers: it avoided discussion as to the prices which could be safely charged: and it diminished the strain on the simple working-men, who were serving an apprenticeship to a difficult business. It further afforded a small inducement to continue purchasing at the store, and persuade others to join it; because everything that quickened the turnover of the store, added to the profits which (after deducting interest on capital subscribed and borrowed) would be available for paying Dividend. And there was yet another and a higher motive: the working classes then, even more than now, were apt to get into the habit of living from hand to mouth; so that they lacked the power to buy outright a solid piece of furniture, or a useful implement. The Dividend has taught hundreds of thousands to know the pleasure of possessing two or three sovereigns, free from any mortgage. This motive operates still; though in this richer age, the Dividend is often applied to defray the expenses direct and indirect of a summer holiday at the sea-side. The Dividend relieves many anxieties of the sick-room: and nearly £100,000 are spent by the Stores annually on education.

II, VII, 1. alert shopkeepers came on the scene; who watched and copied cooperative methods of selling good things cheaply for cash, thus leaving the improvident customer to those of the old-fashioned shopkeepers who still remained. In order to compete with these new rivals, the cooperators had first to learn how much harder a task it was to buy well than they had thought: and then to face the difficulty that the affinities and sympathies of wholesale dealers lay with the "regular" retail trade. So they decided to extend the cooperative principle to wholesale purchases. In the course of time the English and Scottish "Wholesale Cooperative Societies" were set up. They have gradually developed many branches of production. They manufactured in 1913 about eight million pounds' worth of goods: and their total sales, exclusively to retail cooperative stores, amounted to about forty million; that is, about half the total sales of those stores. These Wholesale Societies are owned by retail cooperative societies, to which they sell at current wholesale prices; while the greater part of the excess of receipts over costs, after deducting interest on capital, is returned to those societies as a Dividend on purchases. But the Scottish Wholesale gave till recently a share of the profits on its productive departments to the workers in them[1].

[1] The Society which is now called the English Cooperative Wholesale Society, was founded in 1864, twenty years after the present model of cooperative retailing had been set up at Rochdale; when the total sales of the retail stores were under three million pounds. The cooperative movement is strongest, relatively to population, in Scotland. Ireland is notable for the new vigour of cooperation in dairying, to which reference has already been made. There are also many independent cooperative societies for production; which maintain "Copartnership," under which the workers, as workers, have a share in the control of the work as well as in profits. This high ideal is rejected by the English Cooperative Wholesale, which treats its employees in the same way as a joint-stock company does: the workers in one of its factories have no control over the policy of that factory beyond that which falls to every one of the more than two million members of the retail stores who own the Wholesale. There are many who regard this action as out of harmony with the fundamental principle to which the cooperative movement owes its success: they argue that even though there be some immediate commercial gain in it, it yet is akin to the selling of a birthright for a mess of pottage. In 1892, the able and zealous chairman of the English Wholesale, when asked whether the policy, if complete, would not result in putting all the industries of the country into the hands of Government officials; so that a worker would have no more control over the conduct of the business, in which he was engaged, than the worker in a Government factory has now, replied:—"To a large extent

2. *Some remarks on the strength and the limitations of cooperative trading.* II, VII, 2.

The managing committees of the cooperative societies on the Rochdale model, and of their Wholesales, are for the greater part working-men: and, though they now pay rather high salaries to a few expert officials, their total expenditure on management is far below the aggregate of the incomes (exclusive of interest on capital and insurance against risks) of the owners and officials of private businesses with an equal aggregate of marketing and production. And yet goods made or imported by cooperative methods, and retailed by the same, are not sold conspicuously cheaper (deduction from full prices being of course made on account of Dividends) than similar goods, made and handled avowedly on commercial principles by those "regular" retailers, who give no credit, and confine themselves—as the cooperative stores mainly do—to goods which are marketed easily with a quick turnover.

This result falls somewhat below the sanguine expectations of those, who had thought that the profits of wholesale and retail trade, even under the severely competitive conditions of modern times, left a huge margin over costs; and that therefore an organization which controlled the production of one half of the things which it sold, and bought the remainder wholesale from primary sources, could sell without loss at prices which (Dividend being reckoned in) would be very much lower than those of the regular retail trade. But some at least of the causes, which have prevented that result from being achieved, are now well understood.

To begin with, the giant fortunes, that are made both in production and trade by some men of exceptional genius, impress the imagination: but yet, when such fortunes are added

it would tend in that direction, and the sooner the better." (*Evidence before Labour Commission as a Whole*, Q. 287—290.) In 1913 the work-people employed in the productive departments in the Wholesale numbered less than 16,000: showing an output per head of over £800: this is due to the fact that the work consists largely of flour milling and other work in which very little value is added to the product. Many retail societies have productive branches: but the trades of the butcher and the baker are prominent among them; and consequently they show a large gross output in proportion to work done. See *The Story of the Cooperative Society* 1863—1913, by P. Redfern.

II, VII, 2. together, they are a very small percentage on the total capitals that have been invested in their several branches of business. The returns on large parts of those capitals have been but moderate, while other large parts have disappeared through losses: but those who fail are lost to sight[1].

Next, an army commanded by a committee, has seldom given a good account of itself. Many decisions in the course of business require prompt action, based in large part on intuition associated with reason: the time and strain, involved in proving to other members of a committee that the best course is not that which appears best at first sight, are very great; and only a man who possesses the rare combination of fine and sensitive insight with a strong and even rugged character, is likely to persist and succeed in his efforts to bring a committee composed of ordinary men round to his point of view[2].

Lastly, every successive step in the marvellous progress of the cooperative movement has tended to weaken the relative strength in its counsels of those in whose breasts the original cooperative faith is cherished. It is becoming more and more a huge business managed by men, many of whom are of high natural ability, though few of them have had extensive business training. Its problems are approaching to those of ordinary

[1] The average rate of profits of small shopkeepers is to be found by deducting the aggregate of the capitals that have been lost in the trade from the aggregate profits of those who survive; and dividing the remainder by the aggregate capitals which have been brought into the trade by those who survive and those who have failed. The result thus obtained is on a fair basis for comparison with the profits of cooperative stores made out on a similar plan: but in fact the failures among them are almost negligible.

[2] The Committees of cooperative societies have some privileges as to attendance, with expenses paid, at congresses and other meetings: and sometimes a Committee man who has had his share of them, makes room on democratic principle for another: he thus goes out of office, just when he is beginning to get an expert grasp of its work. The standard of duty is probably a good deal higher among active cooperators than among almost any other non-professional body of nearly equal size; but yet those who are responsible for their purchases are offered bribes, sometimes direct and sometimes indirect, by agents of large mercantile houses. No doubt bribes are seldom accepted; but the difficulty of ascertaining whether they are or not causes friction, and prevents the buyers from acting with that full freedom, which is allowed to his buyers by a strong business man: for he knows that they know that any tortuous dealings of theirs are likely to be soon detected. It is true that joint stock companies and Government Departments share some of these difficulties: but that is another story.

trade in their general character: and though they have taught, and are teaching, some great lessons—especially in relation to the importance of cash payments and a quick turnover—yet many of these lessons are assimilated by alert traders: and thus cooperators find themselves opposed by their own weapons in the hands of keen combatants. There are no doubt exceptions to this rule: but they seem to be of minor importance with one exception.

That exception is that, although the English Cooperative Wholesale Society has been charged by some cooperators, with a lack of adequate sympathy with independent "Copartnership" productive societies; yet on the whole, cooperative trade spends little on advertisement. On the other hand, some sorts of private retail trade are spending lavishly on competitive advertisements, most of which waste much of their force in neutralizing the force of rivals. In America, where they have been developed with more energy and inventive force than anywhere else, it has been said recently by a high authority that it is to the field of cooperative trading on the British plan, which shuns advertising in all its forms, that Americans "may look for very important developments of retail trade within a comparatively few years[1]." Cooperation has not done the impossible: but it has rendered, and is rendering, noble service to the British people.

3. *Other developments of massive retail trading. Grands Magasins, and Department-stores: Multiple-shop Companies, and Chain-stores.*

In 1866, shortly after the foundation of the English Cooperative Wholesale Society, the success of the working-men's cooperative movement prompted some members of the British Civil Service and the British Army and Navy to adopt the name, a considerable part of the method, and a very small part of the principles of the Rochdale stores. The founders were groups of fellow workers, without technical knowledge of retail trade, who cooperated in providing for all willing members of that group a supply for cash of things

[1] Cherington, *Advertising as a business force*, p. 203.

II, VII, 3. similar to those handled by the workmen's stores, of good quality, and at a low advance on wholesale prices. *Esprit de corps*, combined with the commercial benefits offered, brought customers past hundreds of shops suitable for their purposes to an unattractive building in a quiet street. Though free use was made of printed catalogues, etc., nothing was spent on advertisements. Thus in several respects the method was "cooperative."

But after a time they and other "cooperative" stores founded on similar lines, became in effect "Universal Providers" or "Department-stores," worked by joint stock companies, and deriving a moderate profit on their capital from cheap cash sales to almost anyone who applied for membership. The minute element of the cooperative spirit, with which they had started, had evaporated: but they continued to be an obstacle to any attempts at anti-social combination among retailers.

Meanwhile the alert and prosperous population of Paris had offered an excellent market for good ordinary commodities, sold cheaply at cash prices, with but little trouble to the purchaser. Probably English cooperative experience had some influence in moving the founders of the "Bon Marché" and the "Louvre" (about 1852) to develop two unpretending businesses into what soon came to be known as "Grands Magasins." There was much genuine philanthropy in their administration; but they were frankly competitive[1].

France is thus the original home of Department-stores, and they have prospered in Britain, Germany and other countries. But their methods and their potentialities are congruous with American character and conditions, both economic and geographical; and their most notable developments belong to the New rather than the Old World. Some American Department-stores have attracted custom by methods not altogether admirable. But the chief of them appear to have recognized the principle that, though a giant store can, and must, use many expensive means for making its claims known, its best resource

[1] It appears that most of the Grands Magasins were originally connected either with linen drapery, etc. or with furniture; and after increasing the number of branches of those trades which they represented, gradually went out into diverse trades. In the English cooperative societies on the other hand groceries have generally taken a chief place, if not the first.

is in that highest form of advertisement, which comes from the recommendations of one customer to another; and from the inducements which dealings with one department offer to dealings with another[1].

A vast store has many large economies in administration and in buying. It saves especially in ground-rent: for a single first-rate frontage on a good thoroughfare serves as an introduction to many acres of flooring, well lighted from the centre and sides. It does not need to keep a sufficient staff in each department to meet exceptional demands; for some employees are so trained as to be serviceable in each of several departments: each of its motor vans can deliver parcels containing purchases from several departments: and so on. It saves also in buying: for the quickness of its turnover and its general strength make its credit good; and it is able to obtain at least as favourable terms as an ordinary wholesale dealer from the producers, whether the goods are made under contract to a special order or not. But, as the head of a Department-store has a specially large range of marketing to handle, he should not, in Mr Wanamaker's opinion, become a manufacturer himself[2].

[1] Some of them claim to act up to the rule that no small gain should be sought through action, that tends to cause complaint; and that every doubtful question between a customer and a department, shall be decided in favour of the customer: no one is to be persuaded into an unwilling purchase. And a new principle is being adopted by some stores with the highest ambitions, that as a rule no new department shall be opened, till provision can be made for as high-class control and stock as those of "the average exclusive stores" of a similar scope. (See Mr Wanamaker's testimony before the Industrial Commission in 1899, *Report,* vol. III. 454.) The testimony of witnesses for and against Department-stores, gave a full view of the situation: its drift is set out clearly in the official Digest (pp. 17—27).

The economies of time and trouble, and the general conveniences which are offered to customers by the largest retail businesses in London, and on still larger scales in some American cities, may appear to be merely trivial: but in fact they are exercising a considerable influence on the structure of business. Commodious lifts and moving staircases enable a customer to visit without effort or loss of time the equivalent of a large number of different shops.

[2] On the other hand, Mr Selfridge, an American who has set up a mighty Department-store in London, gives (*Romance of Commerce,* 1917, p. 366) a chart of an ideal dry-goods store, which includes a considerable Production Department. He says (p. 365) that an American store already has sometimes fifteen storeys, with two million square feet of flooring, connected by between one and two hundred lifts. He remarks (p. 377) that "window displays are designed, constructed and actually dressed in the studios before they are placed in the windows. They often require months of study, and months of execution."

II, VII, 3. A Department-store may indeed be hampered by the need of numerous checks and counter-checks, which are obstructive in many ways. But a group of men, or even a single man of great energy and insight into character, can dispense with some and make short cuts in regard to others: and so great are its opportunities in the hands of an exceptional genius, that it sometimes rises with meteor-like rapidity and splendour. Experience does not suffice to show how far it may generally be able to obtain adequate successors to those who have created its position and its fame. But, so great is the attractive force of a well-established massive business, that it may continue long to keep most of the ground which it has gained, even in the hands of men of no great initiative; provided they are careful to watch the signs of the times, and to avail themselves promptly and generously of any strong mind with a large imagination, that may be found among their subordinates. While they beat steady time, others will follow in the steps of their own predecessors. New Department-stores, slight variants from the old, will arise: and, unless some new capabilities are shown by the small shopkeeper, the scope for his usefulness seems likely further to dwindle[1].

A Department-store sets itself to concentrate in one place opportunities for the satisfaction of innumerable wants of customers scattered over a wide area: and thus develops by purely commercial force one of the chief purposes which the Rochdale store set itself to attain by a combination of commercial and ethical force. Retail stores cooperate with one another in establishing and controlling a wholesale centre, from which they draw their resources: and their lead in this respect may be said to be followed and surpassed in regard to particular branches of retail trade by "Branch-shop Companies" or "Chain-stores"—the second great group of massive organizations of retail trade on purely competitive lines. For they

[1] But it is thought that "regular" retailers still hold six-sevenths of the whole of the trade of America (Cherington, *l.c.* p. 20). Department-stores and other large businesses have developed a large "mail-order" trade, with distant customers; and thus supplemented the ordinary retail trade of a great part of the United States, and in a less degree of other countries. But though the volume of this business would have seemed incredible not long ago, it is small relatively to that of the total retail trade of country districts and small towns.

aim at bringing near to the doors of vast numbers of customers in different parts of the same town, in small towns, and even sometimes in rural districts, the attractions of a prompt supply of fresh goods delivered from great central reservoirs, with the smallest possible handling by middlemen.

Such a company buys on the most advantageous terms direct from the producer or importer; it sometimes owns factories or at least makes contracts for the delivery of large quantities of goods; and perhaps it imports directly from abroad, or even owns plantations for tea or other commodities. Decisions as to what things shall be bought, and how they shall be priced are made by the central control, with high-class expert assistance. The accounts of each separate shop, including statements of its stocks of all important things, are at the central office. Comparisons of the accounts of various shops will show which are efficiently managed; and will afford an answer to vain excuses; though, of course, allowance must be made for the different facilities for marketing of each individual shop, for the general conditions of its neighbourhood, and especially for any severe competition that it may have to meet, and so on. The activity of the head of each shop, and perhaps of his assistants, is stimulated by the establishment of some sort of connection between their salaries and their sales. Lastly, stock, which does not sell well in one locality, can often be marketed without loss when transferred to another[1].

Appeal is sometimes made by small retailers for sympathy on the ground that the percentage of people who are called on to use their own initiative in one of these great magazines is relatively small; and that the routine and mechanical checks, which occupy the greater part of the employees, are not as conducive to the formation of a strong and enterprising national character, as are the risks and excitements of a multitude of

[1] See some suggestive facts and analyses by Cherington, *l.c.* pp. 171—196. It appears that in 1914 there were in Philadelphia 1260 grocery stores belonging to nine chain-companies. It may be added that in America and elsewhere some independent retailers have grouped themselves into chain-stores for the purpose of buying large quantities wholesale on favourable terms; thus moving very much on the lines of the numerous cooperative societies which peasants and small farmers have formed in Central Europe and elsewhere for buying feeding stuffs, manures, and farm stores generally.

II, VII, 4. independent retailers. Some weight may be conceded to this appeal, in spite of the facts that the occupation of the retailer gives little scope for the highest constructive effort, and does not create cumulative progress in the same way as does the best work of the manufacturer; and that therefore combinations, which sustained the retailer's profit above what would be adequate if his time were well occupied, cause social waste[1].

4. *Influences on the methods of marketing of goods, "branded" with a mark which conveys a guarantee of quality.*

We are now to inquire whether some considerable changes, economic and social, may not be latent in the apparently insignificant fact that an increasing vogue is being obtained, by goods which are so far standardized, that their character is certified by a trade-mark, or other brand. For it has behind it forces which have taken many branches of manufacture out of the hands of small local producers, and given them over to giant businesses, or to strong centres of localized industry. The direct influence of these brands does not always extend to the ultimate consumer. But the retailer of cutlery or cloth knows that he is safe in selling things that bear certain brands: a trustworthy brand gives the maker a good connection, because it enables the retailer, who uses it, to get a good connection. Few men know the source of the cloth of which their clothes are made: but the tailor knows well that his reputation runs no risk when he recommends a cloth from the pattern book of a particular maker. It is however different in regard to food and medicines: fifty years ago biscuits etc. used to be bought from a neighbouring baker; now they come almost exclusively from giant firms who have established high reputations. And American experience, which pioneers in many matters of this kind, suggests that brands and other trade-marks on things for domestic consumption will ere long become an important factor in the spread of large capitalistic control over industry and life.

[1] A law, which effectively doubled the present charges for cabs, etc., would not make cab-proprietors or cab-drivers permanently more prosperous: but it would very much increase the number of cabs which loitered idly in hope of a fare. Of course the trade in artistic products, no two of which are alike, involves the exercise of high faculties; and it is to the public interest that those who do this work well should be rewarded: but such cases are not numerous.

Whereas till recently the process of obtaining a high public favour for a brand was a slow one, it is often cut short in the modern age. For now a wealthy individual, or an alert joint stock company, sometimes starts at once with the devotion of large resources to setting up the most advanced plant for making a thing which seems likely to meet a general want; together with a vast system of advertising its merits to traders and consumers alike by vigorous, various, and well-planned measures. A little more capital may need to be sunk in selling to dealers at prices which enable the thing to be retailed at a very high rate of profit: but when it has won its way, the dealers can be forced to handle it at a low rate of profit[1].

Branded goods occupied a relatively small place in retail trade in the early days of Cooperation: but they were at once turned to account to attract customers, who might be suspicious of the competency of amateur dealers to make good selections of things which could not be well judged without expert knowledge. So cooperative stores, and some independent retailers who sold a great variety of goods cheaply for cash, were inclined to sell branded goods—as well as sugar, and some other things which many customers commonly supposed themselves able to judge and compare—at prices that barely covered expenses; in order that they might act as "decoys" or "leaders" for other sales. But retailers, who preferred to give credit and charge high prices, were aggrieved. They had little defence against the selling cheaply of those few branded goods, which had already

[1] Another generation may possibly see large extensions of methods, still more or less in an experimental stage, by which slot machines may be made to sell not only standardized goods, but fruit and even the hot dishes of a restaurant, each separate consignment being visible through a glass door when an appropriate coin is put in the slot.

Meanwhile some curious difficulties are rising in regard to the ownership of trade-marks. A merchant sometimes designs a new device, and contracts with a manufacturer to work to it by well-known means; then the product should, as a rule, bear the trade-mark of the merchant. Again a merchant in high repute can sell such things as cutlery, made by unknown men, at higher prices if they bear his name, than if they bear the names of the makers. But sometimes one of these makers develops exceptional ability, and his goods add considerably to the value of the merchant's trade-mark: and he may then wish to claim the merits of his advance: but if he insists on issuing his own name or trade-mark, he will need to begin to build up a connection for himself.

II, VII, 4. so strong a hold on the public, that a refusal to handle them would simply drive away customers. In fact the proprietors of such goods sometimes sell them wholesale at relatively high prices, leaving retail prices to take care of themselves.

But a brand, not yet dominant, might be grievously injured by a general unwillingness on the part of dealers to bring it to the notice of their customers: and the "protection" of branded goods on their way to consumers has been developed by American producers into a fine art. On one side, measures are taken to prevent the goods from being sold in poor condition, and thus bringing the brand into disfavour among consumers: and, on the other, "price maintenance" is enforced on wholesalers and on retailers alike, in order to keep the brand in the favour of traders. Similar policies have been pursued, though perhaps with somewhat less vehemence, in other countries[1].

[1] Anticipating a subject which will hold a large place in Book III, it may be observed that the famous official inquiry into cartels, held early in this century (the *Kartellen Enquête*), was occupied for three days with the profits in the booksellers' trade. On the one side it is urged that the skilled bookseller is something more than a retailer: and that many authors would do better for the world in some other occupation. On the other side stress is laid on the poverty through which many authors have to struggle on their way to work, which cannot in any case bring a considerable monetary reward to either publisher or writer; and which yet is so important to the world that lavish subsidies to it would be well spent, were it not practically impossible to administer them rightly on a large scale, though a little is done in this direction by Universities and Learned Societies. It may perhaps be true that a wise use of the retailer's power of combination might have tended to lessen this social discord, if they handled such books at a lower rate than is demanded on popular literature and reprints of books of which the copyright has expired. But in fact the tendency of combination in this case is to discriminate in the opposite direction. No doubt this action follows the path of least resistance; but none the less is it suggestive as to the social influences of trade combinations.

On the other hand, the publisher often performs important services by taking the high risks of loss on scientific and other high-class books addressed to limited numbers of readers—risks which a young and unknown author often could not carry himself: and the few words of advice which the publisher gives to the young author are often of inestimable value.

The controversy as to the maintenance of a high retailer's profit on branded goods, is closely connected with another as to the expediency of allowing "Grands Magasins" to retail a great variety of goods, which has occupied a good deal of attention in France. See Appendix J, 5 as to some other matters connected with the struggle of small shops for their existence.

5. *The great ability and energy, which have been devoted in America to massive retail trade, tend to lower prices: but they are still rather high.* II, VII, 5.

During the last few decades the prices received by the manufacturers for many goods have fallen in America faster than in the rest of the western world; and they are indeed in some cases the lowest that are known anywhere. But the retail prices of nearly all goods in America (the exceptions are almost confined to a few cases in which there are special local facilities for supply) are higher than in Britain and some other western countries. Important causes of this contrast are to be found in the peculiar physical conditions of the United States and in the racial characteristics of her people. Let us glance back at these.

In the course of the notice of the industrial leadership of the United States in Book I, stress was laid on the great market which the homogeneous demand of her vast population offers for standardized goods made by the most powerful plant, under the guidance of the strongest of brains, and handled in great part by sturdy immigrants. Almost every chief raw material is supplied by Nature on easy terms in some part of her area: and many causes have contributed to enable her railroads to offer low rates per ton-mile for the carriage of massive consignments over large distances. Thus her giant single businesses have increased even more rapidly than her largest cities. Many of the immigrants who work in her mines, steel works, factories, etc., are rather highly paid in comparison with most other western countries: but some classes of them work so hard and for so long hours, that they enable the employer to make the most out of his plant; and, though they may exhaust most of their strength in a comparatively short time, the arrival of fresh immigrants prevents the supply of labour from becoming scarce. Also larger use is made of mechanical power in America than anywhere else. Massive production therefore is nearly always relatively cheap there; and it is in a few cases absolutely cheap[1].

[1] The economies of massive production of men's clothing have been carried much further in America than elsewhere: and it is said that fairly well fitting men's clothes can be bought there at a less advance on the cost of material

II, VII, 6. We have seen how massive production tends to foster massive methods of wholesale and retail dealing; while the low rates for massive freights on American railroads have helped powerful wholesale dealers, department-stores and chain-stores: but, though the rates for such traffic are low per ton-mile, the total charge per ton is kept high by the very great distances, which separate the producer from the average consumer of his goods. More important are the facts that the ordinary American retailer has seldom an old-established business, well supplied with capital relatively to its requirements; that he cannot always obtain advances on easy terms; that he generally belongs to a race and social order in which a much higher average level of incomes prevails than in Europe; and lastly that the temper of nearly the whole American people, including even those of foreign birth, inclines to impatience of assiduous care as to small savings on petty purchases.

Each of these considerations goes some way towards explaining the paradox that the nation, which excels all others in the energy and inventive ability devoted to developing the efficiency of retail trade, is also the nation that pays the most dearly for the services of that trade. But there remains a less obvious cause to be considered: it is that much of the modern expenditure on advertising is not constructive, but combative.

6. *Constructive uses of "advertisement" in that original broad use of the term, in which it includes all measures designed to draw the attention of people to opportunities for buying or selling, of which they may be willing to avail themselves.*

Some of the implements of constructive advertisement are prominent in all large cities. For instance a good frontage on a leading thoroughfare; adequate space for the convenience of

than in England: for since many well-to-do people are willing to buy ready-made clothes, the trade in them is of gigantic dimensions, and gives scope for lavish advertising. American "makers and distributors of trade-marked clothing, who spend in some cases upwards of half a million dollars a year on publicity," find their "selling cost per suit less now than before they began advertising. They manufacture and market suits by the hundred thousand"; and they thus even reduce their advertising outlay per sale, as well as costs of "buying, manufacturing, selling, and the handling of reserve stocks" (A. W. Shaw, *An approach to business problems*, pp. 204—5).

employees and for customers; lifts and moving staircases, etc., are all constructive, so long as they do not exceed the requirements of the business. That is to say, the assistance, which they afford to customers by enabling them to satisfy their wants without inordinate fatigue or loss of time, would be appropriate, even if the business were not in strong rivalry with others. But eager rivalry often causes them to be carried to an excess, which involves social waste; and ultimately tends to raise the charges which the public have to meet without adequate return.

Again, printed advertisements regarding particular transactions, such as horses for sale, or hire; contracts to be let out; vacancies, etc., have seldom any considerable combative effect. The sending to customers of samples of a special kind of prepared food or other common product is an effective instrument of combat, the use of which is confined to powerful capitalists: but it is of little avail unless the product is approved; and on the whole it is constructive. Similar remarks apply to the sending out by producers or wholesale dealers, of samples in the charge of persuasive travellers. Again, advertisements in trade newspapers; and, especially such as are largely occupied with technical and scientific discussions, are generally terse, explanatory and constructive: though indeed a powerful firm, whose resources and specialities are well known, may sometimes prefer a few words in impressive type, or perhaps a bold illustration, to an explanatory statement: for that cannot be adequate, and yet confined within narrow limits.

Exceptionally constructive are all those measures needed for explaining to people generally the claims of some new thing, which is capable of supplying a great but latent want. If the thing is in small compass, easily handled, and not costly, samples of it can be distributed in various ways. But if it is expensive, and above all if it cannot be adequately handled without considerable training, then people can be fully informed of its usefulness only by seeing it at work. In such a case as that of the typewriter, when first introduced, efficient demonstration is beyond the scope of any but powerful capitalists[1].

[1] When the idea of a typewriter was first conceived, very few people were inclined to take seriously the suggestion that it could rival the pen in efficiency. It could not therefore be sold by mere printed notices: and the retailers of

II, VII 7. *7. Advertisements which are mainly combative generally involve social waste.*

On the other hand the combative force of mere capital obtrudes itself in the incessant iteration of the name of a product, coupled perhaps with a claim that it is of excellent quality. Of course no amount of expenditure on advertising will enable any thing, which the customers can fairly test for themselves by experience (this condition excludes medicines which claim to be appropriate to subtle diseases, etc.), to get a permanent hold on the people, unless it is fairly good relatively to its price. The chief influence of such advertisement is exerted, not through the reason, but through the blind force of habit: people in general are, for good and for evil, inclined to prefer that which is familiar to that which is not.

The lavish advertiser must deduct his expenses from the gross profits of his additional sales: while the rivals whom he

writing materials were not inclined to master its manipulation. The only practicable method therefore was to show it working rapidly in the hands of expert agents throughout the land. This involved vast expense: but it led the way to even vaster gains. For the typewriter, though a complex instrument, belongs to a class which can be brought so completely within the range of mechanical production, that it can be made on a large scale cheaply: and its uses are now so important that some people would pay £100 for one, if they could not get it for less. Thus lavish expenditure on developing a new want, being based on clear foresight, was well justified by its results to the venturers. And, in a broad view of its social results, there is perhaps no very great cause for regretting that the proprietors of the chief patents for the machines have been able by agreement among themselves to maintain (subject to some partial exceptions) for a long while at £20, the price of things, which ere long will probably be sold at little more than their direct cost of production; and that is reported even now not to exceed £5. If a new and perfectly efficient typewriter could have been produced by a moderate outlay, and without infringing the many wide-reaching patents still in force, a great reduction in price might have come long ago: and in this respect the typewriter, though a brilliant, is not a generally representative instance of the commercial success which is to be obtained by creating a new want and meeting it. For the main constructive acts are often confined to discovering the existence of a latent want, and educating the public in regard to it: these being accomplished, a number of independent routes, by which the want may be met, may perhaps be opened out, all about equally good. Indeed experience of the route followed by the pioneer, may itself furnish quickly hints to fresh minds; and thus lead to the discovery of a new route, which is better than his, and is not covered by his patent, though no one would have been likely to find it unaided. In such a case the pioneer bears the chief burden and others enter into his heritage. There is much suggestion on all these matters in Cherington's *Advertising as a business force.*

ousts lose their gross profits, and thus there enters one element of social waste. It is true that his additional sales may slightly lower his costs of production per unit: but in fact nearly all the products, in the advertisement of which iteration has been carried to extravagant excess, offer occupation for many firms each strong enough to command all the chief economies of large scale production. A second element of social waste, caused by bold displayed advertisements, is the relative obscurity into which they are designed to throw, and do throw, the smaller advertisements of less wealthy men; some of whom may have high constructive faculty[1].

In conclusion it should be noted that academic students and professional advertising agents in America have united in applying modern methods of systematic and progressive analysis, observation, experiment, record, and provisional conclusion, in successive cycles to ascertaining the most effective forms of appeal. Psychology has been pressed into the service: the influence which repetition of an advertisement exerts has been subsumed as a special instance of the educative effect of repetition[2].

[1] Large questions are opened up by the consideration of the dependence of newspapers and magazines on receipts from advertisements. They are thereby enabled to provide a larger amount of reading matter than would otherwise be possible: but this influence does not work wholly for good. In the United States, £50,000,000 a year are estimated to be spent on advertising in newspapers; and £70,000,000 on other kinds of advertising: one periodical received on a long contract £800 for each use of its back outside page. One French house sends out £20,000 worth of patterns of dress materials annually.

[2] The task is more difficult than appears at first sight. It has indeed been shown that test experiments in regard to different modes of advertising a particular product, may be of much service in regard to that product. But the attainment of trustworthy general results seems yet far off. For instance, a number of notices, some on full page, others on half and quarter pages, were set before a group of observers; and the results indicated that the larger notices impressed the eye more strongly in proportion to their size than the smaller ones did. (Munsterberg, *Psychology and industrial efficiency*, ch. XX.) But the indication seems to be inconclusive. For instance, if a person is in need of some particular thing, such as an aid to imperfect hearing, or a folding chair suitable for travelling, his eye is likely to be arrested by even a short notice of it. In such a case small advertisements in many periodicals are likely to give better results relatively to a few displayed advertisements than is suggested by such a test. An excellent account of laboratory study in such matters is given in A. W. Shaw's *Approach to business problems*: and there is much to a similar effect in Cherington, *l.c.*

CHAPTER VIII

BUSINESS ORGANIZATION: THE GROWTH AND INFLUENCE OF JOINT STOCK COMPANIES

II, VIII, 1. 1. *Some of the modern problems of administration on a large scale were anticipated long ago by private and corporate owners of great estates: though they did not often need to balance their incomings against their outgoings closely. The fiduciary element in corporate administration.*

Recent chapters have been concerned mainly with the external relations of a business to other businesses, and to consumers of its products or services: we now pass to consider modern developments of the internal relations of a large business, with special reference to its administration, whether under individual or joint stock control. Several suggestions in recent chapters have pointed towards the growing need for progressive detailed study as a means towards the efficient and economic conduct of business: and the last chapter of this Book will be occupied with applications of such study, to measure the economic efficiency of various methods of working. They can claim at present only a very partial success: and yet they have attained in some directions to a degree of accuracy, which, though far from ideal perfection, is yet much in excess of what appeared practicable in tasks so large and complex even a generation ago. But this tendency of business administration will not come into view in this chapter or the next two: they will be occupied mainly with matters specially relating to joint stock association; to finance; and to the faculties and resources which are required of the head of a large business and its chief officers, in regard both to the general scheme of the business, and to the control of its subordinate employees.

But before settling down to our main task there may be

some interest in considering how far the problems of administration of the present age differ in essential character from those of earlier times. Their forms are certainly far apart: but perhaps they differ in substance less than appears at first sight.

Let us look at the business side of the functions of a great landed proprietor, and especially of one who has no easy access to the assistance of skilled professional business men equipped with the powerful appliances of modern times. Like a mediaeval baron or abbot, he is called upon to carry responsibilities as a capitalist undertaker and as an employer of labour, which may fairly be compared with those of the heads of very considerable businesses in the modern world. He must indeed look far ahead, estimate chances and balance risks when he decides whether to invest resources in (say) opening out a quarry, or setting up an additional mill: and, subject perhaps to some partial customary rights over persons on his estate, he will need to select those who are to superintend each new undertaking. If he is able, industrious, and alert, he will see that all men are put on work for which they are fit; and that each instrument of his resources is carried up to that margin or limit, at which any further employment of it would be inappropriate. On such an estate, everywhere and in all times, there will be found much delegation of authority, and a rough gradation of the difficulty and responsibility of each man's task: the lower rewards generally going to those whose physical toil is severe; and the higher to those who are called on to exercise discernment, judgment, tact, and a power of bearing responsibility, together perhaps with some modicum of initiative. On the estate, as in the modern business, the extent to which specialization, subordination, and the coordination of faculties and of tasks are carried has varied with the general conditions of the undertaking: but the governing principles will be always the same.

It is indeed true that the organization of a private estate is designed to afford gratification to its owner either directly; or through his friends and others to whose comfort, admiration, and perhaps envy, it contributes. If the arrangement of a stable is pleasing, it can be maintained, though the horses might be cared for equally well on a less expensive plan: if a tree is beautiful, it may be spared, although its trunk is not straight enough to make good timber: and so on. That is to say, although the organization of the private establishment gives scope for that scientific management, which attains a desired end by the least costly means; yet the means themselves are generally a considerable part of the desired end; and the end itself is not expressed in terms of money. It is not therefore under as rigorous a rule of arithmetical balance sheets, as is a modern business, which is closely run by competitors working for the same market with similar resources: but the differences between the two are not fundamental.

A somewhat similar freedom from the yoke of an exact balance sheet seems to have been enjoyed by those great merchants of early times, whose financial strength enabled them to gain increasing profits with ever increasing ease, so long as strength lasted and fortune favoured. The power of a Fugger, or even a de la Pole or a Canynge, controlled the fate of monarchs and of nations: and so vast, relatively to the aggregate movable wealth of Europe at the time, were the gains which resulted from their larger transactions, that they had little occasion to spend strength on petty economies. Although there was but little trustworthy information of distant affairs, beyond what could be obtained only at great cost and slow speed from private agents and correspondents, a few of them grasped the main threads of most of the chief business problems of Western Europe.

Even those features of large modern business, which are chiefly associated with joint stock ownership and control, were in some measure anticipated by the administration of powerful monasteries; and of other bodies in which the individual had no exclusive dominant rights. It will be seen presently that the partial supersession of individual by joint stock enterprise has not changed the problems of business administration very greatly. But it has introduced a distinct new element into those problems, as to which a little must be said. Many corporate bodies of to-day, and especially colleges at Oxford and Cambridge, retain much of the spirit of old religious houses. The official Head, if a strong man, has great power; as has the

Chairman or President of a great joint stock company: and as a rule every member of the Governing Body cares for the future efficiency and prosperity of the deathless corporation with nearly the same zeal as if it were his own property. Much of this traditional uprightness of purpose and fine ambition is found among the directors of joint stock companies: the purity of their motives is seldom much influenced by the extent of the pecuniary interests which they and their heirs have in its well-being; though it is true that their active zeal, and the time which they devote to its affairs, in preference to their private affairs, is apt to be influenced by the extent of their interest in the company.

Here it may be observed that the directors of a company are, strictly speaking, employees of it. Except in so far as they are themselves shareholders, they run no risks from its failure, beyond some loss of prestige; and a possible loss of employment, which they share with other employees. The shareholders bear the risks, but delegate nearly the whole of their functions, as owners of the business, to the directors and other employees. But in practice the directors, even though they own but a small part of the shares, are seldom displaced unless they have made grave errors: thus they may be regarded as "the head" of the company, in the sense in which decisions on large issues connected with a business belong to its "head"; though he may delegate decisions on minor issues to subordinates. Of course the directors of a company, like the partners in a private business, often share out among themselves the main control of particular groups of these issues, the collective meeting remaining the ultimate authority in large matters. But more of this hereafter.

2. *The growth of the legal freedom and of the inclination to develop businesses in joint stock: their paramount influence on economic structure.*

It is indicated elsewhere that the term "Joint Stock Company" has had many different connotations in different stages of the world's history[1]. In early times it meant little more than association of a few members of the same family, or a few

[1] See above, p. 36: also Appendix C, 3, and Appendix D, 3.

II, VIII, 2. neighbours having intimate knowledge of one another, who united their resources, or parts of them, for some venture. As a rule the venture was one which required a larger capital than any one of them possessed; or else it involved risks, the whole burden of which was too great for any one of them. Especially were companies needed for many tasks which in modern times are generally recognized as belonging to Government; though the recent development of Rhodesia has been effected for the greater part by a company, which worked with special privileges reminiscent of those of the great Joint Stock and Regulated companies.

The founders of those companies were for the greater part merchants, directly cognisant of the nature of the work to be done: and for a long while the supreme control of the business of each company was largely under the supervision of experienced men of affairs, who owned a great part of the capital: even late in the eighteenth century the great East India Company was chiefly owned by about eighty men, many of whom were in close touch with its administration. It might have been expected that joint stock administration would have spread over English business in the eighteenth century: but several causes retarded its progress.

A chief cause was the misuse of joint stock machinery in the "Bubbles" period (1700—1720). It evoked a law, under which the privilege of trading in joint stock could be obtained only by special charter. So associations abounded that were called "companies," but had no legal status as such. As each member of such a company was liable for all its debts, a prudent and responsible man was unwilling to take a share in it, even though it afforded reasonable prospects of high gains; unless he knew enough of his fellow members to be sure that he would not have to bear a great part of the burden in case of failure. Under the influence of this law only those businesses, which were sufficiently important to obtain private charters, were open to legal recognition in England as joint stock companies: the rigour of the rule was relaxed in 1825 and again in 1844; but the full privilege of Limited Liability was not made general till 1862[1].

[1] The law of Scotland was more liberal than that of England. A common

It has been generally agreed that the vehement fury of speculation during most of the eighteenth century in the few stock exchange securities which were accessible, indicates that the time had not arrived at which more gain than loss was likely to arise from opportunities offered to the general public to hand over the control of their capital directly to businesses, of which they had no personal or technical knowledge. No objection was taken to direct mortgages on real property; which long remained a chief, if not the chief, investment of small funds. But, especially when industry was unsettled by the introduction of new methods, and unknown men were rising rapidly to the front, it seemed to be to the general advantage

partnership could by the law of France obtain many of the advantages of Limited Liability: for the responsibility of a sleeping partner, often a retired member of the firm, who took no share in its application, could be limited, by due announcement, to his share of the capital. Mill strenuously advocated the introduction of this principle of *en commandite*: and many of his arguments still remain valid.

The history of early crises has been much advanced in Prof. W. R. Scott's *Joint Stock Companies to* 1720. Attention was called by Rogers to the violent fluctuations of the prices of stock in *The first nine years of the Bank of England.* Adam Smith regarded banking as eminently suitable for joint stock control: but he had in view the excellent management of local affairs by the joint stock banks of Scotland: and their task was relatively easy, because connection with England enabled them to have nearly all the advantages in regard to foreign trade of an expensive gold basis for their currency; while they turned to the account of themselves and their customers the right of issuing paper money, which a more exacting Government might have claimed for itself. However their splendid work, and the reckless misconduct of many private English banks early in the nineteenth century, forced the door to open for joint stock banks in England: and curiously enough the English banking system has developed on lines, in which routine has a larger place than in that of any other great commercial country. But this runs beyond our present subject.

It may however be relevant to note at once that the Bank of England has gradually led the way towards a management of financial difficulties, which is a pattern for the world: and that its best strength has been derived from directors, who have not been mere nominees of its own shareholders, but have in effect represented the chief business houses of London. It has been the leader; and there has been a continuous independent movement upwards, in regard to the management of the financial affairs of the country, especially in regard to joint stock company ventures. The joint stock companies mania of 1825—6 was far less wild than the South Sea and the Mississippi Bubbles in England and France early in the eighteenth century: and, when an underestimation of the costs of developing the English railway system led to another grievous crisis twenty years later, the credit given was found to have been less intemperate than in 1826. Since then, there has been no crisis as intense, and extending to so large a proportion of the business of the country.

II, VIII, 2. that bankers and other professional dealers in command over capital should act as intermediaries. So they lent, mainly at their own risks, the command over capital, deposited with them, to such manufacturers and others as seemed to them able and trusty: the people were shy of investments in businesses beyond their immediate ken.

The expansion of joint stock companies has resulted in the general democratization of the ownership, as distinguished from the control, of business. England was the only country fully ready for such a democratization on a large scale in the first half of the nineteenth century: and there was gain as well as loss in her being withheld from making the experiment till education and the new means of obtaining information about distant events had rendered the venture comparatively safe.

The concession of Limited Liability to any seven persons, who chose to pay a small fee and register themselves as a company, was made in a law so crudely worded as to invite the most inexperienced and poverty stricken rogues to use it as a means of plundering the public: and the reports of the Board of Trade on the winding up of companies contain many ludicrous tales of petty misdoing by methods which are not yet wholly estopped. But they never covered much of the business of the country; and they are now rare.

Next, we may consider some influences on the substance and on the wording of economic doctrine, which arise from the extension of joint stock company control over a great part of the business of all western countries. Let us look back a little. Not very long ago the representative firm in most industries and trades was a private partnership; which in the course of one or two generations had attained a goodly reputation, of a personal and individual character. Its plant had become larger and more various, until it commanded all, or nearly all, those economies of production on a large scale, that were inherent in the most advanced methods then known for its particular branch of business. Its own (Internal) economies were not great: but it took its part in affording a large market for firms in branches of manufacture, which supplied it with made or half-made materials: and in developing (External) economies of general organization, which gradually became common property. Thus each firm, though of moderate size, might reasonably hope to obtain most of the advantages in production, which would be accessible only to vast businesses, if each had been mainly dependent on its own resources. Under these conditions, a very large capital in the aggregate was distributed over many firms of moderate size, each with its own individual life, its own power of initiative, and its own personal relations with its employees. If any firm became slack in enterprise, or weak in purpose, it passed away and made room for others, with but little disturbance to the industrial organism; just as a forest tree, which has lost its vigour, passes and leaves an opening, through which some strong young plant may shoot up towards the light.

But in the new age joint stock control has become universal in regard to railroads; and it has become general even in regard to manufacturing and other industries, which have an urgent need for alert and versatile administration. In most of these industries a tendency to Increasing Return prevails: that is, an increasing output can generally be produced at a diminishing rate of cost. It is obvious that, under this tendency a firm, which had once obtained the start of its rivals, would be in a position to undersell them progressively, provided its own vigour remained unimpaired, and it could obtain all the capital it needed. In old times there was often much difficulty on this score: but that has diminished greatly during the last three or four generations. It seems therefore that, if there were no other difficulty in the way of the unlimited expansion of a strong manufacturing business, each step that the firm took forwards in supplanting its rivals, would enable it to produce profitably to itself at prices below those which they could reach. That is, each step would make the next step surer, longer and quicker: so that ere long it would have no rivals left, at all events in its own neighbourhood. That condition must of course not be omitted; because the expense of marketing heavy goods at a distance might overbear the economies of large scale production. But for goods, of which the cost of transport is low, and which are under the law of Increasing Return, there might have seemed to be nothing to prevent the concentration in the hands

II, VIII, 3. of a single firm of the whole production of the world, except in so far as it was closed by tarif barriers. The reason why this result did not follow was simply that no firm ever had a sufficiently long life of unabated energy and power of initiative for the purpose. It is not possible to say how far this position is now changed by the expansion of joint stock companies with a potentially perpetual life: but every recent decade has contained some episodes which suggest that it may probably be greatly changed, either in substance, or in the methods by which new life is brought into old bodies.

A private firm without great vigour is sure to die: a large joint stock company has special advantages, many of which do not materially dwindle with age. Its hindrances arising from its routine methods do not increase as fast as the increase in its business, while each step of that increase is likely to give access to new technical economies. And, even if it be somewhat lacking in energy and initiative, it can often utilize (as industrial enterprises under Governmental management habitually do) new ideas and new appliances that have been created by independent workers: and it has special opportunities for the introduction of new blood into its management. It has also this dominating financial advantage, that the salaries, which it pays to its directors and chief managers, are much less in the aggregate than that excess of the profits of a successful private business over the mere interest on its capital, which is required to induce men already wealthy to continue to bear the burden of business.

3. *So wide are the varieties of the arrangements between ownership and control of capital, which are now included under the common name of joint stock association, that almost any class of business can be properly conducted by some one or more of them.*

Every successive decade has brought new developments of the structure of joint stock companies, and their relations with other financial businesses. The chief initiative has come from America. But Germany has contributed much: her legislation in regard to the obligations of the promoters and directors of joint stock companies, if not achieving all that has been claimed for it, has at least indicated a direction in which other countries are likely to move, and have indeed begun to move.

The varieties of joint stock company organization are numerous and plastic: scarcely any business is conceivable which could not be efficiently managed by some one or more of them. When a private firm is thrown into joint stock form, for the convenience of members of the family who are not able and willing to take part in its administration, there is often no real change in its administration: whatever it did well as a private firm, it can continue to do as a company; so long at least as the men at its head are of the same stamp as formerly, and other members of the family do not interfere with them. Again, when a group of wealthy capitalists retain the complete effective control of all the affairs of a company in their own hands, they can act with as much freedom and vigour as if they remained in simple partnership. They may distribute widely among the public preferred shares so arranged as to give no votes; and debenture bonds which of course give none. They may even distribute widely half or two thirds or even more of the ordinary shares: for even two-thirds of them, if scattered in small lots among the public, cannot be brought to bear in a conflict for the control of the company, except by slow preparation: and that can generally be countered in time. There is no sort of business which the Standard Oil Company could not set up, and manage with the freedom of a private firm, if it thought the affair worth the necessary trouble.

The distinctive conditions of joint stock administration come into view only, when the ownership of capital is effectively divorced from its control: so that those, who are in control, have not nearly the same pecuniary interest in its economic and efficient working as they would have, if they owned the business themselves. Its higher officials may watch its lower officials, and its directors may watch its higher officials. But its directors can generally keep their positions by faithful, steady work, without showing special initiative; and they often content themselves with that.

A man of restless constructive force, who finds himself on such a Board, may urge a reorganization of some parts of the

II, VIII, 4. procedure on more advanced lines, or the scrapping of some plant that is no longer in the front rank: but he is not unlikely to appeal in vain, if the change would cause much trouble, suggest some criticism of past management, and be of such a nature that its ultimate pecuniary advantage cannot be proved with absolute certainty. As a separate business man he would make the venture; and, if he were a member of a private firm, he might probably succeed in carrying his partners with him. But the *vis inertiae* of a great company is against him: he can seldom argue the case effectively with numerous scattered shareholders, who do not understand the business. He is therefore inclined to acquiesce, however unwillingly, in the general opinion, that a company, the ownership of whose capital is almost wholly in the hands of the public, must for the greater part adhere rather closely to routine.

For this evil there is a possible remedy; which has been largely adopted in America. The shareholders may decide to give their votes in favour of those who will support the almost autocratic power of some man, or group of men, whom they know to be able, resolute, and perhaps to have a large pecuniary interest in the company. This plan has answered admirably in many cases: but has failed in others. Its success seems to require rather peculiar conditions: and the time has not yet come for a good estimate of the chance that it may prove a generally effective remedy for the malaise to which joint stock companies are liable in their old age.

4. *The obscurity of the affairs of many small companies: the exceptional case of manufacturing companies owned largely by working-men.*

The above considerations tend to show that the ordinary investor can seldom safely buy the shares of a small joint stock business, unless he has personal knowledge of those who control it, or is able to form a sound technical opinion on the manner in which it is being operated. He is therefore, if wise, commonly inclined to seek businesses in which he believes many competent and experienced men hold shares: for then he has some sort of assurance that the manner in which the directors and officials of the company discharge their duties, will be noted by a sufficient number of men, capable of forming a fairly good opinion on it, to give security against grave negligence or malfeasance.

An inexpert small buyer or seller of commodities generally deals at a disadvantage. But the goods of the Stock Exchange are absolutely standardized, to the extent that each security is of the same value as every other of the same nominal amount and the same issue: and the small inexpert purchaser pays almost exactly the same price as anyone else, who buys at the same time. Of course slight exceptions are to be made for dealers, who transact their own business; for powerful capitalists, who make special terms with chosen dealers; etc. But in the main, a small buyer is on the same footing as anyone else, who has the same knowledge and judgment as to the selection of securities to be bought and the time for buying; and information as to a large company is often accessible through the public press. No doubt the strong financier can often obtain early information, partly confidential, as to causes which are likely to alter the price of any security; and he can on occasion take part in strategic combinations for the purpose of moving the price in a direction that will suit his schemes. But yet it is on the whole true that dealings in the securities of large companies tend in the direction of democratizing the *ownership* of capital; while the expansion of private businesses, and to a less extent of companies, tends even more strongly to render the *control* of capital oligarchic.

Attention has already been called to the ability of joint stock companies to dominate the manufacture of staple goods, of which large quantities, alike in every respect, are steadily consumed; especially if the appropriate plant has already advanced so far towards perfection, as to be almost exempt from organic change. Even working-men often have exceptional opportunities for starting and controlling cooperative, co-partnership, and ordinary joint stock undertakings for work, with which they are familiar. Such companies can draw on the specialized knowledge and experience of many operatives, who are themselves at work in the most advanced factories engaged in the same branch of industry, or in others which sell to that branch, or buy from it. And, whereas in a great company, the

II, VIII, 4. shareholders generally pay large salaries to directors, who are expected to bring high technical knowledge to bear in their judgment of the efficiency of its chief officers; these companies, consisting mainly of smaller men, bring much of the requisite knowledge to bear themselves. Their appearance in the midst of our complex modern industrial organism may perhaps help to explain the success of some companies in early times, which seem to have grappled with tasks, that required considerable technical knowledge, without the aid of any elaborate organization[1].

It is to be noted that these companies, and many others of recent origin, issue shares of very small amounts: so that an investor of limited means can increase his holdings gradually, as small savings are made; and he can obtain the advantage, formerly beyond his reach, of distributing his risks rather widely. This change is not without its drawbacks from some points of view: but it suggests developments of economic organization, which the new education and wealth of the working classes may possibly effect ere long.

[1] The following facts are taken from Professor Chapman's *The Lancashire Cotton Industry*; and a paper contributed by him and Mr Marquis in the *Statistical Journal*, 1912. Many cotton spinning factories have been originated by joint stock companies; whereas in most other industries, a new company is generally developed out of a private concern. Cotton spinning, in spite of its simplicity, of course requires a rather large capital; larger for instance than is needed for weaving: therefore profits in it are not cut down much by the competition of rising small men. Good cotton yarns almost sell themselves, and therefore do not demand exceptionally able, alert and enterprising managers: and the simpler qualities are easily tested. Consequently when cooperative spinning-mills have wished to change their constitutions, they have become joint stock companies; whereas cooperative weaving businesses have frequently split up into several distinct private undertakings.

When a new spinning-mill is projected, a large part of the necessary capital is obtained, in an exceptional manner, by loans. They "are nominally at short notice; but they are seldom withdrawn, when their removal would place a business in jeopardy." The rate of interest is very low "because the money is found on the one hand by people, who are engaged in the industry, and feel that there is a real security in contact with everyday experience; and on the other hand by people who are acquainted with local conditions, and to a large extent lend on the basis of personal knowledge."

5. *Temptations of joint stock companies to excessive enlargement of scope.* II, VIII, 5.

Meanwhile there has been a constant increase in the number of people of high principle and sound judgment, who are willing to serve as directors; and among these may be found not a few with good business experience. For indeed in many a large private business the charge of details is assigned to responsible subordinates so fully, that the head need seldom concern himself directly with any but the broader and more fundamental problems; and he is therefore able to give a few hours a week to the service of a railway or other important company. Further, the number of intelligent investors has increased. There are far more people than formerly engaged in business of their own, who yet have spare capital to invest in Stock Exchange securities. Such men often know what information as to the affairs of a company should be demanded: and they exercise a wholesome control over the directors; and over the influences, which unwise or designing shareholders may bring to bear on the directors.

The number of intelligent and upright directors increases. But unfortunately many of them are unable to give the large time and energy needed for obtaining a thorough mastery of the affairs of the companies for which they are responsible: and the chief service, which most of them render to the public, is through their common sense; their power of reading character; and the safeguard which their presence offers against gross fraud or folly on the part of the chief officials, or of a managing director.

This passive uprightness is an important asset: but it does not always compensate for the indolence and blindness of directors, who are accomplices in wrong-doing in this sense that they receive their fees, and yet plead ignorance of matters which a sense of their duty should have caused them to investigate. The Law courts of England, in spite of great recent improvements, appear still to treat this form of wrong-doing too indulgently.

There is one direction in which the extension of its operations by a great company, or by a department of municipal administration, is a source of danger that may be overlooked:

II, VIII, 5. it is that routine work by departments of a large business may expand at the expense of small businesses with greater elasticity and power of origination. The growth of a sense of moral responsibility among the chief technical employees of large concerns may be a partial remedy for this danger: but they cannot always approach a proposal for enlarging an existing department, or starting a new one, without some bias.

That bias shows itself in the tendency of some joint stock companies and municipalities to make things, which it would perhaps have been better for themselves and for others that they should have bought. The temptations in this direction are strong. If the officials can get a free hand in the matter, they enter into the new branch of production with a large capital at their backs. They have no difficulty in absorbing most of the best knowledge that is floating about on the subject. The new department is equipped with the most recent appliances; with the most effective, economical, and labour saving machines. It goes along bravely, wind and stream being with it. It can show a saving on the prices at which the company used to buy the goods now made by it, even after allowing good salaries for those concerned in it. Perhaps some managers with special knowledge of its work will be imported: but many of those engaged in it will be drafted in from other departments, at somewhat increased salaries for themselves; and at the same time making vacancies in their own departments which are filled by juniors. There is a move upwards, and an increase of salaries all along the line, and everyone is pleased. So the movement grows; while a true balance of its advantages and disadvantages is perhaps never made out.

The difficulties arising from the multifarious enterprises of railway and other large companies are sometimes partially overcome by telling off a committee of the directors to be specially responsible for the department; and giving them a free hand in all changes that do not vitally affect the general, and especially the financial, position of the company: and perhaps some of the higher officials may be able to render valuable aid. These are palliatives; but, even with them, divided responsibility increases the temptations to laxity which are inherent in joint stock company management. If the ablest directors are attracted to the subsidiary committee, it may do well: but they might render better service in regard to the main work of the company: for, if they do not do their best in that, the best will not be done: and the work of lateral extensions, such as rolling mills and shops for the erection of locomotives, would presumably be done at least as well by firms that attempted nothing else. It is possible that British locomotives might have nearly the same commanding position in the world as is possessed by her ships and marine engines, if British railway companies adhered more closely to the general practice of British shipowners in buying their ships[1].

6. *The mechanical methods of administration, which are inevitable in a joint stock company, are often mitigated by the professional emulation and the esprit de corps of its officials. Good and evil of the progressive supersession of private businesses by joint stock companies*[2].

The wholesale transference of authority and responsibility from the owners of each business to salaried managers and officials would have been impossible had there not been a great improvement in the morality and uprightness of the average man: for even as late as the seventeenth and eighteenth

[1] We are told:—"Railway manufacturing establishments lack the incentive of competition, the output of the works being designed for service on the system of the owning company. The works trade in a closed and fully protected market, and are therefore not in any real sense commercial enterprises. The result is evident to those who have had the opportunity of inspecting these works, and of comparing their organization and equipment with those of the great joint stock companies of locomotive and rolling stock manufacturers. In the case of new shops the equipment is perhaps equal to that to be found in the shops of the private manufacturer, but there is a tendency, partly owing to the absence of competition, but also arising from the fact that the railway manufacturing establishments are not run as separate enterprises, but are merged in the general railway undertaking, to allow the equipment to fall behind current practice, and to be, to an extent unsuspected by those responsible to the stockholders of the company, quite unrepresentative of modern methods of manufacture. The plant does the work required, and that would often appear to be the sole criterion of efficiency; there is no one whose business it is to count the cost." (Financial Supplement to *The Times*, 23 August, 1911.)

[2] A considerable part of this Section is reproduced from "The old generation of economists and the new" in the *Quarterly Journal of Economics* for January, 1897.

II, VIII, 6. centuries we find the great trading companies breaking down largely in consequence of the corruption and selfishness of their officials. But men, who are above such gross iniquity, as was common then relatively to the few opportunities for it, are yet likely to succumb to subtler temptations; and especially to the temptation to consult their own ease by jogging along quietly in accustomed routes, and avoiding the trouble and worry of new initiative.

The owner of a business, when contemplating any change, is led by his own interest to weigh the whole gain that it would probably bring to the business, against the whole loss. But the private interest of the salaried manager, or official, often draws him in another direction: the path of least resistance, of greatest comfort and least risk to himself, is generally that of not striving very energetically for improvement; and of finding plausible excuses for not trying an improvement suggested by others, until its success is established beyond question.

Again the single owner, responsible to no one, may trouble little about mechanical checks on the honesty of his employees; for he may trust to his reading of human character, and his power of detecting unfaithfulness by sharp verbal inquiries. But the officials of a joint stock company, being themselves trustees for others, can seldom take such risks: and they have little chance of taking them safely. Their accountant's work for every department must be full and precise; and so arranged as to be part of a system of elaborate checks and counterchecks. Such a system is necessarily wasteful of effort, and hostile to elasticity: and here lies a chief disadvantage under which a joint stock company lies in competition with a private firm. But this disadvantage does not increase materially with an extension of the scope of the company's business. A mechanical system of checks and counterchecks, when once introduced, adapts itself almost automatically to enlargements: it of course becomes more complex, but on the whole its cost is not likely to grow faster than the size of the business.

In so far as a system of checks represses elasticity and initiative, it is an injury to the community as well as to the company: and though this injury to the company may not be intensified by an increase in the scale of its operations, some little injury to the community arises from every addition to the number of officials whose character is affected by it. Moreover *vis inertiae* opposes the removal of any check to which people are accustomed, even though it is no longer of much use. For those who remove it will get little thanks for their pains, if their judgment turns out to be right; and they run the risk of great blame, should perverse chance bring a flagrant misdeed, that might have been arrested by the check which they have removed.

If this were the whole of the case, then every new advantage, that modern changes confer on large businesses in their contests with small, would be a source of danger to social progress. For the economies of the large business as against the small are mostly a matter of private concern and bear little further fruit: but the improvement of methods spreads from its first home all over the country, all over the world; and the private gain, which results from it to the inventor, is seldom a hundredth part—sometimes not a millionth part—of the social gain. A tendency to ossification of the social organism might therefore be feared as the result of bureaucratic habits of shirking troublesome initiative, the main benefits of which would accrue to those who had not borne the burden.

From this tendency the world is in some measure saved by the influence of motives other than the desire for pecuniary gain. To begin with, the increase in the size of industries is often accompanied by the substitution of scientific methods for empirical: while a sound basis of scientific technique is largely provided by laboratory work, to which an ever increasing number of elastic and enterprising minds are rising from among the people; being stimulated a little by the hope of gain, and much by intellectual ambition, and the sympathy of other students of science. And, in addition to this general energizing force, a special force somewhat similar to it is coming into play to preserve from stagnation the more exclusively practical side of business management. For business experts are getting more and more into the habit of writing and reading specialist journals, of holding congresses, and in other ways coming under the judgment of one another: and thus the thankless task of attempting an improvement which may after all turn

II, VIII, 6. out badly, and to which a man's official superiors and the public at large may be indifferent, assumes a new shape; since it is likely to be judged by a critical and appreciative audience, who know the technical difficulties of the problem. The most important improvements often remain for years just short of yielding financial profit: but such an audience applauds the clever and bold endeavour even though its financial fruit is not ripe; even though the interest of a manufacturer in charge of his own business might not impel him to use it. Thus the modern intercourse of expert officials with one another is bringing into the business world some part of that great progressive force, which pure science has long derived from the approbation awarded to successful research by audiences fit though few. Such approbation is a reward; and like every other reward, present or deferred, it appeals to elements of our nature that are not the very highest of all: but, partly for that reason, it may be trusted to act steadfastly. It is not only a reward: it is also a sympathy; and sympathy is the one solid and strong force which has in it nothing sordid, and permeates the whole of human nature.

This is more important with regard to joint stock companies than to private businesses. For, when once the ownership of a business has left the hands of an individual, who might attach his chief employees to him by bonds of personal friendship; when once faithfulness to the business has ceased to be enforced by the warm instincts of loyalty, and has been left to the colder support of impersonal duty; from that time forward the moral coherence and strength of the business depend largely on the growth of an *esprit de corps*, of a spirit of loyalty to the business itself. As time goes on, and the name of the business becomes hallowed by traditions of good achievements in the past, the best of its employees find a pleasure and a pride in its success and glory, as they do in that of their country: they love it as a student loves his University, as a soldier loves his Regiment; less heartily perhaps, but yet sincerely. And indeed in many a great joint stock company there arise from time to time managers, who evoke among their subordinates a high regard for themselves; and through themselves for the company: and, when they pass away, an increased tradition of loyalty to the company remains. In this matter also the great long-lived company may stand at no disadvantage relatively to a new company, which has more of the vigour of young blood, but is held together by little beyond a mere cash nexus.

This loyalty is being fostered by a multitude of movements, designed to give the employees a direct interest in the prosperity of the business for which they work: while others aim at developing their intelligence and ability in ways, some of which are likely to promote their efficiency as employees; and some, which are desired only as contributing to their higher well-being, are among the best fruits of the larger sense of social duty which is characteristic of the present age.

America appeared rather late in this field, but she is already a chief leader in it: in particular she has made it clear that when a business takes the form of a joint stock company, it does not thereby lose the freedom to make large expenditure for improving the condition of its employees. This seems to be due partly to a certain generosity of spirit, which has always accompanied the keen pursuit of wealth by her people; partly to the clearness with which her employers recognize the economy of attracting those workers who will get the greatest amount of good work out of the expensive plant which is committed to their charge. They not merely pay high wages, but often also offer opportunities for high grade social gratifications; especially if the work to be done calls for the finer industrial qualities; rather than for that heavy manual work, which Americans prefer to leave to immigrants. Lastly something may be allowed here for the autocratic, or at all events oligarchic, constitution of American companies. As a rule the President may, and indeed must, exercise an authority such as is rare in British companies, though not very rare in some of the more ambitious of the German: and a full control at meetings of shareholders is generally exercised by a few wealthy and able business men, who do not grasp crudely at small savings, but support a far-seeing policy.

We may conclude provisionally that recent developments call only for some mitigation, not for a reversal, of the judgment of English business men that the conversion of a private business into a joint stock company, though occasionally inevitable and

II, VIII, 6. very frequently convenient to those immediately concerned, sometimes acts adversely to national prosperity and industrial leadership[1].

[1] *The Statist* (14 Jan. 1905) gave strong expression to this opinion: "The general rule is that the private owner is more diligent, more assiduous in attention to business, more intimately acquainted with all its details, and better trained for the position he fills, than are the directors of a joint stock company.... They are paid exceedingly badly. Very often a man with a large business of his own, quite sufficient to occupy all his thoughts and all his time, is invited to take part in the management of another large business, and is offered a few hundreds a year as remuneration. Is it seriously expected that such a man will give the same attention to the business of the company that he gives to his own private affairs? Everybody knows that he will not....The successful private firm is eager to have the best advice in every department, and therefore its managers and its secretaries are exceedingly able men, and usually have the full confidence of the employers. But, for all that, the partners are very careful to know all the facts themselves and to watch constantly over the course of business....Consequently, when great firms transfer their businesses to companies, as they have been doing for many years past on a very considerable scale, they are taking a step which, from the necessity of the case, renders it certain that the management will be less competent in the future."

CHAPTER IX

BUSINESS ORGANIZATION: ITS FINANCIAL BASIS

1. *Functions of the promoter in relation to joint stock companies.*

II, IX, 1.

The function of the promoter is to organize industrial cooperation on purely business lines. This cooperation is not of so fine a quality as that, to which the name "cooperation" is technically applied: for it does not assume a conscious working by each for the good of all, and a readiness to sacrifice, when occasion calls, something of private gain in pursuit of a common end, and the working out of a common ideal. But the two forms of cooperation are often divided only by thin partitions.

For instance, a better organization of some branches of dairy farming might greatly increase the net gains of the producer, without involving any injury to the consumer. Cooperation in the technical sense is effecting this in many districts of Europe and in Ireland, though England herself still lags behind. The work might have been done more quickly, if the conditions of dairying had been such as to invite the services of the able business promoter and organizer. But he is seldom able to get a hold of those industries which are chiefly in the hands of small capitalists: they remain undeveloped largely because his help is not forthcoming, and they have not leaders of their own ready for the work.

There are nearly always some businesses with a greater future before them than is generally known: an able promoter may perceive their capabilities, procure the capital they need, bring them into unison, and push them on their way to success faster than they could otherwise have gone. Again, he may find a district, the agricultural or mineral riches of which have lain undeveloped, because the people in possession are neither wealthy nor enterprising: the company which he promotes may bring them a railway, and develop the latent resources by modern methods. Here again the promoter creates a position which is an addition to national wealth: he benefits all concerned, while reaping a good harvest himself.

The services of the promoter are easier, but also less necessary in relation to those industries, which are in the hands of men accustomed to deal with large capitals, and familiar with the modern methods of production and marketing. In such industries indeed the owners of the various properties concerned sometimes arrange a fusion without external aid. But often the initiative in starting a new company, or in fusing existing businesses to form a single great concern, comes from a professional organizer.

He makes it his business to study ways in which new inventions, new methods of production, new developments of demand, or new facilities for transport, offer opportunities for profitable alliances between industries that have had little in common as yet. He watches the wastes of competition between rivals: and, being detached from the details, he is generally able to take a broader view of fundamentals, and to discover their true relations and proportions better, than those whose energies are chiefly occupied with practical work in their several lines.

If he decides to aim at a fusion of existing businesses, he endeavours to obtain from each of them, in return for a small price paid down, "an option," or right to demand the sale of that business to him within a given period; and on specified terms, which commonly include the delivery of both money and securities of the new company. He reckons the extra money required for bringing up to date any plant which is behindhand, and capable of improvement: also structural changes, etc. Unless provided with exceptional resources, he then approaches some financiers. A case having been made out for the conclusion that the company can earn good dividends on a certain capital, the financiers are asked to underwrite a certain part of the securities on that basis. That is to say, they are asked to promise to buy right out a considerable part of the securities of the new company at a price perhaps twenty per cent. lower than that of issue to the public; thus securing the promoter his necessary supply of cash. If the comparison of these two sets of options, the one to demand the sale of properties, the other to demand the purchase of new securities, shows a sufficient margin to himself in cash and new securities combined, he launches his project. The highest demands on his diplomatic finesse are in his interviews with those whose properties he desires to purchase. But his chief expenditure generally goes to preparing the public to accept a high valuation of the new company. There are few who do more to increase the efficiency of labour in creating material wealth than an able and upright company promoter: he forecasts coming developments, and he aids the public to invest their resources in those fields of industry which will yield the best harvest in coming years.

In strong contrast with him is the promoter, whose ventures are commonly chosen; because he thinks he can induce others to believe they have a good chance of success, though he himself suspects they have none; and who is careful to clear out from them before they collapse. Speaking generally however the course of progress is hostile to the fraudulent promoter. The ground-plans of most of his devices are one or two centuries old: perhaps he may, with consummate skill, deck them out in a new garb, and add new details; but the detective forces of organized knowledge in the public press and elsewhere grow cumulatively, and the new elements in his guiles are less in each generation than in the preceding.

During the last few years, however, there has been a great increase of promotions, the leading feature of which has been the assertion that great economies are to be attained, in marketing as well as in production, by very large businesses; especially where they can practically monopolize a considerable market. This assertion contains much truth: but in many cases it is an overstatement prompted by a strong bias. In America and some other countries, vast gains have often accrued to promoters who have succeeded in inducing the public to accept a high estimate of the economies to be obtained by the fusion of competitive businesses. For instance, it may appear that when several businesses of which the aggregate capital

II, IX, 1. value is, say, twenty million dollars, have been amalgamated into one, its net earning power will be so much greater than the aggregate of theirs, that its capital value may fairly be estimated at, say, thirty millions. In this, which is not an extreme case, a few months' work will have put into the hands of the promoter, and those who work with him, a gross sum of ten million dollars: and, in spite of great incidental expenses in securing options, advertising, etc., more than half may be net gain. Such rich rewards have never been reached so quickly as those which have fallen to some dozen or score of promoters of the first rank in America[1].

These gains appeal to the common desire for wealth as a means of mere physical enjoyment; and they appeal, in some cases, even more strongly to the higher and more intense desire for success in great strategical enterprises. They fascinate upright men, who have earned a good reputation by a long career of solid work. And they give unprecedented scope for the use of all those subtle devices for misleading the public which have been developed by successive generations of astute knaves. Meanwhile the contrivances of the law for the defence of the public against them plod with heavy steps some way in the rear; but on the whole are gaining ground relatively to the wayward progress of the evil-doers.

[1] See Meade, *Trust Finance*, p. 196.

Mr Flint, an experienced promoter, stated that in 1900, a year of high inflation, forty-seven of the chief industrial amalgamations paid an average of 13·6 per cent. on the market value of all their securities, including common stock; and 7·44 per cent. on their nominal value: whereas the figures for 37 of the chief railroads were 4·85, on both market and nominal value: and he inferred that the industrials could not be over-capitalized (*North American Review*, May, 1901, pp. 667, 671).

But this inference was invalid. The return to investment in industrial securities was high because many industrials had entirely disappeared from the list, so that their capitalization was not reckoned in to swell the total; while the investor warned by their fate demanded a high premium for insurance against the risks which may yet await the survivors. What the figures really prove, is that the market so distrusted the capitalization of these securities as to refuse to raise their total price much above half of their nominal value, even in 1900, when tempted by the high immediate return of 13·6 per cent. on investment. He remarked significantly that "it is not an easy matter to find a man of sufficient ability and financial responsibility to take up" a new promotion, and that "there has to be a high inducement offered, because it involves a risk and a very high class of work," *Report of Industrial Commission*, XIII. p. 92.

When a fusion is over-capitalized the promoters and their friends gain, at the expense of an ultimate loss which falls on the investors: but this transference of wealth from one set of people to another is mainly a matter of private concern. And investors are learning as they go: in so far as the hopes held out by the promoter of recent amalgamations are unduly high, and are falsified by experience in coming years, the task of his successors will be more difficult.

2. *Some difficulties connected with the valuation of a company, and especially an amalgamation of several companies. Opportunities for, and temptations to, excessive valuation.*

If all the nominal capital of a company represented actual outlay, an approximate estimate of the cost of creating a business might often be formed on that basis. But, as has been seen, much of the nominal capital is often "water": that is, it is issued without any actual payment of a corresponding sum of money. Even if it were possible to ascertain to what extent this has been done, the result would not necessarily be a good guide. For instance, a railway in a deserted mining district is almost valueless; and, if its nominal capital represents its original cost, nearly the whole of it will be really, though not technically, water: and the same is true of buildings or plant which are obsolete, or otherwise no longer well suited for their work. On the other hand, a concern may have bought cheaply a great deal of land, which has unsuspected supplies of rich ore: its nominal capital may in consequence have been increased five-fold, by the issue of additional stock to the original investors; and thus four-fifths of it may technically be water, and yet not be in excess of the true value of the business.

Therefore in estimating the value of a property which he proposes to buy for himself, a reasonable man seldom pays his chief attention to its cost. He forms the best opinion he can of its probable net earning power in future years: he discounts each item with reference to the time that he would have to wait for it. Account being taken of the chance that it may turn out either less or greater than he expected, the aggregate of

II, IX, 2. these items truly reckoned, *i.e.* the "capitalized future net earnings" of the property, is the true value for which he is in search.

Estimates of the future earnings of a business must indeed be based largely on a knowledge of the past. The promoter is sure to take a hopeful view in every doubtful case: and he does not always assist the investor to get at all the facts. For instance, most promotions of new companies, and reorganizations of old companies, are made in the years just before an inflation of credit and prices reaches its bursting point. Those years show exceptionally high profits on nearly all manufacturing operations; and investors discount this fact to some extent, though seldom sufficiently. Part of the apparent profit is commonly due to the fact that stocks in trade, that were on hand at the end of each of these prosperous years, were entered in the accounts at higher prices than similar stocks had been entered twelve months before. Few investors allow for such influences, and indeed the necessary facts are seldom before them.

Again, if a business has been losing ground, a promoter who is reorganizing it, is apt to base his estimates of its success on the average of many years, and to ignore the fact that its recent net income has been small. In the opposite case, he will sometimes base himself chiefly on the profits of the last few years, and give hopes of continued increase: but in fact those interested in the sale of the business may have contrived to defer some expenses which properly belong to those years; and, in particular, they may have let the plant run without adequate renewals or even repairs, till it is nearly valueless. They have even been known to pay out of their own pockets some of its legitimate expenses; trusting to get back five thousand pounds from the investor for every thousand that they have gifted to the business.

The shipping trade affords a good instance. There is, even in peace time, about one year in ten, in which the net earnings of a ship about equal its total cost; but, for every such year, there are several in which a great many ships earn far less than their costs of working. If therefore a promoter selects for his basis a prosperous year, and one in which very small charges have been made to income on account of depreciation, a capitalization at two or three years' purchase may be excessive.

In these cases the excessive capitalization is based on an overestimate of resources. But perhaps an equally common cause of excess is to be found in the assumption that a business which has been created by a man of exceptional organizing or inventive genius, or by one who has a great faculty for anticipating coming movements of taste or fashion, will retain its vigour after a reorganization. This assumption is not likely to be justified, if meanwhile he loses effective control, even though retaining some nominal connection with it.

The natural bias of a promoter to put a high value in his prospectus on the good-will of a constituent company of his proposed amalgamation, is very great in the case of a moribund concern, which he has included only because it might weaken his strategical position if it were left outside, and open to purchase by a powerful capitalist: and several promoters, when giving testimony before the American Industrial Commission, made no secret of their having been forced to buy such businesses.

But in the most notable amalgamations the promoter has occupied himself chiefly with vigorous concerns. He has then maintained that they were capable of paying fair dividends on a nominal capital larger than their present, even if still subject to the wastes of separate administration and mutual competition: and that, if working together under able management, they would yield a large additional surplus. Accordingly he has asked the public to subscribe for "preferred" stock equal in amount to the whole nominal capital of the separate concerns, and has issued also "common" stock to an equal nominal amount. In a few cases the public have been explicitly told that in buying the common stock they were getting nothing but the right to a share in the chance of additional economy and efficiency which the amalgamation would bring. Its ownership of course gives a share in the control of the company: but, as that is of less use to the public than to financiers, the common stock has often been retained largely in their hands. In such cases as these, the movement towards amalgamation is pushed forward by the hope of gains which the promoter and his friends may reap after the conversion, in addition to those rising directly out of it. An increase of nominal capital is sometimes favoured by investors, because they think that a high rate of

II, IX, 2. profits on a nominally small capital may attract new competition, and invite popular jealousy and hostile legislation. But, when carried far, it is apt to injure the credit of the company in the long run: for in a time of depression the stock may fall far below par.

In the case of railways, and other partial monopolies, stock-watering must be jealously watched; because it may be, and in fact has been, used to show that concessions demanded from the company in the public interest would depress its dividends below a reasonable return on its capital: it is not always easy to prove that the capital is watered, and therefore has no right to a large dividend[1]. It may be admitted that every such company charges as a rule the price that will gain it the best net return, whatever its nominal capital may be; and there is no good ground for the common belief that watering capital causes prices generally to be *much* higher than they otherwise would be. But there are many cases in which it screens a harsh use of monopoly power; and, as President Hadley says, "If the directors so arrange their books as to make it appear that money has been invested, which actually has never passed through their hands, they are under a great temptation to make false reports concerning other parts of their business[2]."

Finally, a few minor causes may be briefly noted which tend to promote amalgamation. A local concern must often borrow at a high rate of interest: if it is amalgamated with many others, the securities of the whole find a market on the great Stock Exchanges, and it can borrow more easily. And indeed it is a universal rule that a bond which is part of a small issue always has a rather lower price than one of exactly the same rank which belongs to a large issue; because if the owner should want to sell, a buyer will more promptly be found for the large issue than the small. Again, the launch and the subsequent history of a vast company, like those of an exceptionally large ship, are treated by the newspapers as of general

[1] See below, p. 530 and Appendix M, 5.

[2] *The Education of the American Citizen*, p. 46. German law prohibits the watering of stocks directly: it is ineffective against the purchase at a high price of a business as a going concern, and is largely evaded; but yet its influence has been shown in the high average prices of, and dividends on, German industrial securities.

interest: and the gratuitous advertisement thus afforded is often an asset of considerable value. Again, though publicity generally helps honest dealings; and puts difficulties in the way of some crude forms of dishonesty, it is sometimes used to further the ends of astute and powerful financiers: for it broadens the Stock Exchange transactions, in which there is a harvest to be reaped by those who know in advance whether the next information that is imparted to the public will tend to raise or to lower prices.

Again it often happens that those who control a company want to shake the public out, and acquire a yet greater control of it. They then charge expensive improvements to income account; and prepare a balance sheet, which will show that little or no dividend can be paid: and meanwhile they make large sales of the stock by concealed routes. When the price of the stock has thus been lowered, they quietly buy all that they have sold, and a great deal more. In the next few years it may probably appear that the charges, which had to be made to income account in order to keep the plant up to date, are not very heavy. The greater the attention the public pays to the affairs of the company, the more skill is required for such manœuvres: but also the larger is the volume of amateur and professional speculation, on which toll can be levied by those who can control events, and rumours of events, which control Stock Exchange prices[1].

3. *The part played by banks and other financial agencies in the adaptation of industry and trade to the enlarged financial requirements of the modern age. British banks.*

We have seen how in the joint stock era, the population at large hands over an ever increasing part of its spare resources to be employed in business, without calling in the services of any intermediary. But latterly "banks" (in the broad use of the term in which it includes many classes of financial houses in Germany, and to a less degree in some other countries) have taken a large part, in underwriting and otherwise financing

[1] Much suggestive information on the above and allied subjects is given in Professor Meade's *Corporation Finance.*

II, IX, 3. great businesses, almost exclusively in joint stock form: and from that they have proceeded to exercise a strong control on the general course of business in various ways, and especially by nominating their own representatives on the boards of direction of leading industrial and trading companies: a matter which will call for much attention in the next Book.

Many recent changes have contributed to increase the financial element in the directorate and management of industrial concerns; and, in not a few cases, to relegate those, whose faculty is constructive rather than commercial, to subordinate positions. Not only trade secrets, but even trained industrial instincts, often count for less than they used to in comparison with command over capital, and skill in buying and selling. This would be inevitable even if joint stock company finance did not offer a field for great achievements by relatively small efforts of able and wealthy capitalists.

Thus the movement towards the consolidation of industry under high financial control is strong in many countries. It will suffice to consider three; Britain, where the movement is opposed by tradition and perhaps by national character, and where it is not very prominent; Germany, where its development is perhaps most typical and uniform; and the United States, where the movement has been irregular, but has gone very far in several great departments of industry.

The Scottish banking system a century ago was different from, and in many respects superior to, the English system generally; though it was under greater obligations than it seemed to recognize to the Bank of England, in regard to the maintenance of foreign exchanges: but for the present purpose the Scottish banks may be associated with the English. British banking problems are often discussed mainly in connection with the currency: the present reference to them is concentrated on a single point; and it ignores many matters which would be vital in a broad study[1].

[1] The name "Lombard Street" indicates that England owed much to Italian bankers. Venice seems to have led the way in deposit banking. The Bank of Genoa may perhaps claim to have pioneered giant financial operations for the development of trade.

As is well known, a representative British bank makes its profits, as a rule, chiefly by lending command over capital, most of which has been placed with it by its regular customers: it pays them little or no interest on their capital: but it renders them gratuitously the great services of receiving payments from, and making payments to, all parts of the country. The command of capital thus placed with it constitutes the basis of its "deposits": but another great part of it consists of mere book entries, each of which indicates that the bank has made a loan (probably covered by the placing of some securities in the custody of the bank) to a customer; the loan is not generally taken out at once, but is placed to his credit to be drawn against. Every cheque drawn against any of the bank's "deposits," of whatever sort, must be instantly paid by the bank; which must therefore have a good stock of cash in hand, or at call; together with a considerable holding of bills etc. which automatically give a speedy command over cash. It cannot safely lock up any considerable part of its resources in loans based, directly or indirectly, on the standing securities of any single business, whether a private firm or a company; unless indeed that company be a first-class railway or other concern of vast size and high repute, whose securities can be promptly marketed on fairly good terms to almost any extent[1].

The burden of supplying to any ordinary business, the main body of the capital which it needs, otherwise than for temporary uses, must therefore be left in England to the Stock Exchange, and to financial agencies that are not under obligation to pay on demand cheques drawn against them. The chief of these agencies are "accepting houses" sometimes called "merchant bankers," because some of them first established their position as wealthy merchants; together with several other classes of dealers in credit, who still retain the name of bill-brokers. The currency of each bill is of course short: under favourable con-

[1] The above remarks indicate that a great part, very often the greater part, of the "deposits" of a bank are in effect statements of loans made by itself, or based on loans made by other banks; and therefore these deposits are not to be reckoned in an inventory of the national wealth, in addition to the value of the material properties and business reputations and connections on which they are in some measure based. But yet it would not be correct to take no account of them in such an inventory.

II, IX, 3. ditions, continued credit can be obtained by a series of bills; and the rate of interest charged is low, partly because the lender can speedily recover command of his capital in time of pressure. But, for that and other reasons, a long-period credit would often be more serviceable to the borrower.

A cheque paying bank can seldom safely make a large advance on securities that are not eminently marketable: but the term "large" is relative. The general increase in the size of the business unit, whether a private firm or a joint stock company, causes an increase in the size of the advances for which it is likely to have a legitimate occasion: and a bank, which wishes to be active in important affairs, and at the same time prudent, finds in this general expansion of the business unit a subsidiary impulse, prompting it to consider plans of amalgamation with other banks[1].

This quiet policy has its drawbacks: but it gives stability to a system which is worked on a very slender basis of gold reserve, and is liable to great foreign drains. And, what is more to our present purpose, it offers no inducements to powerful speculators to capture those banks on whose solidity the ordinary business of the country depends: since the resources of such a bank could not be used in financial campaigns. It must be admitted that the banks, while stable themselves, have sometimes been rather niggardly in their holdings of the gold basis of the credit on which their cheque system rests: and that they have not always exercised an adequate organized control over speculative tendencies on the Stock Exchange and elsewhere. The burden laid on the Bank of England should perhaps be shared by them in a rather larger degree. But such considerations bear only indirectly on the question whether the present organization of British banking suffices for all the needs of

[1] The economies, which a bank obtains by an increase in the number of its branches in different parts of the country, are in some respects similar to those which a railway derives from an increase in the number of points, at which it can receive and deliver goods. The transport of command over money effected by a bank involves a prodigious amount of routine work, which does little towards the development of the higher faculties; and it does not tend directly, as the open air work of railway men does, to improve the physical vigour of the race. Possibly the demand for the most mechanical parts of it may be considerably checked by the further development of automatic tabulating, reckoning and printing machines.

industry and trade: before coming to that point, it will be well to look abroad. II, IX, 4.

4. *Relations of banks to industry and trade in Germany and America.*

The French banks have something in common with the quietude of the British. They do not indeed occupy themselves much with transferring payments from one man to another: and the Crédit Mobilier, founded in 1852, was one of the chief pioneers of large industrial ventures. But, with a few exceptions, they have avoided extreme speculative courses: and they have not stretched out their hands towards a concentrated direction or control of trade and manufacture; being perhaps to some extent warned off by that spirit of individuality which we have noted as underlying representative French industries.

In Germany however large capitals and great industrial enterprises are of recent origin and have grown rapidly: the masterly financial genius, and faculty for associated speculative action of the Semitic race count generally for more in the east of Europe than in the west.

Sixty or seventy years ago Germany was not equipped with any organized credit system: the credit banks which then began their work were obliged, as Professor Riesser tells us, "to occupy in the national economy the place held by the maid of all-work in the private household,...and to take upon themselves all or nearly all the tasks which in England are apportioned as a rule, under a strict division of labour," among numerous financial agencies[1].

[1] This quotation from p. 220 of the translation, issued by the American National Monetary Commission in 1911, of Dr Riesser's *Die deutschen Grossbanken und ihre Konzentration*, is the starting point of a long and weighty argument that the form taken by Germany's organization of banking was first, an inevitable consequence of her conditions; and, secondly, on the whole superior to the British system, the claims of which had been strongly urged by the late Adolf Wagner and others. Dr Riesser seems to be mistaken in holding that system responsible (pp. 557 and 848) for the great number of failures recorded in the history of British banks. There have been comparatively few failures of considerable joint stock banks in England; and those few were almost without exception caused by flagrant violations of the principles of the present system.

II, IX, 4. A chief part of their work consisted in granting short-term credits, such as have been given in one form or another to business men by almost every sort of bank: but the credits had to be renewed, and gradually were merged in long-term credits; and these in their turn developed into the issue of shares and bonds. "By such an issue the connection between the banks... and industrial production is drawn so tight that they are thereafter joined 'for better or worse.' Sooner or later this connection finds further expression in the appointment of members of the bank directorate to the supervisory council of industrial enterprises....This practice is virtually caused by the necessity for the banks to maintain the influence, which they have gained through the issue, and to retain such permanent control.... Conversely 'captains of industry' are appointed as members of the supervisory councils of banks; where as a rule they have much less influence than the representatives of banks in the management of industrial companies[1]."

The German great banks are, as a rule, remarkably well managed. But they are also inclined to ventures which have something of American boldness: and some good judges think that they are inclined to venture beyond their strength; especially by carrying to excess the locking up of their capital in loans, which cannot be called in under grave emergency. It is however claimed that their intimate association with large industrial movements keeps them alert: that they earn a higher rate of interest on their advances and can pay higher interest to their depositors than they otherwise could; and that they can in some cases undertake the flotation of new securities at lower charges than would be required by English financial houses[2].

No doubt there were very many disgraceful failures of private English banks, when the Bank of England's monopoly of a joint stock constitution was still in force: for that monopoly deterred many responsible people from taking part in banking; and it gave an indirect premium to petty traders who opened "banks" without system and without resource.

[1] Riesser, *l.c* pp. 336—7. He gives a long table of representatives of banks or industrial companies; a point to which we must return in Book III.

[2] Some highly coloured, but instructive, observations on Germany's banks, her study of markets, and her commercial penetration, will be found in Prof. Hauser's *Germany's commercial grip of the world.*

The Social Verein published a remarkable set of monographs on the dis-

The consolidation of banks proceeds apace in Germany, as in England. Its motives are partly the same: they include economy in the transmission business, and in the keeping of cash reserves; together with a greater independence of the varying fortunes and activities of particular fields of investment. But in addition, a German bank consolidation has generally some connection with the needs and opportunities of some industry in which one or more of the banks concerned has a special interest. Thus the power of the High-finance, embodied in the great banks of Germany, is becoming an *imperium in imperio*. It is fostering cartellization in every branch of industry, and in this and other ways it is helping the commercial element to obtain the upper hand over the constructive, faster perhaps in Germany than anywhere else: but more of this later on[1].

turbances in German business (*Störungen in deutschen Wirthschaftsleben*) at the turn of the century; and one of these relating to the influence of the great banks, by Dr Ernest Loeb, brought out the facts that most of the banks took what proved to be too optimistic a view of the situation in 1899; but that the older banks were generally more cautious than their newer rivals, and especially than those which had recently increased their capital very fast (*Schriften*, No. 110, p. 313).

[1] Herr Calwer, who is friendly towards cartellization, frequently calls attention to the influence which the banks have exerted in promoting it. And yet he complains, *Handel und Wandel*, 1900, p. 155, that great banks arrive at mutual understandings which enable them to regulate prices in the money market very much as an ordinary cartel does in the market for its own special wares. "Berlin High-finance unquestionably dominates the most representative and the largest businesses in every branch of production." He gives the titles of the chief of the 350 large industrial companies in which one or other of seven banks named by him has a seat on the directorate. This matter is discussed from another point of view below, pp. 566—570.

The position that a country, poorly supplied with capital, is almost compelled to look to its banks for aid in speculative business; but that Germany has reached a stage at which some of her banks might with advantage devote themselves more exclusively to the narrower affairs of deposit and transmittance, is taken by Dr Adolf Weber, *Depositenbanken und Speculationsbanken*.

It is however noteworthy that in Silesia the iron and steel industries are in the hands of wealthy families, who dominate the banks; and that even in Westphalia, where expansion has been more rapid, the chief industrialists are becoming independent of the banks. Prof. Schumacher (in Schmoller's *Jahrbuch* for 1906) notes this, and attributes it in part to the fact that few bank officials have been found capable of conducting large enterprises.

This picture of course relates to conditions antecedent to the great war. The changes in it, which may result from the destruction of capital and other influences of the war, are not to be foreseen.

II, IX, 4. Passing to the United States, we find the concentrated force of capital even more striking there than in Germany. But its organization has been less bureaucratic, less symmetrical, and more fitful in its action. According to common repute, there is no set of bankers and banking officials that is shrewder, more alert, or more generally capable than those of New York: but the banking system, as a whole, has lacked something of that symmetry and caution, and perhaps also that restraining influence of public opinion, which older banking systems have derived from their slow growth and their respect for traditions. Traditions indeed are to-day little better than fetters in some branches of business: but they are supports rather than fetters in banking; where the welfare of all requires imperatively that the enterprise of each should take account of considerations other than those enforced by the letter of the law, and his own immediate profit. The absence of such traditions has been emphasized by the predominating power in American finance, exercised by a relatively small group of men, who have combined the ownership of vast wealth with the ambition to show a Napoleonic faculty in its use. They have owned some private banks, which take a leading part in great financial operations; and they have controlled some large joint stock banks. But the greater part of their fortunes has been acquired by constructive and strategic faculties; which have been applied to railways, to mining, or to manufacture, or to all combined. The peculiar conditions of American business and finance caused at one time some anxiety lest an implicit "trust" or combination of financiers should dominate the business of the country: that fear seems to have been definitely laid by the great Federal Reserve Act of 1913[1].

[1] That Act aims at preserving the full freedom of enterprise of all classes of banks, in so far as their action does not indirectly make for general instability of credit: and at keeping only such control over them, as is necessary for combining a solid basis of the currency with adequate elasticity in times of need. This control is to be exercised in the main by the Federal Reserve Board; which is so constituted as to secure in explicit terms recognition of that supreme obligation of the banking community to the general business community. This has been in effect, though not in form, obtained by the predominance of representatives of general business on the Board of Directors of the Bank of England: the influence of Government is however greater and more direct

But no banking reform can remove some of the dangers which are inherent in the power of very rich men, who have not retired into the quietude which is preferred by most of the wealthy families of old countries, but are still eager for the excitements of the chase in the hunting ground of Wall Street. Their power is increased by the facts that absolute control of a joint stock company is given by the possession of fifty-one per cent. of its stock, or sometimes even only of special issues of its stock; and that, as has already been observed, when a great part of the stock is held in small lots by people far removed from one another, one-third or even much less of the whole stock will give practically safe control. Now, if as often happens, one company holds a controlling share of the stock of another, then those who control the first control the second: and an investment of one million in the first may give control of four millions in the second, or even more. Next, the changing conditions of life are making it desirable to employ companies, rather than to ask private friends, to act as trustees for property: so "trust companies" (not to be confounded with "trusts") have been founded for this purpose; and they, together with insurance companies, hold large quantities of shares in railways and industrial concerns. Now it is comparatively easy either to control these companies directly (for of course their own stock is not very large); or to make terms with their directors, and to command the voting power given by the shares which they hold.

Last, but not least, "communities of interests" are constantly created for various purposes, more or less permanent, by informal agreements that the Board of Directors of each of several great companies is to include some members of each of the other

in the American, than in the English, control of the gold reserve of the country.

It is to be observed that the movement towards the aggregation of banks into large units, each having many branches and sub-offices, which has been conspicuous in England and Germany, has not gone far in America. There are a few powerful banks, chiefly in New York: but conditions somewhat similar to those of England early in last century have promoted the growth of an immense number of small local banks: and the new law, which gives somewhat increased security for their good guidance, seems likely to maintain a notable diffusion of the minor forces of finance by the side of intense concentration of its main forces.

II, IX, 5. Boards: and this often acts as an intermediate stage to an interchange of the holdings of the several companies. If this interchange is complete, the result is in effect a fusion of the companies: if it is partial, it forms a strong bond between them, which is not very likely to be dissolved. Thus the total indirect control, which the great capitalist groups exert, becomes very extensive; insomuch that campaigns in which either side is equipped with an effective voting force, amounting to several scores or even hundreds of millions of dollars, are very common.

5. *Suggestions that Britain's industry and trade might derive material assistance from powerful and prominent financial institutions, which would supplement, and cooperate with, her great banks.*

We now resume the consideration of the British banking system. Its unrivalled efficiency in those tasks, to which its chief energies are devoted, has some defects of its qualities. Its general rule, that credits must be covered by handing over marketable securities to the custody of the bank, is a necessary condition for the maintenance of its power to meet any sudden and violent call for return of funds given into its charge. But this rule is relaxed in special cases: for otherwise the banking system while working largely with capital placed in its custody by men of but small means, would be compelled to refuse aid to any whose total capital did not overflow the most urgent needs of their business; except in so far as it can be obtained by discounting bills, a process not always convenient.

The private banker whose life was spent in one locality was able to ascertain the characters, habits, and prospects of his neighbours more thoroughly than is possible for the branch-manager of a great bank, who is often almost a stranger to the locality: and therefore loans on "personal" credit to businesses which are not strong, are perhaps rather scantier, and yet not more safe, than they would be, if a considerable number of the smaller private banks could hold their own. But, as Bagehot argued in his epoch-making *Lombard Street*, 1873, the trend of events has moved increasingly against them since about 1850. The borrower must therefore be content with the reflection, that, when he can supply the needed security, he is certain to obtain immediately almost unlimited funds at a rather low rate of interest: and thus a little evil is mingled with the great good effected by the consolidation of banking interests[1]. II, IX, 5.

Larger issues are now being raised by the question whether this consolidation has made full use of its strength. Great banks do nearly all the work that used to be done by small banks, with ever increasing efficiency. But, it is asked, whether they should not approach some larger tasks, which were beyond the reach of smaller banks; and which, as the experience of Germany and other countries has shown, are within the reach of great banks.

In particular it is suggested that, in this age of rapid progress, attention needs to be directed to ventures that show a promise of becoming strong, at least as much as to those which are already strong: and that some enlargement of the scope of the work of giant banks in this direction would be of public service. A little may perhaps be effected by the direct action of great banks of the ordinary type: but there seems to be a large and rapidly widening scope for prominent and powerful financial institutions, which would be called "banks" in other countries; though, to avoid misapprehension they should avoid that title in Britain. For instance it seems to have been fully established that prompt and strong assistance is not always to be had for such inventions and other new ideas, as are in the minds of men whose financial position is not already strong; and who do not know their way about the City of London. In Germany, on the other hand, "the pioneer would take his proposal to one of the great banks with an Industrial department; and the proposal would immediately be put before experts, scientific and technical, well known to the bank and thoroughly trusted who (on the assumption that the proposed business was really good) would report well on it, *and would be believed*[2]."

[1] The benefits of a fusion of banks already strong are perhaps greatest when a bank in a residentiary district finds an outlet for the savings of its clients by alliance with another, whose chief connections are with industrial districts, greedy of capital. And a recent fusion of a colonial bank with a British bank promises even larger advantages of the same kind.

[2] From a pamphlet by Mr William Olsson, a Swede who has had exceptional opportunities of comparing the methods of high finance in Germany, Britain and other countries. Some account of it is given in *The Economist*, 5 Feb. 1916.

II, IX, 5. Of course work of this kind is done in London by various financial houses: but their scientific and technical equipments are not organized on as massive a scale as those of (say) the Deutsche Bank. Some of them are powerful: but they do not seek prominence; and the guide posts, which might point the inexperienced inventor to them, are not as clear as those which point to a great bank. These and other considerations have led to the establishment of "The British Trade Corporation" starting with an initial capital of £2,000,000. Its chief immediate purpose seems to be the granting of relatively long credits to merchants and producers engaged in business over-seas; so that they may be on equal terms with competitors, who are aided by foreign, and especially by German banks. But, though this be the most pressing matter at the time, the largest scope for institutions similar to it, is likely to be found in connection with the development of industry at home: for, if recent developments may be taken as true indications of the future, a great part of the material plant of many industries will need to be recast in each coming generation. And indeed the Prospectus of the Trade Corporation points in that direction:—"There exists to-day no large financial institution possessing an industrial department or an organization for study and research into new ideas and inventions, which is specially equipped to examine and nurse new schemes or developments until sufficiently proved and ripe for public investment. The Corporation will make this a special feature of its business, and will aim at becoming a link between British industry and the British investor."

Its affairs are in such strong hands that it is not likely to over-reach its strength. But so many and so large are the suggestions already made for the work to be done by it, and similar institutions, that their accomplishment would need the locking up of capital amounting to many scores of millions of pounds: therefore, these financial institutions must speed on its way to the Stock Exchange many a venture which they will be unable to support permanently[1].

[1] The foundation of the Corporation was the chief immediate result of the appointment in 1916 of a very strong Committee of the Board of Trade, with Lord Faringdon in the chair. The following passages are taken from its Report—"There exist to a considerable extent at the present time in this country

the machinery and facilities for the finance alike of home trade and of large over-seas contracts, and for carrying through much of the business which has been done by foreign banks. The British banks afford, we believe, liberal accommodation to the home producer. British bankers are not shy in making advances on the strength of their customers' known ability and integrity, and the charges for accommodation are we believe often lower than the corresponding charges in foreign countries. Similarly, the Colonial Banks and British-Foreign Banks and Banking Houses render immense assistance to British trade abroad; and certainly in the Far East and in many parts of South America British banking facilities do not fall short of those of any other nation. We find also that, in the case of large contract operations, British contractors with the assistance of Financial Houses have in the past been ready to provide large amounts of capital, and to take considerable risks in connection with the operations which they have undertaken.

"Our arrangements, however, are faulty in our not co-ordinating many of the facilities mentioned in the previous paragraph. We recognize also that the British manufacturer may be frequently in want of finance of a kind which a British Joint Stock Bank with liabilities as above described could not prudently provide, whereas the German Banks in particular seem to have been able to afford special assistance at the inception of undertakings of the most varied description, and to have laid themselves out for stimulating their promotion and for carrying them through to a successful conclusion."

"Foreign banks have, in most of their operations, adopted the course of forming syndicates to undertake any business of considerable magnitude. They have headed such syndicates and they have taken the labouring oar in connection with investigations. The members of the syndicate have generally included other banks: and associated with them have been those who were particularly interested in the class of business proposed to be done. These syndicates are formed after the first superficial enquiry has satisfied the banks that there is apparently a good business to be done. Directly this point is reached, the expenditure in connection with thorough investigation is on account of the syndicate. If the business is ultimately proceeded with, the profits or losses on the wind-up of the business are shared *pro rata* after allowance to the bank for management. Some such procedure should be followed here. It would enable the Institution to undertake business of a comprehensive character, and its 'imprimatur' would have value when issues were made to the public."

The Report suggests also that the Institution should receive aid from Government Officials; especially from Commercial Attachés and Consuls. It is further suggested that each such Institution should be specialized for particular localities or for particular large groups of industry: also that the present great banks, either collectively or in groups, should own the capital of one or more such institutions; each of which should have a highly organized staff of technical advisers. In that case, a business man with a new idea, but without special technical or financial experience, might get advice through his own bank from experts of the Corporation: and, if they reported favourably on his idea, his way to needed financial aid would be made smooth. But such suggestions have to run the gauntlet of much criticism and perhaps some hard experience. Expert technical guidance on some matters can be better obtained by the associated efforts of particular branches of industry, than by aid of financial institutions: but this matter belongs to the end of Book III.

CHAPTER X

BUSINESS ORGANIZATION. ITS TASKS AND REQUIREMENTS OF FACULTY

II, x, 1.

1. *The value of a machine to a business can be calculated on the basis of its efficiency for its immediate work. But the value of an employee must be estimated, partly by instinct, with a view to the probable development of his capacities: and the difficulty of this task is increased by the conditions of modern business.*

Although human nature is nearly the same now as of old time, while the plant and processes of almost every industry have changed fundamentally more than once during the last five generations; yet the problems which the head of a business has to solve in relation to its personnel have changed and are changing their character much more completely than those which he has to solve in relation to its plant and processes, except in a few industries. For his plant and his processes are always under his eye; and though he must trust to second-hand information in regard to many of their details, yet any information that he needs is always to be had with certainty and precision. On the other hand a certain and precise knowledge of the characters of employees by close contact and continuous observation, such as prevailed in the small workshops of former times, is not to be had at all: and the head of a large modern business must delegate to others nearly all responsibility in regard to the greater number of his employees. He is indeed directly responsible for the choice of his chief subordinates: he needs quick insight into character, and some power of influencing it; and he must exercise this insight and power largely in calling to his assistance men who are possessed in various degrees of like endowments.

The relations of an employer to his employees generally contain some elements which have little connection with business: and, even from a merely business point of view, account is to be taken of the fact that the trust, esteem and affection of his staff are a valuable business asset, of a kind which his machinery cannot supply. But, for the moment, we are to watch him when considering how much it is worth his while to pay a certain employee, from nearly the same point of view as that from which he would consider how much it is worth his while to pay for the use of a certain machine.

When the master manufacturer was the leader and perhaps the most skilled artisan of a workshop, assisted by a few workers of various ages, his instincts had full opportunity for putting each one to the task appropriate for him within the narrow range of the shop. There was no subtle analysis of character and its potentialities: but experienced instinct carried far. Education by imitation began in early youth, when mind and body were most plastic: and the experience of rowing and other athletic exercises, has led the way towards many modern improvements in school education: an hour's rowing behind a first-class oar teaches more than much verbal exhortation[1].

For great good on the balance, but for evil in some degree, the boy now remains at school till his susceptibility to the supreme educational influence of imitation has been somewhat dulled: and meanwhile the scope for boy labour in those occupations, which used to afford the most excellent training, has greatly diminished, for the work is done now mainly by machines. Some compensation for these losses is found in the movement for technical education in continuation schools: but, since those, whose example is to be followed, are relatively few in a school, though they are numerous in workshops, imitation in it has to yield the first place to formal instruction. On the other hand the boy's general faculties are now more highly developed when he comes into the workshop: and there is more material to work upon in the selection of the most fitting

[1] Prof. W. D. Scott, in his suggestive study of means of *Increasing human efficiency in business*, puts the educative influence of imitation into the foreground.

II, x, 1. task for him. In businesses of small, and even of medium size, each employee can be to a certain extent treated as an individual human being: his strong points and his weak points are known; and his latent efficiency may be evoked by a word or two of authoritative advice on one occasion, and a tentative change in his work on another. The methods of school education have improved greatly, and tend increasingly to strengthen the children's minds. But to this general statement there is one deplorable exception in English-speaking countries. In learning by rote the vagaries of English spelling, as misleading historically as they are tedious in practice, no constructive faculty is strengthened. A rational system of spelling might set the equivalent of at least a year's work in elementary schools free for drawing, and for studies of nature: these would sow germs of the faculties of observation and reasoning; and thus prepare the mind in elastic youth for the work and responsibilities of after life. The divergence of pronunciation from spelling presses on all classes of the population: but it is most oppressive to those classes whose school-term is short[1].

As a rule, there is no one in a large business who has at once the authority, the opportunity and the interest that might empower and impel him to make a careful study of the abilities and aptitudes of each employee in the lower grades; to direct those abilities and aptitudes to their most appropriate work and educate them in it. Foremen and other subordinate officials have some interest in getting the most work that they can out of each man as he is; but they seldom take account of what he might possibly become. This is one cause of a certain tendency on the part of the less energetic members of a trade union to press for a somewhat high standard of pay for an amount of work, that is far below the maximum which they can easily

[1] Of course it would need to be framed by a convention of men of high philological and educational authority, appointed by the Governments of English-speaking countries. It would not aim at forcing the written language into exact conformity with any one variety of the spoken: but it would seek a mean position, that represented fairly well the common usage of the English-speaking world: and a spoken language, in ever closer correspondence with the new written language, would in the course of a generation become the general language of international intercourse. The notion that existing spelling has a sound historical basis is of course erroneous.

accomplish; and to be relatively indifferent to a prospect of high rewards for enlarged efficiency. II, x, 1.

Increasing attention is being paid to this evil by far-seeing and public-spirited men in control of large establishments. Some of them make it a rule that failure to succeed in one kind of work shall not be taken as ground for dismissing a willing worker; and that he shall first be tried in work of other kinds. "By such shifting the right place can often be found for him. Young people, to whom in spite of long trial and the best will it seems impossible to supply certain automatic machines, become excellent workers at much more difficult labour in the same establishment. Women, who are apparently careless and inattentive when they have to distribute their attention over a number of operations, do high-class work when they are engaged in a single activity; and in other cases the opposite is reported." But as things are the operative who is a failure at one task, seldom has any opportunity for showing his strength in other work: he is simply dismissed, and his fate in his next employment may be no better[1].

Again there are some exceptional works in which the standard of intelligence required of nearly all the operatives is so high, that labour becomes an education. A splendid instance of this is the Zeiss glass works, which, under the noble guidance of Abbé, steadfastly pursued ideal perfection in manufacture, secure in the confidence that good work would bring adequate profits. He knew that "in order that an article may really excel, it must be the outcome of thorough theoretical knowledge, combined with great technical skill"; that is, when "everyone participating in the manufacture devotes his whole experience, intelligence, and time solely to the production of this one article." But he "recognized that even this principle of the subdivision of labour has its limits."

For he gradually found that, while the works were making nothing but microscopes, "the worker suffering from the mono-

[1] Something may be accomplished by direct applications of science. But from the time of Owen down to that of yet living leaders of industry, such as those whose endeavours and achievements are recorded in Meakin's *Model Factories and Villages*, the chief pioneers of progress have been plain men, whose enthusiasm and ardent sympathy have been guided only by instinct and business judgment.

 tony of always having to work in the same groove whether with the hand or brain, has his mental vision thereby dulled for anything situated beyond his own narrow horizon, and loses the power of utilizing at the right moment for his own particular purpose, anything lying a little beyond his ordinary everyday path." So, true to the proverb "to rest is to rust," he multiplied the products of the works, and let in fresh air past the barriers of monotony[1].

But in spite of such broad movements, the large majority of employers and their officers are still apt to keep philanthropy and business in different compartments of their minds: partly because, though the aggregate profits of business are large, they are a diminishing percentage on outlay. In some uniform industries this percentage is very low; and it might indeed be wiped out by a comparatively small increase in outlay, unless it was in some degree remunerative from the purely business point of view. This consideration suggests the great social importance of evidence that has recently been collected to the effect that much of that care for employees, which has been prompted in the past mainly by altruistic motives, is commercially profitable.

2. *Faculties needed by the head of a large business; and by its chief officials.*

The following observations are so worded, for the sake of simplicity, as to apply specially to the case of a business, owned and controlled by a single individual: they imply throughout the possibility of maintaining unity of purpose and continuity of policy. They apply to a company, the "head" of which is a Board; provided either tradition or the predominance of a single masterful mind and will enables the Board to act coherently, in spite of some divergence of temperament and interest among its members.

The tasks of the head of a large business are heavier than those of a small one, and yet they may be fewer in number. For

[1] The German proverb is "*Rast ich, so rost ich*": but his work was not complete till he had shortened the hours of labour and made other provision for the rest, which is recuperative and develops energy, under the variant proverb "*Rast ich, so rüst ich*"; *i.e.* "To rest is to prepare" (Auerbach, *The Zeiss Works*, pp. 5, 6, and 113).

he must delegate multitudinous business details to others: and the details even of a small business are generally more numerous than the broad problems of a large one. He is primarily responsible for the general plan of the business: but second in importance only to that is his selection and quiet control of officials who are responsible for details. In a very large business he may indeed delegate the greater part even of that responsibility to chief officials: but he bears the weighty task of reading the characters of strong men: and therefore he must be very strong. Meanwhile the study of the organization and policy of his business is likely to require a larger originality, and a wider outlook than are needed for similar tasks in a business of medium size. Let us go into some details.

An adequate supply of capital being assumed, the chief requisites of the head of a considerable business may be classed as (*a*) judgment, prudence, enterprise, and fortitude in undertaking and carrying risks: (*b*) an alert acquaintance with appropriate technique; and some power of initiating advance: (*c*) a high power of organization; in which system plays a great part, but "always as a servant, never as a master": (*d*) a power of reading character in subordinates; together with resolution, tact, trust and sympathy in handling them: (*e*) prompt diligence in assigning to each the highest work of which he is capable, or can be made capable within a moderate time. All these qualities are needed in the head of a business of even moderate size: and, if it is to be thoroughly well administered, all of them are required more or less in its chief officials; for the head cannot be directly in touch with details. He needs men immediately under him who would be capable heads of small businesses: but their tasks are lighter than his, because the range of the responsibilities of each of them is narrower than his. He must hold all departments in view; partly because he needs frequently to revise his estimate of the energy, ability and integrity of each departmental chief; but mainly because the changing courses of industry and trade require continual alert watching of the mutual relations and proportions of the various departments of the business. This task belongs to the head alone: it cannot be delegated; though work preparatory to it is often shared out among several directors of a joint stock company, and even among trusted

II, x, 3. chief officers of large businesses generally. In the case of a giant business the responsibilities of the chiefs of particular establishments, and even of particular departments of one establishment, may be as heavy, and almost as wide-spreading, as those of the head of an independent business of moderate size: though some large questions of organization, and nearly all large questions of finance will be ultimately determined by the head of the whole business.

3. *The education of business faculty.*

As will be argued presently, constructive genius of the highest kind seldom owes much to education: but, with that exception, all orders of business ability may be fostered by appropriate preparation in early years. The circumstances, which have impaired the forces of British education in past times, have already been indicated[1]. But a little may fitly be said here as to the functions of education in promoting the alertness, sense of proportion, and strength of reasoning which are required in business.

The main point is that the chief function of education is to "educate" faculties, that is to bring them out and develop them. A great part of the instruction, given in most schools and many universities, imparts information, with scarcely any education in the true sense of the term: much of it even tends to hinder the movements of faculty by clogging it with inert matter. For indeed a man, whose own mind is stagnant, can impart knowledge without effort: but the education of faculty is a task which calls for vitality and initiative on the part of the educator. Therefore paths of least resistance have commonly been sought in many classes of schools, especially where the teachers have been few in number relatively to the pupils; and even to some extent in universities. But continuous description and explanation tend to deaden the minds of the hearers; and should not find place in oral instruction except for some urgent reason[2].

[1] Above, pp. 95—99.

[2] Injury is done by the continuous reading aloud of matter, which could conveniently be printed, and is perhaps already accessible in good text-books. The students should be required to read such books; and any explanation given in lecture should be supplemented by occasional questions pointing towards the next step in description, in explanation, and above all in reasoning. There is something to be said for a plan, under which the lecturer prepares beforehand

The higher branches of education in America lagged for some time a little behind the best European methods: but their rapid advance in recent times has brought them into the first rank, at all events in those studies which look towards the future rather than the past: and Britain may profit much by some of her suggestions. The character of the German people differs from that of Americans and Britons. It has more patience and steady assiduity; so that methodical, orderly procedure in school and college has peculiar attractions for them. The splendid organization of their *Real* schools and colleges, devoted to the direct preparation of youths for the practical work of after life, is specially suitable to their temperament: and any danger to intellectual individuality, which it might threaten, is in great measure warded off by the abundance of their Universities, in which high ideals of study are maintained. But Britain's Universities are still rather few: and, partly for that reason, the new desire for education, as a source of strength in industry and trade, might conceivably be turned to but indifferent account, if German *Real* education were too closely followed. Fortunately however the last few years have seen an increasing tendency on the part of the British Government and people to seek in such matters the counsel of leaders of scientific study: and in that tendency there is safety[1].

sufficiently to require to use only a few notes as guide-posts: he then thinks the matter out as he goes, and *gets his class to think with him.* If he strays into an unpremeditated illustration or inference; the class, seeing the effort of his mind, and stimulated to work with it, will have their strength brought out more in a few minutes than it would be in an hour in which information is loaded into their minds as goods are loaded into trucks. If they seem bent on passive entries into note-books, they may be forced into an active and even critical attitude, by the quiet insertion of an inaccurate statement, or invalid argument, into the lecture; and by questions being asked about it.

The importance of developing power, rather than knowledge, is well urged by President Hadley, *The Education of the American Citizen*, pp. 175—190.

[1] A notable article on education for business men (*Unternehmer*), in Schmoller's *Jahrbuch*, 1916, complains however that German Universities themselves devote too much attention to preparing those, who aim at employment under Government, for official examinations. The writer insists that the education of business men should be more free; and bring them more into contact with those whose minds and associations are less distinctively official: it should include some study of economic science. The subjects of this Section are considered further in Appendix K.

II, x, 4. 4. *In periods of economic reconstruction there is an urgent demand for creative faculty; and those who come to the front, seldom owe much to any formal preparation for their work.*

"The poet is born not made." The original meaning of the word *poet* is "a man who creates": and it is a commonplace in University life, that while the merely able man's success depends greatly on the teachers into whose hands he has fallen, the man of genius is fashioned mainly by himself. In like manner it seems to be true that the man, who proves to be endowed with business genius, has seldom owed very much to formal education. The peculiarity of his mind does not lie in the power of doing any one thing in particular. He penetrates quickly to the root of each of the many conditions of success in the attainment of a proposed practical end: he coordinates them, moulding and combining them anew. He formulates large schemes of operations, measuring their risks, and facing steadily those which his judgment approves. He may not have the faculties needed for scientific research, or even for highly specialized invention: even if he has them, he can hardly give them full exercise without blunting the edge of his energy in that work which bears most directly on his immediate end. But he watches all new thoughts and inventions which point to that end; and he is quick to adapt them, or to cause them to be adapted, for his special uses. These considerations were most strikingly illustrated by American industry in the phase in which it was about a generation ago.

But the earlier history of British industries was on similar lines; for, as we have seen, the leaders of those industries in the last quarter of the eighteenth and the first quarter of the nineteenth centuries were mostly rugged men, with a much narrower outlook than that of most of the later leaders of American industry; but with like self-reliant, self-contained characters. A bold, vigorous use of the newest machinery and methods put them for a time beyond the range of competition by those, who were much occupied with careful attention to details and the teachings of long experience. The stream of inventions never slackened; but yet, when the main outlines of the new methods were fairly settled, machines with the last improvement but one could hold their own fairly well. From that time forward strong self-reliant energy lost some of its importance relatively to a sedulous care for detail; and also to careful account-keeping and other irksome matters, in which organized experience is more serviceable than quick flashes of individual initiative. Consequently, before businesses began to fall largely under Joint Stock ownership, they again became hereditary. The son of a manufacturer profited by traditions as to things, methods and persons handed down to his father; and a youth who rose from the ranks into business had to overcome more difficulties on his way than during times of revolutionary change.

Those who held the chief places in American industry at the end of the nineteenth century, had lived through a period of transformation similar to that which British industry had undergone several generations earlier. Thus, as already noted, Mr Carnegie sets out a long array of leading industrial businesses, which have been founded in America during the last two generations by mechanics, clerks and office boys; and of great commercial houses that have been founded by clerks and office boys: but he can make only a short list of those which have been founded by men whose early lives were spent under easy conditions[1].

[1] He concludes: "Neither capital, nor influence, nor college learning, nor all combined have proved able to contend in business successfully against the energy and indomitable will which spring from all-conquering poverty." He lays stress on the fact that an alert office boy has opportunities for reading the characters of all conditions of men; while the lad who lives at home, at school and in college till he is twenty-two is often brought into direct contact with only one thin stratum of human character. Mr J. D. Rockefeller's account in his *Reminiscences* of the education, which he got by keeping his ears open while doing menial work in the office of a small business, is very illuminating. It is however to be remembered that the percentage of the mechanics, clerks, office boys and others, who have used these advantages as ladders, by which to climb to the highest posts of business, is not very great: it may be less than that of the college lads who have turned their connection with business to good account.

Mr Archbold, a vice-president of the Standard Oil Company, ascribes Mr Rockefeller's success to the marvellous "power of control" by which he "can so draw together the best men in mechanics, in executive work, in buying and selling, that they work as a unit."

Mr Gates, who ultimately became a chief leader of the iron and steel industry, was put into a responsible position, though without any experience in

II, x, 5.

5. *The increasing scope for trained faculty and methodical organization of detail in industry and trade.*

Opportunities for economic reconstruction, offered by the opening out of unknown Continents and of new communications between old Continents, belong in great measure to the past. And, though it is true that the industrial evolution caused by the advance of technique during the last few decades has been much more rapid than at any other time; yet the leading characteristic of modern advance is its increasing dependence on faculties and aptitudes that need to be developed by patient study, if not by some sort of academic discipline.

Even on the side of business speculation we find that individual initiative is being in some measure supplanted by agencies, which give great scope to alert diligence combined with moderate natural ability and resource. The ordinary newspaper press and special trade journals now supply at a nominal cost detailed information on nearly every affair, in which a business man is interested; and he can supplement it more quickly than formerly by confidential information as to any matter of private interest. He can, if he will, know all that is happening at home and abroad in regard to things in which he is interested as buyer or seller; what new sources of supply are being opened up; what new demands are growing and which of them are likely to be permanent; what new technique is being tried, and how the trials are going: what new uses of by-products are being developed; and what progress is being made by industries cognate to his own, on which its progress may largely depend. In these and other ways the new age gives ever increasing opportunities to the business man to strengthen his enterprise by making good use of information, which is generally accessible, but yet cannot be

business, because Mr Rockefeller had observed that he showed capacity in his work for the Baptist Education Society: and later on, Mr Gates appointed Mr Bowers, "an honest, enterprising, keen and thrifty man," but one without any experience in the management of shipping, to control the company's fleet of lake steamers. The splendid career of the electrical works of Siemens and Halske owed much to the decision of Halske to call to his aid the artillery officer Wiener Siemens, who had then no knowledge of the business. And the Zeiss works profited in like manner by annexing the University professor Abbé.

turned to account without some mental effort; and if he does not avail himself of them, he must make way for more alert competitors. II, x, 5.

Moreover the man whose originating ability, though considerable, is not of the first order, must depend largely on a careful study of the best results that have been attained by others. For otherwise he may be outpaced by those who have scarcely any high initiative, but can bring to bear on their work a sound trained faculty in thinking clearly; and who have learnt under good guidance how to turn to account the multitudinous knowledge, which modern resources place at the disposal of those who seek them rightly. This training is not necessary for the man of high natural genius: he is eager for work in which his great strength tells, and has too much self-respect to refuse helpful guidance from any source: but a man of less exceptional ability, whose mind and character have not been disciplined, is apt to humour a false pride by a partiality for his own devices. Thus America, while following the lead of Germany in the subtler technical applications of science, is pioneering applications of a broad University training in the conduct of business. As Mr Carnegie says:—"the trained mechanic of the past, who has hitherto carried off most of the honours in our industrial works, is now to meet a rival in the scientifically educated youth, who will push him very hard indeed.... The mechanic is disposed to adopt narrow views of affairs, for he is generally well up in years before he comes into power; while the scientifically trained boy has no prejudices, and goes in for the latest invention or newest method, no matter if another has discovered it[1]."

[1] There is much helpful suggestion in the contrasts drawn by Dr Youngman, *Economic causes of great fortunes*, between the origin of representative fortunes in three stages of American history, viz. (1) John Jacob Astor's many sided work, on lines not very different from those of the eighteenth century; (2) the powerful, if often malignant, Stock Exchange speculations of Jay Gould; and (3) the even stronger building up of "group fortunes" by quiet incessant, financial operations, not always above criticism from the social point of view; but in which "constructive speculation" has predominated on the whole. His study points to the conclusion that there is no one route by which even any one great fortune has been reached; and that versatility, as well as imagination, judgment and assiduity have been conspicuous in the making of every sort of great fortune. See also Dr Watkins' *The growth of great fortunes*.

II, x, 6. 6. *The organizing faculty of a masterful mind can sometimes make itself felt over the whole of a large business, even when owned in joint stock; largely through its influence on well-chosen chiefs of departments.*

The position of an able man, conducting a business which he owns, is very strong in industries in which almost the maximum of efficiency can be attained by a comparatively small capital; which are constantly changing their form; which require restless care and initiative; and in which the selection of the right man for any post of responsibility is too critical and difficult a task to be performed adequately by salaried officials.

A business owned by one man seldom offers scope for quite the highest forms of organization. But under modern conditions, and especially in the New World, a man of exceptional genius may build up so large a business, while he is still in the prime of life, that it becomes an organic whole, more complete, more carefully organized, and more efficient than any which could have been created, before steam and electricity and large mobile stocks of capital had quickened the growth of great enterprises. All its various departments are coordinated; means are nicely adapted to ends; and human capacities are adjusted by sympathetic insight to their several tasks. Only a little of this harmony is sacrificed, and fresh strength is generally gained, when the head of a business takes to himself fitting partners; and even when the partnership is turned into a joint stock company with limited liability, with the understanding that its shares are not to be put on the market, but to be held by those who are actually conducting its affairs. Under favourable conditions such a business may flourish for many years, as is shown by much experience in England and other Western countries. So long as the men who have made it remain at the helm, it is likely to retain nearly all the energy and resource of individual management, combined with greater breadth and solidity. For such men are able to decide freely each question on its merits. They can boldly invest large sums in improvements, the importance of which is not obvious to the onlooker, but which will bear rich fruit in due time. They can throw away plant that is almost new, if more efficient plant has just been invented; for they are in no fear of the censure of shareholders, who cannot understand either the merits of the new plant, or the conditions which made the purchase of the abandoned plant reasonable at the time[1].

But this brings us back to the difficulty suggested at the beginning of Section 2, that continuity of policy, and unity of purpose are not always to be had on a Board of Directors; especially in a business, which can get but little guidance from tradition. In fact, a joint stock company, when exceptionally progressive, generally shows the impress of an individual mind and character. This is marked in the railway history of England: and in America the president of a railway system of some ten thousand miles, especially if he and his friends hold a considerable part of its stock, may fashion the railway, and even to some extent the district which it serves, largely on his own model. But after all, the main work of a railway is relatively uniform and amenable to routine methods: it may flourish if that is well done, even though its minor departments are not highly efficient. The difficulties of centralized administration are greater in vast manufacturing undertakings[2].

The creation of vast businesses involves great risks unless there be good reason to expect that men competent to manage them will be forthcoming. It is often assumed that they are sure to be forthcoming: but history gives little support to this belief. "There are many who can manage a million dollars, few who can manage ten million, and next to none who can

[1] This arrangement may be adopted in order to enable some members of a partnership, or small company, to retire from active participation in the business and to limit their risks to their holdings:—a plan which may work well if the active members are strong, and the passive members give them a free hand.

[2] Sometimes the inevitable difficulties of vast size are increased by making provision for the heads of secondary businesses which have been absorbed in order to strengthen the strategical position of a great amalgamation.

Centralized administration of railways has always owed much to the telegraphic communication which the exigencies of the traffic require to be maintained even with the smallest station. But the telephone is more efficient than the telegraph in enabling the chief to read the character of his subordinates, and it is lending its aid in a special degree to scattered branches of a manufacturing business. It enables, for instance, the chief chemist to be largely responsible for the chemical side of the work of the branches: this promotes order and economy in the first instance, but may weaken the character of his assistants.

II, x, 6. manage fifty million. The mere work of centralized administration puts a tax on the brains of men who are accustomed to a smaller range of duties, which very few find themselves able to bear[1]."

[1] Hadley, *The Education of the American Citizen*, p. 42. Evidence to a similar effect was given before the Industrial Commission by eminent promoters of the tendency towards industrial consolidation. Mr Flint, an authority of almost unrivalled experience, admitted that a consolidation, that can be worked efficiently by "an intellectual giant," may be in great danger in the hands of anyone else (*Report of Industrial Commission*, vol. XIII. p. 84). In the *North American Review*, May, 1901, he said: "Had A. T. Stewart been a member of an industrial combination at the time of his death, of which combination John Wanamaker had also been a member, the business of A. T. Stewart & Co. would never have declined." But this takes no account of the chance that Wanamaker's full faculties might not have developed under such conditions.

Mr Schwab, who was then President of the United States Steel Corporation, told the Commission that the limit of a single man's power of controlling a great concern had not been reached: but he admitted that "it is a matter of the greatest difficulty to-day to hire administrative ability sufficient to run a concern without loss." And, so far from laying great stress on the economy of unified administration in a very large business, he "was careful to throw the whole responsibility for the results and the manufacture upon the subsidiary organizations." He thought it better in the long run to put three rollings under the independent controls of three men, than to put all under that of the ablest. He set the three to rival one another; and thus in effect supported the principle of competition against that of monopoly. He described the U.S. Steel Corporation as "largely a clearing house for information" between the presidents of the subsidiary companies. Each is allowed to make bargains freely with the others: and "each company is so interested in its own business that it is hard to get them to make bargains, each wants to drive so close a bargain with the other." But of course all are ultimately controlled by the power, which the possession of the majority of the shares in each subsidiary company gives to the central administration, of displacing at the next annual meeting any director or other officer who does not fall in with the central policy: and Mr Schwab told the Commission that Mr Carnegie had started by forming a separate company for each branch of his business, while he himself of course retained a controlling interest in each, corresponding to that which is held by the central administration of the U.S. Steel Corporation: but at last Mr Carnegie fused all these companies into one; because he considered it was not for the good of the whole that those in (say) the coke department should have their own special interests to look after, when a contract was being arranged between it and (say) the steel department. (*Ib.* pp. 493, 450—3, and 463.)

CHAPTER XI

BUSINESS ORGANIZATION: APPLICATIONS OF SCIENTIFIC METHOD

1. *Movements towards the general application of scientific methods in business administration were pioneered by studies of cost-accounts.* II, XI, 1.

We have seen how modern industry is compelled to make increasing use of the results obtained by professional students of science; and even to set up great laboratories for the intensive study of particular scientific problems, which lie in the course of its higher developments. We are now to consider recent developments of an old tendency to apply scientific methods to the organization and administration of business as a whole. The tendency to the use of systematic analysis as an engine of business, first attracted general attention as the result of dissatisfaction with the crudity of customary methods of making up "cost-accounts"; that is, accounts which claim to show the total charges to be attributed to each particular class of product. Incidentally progress was made in the easier task of enabling the accounts of a large business to act as a substitute for the eye of the master of a small business, in regard to the prevention of waste.

Absolutely exact cost-accounting would of course require that the path of each element of material, on its way to becoming a finished product, be traced sufficiently to show how much of it was embodied in the product, how much was consumed in the process, and how much was wasted or otherwise lost, and so on. In ordinary practice such matters are of course not set out fully in the accounts; but foremen and other officers are intrusted to see that material is not

II, XI, 1. wasted, and that the operatives give a fair return for each hour's wages. Such checks as are applied are commonly rather general in character. Experience is trusted to show about how much consumption of material, and expenditure of labour is required for a given output of any kind: a certain normal allowance is made for wastage; and any considerable excess can be met by a special inquiry. Also, when several works in the same ownership are engaged on the same process of manufacture, the supreme control can infer, from a comparison of their accounts, which of them is the most economically and efficiently managed: such comparisons tend to strengthen large aggregations of business on a side on which they are apt to be weak. For indeed the personal observations, and the instinctive judgments on matters of detail, which are within the competency of a small master "whose eye is everywhere," are chief sources of his strength. They enable him with but little effort or outlay to exercise so effective a check on sluggishness and waste, that a large business, conducted on traditional lines, cannot attain to it even by lavish expenditure[1].

In a large business the vigilance of trusty officials may furnish an adequate safeguard against some wastes: but there are many for which no check seems possible except that furnished by a comparison of written records of the various sides of each transaction. This is one of the tasks of the science of accounting,

[1] This fact was impressed on me in one of the tours which I made formerly in the manufacturing districts of England and some other countries. I may record the extreme instance of the owner of a lock factory, employing some thirty hands. I was directed to him as one whose goods were of high quality, and commanded a price somewhat above the average. His method of working without any clerks, and with but few written accounts, was instructive. His materials were all under lock; and the keys were never out of his control, except when he left them with his sister during his absence from home. He gave out to each man from time to time such material as was appropriate; and he knew without consulting books whether the man made good use of it. He knew this partly by general reasoning, and partly by observation: for in constant presence among the men, he had learnt to measure narrowly the skill, diligence, judgment and carefulness of each. He knew, without any aid from records, almost exactly what each thing produced in his factory had cost him, and therefore what rate of profits he was making on each class of his work: for, his work being all of one kind, he could frame his estimates of indirect outlay on each task by means of his knowledge of the direct outlay on it.

which has received a very high development during the last few generations. But its finest work is too laborious, intricate, and costly to be appropriate to any but very strong businesses: and in fact the check, which accountants exert on waste, has often been limited to ascertaining that the entries made in a broad statement of one side of the work of a business correspond to those made in a similar broad statement of another side. Even now they often merely apply a few broad rules, which represent broad results fairly well, while making no pretence of being adapted closely to the special circumstances of each individual case.

Gradually however increasing attention has been paid to the actual extent to which each process of production has laid under contribution, directly or indirectly, the several material resources and human energies belonging to the business: and, in so far as this is done, opportunity is afforded for ascertaining which of its elements have yielded the best results, and where there has been any waste. It is for instance ascertained how much use was made during the production in question of each class of plant: account is taken of the cost of that plant, its wear and tear, its consumption of power; and in some cases even of its liability to rapid depreciation, in consequence of the dependence of the demand for its services on evanescent fashions, etc. Similarly the charges to be set against any particular product on account of storage accommodation, and expenses of internal movement, are specially examined, in cases in which these charges are likely to be exceptionally light or exceptionally heavy: for it is obvious that goods which occupy little space, but demand much high grade labour, are easily marketed and are made of expensive material, ought to be charged on these accounts at a low rate relatively to their prime costs; while a high rate is appropriate to things which have the opposite characteristics. Again an hour's work of a machine for which there is but little appropriate work must be charged more highly than that of a machine which is seldom idle: machines, that do little work, are often engaged on things that are not in general demand; therefore sell slowly; and have high traders costs on the turnover: and so on.

II, XI, 2. 2. *A general view of the aims and methods of the movement that goes by the title, "Scientific Management."*

A little while ago no one would have been likely to suggest that it would be profitable to keep elaborate records of every detail of the expenditure of material and labour in a factory with a large and various output. But a scheme has been already brought into operation on a considerable scale in America, under which it is claimed that such records are obtained as by-products of a movement for applying to the mental work of business those general methods of extreme subdivision and specialization of labour, which have greatly increased the aggregate efficiency of manual labour[1].

Its chief originator was the late F. W. Taylor: it was developed, with some variations from the original plan, by Mr Emerson, Mr Gantt and others; and it has now a powerful band of constructive advocates. It does not claim to set up a science of business: that is not yet in sight, and perhaps it is unattainable. But it has in great measure made good its claim to carry the application of scientific methods to the broader problems of business, much further than they had been carried before. Many of its chief proposals have been applied by able business men in past times, and especially in recent decades: but it has given them such coherence, and power of progressive development by aid of organized records, that it seems likely to influence economic advance on many sides; even though it may be found that some of its claims are pitched too high, and that some others are opposed by too strong drifts of opinion and sentiment, especially among British operatives, to be likely to meet with general acceptance in the near future.

The present Volume is concerned chiefly with the business point of view of industry and trade: but their human aspect must be made prominent in the present chapter. For Scientific Management is in the main a method of redistributing and reorganizing the functions and the mutual relations of the personnel of a great business, with the purpose of increasing aggregate efficiency by narrowing the range of responsibility of

[1] Some explanation on this subject is given at the end of the following Section.

most of its employees, and bringing careful studies to bear on the instructions given in regard to the simplest manual operations.

The chief outward token of the new plan is the elaboration of a system of cards so full, and so carefully organized that the central control shall have a firm basis for arranging the details of its work. Other cards, partly duplicates of cards which remain with the central control, pass downwards through heads and subheads of departments, and minor officials; while some reach the manual operative. They cover very many details, of which no record had been kept previously even in the most highly organized businesses: but almost all of those details, which an expert cost-accountant desires, are entered on some classes of them. It is claimed for instance that the cards, issued for the purpose of insuring that each department and sub-department shall be always supplied with the material needed for uninterrupted work, afford automatically a basis for reckoning the obligations under which a cost-accountant would need to put them; and the special purposes of those obligations. Meanwhile the cards, being passed from hand to hand, may discharge various executive functions in all departments of the business; whereas entries in ledgers, or on cards designed for exclusive use in the office, have a much narrower sphere of influence[1].

3. *The chief responsibility for the affairs of a great business in Scientific Management is intrusted to a Planning Department: and this, together with the higher control under which it works, develops the organization of the business according to "function" rather than "line."*

Thus one main drift of Scientific Management is towards concentration, combined with specialization of control in regard to all matters that require thought and judgment: a second main drift has its chief origin in studies of machine tools, and of the relative efficiencies of various manual operations. The

[1] Some tendency to underrate previous progress can often be noted in a bold strong new venture: and models of entries in ledgers and other office records, which seem to anticipate some cards that are prominent in the new movement, may be noted in as old a book as *Factory Accounts* (by Garcke and Fells, London, 1887).

II, XI, 3. result of the second may be epitomized in the phrase that traditional methods of work, and especially of manual work, are "excellent servants, but not good masters." They are the heirs of the progressive experience of ages: and it would be foolish to attempt to build up new methods without care for the many fine and subtle indications that are latent in the old. But nevertheless the promoters of Scientific Management have shown some surprising instances of economy of effort, obtained by the suggestions of an expert in mechanical science; and by practice, working on the basis of traditional methods of manual work.

These two drifts, the one towards extreme subdivision of mental effort, and the other towards the bringing of specially trained intelligence to bear in turning to account the traditional methods of ordinary labour, have issued almost necessarily in a proposal to set up a "Planning Department"; which has the duty of making provision for every need of every operative who will be called upon to contribute to any process of production. This proposal, though not the starting point of the movement, is the best starting point for a general description of its influence on business administration. The movement is in effect a bold effort towards the progressive application of analysis, observation, experiment, and reason to a class of problems which have until recently been in the hands of men little addicted to analysis; and in which much virgin soil awaits, even in old countries, those who bring powerful methods of thought to bear on it. But America offers an exceptionally large scope for the movement: for her problems are newer and her artisans have less set habits and traditions than those of Britain, or even of Germany; and her business men, if less sedulous students of science in the narrower sense of the term than those of Germany, have developed a more conspicuous faculty for the application of laboratory and other scientific methods to the larger problems of business administration.

The movement has not escaped the danger of exaggeration by enthusiastic adherents: but its chief leaders regard it as a development on a large scale of certain well-known principles. They urge that progress has been most rapid, where experience in bulk has been supplemented by well-considered experiments in detail. They lay stress on the two facts that every business has some problems of administration to solve, which are peculiar to it, just as it may have occasion to use some special machines; and that most of its problems have much in common with many that have to be faced in other businesses[1].

The exigencies of an army in the field require that complete authority be given to every officer, commissioned or non-commissioned, in regard to all doubtful matters, as to which no instructions from a higher authority are available on the spot. But the organization of the army as a whole, in preparation for war and in war, is committed to a large staff, consisting of many departments, each specialized on a distinct *function*, under a supreme control. Traditionary business arrangements, it is urged, follow the order of "line organization," in which each one receives all his instructions from the same superior; though the exigencies of a campaign, out of which this order arose, have seldom any existence in a compact business, however large: "staff" or "functional" organization is more efficient under favourable conditions, such as are often found in large businesses. The particular details of staff organization must vary from one industry to another. But the same underlying principle applies to all: and we may with advantage follow Taylor in taking large engineering works as representative of conditions in which the advantages of Scientific Management carry furthest.

On his plan the central office under the immediate direction of the head of the business (practically the old counting house rearranged) deals with questions of general policy, especially in regard to sales: as, *e.g.*, what things to make for stock, what

[1] Some of the adherents of the new scheme have indeed brought it under the suspicion of being "top-heavy" by proposing to apply it to small businesses, for which it is not designed. Perhaps there have also been some departures from Taylor's position that, in its essence, the movement is one for the supersession of unreasoned routine by elastic methods; to the concoction of which there have gone three parts in four of analysis, the remaining fourth being common sense. The thought and experience of half a generation have already brought out a number of variations on the original proposal, chiefly tending to soften its rigid outlines; and in particular to mitigate the severity with which the personal relations between the operative and those from whom he took his instructions were at first subordinated to the technical.

II, XI, 3. orders have to be accepted, and so on: it procures cost-estimates by aid of the lower departments, and information as to prices to be obtained by sale in different markets from its agents and other sources. When it has decided that a certain thing is to be made in any quantity, the Engineering and Drafting room, or rooms, develop their rough estimates of quantities, and prepare complete working drawings. All this is according to customary routine: but under Scientific Management details are worked out in advance; partly in order that working "instruction cards" may be prepared for every operative.

These instruction cards represent the combined work of several men in the department, each of whom has his own function. One is a specialist on cutting tools, and the use of slide-rules in regard to speeds. Another knows the best and quickest motions to be made in setting up the work and removing it, etc. A third gives the proper time for each element of the work. All these details are written on a single card[1]. "A ticket made up in the central planning department, when combined with the instruction card, serves to plan the work in advance; then it is used to control the order of work by being placed on the bulletin board....On this ticket is stamped the time at which the work begins, and when it ends. It checks off the progress of the work on the route-sheet. Then it goes to the accounting department, from which the man's pay is made up. It is then redistributed and furnishes the labour cost of the particular operation on the cost-sheet of the job. From cost-sheets similar to this are summarized not only the cost on all jobs, but department expenses and charges, which appear in each four-week period statement[2]."

A little will be said in the next Section as to the nature of

[1] The "instruction card," in an engineering shop, instructs "both the executive bosses and the men in all the details of their work. It tells them briefly the general and detail drawing to refer to; the piece number and the cost order number to charge the work to; the special jigs, fixtures, or tools to use; where to start each cut, the exact depth of each cut and how many cuts to take; the speed and feed to be used for each cut; and the time within which each operation must be finished." This description of course refers to work that is not of a routine character. A few words on the card suffice in regard to familiar repetition work.

[2] See p. 126 of the *Report of a conference on Scientific Management* held in 1911 at the Tuck School of administration and finance.

the economies of manual effort which are claimed as resulting from the application of analysis, experiment and measurement to common operations. Assuming these economies to be highly important, the following general positions are laid down: "If practicable the work of each man should be confined to the performance of a single leading duty....All possible brain-work should be removed from the shop and centered in the planning or laying out department, leaving for the foremen and gang bosses work strictly executive in its nature....Each man must learn how to give up his own particular way of doing things, adapt his methods to the many new standards, and grow accustomed to receiving and obeying directions covering details large and small, which in the past have been left to his individual judgment....The high priced mechanic needs (even more than the cheap labourer) the cooperation of men better educated than himself in finding the laws [appropriate for guiding him in his work], and then in selecting, developing and training him to think in accordance with these laws[1]."

In the new system, as in the old, orders seldom go past subordinate officers: each man receives them from someone immediately above him. But, whereas the operative was under the exclusive direction and influence of a single foreman for nearly all purposes; under the new system he takes orders in regard to different sides of his work from eight (or some other considerable number of) specialized foremen, commonly called "bosses." Each boss acts as technical guide over a rather narrow area for a large number of workmen; and therefore his relations to each of them are so slight and impersonal, as to

[1] See Taylor, *Shop Management*, pp. 98—100 and 113; and *Scientific Management*, p. 97.

Emerson's method differs from Taylor's mainly by maintaining "line" foremanship as far as possible: his "functional" experts are relatively few; and every foreman or other officer in each line has access to an appropriate expert in any difficulty: the expert instructs the line officer, who passes on the instruction. Time alone can decide between the two. Taylor's method seems to have as yet the greater number of adherents: but yet it is said that the full system of functional foremanship has seldom been installed, and when installed has in some measure yielded to a return of the old military order. Differences among the systems of Taylor, Gantt and Emerson, the chief leaders of the movement, are implicit in their writings; and are set out in many books; for instance Thompson, *l.c.*; Drury, *Scientific Management* (where there are some interesting personal details); and Hoxie, *Scientific Management and Labor*.

II, xi, 3. have little control over his general conduct. A special "shop disciplinarian" is therefore invoked in case of his wrong-doing. Such a system, when thoroughly set up, and worked by able and enthusiastic adherents, may not improbably turn the existing faculties of the operative to the best account in the production of material wealth. It is not irrelevant to remark that international comparative statistics show the output per head in engineering industries generally to be a great deal higher in America than anywhere else; though it is true that much of this difference is due to her extended use of standardized mechanical processes. There is a notable excess in the horse-power that aids each thousand operatives in America even over that which prevails in Britain[1].

In so far as the cards relate to payments for labour and consumption of material, they afford a direct check always available against waste and other forms of leakage. In so far as they can be used to show how much time of any particular machine has been given to the job, they contribute to an accurate estimate of the cost of each product; on the assumption that an hour's work of any machine is to be charged at the same price to every class of product on which it is used[2].

[1] The shop disciplinarian "sees that a complete record of each man's virtues or defects is kept." He has much to do with readjusting wages: and he should be "peace-maker" (Taylor, *Shop Management*, pp. 103—4; following a luminous account of the functions of the seven other "bosses"). Mr C. Bertrand Thompson says that "the time study and instruction methods of Scientific Management have increased the output of hand operatives from 10 per cent. to about 300 per cent., the majority of cases lying between 60 per cent. and 100 per cent." (*Q. J. of E.* Feb. 1915, p. 278). But he points out that these results involved elaborate organization: and the expense of that organization may have outweighed the savings on the cost of manual labour in some cases. It may be added that the personal influence of able exponents of the new system must have counted for much.

[2] Parkhurst, *Applied Methods of Scientific Management*, goes into this matter in some detail. The time clerk's card, aided with appropriate clocks, shows the time which each man (known by his number) is allowed for a job; also the time, during which he is to use a certain machine for it. The cost clerk's sheets show all materials requisitioned from stores or outside purchase for the job: and also all charges actually made for labour spent on it. "All time posted on the cost sheets is distributed into a daily wage distribution book, which agrees with the similar entry made daily by the time clerk, so that the time card coupons from which these postings are made, are sure to agree with the total on the man's time cards, as shown by the time clock. A limit of error, not to exceed four hours in time, or one dollar in money, or both, is allowed to

The planning department arranges that nothing shall go into store or leave it without records, so made out as to check one another automatically: that material shall be ready for every job, and yet not be stored in excess; that each job shall be pressed forward according to its relative importance, that every class of machine shall, as far as possible, be in fairly constant employment; and, of course, that the total "route" traversed by each product during manufacture shall be short and easy. The men in the shop follow their instructions; they are not required to use any forethought, or any considerable discretion[1].

Probably another generation must pass before experience has taught how much of this vast detail is worth what it costs: and in particular how far it is expedient to use the instruction cards as a basis for exact accounts of all operations and their costs. No doubt the same restless genius which has brought Scientific Management to its present high level of achievement will improve it progressively; till all the more obvious criticisms on its general scheme will have become obsolete[2].

II, XI, 4.

4. *In Scientific Management it is arranged that, as far as possible, each frequently recurring manual operation shall be made the subject of elemental time studies, conducted under favourable conditions by highly trained observers, who seek guidance from the traditional practice of skilled operatives.*

A movement making for large change is seldom both entirely new, and very important. It is not likely to be very important

go uncorrected per week" (*ib.* 3 G). Stress is laid on the fact that the records of the stores clerk afford an exact inventory up to date, without the cost and disturbance of periodical stock-takings (*ib.* 3 F and 5 A).

[1] A little may be added as to the work of the route clerk. He makes out a "next-work order" for each piece needed for any job: and in this he is guided (subject to certain technical considerations) by the geographical conveniences of the order of movement; and by the extent to which the several machines happen to be busy. Information on this last point is supplied to him by the order-of-work clerk. He is present at the factory board meetings, so that he may learn the relative importance of the different jobs, and bring the various parts through for completion in the proper time. All next-work cards are received by him; and the order, in which he arranges them, decides the order in which the foremen take them out and act on them. For further details, see Taylor, *Shop Management*, pp. 110—120; and Knöppel, *Installing efficiency methods*.

[2] Influences of the movement can be traced in many directions. For instance Mr Selfridge's "Organization Chart of a twentieth century Department Store,"

II, XI, 4. unless it has its roots in broad principles of human or material nature: such broad principles have often suggested ideas, which have been forgotten because they were not ripe, or because the time was not ripe for them. In a later age they are thought out anew, and attract general attention by their own strength and by the favour of circumstances. One of the chief ideas of Scientific Management was worked out a considerable way by Babbage in the middle of last century; and, for good reasons, he took as his chief illustration the common task of shovelling earth, which Taylor was to use for the same purpose later on[1].

with some 4000 employees, shows seven managers of departments. Four of these are specialized vertically on the line system. But the Managers of Staff, of Systems, and of Expenses, are functional, and are responsible for particular sides of the whole business. The duties of the last of these are delicate: he is to make suggestions for economy wherever he can see room for it.

[1] Babbage says: "In taking a comprehensive view of any subject, it is very desirable to throw into the shade all its minor points: but, in estimating the consequences of any set of facts, there is another condition which must be fulfilled, before we can arrive at accurate conclusions. If we are about to neglect a cause on account of its apparent insignificance, it is *essential* that it should not be one of frequent recurrence." He remarked that the weaker of two men, engaged on shovelling earth, could do more work than the stronger, provided he had made a more careful study of his work, and had hit upon a better weight of earth to be raised at each stroke, a better number of strokes to be made in an hour; and better weights, sizes and forms for his shovel and his barrow. He further argues that, "if a labourer inconsiderately lifts his shovel but an inch or two more than is necessary to throw its load into his barrow, although the exertion of force is trivial in each instance, its repeated occurrence during the whole day will produce at its conclusion a very sensible difference either in fatigue or in the amount of the work done. Napoleon is said to have remarked of Laplace, when he was Minister of the Interior, that he was too much occupied with considering *les infiniment petites*. To dwell upon small affairs, which are isolated, is not the province of a statesman: but to integrate the effect of their constant recurrence is worthy of the greatest." And he lays down clearly the great maxim, which has guided most of the best work of students of economics as of other sciences: "One of the most important processes in all inquiry is to divide the subject to be considered into as many different questions as it will admit of, and then to examine each separately; or, in other words, to suppose that each single cause successively varies, while all the others remain constant." (See his little known, *The Exposition of 1851*, pp. 3 and 4.) Mr Thompson justly remarks (*Scientific Management*, p. 6) that, though the modern movement in the same direction as Babbage's thought owes nothing directly to him, yet "the extension of specialization beyond manual labour to mental labour, which is at the basis of the Taylor doctrines of functional foremanship and the separation of planning from execution," was suggested in Babbage's well known *Economy of Manufactures*. Reference has been made (above, p. 224) to the fundamental

A great deal has been learnt as to what education can do and cannot do for the workman, since Babbage proposed that improvement in such methods should be sought by education: the workman must "when a boy have been taught to examine *separately*" the details of his work. More is known now than then as to the extent to which a thorough education of the masses of the people can contribute to industrial efficiency, as well as to the elevation of life: but experience has also shown that mere education cannot easily fit a man for such complex tasks as are demanded by the leaders of Scientific Management. Moreover their judgment has perhaps been a little biassed by the contrast between the intellectual agility of the class and race to which they belong, and the crude physical strength of many of the manual workers whom they direct. They therefore propose to build themselves on the foundation laid by tradition and the individual intelligence of the worker, but not to make great demands upon it.

Further they urge that the fallibility of tradition as a guide is evidenced by the multitude, "fifty or a hundred," of traditional methods of performing almost every manual operation: and that, on the other hand, the fundamental accuracy of traditional guidance is shown by the facts that almost all traditional methods conform to the rules that rhythmical movements are physio-

idea of his famous chapter on "The division of [manual] labour": his less known chapter on "The division of mental labour" ends with a eulogy of the partial system of functional foremanship which already prevailed in mines.

Babbage and Taylor were similar in other ways. Babbage spent much of his life in working on his "Differential Machine," for mathematical calculations, —probably the most marvellous mechanism ever devised: his analysis of the cost of making pins is quoted in a Report of a Committee of American Engineers, 1912, reprinted by C. B. Thompson, *l.c.* pp. 171—2.

Taylor having been impressed by the haphazard adjustments of cutting tools, and the machines in which they were set to their tasks, resolved to find general principles which should govern the shape of the tool; and also the relations between the amount of power supplied to the driving tool, the rate of its movement, the rate of feed of the material, the depth of the cut to be made and so on. He claimed to have connected these elements by mathematical formulae; which, when embodied in a set of four special slide-rules, will enable engineering artisans to obtain at once the adjustments most suitable for any particular case. His expenses during the twenty-six years spent on this task, in the course of which he cut four hundred tons of metal into chips, were defrayed by ten industrial companies: and it appears that the result amply justified the outlay.

II, XI, 4. logically advantageous; that economy of nervous stimulus is attained by avoiding the use of large muscles when the work can be done efficiently by small muscles; and so on. They have set themselves to "induce each workman to use his best endeavours, his hardest work, all his traditional knowledge, his skill, his ingenuity and his goodwill—in a word, his 'initiative,' so as to yield the largest possible return[1]."

These general principles can be most easily apprehended by a detailed instance: and none better can be taken than that of shovelling; which, as has just been said, Babbage and Taylor have alike recognized as combining the advantages of familiarity, definiteness, and a greater complexity of movement than is generally recognized.

Two first-class shovellers in a business, that employed many, were invited to work for two or three months, on the understanding that, while complying with instructions, they should receive double their usual wages. A man stood over them all day with a stop-watch; so as to find out how much they did in a given time, with varying shovels and loads and periods of rest. The bargain with them was that they were neither to hurry, nor to "soldier," but just to go at their ordinary fair pace. Patient experiments ultimately brought out a standard weight of twenty-one pounds for each lift: a standard lifting movement in which the shovel rested on the left leg, and the weight of the body was thrown on the right arm so as to start the weight of the shovel upwards by its own fall. Then the standard wage rate per ton raised was so adjusted that a first-rate man, not one of exceptional excellence, would earn when working on the new method nearly two dollars; that is about half as much again as had been ordinarily received in the district for shovelling work: but for all that the use of the left leg as a fulcrum does not seem to become general in shovelling.

After standards of the mode of handling the work, of the amount done by a high-class shoveller, and of the payment for it, had been thus settled; the next step was to set up an office, in which three college men with their clerks and assistants,

[1] See Taylor, *Scientific Management*, ch. II, and Münsterberg, *Psychology and Industrial Efficiency*; also Bücher's *Arbeit und Rhythmus*.

planned the work for each of the 500 workmen employed in the business, at least one day in advance. Each man in the morning got a slip of paper telling him what shovel to get from the store-room, and where to begin work; while a second paper told him what wage he had earned according to the new standards. If that wage fell much below the standard wage, a "teacher" was sent to improve his methods: if he was obstinate he was dismissed: if he was weak, he was tried at another job. In the result the average earnings of those who remained at the work were sixty per cent. higher than those of the earlier and less carefully selected group had been: but the combined costs of the work and its organization had been halved[1].

The method of time studies is in the main unaltered when a particular job in an engineering workshop is the subject of experiments. An intelligent and willing artisan is selected, and a specially qualified officer set to superintend him. The job has been considered beforehand, and analysed into its various elements. All necessary provision of appropriate material, tools, etc., are ready to hand; so that he is not required to make any movements save those which belong necessarily to the job, and is never held up for want of any requisite. He is induced to work hard, but not so hard as to overtire himself: for his output is wanted to be representative of that which can be maintained steadily by workmen generally; provided, of course, they are supplied with the same standard appliances and subsidiary care, as have been prepared for him. A full record is made at each observation of all details; such as the sequence of operations, the tools and their adjustments, and the speeds, feeds, cuts, etc., employed: these may throughout follow a standard; or they may be varied from one experiment to another; the times being taken in every case with a stop-watch.

The superintending officer has perhaps made many such studies of elementary motions or groups of motions in regard

[1] Further details will be found in Taylor's address to the Tuck School Conference, 1912; and in his *Scientific Management*, pp. 65—77. He "had never met a shovel-contractor to whom it had ever occurred that there was such a thing as a science of shovelling."

II, XI, 4. to similar work. He takes account of them, and of similar studies recorded by others: and he looks at the physiological and psychological elements of the whole, as well as at the mechanical. Thus he is able from time to time to make suggestions for changing the method of various movements and perhaps their order: and he continues to experiment till he can no longer effect any further economy of effort[1].

[1] When systematic stop-watch observations of a number of miscellaneous jobs have been made, an almost incredibly large part of the workers' whole time is found to be taken up with minor elementary operations, which are often but little heeded; such as raising different things from floor to machine by hand or crane; and again clamping with different sorts of clamps and bolts. Elemental times for such actions have very wide application, not only in almost every workshop, but also to many different classes of work in each. Mr Sanford E. Thompson, whose investigations formed the basis of the detailed account of time studies (*Shop Management*, 149—158), reports later that there are "instances of data, taken in Philadelphia on the manufacture of one type of machinery, being used in Boston for the manufacture of an entirely different type" (*Journal of Political Economy*, May, 1913, p. 380).

In these studies experiments are made as to the periods of rest, which are found most conducive to lasting efficiency in work which puts great strain on particular muscles or nerves. They sometimes extend to minute motions, too small to be recorded by an ordinary watch, but yet important in the aggregate. Mr Gilbreth applied to them "a motion-picture apparatus, including in the field of vision a large faced clock, the rapid movements of whose hands record small divisions of a second. In the back-ground is a close net-work of fine lines." The result can be read with a magnifying glass; so that, "even in the nimblest work, an expert can detect false motions, and tell the worker which of his various ways of working are the most efficient."

As might be supposed, the practical applications of this method in business are more interesting than important. But it has recently proved of excellent service in helping soldiers who have lost a limb, or are otherwise crippled, to do industrial work. It enables many customary motions to be eliminated, and others modified; so that, for instance, a man who had lost both his arms has been taught to drive a motor car safely at 100 miles an hour. (*Times Engineering Supplement*, December, 1916.)

CHAPTER XII

BUSINESS ORGANIZATION: APPLICATIONS OF SCIENTIFIC METHOD, CONTINUED

1. *The principles of Scientific Management lead up to a careful analysis, partly on lines which have long been followed in some British and other industries, of the notion implied in the term "a standard rate of wages." A claim to be working towards "absolute" standards.* II, XII, 1.

The problems of remuneration of labour, so far as appropriate to this work, belong to its second Volume: but there seems to be an advantage in making a few observations in the present place on the attitude of Scientific Management towards some of them. Although the general tendency of the increase of knowledge and the improvement of communications has been to facilitate contracts, yet the bargaining between employer and employee as to the amount of work to be done, and the wage to be paid for it, has become in some respects less easy and less free than formerly. An operative, who worked more strenuously than was the custom, was always likely to be rebuked by his shopmates. But now he is likely to be called to account at a trade-union meeting, and incur grave censure: for it is argued that his example will tend to make a bad precedent, from the operatives' point of view, in regard to the work expected to be done for a given wage throughout the district, and even beyond.

The method of payment by piece is preferred in most industries by employers; and, for various reasons, it is increasingly tolerated, and even in some industries insisted upon by employees. But the spread of a uniform piece-rate throughout a large district introduces a new social discord: for a fixed

II, XII, 1. rate of payment for work done under varying conditions yields a varying, and not a uniform, rate of remuneration for a given amount of good work. In some shops the plant is the best attainable; and every provision is made for the regular supply to each artisan of work to be done, and of the implements and materials which he needs: the piece-rate required to enable a man to earn good wages in them is lower than in others, which are ill managed. The alert employer is therefore liable to be held to piece-rates so high as to give him little or no reward for his enterprise and energy: an improvement which costs £100, might yield him a return of £200 if he were free to lower the piece-rate to a level which enabled the same wage as before, or even a little above it, to be earned by equal exertions; but, if he must pay the old piece-rate, he may lose nearly the whole £100. The pressure of a standard piece-rate, without provision for standard conditions, hampers some of the best businesses. It retards industrial progress in England and some other countries; in spite of the fact that with a uniform piece-rate the employer, whose plant and methods are the best, can generally secure an abler and steadier set of employees than the average.

America has suffered relatively little from this particular evil. For her conditions change so rapidly that fixed rates of any sort have seldom a very strong footing: her employers are specially alert and resolute; and—the chief cause of all—the workers in her great industries, being of many races and generally strangers to one another, have as yet but little cohesion. These same conditions have aided the endeavour of the leaders of Scientific Management to introduce standard rates of remuneration for work done under standard conditions; and to make provision for increase of the payment, wherever the conditions fall short of the standard set for them.

And yet the most important successes in the attainment of "standard rates of pay by piece," in this the only true sense of the term, have their origin in different and nearly opposite circumstances. They are found in industries in which almost precisely the same task has long been performed by many thousands of workers in almost the same way. Especially in the Lancashire cotton industry the standard piece-rate of wages is a true standard rate: for experience has gradually set up understandings as to the allowances to be made in regard to both quantity and quality of output for particular shortcomings in plant, material or other elements. If an operative thinks that insufficient allowance is made on these accounts in any case, an official of his Trade-union is called to arbitrate, with or without the presence of an official of the Employers' Federation. In many cases the judgment of the Trade-union official alone is accepted: if both officials are summoned, they nearly always agree, and their decision is adopted without demur. This standard is in no sense an "absolute" standard: it does no more than to insure a fair approach to uniformity of remuneration to equally efficient workers in different factories. The enterprising employer is rewarded for his good deeds, and so is the skilful and energetic employee: there is an almost perfectly level rate of real remuneration throughout each subdivision of the industry.

The method is excellent within its limitations. Being based on the experience of the past, it is not fully applicable to industries whose technique changes rapidly. And of course it does little towards answering the questions whether the levels are equitable, as between various classes of those interested, and especially between employers generally and employees generally; and whether they are those best calculated to promote human well-being and to accelerate economic progress. The only substitutes for answers that are available practically, perhaps about the only substitutes for which human nature is fully prepared in its present stage of evolution, are in the arbitrament of conflict, actual or threatened, between the organized forces of employers on the one side and employees on the other: the relative strengths of these forces being influenced from time to time by strategical devices, and accidental incidents. But the controlling force in the background is exercised by the fact, that if profits in any industry are abnormally low relatively to the faculties and the capital required for working it efficiently, employment will dwindle, and therefore the standard of wages must come down: while conversely, if that standard falls materially below the level of wages in occupations of similar difficulty and strain, employers will ere long be so

II, XII, 2. stinted of labour, as to have no strategical defence against a strike for a rise in the standard.

The standard wage for each manual labour task, which Scientific Management would set up, is in like manner liable to be altered by changes in economic circumstances, which may tend to strengthen or weaken the strategic force of employers and employed, whether organized or not. Nevertheless the standards toward which Scientific Management is working have real, though very narrowly limited, claims to be described as in some degree "absolute." For, in the first place, its standard rates depend in a less degree, than do those reached by older methods, on specific customs relating to each particular task: and, in the second place, they claim to have a foundation in the mechanics of elemental movements of the human body, the measurements of which have something of that aloofness from irrelevant accidents, which belongs to laboratory experiments. Let us look back a little.

2. *Suggestions that very high efficiency of plant can be obtained without overstraining the operative in charge of it, by supplying him with high standard conditions of work, and causing his remuneration for each job to increase with every increase in the speed of its performance.*

Scientific Management approaches the problem of remuneration for manual labour by the reflections that time-wages give no direct stimulus towards efficiency; and that piece-rate wages err by yielding the same payment to two men, using similar plant for the same job; though one of them has occupied his plant with it for a day and a half, and the other only for a day. It insists that the importance of setting up a direct connection between an operative's remuneration for a job and the shortness of the time during which he keeps his plant occupied on it, grows with the present rapid increase of the costly plant, for which he is responsible. Moreover the life of many kinds of plant is being rapidly shortened: high-grade plant is seldom worn out; its power of work lasts longer than its claim to be the most efficient of its kind, and the additional wear and tear caused by keeping it more fully at work is almost negligible. These facts are indeed at the base of the "Rowan" and other simple systems of remuneration, which have already some vogue in Britain[1].

But Scientific Management claims that a change in the mode of reckoning remuneration does not suffice: there is needed in addition a "scientific" ascertainment of the time which the job requires when performed with standard provision of accessories, and by a workman of fair average ability. It therefore starts each problem of standard wage fixation by arranging the conditions of the operative's work in all details, and by so instructing him as to his method of work that he is able to get more out of his plant, without undue effort, than he could otherwise. It sets its standard time by observation of the work of a willing operative of fair, but not exceptional ability; it sets the standard wage which corresponds to that standard time, a good deal higher than that which the same man would get if employed in the ordinary way; and finally it increases the wage for the whole of his job for every diminution below the standard of the time during which he detains his plant on it[2]. It claims that standardization of the conditions and methods of work secures the employer against the danger of finding himself unable to keep any promise that he may have made that the rate of remuneration, when once settled, shall not be lowered, unless some definite change in technique, or the auxiliaries, or the general conditions of the labour market renders obsolete the basis on which the standards were set up. Professor Hoxie, "Investigator of Scientific Management for the United States Commission on industrial relations," amassed a vast amount of information on this and similar subjects from operatives and

[1] Diagrams illustrating the working of the schemes of remuneration on this plan, proposed under Scientific Management, the Rowan scheme and others are shown in *A rational wages system*, by Henry Atkinson; and their several principles are explained by C. B. Thompson, *l.c.* pp. 684—705.

[2] Under the Taylor system the operative is penalized severely if he takes more than the standard time, but rewarded highly if he takes much less. Gantt and Emerson are gentler towards rather low efficiency; and not quite so liberal towards that which is high. The terms of the definition of a standard wage for a standard task under standard conditions allow in effect for reconsideration of the money-wage in consequence of an established change in the purchasing power of money.

II, XII, 2. employers; and he holds that this claim of employers is substantiated, though many others are not[1].

The leaders of the movement are emphatic in their assertion that "strenuousness is the opposite of efficiency": if a man is tempted (save in some exceptional emergency) to be strenuous, that proves that the preparation for his work has been inadequate, and not on the lines advocated by the leaders of the movement. They have indeed gone beyond most other students of business administration, in their sedulous applications of the teachings of advanced modern physiology and psychology as to the increase of efficiency which may result from appropriate rest, relaxation, and amusement[2].

Some opposition to the movement has arisen from the erroneous notion that it proposes to put so great a strain on the worker as to exhaust him in a few years. The employer, it is supposed, may find his advantage in paying strong men highly for turning his expensive plant to the best account; but the wages so earned will really be at the cost of their future efficiency: and that cost will fall on them; for the employer will meanwhile have filled their places by others whose fresh strength he will shortly exhaust. There seems to be no good ground for this charge; though, no doubt, some unguarded phrases as to the real cheapness of the exceptionally vigorous labour with which the new scheme is to supply the employer are partly responsible for the misunderstanding[3].

It is admitted that the plant which an operative controls, is to have no rest: but it is urged that the time, which under otiose management he often spends in arranging for the con-

[1] Hoxie, *Scientific Management and Labor*, p. 84.

[2] They have characteristically tabulated the numerical results got from a study of the strain involved during every second in which a heavy weight is carried: they show that in such cases, many periods of rest combined with rather rapid movements during less than half the working day, gave the best result. And again that when pig iron is being handled (each pig weighing 92 pounds) a first-class workman can only be under load 43 per cent. of the day. Of course, the lighter the load, the greater the percentage of the day in which activity is advantageous.

[3] Probably too great stress has been laid on the fact that at Bethlehem Steel Works, under Mr Taylor's management, "the tasks were all purposely made so severe that not more than one out of five labourers (perhaps even a smaller percentage) could keep up" (*Shop Management*, pp. 54—55): that was exceptional, and its example has not been followed.

tinuance of the machine's work, is to be given to keeping the machine at work: his occupation is not intensified, though that of his plant is: the various specialized "bosses" see to it that he has nothing else to do. Strain on the worker is to be shunned for business reasons, as well as humanitarian: and heavy work is to be done by carefully picked men, who can do it without strain. Every man is to be carefully selected as appropriate for the work he is to do, whether it be heavy and suitable for an "ox-like" man, or light and needing agile fingers and delicate care: he is to be specially taught how to do that work: and he is to do no other. The standard price for the work is to be set at such a level that a willing, good, but not exceptionally able, worker under standard conditions will earn as much as he did under the old conditions; though his output is considerably lower than that which emerged in the standard-making experiments. So far all seems well.

But doubts begin to rise, when advocates of the new order hint that no room can be found in it for any worker who is not somewhat highly endowed with manual energy; that a great part of the mental work, which used to be committed to operatives and foremen, will be absorbed by the Planning department; and that nearly all the machines of an engineering shop may "be run by men who are of smaller calibre and attainments, and are therefore cheaper, than those required under the old system[1]." They are, no doubt, justified in saying that the ordinary man underrates greatly the amount and the difficulty of the work, he can do under the best conditions; and that their method will progressively enable him to increase that work without overstraining himself. But there seems to be at present no considerable body of experience at the back of their sanguine expectation, that the new system will overcome the difficulties, with which modern business has to contend, in organizing the work of those operatives, who are not marked out by exceptional energy and individuality as specially adapted to it.

It is true that under the new system, working with the freedom which is allowed to it by the special conditions of America, unskilled labourers of good physique and moderate

[1] Taylor, *Shop Management*, p. 105.

II, XII, 3. natural intelligence are educated in certain narrow tasks; pushed into work which used to be regarded as appropriate to skilled artisans; and enabled often to earn very high wages at them. It is true that the ablest of the artisans, whose places are thus filled, are promoted to still more highly paid work as special "bosses," if not to yet more responsible posts; and that some of the works, in which the system is fully developed, have an output exceptionally great in proportion to the number of their employees, and are making very large additions to the aggregate production and wealth of the country. These are great achievements: and yet we are bound to reflect that the effects of taking away from the operative any duty, save that of carrying out his instructions carefully, are not likely to be altogether good.

The system has indeed been defended against the charge of monotony, by reference to the fact that the endeavour to work up to a high standard of output keeps the mind active. But that sort of activity is not educative: it may even prevent the mind from getting the rest during monotonous work, which might fit it for taking part in those higher activities of mind and spirit, which used to belong almost exclusively to the dominant classes and now belong to the entire people. It is true that leisurely walking is often an aid to thought, partly because it is monotonous: but walking up a steep hill under a heavy load, though equally monotonous, is not conducive to mental activity: and Scientific Management, though averse to strenuousness, requires attention to be kept close to the work. But yet there may be more force in some of the pleas advanced in defence of the treatment of labour under Scientific Management than appears at first sight: let us look more closely into the matter.

3. *General relations of Scientific Management to the remuneration of manual labour and to the democratic control of industry.*

The movements which are classed under the name Scientific Management had to overcome great obstacles. Many sound reasons and more prejudices in favour of established methods were urged against them. If no step had been taken until all objections had been answered to the satisfaction of the objectors, progress would have been slow. Strong resolution has been needed and has threatened to bring the movement under the suspicion of autocratic tendency.

This danger has indeed not been entirely overlooked: the leaders of the movement have themselves pointed out that the scientific establishment of standard elemental times, could be undertaken by employers and employed acting together, through joint committees, or otherwise. Undivided responsibility and prompt autocratic decision were indeed necessary at first: but, though they will always facilitate progress in some directions, they are no longer necessary. There is no fundamental obstacle to their being so developed as to meet all the reasonable needs of working-men who are gregarious in habit, with a bias towards collective action; and who have but moderate ability and but a moderate desire for hard work.

The difficulties in the way of a democratic adjustment of standards for the wages of work under standard conditions are moreover increased by the incessant changefulness of methods and of plant. It has already been observed that the trouble is not greatly felt in the Lancashire cotton industry in which the products are relatively uniform, and the plant has been settling down towards its present shape during a century. But in industries that are new, or are being rapidly transformed, standard conditions must be incessantly changing; and allowances for deviation from them may probably be demanded in so many cases, that to deal with each by democratic procedure will, for some time at least, be scarcely practicable. It is to be remembered that a chief ground for holding the new method to be "scientific" is that in such cases an estimate of the effort required for any piece of work can be based in part on previous stored-up records of elemental times: but this is a highly complex matter: and the organized removal of all need for the use of individual discretion from the operative, which is a main feature of the movement, is not a good preparation for so extremely arduous a task. There is however another side of the matter; and we shall see that an alert workman may find under Scientific Management considerable opportunities for obtaining insight into administrative problems, with which

II, XII, 3. the ordinary working-man is seldom much concerned, unless he be in a cooperative or a copartnership factory[1].

The leaders of Scientific Management claim that, on the balance, it develops the intelligence of the workers: that it "trains them mechanically as they were never trained before, energizes them intellectually, and extends their opportunities for advancement; and it gathers up and systematically *transmits* to the workers all the traditional craft, knowledge and skill which is being lost and destroyed under the current industrial methods." They assert further that in fact promotion is exceptionally rapid under Scientific Management; and that efficient operatives seldom move from under it except to take posts of high responsibility elsewhere. There is no doubt that the Taylor system of remuneration attracts workers of exceptional capacity, and deliberately penalizes those who are incompetent; and there is no reason to question the statement that promotion is rapid under it. But trade-unions assert that "it looks on the worker as a mere instrument of production, and does not tend to develop general or long time efficiency": and far from being grateful for its supplying them with the quintessence of the experience of the ablest workers; they complain that it "tends to gather up and transfer to the management all the traditional knowledge, the judgment and the skill, and monopolizes the initiative of the worker in connection with the work." They claim also that it greatly increases the number of "unproductive workers"; *i.e.* those engaged in clerical work, and often squeezes out of the workers vast overhead charges.

[1] Professor Person, the Director of the Tuck School, told the American Economic Association: "It is possible to conceive of the time when the management of a business and a board from the union shall together make the time studies, set the task, and determine the differential rate; and then the board turn to the members of the union, and say, 'The rate is just, even according to your respective abilities.' Under scientific management one element of trouble in the bargaining between management and labour, a lack of knowledge of the facts, would be absent. Scientific management determines with extraordinary exactness the facts of production under any given conditions. Labour when it knows the facts is reasonable." But representatives of labour are not to be satisfied that Scientific Management acted fully up to its profession of putting no unreasonable pressure on the operatives. See for instance the contributions of Mr Tobin on behalf of the Boot and Shoe Workers' Union, pp. 204—238. See also the discussion of Scientific Management on Mr Cadbury's initiative published for the Sociological Society in 1915.

On the other hand, leaders of the movement claim that it does away with the need, under which manual workers have previously lain, for the support of collective bargaining in regard to their remuneration. But this is not admitted by the trade-unions: and the careful investigation of Prof. Hoxie points to the conclusion that "even where the employers have no special autocratic tendencies...the workers have no real voice" in the conditions of their employment; and that "with rare exceptions democracy under scientific management does not and cannot exist apart from unionism and collective bargaining[1]."

4. *Though the wage systems of Scientific Management give small scope for collective action by employees, its open methods of planning may do a little towards fitting manual workers for the responsibilities of democratic control.*

In Britain, though not in an equal degree in America, industrial traditions are powerful. Class consciousness is cherished by the manual worker with an almost religious fervour, which commands respect; even though a more penetrating knowledge of the questions at issue might often convince him that a claim made on him in the name of duty to his class, is not truly in the interest even of that class. It seems therefore probable that, while Britain may derive great and almost unmixed gains from the technical adjustment of each worker's plant, methods of work, and auxiliary conditions to the highest standard which Scientific Management can devise; yet adjustments of a standard

[1] Hoxie, *l.c.* p. 109. The above description relates mainly to the Taylor system; from which the Gantt system differs little. Mr Emerson's attitude is more sympathetic than Taylor's; but even Prof. Hoxie's careful comparison of the two (*l.c.* pp. 152—168) leaves some matters obscure. Emerson says indeed that "What can be done in an hour [with standard plant and subsidiary arrangements] is for neither the man nor the employer to determine. It is as technical a problem as calculating an eclipse. The share of the worker in the gain, as cost-efficiency increases, is a proper subject for bargaining" (*Tuck School Conference Report*, p. 104). And, though he is not always consistent (see Hoxie, p. 165), it seems that he is in large measure tolerant of trade-union cooperation in the bargaining; as to which there is great difficulty under Scientific Management, even with the best intentions. The Taylor system proposes to welcome it: but asserts that it makes "collective bargaining and trade unionism unnecessary as means of protection to the workers" (*ib.* p. 147); while the unions assert that it "makes collective bargaining practically impossible, and destroys the union spirit and organization" (*ib.* p. 177).

II, XII, 4. task and a standard wage can seldom be satisfactorily arranged by employers alone. Representatives of the manual workers must, as a rule, be able to take part in them. This cooperation may be facilitated by the present movement towards the setting up of joint committees of employers and employed for each industry as a whole; for each important branch of it; and, in appropriate cases, for individual works. Such cooperation is likely to be the more effective, the more the workers understand that, though the immediate interest of any particular class of workers may point towards easy-going methods of production, the working classes as a body have a very strong interest in the efficiency of those businesses, to which the methods of scientific production are most likely to be applied. Let us look into this.

The growing power and intelligence of the manual labour classes go far towards overcoming the difficulty, which everyone has in some degree when he attempts to measure the abilities of men who are abler than he is. This difficulty has hindered the progress of cooperative production and of profit sharing; though both of those great movements have helped towards a general understanding of the dependence of industrial progress on the provision of expensive plant by private capital: the State has been a borrower of capital; and is not likely soon to be able to provide it for ordinary business. Therefore considerable credit may be given to Scientific Management for the contribution—small though it may be—which its methods make towards enabling a thoughtful manual worker to form some sort of independent judgment on the course of a business, in which he is employed.

In works, which are organized on the ordinary plan, the manual worker is seldom in a position to read the motives of those who issue orders affecting his work; for the general plan of the operations is not conspicuous. But under Scientific Management organized planning is done in the open and made prominent by series of "instruction cards"; each of which, whenever it comes into the hands of a thoughtful man, may suggest to him something of the purposes and methods of those who have constructed it. Comparisons of different sets of cards may further suggest comparisons of the abilities of different sets of officials; and, in these and similar ways, some small insight into the higher problems of administration may be gained, by aid of the thoroughness with which planning in all its branches is worked out and made manifest. Thus, though it be true that Scientific Management diminishes the need of the operative for resource and judgment in small matters, it may help him at first a very little, and afterwards a good deal more, to estimate the characters of those who bear large responsibilities. Unless and until he can do that, democratic control of industry will be full of hazards. For a people which endeavours to rule its rulers, without being able to enter into the difficulties of the work to be done, is apt to fall under the guidance of plausible speakers. In such case, what appears as democratic control becomes in effect haphazard oligarchy.

American methods of Scientific Management will need to be somewhat modified, before they can obtain a very wide acceptance in British industry; where—it must be repeated—sectional solidarity has an intensity that does not exist at present amid the rapidly changing technical and racial conditions of American industry. But it happens that, at this very juncture there is growing up a strong movement, the leading ideas of which are embodied in the well-known "Whitley Report." It proposes that employers and employed shall discuss matters of common interest, first in "Works Committees" of individual factories, etc., and afterwards in District Industrial Councils, the members of which are elected by Works Committees; while still larger National Councils are to be elected by the Local Councils. This movement is already being turned to account in developing some of the leading ideas of Scientific Management under the organized joint direction of employers and employed[1].

[1] The Whitley Report substantially adopts the "Outlines of a settlement" which are set out at the end of a *Memorandum on the industrial situation after the war*, issued by the Garton Foundation in June, 1916—a document of singular constructive force, but inadequately known. The issues here raised belong to the study of the influences of industrial organization on social well-being, which is proposed to be included in a companion volume to the present on *Industry and Trade.*

But one or two suggestive facts, taken from a *Report on Works Committees*, published in March, 1918, by the Ministry of Labour, may be mentioned. One firm reports that "the management discusses with the [Works] Committee, or those of it concerned, changes of process, while the men according to the

II, XII, 4. The tendencies of the age are, no doubt, towards increased solidarity of those engaged in any industry: the employers act together in various degrees; and each class of employees also act together rather more closely as a separate group as to some matters and in alliance with other groups as to others. Such movements may be productive of great good to the particular industries, or groups of industries concerned; and to the nation as a whole. They are signs of healthy vigour; but they also suggest grounds for anxiety. For grave and far-reaching injuries to the common weal might arise if strongly organized joint committees of employers and employed in industries, or groups of industries, which controlled important products, were tempted to use their power in the furtherance of their sectional interests. There are many ways in which such a policy might benefit, at all events for a decade or more, those who set them up; while their gain, easily visible, might probably be much less than the aggregate loss, which the nation as a whole would suffer in ways that cannot be easily traced.

Some light is thrown on these matters in Book III; which is given to a study of the good and the evil, the strength and the weakness of those combinations and aggregations in industry or trade, which develop monopolistic tendencies, whether of set purpose or not.

view of the management 'have helped the management in many cases on knotty problems of output, and have made suggestions, which were acted upon.' ...The system of base time for premium bonus work prevails throughout the works: and if the base cannot be settled between the foreman of the department and the workmen, the matter is brought by the Convener and Shop Steward of the department before the management" (p. 58).

Again another firm describes (pp. 59—65) its *system for fixing piece-work prices by continuous arbitration.* "One of the greatest objections to present piece-work systems is that the employer works out the price in secret, writes down the time on a card, and then settles the price....The following is the agreement reached between the principal Union of metal workers and ourselves:—On getting out a new job we would calculate the feeds and the speeds, which were suitable for the tool, on which the job was to be performed; and then put forward the time to the man who had to do the job." If he objected he could "go to the Time Study Office" and talk the matter out. If no agreement was then reached, the matter would be referred to a Committee consisting of the workman himself and two others "selected by him, who are operating the same type of machine, or whose work is closely allied to the work in question"; together with three representatives of the firm. If still no agreement was reached, new studies of the matter are to be made.

BOOK III

MONOPOLISTIC TENDENCIES: THEIR RELATIONS TO PUBLIC WELL-BEING

CHAPTER I

VARIOUS INFLUENCES OF MONOPOLY ON PRICES

1. *Introductory.* III, I, 1.

The first chapter of the preceding Book contained a broad sketch of the relations between production, consumption and value, on the supposition that the production of a commodity is not restricted by exclusive privileges or advantages: and that consequently, if its supply runs so short that its price is considerably above its expenses of production, an increase of supply will be speedily caused by the high profits held out to those who can bring more of it to market. And the chapter ended with an indication that a companion to that sketch would be presented here, designed to show the nature and extent of the modifications in the problem of value, which may result from the exclusive possession by a single person, or by a group of persons acting in concert, of facilities for producing the commodity. The sketch, contained in this chapter and the next, is of the same character as its precursor; and may for the same reasons (see p. 181) be omitted by some readers.

The contrast between the subjects of this Book and the last is commonly described as the contrast between monopolistic and competitive conditions. This description may often serve on account of its brevity; but it is open to misconception. For, as we shall see presently, the fiercest and cruellest forms

III, I, 1. of competition are found in markets which are no longer quite free, but have been already brought in some measure under monopolistic control. In a truly open market, competition is often constructive and not ungenerous. But, when a giant business is striving to attain a monopoly, or to repel rivals from ground which it wishes to make its own, it is under strong temptation to use ferocious and unscrupulous methods to compass their undoing.

The central fact of the problem of value under competitive conditions is (see II, I, 3) that scarcely any important result is true in regard to both short periods and long: a great part of the many barren controversies, that have raged on the matter, results from attempts to refute statements relating to long periods by others relating to short periods, or conversely. Speaking broadly we saw that the fluctuating pressures of demand on the market are the chief causes of temporary movements of prices for most things, except those that are derived from the harvests of the land or the sea: but that in the long run the governing force is the relation of cost of production for various annual rates of supply to the prices at which those rates of supply can be marketed. A chief cause of the apparent differences in character between the price movements of different commodities lies in the fact that a period, which is long relatively to the conditions of supply of one thing, may be short relatively to those of another. Ricardo quaintly said "I do not dispute the influence of demand on the price of corn, or on the price of all other things: but supply follows quickly at his heels, and soon takes the power of regulating price in his own hands; and, in regulating it, he is determined by the cost of production[1]." Thus the answer to the question whether variations in demand, or variations in cost of production, exert the stronger influences on value under competitive conditions in a given time, depends mainly on *the ease with which supply can alter its pace*.

Similarly it will be found, generally speaking, that the ownership of exclusive facilities for production or trade in the modern world does not always suggest to a man of sound judgment that he should pursue a severely monopolistic price policy. On the contrary, he will keep a watchful eye on the

[1] See Dr Bonar's edition of *Ricardo's letters to Malthus*, p. 179.

sources of possible competition, direct or indirect. If it appears that those sources are likely to prove large and strong; and that the pace at which competitive supply runs, is likely to become considerable before long: then he will not make full use of his power, but will adjust his prices to obtaining a firm hold on the market before he can be caught by competitive supply "following quickly at his heels."

It will in fact presently be seen that, though monopoly and free competition are ideally wide apart, yet in practice they shade into one another by imperceptible degrees: that there is an element of monopoly in nearly all competitive business: and that nearly all the monopolies, that are of any practical importance in the present age, hold much of their power by an uncertain tenure; so that they would lose it ere long, if they ignored the possibilities of competition, direct and indirect.

This interlacing of monopoly price policy and of competitive price policy has indeed always existed. But it needs more careful study now than formerly: and this for several reasons. The temper of the age is increasingly analytical; while the contrast between the influences of cost of production on competitive and on monopoly values is more complex than it was when the foundations of modern economic science were laid. Again, though the progress of analysis has taken nothing of importance from the foundations which were then laid, it has built much upon them; while the progress of events has brought into prominence many considerations, which might reasonably be neglected for the practical purposes of business at that time, but which the modern student is bound to examine with some care. It is to be remembered also that, independently of the general study of combination and monopoly on which we are engaged just now, the relations between monopoly and competition prices have, now more than ever, a large place in problems of international trade.

Stress must be laid on the fact that absolute monopolies are of little importance in modern business as compared with those which are "conditional" or "provisional": that is, which hold their sway only "on condition" that, or "provided" that, they do not put prices much above the levels necessary to cover their outlays with normal profits. If they did, then competition

III, I, 1. would probably make itself felt; unless stayed by authority, as is the case with patents, copyrights, and some rights of way. The supply of water, gas, or electricity to any locality cannot be distributed over several rivals: for, to say nothing of its wastefulness, that would involve so many encroachments on, and disturbances of roads, etc., that it could not be tolerated. The greater part of the postal system is an absolute Governmental monopoly almost everywhere: though there is some lack of uniformity in relation to the collection and delivery of parcels and other matters. Again in some countries railway work is an absolute Governmental monopoly: and in other countries there are many patches of practically absolute monopoly in railway traffic. But many monopolies, which seem absolute, are yet to some extent liable to be assailed by indirect routes; and are incomplete and subject to the "condition" that the monopolist makes no such extreme use of his power as will induce others to force their way through obstacles and set up effective competition.

These obstacles are mainly of two kinds. The first is the necessity for sinking much capital and effort in setting up the plant and organization, suited for competing on nearly even terms with a strong business, already in possession of the field. Few are able to do it: and fewer still are willing to take the heavy risks involved in it. For this reason some kinds of monopolies, which even a generation ago would have been properly classed as provisional, have now become so strong as to give grounds for raising the question whether authority should be called in to exercise a control, which competition might have been trusted to do in earlier times. This cause of increase in the strength of monopolies in industry and trade, is a main subject of the present Book.

The second obstacle to the setting up of efficient competition with a business, that has acquired a conditional monopoly, is the *vis inertiae*, the opposition to change, which is inherent in human nature and in human conditions. It is being continually diminished by the influences of modern technique, no less than those of modern habits of thought and life: and accordingly some monopolies, so strongly fortified by large capitalistic resources, advanced methods, high ability and large business connections, that they would have been practically impregnable not long ago, are now often quickly impaired[1].

The industries of transport by land and sea have together occupied more of the thought and energy of the populations of the civilized world than any other, except agriculture. Agriculture has indeed been always a chief source of great fortunes: but the owner of a large landed property has seldom extended his direct control over the whole of it. The concentrated control of large movable capital was pioneered by merchants; though much the largest aggregations of fixed capital were to be found in public highways, until railways began to dispute that place with them. The industries of transport by land and water have frequently changed their methods: but their history is in this sense continuous, that the services rendered by them have been more homogeneous, definite and uniform in character throughout the ages than have been the products of any other group of industries, except perhaps agriculture: and contests for dominion between the methods of competitive and monopolistic organization have developed with more continuity, and can be studied now more closely in them than elsewhere. Britain is the chief inheritor of traditions in regard to the sea: but with regard to railways America has recently taken the lead in the constructive study of the complex relations of competitive and monopolistic policies to public interests; and a large place is given to the results of these and kindred studies in the present Book.

2. *The monopolistic element in the policy of cartels, and other regulative associations of independent producers or traders, is a chief instance of the interpermeation of competitive and monopolistic policies.*

Monopolistic aggregations have often been slow growths from small roots; and have expanded under the influence of constructive business enterprise, with little or no thought of monopoly, till they had attained great strength. Monopolistic

[1] Monopolistic policies give scope for important uses of high analytical methods. Cournot led the way: and among those who have made chief advances in it Professors Edgeworth and Pigou are prominent. Readers are referred to their masterly work for an intensive study of the theory of monopoly.

III, I, 2. federations, which are increasingly described by the German name "Cartels," have their roots deep in the past, where the spirit of comradeship was often as potent, as the desire for the monopolistic regulation of prices. It seems probable that the total influence exerted on prices by monopolistic associations has been greater than that exerted by monopolistic aggregations.

Understandings and associations for the control of particular markets have prevailed in almost all times and places, and have been prompted by nearly the same motives as are at work to-day. In primitive civilizations people of the same calling or the same locality have generally acted together by habit and instinct, rather than by any formal convention. And, though the overt action of gilds, and other trade and professional associations, has often shown deliberate and elaborate strategy in dealing with the outsider; yet a great part of that collective selfishness, which is thinly covered by some unselfish devotion to the interests of a trading group, has worked through tacit and indefinite understandings[1].

In the modern age human nature remains very much as it was in former times: but intellectual habits and methods have changed fast and progressively. The old associations of neighbourhood and a common occupation have still considerable force: but new developments of critical and analytical faculties have caused men increasingly to submit their instinctive tendencies to the cold arbitrament of numerical estimates. The gains and the losses, in money and in ease, which are likely to result from any plan of combined action, with its attendant discipline and curtailments of individual freedom, are weighed against one another; and, if the balance of advantage seems to lie with organized regulation of marketing, a cartel or other association is set up for the purpose. Its immediate and overt aim is to maintain prices in particular markets against inconvenient competition: and especially that of competitors who desire to force their way into those markets by selling goods at, what appears to be. less than their full costs.

[1] The obvious, but important fact that, if the price of a thing which several persons are able to produce, is to be kept much above its cost of production, the inducements to combined action will be cogent, is shown with the aid of diagrams by Prof. Colson, *Cours d'économie politique*, vol. I. ch. III.

Even a man, who occasionally acts somewhat in the same way himself, is apt to regard all such intrusion on his own particular market as "unfair." If his ways are old-fashioned, and his costs are high, he may even regard as unfair the selling at prices, which yield some profit to others, whose plant and organization are superior to his. Thus he is prepared to give a ready ear to suggestions that he should take part in a defensive association or federation, the members of which undertake not to sell at unfairly low prices in a certain area; and to oppose any intrusion of unfairly low priced goods by various strategical devices: the chief of these are underselling the intruder in his own particular markets, and boycotting those who supply his wants. "Defensive" combinations of this kind make out a claim to be morally right: and those, who are in need of defence, eagerly endorse the claim; even though the assailants differ from themselves only in being more able and better equipped with appropriate plant and method. The strength of purpose thus obtained is often developed by combat, and by common exertions for overcoming difficulties. After a time they think less of the defence of markets, in which they had already established themselves; and more of extending control, by alliances and otherwise, over wider markets. If they yield to this temptation, they are on a steep and slippery incline, heading towards a federated monopoly; which is often uncompromising in purpose, though probably limited in extent[1].

There are three classes of producers who are not tempted to restrictive combination: those who produce for their own consumption; those who produce things for sale in a large open market in such small quantities, that current prices will not be appreciably affected by anything which they may do or abstain from doing; and lastly the owners of absolute monopolies. The first two classes have indeed grave anxieties: short harvests may inflict hardships on those who rely on the produce of their own farms: glutted markets may grievously distress the small producer for sale; and even the absolute monopolist must think and contrive a great deal if he is to make the best of his property. But on none of these people does the burden lie of guarding

[1] In this connection reference may be made to the first chapter of the previous Book, and especially its last paragraph.

III, I, 2. watchfully against the encroachments of others. That burden lies on those who have to defend a market which is open to attack: it is the heavier, the greater is the value of the partially monopolistic advantages which they hold in it, and the greater therefore the eagerness of others to intrude.

When discussing the costs of marketing (above, pp. 271—3) some explanation was offered of causes which lead the seller to court the favour of the buyer in regard to particular transactions, especially in retail trade: although in the long run consumers would suffer more from a restriction of their supplies of urgently needed goods, than producers would by being driven to another occupation. That explanation being assumed, it may be added briefly that combination tends to aid sellers more than buyers in regard to immediate transactions. For, under ordinary circumstances, if a buyer passes from one seller to another, the seller loses his normal profit, while the buyer is likely to get his needs supplied without difficulty and possibly at some extra advantage; but, if combination has so fixed prices that the purchaser cannot expect to improve his position by passing to other sellers, he is likely to accept the first seller's terms without demur. This consideration suggests that monopolistic combinations are likely to be more frequent among sellers than among buyers: and that such combinations as are effected among buyers are, for the greater part, evoked as defensive measures by combinations among sellers. We shall find that this is the case in fact.

It will appear also that in the long run combinations of buyers are on about equal terms with combinations among sellers; except when a combination of sellers controls the chief effective sources of supply of a necessary raw material. The most necessary raw material is that of staple foods. Governments have often been called on to intervene between unorganized consumers and organized dealers in grain: and, as the world-war has reminded us, when ordinary markets are partly closed by military operations, authoritative intervention may be required in regard to dealings in many things besides muniments of war.

3. *Price policies of monopolies, absolute and conditional, in regard to immediate net revenue and to prospects of future development.*

In the remainder of this chapter the monopolist will be supposed to make only one product for sale; and to supply it to all purchasers at the same price, subject only to such variations as may correspond to varying costs of delivery. More complex issues will be opened out in the next chapter.

Unconditional natural monopolies, such as those given by the possession of a unique mineral spring or vineyard are relatively rare. The possession of the only coal-mine in a district may give its owner an almost unconditional monopoly there, because coal cannot be carried great distances by land cheaply. But it has already been observed that, as a rule, unconditional monopolies are the products of authority: they were very common in early times: but now almost the only relics of them are designed merely to prevent people from infringing the reasonable rights of others in their own productions.

Reference has also been made to the monopolies that some trading companies acquired long ago in regard to spices, salt, and other flavours, which contribute much to enjoyment; but are yet consumed in so small quantities, that a ten-fold rise in price above the cost of obtaining them in a free market makes no very great demand on the purses of customers. When the Dutch, having obtained a monopoly of the trade of the Spice Islands, found it to their advantage to burn a great part of the crop after a large harvest, they were sounding the keynote of extreme policies of absolute industrial monopolies.

Dunlop's simple valve for keeping the air in a cycle tyre at high tension added much to the value of a cycle; and therefore the licence to make use of it could be sold at a considerable percentage on the price of a costly cycle, that is at many times its own cost of production. Again, Coats' trade-mark on sewing-cotton is of exceptional value; because if a person were to experiment with a cheaper sort of thread, which turned out badly, the saving of a halfpenny on thread might so damage expensive costumes, etc. as to cause inconvenience or loss of trade reputation worth many shillings, or even pounds: thus the

III, I, 3. unique position, which Coats' Combination holds among British monopolistic businesses, results in part from the fact that its products constitute a small but essential link in processes of production which are in the aggregate of very great value.

It will be convenient to refer occasionally to the amount of the profits, which a monopolist is enabled to make by setting his price above that which covers his full costs of production; in which are to be included of course allowance for risk and depreciation, and for the remuneration of his own work in connection with the business. This may be called the *monopoly net revenue*, which he will get from the adoption of that price. Speaking generally the price, at which he offers his goods, will govern the amount of his sales; and therefore of his total costs of production, as just described. His monopoly net revenue will be the excess of his receipts over those costs. The higher he sets his price, the less he will sell: and therefore if his costs of production are always in the same proportion to his output, his monopoly net revenue will be greatest for that price, which makes the number of units sold, multiplied into the excess of his price over his costs per unit, to be the greatest. Speaking generally again, his inducement to keep his price rather low in order to increase the demand, will be stronger if his costs of production per unit diminish with increased output, as is the case in manufacturing and other Increasing Return industries, than in Constant Return industries: and it will be least of all in such a case as the production of a wine of unique flavour, which can be raised only from a small area.

His monopoly revenue is the excess of his receipts over his outlay with normal profits: and his aim may be to fix his price (and therefore the amount of his sales) at that level which will yield him for the time the highest gains: that is at his *maximum net revenue price*. This is often inadequately expressed by saying that the owner of a monopoly aims at the highest charges "which the market will bear"; or, if a railway is under discussion, at the "highest charges which the traffic will bear." Sometimes the same notion is thrown into a negative form without real change of meaning, and it is said that the monopolist will take care in his own interest not to charge more than the market will bear. But all these phrases lack definiteness. For the market will bear a great many prices though it will contract its demand as the price rises; whereas a competitive market will seldom bear permanently any price which does not correspond to cost of production. What is really meant is that he attempts to select a price which will just not drive away a large body of customers, or even prevent him from attracting them. For this purpose he needs to study the elasticity with which demand will respond to a low price, as well as his costs of production[1].

4. *Benefits which the public may derive from a far-seeing use of monopolistic power under certain conditions.*

Selling at a price lower than that which would maximize the immediate net revenue of the monopolist, in order to familiarize consumers with his product, is an investment of capital in the expectation of deferred gains; and indeed it may be regarded as a particular form of the investment of capital in lavish advertising. All such expenditure, if well devised, facilitates further advantageous extensions of plant and further subdivision of labour, which tend to reduce costs; and it may lead to so great a reduction of costs that the price, which will maximize his net revenue, will fall below that originally adopted

[1] A numerical example may be helpful. Suppose 10,000 units of a product are being produced at an outlay of 6*s*. per unit, and sold at 9*s*.: thus yielding 30,000*s*. for total profits, *i.e.* for ordinary profits, together with additional monopolist gains. Suppose that twice the number can be sold at 7*s*., the demand being elastic. The profits will then rise to 40,000 shillings, if the outlay per unit falls to 5*s*., under a tendency to Increasing Return (though it would have fallen to 20,000 shillings if the outlay per unit had been constant). If however the demand had been less elastic, so that 20,000 could not be sold at a higher price than 6*s*., then it would not have been advantageous so to enlarge the plant as to produce 20,000.

It may be well to observe that as the monopolist will, in his own interest, be inclined to favour things that conform to Increasing Return by low charges, in order that he may increase their consumption, and gain the economies of production on a larger scale: so it is a general rule that, *other things being equal*, the Finance Minister should press on products of Decreasing Return industries rather than on products of Increasing Return industries. For a tax on either class tends to diminish consumption: and therefore to lower the price of the untaxed product in the first case and to raise it in the second. Thus the tax raises the price against the consumer by less than its own amount in the first case and by more than its own amount in the second. The above argument, in relation to taxation, is illustrated by diagrams in my *Principles*, Book V, XIII, 4.

III, I, 4. as an investment for future reward. His net revenue may continue to rise, while his price continues to fall.

Again, though a trade association may undertake a part of the expense of bringing to the notice of the public a product in which its members are interested; no one of many producers of the same thing may have an adequate interest in pushing its claims on the attention of the general public, unless his contiguity with them, or some other cause, may be likely to turn their custom in his direction. The far-sighted monopolist, on the other hand, is constantly considering what new advantages he can afford his customers, present and prospective, which will remunerate him in the long run, even though they reduce his monopoly revenue for the time being: a new suburban railroad sometimes makes temporary concessions, such as cheap or even free season tickets, to induce builders to erect houses in its neighbourhood. Or again a monopolist may go to some expense to aid people in turning to good account what he has to offer[1].

In all such cases the monopolist expects to obtain a large share of the whole benefit that will result from calling the attention of consumers to a commodity that will serve them well; from offering it at a price that will attract them to it, and generate habits of familiarity with it; and from aiding them to use it to the best advantage. In fact he makes a compromise between the prices which he would charge, if his sole object were to increase his immediate revenue; and that which he would charge, if he counted a benefit to consumers as of equal value with a similar benefit to himself.

A great monopolist railway in a new country sometimes finds itself in a position somewhat similar to that of a monarch whose prosperity depends on the well-being of his subjects, which

[1] The care and expenditure which the monopolist owner of a trade-mark, patent, or other speciality devotes to arousing the public to its claims have been considered in II, VII.

A purveyor of night-lights has sold at a very low charge an apparatus for enabling the light to maintain a supply of warm food. And—to take a larger illustration—some railroads in the Western States of America, finding that the badness of the local roads made the cost of transport between farm and local railway station a considerable addition to the freights for long distance traffic, set themselves to educate the farmers in road making: a fully equipped train with a road-engineer and gang of navvies was sent to a station, to stay there till a short piece of road had been made gratis, as a model to be copied.

in its turn is highly sensitive to his care for or neglect of their interests. In such a case the monopolist or the monarch may act in almost the same way under the influence of shrewd business calculations, as he would if his chief aim were to benefit his customers or his subjects. A monopolist's inducement to move in this direction is especially strong if the cost of a large output is relatively less than of a small. It may then be worth his while to sell temporarily at a price below the cost for a small output, and therefore at a loss; looking for his reward when the demand is large, and his costs relatively low. He cares little at what cost a temporary increase of output can be made: his concern is to know at what cost he will be able ultimately to meet the increased demand which he is proposing gradually to develop; it being assumed that he feels confident that his hold on an elastic market will last long. The length of time required of course depends on circumstances. If it were possible to adapt the duration of each patent grant to its peculiar conditions, the public interest would call for a specially long period for patents relating to processes to which the law of Increasing Return applied strongly, but in which its effects are slowly developed.

It is to be noted that, however far-sighted a monopolist is, he may be unable to abstain from grasping at quick returns, if his capital is small, and his credit is poor. An outlay for distant returns which would be profitable, if he could borrow at five per cent. per annum, may be impracticable if he must pay ten per cent. The same difficulty often cripples the energies of an able poor man engaged in competitive business: but if he does not occupy a fitting place, that place may be filled by others. On the other hand the best ideas of an inventor are often lost to the world, because he fails to induce a sanguine estimate of the value of his invention among those who could supply him with capital.

But too much stress has sometimes been laid on the influence, which the rate of interest exerts on the inclination of a monopolist to subordinate his immediate interests in a large net revenue to the development of his resources in such ways as may enable him to make great gains in the future; and meanwhile to supply his products at a price not much above their

III, I, 4. present cost of production, and possibly even a little below it. This consideration is important; but it is not confined to monopolistic businesses: it applies in some degree to almost every business in an Increasing Return industry. The fall in the rate at which additional capital can be obtained for making expensive experiments, for setting up costly appliances which may specialize and economize labour and so on, has been a chief promoter of that progress, which has greatly increased the command of all, and especially of the working classes over conveniences, comforts and luxuries, that were either unknown, or else the exclusive perquisite of the rich in earlier times. The monopolist of a product has no monopoly of this tendency; but, no doubt he is often in a position to make large use of it: and, in so far as it inclines him to sell at low prices, in order to develop a future consumption which will accrue directly to his benefit, the consumers of his product enter at once into benefits, which would otherwise have been deferred till the technique of its production had been considerably advanced. In this respect therefore the public has an exceptional interest in the supply of large resources to an enterprising and public spirited monopoly.

But on the other hand its strength, if excessive, may become a source of national danger. For instance, the coal industry, especially in alliance with the iron industry, might conceivably attain to a monarchic authority throughout a whole country almost as unchallenged as that of the sole railway system in an inland district of a great continent. England was the first to feel this danger: it has been considered in America; but it seems to be more nearly imminent in Germany than anywhere else. The public spirit of American railroads has been stimulated in some directions by legislative and administrative intervention, actual and projected; and similar intervention may be needed in an increasing degree with regard to the few other monopolies that threaten to be both lasting and strong.

But, after all, the most powerful protection to public interests against the possible lassitude and exactions of railway officials and shareholders has not come from Government. It has come from the increasing force of indirect competition as regards railway services. They have seemed ever to be on the point of escaping from competitive influences; and to be able to adjust their charges to what the traffic would bear with even less regard to cost of service: but in fact the indirect influence of cost has incessantly asserted itself to a degree that could not have been anticipated when Stephenson more than half-a-century ago said, with reference to railways, that "where combination is possible, competition is impossible."

Many of those manufacturing aggregations, which are commonly regarded as monopolies, are in considerable danger from the indirect competition of businesses, which seek to attain ends similar to their own by other routes. This is a danger which is often overlooked, till the new method has already established a firm position within what was thought to be the special territory of the monopoly, and has even introduced some changes in the habits of consumers which cannot easily be reversed. For instance, a high price of gas in some places, in which gas was regarded as having a monopoly, has been reduced under the influence of growing competition from petroleum and electricity: and more recently improvements in electric light have been stimulated by the economy of improved incandescent gas-mantles.

Another illustration may be taken from the case of the partial monopoly of a trade-union. About the year 1880 the masons' union made so harsh a use of their power, that builders were unwilling to bind themselves by penalty to finish in a given time any contract that involved much stone work. So English architects set themselves to substitute the effect of shadows thrown by varied forms of brickwork for that relief to the monotony of buildings, which they had sought in the use of stone work. As a result, their command over brick as an effective material has increased fast; while there has not been a corresponding improvement in their command over stone. Thus English architecture is in some respects richer, and in others poorer, than it otherwise would have been: but perhaps another generation will elapse before the number of skilled masons in England is as large as it would have been if their union had shown more moderation in 1880.

CHAPTER II

VARIOUS INFLUENCES OF MONOPOLY ON PRICES, CONTINUED

III, II, 1. 1. *Partial shiftings of burdens imposed on monopolies.*

The imposition of a tax is commonly taken as representative of the many various burdens which may be imposed on a monopoly: and we may follow that plan. The burden may be caused by a partial failure of supply of some material or labour needed by it; or by onerous conditions of working imposed on it in the interests of public health or by other causes. But so far as the questions now before us are concerned, such burdens have the effect of increasing its costs, or otherwise lowering its revenue: and such effects are conveniently regarded as equivalent to the incidence of taxes imposed specially on it.

If a tax is set on anything that a man uses in business, he endeavours to recover the tax from his customers by putting up the price of what he sells. Others in the same business do the like; and a part of the burden of the tax is thus shifted "forwards" on to consumers. In consequence they are likely to diminish their consumption of his products: and therefore he diminishes his purchases of materials and other things. Thus a part of the burden is probably shifted "backwards" on to those from whom he buys; and they in their turn are likely to shift a part of that part backwards on to those from whom they buy: and so on. Similarly, if those who purchase his products, require them for use in business, they are likely to shift a part of the burden a second time forwards on to their customers. If industrialists and traders are alert, and but little under the influence of habit; and capital-supply is highly organized—in short, if the general economic conditions are fluid—the shifting will be rapid:

the more viscous they are, the slower and less complete will the shifting be. Monopoly tends to resist adjustments of means to ends, but in ways rather different from those of simple viscosity or immobility: and its action in presence of a new tax, or other disturbance varies with the nature of the attack made on it[1].

If a tax on an absolute monopoly is levied either as a fixed sum, or as a percentage on the net income derived from it, the monopolist will be in a position from which no escape can be found by raising his price. He is supposed already to have put the price so high, that any further rise might so lessen his sales as to lower his net revenue: and a tax, which is not adjusted to the amount of his sales, or the price at which he sells, cannot be evaded by a raising of his price: for that would threaten his net revenue. If the tax is fixed in amount, he will simply pay it out of a smaller net revenue: if the tax is assessed at, say, a tenth of his net revenue, he will retain nine-tenths of that smaller revenue for himself instead of nine-tenths of his full original revenue[2].

[1] The general principles which govern the shifting of the burden of a tax from its point of first impact were clearly set out by Ricardo: and subsequent analysis, partly in mathematical form, has greatly developed his work. Our present knowledge does not supply a sufficiently firm foundation of ascertained fact, especially in regard to the ever varying plasticity of industrial and other economic relations, to enable this reasoning to reach exact practical conclusions. Analysis may however indicate broadly the nature of the shifting that will result on various definite assumptions as to the fluidity, the viscosity, or the rigidity of the several elements: and in this direction there seems to be hope of yet further progress.

Where everything is either absolutely rigid or absolutely fluid, a knowledge of the tendencies of change points clearly the way to a knowledge of their results. But in fact scarcely any economic element is either absolutely rigid or absolutely fluid: nearly every one is more or less viscous. If the viscosity is slight, reasoning based on the assumption of perfect fluidity, may be fairly applicable to most problems that range over long periods of time. But, if the viscosity is great, tendencies, indicated by present conditions, may work slowly: and thus may not have completed their work before new conditions have come into being, and set up different, perhaps even reverse, tendencies. Indeed uncertainties in regard to this viscosity are a chief cause of the limitation of the scope of pure reason in real economic problems.

[2] Nevertheless the common opinion, that such a tax is likely to cause the monopolist to raise his price, is not without some justification. For the monopolist might probably raise his charges, and attribute the rise to the tax. The rise of price would diminish consumption, and therefore the number of employees needed for his work: he might probably dismiss some, and lower the wages of

III, II, 1. On the other hand a tax proportional either to the amount of his output, or to his gross revenue (that is the amount sold multiplied into the price) would give an inducement to the monopolist to lessen his output and raise his price. For by so doing he would escape a part of the tax: and thus the excess of total receipts over total outlay might probably be increased by a diminution of output, though before the imposition of the tax it would have been lessened. As a consequence of the diminution of his output, he might probably be forced to dismiss some of his employees, and be tempted to lower the wages and salaries of others. In these ways a part of the burden of the tax would be shifted to other shoulders: and, in so far as he diminished his purchases of plant and material, some share of the burden would be diffused over a still wider area[1].

The case of a conditional monopolist is rather different; chiefly because any tax, levied on him, would be likely to be levied, in some degree at all events, on any present or future competitors. He would therefore reflect that he might set his price rather higher than had seemed safe before, without attracting much new capital into his special province. That would be true, even if the tax were of fixed amount, or assessed on his net income: and if it were assessed on his gross income, or on his output, he might perhaps raise his price by nearly the full amount of the tax.

others; always throwing the blame of the change on the tax. It would then appear that he was shifting a part of the burden of the tax on to his employees and another part on to his customers. But the appearance would be illusive. The tax did not give him any new power to gain by raising his charges. It was always open to him to raise his price, to stint his production, and to take advantage of his diminished need for labour to force down wages temporarily at least. He did not take that course, because on the whole he reckoned the price already chosen to be the most advantageous to him; and the tax if immovably fixed would have made no alteration in any of the data on which he founded that conclusion. The only change made by it was to give him a motive for impelling his customers and his employees to intervene between him and the Public Treasury.

[1] The observations in the previous footnote apply to this case also. The analytical side of the subject of this Section is developed with numerical and diagrammatic illustrations in my *Principles*, V, XIV, and in the corresponding Mathematical Appendices.

III, II, 2.

2. *Influences which various degrees of monopolistic advantage may exert on the distribution of the burden of the general costs of a business among the several groups of its products.*

We must here revert to the consideration that, when a business produces more than one thing, the costs which are incurred on account of each several process of production cannot be definitely ascertained. The costs in view in such a case are not the prime or "out of pocket" expenses, directly incurred on account of a particular small order or contract. They consist of a share of the general costs of the business; due provision being made for keeping the plant in full repair and of suitable capacity for its work.

We have seen[1] that, when the common costs of a group of products are so intimately associated, that each of the products can be produced to good advantage only in association with some or all of the others, then the problem is assimilated in some degree to that of "joint products," such as mutton and sheeps' wool, the production of which cannot be separated; though the relative proportions of the several products may be varied. In this case the distribution of general costs becomes somewhat arbitrary. But the economy of producing (or marketing) together several different products, which can conveniently be handled "in common" by the same plant and organization, though often considerable, is seldom over-mastering. Consequently, if any one of those who produced several varieties of such goods were to try to place on any one variety much more than its due share of the general costs of his business, he might probably find himself undersold by someone who specialized on that variety. Therefore the freedom which he has in distributing those costs, though real and important, is rather narrowly limited: he cannot afford to leave out of mind the principles according to which the general costs of a business are ordinarily distributed among its various products, nor to depart far from them.

The monopolist is bound by no such fetters. He may indeed need to watch the prices of products which, though different from his, might displace some of them, if his were not easily to

[1] Above, II, I, 5.

III, II, 2. be had: but in the main he has to consider only how to increase the amount by which his own net profits exceed those of ordinary businesses.

Let us take the case of an absolute monopoly, which has already established its market, and has no exceptional reason for sacrificing present income for the sake of a distant future. Of course its owner will not undertake any new outlay, unless he has a fair prospect of recovering it with at least normal profits from the sale of his products. First let us suppose that the outlay is expected to improve their quality, and to enable him to charge higher prices for them, while maintaining or perhaps even increasing their sales; he will then consider which groups of them can bear the greatest increase in price without considerably checking demand; and he will make them carry the chief part of the expenses of his new outlay. If, through political or other pressure, he is prevented from raising the price of any one, he will conclude that he must throw a larger share than he would have wished on other products; or, in an extreme case, abstain from the projected outlay.

Let us now pass to an absolute monopolist who has reason to believe that he may greatly develop the market for some of his products by selling them a good deal below the prices, at which they would yield him the largest net revenue in the present. He may of course reckon that, with a larger output, he will have lower costs of production per unit; so that ere long the prices which will yield him the maximum net revenue, will be as low as, or even lower than, those which he is now charging. Thus the price policies, which he adopts for different products, are partly dependent on one another. If he receives less than he expected from one product, he may be unable to sacrifice as much immediate revenue for the sake of future gains, as he had proposed: and he may raise some of his other prices. Similarly, if a tax were imposed on one of his products: he would then be likely, in effect, to throw more of the burden of the general costs of his business on other products[1].

[1] If the taxed product were a "joint product" in the narrowest use of the term with some other that he made; then the lessening of the sale of the first, caused by the tax, would tend to diminish his output of the second; and he would almost certainly raise the price of that.

The conditions which may call for such action on the part of an absolute monopolist are indeed rather infrequent: that is not of much practical importance, because absolute monopolies are rare. But such conditions are common in the much more numerous group of conditional monopolies. For suppose a steamship company, or a large manufacturing company of any kind, has attained a conditional monopoly in a certain area. It will consider the danger that the high aggregate profits which it is making on its business as a whole, are likely to tempt new rivals into its area. If a new tax or some constrictive regulation is imposed on one group of its services or products, it may assume that potential rivals would make account for like treatment, and regard the prospects of making high profits on a competitive undertaking as less bright than before: and in consequence it may probably raise its charges for some services or products, that are not affected by the new legislation, a little nearer to the levels, which would give the maximum net monopoly revenue. Of course it would not raise them above those levels.

More complex issues are raised when a monopolist's product is sold in several markets, in some of which the demand for it is elastic, and in others inelastic: for he has stronger inducements to lower his price in the former than in the latter. Again, one of two markets, otherwise similar, may be at a much greater distance than the other; and, if his own charge is the same for the two markets, the price of the product when bearing high costs of carriage may be almost prohibitive; though the lower price at which the nearer market obtains it may not be too high. This is one of several causes, legitimate and illegitimate, making for price-discriminations in monopolistic policy.

3. *Unequal or "discriminating" charges for the same goods or services delivered under dissimilar conditions may be a part of a reasonable, and even of a constructive policy: but the line of demarcation between these and others, which aim at the destruction of inconvenient rivals, is often hard to be drawn.*

So far it has been assumed that the monopolist sells to all purchasers at the same price. But it may be that his goods or

III, II, 3. services are in such urgent demand from some groups of well-to-do customers that their purchases will be but little diminished by a great rise of his prices. Meanwhile other groups may be unwilling or unable to make considerable purchases at any but a low price: they may have convenient access to some tolerable substitute; or they may be relatively poor, or finally have no great occasion for the things he offers. Unequal conditions of these kinds are to be found in connection with the retail supply of many classes of goods.

In such cases it is generally the rich, who are charged the higher prices. But in large commercial transactions, especially in regard to transport services, any differential treatment that is made, is likely to be in favour of the more powerful customers: and this fact has contributed largely to a hostile attitude towards railway discriminations generally, which was very prominent not long ago, and has considerable strength still.

This attitude in its turn has fostered the opinion that if a railway, or other partial monopoly, were forced to charge the same price to all, that price would be lower than the average of its charges had been when it was free to vary them to suit its own advantage. There are some cases in which this result would follow. But in other cases the monopolist would simply dispense with those of his sales, which could only be made at a low price: with the result that some of his customers would be seriously prejudiced; and the uniform price, which he charged, would probably be higher than the average of those which he had previously charged.

Whether the first or the second of these results follows, depends on the relative capacities of the markets for which he judges high prices to suit his purpose the better, and those for which he prefers low prices. For instance, in rural districts the only good artificial light to be had is that of mineral oil; in urban districts where gas or electricity is accessible, scarcely anyone would use oil if it were dear. If then the supply of oil were in the hands of a monopolist who was able to discriminate, he would charge a high price in the first set of districts, and a low price in the latter. If he were prevented from discriminating he would consider whether the custom of the urban districts was worth retaining at the cost of charging a low price in the country. This would depend on the volume of the urban demand; and on the relation between the low price, which alone it would bear, and his costs. If the urban demand at a price considerably above cost of production were very great relatively to that of the country, his single price would be a low one. If not he would prefer sales in the country at a price which gave him a large margin of profit; and, abandoning urban markets, he would charge a higher price than if he were able to discriminate.

But unfortunately a discrimination, which belongs to legitimate constructive business, is not always capable of being distinguished clearly from one, which is strategic and may involve danger to the body politic. A strategic discrimination nearly always has some constructive value; and its apologists naturally put this into the foreground. It often happens that they alone have the knowledge required for assigning to these two elements their true relative values. The public, in doubt, may be compelled to acquiesce in some discriminations, the real purpose of which it suspects to be destructive: while it must prohibit others that may be constructive under some circumstances, but also may be applied to evil uses by routes which it is not easy to trace[1].

This matter is becoming increasingly serious with the con-

[1] This difficulty may be illustrated by an extract from the Report of the Commissioner appointed in 1904 to inquire whether the great firms engaged in the beef industry had been acting in violation of the public interest. He refers to the charge that they had injuriously undersold local dealers in small towns by exceptional prices at the season when the local supply was largest; and gives (pp. 80, 81) Mr J. Ogden Armour's defence:—"On account of local conditions we have frequently been obliged to sell meat products at a loss in certain sections for certain periods of time in order to keep our branch houses running. There are, for instance, certain markets in Ohio which, during part of the year, are supplied largely with local cattle grown in the neighbourhood. Of necessity the prices at that time are not good, and the volume of our business is cut down. We nevertheless continue to sell some beef, because we have our investment there and a staff of men, so that the expense goes on constantly, and because we have a certain line of trade which we must keep on our books. We cannot close up one month and open the following with any success. The practice of selling at less than cost has not been pursued in any case with a view to obtaining a virtual monopoly of the supply of any meat product, nor has it in any case resulted in securing to this company any such monopoly in any part of the country." No one can question the *prima facie* validity of the defence: but those who have suffered from the underselling while not definitely asserting that "a virtual monopoly" has been aimed at, may doubt whether the chief motives of the underselling have been made public.

III, II, 4. tinual growth of vast capitalistic aggregations. Thus, returning to the case of mineral oil, let us suppose that the greater part of the trade in it throughout a large district had fallen into the hands of a company, which desired to make its monopoly complete. It might watch for the appearance of competitors with small means; and if allowed to discriminate it might destroy them by selling at a very low price in their immediate neighbourhood. But it could not afford to adopt this price everywhere: and if forced to maintain a single price (after due allowance for differences in costs of delivery), it would reach uniformity by ceasing to sell any oil at a very low price: that is, by raising the average price of its sales. And yet this result might be more in the public interest in the long run than that which would follow from opening the door to malignant discrimination; which might begin by suppressing nascent competition, and end by raising prices generally, though not necessarily to a uniform level, throughout the whole district.

4. *The relations between two monopolies each of which is dependent on the services of the other. Buyers' monopolies. Local and other partial monopolies in multiple ownership.*

If the product of each of the two monopolies is useless without that of the other: if each is absolutely free from the competition of any possible substitute, and the owner of each is able and willing to wait for any length of time; then there is no possible issue to the contest between them for the upper hand; unless it be found in the good nature and sense of one or both. This case has, of course, little practical interest: for the shortness of human life, the changing conditions of demand, and the development of technique have nearly always loosened some one or more of the foundations of any conflict between monopolists, which has appeared to have no solution. Nevertheless any such contests which appear likely to last long, may be of public concern, and give occasion to anxious thought on the part of responsible statesmen.

It is customary to regard the employer as the buyer of labour, and the employee as the seller of it. But a well-known boast of exceptionally powerful trade-union officials is that they practically control their whole industry, and allow the employer just as much as they consider necessary to keep him at his work: they claim to be the buyers of the employer's services. The industry is of course dominated by long established routine: a similar boast could not be made in an industry, in which no moderate success could be obtained by an employer, who lacked the faculty and the opportunity for constant readjustments of his methods, and for casting away plant which became obsolete long before it was worn out.

This illustrates the principle that when the services of two sets of people are required for producing a certain result, and neither can be turned to any considerable use unless it has the aid of the other, then it is a matter of small importance which of the two receives the price for the common product, and pays the other for his share of the work. What is important, is the question which of the two is in the better position for bargaining.

Again a railroad serving a purely agricultural district of a new country, must look to freights of farm produce as its main source of revenue; while the farmers are dependent on sales, which they cannot make without the aid of the railway, for the whole reward of their labour beyond their own food. If the railway is strong and uncontrolled, it may in effect say to the farmers either, "We will sell to you or to any purchaser from you, our services at rates that will leave you a bare living," or "We offer you a price for your produce, which will give you a living. If you refuse it, we will not carry your produce at any rate which it can bear." The results are the same in the two cases, though in the one case the railroad appears as a monopolistic seller and in the other as a monopolistic buyer. In either case it would probably have the upper hand, because it could afford to wait.

If, however, the farmers were able to combine and make a railway to reach the ocean, or navigable water leading to it, they might send their produce to markets hitherto inaccessible to them: and, acting in combination, they might refuse to buy any transport from the railway (or, which comes to the same thing ultimately, to sell any produce to it) except on terms only just sufficiently favourable to it, to keep it in business.

Again, consider cartels, each of which controls a stage of a

III, II, 4. single branch of production: as, for instance, that of drawing the wire of which wire nails are made, and that of making the nails. In this case it is possible for those engaged in either stage to undertake the other also. Movements of this kind are going on in all countries, but especially in Germany: they indicate that, though the buyer generally has the upper hand of the dealer in the ordinary course of trade, a combination of sellers frequently dictates terms to a combination of buyers: and, if the buyers are not ultimate consumers, the public may suffer a two-fold burden.

This leads to the remark that, if each of two monopolies is essential for the performance of a given public service, and if there is no chance that any effective competition will be offered to either, then it is generally in the public interest that they should be amalgamated. For when separated, the benefit of any outlay, made by either for the improvement of its efficiency, will accrue partly to the other, until new terms for the division of the earnings of their joint work have been agreed on: whereas a single monopoly would get at once the whole reward of its enterprise.

Monopolies of this class are, however, seldom as absolute and permanent as they appear; and it may be important in the public interest that doors should be left open for the appearance of competitors. Suppose for instance that a line of steamers runs between two ports, each of which is served by only one railway: the immediate effect of a purchase of the steamers by one of the railways might probably add to the efficiency of the service without any increase of cost; and, possibly even at a lower cost. But yet such a purchase might in the long run be contrary to public interests, unless Government exerted a strong influence on the railway to prevent it from making harsh use of its monopolistic power. In the long run, it might have been better that the steamers, in independent hands, should have offered inducements to a second railway to make connection with them at the same, or some other, port[1].

[1] The Railway Act of 1854, clause 30, ordered that a railway company, when authorized to set up a line of steamers, should be required to charge the same fares to passengers on the steamers, who travelled by rival lines, as it charged to its own passengers: and the Act of 1883, clause 30, authorized any port

Sometimes a conditional monopoly is held, not by a single owner, but by a group of owners; who may act sometimes independently of one another, and sometimes in more or less stringent association. Many such *monopolies in multiple ownership* are local: others are national, and they will call for careful study in connection with the policies of international trade. Others are based on common interests in some branch of industry or trade; which is indeed open to all, but is yet a partial monopoly for the time at least of those actually engaged in it. The most prominent instances of these are cartels, the members of which act in unison. But there are other cases of monopolies in multiple ownership; where the bond of union is very slight. They are largely associated with localized ownership of property: taxes (or rates) levied on them are often spent mainly for their benefit, and are not "onerous": something is said about them in Appendix L. But an imaginary illustration, more appropriate to this chapter, may be given here.

Suppose that there are several patents, all about equally effective for making a thing; and that there is no good method available for making it, which does not infringe one or more of these patents: also that the various patentees do not agree on terms of fusion. Each might look to get a certain monopoly revenue in excess of normal profits on his capital (remuneration for his own work being included); and push the sales of his goods at the expense of his rivals. If the industry yielded a more than proportionate increase of product to increased labour and capital, the well-known conditions of unstable equilibrium would arise: each would hope by increasing his production to undersell his rivals, and thus gain the power of still further underselling them with increased profits to himself. Thus, from a purely abstract point of view, it would appear that the

authority to claim a hearing of the charge that the railway company, or companies, which served it, placed it at a disadvantage as compared with any other port served by the same company or companies.

A somewhat similar critical case arises when the products of one place A, can be best marketed at another place, B, on the same railway. Then the carriers are likely to say that "the value of their service" is shown by the excess of the B prices of those products over the A prices: while traders will justify their B prices by reference to the carriers' charges. Circular reasonings of this kind will be found to add to the inherent difficulties of many problems of semi-monopolistic production, trading and transport.

III, II, 4. strongest competitor would ere long outbid all his rivals by selling close to mere cost of production, or even below: and reducing the problem to one of simple monopoly. But, in the real world, increase in the size of a business goes with increase of age, which is often a source of manifold weaknesses; and no violence is involved in supposing that several firms with about equal economies of production remain in competition. Then if a tax fixed in amount were levied on each business, the burden of the tax would remain on it, provided of course the tax were not sufficiently heavy to put a stop to the business: and the same would be true of a tax proportionate to the net monopoly profits of the business. On the other hand a tax proportionate to the amount produced, or to the gross receipts of each business would diminish production; and parts of the burden of the tax would be shifted on those who bought the product in question, and on those who produced the materials and plant needed by its producers.

CHAPTER III

COMPETITION AND MONOPOLY IN TRANSPORT

1. *The interpermeation of competition and monopoly, illustrated by the simple case of traffic at a small ferry.* III, III, 1.

Man can create thought: but he can only move matter, readjust it and bring it into position for being affected by Nature's chemical and vitalizing influences: there is indeed a large element of simple transport in mining, forestry and even some manufacturing industries[1]. But yet the "transport" industries, which undertake nothing more than the mere movement of persons and things from one place to another, have constituted one of the most important activities of man in every stage of advanced civilization.

Transport is a common need of nearly all persons and nearly all goods. Speaking generally, each transport agency can carry almost anything in its special area; and it thus differs from a cotton spinning mill, the plant of which cannot be used as a whole for any other purpose than its own. But much of the plant of an engineering establishment often takes part in the making of hundreds of various products. No doubt there is much variety in the handling appropriate to them: but a similar variety is often met in the handling for transport of various things; as, for instance, human beings and live animals; coal and gold; lumber and perishable fruit. Thus the services rendered by transport agencies are so much more uniform in character than those rendered by most other industries, that the varying relations of monopoly and competition can be traced in them, with less intermingling of technical considerations peculiar to them than in the case of any other great group of

[1] See above, II, I, 2.

 industries. They are therefore used to set the keynote of the present Book.

As was indicated at the beginning of this Book, the most prominent instance of the interpermeation of competition and monopoly in the modern world is to be found in railway traffic. But the advantages which a railway company derives from the exclusive occupation of a great thoroughfare have very little counterpart in other industries. Accordingly it is best to start with industries of transport on open ways by land and water: for competition penetrates into them further than into the railway industry.

The main outlines of the problems of transport are presented in their simplest form in the case of a small ferry. For the journey being short, the same boat generally carries passengers and all manner of goods: there is no occasion to make special provision for things that need to travel quickly, or require careful packing or tending. Thus the ferry differs widely from a shipping line and a railway: but yet its management sometimes raises issues, which are prominent in railway literature.

For instance, a ferry-boat with only half its complement of passengers could take a few more without appreciable cost. When therefore we say that free competition among ferry-boats, where there is no monopoly, tends to make the charges equal to the cost of service; what we mean is that it tends so to adjust the supply of ferry-boats and their charges to demand, that the earnings of a boat give normal remuneration to the capital and labour invested in it: competition adjusts charges, not to the cost of carrying any particular passenger, but to the *whole process* of ferrying for goods and passengers alike.

If the boats carried only passengers, each passenger might fairly be said to have cost the annual expenses (including profits and depreciation) of working a ferry-boat, divided by the number of passengers carried in the year. This is a simple instance of the general proposition that the cost of production, with which economic science is concerned, is scarcely ever that of a single unit; it is nearly always that of a whole process. The cost of a particular copy of a book or a particular ice, like that of carrying a particular passenger on such a ferry, must be inferred from the cost of the whole production. A book left on the publisher's hands, or an ice which a vendor takes home on a hot day, corresponds to a vacant place in a ferry-boat or a railway train: the prices of those things which are marketed must cover the costs of production of those which are not marketed. The fact that a train can carry an additional passenger without appreciable cost to it, has sometimes been alleged as a distinctive feature of the railway industry: but it is only a strong instance of a general rule.

Again, on the ferry-boat, as on the railway, there is no simple rule for dividing out the costs between passengers and goods. If the space occupied by cargo could not in any case have accommodated passengers, the division would, for the time, be arbitrary. But the structure of a boat can often be so modified as to change the proportions of the accommodation which it offers for passengers and cargo: and then the additional cost required for constructing and working a boat to carry rather less cargo and rather more passengers, or *vice versâ*, affords the basis on which free competition could divide out cost and charges in the long run between the two kinds of traffic. In such matters the tendency to experiment, which is innate in human nature, will sometimes try various arrangements: but more often there is an inert acquiescence in a traditional shape of boat and a traditional distribution of charges.

If all the ferry-boats connecting an island with the mainland are in the hands of a single owner, with absolute permanent monopoly, unfettered by any regulations, his charges may probably be adjusted to "what the traffic will bear," in the sense of yielding the maximum monopoly revenue. But he may be in some measure influenced by considerations other than those of immediate gain: and in the extreme case in which the island belongs to him, he may reflect that charges, which appreciably diminished its attractions for residence and for business, would so retard the growth of population and the investment of capital in it, that he would lose in rents of agricultural and urban land, and in other ways, more than he gained from high charges for the ferry. He may therefore lower his charges a long way towards those which would afford the *maximum total benefit*: that is, the sum of the net benefits which he derives directly from the ferry;

 together with those derived by the islanders from the journeys which they would take, and from the business which they would carry out if the ferry charges were low, but which they would forego if the charges were high. If he owned only a part of the land, he would not, as a matter of business, lower his rates very far: he might however adopt a "Compromise" set of rates, lower than pure monopoly rates, but higher than those which he would adopt if he regarded his own interest as substantially one with that of the islanders.

2. ***On the open high road some kinds of traffic show traces of monopoly, and of the arbitrary distribution of general costs: but competition keeps the charges for the main bulk of heavy traffic close to its actual costs.***

The problems of a carrier on a route, which offers insufficient employment for more than a single cart, resemble those of a ferryman in like case. So long as he does not set his charges so high as to invite competition, he has a partial monopoly; and he may put a rather high charge on any service, which is desired by people who can afford to pay well, and have no convenient alternative: though those services, which farmers and well-to-do people can discharge easily for themselves, will not bear a high rate.

More interesting are the problems of services by coaches, working with fixed time tables, and carrying mails, passengers and light parcels. Their equipment involves large expense, and many journeys that hardly pay prime costs; and, partly for these reasons, their charges are arranged in some respects on methods which are commonly regarded as characteristic of monopolistic railway policy. A coaching firm can adjust fares for passengers inside and outside, and for parcels, to that which each sort of the traffic will bear without greatly shrinking. If it finds that this arrangement of charges, leaves part of its accommodation idle, while another part is over burdened, the shape of the coaches can be gradually modified to suit the changed conditions: or supplementary vehicles can be employed.

Again, the conflict of interests between long and short distance railway traffic is commonly associated with railway monopoly: but it may exist on the highway, in a place where the total demand for the services of public passenger conveyance is small, even though there be no monopoly. If there are two or more roads (but no railroad) connecting two towns, the coaches serving them will choose the shortest. Those who live on a longer route will however desire facilities for travelling both locally and to and from each of the towns: but their traffic may probably not suffice to give fairly good occupation for a single coach; therefore, if a coach is put on that route its charges per mile may reasonably be higher than those on the main route. But that coach could not attract passengers for the through journey without carrying them at somewhat lower fares for the whole journey than are charged on the main route; and therefore at a much lower charge per mile than for local traffic on its special route.

The competing coaches on the main route may acquiesce in that arrangement. But if those who live on the longer route find themselves charged more for a long stretch of the journey between the two towns than is charged for the whole distance between the towns by their route, a feeling of grievance arises; which is not easily to be allayed by argument, though in fact it is not well founded. Such cases are rare: but somewhat similar cases of reasonably high charges for short distance traffic have been given great prominence in discussions of public policy as to railways; as we shall see.

Passenger omnibuses in London passed long ago out of the hands of small firms into those of considerable companies. After a time the companies divided out the traffic between them in peace, broken occasionally by violent fights[1]. With the advent of motor traffic, there has been an increasing advantage in being able to keep a large general reserve which could come to the aid of any particular district, in case of exceptional demands by the public or breakdowns of the plant: thus combination grows.

[1] They made common cause against interlopers; and there was an office at which a list of fees was kept, each corresponding to the price which must be paid for leave to run an omnibus on a particular route at given hours of the day. Of course any omnibus might start without paying the fee; but if it did, it would be "nursed" by one running just before it, and another just behind it; with orders not to spare the horses, but to cut in between the intruding omnibus and its passengers.

III, III, 2. But in cities of the first rank the competitive activities of tramways and motor-cabs are supplemented by those of underground railways. The recent amalgamation of London underground railway, tramway, and omnibus companies gives scope for great economies and enlarged conveniences for travellers. It may prove a great public benefit so long as those in control are able, energetic, alert to seek improvements in technique; and to promote subordinates, with true insight into their qualities of mind and character. But, should any slackness supervene, the monopolistic power of the amalgamation may raise demands for authoritative intervention, and thus increase the burdens that tend to impair the efficiency of Government in that work, which it alone can do.

Again, much of the collection and distribution of large and small parcels over a very wide area, though open to everyone, falls necessarily into the hands of one or more powerful organizations: it is in fact of a scope too large to be perfectly managed by any force less than that of the universal State post. Thus the long-distance-distribution of light parcels, letters, etc., has fallen almost wholly into the hands of public and private bodies with large resources[1].

Far different is the case of the transport of heavy goods by road in large quantities. Everyone who habitually sends whole wagon loads of any sort of goods, either keeps his own wagons for the purpose; or makes a contract for the work on competitive terms, close to actual cost of service, with some firm that is specially equipped for such work. The recent improvement of the surface of main roads, and the development of wagons and even small trains propelled by steam or internal combustion along the roads, introduces a new competitive element into

[1] The divergences between charge and cost of service for postal services are indeed grotesque. For instance, the charge for sending a book by post a mile or so from one part of the same postal delivery system to another, is the same as for sending it from any part of the Postal Union to any other, though the two may be ten thousand miles apart. Perhaps motor wagons may redress some of these anomalies; the charges for the delivery of parcels over small distances being reduced to much lower levels by the activities of private companies. These companies are however not unlikely to develop after a time monopolistic tendencies. A comparison of the practice of the Governments of Western Europe in this matter with that of American Express Companies in regard to the collection and delivery of parcels is not favourable to private capitalistic organization.

the charges made by railways for carrying goods in bulk over medium distances; of which more hereafter[1].

3. *On the ocean as on the land, charges for the carriage of heavy goods in bulk are governed mainly by the costs of the services rendered; while the charges for quick transport at fixed times are in great measure adjusted to demands for the services rendered.*

Britain is the chief home of the shipping industry. The capital, which she has invested in it, is indeed small relatively to that invested in her railways: but her prosperity depends on the smooth working of her shipping industry in an exceptional degree. Norway, New Zealand and Japan also have predominant interests in the sea: but Britain for the present pioneers the way in shipping problems. The best study of monopolistic problems in shipping is that made by the British Royal Commission on Shipping Rings (1906—9): and, as these problems resemble monopolistic problems in general industries more closely than do the problems of railway monopoly, it is fitting that prominence should be given to them here.

Sailing ships used to lay themselves out mainly for cargoes: though they were generally ready to take a few passengers. They might have fixed times for starting; but they could not have even approximately fixed times for arrival at the end of long voyages, and they offered but few amenities: scarcely anyone took a long voyage unless for urgent business. But the economy and efficiency of large steamships have offered increasing inducements for taking long voyages on even slight occasions: and this change, together with the growing demands and resources of the chief post offices of the world, has called into existence great fleets of swift steamships, which make it their first business to attract passengers, and in some cases mails: their second aim is to attract such cargo as can afford to pay relatively high charges for sure and quick transport[2].

[1] See below, pp. 500—506. Attention has been called (above, p. 297) to the advantage, which a giant retail business is obtaining over local shopkeepers through its power of delivering its goods by a "fleet" of motor wagons: but the issues raised thereby are of a different order from those now in view.

[2] When business activity is high in America and low in Europe, a million emigrants may go westwards in a single year; and a considerable number of

III, III, 3. The chief advantages which a great "Line" offers to shippers, besides quick transit in well-appointed and secure ships sailing at short intervals, are implicit or explicit guarantees as to the care with which the cargo is handled, and as to the stability of the charges made. These advantages are of some importance in regard to light goods, and small consignments of all sorts of goods. Light goods, which are liable to damage by careless treatment, are not readily consigned to the charge of an unknown person: but the shipper knows that a great Line cannot afford to let them be handled negligently, and he often does not even concern himself to inquire by what vessel they will travel. The more frail and valuable his goods are, the more highly he prizes this speed and security, and therefore the higher is the rate which "the traffic will bear" for them. Again, many foreign buyers desire to have prices quoted to them for delivery at their own ports. It is true that in the case of any particular large consignment, the charge to be made on this account can be ascertained by telephone and telegraphed to the buyer: but for minor consignments, and especially for those advertised in price lists addressed to small buyers, there is an urgent need of charges fixed some time in advance[1].

them return when the conditions are reversed. It is true that the great "Liner" has no exclusive hold on emigrants and others who are content with rough accommodation, provided the charge for it is low. But the carriage of a thousand emigrants on a lower deck of a great ship can be effected very cheaply: their food is inexpensive, and they pay little more highly for space than does first-class light cargo: they even yield a higher rate of net profit on their direct costs than do first-class passengers. In the main the carriage of emigrants belongs to the great companies: expensive organization is required for collecting full loads of emigrants.

[1] This is a matter which has more influence on the courses of international trade than is generally known: its importance is increased by the almost universal tendency of the present age towards keeping ever smaller stocks of each of an ever increasing variety of goods; and replenishing the stocks by small orders at frequent intervals. Liner freight rates are at so much a ton by weight, or "measurement"; the latter being taken at forty cubic feet: that method is chosen in each case which indicates the higher charge.

Differences in value and ease of handling have led to the placing of glass ware in crates in class IV, with clay, chalk, crude forms of iron, etc.; while iron chains, oak boards, etc., were in class II and copper in class I. The rates for class I were nearly twice as high as those for class IV; but as glass pays by measurement, a ton *weight* of glass pays at least as much as a ton of copper. It may be added that shippers complained of the scarcity of information on such matters; and that even the Commission's inquiries met with but little response.

But these advantages are of relatively small importance to the shipper of common goods in bulk, such as grain, coal and other minerals, cotton, jute, wool, etc. The shipper of such things generally finds it to his advantage to hire, or "charter" one or more cargo ships for the purpose. A great part of the transport of all these things, and especially grain and coal, is done by "Tramps"; that is vessels which have no regular route and no fixed times of sailing, but ever seek those ports at which they are most likely to get good freights. This work corresponds to that of carts on the high road which carry things in bulk. Lines of ships, like lines of coaches (where there are no railways), carry passengers and small parcels[1].

The freedom of movement of Tramps, and their variety of size and speed, enable them to supply whatever accommodation any merchant happens to want, without asking him to pay for capacity or speed that he does not need: and their position is in some respects impregnable. They do not indeed keep freights steady: because harvest variations, and fluctuations of general credit cause the total demand for shipping all the world over to vary greatly from year to year; while the demand at any one port may change violently with but short notice. A shipper anxious to hit some market, where the price of his grain is a few shillings a quarter higher than he can expect if he misses that market, may be willing to pay 10*s*. extra per ton in order to catch it; and that is a very large addition to the ordinary Tramp rates for most voyages. On the other hand, when accident or miscalculation has brought to a port a tonnage much in excess of the cargo available, Tramps will carry freight at a merely nominal rate in a direction in which they expect to find good employment. But in spite of these great fluctuations

[1] Of course the terms "large" and "small" are relative to the agencies used: a small consignment for a ship would often be much too big for the largest wagon. It requires an effort to apprehend the difference in scale between the traffic of the ocean and that of the land: and some illustrative figures may be of interest. The cargo of a small ship, if set on horse-drawn wagons, would occupy several miles of road: that of the largest ship of the present time would occupy about fifty miles. An efficient modern ship of 5000 tons net register, capable of carrying more than ten thousand tons, will consume but two tons of coal while steaming for an hour at the rate of about nine knots. That is, the consumption of coal fuel needed for carrying one ton a hundred miles is about three and a half pounds; costing less than a half-penny.

III, III, 3. from time to time, the average costs of carrying the great mass of heavy ocean traffic are kept down, directly or indirectly, by the competition of Tramps very close to the actual costs of the cheapest method of transport that has ever been known. Thus it may be said that, as a rule, the prices current at ports of delivery for goods carried in bulk exceed their prices at ports of origin on the average of a decade (in which there has been no great war or other violent disturbance) by amounts that are just sufficient to cause the supply of cargo vessels to keep pace with the increase in quantity of heavy freights that are seeking tonnage[1].

Of course the degrees of control over cargo rates which are exerted by Liners and Tramps respectively vary with the circumstances of each course of trade. The tonnage passing between Europe and North America annually exceeds that in all the rest of the trade of the world. But it is largely occupied with passengers; and there is so much empty carrying space in the holds of many Liners that the regulation of cargo rates by them is impracticable: they often underbid the Tramps. Again the coasting trade of Britain is so much controlled by railway competition, and so intimately connected with small local affairs, that it also is not regulated. Again the tonnage required for the trade to Europe from Argentina, Australia, and some other countries is much in excess of that furnished by Liners; and rates are practically governed by the supply of Tramp tonnage relatively to the demand: but more of this a little later[2].

[1] Various estimates give to "Tramps," in the broad use of the term, from five to eight-tenths of all the existing shipping. Agreements among them as to rates are rare; for it seldom happens that any one of them has a special interest in any particular route. On the other hand there are signs of the appearance of great lines of cargo steamers, with strong capitalistic backing: and, partly for this reason, it seems possible that the conditions of heavy cargo traffic may approximate in some degree to those of passenger and light cargo traffic. The charges made during the world-war of course belong to a class by themselves.

[2] The influence of Tramps is now strongest in grain trades, and especially in the wheat trade. Of course coal cargoes are vastly heavier in the aggregate than grain cargoes. But coal is often used by outgoing Liners and cargo-ships to make up their loads: sometimes it is used for the return journey either by the ship itself or by another belonging to the same owner; sometimes it is left at a coaling port. Consequently no attempt is made to regulate the freights

4. *The growing concentration of a large part of the oceanic passenger and light goods traffic in the hands of a relatively small number of powerful companies; groups of which often act together in "Conference."* III, III, 4.

We saw in Book II how the progress of technique not only increases the size of the plant which can be worked by a given number of men, but also increases the efficiency of powerful plant more than in proportion to its cost; and how these changes tell on the side of the large business relatively to the small. We saw also that these influences of progress have been specially conspicuous in the building and mechanical working of giant ships. Moreover such ships can afford a high class of professional service, including that of wireless telegraphy by night as well as by day, and other amenities. These direct influences, tending to strengthen the companies that are already powerful, are indirectly supplemented by geographical causes which concentrate the best part of a country's trade in a small number of ports, and thus further promote the expansion of a company that is already powerful. For large ships need deep entrance channels; and powerful mechanical appliances, that will load or unload several thousand tons in a single day: a small port cannot do this unless aided by some public authority, or by a railway that reaches the ocean at that port. Railway enterprise and geographical causes in America and England, but notably not in Germany, have opposed important resistance to the overmastering predominance of a few great ports.

This geographical concentration is both cause, and effect, of a continual increase in the range covered by a great shipping Line. Partly by amalgamations or working agreements with other Lines, and partly by setting up subsidiary lines of its

for coal: the supply of tonnage at coaling ports is generally much in excess of the demand.

Both ordinary Liners and Tramps are yielding some ground to lines set up by great railways to ply from ports served by them: also to lines specially adapted to carry oil, or perishable fruit or cattle. These last can often carry passengers advantageously; for cattle and perishable fruit as well as human beings, need speed and some care in handling. Those that bring butter, fresh fruit and vegetables from the Continent to England are very swift; and, even when they arrive at night, their cargoes are often unloaded and sent off by quick trains, so as to reach the industrial districts the next morning.

III, III, 4. own, it is able to take efficient measures for attracting custom: and it thus gets the better of any competitor, who follows the old easy-going plan of waiting to be sought out by those who have cargo to send. Its position is strengthened by its ability to collect, on through bills of freight, cargo from almost any port on one long line of coast, extending perhaps along several countries; and to deliver it at almost any port on another long line of coast: the equipments of the great ports, between which its main lines run, facilitate transhipments, when necessary. On both its main and its subsidiary lines, it is likely to make use of cargo steamers, of various sizes, as occasion demands: and it may even make some use of Lines of cargo steamers, with fixed time tables. It generally owns some of these steamers; and "charters" others by the year or for particular tasks[1].

A great company owning or controlling some fifty steamers of various sizes is able not only to pick up and deliver freights at many ports, but also to adjust the tonnage which it is running on any particular route to varying demands. It can advise any of its customers, who have about equally good access to two or more ports, to send their cargo to that one from which one of its vessels is on the point of starting for the particular destination which he desires; it thereby obtains some of the economies possessed by a giant business, such as the United States Steel Corporation, of being able to direct any particular order to that one of its plants which has at the time the best facilities for it. As a canvasser for custom it has some of the advantages of a Branch-shop Company[2].

[1] By these means it escapes the necessity of carrying heavy cargo in bulk on expensive ships, with high coal consumption; unless indeed the ship happens to need ballast. Such things as steel rails are often taken at rates even lower than those generally charged by a cargo ship, for they serve instead of water-ballast: in fact, before the days of water-ballast they were said to be sometimes carried gratis.

[2] It may be well to go into some details as to the position which the chief German line had reached in 1913; after having absorbed many others, and formed a close alliance with its leading rival. A great part of the trade of the central and western States of North America has about equally good access to the sea at any one of several great ports on the coast line between the St Lawrence and the Mississippi: and a large part of the whole American trade with Northern Europe has a nearly even choice among several ports in Britain, France, Belgium, Holland and Germany. The Hamburg-Amerika line, working in unison with the Norddeutscher Lloyd of Bremen, had attained in 1913, an absolute control of the

The great lines generally have sufficient space for all the high grade cargo that is offered. If it comes forward in unusual quantities, they make room by declining lower grade freight; and consequently their charges for high grade freight are liable to less fluctuations from passing accidents than are the charges for low grade cargoes in bulk. On the other hand the standard charges made by Liners are not governed by large economic forces as directly as are the average freights paid to Tramps: they are governed by the estimates which a company or a Conference forms of the net revenue to be derived from various rates of charges; the highest rate being chosen, that will not greatly check the normal flow of trade into their hands. But charges may be oppressive to those who pay them, without exceeding the limit suggested by this rule. And against such charges, the starting of an effective independent line of steamers being generally out of the question, the only remedy is to be found in expressions of public opinion, which may culminate in an agitation for the intervention of Government.

Thus the general trends of the technical and financial developments of the shipping industry favour the extension of partial and conditional monopolistic control over an ever larger portion of its work. There is a constant increase in the variety and the importance of the services which a giant company can render to innumerable customers; few of whom could find any tolerable substitute for its assistance, unless from the appearance on the scene of a rival company of similar scope and strength. The immediate result of such an arrival is usually a fierce rate-war: the deferred result is often either a fusion of the two companies,

direct trade of Germany in the Atlantic Ocean. But the competition of lines serving other ports of North-Western Europe remained strong enough to insure a moderate use of that power, in regard to transoceanic trade: and, in order to suppress that, it was said to maintain, in conjunction with its allies, a "fighting fleet" of nine ships valued at £300,000 for the purpose of fighting opponents and "nursing" them out of existence.

According to the *Report of a Committee on the Shipping and Shipbuilding Industries*, 1918 [Cd. 9092], p. 95, nearly all the German lines were associated before the war in a *Rhederei-Vereinigung*. "A Contract with any one of these lines was a Contract with the group." Germany's concentration of her chief trade in two associated ports is an aid to the organization of her shipping trade, though an injury to her industries.

III, III, 4. or else a "Conference" between them. The Conference sets up a common schedule of rates, while leaving for the time some room for competition as to prompt action, and other facilities and amenities. But this competition generally fades away rather quickly; very few vestiges of it being left, even before the complete fusion of the two has been effected. Such a fusion is not unlikely to be made the occasion of a further fusion with one or more other companies, whose routes overlap more or less those on which the competition was first set up; for the power and the appetite for extension are apt to grow with every increase of it.

A great company or a Conference of companies thus obtains control, which is not indeed absolute, but is yet practically undisputed for the time, of all that part of the trade of its special area, that is not suitable for Tramps. It can therefore act very much as though it had an absolute monopoly of that trade: that is, it can distribute the general costs of its business as may seem best in its own interest, and charge the rate that will yield it the highest net gain for each service, account being taken of the urgency and elasticity of the demand for that service.

There is however less that is arbitrary and accidental in the apportionment of charges for ordinary consignments of different sorts of goods than appears at first sight. Long established usage, based in some degree on sound reason, has set up the general principle that goods are to be classified for high or low charges per ton (by weight or measurement) roughly as their values are high or low; provided the difficulty and the risk of handling are about equal. The several classifications set up by different companies and Conferences differ in detail, according to the conditions of the routes of trade with which they are associated: but all conform to this general principle, which came to be regarded as reasonable or "natural" long before the shipping industry entered on its present phase; and will probably be so regarded long after that phase has passed away. It is maintained in great measure even in an eager rate-war for the exclusive or partial occupation of any area of trade: rates may be lowered generally; but a proposal to carry first-class goods at fourth-class rates would be regarded as short-sighted even during the heat of the combat.

But though there is relatively little that is arbitrary in the classification of goods by a Company or Conference, a somewhat high charge can generally be put with safety on any particular class of traffic, which has not sufficient volume to attract a competitive service, and is not suitable for the Tramp. It runs indeed a considerable danger of inviting opposition from an independent Line promoted by shippers, or from an existing Line which is called by them to their aid; if the general level of its rates is much in excess of that needed to cover its costs with good profits. But, in spite of the keenness of modern commercial competition, this danger to it is being diminished. For not only is there a rapid and ceaseless increase in the capital outlay required for setting up a new Line, or even a branch of an old Line, on a scale sufficient for effective competition: but further, in spite of occasional wars on a great scale between Conferences, their mutual understandings and alliances have grown almost as fast as the resources under the control of each of them. This fact indeed contributed greatly to that feeling of unquiet among shippers, which evoked the "Royal Commission on Shipping Rings" (1906—9)[1].

This association of Conferences is a matter of but little direct concern to the Tramp: for she has no fixed route and presents no good target for their artillery. So they turn their attacks not on her, but on any who make use of her for work which they are ready to undertake: they think it an unfair competition for the Tramp to come in when things are good and drop out again when things are bad. They are not able to eliminate the "fitful tramp" from the regular trades: but their weapons are turned against anyone who sets up a regular

[1] The *Report* of the Majority of the Commission, § 35, states that "each Conference has its own area; and in certain cases, where several trade routes intersect or adjoin one another, the various Conferences have understandings or agreements with one another to respect each other's spheres of influence. This is especially evident in the trade with India and Ceylon, which is in the hands of a group, or family, of Conferences, related to one another, members of each of them being also members or part members of other Conferences. Such interdependence secures a harmony of action in the working of these various bodies, and it prevents the clash of interests which might ensue, were Conferences free to engage in mutual competition." Also two groups of Conferences, which serve the same area, generally abstain from encroachment on one another, "no doubt from fear of retaliation."

III, III, 4. Line of cargo steamers, which may divert traffic from the Conference[1].

It is of course possible that the economy and efficiency, which can be attained by a vigorous and unselfish use of monopolistic power in such a case, may on the whole be to the advantage of the public. The absolute monopolies granted to England's early Joint Stock Trading Companies have already been recognized as working for the general good, so long as the special conditions which had called for them, were still in existence: and the conditional monopolies possessed by some modern shipping Conferences claim to render some important services. No doubt (as was seen in Book II) some wastes of competition are conspicuous in the struggles of almost every class of producers, and of wholesale and retail dealers: and it is obvious that very far-reaching wastes are likely to be caused by rate-wars between competing Lines of steamers. The public undoubtedly gains something from agreements which keep rates steady, and enable producers and merchants to quote prices, cost of delivery at a distance being included[2].

The leaders of the Conferences claim that these ends are achieved by them, and cannot be achieved otherwise. They claim also that their charges are not in excess of those which are needed to yield fair profits to a well managed company in

[1] These statements are taken substantially from the evidence, not always very willing, of Mr Byron, representing the South African Conference, whose affairs occupied a large part of the attention of the Commission (see Q. 15,374—9; 15,470—5). He further admitted that "the business man in South Africa has no choice: he must come to the Conference, unless he chooses to charter vessels" on his own account (Q. 15,736—7). And yet it was maintained with some persistency that the Conference had no monopoly. Thus Sir Donald Currie said (Q. 15,016): "The whole truth is that Conference Lines have not any monopoly at all." Mr Byron asserted "emphatically" that the Conferences have not "by virtue of this system of rebates anything like a monopoly.... That lies at the root of [my] argument" (Q. 15,270—1). But he was gradually forced to admit that what he meant was that "there is not a complete and absolute monopoly....There is something of the nature of a monopoly; that goes without saying." In answer to the suggestion that "the very object of the deferred rebate system is to create a monopoly," he says "undoubtedly it has that tendency," and that "the object of it...is an actual monopoly" (Q. 15,493—8). These quotations illustrate the difficulties inherent in the common elusive uses of the term "monopoly."

[2] But shippers complain that, though the Conferences publish their rates for each class of goods, they seldom publish their classifications.

a normal year: and that the means, by which they exclude the competition of interlopers, are reasonable in themselves. A judgment of these claims must turn in some measure on the nature of the weapons, with which they combat interlopers. The chief of these has recently been that of "Deferred Rebates" which, as already said (p. 234), raise questions similar to those of the "tying clauses" in boot and other industries.

5. *The uses of Deferred Rebates as a means of insuring the loyalty of a shipper to a steamship Company or Conference; and their abuses.*

The system of Rebates or discounts to those who deal exclusively with a particular company is very old: but the plan of withholding the rebate for a long time, in order to keep the shipper in what he regards as bondage, was begun late in last century and soon became general in the outward trades. For reasons already explained the homeward trades from the East and South generally include so much cargo which is specially suited for Tramps, that regulation of the rates in them is impracticable: but the exceptional lightness of the homeward trade from South Africa made it amenable to regulation.

A Memorandum, submitted to the Commission on Shipping Rings on behalf of the South African Conference, contended that "the facilities and advantages offered by the various lines, which enable shippers and importers to carry on their business with regularity year in and year out, carry with them a moral obligation on the part of shippers to support the regular lines." This obligation is said to be recognized by many shippers: but in order to bring pressure on others, the Conference Lines have set up a "bargain" with their merchant customers, which in effect says: "We will provide you with a regular and sufficient service, if you, by giving us all your business, will afford the demand essential for that supply."

This contention is not *primâ facie* unreasonable: for it is of course a common practice to make lower charges in some cases to regular than to irregular customers: an annual railway ticket likely to be used for six hundred journeys may be sold for the equivalent of two hundred ordinary tickets, or even less: and shopkeepers at a summer resort may fairly charge rather

III, III, 6. higher prices to summer visitors than to permanent residents. But some actions, which are harmless in ordinary cases, may work injuriously when backed by monopolistic strength. And it is an open question whether the principles by which the general obligations of common carriers are governed, should not exclude the right of a company to use its sole possession of facilities, which are specially important for some kinds of traffic, as a means of compelling other kinds of traffic to be sent by it. The old notion, that a common carrier had obligations to the public, was associated with the notion that he often has some sort of local monopoly, as has already been urged: and coercive measures by great Lines, have certainly grown with the growth of their monopolistic strength[1].

6. *Some general inferences. The functions of an authoritative Commission of inquiry in compelling publicity; and in promoting measures for the interests of the general public on matters, which cannot be fully understood without expert knowledge.*

We may pass to some inferences which the *Report of the Commission on Shipping Rings*, 1909, suggests as to the nature and limits of the profitable intervention of Government in regard to uses of monopolistic power by a great aggregation or confederation in an industry, which must maintain a large scope for the untrammelled exercise of free initiative. We are to see presently how American experience is pointing towards a larger use of permanent regulative Commissions in regard to industrial aggregations of all kinds, in order to grapple with the ever

[1] *The Economist*, January 5, 1918, quoted, as recently issued, a manifesto by the Council of the Associated Chambers of Commerce, in which the system of shipping rings was condemned on the grounds, among others, that "it develops into a restraint by coercive means of British manufacturers and merchants: and that, even if not so designed, it tends to the crushing out of competition in ocean sea carriage by British tramp steamers": also that it tends to restrict the formation of new lines; to "maintain artificially high freights"; and to "make agreement with foreign shipping lines to the prejudice of British traders, who are not members of the Conference lines." From another point of view a representative of Manchester warehouses had complained that, though the war had stayed the preference which Conferences had secured to some German export trade, they still caused an immense quantity of Manchester goods to be shipped *viâ* Liverpool or London, which obtained exclusive favours from the Conference. See *Economist*, Dec. 1, 1917, pp. 871 and 885.

increasing power of destructive competition, which is being acquired by concentrated capital. But, with some partial exception for railways, Britain has not yet felt a great need for such drastic action: and, from her point of view, exceptional interest attaches to investigations of particular difficulties by the authoritative Commission on Shipping Rings.

We are told how representatives of the Conferences confidently asserted on their behalf that "self-interest is an adequate safeguard, and that a Conference could not exist very long" if it were to "use its position for the exclusive use of its shareholders, and to the prejudice of its customers." That is probably true: so extreme a policy would be "suicidal." But the public interest may suffer much from a selfish use of power that is less extreme. A prudent ruler of a conquered province will not adopt such extreme measures as are likely to incite rebellion, or an appeal for external intervention: but he may be glad to draw a goodly revenue for himself, and to cover the expenses of a strong military force against any who might challenge his dominion. A Conference may be tempted in like manner to incur great expense for strategic purposes; and to throw a considerable part of that expense on its customers. If its exclusive hold on the traffic had been absolute and permanent, it would have set the charge for each service at that level, which would yield the maximum net revenue: and, when it incurred any unforeseen expense, which could not be affected by any alteration in its charges, it would have written that expense off out of the value of its property, and kept its charges unaltered. As things are, its monopoly being conditional and not absolute, it is not likely to have ventured to put its charges up to the highest monopoly levels: but it may on the whole conclude that its position will be less endangered by raising its charges a little nearer to those levels, than by stinting expenditure for the confusion of any assailant whether actual, or merely anticipated. This indeed seems to have actually occurred[1].

[1] For instance, shippers represented to the Commission that the number of ships kept up by the South African Line was in excess of the needs of the traffic; and that the inconvenience to them caused by the removal of the superfluous ships (having of course in view the fact that Tramps would respond quickly, though perhaps not at very low charges, to any unexpected increase of heavy freightage) would be less than that caused by paying the charges, which the Company found necessary in order to cover their outlay with profits. But

III, III, 6. The problems of the shipping industry are remarkable alike for their magnitude, and for the multiplicity and complexity of their detail. The carriage of goods a certain distance in a certain time and with a certain amount of careful handling, is a definite thing from a physical point of view; but, from an economic point of view, it varies with the nature of the route to be traversed; with the changing conditions of demand and supply on that route and on the return journey; and some other considerations. It is therefore not suitable for minute Governmental control, and still less for Government undertaking. But nevertheless Government has distinct functions in regard to it, when in a healthy condition, and still more when it has fallen into malaise of any sort.

The chief successes of the medical treatment of bodily ailments have been achieved by measures which tend to give free play to the remedial forces of nature. The chief of the remedial forces of nature in regard to human action is knowledge: and nearly all beneficial intervention of authority in social troubles begins with the acquirement and publication, voluntarily or under compulsion, of information, which some of those interested in the conflict are not likely to offer spontaneously. Many exaggerated complaints, when formulated under pressure, and set out in clear light, shrink up even before they have been answered. And, on the other side of the case, upright men are often half-way converted towards removing such just grounds as there may be for complaint against their conduct, by reading a well-informed and well-balanced statement of those grounds; and knowing that an impartial public is forming its judgment on them. In this and many other ways a careful authoritative inquiry, with publication of the evidence taken, goes a long way towards removing sources of social harm; though it may have no legal power of compelling answers from recalcitrant witnesses, and its specific recommendations in regard to authoritative intervention do not carry very far.

to this Sir Donald Currie (Q. 15,214—6) answered:—"We do not know when busy times may come; and, if our tonnage were reduced considerably, we would not have the steamers there, and somebody else would put on the steamers." He did not attempt to prove that such a result would have been injurious to South Africa, and that therefore she might reasonably be asked to contribute towards the expense of preventing it.

Much helpful knowledge comes to a Commission of Inquiry spontaneously. For there are nearly always two, often more, sets of persons who have intimate technical knowledge of, and strong interest in the subjects investigated by it. Each set puts out its own case vigorously, and spares no effort to bring to light any flaw in statements or arguments that make against it: and thus, so far as the trade interests of any important group of people in the country are concerned, the Commission may sometimes rest content with keeping a fair field for all combatants, and sifting out the vital from the secondary and even irrelevant issues that may be raised. But the interests of those who can offer careful, well-informed, and well-organized evidence are often less important in the aggregate than those of the public at large; who seldom have the special knowledge required for ascertaining exactly where lie their interests in the matter under discussion; or the organization required for setting out their case. The Commission is required to take some initiative in regard to the interests of the non-vocal multitude, in order that it may present a well-balanced picture of the whole position. Thus one of the chief services rendered by public inquiries in various countries (especially in regard to such complex problems as those connected with conditional monopolies) lies in their presenting the points of view of able men; many of whom have no personal interest in the subject under discussion, while they have yet a familiarity with its general scope, and even with its more important practical details, such as seldom can be attained by any save those whose judgments are apt to be biassed by their own special interests. The main Report often lays chief stress on the questions at issue between those most directly interested in the subject under investigation; and sometimes the indirect interests of the public at large are specially considered in Minority Reports.

III, III, 6.

Thus a strong minority of the Commission on Shipping Rings called attention to the fact that the persons *immediately* interested in the policy of the Rings are not those on whom its main effects are likely to fall in the long run. They are "the merchants who buy goods in one country and sell them in another; and they can generally readjust their dealings to suit the rates of freight, and in this way transfer the direct loss from

III, III, 6. excessive rates of freight, or other increase of charge, to the producer or the consumer....The producers and consumers, who are really more interested in the question than the merchants, are affected only indirectly as a whole, and they have very little power of combination for such a purpose as meeting and counteracting the combination of Shipping Rings[1]." These remarks point to the conclusion, which the much larger experience of America in such matters tends to support that, where a powerful monopoly is threatened a body of experts should be set to inquire *ne quid detrimenti Respublica capiat*; and to suggest remedies to be enforced by appropriate authority: as to which more will be said later on[2].

[1] *Report*, vol. I. p. 97.

[2] Traders often rejoice quietly in the imposition of increased taxation on a thing in which they deal, if they have good reason to believe (1) that the demand for it will not greatly shrink in consequence of an increase in its price; and (2) they are sure that all their competitors will pay the same price: for they then expect to pass on the tax, augmented by profits for themselves on it, to the consumers. Accordingly shippers welcome certainty as regards the rates charged for their cargo, even if the rates are somewhat high: and they regard with satisfaction the promise by a Conference, that so long as loyalty to it is secured by deferred rebates or other means, the shipowners will never carry cargo on their own account. But that undertaking, though eminently agreeable to the shippers, tends *primâ facie* at all events to increase the costs, which the non-vocal public will pay for the services they need.

The Majority Report of the Commission on Shipping Rings recommends that "where it appears to the Board of Trade that there are good grounds for believing that important national or imperial interests are affected" the Board of Trade shall have power to institute a special inquiry; and, if it thinks fit, to present a report on it to Parliament. The Minority Report goes further; and recommends that "the Board of Trade should be free to direct an inquiry ...when it appears that important public interests (including those of consumers and producers) are affected by the action of Shipping Companies," and that it should report to Parliament promptly the main results of such inquiry.

The Majority give support to the claim that the services, which Liners render and the public need, could not be maintained without monopolistic control. But their reasons are disputed by the Minority with agruments so strong, and based on answers to such searching questions by themselves and some other members of the Commission, as to seem to incline the balance of evidence against that claim.

It may be added that the South African Conference, partly under pressure from the Union Government, has given up the system of rebates for the time at least; and substituted an arrangement, under which the merchants agree to confine their shipments to the regular Lines engaged in the trade; while the Lines undertake to maintain their services, at uniform rates of freight mutually agreed upon. This arrangement has however been charged by some shippers with effecting abuses similar to those imputed to the system of rebates.

CHAPTER IV

COMPETITION AND MONOPOLY IN TRANSPORT, CONTINUED

1. *Introductory.* III, IV, 1.

It has already been observed that, the advantages which a railway company derives from the exclusive occupation of a great thoroughfare have little counterpart in other industries: and for that reason the study of transport industries for the special purposes of this Book has begun with problems of transport on open courses on land and sea. But incomparably the largest and most instructive experiences, which the world has had of semi-monopolistic power, sufficiently strong to raise problems of public interest, have related to railways.

The tendency towards combination, or cartellization, which we have seen in the development of shipping companies, is now showing itself increasingly in railway combinations and agreements; and yet the main substance of railway problems resembles that of problems of giant manufacturing businesses, which have not come definitely under the dominion of a cartel: for each railway has still a strong, almost absolute, monopoly of some local traffic. But long distance traffic, especially for goods, is on the increase; and this opens ever new competitive activities; in ever-shifting relations with combination. This in its turn has awakened new jealousy, and evoked authoritative restraint. Thus few important railway problems can be solved by reference to the abstract principles of pure monopoly; but there is no other field of economics in which problems of conditional monopoly are so numerous, so large, and so various.

The study of railway science has now its chief home in America. Nowhere else are the financial aspects of railways so

III, IV, 1. prominent: nowhere else would railways, acting in uncontrolled concert, have so complete a mastery of the whole resources of the country; or so despotic a power of deciding what districts should flourish, and what should languish. But the people have been little inclined to let such giant strength work uncontrolled. Railways have been the chief mark of popular criticism, just and unjust: tyrannical exactions have been met by organized mob-violence: and the thoughtful American has been put on his mettle to consider what part of a railway's freedom to do as it liked with its own was reasonable, and what part threatened commercial and even social stability[1].

For a long while the light thrown on railway problems did little more than make darkness visible: but gradually some leading principles emerged which served as guiding lines through many difficulties. An Interstate Commerce Commission was set up: Massachusetts and other States had Intrastate Commissions to regulate local traffic. Recently a great number of shrewd minds, with and without special technical knowledge, have considered complex railway problems with care: and the expert American literature on the subject, official and professional, is of exceptional volume and authority.

Britain and the United States are alike great industrial countries, with the strength and the weakness that comes from popular government; and thus their administrative problems have a closer kinship with one another than with those of any other great industrial country: for neither of them needs to put military considerations in the forefront of her railway policy; and each of them governs her own Government.

But the physical conditions of the two are wide apart. They cause goods traffic to predominate over passenger traffic, and long distance traffic to predominate over short in America: and in Britain they reverse these proportions. Again, British railways have paid higher prices for their land than any others; while American railways have obtained much of it gratis, and

[1] I attended a "Granger" (*i.e.* farmer-in-revolt) meeting in San Francisco in 1875, and one of socialists at Frankfurt a year or two earlier. In both the discourse ran chiefly on "the enemy." But in Frankfurt, the enemy was capital, in San Francisco it was the railways; though in other respects the two discussions were much alike.

have often received direct subsidies, chiefly in the form of land. Again, British railways settled down to quiet policies in the middle of last century; but violent financial struggles for mastery clouded American railway history during most of that century, and have even trespassed on this. For these reasons, it seems best to follow the course of British railway policy in the present chapter, with but little attention to parallel details in American railway history: though, in matters of fundamental principle, guidance must be drawn largely from American sources.

Next in importance to the railways of America are those of Germany. There is a notable contrast between the financial success of Governmental ownership of railways in Prussia, and its comparative failure in every other part of Germany; as in all other countries in which it has been tried without some exceptional advantage. The chief causes are to be found in geographical conditions[1].

It might have been expected that Prussian love of order would have evolved a uniform rate of charges for a given amount of transport of a given quality over a given distance. But the practical exigencies of traffic in various regions gradually

[1] A great part of the population of Prussia lives near the level of the sea, in land so flat as to require but few tunnels; and not many railway cuttings or embankments. She bought her railways cheaply before the strength of Westphalian coal and iron from Luxemburg, Lorraine, etc., combined with other causes, had enabled the country to rise from relative poverty to wealth. None of these advantages accrued to the other States which own their railways: in some of them railway making met with natural difficulties as great as those which have increased the cost of British railways. And, what is of even more importance; by far the greater part of Germany's external trade, as well as of her own heavy internal trade in coal, passes over Prussian lines to Hamburg or Bremen, or to Russia. In these respects the finance of Prussian railways has a unique advantage. If the whole of the railways of the southern half of Germany had come under an excellent Governmental control, they could not have fared well in the face of Prussian control of the northern half. Some of these considerations are emphasized in Prof. Schumacher's instructive eulogy of Prussian railways at the memorable congress in 1912 of the British Royal Economic Society. He says that "in the lesser German States the nationalization of railways has proved a bad bargain....In Bavaria, Baden, Würtemberg and Saxony they yield only about one half the rate of revenue yielded by the Prussian railways. Würtemberg even shows a deficit on its railway working returns" (p. 46). It may be added that the German railway returns, which are reproduced in a H. of C. paper 1913, No. 287, are not easy of interpretation: for the capital accounts of German State railways do not always disclose all the facts: in some cases the railway debt is not even clearly distinguished from the general State debt.

III, IV, 1. broke up the simplicity of the original design. Allowance is now made for water competition; for the needs of particular industries, general and local; for competition with routes in which external railways bear a dominant share; and for special rates in favour of the export trade, and the final result is a highly complex table of the freight charges levied on the most completely homogeneous great system of railways in the world. The Prussian Government has set up a number of Councils, in each of which leading business men of a Province can urge concessions to particular local interests; and their suggestions are generally adopted. This in Prussia, as well as in Britain and America, monopolistic tendencies are restrained in great measure by indirect competitive tendencies; and, where their course might otherwise run freely, they are curbed and directed by authoritative control, more or less under the influence of general business opinion. We shall return to this class of consideration later on[1].

In Britain the relations between monopolistic, competitive, and authoritative influences have changed with the development of the railway map. In very early stages, most of the traffic of each railway has been free from the competition of other railways; though it may have suffered a good deal from the competition of other methods of transport. In the next stage, competition among railways has directly increased: but a little later on, that has often fallen into the background; though indirect competition of various kinds has taken its place to some extent. But meanwhile general attention has been called to the evils that might arise from concerted action by all the chief railways serving any one district: and railways have been restrained from all extreme uses of monopolistic power; if not by actual authoritative edict, yet by the fear of inviting it.

[1] A good account of the German Advisory Railway Councils is given in the *Report of the Board of Trade Railway Conference*, 1909 [Cd. 4677], pp. 83—92, and 109—112; where they are described as "exercising, if not actual, yet a certain moral pressure on the authorities." They have contributed to the multiplication of special (*Ausnahme*) rates, which in 1906 already covered nearly two thirds of the goods traffic on Prussian railways; so that, in spite of some efforts at simplification, there were nearly a thousand different rate-books in operation (*ib.* pp. 98—105).

III, IV, 1. It may be said that the British railway industry pioneered the path of public policy in regard to the authoritative defence of general interests against the abuses of overmastering strength. Its problems are unlike those of any other great country; though those of Japan and New Zealand may develop on somewhat similar lines. For it has no heavy through traffic: and, with a partial exception for coal, it has comparatively little heavy internal traffic. It has been deprived of much specially remunerative traffic by coasting steamers: and in return it has taken from canals traffic which they might have been able to work more easily than it can. These two considerations are often ignored: but they will be found to explain the chief peculiarities—good and evil—of British railways, and something must be said about them.

The foundations of modern railway science were firmly laid by Lardner's *Railway Economy*, 1849. He attributed the complexity of its problems mainly to "the variety of the services rendered by a railway, and their remoteness in time from the outlays involved in its construction." But, when he wrote, not very many miles of well made railway line had been at work for more than a single decade: and since his time light single tracks have been displaced by ever heavier double, triple and quadruple tracks: short cuts have been made, sharp corners have been rounded off, and steep inclines have been moderated. Each successive generation has regarded the representative type of railway of its own times as fit to exercise an enduring monopolistic sway within its own region; but in fact new developments have demanded new provisions: broad details are ever changing, though fundamentals remain nearly as they were in 1850[1].

[1] Lardner's work is a fitting companion to Babbage's *Economy of Manufactures*, 1832. Each of them set the main principles of an important branch of applied economics with so much constructive genius, that subsequent study has confirmed them, even more than it has enlarged them; while some of their results are often ignored even now. There are few controversialists on either side of the dominant railway issues of the present time, who might not learn much from Lardner. His work is thoroughly English: but the chief obligations which he records are to analytical studies made in Belgium and France.

The slight touches of mathematical reasoning which are to be found in early books on railway science, have been greatly developed by Launhardt, Colson, and others. The brilliant work of Edgeworth and Pigou has special claims

III, iv, 2. 2. *The configuration of Britain and the habits of her people are responsible for the fact that most of her goods traffic consists of small consignments, carried short distances; and therefore at high average costs per "ton-mile."*

Railways grew out of difficulties of heavy transport (especially when mud was thick) at mines, quarries, docks, etc. The motive power was supplied at first by men or horses; and afterwards by stationary engines: and it was long before railways attempted seriously to compete with inland water traffic, drawn by horses, for the carriage of common products in bulk. They sowed their wild oats in "the forties"; and during the subsequent seventy years have progressed quietly, doing great things, but making little history. A short account of their early struggles is given in Appendix M, 1: we may pass at once to the immediate antecedents of present conditions.

The most profitable part of the work of almost every railway system is its goods traffic: and the most profitable part of that is the carriage of great loads over great distances without break of bulk. For though the charges per "ton-mile" (that is, for carrying a ton the distance of a mile) in such traffic are nearly always exceptionally low, its costs are even lower in proportion. There is little or no shunting; the consumption of coal, and the expenditure of labour are low relatively to the ton-miles accomplished; and a much larger volume of goods traffic of this kind than of any other can pass over a line in the twenty-four hours.

The ocean is now a mighty purveyor of such traffic to the railways of North America; and in a less degree of Central

on English readers. But their route is not followed here: for mathematical analysis cannot easily be applied to *conditional* monopoly: it is almost constrained to start with the hypothesis of *pure* monopoly, and gradually to introduce successive limitations, corresponding to the various limitations and restrictions which are imposed on railways by various circumstances, and especially by the guiding and restraining influences of public opinion and authority. On the route taken in the present chapter and the next, railway problems are seen in the first instance as concerned with conditional monopoly; cases, in which monopoly is in effect almost absolute, being treated as exceptional. Each route for the study has its own advantages: the two should meet at the end; as do the Eastern and the Western routes to Australia. The route followed in these chapters seems the most appropriate to the general purposes of Book III.

Europe. But the like services which it renders to English railways are relatively small: and they are diminishing under the rapidly growing economy and efficiency of steam coasting traffic. In early days, traffic between the eastern and western coasts of England had gone frequently by canals, rather than by sailing ships; although the canals were narrow and shallow, and had to pass watersheds many hundred feet high, by tedious locks: for delivery by canal boat was often quicker, and more capable of being guaranteed true to time than was delivery by sailing vessel. One of the first achievements of the relatively slow and costly paddle steamers of the second quarter of last century was the complete defeat of canals in this trade. For a while the railways made a strong bid against the steamships: but the ships increased in speed and economy so much faster than the railways did, that they quickly took over nearly all of that trade: and very little long distance heavy traffic was left for the railways, except that in coal to inland consumers[1].

Meanwhile the number of great industrial and trading centres, from which wholesale and retail dealers can draw supplies, has continually increased, as was noticed in Book II: and the growing changefulness and imperiousness of demand have caused the stocks, which dealers hold, to diminish relatively to the number of different things in them, and in many cases to diminish absolutely. Consequently wholesale dealers occasionally, and retail dealers habitually, have found themselves in need of small consignments sent at short notice. Many of these travel as parcels by passenger train; but the remainder are an increasing part of the goods traffic. With ever lessening

[1] It is indeed true that, though London has good access to the sea, yet half her coal comes now direct by land. But it is to be remembered that many seams of coal, which were near tidal water, were for that very reason exhausted long ago: and a great part of such coal as can easily reach the sea is exported. If coal has to travel by railway to the sea, and again from the sea to the consumer; then, even though the railway journeys be short, the cost of double transhipment is likely to give the advantage to coal sent in wagons direct from the mine to the consumer, or at least to a railway station in his immediate neighbourhood. Gas and electricity companies and other large consumers of coal often seek tidal water in London and elsewhere. But small consumers draw nearly all their supplies from railway stations; the cost of local delivery, though perhaps the lowest attainable under present conditions, being high even for short distances.

III, IV, 2. competition as to charges, railway managers have set themselves to attract traffic by speedy delivery: they have sent off each consignment as soon as it arrived; often even giving it a truck to itself, if there was nothing else going to the same destination, unless it was very small indeed. So they are loath to bring the large wagon into general use; although, when full, it weighs less in proportion to its freight; occupies less space on the line, and is more economical in other ways than a small wagon. And, partly in order to lessen the total time occupied in the journey of a consignment from sender to receiver, the railways perform themselves, and include in their ordinary charges, some services, which elsewhere are left to the individuals concerned or subsidiary transport agencies: this practice causes the charges made on British railways to appear higher, relatively to those in other countries, than they really are.

These and similar causes have given a peculiar character to English railways, which differ from those of other great industrial countries of Europe somewhat in the same way as those differ from the railways of America. Wherever much long distance heavy traffic must go by railway, plant and charges are adapted mainly to its requirements: and heavy engines draw long trains of large wagons loaded with freight; which pays high charges per ton for each average journey, but very low charges for each ton-mile (that is, for each mile that each ton is carried). An American train often carries more than a thousand tons in fully loaded wagons, holding from thirty to fifty tons, for more than a thousand miles with scarcely any break of bulk. The majority of British goods trains, other than those loaded with coal, are made of small wagons destined to deliver a multitude of consignments, averaging some two or three hundredweight, or even less, at a multitude of stations.

Hence arise two results, which will occupy our attention a good deal. Competition for traffic between two British routes, whether each be wholly by one railway or made up from portions of two or more, turns more upon the incidental conveniences offered by the several services, and less on the charges made per mile, than is the case in many other countries and especially in America. And secondly, statistical records of the average charge per ton-mile of goods carried, if ever they should be collected for Britain, would show a much higher level than those of many other countries: partly on account of the special facilities, to which British railways are forced to devote much money and care; partly because the heavy charges, which forwarding agents make in other countries for similar work, are apt to be left out of account in international comparisons. These agents often delay consignments till they have enough for a single destination to enable them to claim a lower rate of charge than that for small consignments. An Englishman generally prefers a prompt service to one that is rather cheaper. Perhaps this preference is sometimes carried unreasonably far: but a fair comparison of two railway systems in regard to efficiency and economy requires that full allowance be made for economy of time[1].

3. *Britain's railway map shows the fortuitous results of competition; and her passenger service is very costly: but the economy of time resulting from frequent rapid services on parallel lines is perhaps worth more than its cost.*

We may next consider the rule that density of population shortens the average railway journey; and raises the benefit which the public derive from a great choice of trains, in comparison with that which they get from low fares and low rates for the transport of goods. At the same time, it enables charges for the cost and upkeep of the permanent way to be divided among a great number of passengers and tons per mile: it therefore allows the direct costs of hauling each passenger and ton of goods a mile to be rather high without lowering the dividends of the line. Advantage has been taken of these conditions throughout the industrial and trading districts of England and Scotland to set up a greater number of trains, and especially of fast trains, than are to be found in any other area of equal size in the world. Nowhere else are there so many pairs of points between which the passenger has a large choice of the time of day at which he will start on his journey, and yet travel at an average rate exceeding forty miles an hour. Nowhere else are small packages collected and delivered over

[1] Methods of obtaining economy in money costs, without losing economy of time, are considered below, pp. 490—1.

III, IV, 3. so many considerable distances within the twenty-four hours, even at the cost to the railway of sending off wagons with but light loads: nowhere else are so many express fish and milk trains run, though the quick and secure transport of perishable food over long distances has been brought to a high degree of perfection by American railroads.

The compactness of the industrial districts of England and Scotland, combined with the manifold railway access which each district has to various sea-ports, has made competition for traffic of this kind very eager. In the result there has been a constant tendency to agreements as to charges: and these agreements have been promoted by the intervention of Government; even while a chief motive of the Legislature was the desire to maintain competition among railways, and to check the movement of the railway system as a whole in the direction of firm monopoly. Parliament has always favoured the fusion of lines which make a continuous whole, and regarded parallel lines with some suspicion; but some parallel lines for which there was no good reason, when they were made, are now fully employed.

The intensity of some kinds of goods traffic, and of almost all kinds of passenger traffic between chief centres of population has contributed to the concentration of the greater part of Britain's railway system in less than half of her area: and it has been justly observed that the forethought of a strong Government might have effected a somewhat better distribution. But under modern conditions, densely peopled districts exert a preponderating influence on Governments, even of a somewhat absolute character: stress is laid on the fact that trainloads are often very light in districts in which the passenger train mileage in each hundred square miles is very small. It is noteworthy that, the railway map of Prussia, under by far the most efficient governmental management in the world, shows alternations of dense and sparse networks somewhat similar to those of England's map: and this is in spite of the fact that many Prussian railways in sparsely peopled districts were made almost exclusively for strategic purposes.

Again, when two considerable railway centres *A* and *B* are connected by parallel railways, some waste may be caused by running express trains on both routes: and the cessation of such waste is one of the more prominent advantages which are sometimes anticipated from a fusion of the two lines, whether in private or Government ownership. But there seems to be no very great waste in such duplication; except in a few cases, in which the trains on both routes are inadequately filled, and run between *A* and *B* without stopping. It more frequently happens that some of these express trains stop at one or more important secondary stations on the way. Suppose *C* to be such a station on one of the lines; then it will probably be arranged that a slow train arrives shortly before a quick train stops there; so that passengers from small stations intermediate between *A* and *C* travel quickly between *C* and *B*. Similarly passengers, starting from small stations between *B* and *C*, travel quickly between *C* and *A*[1].

4. ***In regard to short periods most of the costs of a railway are "fixed"; but large problems of railway policy relate chiefly to long periods, in regard to which much fewer costs are fixed.***

Passing from general considerations relating to the structure of British railways, we may now enter on the large and difficult problem of the relation between costs and charges in the railway industry, regarded as one of conditional monopoly.

[1] Parallel lines are sometimes deliberately arranged by a single company. Great Western expresses between London and Exeter have three routes: one through Bath, another through Badminton, and a third through Westbury. It is doubtful whether any waste is involved by the fourth parallel route of the South Western through Salisbury: and North Devon would have suffered much if that route had not been continued to Plymouth through Okehampton. There are no long parallel lines in Britain so near together as those that run on the right and left banks of the Rhine for more than a hundred miles, being in sight of one another for the greater part of the way: they are two of the busiest lines of the great Prussian system.

The Great Eastern and Great Northern lines are parallel between London and Cambridge. But Cambridge is the focus of many lines; and some Great Northern trains are arranged to arrive at or leave Cambridge at about the same time as Great Eastern expresses; so that Norfolk and other Eastern Counties may have good connections with Hertfordshire and neighbouring districts. As a rule the two sets of express trains supplement one another: and if their number were much diminished, the small gain in net income to the combined companies, would probably be of less value than the loss of time and convenience to those whose engagements give them occasion to move between London and Cambridge.

III, IV, 4. It is true that when once a new railway has a fully equipped double track, it can carry a great deal of traffic without further outlay on its permanent way, and with but little further outlay on buildings: though of course it must increase its rolling stock, and almost every class of its employees. It is true therefore that its costs are less dependent on the extent of its business than are those of a shipping company, which makes use of public docks: and invests nearly all its capital on vessels that speedily deteriorate, even if they are not rendered obsolescent by technical advances. A large ship is no doubt very economical of working, provided a full cargo can be found for it. But the total costs incurred by a railway for a small traffic per mile are generally very great, while those for a dense traffic per mile are generally low: and there is no equally striking contrast between the expenses per ton or passenger mile of a small line of well chosen ships, and those of the most powerful line. It will however be found on examination that tendencies to Increasing Return are strong only at certain stages of a railway expansion: and that similar tendencies are found at corresponding stages of the growth of a business in industries which are not, in any special sense, Increasing Return industries.

Consider for instance the case of a printer, who is equipped with a varied up-to-date plant and staff, but is slack of work: the gain of an additional order may be worth to him nearly the full price that he would get for it, after deducting the cost of the materials. And yet, if his normal output doubled, he might probably need almost to double his plant and staff: he would not reap any great additional economies from more highly specialized plant or staff, utilization of waste products, etc.: that is, he would not reap many additional economies of those kinds which are giving the upper hand to a giant firm in steel and some other distinctively Increasing Return industries. Therefore although a particular order may be taken, without allowing for more than out-of-pocket expenses; yet, speaking generally, orders are to be charged with their appropriate share of the cost of setting up, or it may be enlarging the printer's buildings, plant and staff: and the same is true in great measure of railway work. That is to say there are alternating stages in the evolution of the traffic on a railway. When it is first

III, IV, 4.

opened, it commonly has an equipment expected to suffice for several years, without calling for any very heavy expenditure. It has at first very little traffic; perhaps hardly sufficient to cover working expenses, without making any contribution to interest on the capital invested. During that stage, every addition to the traffic adds much more to the revenue of the railway than to its costs: and it may be said, without greatly forcing the use of words, the railway is an Increasing Return business. But after a while the traffic begins to outgrow the equipment of the railway; and then no more can be carried efficiently without great outlay: while that development is in process the railway may be described, without greater forcing of the use of words than in the preceding case, as a Diminishing Return business: and so on[1].

It may be well to go into some detail in regard to this. Of course it is, generally speaking, no true economy to build a line with steep gradients or sharp curves, or even on a circuitous route, if there is any considerable chance of its being required in the course of a generation to do important work. But nearly all the other outlays, which belong to a first-class railway, may well be avoided when building in a sparsely peopled district.

A single line, with few and short sidings, scanty ballast and light rails can be built and equipped cheaply. It may be closed at night; and at a very small station two men can do the whole work, including the signalling. As the traffic increases, the efficiency of the railway can be increased gradually: and

[1] This point has been developed by several writers and especially by M. O. Lorenz in the *Harvard Journal of Economics*, Feb. 1907 and Feb. 1916. He quotes from President J. J. Hill of the Great Northern Railway, U.S.A., speaking in 1907: "The traffic increases wonderfully, but the railroad facilities have not been able to keep up the pace. That is why to-day your business in some respects is paralysed, while you cry aloud for transportation help. Long paralysis means slow death. The fact is probably forty per cent. of your business to-day is without any facilities to handle it."

The fundamental importance of the element of time in all discussions of the lines of division to be drawn between (1) fluctuating operating expenses, (2) constant operating expenses, and (3) fixed charges, is explained in great detail, with special reference to American conditions, in W. J. Ripley's excellent *Railroads*, vol. I., especially pp. 61—66. "Everything depends on the length of time under consideration." Compare his long period chart (p. 66) with those for short periods (p. 100).

III, IV, 5. thus its capital cost can be kept in fairly close relation to the work it has to do, and the income it can earn. But the increase in expense makes some great jumps: as for instance as soon as it has been decided to have two lines instead of one, or three or four instead of two; or to keep the signal-boxes open by night; or to make the permanent way, including the bridges, solid enough to carry heavy locomotives at a great speed. None of those changes can, as a rule, be made piecemeal: and after each of them, the efficiency of the line is so much increased, that it can carry more additional traffic, than it is likely to have for some time, without any appreciable addition to its expenses on account of the permanent way.

These general considerations are sufficient to show that the permanent way and its equipments are not even approximately, definite entities, made once for all, and "fixed" independently of the traffic. If further evidence were needed, it would be supplied by the fact that in the thirty years 1882—1912, the "paid up capital" of British railways increased from 768 million pounds to 1335 million pounds; though their aggregate length had increased only from 18,457 miles to 23,441.

In one sense indeed it is true generally that the density per mile of the traffic of a railway system increases with its length; and that therefore the larger it is the lower the rates at which it can profitably work. For if an extension *B* is added to a railway *A*, the traffic on the united lines exceeds the sum of the traffics that there would have been on *A* and *B* separately by the traffic between *A* and *B*. But this consideration is more than outweighed, in a country already well supplied with railways, by the fact that the natural courses of the chief traffic have been occupied by the earlier lines.

5. *The direct costs of particular passenger services.*

The business of a railway consists of two main branches, goods traffic and passenger traffic. Goods traffic is the more interesting for our purpose; but it is also the more complex. For much of its cost is due to terminal services, which are of a different order from those of mere transport: and while, as a rule, the fare paid by a passenger is of no concern to anyone but himself, much of the trouble connected with charges for goods traffic arises from the fact that the charge paid by producers or traders for the transport of any class of goods is a matter of concern on the one hand to those who desire to use the goods, and on the other to those who offer competitive goods from the same, or from different, sources of supply. We will therefore begin with the direct costs of passenger traffic.

III, IV, 5.

The unit of charge is as a rule (subject to exceptions for season tickets, organized excursions, etc.) a single or double journey for a single person: but the smallest unit of cost of service is that of a passenger wagon[1]. There is no means of ascertaining beforehand how much dead weight will be carried for each passenger in any train (save in a few cases, such as those of trains which bring every week day the same crowds of workers to go on duty at, say, nine o'clock); and the accommodation provided is adjusted to the probable demand for it, a large margin being generally allowed for unforeseen contingencies. Therefore the direct cost of a passenger must generally be taken to be that fraction of the total cost of hauling a wagon, which corresponds to the average number of those who travel in the same class of carriages with himself, in trains which run under similar conditions to his. This last qualification leads to the next point.

As it makes scarcely any difference to the cost of a railway whether any carriage in a train, that is made up ready for running, is full or not: so the addition of an extra wagon to a train, which is bound to run, adds to the total costs of the train, nothing but the wear and tear of that wagon, and the consumption of a little extra coal. Therefore speaking generally the wagon unit of cost is to be regarded as a proportional part of the next larger unit of cost, that of a train.

It used to be held that a fast train cost more than one which made many stoppages on the same route. This was partly because an engine that could travel fast, was very expensive: but improved methods of exact mechanical engineering have reduced this difference; and it is now understood,

[1] It is true that when some of the wagons contain compartments of more than one class, it is possible to meet slightly increased demand on the part of any class of passengers by substituting a long wagon for a short one. But, for the sake of simplicity, these and similar trifling details will be left out of consideration.

III, IV, 5. that a train travelling forty or fifty miles an hour with but very few stoppages, is less costly than one that makes frequent stoppages, and is yet required to attain a good pace between each pair. Therefore the practice of charging additional fares for express trains has declined, especially in Britain; and the direct cost of a passenger train may be taken as varying generally with its total weight and length of journey. But a train which runs at a time, when the line has more traffic than it can conveniently accommodate, may be held not to pay its costs unless it is fairly full: as a rule, the trains that do run at such times can earn large revenue even at low charges; and these opposing influences have led to some curious anomalies[1].

The total charges that belong to the passenger service, including the transport of such parcels as go by passenger train, consist of the direct costs incurred on current account for passengers, parcels, rolling stock, stations and employees; together with interest on all outlays for those that are to be charged to capital account: also with appropriate shares of the general costs of signalling; and of the making and maintenance of the main way, and of such sidings as are not exclusively used by the goods traffic. But the distribution of these general costs between the passenger and the goods divisions cannot be brought under any fixed rule. As a starting point it may be supposed that they should be divided roughly in proportion to the direct costs of the two divisions: with some special allowance for costs that are incurred more for one service than another; and especially when one pushes the other aside. For instance passenger trains crowd goods trains off the line at certain hours of the day, while goods trains in return have almost exclusive possession in the centre of the night.

To pass to some points of detail:—it is often said that the tendency of the age is towards increased subtlety of differentiation between various classes of goods that travel on the same line of railway: but, in so far as this is true at all, the cause will generally be found to be some new differentiation in the services required for different things. In passenger traffic on

[1] Something is said about them in Appendix M, 2.

the other hand the tendencies of the age are clearly in the opposite direction. In early times indeed everyone had a definite rank: when he travelled he received accommodation according to his rank; and he paid for it proportionately, unless indeed he exacted it without payment. The first English railways went on this plan: those who were unable to pay high charges were forced to travel in great discomfort: and express trains were practically reserved for the gentry, partly because it was thought that quick transport was very costly; until, with the advance of railway technique, it was found better to attract all classes of passengers between principal stations into fast trains.

Thus one form of differential charge, which was long customary, has practically disappeared from British railways. Meanwhile the amenities of third class travelling have been greatly increased; and it has become necessary to provide first class passengers with so much free space, that the actual cost of the haulage needed for earning a given sum from first class carriages has become greater than for third class; though of course the net earnings on each hundred passengers are greater for the first than for the third class. In several other ways differential charges for passenger traffic have diminished; and an elastic demand has been met by increasing accommodation and specially low fares, even under conditions which made the direct cost of haulage more heavy than usual.

These considerations tend to show that the reasonableness of the fares charged by a railway cannot be judged even approximately by mere reference to the rates per mile in each class: for the services of one railway may be so much more advantageous to passengers than those of another, that they are really the cheaper, though at higher charges. Speed and frequency of trains, spaciousness and ease of carriages, allowances of free luggage, etc. are benefits for which extra fares could be charged reasonably; in the same way that a higher rent may be reasonably charged for one ten-roomed house in which the rooms are large and well appointed, than for another which is also classed as a ten-roomed house but cost much less to build. Again, a line built in a mountainous and difficult district, where traffic is scarce, may charge higher rates for a service inferior in comfort or efficiency to that of another in a rich, flat, densely peopled district: and yet be in effect the cheaper of the two.

But so great are the advantages of simplicity and uniformity that, with a few divergences in exceptional cases, the charge of a penny per mile for ordinary third class traffic is universal on British railways; it being understood that, where there are competitive routes, the mileage is reckoned as by the shortest. Thus practical expediency has brought about a rigidity of rule, which would have been resented if imposed on the railways by authority.

6. *The direct costs of particular goods-traffic services.*

As a single passenger is the ordinary unit of charge on his side of railway business, so is a single consignment the unit of charge on its side: and, as in passenger service so in goods service, the direct cost of the appropriate unit of charge, is derived in the first instance from that of a wagon unit (or, in the case of a large consignment, of several such units), which again is generally derived from that of a train unit. And the general costs of service are shared out over particular direct costs on a similar principle, or lack of principle, in the two cases. But there are some broad contrasts between goods and passenger services, from the points of view both of the railways and their customers, on which a little should be said.

To begin with, there is the consideration that goods traffic bears a closer resemblance to manufactures than passenger traffic does: because the carriage of goods, like the work of a factory, is only one link in a chain of production; whereas a passenger journey is, as a rule, complete in itself. Consequently the immediate, though not the ultimate, interest in the freights charged for any kind of goods is generally concentrated in a relatively small number of people, who trade in those goods as buyers or sellers. But the interest, both immediate and ultimate, in passenger fares is diffused over the whole population; and therefore it seldom gives rise to keen sectional conflicts, such as are found in the relations between those engaged in successive stages of the same long process of production; especially if they are organized in cartels, or so-called "trusts," and other giant businesses. Accordingly, freight rates are subject to an eager, alert and well informed scrutiny, which is seldom brought to bear on passenger fares: and, as it happens, though discrimination between passengers according to their rank has been rendered impracticable by the obsolescence of definite lines of social cleavage, the discrimination of goods according to their rank has become a very important matter to the carrier: and it is not very difficult.

Again, a passenger who desires to travel between two points *A* and *B* is concerned only with the charge levied on him: he does not care whether it is greater or less than the charges levied on other people who travel between either point and some third point. But the producers and dealers who live in *A* are often deeply interested in the relation which the railway charges, levied on the goods which they send to *B*, bear to those levied on rival goods, which come from *C*, or *D*. In fact, there is much truth in the saying of an experienced railway official, that when a trader or a locality complains that railway rates are too high; what is really meant, is that the rates charged to some competitive person or locality are too low. For, as has been already observed, neither producer nor trader is very much affected by a tax or any additional charge laid on him, provided that everybody else, who supplies the same market, is subject to the same burden: the main burden falls on the ultimate consumer, though the businesses of producer and trader may be a little curtailed.

Again, in a small country such as England, which has sufficient traffic to require its chief lines to be kept open at night, the goods service presents in one respect simpler problems than the passenger service. For the passenger insists on choosing his own times for travelling: and these are, for the greater part, times when the line is crowded (unless the journey is long enough to give time for a fair night's sleep). But the shipper of goods requires nothing more than that they should travel safely, and be delivered without great delay: he does not care whether they go in a fast or slow train, or what stoppages they make by the way. So far from objecting to their travelling by night, he rather prefers it; at all events in a compact industrial district, where goods collected by a railway towards

III, IV, 6. the end of a day's work can be generally delivered before noon on the next day. This convenience is partly cause and partly result of the British practice of making up numerous trains, of small wagons, many of which are not nearly full; so that one can be dropped at each considerable station to be unloaded at leisure. The proportion of dead weight to freight in these trains is very high: but they enable work to be done without very much night labour between two working days, which in most other countries is spread over at least twice as long a period. And thus in goods traffic, as in passenger traffic, *British railway services rate economy of time to the customer much more highly in comparison with money costs, than other railway services do*. Let us pass to another contrast, that between railway and shipping services.

The special services with their corresponding costs, which steamship lines render to valuable goods, consist chiefly of more rapid transit, with a regular service of ships insuring prompt despatch. These advantages play a relatively small part in railway goods traffic: for distances are short, at all events in small countries, and there are frequent and regular services on main lines for all sorts of traffic. Steamers charge light goods according to volume. Railways do not: they simply put goods that occupy much space in proportion to their weight into a "higher," that is more highly taxed class: machines for instance are in a high class when fully set up, and in a low class when their several parts are closely packed in square cases.

English railways generally undertake cartage for everything, except minerals and other things, which come in great bulk and are carried at very low rates. Costs are incurred and corresponding charges are made for "terminal" expenses of various kinds, with extras for covering and uncovering, loading and unloading. These costs and charges are not always very heavy absolutely: but they are large relatively to actual costs of haulage, especially in short distance traffic: consequently unless terminal charges of all kinds are separately entered, the total charge per ton-mile must be very high for small distances, and gradually diminish, as the distances increase[1].

[1] The direct cost of carrying the same class of goods per ton-mile has been found, other things being equal, to vary generally as the square root of the

Accordingly railways in every country arrange that the charge for each consignment per ton-mile shall be greater for small consignments than for large, and for small distances than for large: administrative economy requires the rates of charge to be grouped into several broad classes. The charges for each sort of goods are in some measure adjusted, with general consent, to the average of the total consignments of them which make the same journey, and give scope for making up fairly full wagon-loads, if not train-loads; and again to the costliness of any special wagons needed, and the ratio of their weight to their carrying power; and again to the outlay and care needed for preventing depreciation of the goods and injury by the weather. Account may also be taken of the fact that wagons specialized for one sort of traffic are apt to be expensive, to travel often empty one way; and in some cases, to be idle during a great part of the year.

To conclude:—a fairly old railway, holding the greater part of the transport of a compact industrial district, is likely to have so completely adjusted its appliances to the traffic, that each of them is well occupied; and does its work so economically, that any addition to that work would have to carry nearly full costs. In such a case cost of service could automatically become the chief regulator of railway charges; and some American writers are inclined to think that, ere many generations are past, railways will in their own interest cease to concern themselves much about the various values of their services to particular classes of traffic; but will levy nearly the same charges for all services that make equal demands on their plant at equally busy seasons, and require equal direct or "particular" costs. Mr M. O. Lorenz argues cogently that while *value* of service is likely to continue long the chief regulator of prices in the sparsely peopled districts of the Southern and Western States of America, *cost* of service shows signs of taking the first place in the Eastern States[1].

It has already been said that Scientific Management is but one exceptionally vigorous and sanguine embodiment of

distance. (See Ripley, *l.c.* I. p. 103.) But this empirical rule might easily be set aside by changes in organization and in technique.

[1] *Quarterly Journal of Economics*, Feb. 1916.

III, IV, 6. the fundamental idea that the progress of the science of business, as of all other sciences, depends largely on the clearness and precision with which the achievements of one generation are recorded so as to form starting points for those of the next. The trained instinct of a business man of high genius will no doubt often see at a glance a clear way through problems, on which even the most voluminous statistics could give but little guidance.

But, as was urged above (II, II, 2), the printed figure remains; and cumulative progressive knowledge based on organized records of observed facts supplies the material on which modern constructive faculty works. Its province is to perceive how the slight and indirect lights, thrown by mere numerical records, can be so utilized, in combination with lights drawn from their sources, as to cause realities to fall in their proper positions relatively to one another, and to set on one side hasty inferences from limited observations.

No doubt untutored critics are apt to be misled by international comparisons, which discuss ton-miles, wagon-miles, and train-miles, on the supposition that each of these terms means nearly the same thing always. But American railways have lived down such difficulties as these; and are turning to ever better account the publication of the information; which the Interstate Commerce Commission, with full support from public opinion, requires them to publish[1].

Some reference has already been made to various policies for the distribution of the general costs of a railway among the charges for its various services. But we have come to the point at which these complex and thorny matters must be considered more closely.

[1] Something more is said on this subject in Appendix M, 4. The present is not the proper place for investigating the relations between employers and employed in conditional monopolies. But the charges, made by British and Continental railways, cannot be compared fairly without reference to the high wages which British railways pay. An Act, passed in March, 1913, provided that a rise in their charges might be justified on the ground that it was needed to cover outlay on "improvement in the conditions of employment of its labour or clerical staff."

CHAPTER V

COMPETITION AND MONOPOLY IN TRANSPORT, CONTINUED

1. *The distribution of the general costs of a railway over its various services.* III, v, 1.

The present chapter is mainly concerned with the application to railway problems of the general principles, already discussed, relating to the good and the evil of price-discriminations by semi-monopolistic businesses. This inquiry, especially in so far as it relates to geographical discriminations, runs up into the question of Government control of railways and of their relations to other agencies for internal transport; as to which something is said in Chapter VI.

In the present chapter, as indeed throughout, reference is made to normal conditions, such as those which existed before the world-war: they were the basis on which earlier drafts of the present Volume were written; and no account is taken of the abnormal conditions which have arisen during the war, save where an express reference is made to them.

When price is governed by active and unrestricted competitive production, the highest price that the market will bear is the equivalent of the cost of production; provided the commodity in question is in fact, or can conveniently be made, the chief product of a well-equipped business. But the case is different, where several products have a joint cost of production, in the strict sense; so that it is almost impossible to produce one without producing the others. For then the division of the costs between them is governed by the relative volumes and intensities of the market demands for them; subject to the condition, that if the processes of production can be so

III, v, 1. modified as to vary their relative proportions, then those proportions will be modified in accordance to the relative market demands; and prices will be modified accordingly. Thus, before mutton could be brought across the equator in cool chambers, the wool of Australian sheep was developed at the expense of the mutton; though, in breeding British sheep, the first consideration was the rapid maturity of a heavy carcase. In such adjustments monopolistic and competitive policies run on similar lines: what differences there are between the two are relatively unimportant.

We have seen that manufacturers, traders, and shipping companies, who offer a variety of commodities or services, are seldom able to set a large share of general costs on any commodity or service, on which well-appointed businesses can conveniently specialize: but in regard to all others they have great freedom. Their normal practice is to adopt some distribution of the general charges provisionally: to make slight tentative variations in the distribution—sometimes with reference to particular transient conditions, sometimes with the purpose of improving their permanent policy. A strong monopolist business has a free hand in making such experiments: but its action in this respect differs only in degree, not in kind, from that of almost every considerable alert manufacturer and trader.

Just as independent competitive manufacturers and traders distribute their general costs over various classes of goods, somewhat arbitrarily indeed, but yet ultimately very much on the same plan; so it has been found that "there exists surprising similarity in the methods employed by different railway companies in apportioning certain common or overhead expenses. This similarity appears to have been brought about without previous conference and agreement; and is apparently the result of similar conclusions arrived at by men working at the same problem independently of one another." It appears that this agreement, liable to vary as it is from one country to another, and to change in some degree from decade to decade, is yet sufficiently definite to serve as a basis for "public policy expressed in most general terms, leaving the detailed application to administrative action and judgment." Such appear in effect to be the main principles governing the British Railway Commission and Board of Trade; as well as of the Interstate Commerce Commission, on whose behalf they have been thus formulated[1].

From a purely abstract point of view, it might seem proper to assign to each service its own direct costs, together with a proportionate share of those which belong specially to services of a like kind with itself; and another proportionate share of those which are common to the whole railway. But for practical purposes, account must be taken of the universal custom of putting lower charges on goods that could not be carried at all at rates, which have but little constrictive effect on traffic in more costly goods. Accordingly a charge for any service is not regarded as discriminative, so long as it includes shares of general costs proportionate to the charges which are commonly levied for similar services in regard *to goods of the same kind* on the railway in question, and on others working under like conditions. Such conclusions are based on a broader foundation of experiment and experience than most of those which are adopted as rules in practical life. They are not final of course; and must in the long run be modified by the assault of experience which is growing slowly in breadth, and fast in organized analysis, record and reasoning: but they hold the field for the time.

A preliminary difficulty arises from the distinction between the cost of handling freight at its points of departure and arrival; and the cost of moving it when it is in its wagon. The first cost is approximately the same for similar consignments,

[1] By Mr B. H. Meyer at the meeting of the American Economic Association, in 1913. Professor M. B. Hammond suggests that it matters very little how a merchant or a manufacturer starts his distribution of general costs. He may apportion them "to labour costs, or to the cost of the material; or, even more loosely still, according to floor spaces, or according to the amount of sales or the number of employees." After a while he will get from any starting point to nearly the same conclusion; since "by carefully comparing the rates of growth of the various departments with the growth of his profits, he is able year by year to correct his former standards of measurement....In applying the comparative method of determining costs and of fixing charges in accordance thereto, it would seem that the Commissioners and the railway officials have been merely pursuing the methods generally known and accepted by most careful business men." (*Quarterly Journal of Economics*, Nov. 1910, p. 66.)

III, v, 1. whether destined for a short or a long journey: the second varies nearly with the length of the journey, but is rather less in proportion for a long journey than for a short. Here it is necessary to recall the contrasts between the charges for large and small consignments, and for long and short distances.

First, as to the terminal charge: it must cover direct costs, together with a share of general costs; all being roughly adjusted to the labour of handling done by the servants of the railway, with extras for such special tasks as that of protecting the consignment from the weather by a waterproof covering. These terminal charges are independent of the distance to be travelled; except in so far as a long journey may call for any precaution, that would be inappropriate for a short one: they are of course at somewhat higher rates for small consignments than for large.

Secondly, that part of the charge, which relates to moving, covers direct and indirect costs. The direct costs of moving are proportionately higher for short distances than for long. And they are much higher for small consignments than for large: because full truck loads can be sent through to their destination, without further handling; while small consignments must often travel in partly empty wagons, at the expense of much "dead weight"; or else call for much special handling and delay on the route.

With so great an economy to the railway in performing a large task relatively to that of performing a small one, it is inevitable that there should be some corresponding lowering of proportionate charges in favour of the large tasks: and, as large tasks are generally undertaken for large capitalists, there appears to be some discrimination against the small man. But in fact it seems certain that the shares of general costs, which are charged in addition to direct costs, often bear a lower proportion to those direct costs in the case of small tasks than of large.

Hence it might be inferred that the large trader, and not the small, has ground for complaint of discrimination unfavourable to him: but this contention, though plausible, seems to be invalidated by the fact that the charge for the large task gives a less excess over direct costs, and thus contributes less to the net revenue of the railway, than would the aggregate charges for an equal aggregate of work divided up into small pieces. Whatever nominal discrimination there be in favour of the small consignment, is therefore not injurious to the railway; and it is generally approved. This illustrates the great difficulty of laying down definite rules for deciding whether there is any element of undue discrimination in charges made for services that are similar, but not identical.

There are some large classes of discrimination as to which judgment is even more difficult. Many of them, which can be defended by plausible arguments, will need a little study: but we may first note, and put aside, distinctly vicious discriminations, due to corrupt practices by some railway officials, or to violent action by powerful capitalists: they have done much to excite prejudice against differential charges which are really reasonable. For instance in the tumultuous development of American railways in the latter part of last century public anger was roused by the pressure, put by powerful customers on various railways, to grant them concessions out of all proportion to the economy to be derived from the large size and steady flow of their consignments. Some of these concessions were open, some secret: some were made honestly in the apparent interest of the railway; some were obtained by corrupt payments to particular railway officials, or by other malign courses. Such cases are however now rare and relatively unimportant: the sensational chapters in railway history, for which they provided material, are no longer of general interest[1].

[1] To take extreme cases of pressure put on a railway:—a giant business sometimes made a demand on a railway for exceptionally low rates, supported by a threat to make a branch line to connect its works with a rival trunk line, or even with the sea-board. And a group of financiers, or even a single powerful financier, having large interests in each of many concerns, would give a railway to understand that, if it did not yield a concession to one of those concerns (which perhaps had no access to rival lines), the railway would lose a good part of the traffic of other companies which had access to several lines. Concessions of this kind were seldom secret.

But others were secret and dishonest. Thus packages consisting mainly of goods, which according to the recognized classification ought to be charged at a high rate per ton, would be billed as consisting solely of low-rate goods; and the railway would not trouble itself to inquire too closely. Warehousing charges would be omitted, or trucks would be allowed to be used practically as warehouses by the agents of a favoured business: while the goods in which a rival business was interested would be habitually delayed; and at critical times even

III, v, 2. 2. *Discriminating concessions to particular industries and trades in regard to charges and services are mostly local; and they are often much influenced by competition between industrial and trading districts, served by different railways.*

It has already been observed that the public at large seldom concern themselves about railway freight charges: and that the alert attention of producers and traders is generally directed to the *relative* rather than the absolute, amounts of those charges; for, so long as each is sure that all his competitors, far and near, are subject to like charges, he is generally content. In so far therefore as agreements among railways weaken the motives which prompt producers and traders to vigorous action in such matters, they deprive the non-vocal consumer, who bears the ultimate burden of any high rates, of a chief defence; and they thus throw an ever increasing responsibility on public authority to intervene in the general interest. For instance, if the whole of the flour consumed in the North of Scotland came from Glasgow mills, then high railway charges on flour, passing from Glasgow to the North of Scotland, would be of little importance either to the Glasgow millers or to the bakers in North Scotland: the public alone would suffer, and they would scarcely know to what extent they suffered, or how to seek a remedy. Similarly, if a combination among the Glasgow millers kept the price of flour somewhat high relatively to that of wheat (effective competition from other mills being absent), the local bakers would raise the price of bread either directly, or by a change in quality, and would pass unscathed. The public would suffer: but they are not vocal, unless strongly aroused; and probably they would not be.

Often however agriculturists, or some other class of producers or traders in any locality, see that lower rates would give them an advantage in any market, where they are brought into competition with producers or traders of another locality, who are not subject to the same set of railway rates: and then

covered up on side tracks by so heavy a block of other trucks as to be practically inaccessible. Free passes would be given, not merely to regular business "travellers"; but to others, who had no special claim, but whose interest it was desired to enlist.

sufficient driving force is supplied to attract attention. If the locality affected is large, and the special interests concerned are strong, the issue becomes one of national importance. A notable instance of this was the complaint made by British agriculturists generally, that the railways carried imported produce from Southampton and other ports, at much lower rates than they themselves were charged when sending their produce to London and other markets[1].

On the whole, controversies in regard to Preferential rates are declining in interest. There is much truth in the statement frequently made that a railway is often prevented from lowering a charge, which would benefit a certain local industry or trade without material loss to the railway; because it fears that such action would invite complaints from some other district, in which a similar concession could not be made without much loss. Since preference in the character of the services rendered

[1] These complaints were investigated by a strong Committee of the Board of Agriculture, whose Report [Cd. 2959], 1906, is a chief source of information on the subject of Preferential Rates, so far as this country is concerned. It brought out clearly the tendency of long distance traffic, especially in connection with international trade, to be sent in large quantities direct from a port, or other lading point, to a single market; and in packages so arranged as to travel easily and occupy the least possible space, so that the cost per ton-mile is very much less than that of ordinary local traffic. A little education in railway technique would remove many of the wastes and other troubles involved in such traffic; especially by inducing cooperation among producers in the same locality, so that each one's small consignment might earn the benefit of the low rate for a large consignment: whereas in fact (*Report*, p. 32) a grower will often split up his consignment and "send it to different salesmen, in order to find out who gives the best prices." The Report tends to confirm the impression, previously prevalent, that in such complex matters as complaints of harsh treatment or undue preference by a railway, an expert handling of the case is necessary even before a sympathetic tribunal. A shrewd, but untrained, exponent is apt to state his case badly; and, by losing it, to injure others who have grounds of complaint similar to his. The Board of Trade exerts itself to lessen this evil by informal conciliation; by clearing away misunderstandings; and by putting such pressure, as lies within its power, on a railway that seems to be acting harshly. But where recourse to the Railway Commission is necessary, the costs are said to range between £21 and £2000 (*ib.* p. 28). The *Report of the Board of Trade Railway Conference*, 1909 [Cd. 4677], p. 4, however suggested a scheme under which the Registrar of the Commission might have provisional authority for dealing with small cases by less expensive methods. Statements of the cases for and against the railways respectively will be found in Pratt's *Railways and their rates* and Waghorn's *Traders and Railways.* A short balanced statement is given by Williams, *The economics of railway transport.*

III, v, 3. cannot easily be made the ground of complaint, this consideration increases yet further the tendency to compete by improvements of service rather than by lowering of charges. Such escape from restraint on competition works for good in many ways; though its benefits are less frequently considered than the increased charges, which it entails. It is one of many causes, which makes the fares and rates for freight on British railways appear higher relatively to those prevalent in most other countries, than they really are.

For instance, even when railways have no direct contact with one another, or they have deadened competition by agreements made for their own convenience, the rivalry in industry or trade of the regions which they serve sometimes introduces rough but invigorating breezes of new contests. Thus Grimsby's connection with the manufacturing districts lies with the Great Central, while that of Hull is mainly controlled by the North Eastern: and, so long as Grimsby was little more than a fishing port, either railway was in a rather easy monopolistic position. But when the great new dock at Immingham, close to Grimsby, was opened, the two railways roused themselves to new activities[1].

More generally, if two districts, *A* and *B*, are in keen competition with one another for supplying a common market with their special goods; and *A* has grounds for thinking that *B*'s railway connections with it are better served than its own, a movement throughout *A* is speedily organized with the purpose of bringing its railway up to the level of that of *B*. The movement is likely to be successful: for in such a case the interests of the railway and the district are closely united.

3. *The good and evil of the concession of specially favourable railway rates to particular districts, whose geographical positions are somewhat unfavourable.*

In so far as the rival interests of producers or traders in different localities keep the railways, which respectively serve them, alert and progressive, the result is almost wholly good. But complex questions of public interest are raised, when local pressure causes a railway to carry the traffic of a district, which is in eager competition with others, at rates that do not bear

[1] See W. A. Robertson, *Combination among railway companies*, pp. 92—3.

their full share of its general costs: for it is likely in consequence to reduce its facilities or raise its charges for other traffic, in regard to which it has a freer hand. This is, as has already been observed, a consequence of the fact that the railway has not an absolute monopoly, but one conditioned by the pressure of public opinion and public authority. For if its monopoly had been absolute in the districts, which were more specially under its control, it might already have set its charges there at those levels which would yield the maximum net revenues: and in that case it could not improve its position by raising those charges.

Railways, like every other great economic agency, and sometimes more than any other, take a part in fashioning the geographical distribution of population in general, and of industrial centres in particular. Facilities offered by them help some industries to be carried on in country districts; perhaps by independent workers in their own homes; perhaps by giant businesses, equipped with the best appliances, and with special departments for meeting such of their needs as in earlier times would have been met by subsidiary industries. Again industries which, even under modern conditions, gain much from the neighbourhood of allied industries, are enabled by the railways, for good and for evil, to concentrate themselves in large cities, and to send their goods to be consumed at distances averaging several hundred miles, in some countries, from the point of production.

In so far as this localization is effected by an even-handed increase of facilities, and lowering of charges for transport, there is strong *primâ facie* reason for believing that it conduces to the public good: for ease of movement, even when no part of a deliberate and far-seeing public policy, is likely to be beneficial, because it develops new opportunities. But the case assumes a different aspect, when account is taken of the interest which every railway, however just its methods and purposes, has in increasing its share of the total services which enter into the production of commodities in general.

For instance, "railways are giving exceptionally low export rates from the manufacturing districts in the North to London, in order to get the traffic on to their lines from London to the

III, v, 3. North, London being thus favoured in competition with other ports nearer to the manufacturing centres[1]." There is much to be said for such an arrangement: but there are reasons for doubting whether the principle which underlies it, is one which can be applied extensively without ultimate injury to the public.

It is obviously to the general interest that sources of supply should grow up as near as possible to centres of consumption; subject to the condition that, where one source has a natural advantage in climate, mineral resources, or deep-set human aptitudes for a particular industry; it may be advantageously developed even at the cost of somewhat large expenditure of labour and material on marketing its products. And it may further be conceded, that when an industry has grown up in a district, under the influence of advantages which have been deprived of their force by changes in technique or other causes; a beneficial railway policy may, temporarily at least, grant to it relatively low transport charges in order to mitigate its misfortune. But in practice it is difficult to afford this relief to a particular group of producers or traders without encouraging the expansion of industry and trade in unsuitable places.

Care is needed, in the national interest, to preserve the full energy of the *Vis medicatrix Naturae*, which promotes migrations from districts in which the output of effort and its reward are on the decline, to those in which effort can be of more service. When, for instance, the chief cause of the weakness of any district is its failure to keep pace with more alert, energetic and capable efforts elsewhere; then only harm arises from any check to the stimulus which it might derive from the pressure of competition. In America it has been found that the desire not to charge more than what a weak district will bear, while charging to a strong district nearly all that it will bear, has led to extreme policies of "keeping everyone in business." This plan, though often conducive to high aggregate railway revenues, may be contrary to the public interest: "the final result has oftentimes been that the carriers have entered into arrangements, whereby they agree to equalize the advantages of com-

[1] W. A. Robertson, *l.c.* p. 93.

peting towns, by fixing rates in inverse ratio to the natural advantages of these towns[1]."

The Interstate Commerce Commission has consistently maintained that its mandate requires it to act on the principle, that "each locality is entitled to the benefit of all its natural advantages." It has been loath to admit such claims as that of Boston for rates to and from the West, approximately equal to those of other ports which have shorter connections with the West. (Boston herself owned so large a share of the railways which wanted to charge but a small part of their general expenses on the traffic with the West, that her wish might have been granted without throwing much of that burden on other shoulders.)

The task thus undertaken is of the greatest difficulty. The interests of the railways concerned are always ably advocated; and those of particular localities and particular groups of producers or traders commonly are. But those of the general public will not be adequately urged, unless it be by a strong specialized representative of the Government. The British Board of Trade is moving a little in this direction. France has formulated her policy with wonted clearness: the Minister of Public Works, acting with the advice of his Consultative Committee, rejects any rate, which appears to make undue discrimination, or to draw traffic away from any other railway, or to ruin the business of coasting steamers or canal boats; and strives so to adjust the tarifs of competing districts, as to secure to each "the natural advantages of its location." His work is in some degree simplified by the fact that nearly the whole of France is divided out into several large triangles, having a common apex in Paris: each of them being in unchallenged occupation of a single railway. But the State has the ultimate reversion of their property; and meanwhile it exercises a very effective control over their relations with the public: and indeed France is compelled to keep a tight hand on her railways in time of peace, in order to be prepared for war.

[1] Prof. Hammond, in the *Quarterly Journal of Economics*, Feb. 1911, where a full study of these matters will be found. His series of articles on "Railway Rate Theories" is the authority for several statements that follow as to the action of the Commission.

III, v, 3. Prussia has worked on similar lines, in ever closer touch with German railways other than her own. Her Minister of Public Works, with his General Advisory Council, has indeed for his chief aims the advance of national interests in production and trade; and especially the support of Prussian sea-ports and railways against foreign rivalry. But the claims of each locality for favourable treatment occupy much of the time of the General Council and of nine Local Councils; and they are largely responsible for the great number and complexity of the special (*Ausnahme*) railway rates of Prussia[1]. The practical issues connected with these problems are on a much larger scale in America than in any other country: the abuses connected with them have been particularly bold; and the investigations evoked by them have attracted an unsurpassed amount of thorough scientific investigation on the part of professional students and public officials. America has followed the common practice of making exceptional railway rates to meet the competition of water routes: and the great distances which much of her goods traffic must pass, for the purposes of domestic as well as foreign trade, combined with other circumstances, have caused this practice to give a certain twist to much of her railway policy. For instance the charges to places which had water communications were often lowered below those to intermediate places. This provoked complaint and was forbidden: but the results were complex, and not altogether satisfactory. Something is said of them in Appendix M, 3.

It is indeed a grave question whether the practice has not been carried too far. The rules of the Interstate Commerce Commission have formally allowed railway rates to be reduced so far as to *meet* water competition, though not so far as to *extinguish* it: but they do not seem to arrange that, if a railway oversteps this limit, it shall be punished, by being prohibited from raising the rate above the level which it had chosen for its destructive strategy.

The majority of the British Commission on Inland Waterways (1906—9) expressed a hope that it might be found possible to enact that a railway, which lowered its rates in competition with carriers on an inland waterway, should not raise them

[1] See above, p. 448.

again until it had shown a good case for its action. But, with less caution, the Act of 1894 had put difficulties in the way of a railway's restoring an old charge, even if reasonable, when once it had adopted a lower charge. The intention of the Act may have been to restrain any lowering of rates for the purposes of a campaign. But in effect it hindered also reductions which were part of a constructive policy in the public interest, and often necessarily tentative: so it did mischief: it was in abeyance during the Civil War and it seems likely to be repealed.

This is an instance of the inability of mere legislation to cope with such practical issues, as those concerned with traffic: it can act efficiently only through an administrative body, which can go into the details of each particular case; and even pronounce judgments as to motives. Much railway legislation has worked badly because it resembled the old rule that anyone who killed another should be put to death himself: in modern times he is acquitted, if he can convince a jury (or other authority) that his motives were only those of legitimate self-defence. Railway competition with water routes should in like manner be subject to the ordinary rules against monopolistic underselling: any lowering of railway charges should be stayed by administrative authority, when the evidence indicates that its aim was to destroy competition. The question whether it is consistent with the public interest that a railway should be at liberty to "dump" its services at less than *full* cost price, in order to drive a carrier by water, or any other troublesome competitor, out of business, resembles in many respects such questions, as whether the Standard Oil Company shall be at liberty to sell its oil in certain districts at a very low price, in order to extinguish local competition, and clear the local markets for its own products at monopoly prices—a class of problems which we are soon to consider.

4. ***Improved railway administration has narrowed the field in which the authoritative regulation of particular rates is required. Estimates of the costs of particular services are relegated to secondary, but useful work.***

We may now resume the substance of the preceding arguments and bring them to a focus. We have seen something

III, v, 4. of the justification of the general opinion, which has been endorsed by the Interstate Commerce Commission, that railway companies everywhere apportion their general costs in nearly the same way. Indeed this opinion is in harmony with the results of experience in even wider fields; and a somewhat similar distribution of general costs prevails in many industries and trades, which handle several various products, even though there is no monopolistic control of any of them. The broad influences of public opinion, and the ever widening experience, and sense of responsibility of the leaders of the railway industry have done much to bring about this result by authoritative regulation in Britain and other countries; each country proceeding on her own lines, but all moving in similar directions. Regulation has become careful in general scheme and in detail, and the force of public opinion behind it has increased: therefore its action has become ever more important and stronger; and at the same time more subtle and more delicately shaded. Precedent has grown into precedent: decisions have proceeded with ever greater ease, certainty and precision. But yet there is more new work on the anvil now than at almost any previous time: the call for vigorous, but moderate and well considered, action by the regulative authorities increases with their strength[1].

In particular, there is almost universal agreement that railway charges cannot be adjusted to particular costs; and that they should not be so adjusted, even if they could. But questions relating to absolute and relative costs continually arise, very often on the initiative of the railways themselves: and organized knowledge, based on systematic studies, is rendering it ever more possible to make fairly confident, though carefully limited, statements in regard to them. The Interstate Commerce Commission often sets up independent investigations, when

[1] This is excellently shown in regard to America by Prof. McPherson who has set out (*Railroad freight rates*, pp. 399—404) in parallel columns "the complaints of 1886" and "the condition at present" in regard to each part of the field. In almost every case the greater part of what was formerly under dispute is now common ground to all: and attention is given chiefly to points which, though important in their way, could not attain prominence earlier. It is to be hoped that a similar table in parallel columns will be made out in regard to British railways.

railway representatives defend rates, that have been impugned, by arguments based on cost of service. Such cases are apt to occur, (1) where any special service is performed and obligation incurred by a carrier: (2) where a rate complained of is judged as to its reasonableness by comparing the *ascertainable* costs of transportation of other commodities, whose rates are believed to be reasonable: (3) where comparison is made with costs on other roads or on other parts of the system; and (4) where comparison is made between rates for car-load lots, and for smaller lots. In particular the Commission insists generally that in the fixing of relative rates on articles strictly competitive, such a relative rate should be fixed for each as corresponds to the difference in cost of service, if that can be ascertained.

On the whole, the public interest in railway discriminations has somewhat diminished. Those which can be condemned as secret and corrupt, are rare. Those which are based on broad considerations of policy, and especially regional discriminations, are changing their form: the part played in them by individual interests is becoming small. And, though local interests have much to say about them, the substantive questions at issue seldom have much to do with railway technique.

To conclude:—the task of regulating such discriminations as remain, would be much lighter, if it were not that the motives of two discriminations similar in outward form may be very different: one benign, the other malign. To distinguish between them requires the same judicial and penetrative faculties that are required by judge and jury in combination, in order to decide whether the motive of a certain action was malignant or fraudulent. But it also requires an intimate knowledge of the methods and motives of railway and general business policy. Some discriminations are paternal sacrifices for the benefit of weak industries, from which the railways hope to reap their reward in due time. Some are strategical movements for the capture of traffic, which otherwise would not come to them; and these occasionally have in the background an evil purpose of destroying competitive routes, in order to strengthen a monopoly. And these evil motives for discrimination are not only subtly disguised; they are apt to be interwoven with others that

III, v, 4. command respect. Human nature is composite; and the faculties required for conspicuous success in the President of a great American railway, or the head of any other large business, are scarcely ever to be found in a man who does not take a noble delight in seeing things prosper under his hands: even if he be somewhat unscrupulous in his modes of warfare, he is glad when his manoeuvres have a side effect in "making two blades of grass grow where one grew before." A discrimination which he sets up, in order to give much needed aid to a struggling district, may come to be developed for the sake of the harm it will do to an obnoxious rival: but the original motive continues to work. When defending his action, he lays stress on that motive: and the half truth, skilfully handled, impedes the search for the other half. Therefore, although the task of specific regulation becomes lighter in many ways; there is no diminution of the need for such automatic control of railway charges as may result from the development of traffic by road, motor and inland waterway in Britain and some other countries: a matter to be considered in the next chapter.

In America increasing attention is appropriately being paid to the broad question whether railway rates as a whole are higher than is necessary in order to yield a reasonable net return on the capital *bonâ fide* invested in railways. A little is said on this subject in Appendix M, 4, 5.

CHAPTER VI

COMPETITION AND MONOPOLY IN TRANSPORT, CONTINUED

1. *Changing attitudes of the British people and Government towards the amalgamation of railways; the line of division between continuous and competitive railways being meanwhile almost blurred out.* III, VI, 1.

The high profits and the even more exalted expectations of English railways about 1844, when they had mastered their chief difficulties, and had still much virgin soil on which to expand, caused a Parliamentary Committee to advocate their purchase on terms which now seem extravagant[1]. But exactly at that time the public was becoming convinced that, even if the principle of "protecting" home industries by taxes on imports were accepted, the almost incredible folly of the details of the old Protective tarif indicated that the forte of the British Government did not lie in business. Also, as regards railways, people had been offended by the contradictory decisions of Parliamentary Committees; and by the inability or unwillingness of Parliament to check the heavy expenditure of money, not always through clean channels, which was required to secure the acceptance of a Railway Bill, even when its proposals were clearly in the public interest. Public opinion increasingly favoured the view that the function of a constitutional government was to legislate, and perhaps appoint administrative authorities; and that it should not readily engage directly in business undertakings which were within the scope of private enterprise.

[1] A little is said about this project in Appendix M, 1.

III, vi, 1.

For a time there was hesitation: but gradually it became generally recognized that Government cannot exercise effective control in such a case by merely passing laws to be enforced by strict verbal interpretation in a Court of Law. After many experiments it has set up a permanent Railway and Canal Commission; of which the President is an eminent lawyer, whose decision on points of law has been generally accepted: but his colleagues have been men of affairs, with trained instincts for handling large practical issues. The Commission has seldom been called on to act, unless one or more of the parties concerned in any doubtful matter has been unwilling to accept a decision reached by the Board of Trade, in regard to it. The Board, in effect, has decided what provisions shall be made by the railways for insuring public safety. But in other matters it acts as conciliator between conflicting interests: it avoids indicating its own conclusion, unless and until its efforts at conciliation have failed; but that conclusion when given is generally accepted, even though it has not by itself the force of law.

Whether the settlement of a disputed point is attained by the Board without friction, or by the aid of compulsory authority in the background, the scope of the settlement extends in effect to other railways besides those immediately concerned; and thus has much of the force of a general regulation. Every such general regulation tends to diminish the number of conflicting interests among railways: it often both invites and facilitates agreed action among them. They have thus found themselves increasingly making common cause in defence of common interests against common troubles; and the way has been prepared for the mitigation of competition, and the strengthening of tendencies towards combined action. In short the only provision that exists in Britain for dealing with public interests in large railway issues is somewhat fortuitous in initiative, and amateurish in study, as compared with that called forth by the needs of America.

The Parliamentary Committee of 1853 seems to have been the first to lay special stress on the danger to be anticipated from the monopolistic tendencies of agreements among railway companies, as distinguished from the simple monopoly of each railway along its special route. Stephenson's celebrated, but vague, dictum that, "where combination is possible, competition is impossible" was gradually being developed towards its modern more exact form. Thus developed, it indicates that the tendency towards combination is so strong as to be almost irresistible, when (1) each of the chief businesses concerned is so large as to be beyond the strength of ordinary capitalists; (2) the interest of each tends towards the adoption of about the same policy, in regard to the public; and (3) the interest which each has in conducting an aggressive campaign against others is relatively small. Competition is often weak when these conditions are not completely filled; and when they are, it is suspended. It is indeed full of resource; and, beaten on one front, opens a new campaign on another: but combination is also alert; and, if favoured by circumstances, endeavours to reassert its dominion on that front also: action and reaction continue without cease.

For instance Parliament had encouraged the fusion of consecutive lines, and discouraged the fusion of competitive parallel lines: but time blurred the distinction between the two classes. The broad contrast between them may be put thus: The consolidation of two or more railways that feed one another, and find a market for one another's services, corresponds to the consolidation of blast furnaces with mines on the one hand, and rolling mills on the other. The consolidation of parallel lines corresponds rather more nearly to that of neighbouring rolling mills, or neighbouring blast furnaces. But blast furnaces which do not own mines, run a risk of being cut short of supplies when most needed; and in the alternating periods of depression they may wish they could use up their products in their own manufacturing works: while neither of two railways, that can feed one another, is likely to be backward in doing so; unless indeed it falls into the hands of a rival that parallels the other[1].

The sharpness of the contrast between consecutive and parallel railways has however been blurred by the expansion of great railways, which has brought each into competition with its neighbours for some traffic that used to be under single

[1] A striking instance of this was the contest between the Great Western Railway and the South Western for control of the Cornish lines from Plymouth. The Board of Trade compelled the victorious Great Western Railway to allow all reasonable facilities to the South Western: but the upper hand is still that of the victor.

III, VI, 1 dominion; and has enabled it to pass traffic to, and receive traffic from, railways, or at least particular branches of them, with which it had not been in contact previously. The London and North Western Railway is still known on the Stock Exchange by its old name of the Birmingham Railway; and it formerly had no competition with, and no inducement to combine with, others that ran to Bristol, Doncaster, etc. But it is now in competition with the Great Western for much traffic with Wales, while, in competition with the Great Northern, and to a less extent with other railways, it is indirectly concerned with through traffic between England and Scotland. These fusions of consecutive lines, often directly fostered by Parliament, have greatly diminished the total area in Great Britain, which is dependent on a single railway for most of its communications: and competition has obtained ever widening opportunities for its tendency to stimulate the energy and alertness of railway authorities in consulting the interests of the public. Fusions of consecutive non-competing lines into larger groups of competing lines have indeed been followed by understandings and pooling among those groups: and these greatly reduce the pecuniary gain that any one of them can reap by attracting traffic away from its rival. But the staff of a railway has often a lively interest in so increasing its prestige that the public speak well of it, and give it a preference over rivals which offer somewhat similar accommodation at the same cost and thus enterprise is sustained. Some of this energizing force would be lost if fusions extended so far that a comparatively small part of the population had the opportunity of comparing the methods of different companies. Of course it would be absolutely lost, if all the railways were owned by the Government: a vital matter which is sometimes overlooked. Such considerations as these might be set aside, if the additional technical economies, to be obtained by further fusions, were very great: but they are certainly less than appears at first sight; and the chief of them can be obtained by less extreme measures[1].

[1] Compare II, VIII, 6. P.S. Jan. 1921. The Ministry of Transport recently issued a scheme "For the organization of transport undertakings, etc." [Cmd. 787] under which railways would be associated in six groups: and on 8 Dec. 1920 the Railway Companies Association published a letter to the Minister of Transport, approving the general lines of the scheme, but suggesting a few changes in detail.

2. *Many economies, which are commonly regarded as appertaining only to railway fusions, can be obtained by particular agreements for cooperation; or for pooling certain classes of traffic, or of wagons.* III, VI, 2.

Of course amalgamation reduces the work to be done by railway Clearing Houses: but, so far as the central administration is concerned, it seldom reduces expenditure much. For indeed the large problems of a far-spreading railway are sufficient to occupy the energies of an able staff; and some loss of efficiency may result from concentrating the care of an ever increasing number of problems on a single office. Again the multiplication of services on competitive routes is wasteful only when there is not sufficient work to be done by the parallel trains: but, as we have seen, such trains are run chiefly at hours at which the traffic on each line is heavy; and many of them would be needed if the two lines were under a single control[1].

Moreover many of the economies, which were supposed inherent in amalgamation, such as combined action for carting freights, and for establishing numerous receiving offices in populous districts, are now obtained in great measure by mere agreements among railways for cooperative work: these often enable equal conveniences to the public to be attained with less cost than before, or greater conveniences with equal cost. Such are the granting of running powers over a part of its line by one railway to another, which has special need of it; or, in some cases, the leasing of a line to another, with whose general traffic it fits in better than with that of the owner: and again the making and working of secondary extensions on the joint account of two or more great railways. Most of these agreements require no sanction: and the tendency towards them is

[1] It is true that a further lengthening of long distance trains would effect some direct economies; and that most of the platforms at which they would stop are already long. In America the passenger generally leaves his luggage to be sent after him by an express service; and the distances are great: and therefore very long trains are highly economical. But in England, where distances are short, and the passenger must wait till he secures his own luggage, the case is rather different: for vexatious delays, the economic importance of which is ignored by many writers on railway matters, must be caused by a great further lengthening of trains, unless so vast a staff of porters is kept on hand that their time cannot be well occupied.

III, VI, 2. indirectly facilitated by the action of the Board of Trade; which is continually urging uniformity as to the equipment of railways, to provisions for safety, to the classification of goods, and other matters[1].

Thus mere cooperation can attain, with little less economy, many of the ends for which fusion is sometimes sought; and without lessening the scope for initiative by independent lines. And if, as often happens, the community of work between two great railways extends only to a particular part of either line, the chief economies of a fusion can be attained by "pooling" the traffic on those two parts. The general plan of such a pool is that the earnings of the traffic in each year are to be thrown into a common fund; each railway being however allowed, in effect, to deduct the direct expenses to which it has been put in "moving" its part of the traffic concerned: the pool is then divided out, without any reference to the share of that traffic which any particular railway has carried, and simply in the fixed proportions agreed on at the formation of the pool. Those proportions are of course based in the main on the shares which the several railways had in carrying that traffic in the years preceding the formation of the pool: and, if the pool is certain to endure, no member of it has a special interest in running more trains, or providing any other accommodation, beyond that which is thought advisable by the others. If it is not permanent, each member may—as members of cartels habitually do—endeavour to enlarge its own connection; in order that, when the renewal of the pool is under discussion, it may be in a position to claim a greater share of the traffic[2]. But the

[1] Agreements to allow return tickets, sold by one of two associated lines, to be used on the other, do not necessarily come under this head: for the return halves can be collected and exchanged, with payment for any excess either way. But the extension of a similar privilege to season tickets, as to which no such reckoning can be made, is an advance towards constructive cooperation by businesses, whose finances are not connected by any direct bond.

[2] Already in 1850 much traffic between England and Scotland was pooled: and many minor agreements of a similar nature were made. Difficulties in regard to obtaining through traffic over other lines without a special agreement, had played some part in this tendency: but they were removed by the Act of 1854, which resulted from the Report of the great Committee of 1853, and enacted that the several companies should give reasonable facilities for traffic on their lines, and accept and forward through traffic from and to other com-

scope of such endeavours seldom reaches far, at all events in Britain. III, VI, 2.

The chief wastes, at present resulting from divided ownership of the means of transport by rail in Britain, seem to be connected with the travelling of empty and half-filled goods wagons, and with the shunting of wagons. No organization can do much to reduce the number of empty wagons on their return to coal-fields; though improved organization of the coal trade, such as has been enforced during the war, may reduce the average length of the journeys of coal wagons, whether full or empty. The war has also brought into prominence the economies that may be effected by a great extension of the common practice of pooling, or "common use" of, the wagons used in certain classes of traffic: and it is to be hoped that the practice will be largely extended in times of peace by arrangement, fortified perhaps by special legislation[1].

The wastes involved in the shunting of wagons are necessarily great, relatively to the amount of transport, in a small, densely peopled country such as Britain: a goods engine often travels further in shunting operations than in actual transport. Some of this waste could be saved by a general pooling of wagons: but the only thorough remedy appears to be the setting up of shunting stations with overhead gear, by which a wagon can be

panies' lines, and grant no undue preference. See W. A. Robertson, *Combination among railway companies*, p. 12.

[1] The *Times Trade Supplement*, July, 1916, reported that three groups of companies had made such arrangements. The first consisted of the Great Western, Lancashire and Yorkshire, North Western, Midland, and North Eastern: the second of the Great Central, Great Eastern, and Great Northern: and the third of the Caledonian, Glasgow and South Western, and North British. Over 200,000 wagons were thus pooled by the first group: they were almost exclusively of simple construction, adapted for general use: provision was made without difficulty for readjusting the balance, if any one railway happened to get either much more or much less than its proper share. The plan of setting up a separate company to own all the wagons, and charge each railway according to the total use it made of them, has many attractions. Its possible advantages are illustrated by the conveniences, which all concerned have derived from the provision by the Armour Car Liner Company of well equipped refrigerator-cars for perishable food, and of stock-cars for carrying cattle and tending them on the way. It is true that serious charges have been brought against that company of excessive use of its monopolistic power. (See Ripley, *l.c.* vol. I. p. 194; and a defence of the company in *The packers and the people* by J. Ogden Armour.) But the company now suggested might be owned, for the greater part, by the railways themselves.

III, VI, 2. lifted from one pair of rails and set down on another parallel line; as seems to be done to a considerable extent in Prussia. It is there combined with the use of detachable "bodies," which can be lifted by cranes and transferred from one "chassis" to another: this is commonly done in regard to passengers' luggage when booked through from London to Paris *viâ* Calais[1].

Much economy has been effected by united action in regard to the collection and delivery of goods by several railways, having stations in the same town. Some competent authorities have advocated the general adoption in Britain of a plan, that is in favour elsewhere, which hands over the collection and distribution of all minor goods traffic to independent carriers. Such carriers cart for all railways; they obtain as a rule from each railway the relatively low rates that are charged for wagon-loads. They are thus able to meet a great part of their own expenses out of the difference between those rates and the rates that, without their intervention, their customers would pay for small parcels; and there is much saving of railway work.

There appears to be solid foundation for the suggestion that a railway, contending with others for the favour of the public generally and traders in particular, hurries forward all goods committed to its charge, even though a couple of days' delay might seldom cause considerable inconvenience. This waste could, no doubt, be stopped by State railways, which would naturally tend towards the easy Continental practice of making all small consignments wait till they can be carried conveniently. But that remedy would be less in the public interest than such a combination of the British and Continental methods, as would provide that anyone who had special reasons for prompt service, should mark his consignment accordingly; the railways being free to hold up all other small consignments for (say) a couple of days, in order to make up fairly full wagon-loads. This could be arranged by agreement among the railways themselves; if,

[1] This separation of the body from the chassis plays a prominent part in the suggestive, if too heroic, scheme of Mr Gattie for concentrating as much as possible of the goods traffic of each great railway centre in a single huge station. There would be several floors above ground, chiefly occupied in sorting; and several floors below ground for the accommodation of trains. Through lifts and overhead rails would enable each package to be delivered direct into a wagon on road or rail that would go straight to its destination.

as seems probable, such a course should, after investigation, appear advisable.

Abuses of monopolistic power on the part of railways demand now but little attention from the Railways and Canal Commission: and its constitution might perhaps advantageously be altered, so as to fit it better for the work of constructive statesmanship: its semi-legal functions are still important, but the new age calls for work of a wider scope. It might devote special attention to opportunities for such constructive cooperation among railways as would increase the economy or efficiency of railway work; while taking care that a fair share of the gains, thus arising, accrue to the public.

British traditions call on Government to concentrate its chief energies on guarding the public against oppressive action or inaction, on the part of private individuals or corporations. If it undertakes business enterprises, which could be effectively carried out by private agencies, it ceases to be in a position to judge the conduct of such enterprises: while the great amount of its energy which is given to such enterprises tends somewhat to diminish the efficiency with which it discharges its supreme function as guardian of public interest in general. But yet there are some special reasons for direct intervention by the State in the transport industry, based partly on extensions which modern developments of technique have made of familiar reasons for the ownership of roads by the State: these will be considered in the following Sections.

But first it may be observed that inferences sometimes drawn from the State control of British railways during the world-war, as to the efficiency of permanent ownership and control seem to be misleading. Reference has already been made (above, II, III, 4) to the beneficial influences which the war has exerted in speeding up general standardization, especially in mechanical industries. It has brought innumerable establishments under a strong control. Plant has been kept constantly at work: the Government has been able *in its capacity as sole purchaser* to arrange that operations shall be so multiplied in number and simplified in character that branches of production, which had previously required the judgment and manual skill of a special trained mechanic, could be handled by an unskilled

III, vi, 3. adult, and sometimes even by a child. This work has been done under the authority of Government: but nearly the whole of the brains, by which it has been directed, had been developed under the stimulating influences of free enterprise: this vital consideration is often overlooked.

Unification of railway control under the single authority which directed the production and marketing of most of the more bulky products, which railways handle, has had unique results. It has enabled trains to be long and trucks to be full; and has thus achieved great economies; but in other respects the technique of the industry has remained unchanged. Meanwhile the work of administration has remained in the hands of those who had done it before: the credit of its excellent work, and the blame for many of the mistakes that have occurred, accrue to management by private enterprise, and not by the State. There has of course been no account of the total cost of this work: for both rolling stock and permanent way have necessarily been allowed to fall into poor condition: passengers have submitted to discomforts that would not be borne readily in ordinary times; while delays and restrictions of goods traffic have been regarded as inevitable.

3. *Far-reaching intervention by Government in railway affairs is at once relatively easy and urgent. State ownership of railways.*

The dominant characteristic of the railway industry is the exceptional prominence of routine in its administration as well as in its technique. Attention has been drawn to the general rule that, when once a business has outgrown the scope of private ownership and passed into joint stock, a further increase in its size makes relatively little increase in its dependence on mechanical methods of management: this rule applies to railways more strongly than to most other industries. Again, a public authority, when intervening in the railway industry, will receive more assistance from the people themselves than would be possible in almost any other industry. For the people are the purchasers of the services rendered by railways; they can form a fairly good opinion as to whether those services are well performed, and they can set out their grievances simply and clearly. They cannot indeed generally form a direct judgment as to the inherent reasonableness of those charges: but they have fair opportunities for making comparisons with charges for similar services at home and abroad; and even for making some allowance for differences in the conditions under which the services are rendered. Moreover railway technique is now very far advanced; and it is, for the greater part, internationalized. Every considerable step forwards, made in any part of the world, is quickly followed everywhere: and even a semi-comatose bureaucratic spirit could not greatly retard progress in a western country, while other countries were advancing rapidly[1].

Again it is a characteristic of railways, as of all transport services which publish their time tables, to keep steadily on their course without paying much heed to fluctuations of general credit and commercial activity. Extra coal trains will be run in winter, and extra passenger trains in summer: profits will increase when general credit is good, and shrink when it is bad: but there is very little change in the work to be done of signalmen, porters, and even shunters and engine-drivers; the aggregate employment offered on the line, otherwise than in new construction, remains nearly constant. Again, though railways are a good deal affected by the price of coal, there is no other raw material which they purchase largely for working purposes, as distinguished from repairs and additions to plant: and partly for this reason, they have little temptation to vary their charges from year to year in accordance with the general fluctuations of prices; and they could not make such changes from week to week. This natural stability is tacitly assumed as the basis of all discussions regarding the authoritative regulation of railway charges.

For these, as well as for political and administrative reasons, railways in an autocratic military State are much subject to military discipline; and indeed the chief station-masters are

[1] But lest anyone should think that uniformity and simplicity of charges would rule under State ownership of all railways, reference may again be made to the thousand rate-books of the Prussian railway-system. (See above, p. 448 fn.) A good deal of intriguing and discussion must have preceded concessions, which have sometimes caused rates from Frankfurt to Constantinople *viâ* Hamburg to be less than those for goods sent from Frankfurt to Hamburg, for use there (*Frankfurt Consular Report* for 1909, p. 45).

III, VI, 3. often retired military officers. Sir George S. Gibb lends his high authority to the common observation that "no country has ever adopted State ownership of railways from theoretical considerations. In each and every instance there were some practical reasons, based on military necessities, or concrete and pressing economic conditions, to meet which State ownership was accepted, not as a system desirable in itself, but as an expedient which, in the circumstances, was considered to be the best practical solution of difficulties which stood in the way of the satisfactory development of railways[1]."

The general position has been summed up by Mr Acworth, whose authority is perhaps greater than that of any other Englishman, who is not himself a great administrator of railways. He says that an exhaustive inquiry would "show that State railway systems very rarely pay their own way;...that State purchase of private undertakings is nearly always a financial failure;...that the private railways have to their credit almost every important invention and improvement; that, if it is a question of efficiency and economic operation, comparing like with like, the companies easily beat the State-owned systems; that it is on the private lines that, once more comparing like with like, the lowest rates and the cheapest fares are to be found." But for all that, he holds that State ownership will come soon. For, owners of railway property know that the State seldom buys a property without paying more for it than it is worth. The higher officials of the railways have no cause for anxiety: most of them will continue with at least as high salaries, and somewhat higher prestige. And the rank and file will be able to bring such pressure to bear at the polls, that political considerations will be apt to weigh in matters, that ought to be decided on technical grounds in the interests of the population as a whole, and protected from bias by the special interests of any one section of the people[2]. Some developments

[1] See his address on *Railway Nationalization* delivered to the Royal Economic Society in 1908. It appears that the railways of Switzerland and Belgium were nationalized, in order to prevent their being controlled by foreign holders of their securities. As to Prussian railways, see above, p. 447.

[2] The paper of which the above is a summary, was read by Mr Acworth at the Congress of the Royal Economic Society, 1912, to which reference has already

of this matter, which appeared as this chapter was passing through the Press, are noted below, Appendix M, 2. III, vi, 3.

It is true that the control would probably be vested in a permanent Railway Board, which would act independently in minor matters: but Parliament would hardly be able to avoid passing on to the Government any strong persistent pressure, which might be brought to bear by a million voters, male and female, having a direct interest in a large issue relating to their work: and that might be a great evil in itself, and the harbinger of others like to it. The well-to-do classes generally, and the landowning classes in particular, have no doubt used their political power in the past to further their own material interests; and of course some special legislation in the interest of the manual labour classes is to be welcomed as redressing old injustices, and preparing the mass of the people for a larger and higher life than has yet been theirs. But such movements seem to be beneficial and wholesome only when broad. If particular groups of the people look on the polls, as opportunities for advancing their own sectional interests, rather than for rendering an upright and dutiful service to the State, the Mother of all, then the nation as a whole will become less noble, weaker and ultimately poorer: there is some truth in the

been made. At the same Congress, M. Leroy-Beaulieu showed that the railway recently acquired by the French Government had been worked at a heavy loss; chiefly in consequence of the rigidity and lack of initiative shown by its officials, and the political pressure put on it to find places for many more subordinates than were really required for the service. On the other hand Professor Mahaim, of Liège, contended that the acquisition of Belgian railways by the State had conferred such great benefits on the whole people, and especially on the working classes, by low charges and abundant services, as to outweigh its failure to yield a good financial return. Financial statements are obscure: but it appears that they make scarcely any profit beyond what is needed to pay interest on the price of purchase of the original relatively small network of lines: and that they would show a considerable deficit if they did not charge to capital many things, which private railways rightly charge to income. (See the qualifications in Mr G. Seebohm Rowntree's eulogy of railway aids to the Belgian people, *Land and Labour*, pp. 287, 288.) Their services are not of as high quality as those of the British railways: they pay very low wages, beginning with three francs a day: the lie of country has made their cost of construction exceptionally low: they are supplemented by water communications, which leaves them free to give all their strength to remunerative traffic; and especially to the large and highly remunerative transport of passengers and merchandise from Antwerp, Ostend and other ports to Germany, Switzerland, Austria and Eastern Europe.

 saying that under a democratic constitution, "State railways corrupt politics; and politics corrupt State railways." The fear that political influence may distort the course of promotion, is one of many causes that tend to make seniority dominant in public offices: and this may be of great importance in railways: for hitherto "exceptional ability has generally risen from the ranks[1]."

Almost every extension of Governmental activity brings with it good and evil, both economic and political. The political side is foreign to the main purpose of the present study: but it cannot be wholly ignored. For, when proposals for large changes in the field of economics are prompted partly by political motives, then they are likely to bring about results which will not be satisfactory from the economic point of view, and will perhaps introduce morbid elements into politics. These dangers are specially great in the case of developments which have had a chequered history. For the political advocate can select an abundance of strong cases all telling on his side, whichever that may be: and those to whom he presents his side of the shield, often fail to get a view of the other side. Thus when any particular technique has worked through difficulties to success, leaving on its path the wreckage of much brave and able enterprise; then there is a good opening for the suggestion that the State should annex the benefits arising from it. These suggestions are seductive; and but little thought is often given to the risk that the dominant technique may be surpassed by later enterprise, or lose part of its value in consequence of broad changes. Such risks are ever in the mind of the ablest business men; but they are apt to be neglected when economic considerations are dominated by political. It is therefore necessary to scrutinize the assumption, which is latent in suggestions for the nationalization of railways, that their present predominance as agencies of transport will remain unimpaired. The following Sections suggest that new developments may possibly diminish the share of the total traffic of a country, which falls to railways;

[1] This statement is made on the authority of Mr Dent, General Manager of the South Eastern and Chatham Railway, p. 162 of the Jubilee Number of *The Railway News*, 1914, a compendium of information, to which this and the preceding chapters are much indebted.

but that they may yet tend on the whole to strengthen rather than weaken the case for the nationalization of railways.

Simple and uniform as is the business of transport, the opinion held by one generation as to the dominance of a particular method of effecting it, has sometimes been abandoned by the next. We have seen how the shares of some English canals were selling at several times their normal value, shortly before railways obtained an almost complete victory over them: and not much later (in 1844) Parliament approved terms of purchase of railways, which were indeed never put in operation, but would have proved a grievous burden to the nation if they could have been carried into effect[1]. And only a few years ago much exultation was shown as to the success of the municipalization of certain tramways, which are now declining in favour relatively to motor vehicles.

4. *Causes and consequences of the present weakness of British canals. Heavy goods traffic is controlled by railways and waterways in a great part of North-western Europe; but by railways alone in Britain.*

It is conceivable that inventions, which have already been in some measure adumbrated, will enable a "helicopter," or other aircraft, to rise perpendicularly from a small garden, and descend again into it: in that case, railways may lose much of their best passenger traffic, and the dissociation of residentiary districts from centres of industry and trade may be rapidly advanced. No equally sensational change appears likely soon to disturb railway goods traffic: but the advent of motor lorries and other wagons, working easily on modern roads, especially when tar-paved, may perhaps remove the chief obstacles which the configuration of England has offered to the development of an efficient system of internal water traffic: and this may greatly affect railway goods traffic for good and for ill. Up to the present, England's industries and trade have been set at a great disadvantage relatively to those of many parts of North-western Europe, as a result of the decadence of her canals. Only a small part of this loss has been covered by the gains, which her railways have derived from carrying traffic that could have gone

[1] See above, p. 483; and Appendix M, 1.

III, VI, 4. better by water: and it will presently be argued that in the long run her railways might gain from organized cooperation with canals, aided by fresh developments of road transport.

The early phases of the contest of British railways with canals have already been indicated: it was practically decided as soon as locomotives could be made powerful enough to draw heavy goods-trains. Canals might have continued to do good work, if they had been constructed on any general plan. But few long journeys by canal could be made, without passing through hilly country, where numerous locks were required: a lock that will hold a large boat is very expensive; and hilly districts were generally content with provision that sufficed only for small boats. In fact nearly every canal was made chiefly for local traffic. The occasion was one in which a far-seeing strong Government might with advantage have intervened: it might have required that every canal, whose position suited it for use in a national system, should from the first be adapted to barges of considerable size; for the superior economy in horse and man power of moderately large barges was well known. In suitable cases the State might have defrayed part of the expense of a canal, in return for a deferred claim on the income that might ultimately be earned. As things were, the numerous companies, that were responsible for individual canals, seemed perversely to ignore one another's practice: and the strong Royal Commission on Canals and Waterways, 1906—9, found that some companies had made provision for boats of moderate size by long narrow locks, and others by broad short locks; so that many journeys were possible only for boats that were both short and narrow, and therefore very wasteful of the labour of man and horse.

Further, nearly all concentrated British industries had sought hilly districts, first for the sake of water power, and afterwards in order to be near coal measures; and therefore few easy tracks could be found for busy canals except along valleys. Side arms, to right and left of a main track, soon met with high ground; to be traversed only through multitudes of locks or through tunnels. Tunnels were often the more economical in the long run; and they were numerous, but caused great delays. Long distance heavy traffic by canal never had a fair chance; and canal work in England was seen at its best only in a wide-spreading home of great industries, such as that of which Birmingham is the centre.

But the great majority of the Commission were not content with so poor a result. They reported that "numerous industrial establishments have settled on German waterways; and that agricultural co-operative associations have established stores on them for the collection and distribution of goods, especially near Berlin....Cheapening the transport of coal and other low value traffic has increased the trade, industry and wealth of Germany; and indirectly the revenue derived by the railways from passenger traffic and higher class goods....Had it not been for the improvement of the waterways, it would have been necessary to spend more money on railways and on goods stations and sidings in districts where the cost of land is high, without probably obtaining an equivalent return in additional traffic." Encouraged by the might of great rivers German canals are being adapted for six hundred ton barges; while those of France are making provision for three hundred ton barges. In both countries the goods traffic by inland waterways is increasing much faster than that by railways[1].

[1] French canals are public routes, open to all: and the charges for freight on them are about a farthing a mile generally; but only two-thirds of a farthing on the more frequented lines. In Germany it is intended that the waterways should pay interest on their capital cost; any surplus being devoted to reducing the capital. But German opinion tends to the conclusion that the water-traffic benefits the railways a little and the country a great deal; because it prevents the railways from being overloaded with traffic that can only bear very low charges, and thus sets them free for more remunerative work: "traffic on waterways has been fostered by light railways and connecting lines, built with State aid for that purpose." (See the *Final Report* of the Commission [Cd. 4979]; especially pp. 118 and 122.) Mr F. R. Conder, a pupil of Brunel, told the Select Committee on Canals, 1883, that the British railways would have at least £7,000,000 added to their incomes, if they threw their heavy traffic on canals. See their Report [Q. 2397]: the detailed statistics, on which he founded his estimate, are given in its Appendix 12.

The literature of this subject is large: but special reference may be made to *Garden cities and canals*; in Appendices to which Sir John Brunner gives weighty counsel based in part on his own experiences.

The traffic on the canals that connect the great inland seas of North America is enormous, though it gives no good guidance for British conditions: but canal nets in some districts, as for instance in the neighbourhood of Chicago, may develop on lines adapted to the conditions of a small country. Reference may be made to a discussion on Inland Waterways, reported in the *American Economic Review*, April, 1911.

III, VI, 5. England is indeed weak in this respect that, being an island, she has no opportunities for such large schemes as are open to Continental countries. The six hundred ton barge canal, which has been made on the basis of the river Main from Mainz to Frankfurt, may become a most lucrative investment to Prussia, if ever the scheme to which it belongs is completed. For then six hundred ton trading vessels (to say nothing of submersible and other ships of war) will be able to cross the watershed between the Rhine and the Danube; to carry Prussia's products, iron and manufactures at very low costs to Austria, the Balkan States, the Black Sea and the Mediterranean; and to carry back grain and raw material. But England and, in a less degree, Scotland have some special advantages which may ere long be greatly developed by the aid of modern technique.

5. ***The relations of Britain's railways to heavy goods traffic may possibly be considerably modified by her exceptional facilities for the cooperation of road motors with her canals, and for electric haulage on her canals.***

There are reasons for thinking that the importance of British waterways has been underrated in the past, chiefly because they have lacked adequate auxiliaries. Consequently but little attention has been paid to the fact that the services rendered by a network of canals are far from being limited to those rendered by railways. They include some of those rendered by public roads, which yield no money revenue; but which are of as much importance to the economic well-being of the country as those of railways.

Anyone can set up a business at almost any point he chooses on a high road; and can have goods delivered to it and taken from it by carts; which may stand at his door, provided they do not obstruct the free way. In like manner even a man of small means can set up a business by purchasing a plot of land on the bank of a canal; and his goods can be delivered direct to it and taken direct from it. If his business extends, he can have a bulge made on the canal, which will give him at small expense the benefits of a private dock, or railway siding. On the other hand the stations of a railway must be at considerable distances from one another, averaging perhaps three or four miles: and though a strong capitalist can obtain a private siding, he can do this only at so great expense, and under such onerous conditions that very few businesses venture to do so[1].

Again, a canal, that is not much burdened by locks, will carry a continuous stream of traffic in either direction, just as a public high road will; whereas a railway must allow for long intervals between consecutive trains. Therefore the growth of population and traffic will seldom call for a broadening of the canal similar to the substitution of four tracks for two on the railway: and "trains of barges" may carry large loads, even on a canal, that is not adapted to very large barges.

It is to be noted that the diminutive scale of Britain's geographical features brings many of her industrial centres, which are not easily to be approached by waterways, into close connection with them by motor traffic. A road, with lines of motors moving in opposite directions, will carry more traffic than a railway can; and motor wagons can pick up and deliver goods much more easily, and under many more conditions, than a railway can. Wherever a road comes near to any part of a busy network of canals, contact can be made between water traffic and road-motor traffic: and since the points, at which goods can be delivered or received, may be ten or twenty times as numerous on a hundred miles of canal as on a hundred miles of railway, nearly the whole area of England may ultimately be in easy contact with canals, at lower charges for heavy traffic than those at present current. The immense capabilities of motor wagons had not been fully developed when the Commission on Inland Waterways settled to its work: but it now seems clear that their aid may enable a relatively small number of canals to carry a very large traffic economically and conveniently, provided that effective traction on the canals can be obtained easily.

Recent experience shows that this can best be achieved by means of central electrical stations, with wires extending from each over many miles of canals: and for this purpose England

[1] The Board of Trade Conference of 1909 arranged a "model private-siding agreement" (*Report*, pp. 7—9): probably few people, without special experience, will anticipate the length, intricacy and troublesomeness of the provisions and restrictions, which are required in the interests of the railway and of public safety.

III, vi, 5. and the Southern half of Scotland have greater facilities than any other area containing a like industrial population[1].

Such traction has the incidental advantage of adaptability to single boats and trains of boats of various sizes: it would reduce to a minimum the wastefulness of the relatively narrow canals, which alone are suitable to the orographical conditions of this country. Electric power could be applied on occasion to work the lifts, which may perhaps supersede locks, at all events in districts in which, as in the English Midlands, the supply of water power sometimes runs short. In any case electricity would be a helpful adjunct to water power. It might be supplied, as in Prussia, to factories near the canal, and increase the beneficial tendency of well-appointed canals to check the intensive concentration of industry:—a tendency, which threatens to deprive children of opportunities for invigorating play; and to deprive young and old alike of the opportunities, which abundance of open space offers for invigorating exercise and refreshing repose.

Electricity is unrivalled as an agency for transmitting energy from place to place; and, for that and other reasons it is likely to exert an increasing influence over the structure of transport industries on land and inland water. Also, in its larger developments, it requires way leaves; and is therefore specially beholden to State recognition, and is even in some degree adapted for direct State control. Moreover the six hundred bodies, reported by a Committee of the Board of Trade in 1918 to be generating electricity for public purposes in Britain, employed so many different frequencies that cooperation among them was impracticable. The Committee therefore recommended that a Central Authority should fix standards for the whole country

[1] This plan is already largely used in Prussia; the towage being effected by motors running on tracks on the banks. But there appear to be some reasons for thinking that it may be superseded by, or combined with, a plan that has long been in use to enable heavy vessels to make way against the stream of the Danube, which is some places runs at the rate of seven miles an hour. The plan is to let a strong chain lie free at the bottom of the water: a vessel picks it up, passes it round a windlass (which may be worked by steam power or by electricity); and of course drops it at the stern.

and set up a separate District Electricity Board in each district into which the country should be divided for the purpose. The adoption of a scheme of this kind would facilitate, and be benefited by, the use of canal banks as routes for main wires; and as sites for electricity stations; except in cases in which the generating plant could be advantageously set up in a neighbouring coal-area. This arrangement might be set on foot at once: the full development of a canal system in association with electricity might gradually go far towards enabling Britain to maintain her high place as a leader of industry, in spite of her great inferiority in natural resources to several other countries.

Coal is the chief source, other than the qualities of her people, of Britain's economic strength; and her coal is rapidly disappearing: it is said that she possesses only a fortieth part of the coal known, even now, to exist in the world. Slow transit in water consumes less energy than any sort of traffic on land. And, when account is taken of the inevitable waste of force which is involved in shunting a train, whenever it needs to be broken up, an additional argument is supplied in favour of slow canal transport of coal and other heavy goods; among which chief places must be given to some agricultural products and requisites. The cheapest method of obtaining power from coal for widely diffused uses is to generate it in large quantities, so as to be able to utilize all its by-products (waste smoke being of course eliminated); and to sell it to every class of consumer. Revivified canals would be among the chief consumers of power: they could bring coal by the cheapest means to sites where land was easy to be obtained; and the power which they provided for their own use along their courses, could be made the foundation of electric supply systems for all those parts of the country that are adapted for canal traffic[1].

[1] Movements in this direction might be commenced at once by individual canal companies: but they should be such as would fit in with a comprehensive national scheme, when Government is ready to take that in hand. Specially opportune is the suggestion by Sir R. H. Inglis Palgrave (*Quarterly Review*, Jan. 1918, p. 146) that financial advances for developing canals, though not fitting for ordinary banks, "would be well within the scope of the British Trade Corporation": for that might properly insist that nothing should be spent on half measures that fell below the minimum indicated by the Commission on Inland Waterways.

III, VI, 5. The Commission on Inland Waterways received evidence as to the delivery of coal from the colliery direct into square steel boxes, floating on the Aire and Calder canal. Each of these "compartments" holds forty tons; and thirty of them make a canal train, which is drawn by a tug: they are put on board ship at Goole. In this very successful venture the chain of traffic is complete without aid from a railway: but it seems to contain the germ of a method by which transport by road motor, railway, and canal may be worked into organized unity, with the result of greatly lowering the costs of handling traffic. The method may be seen in the plan on which luggage vans for cross-channel traffic, and many furniture removal vans, are arranged. That is, the receptacle of goods is an independent large box, which could be secured either to a flat railway wagon, or a motor lorry. Of course it could be deposited on the flat bottom of a barge; or it could even be made to float[1].

It has already been noted that Prussian railways have made the "bodies" of some rolling stock detachable from their chassis so that they can be moved by cranes from one truck to another, and thus very greatly diminish the waste of time, and especially of coal, in shunting from one railway track to another. The general adoption of that plan would greatly facilitate the arrangement of through transport of the "bodies" by railway, road motor, and canal, in such proportions as might be most economical, from factory to factory, to merchant's warehouse, or to ship.

As to the important question of the relative costs of canals and railways the following results seem well established:—Of course a railway is not forced to follow contour lines as closely as a canal must; and it therefore needs less mileage than a canal does to connect any two points, except in very level country. The cost of production of its bed is, as a general rule, less than that of a canal of equal breadth: but there is scarcely any amount of

[1] In the course of time it might probably be found that agricultural land derived greatly increased value from direct access to a canal, or even to a shallow and narrow dyke that would hold a boat just able to carry such receptacles to a canal, or other waterway. It is well known that the interchange of soils between land where it is too heavy, and land where it is too light, would often add greatly to the fertility of both: but that generally requires long journeys, and its cost hitherto has been prohibitive save in exceptional cases.

traffic which a fairly broad and deep canal cannot carry: whereas a railway often needs four tracks for its main line, and many tracks in the neighbourhood of stations. The expense of locks (and even of the much more economical lifts) is sometimes a heavy burden to a canal. But it has little or no need of signalling apparatus: and the buildings, that may be needed on its banks for the development of a large and frequent goods traffic, will mostly serve also as private warehouses. The upkeep of a canal generally costs much less for management, for maintenance and for wages than that of a railway does: canal banks need care; but water does not wear out as railway lines do. The cost of floating stock is much less than that of rolling stock of equal tonnage: it has much less wear and tear and needs much less power for haulage. It is however true that, *under the present conditions of British canals*, the labour directly employed in transporting a given quantity of cargo a given distance is greater on them than on a railway: though indeed engine drivers and guards form only a small part of the employees of a railway.

To sum up and conclude:—The volume of transport, for which accommodation is needed, increases without cessation; and, so great are the difficulties of widening a railway in a crowded district, that it cannot always increase its work, where most needed, save at enormous cost. The quickest trains necessarily stop only in crowded centres; and, in this and other ways, their influence tends towards an ever increasing intensity of centralization of the population. On the other hand canal and road-motor traffic make for decentralization; and in association they may relieve railways of much heavy traffic.

But the revival of canals can be effected only by the State: much capital will be needed for it; the war has deprived national securities of that scarcity-value, which enabled them to be marketed at a very low rate of interest; and to that extent it would somewhat prejudice any overtures made by the State for the purchase of the railways. But this consideration may probably be of less solid importance than the reflection that organized cooperation of traffic by railway, canal and improved road might be easier and more effective, if the railways (with their plant), together with roads and canal routes, were in a single hand. The

III, VI, 5. operation of canals like that of roads would be open to all, subject to appropriate conditions, and charges for the use of locks, etc.: those who worked on them, not being State employees, would be under no special temptation to use the franchise for personal gain, instead of as the means by which they could discharge their duty as citizens. These observations have ventured on dangerous ground: but greater risks are taken where no attempt is made to forecast the future, while considering methods of action or inaction that will largely affect the future, than by straining inadequate eyes in reading such faint indications of the future as can be discerned by them.

The case for canals has perhaps been prejudiced by comparisons in their favour based on too exclusive regard to the costs of working them, even when the charges for their use make no attempt to defray the costs of making them: railway charges are expected to cover costs of working and costs of railway building. On the other hand a railway cannot, and a canal can, render innumerable services similar to those rendered by a public highway. The abolition of tolls on highways is now universally recognized as good policy; because the revenue yielded by them would be small in comparison with the excess value of the services rendered by a free road over those rendered by a tolled road: the country would be in a poor way if no roads were made save those, the tolls on which would cover the expense of making them and keeping them in repair. The State has constructive duties in the matter: and it is likely to have important regulative duties, if monopolistic combinations should arise to control through rates by road, canal and railway. This consideration affords a small subsidiary argument in favour of the nationalization of railways[1].

[1] While this chapter was passing through the Press, a Committee of the House of Commons on Transport (H. of C. 1918, 136, p. 10) reported that "unification of the railway system is desirable under suitable safeguards, whether the ownership be in public or private hands; proceeding by any of the following routes:—(1) Further amalgamation of railway companies as a step towards unification; (2) Unification accompanied by private ownership and commercial management. (3) Unification by means of nationalization; followed by (*a*) Establishment of a government department to manage the railways; or (*b*) Constitution of a Board of Management not directly represented in Parliament; or (*c*) Leasing of the system to one or more commercial companies."

CHAPTER VII

TRUSTS AND CARTELS: AMERICAN EXPERIENCE

1. *A review of some general causes of the recent rapid increase of giant businesses, independently of any monopolistic purposes. The poverty of British statistics; the wealth of American.* III, VII, 1.

America has taken the lead in the development and control of vast individual businesses, or Trusts, having monopolistic tendencies: and Germany's Cartels afford the best illustration of the good and evil of sectional associations in industry and trade. Trusts and cartels have so much in common that they cannot with advantage be considered separately: but this chapter and the next are mainly concerned with trusts; while Chapters IX and X are mainly concerned with cartels. As has already been indicated[1], trusts are the results partly of horizontal, partly of vertical expansion: but cartels are in essence horizontal associations: though they may indeed occasionally expand vertically by coalition throughout successive strata of the same industry, or otherwise.

It will be well to begin by bringing together some observations made in Books I and II which are relevant to our present inquiry. In Book I we saw that massive capitals in the hands of mediaeval potentates, political, military, and ecclesiastical, were mainly used for the support of large establishments belonging to their owners; and that the capitals to which the modern methods of production and trade owe their origin, were almost exclusively those of traders. The first prominent uses of capital in the organization of English industry, were seen when "under-

[1] See pp. 215—217, where something is said of curious changes in the meaning of the American term "Trust."

III, VII, 1. takers" sought out domestic workers in various parts of the country, who had but little capital of their own; supplied them with material and instructions for its use, and marketed their products. Shortly afterwards the invention of textile and other machinery, suitable for being worked on a large scale by water power, set on foot the direct capitalistic ownership of all the appliances of production, except only the property that every free labourer has in himself. Thenceforward leadership and control came increasingly to those countries, and to those individual manufacturers in each country, who could invest capital without stint in expensive plant.

Book II was occupied with the causes that have made for the expansion of the business during recent times, in so far as they arise mainly out of the pursuit of increased economy and efficiency in production and marketing. Its general drift was to the effect that, though technical advances in manufacture, in the transport of goods, and in telegraphic and telephonic communication, have caused a continuous increase in the scale of business operations; yet each decade has had its own upper limit to the size, needed for reaching nearly the maximum economy and efficiency in each branch of industry. This general rule was seen to be liable to several exceptions, one of the most interesting of which is found in the dye industries; where progress consists mainly of innumerable relatively small developments of a few master ideas. For these developments can be effected in large laboratories whose processes are secret; so that increased size creates increased power, which takes automatically a somewhat monopolistic form. The new devices could be patented; but secrecy is a more effective check on imitations that are suggested to rivals by a new product; which, not being exact imitations of it, do not infringe its patent.

Meanwhile there has been a steady tendency towards specialization of work and of plant; and—so far as trade union regulations allow—to so complete a classification of employees according to their general ability and their specialized skill and aptitudes, that no one works at any job which could be adequately performed by one of inferior or less appropriate aptitude: and that every foreman and nearly every superior official has just those responsibilities, which will give fair scope for his particular faculties. These tendencies have constantly increased the size of the Representative business unit—that is, of the unit whose costs of production exercise so great an influence on the amount that will be forthcoming to meet any given market demand, that they play a prominent part in the regulation of price under competitive conditions. Formerly the difficulty of obtaining adequate supplies of capital restrained the expansion of the Representative business within narrow limits: but this restriction has almost disappeared under the influence of the ever-growing volume and fluidity of the resources of that market for the command over capital, which is commonly called the Money-market.

And yet, in spite of this elasticity, the influence of technical economies on the expansion of the business unit tends to weaken after a certain size has been reached; partly because the specialization of plant, and the substitution of mechanical forces for that of the human hand, increase the standardization of products; especially in those engineering and other industries, which are ever changing most rapidly under the impulse of technical progress. Hence there arises a certain reversion to earlier conditions. The business of the capable merchant could expand rapidly, and almost without limit, in times when those industries, which preceded modern manufacture, seldom gave scope to considerable capitals: and in the present age the tasks of marketing offer ever increasing scope for vast aggregations of capital. These tasks will be found to give the keynote to the present phase of the development of trusts, and of cartels.

The population of England has been much occupied with large capitalistic production for a far longer time than has that of any other country. The Newcastle Coal Vend anticipated on a great scale many of the policies of German cartels two centuries before they came into existence: and the first monster coal and iron works, dominating a whole country and spreading out their influences far beyond, were founded in Liège by Cockerill, an Englishman. But yet, what seem to be the most characteristic features of the present and coming tendencies towards monopolistic aggregations and federations, are to be sought elsewhere. The total information available as

III, VII, 1. regards British industrial monopolies is very small in comparison with that relating to American trusts. Scarcely any of it has passed through searching investigation, comparable to that which has revealed many of the cherished secrets of American trusts; and has substituted correct information for that which some of them had published. Nor do British trade associations generally rival German cartels in the control of the marketing of particular classes of goods on lines sufficiently firm, and yet elastic, to dominate for good and evil the courses of national industry and trade.

Trusts in Britain are of course subject to the rather stringent regulations as to the publication of their affairs, which are imposed on all Limited Liability Companies: but it has not been thought necessary to obtain much further official information about them; and that which they supply is liable to fall short, at critical points, of the requirements of public interests. The causes of this deficiency are not wholly to be regretted. For many industries, which have sprung up like mushrooms in younger countries, are mainly controlled in Britain by firms, whose traditions go back for several generations, and which are therefore disinclined to sudden changes, and violent courses of strategy: while attempts to make an anti-social use of monopolistic strength in manufacture would generally be frustrated by the arrival of competitive foreign goods in British ports, whence they could be easily distributed over the whole of the small area of the country[1].

British official statistics were cast in a relatively good mould in the middle of last century: but for many decades they followed tradition closely; and they have now much lee-way to make up. An important new departure was made by the *Report of the Census of Production in* 1907; which goes a long way towards giving the needed information in regard to that year. But it had not the advantages of consecutive records and long experience:

[1] This statement, which was in print before the war, is left standing. But the Ministry of Reconstruction has appointed a Committee on Trusts, which is receiving much information, partly confidential, on which to base an opinion. This may be the first step towards more vigorous action, should circumstances require it. Confidential bureaucratic inquiries, at their best, are however a poor substitute for published testimony, which invites rebutting evidence from those who are in a position to detect errors or suppressions.

and it was limited in several ways. The gap may be in some measure filled, so far as our immediate purpose is concerned, by some American statistics which will be found in Appendix N.

2. *Associations and agreements of various sorts prepared the way for the rise of trusts in America.*

We start from the position that nearly the maximum economy of production can often be attained by a well organized business of moderate size: but that the task of marketing efficiently over a large area makes demand for almost unlimited capitalistic resources, unless it is facilitated by association with others engaged in the same industry. Associations for various purposes, some constructive and some mainly strategical, some temporary and some permanent, some overt and some secret, anticipated the rise of trusts in America; and were often the foundations on which trusts were laid. These associations are known as "pools," because they pool some part of the interests of those concerned. Thus the term is now of broader scope, than when we saw it used in connection with agreements among English railways to throw the whole of the receipts for certain portions of their traffic into a common purse, after deducting only the mere direct costs of moving them. In fact it covers as large a variety of consorted arrangements among possible competitors as do the elastic terms "Cartel," and "Syndicate"; of which more hereafter.

Pools might have expanded almost as freely in America as cartels have done in Germany, if they had not been opposed by the Common Law which had come from England with the "Mayflower." For many generations the supply of capital in the country was scanty relatively to the demand, which her vast natural resources made for it: the growing efficiency of English industries, equipped with more expensive plant than a young country could afford, made Americans anxious to see the rise of corresponding industries at home; and aggregations relatively large, though very small in comparison with present standards, were welcomed for their constructive power. But pools and other combinations for the regulation of prices inherited the jealous suspicions, to which combinations of engrossers and others had been subject in the Middle Ages.

III, VII, 2. This is perhaps the explanation of the paradox that the Common Law was habitually invoked for the repression of temporary combinations in restraint of trade; while little attention was paid to the threatening power of permanent growths and fusions of great businesses. That repression was sometimes extreme: and advocacy of yet stronger measures provoked a reaction; some of the exponents of which proclaimed the sovereign efficacy of absolute free competition with an exaggeration, that rivalled that of the early popularizers of Ricardian economics in England and France.

But in the last few decades America has developed the scientific application of economic doctrines to many practical problems, with great energy and thoroughness. More perhaps than any other country, she has learnt that general propositions in regard to either competition or monopoly are full of snares: and that some of the most injurious uses of monopoly, being themselves extreme forms of competition, are not to be restrained by the advocacy of free competition. Consequently she is now engaged in leading the world in the very difficult task of restraining such methods of competition, as are aimed at narrowing the basis of competition. Nearly all such methods come within the scope of prohibitions of "unfair" competition: there are many difficulties in the interpretation of the term "unfair" in this connection, with which a Court of Law cannot deal without aid; but the needful aid can be supplied by the organized systematic studies of *permanent* authoritative Commissions.

The first critical point was reached when public attention was directed to the "Trust," in the original use of the word, set up in 1882 by Mr Rockefeller and others for controlling the trade in mineral oil and its products. It was formed by an agreement among the shareholders of a number of oil companies to make an irrevocable deposit of their voting power with nine Trustees, who would administer the whole as one concern. The plan had two advantages. The trustees had unhampered power; and yet they evaded the responsibilities, which were imposed by the law relating to "corporations" (that is, joint stock companies) on their directors.

This advantage caused many groups of businesses to be

consolidated into Trusts: but public opinion was strongly moved by the danger that the Trusts might become powerful monopolies. And the attempt to exercise the privileges, while evading the legal responsibilities of corporations, evoked the "Sherman Anti-trust Act" of 1890. It condemned under penalties every attempt to monopolize any part of interstate or foreign commerce; and made contracts in restraint of such trade illegal, whereas before they had only been non-enforceable: and "Trusts," in the original sense of the term, were dissolved.

III, VII, 2.

The movement, of which those Trusts were an expression, was temporarily checked, not so much by the Act itself as by a violent collapse of credit, caused by the fear that debts might be repaid in a depreciated currency. But that danger quickly passed: and, the industries of the country being in a substantially sound state, the reaction from the previous gloom resulted in a great outburst of activity with rapidly rising prices, and an almost unparalleled volume of profits. The public is always apt to exaggerate the importance of a short series of years of high profits; and to estimate the capital value of a business on the assumption that such profits represent permanent prosperity. This general tendency was strengthened by the accident that, just at that time, several giant businesses were being developed with remarkable success by the men of genius, who had created them. The technical economies of production on a very large scale in heavy iron and steel, in mineral oil, in beef products, in agricultural implements, and in some other things were attracting general attention. They were emphasized, and exaggerated by constant repetition of cases in which large scale production and dealing had exceptional advantages: and thus, by honest as well as by interested teachings, the general public was prepared for the belief that, if the chief businesses of any kind in any market were united, the net income and the true capital value of the consolidation would much exceed the aggregates of those of the original businesses.

Consequently, the promoters of a consolidation were eager to buy businesses, that might compete with it; or even be used by an opponent as a basis of operations against it. They had little interest in keeping down its total nominal capitalization:

III, VII, 2. for their main aim was to dazzle the investing public with a show of a sufficient domination of the industry concerned, to be able largely to control prices; though of course they made no overt attempt at monopoly. Thus they often bought at high prices establishments, which it was found best to close on account of bad location or inefficient plant.

They endeavoured to evade decisions of the law-courts which had condemned "Trusts" (in the original use of the term) by putting the whole, or at least a working majority, of the shares of the constituent companies into the hands of a small number of men, under the form of a "Holding Company": these men controlled the policy of the whole, and in some cases administered a part of it. But Holding Companies were declared by the Courts in 1904 to contravene the Sherman Law: and they were dissolved. Thus the campaign against Trusts, in the old sense of the word, seemed to have been brought to a successful issue: but in fact it had merely changed its form. In suitable cases the companies, whose securities had been held by a Holding Company, were fused, in one way or another, into a single giant business. We now leave Trusts in the earlier uses of the term, and consider only giant agglomerations of business.

An estimate made in 1904 allotted a capital of about seven thousand million dollars to industrial trusts. About half that amount was assigned to "franchise trusts"; that is water, gas, electricity, tramway and other undertakings, which make exceptional use of public highways. The nominal capital of a third group, that of railroads, was about equal to that of the other two together. A fourth group consists of financial businesses: but the power which they wield would not be adequately represented by their capital even if it could be ascertained with tolerable accuracy; while of course much of it consists of holdings in other "trusts" and has therefore been reckoned already[1].

[1] A Committee of the House of Representatives in 1913 enumerated over two hundred consolidations, each having some degree of monopolistic strength. An estimate, given in the Report of the U.S. Census of 1900 (vol. VII. pp. lxxv—xcii), indicates a large percentage of failures among the early combinations; and Mr C. N. Fay, an apologist of trusts, gives particulars of "the failure of combination to monopolize," and even to succeed financially, in his suggestive *Big business and Government.*

In 1890, the Sherman Law, not having taken effect, the word "trust" was

The large majority of industrial trusts are of course to be found in those manufacturing industries, in which an increased scale of production brings with it increased economies. But in fact they do not owe very much of their power to that advantage: for, with some exception for the steel industries, a capital very much less than that required to dominate the market, will suffice to obtain every important advantage that belongs to production on a large scale. Nearly all the chief trusts in the group, now to be considered, owe more to the economies of marketing on a vast scale than to those of production on a vast scale. But these and similar matters can be presented most vividly by brief sketches of some leading trusts.

One rule alone is almost universal. It is that each great industrial trust has owed its origin to the exceptional business genius of its founders. In some cases the genius was mainly constructive: in others it was largely strategic and incidentally destructive; sometimes even dishonest. But in general there seems to have been present a notable power of visualizing the future. The Duke of Wellington, speaking before the day of aeroplanes, said that a chief business of his life had been to construct mentally the view of the enemy's position on the other side of intervening hills; and the founders of great trusts have been eminent, even among able business men, for their power of anticipating future relations between productive resources and market requirements.

3. *The basis of a firm but wisely limited control of monopolistic tendencies in American business is provided by systematic official studies. The experience thus gained gives valuable guidance as to some urgent problems of British industrial policy.*

It is argued by Americans that the vagueness of the Common Law is on the whole a source of strength. Definite and

still used in its early sense; and the present writer told the British Association that their future seemed to him doubtful. They were in fact vanishing. But a recent writer has authoritatively condemned that prognostication, under the impression that it applied to "trusts" in the very different present use of the term.

III, VII, 3. precisely worded Statute Law is adjusted in matters of detail to the circumstances of the time at which it was made; and cannot be readjusted to new conditions without fresh legislation. Common Law, on the other hand, is interpreted by progressive, judicial decision in accordance with the conditions of each generation, in so far as the Supreme Court, under whatever name, feels justified in setting aside inferences drawn from previous judicial decisions: thus the Common Law is constantly being created, while being only interpreted nominally. The faculties required for this work are not specially legal; but they are in great measure trained by the lawyers' close contact with the affairs of business life, and their relations to public interests: while the decisions of the higher tribunals, by which most of this legislation is effected, indicate a statesman's faculty of discovering and conserving the true interests of the public, even when not directly represented in court. The habits of life of Anglo-Saxon peoples fit them in an exceptional degree for alert exercise of the mind, without much special training: but experience has gradually shown that, as the public interests in business become larger, while business itself becomes more complex, a chief task of practical sagacity is to discover the directions in which it needs to be supplemented by systematic studies, and to organize those studies.

Since the operations of transport are to a great extent standardized by natural causes, their policies can be subjected to some external control without adding greatly to those restrictions on the initiative of railway directors and managers, which are imposed by Nature herself. This control is specially appropriate; because a railway, or group of railways, has something of Governmental power within its own domain; and therefore the work of a Board of Trade or a special Commission in regard to the regulation of railways is fairly homogeneous and relatively simple.

But industrial monopolies are of very various characters. In many branches of production technique changes rapidly; and the methods and purposes by which particular aggregations or federations seek to control prices, are ever presenting new developments. A great trust starts with expert knowledge of its own business; it can hire the most expensive expert witnesses to support the arguments of its highly paid counsel—themselves in some measure experts—on technical points. Against so strongly fortified a defence little can be done by a relatively small and impecunious business, which thinks itself aggrieved; and still less by the inarticulate public, which may be the chief sufferer in the long run. A complete remedy for this social hurt is not to be had: but a long step towards it was made by America in 1903, when Congress set up the Bureau of Corporations to investigate such cases, to enforce a limited degree of publicity, and to make recommendations[1].

The success of the Bureau of Corporations in checking abuses of monopolistic power by merely publishing the results of its investigation of them, encouraged Congress in 1914 to raise its status, under the name of the Federal Trade Commission, to a level with that of the Interstate Commerce Commission: and at the same time to pass a second (the Clayton) Anti-trust Act; which strengthened the provisions of the 1890 (Sherman) Anti-trust Act, for the enforcement of which the new Commission was to have a care. That Act declared in general terms several practices to be "unlawful" when, but only when, "the effect" of any one of them "may be to substantially lessen competition or tend to create a monopoly in any line of commerce." The word "substantially" is perhaps not exactly suited to the purpose of the Act: and the use of the term "unfair" competition in other parts of the Act, as well as the interpretations of it by the Courts, recognizes that the mere expansion of an ably managed business must necessarily contract the area, over which the competition of other businesses in the same industry can

[1] It authorized the Bureau to investigate "the organization, conduct of and management" of any appropriate business corporation; "together with such information and data as will enable the President of the United States to make recommendations to Congress for legislation for the regulation of such commerce." This information "or as much thereof as the President may direct, shall be made public." Some of the evils sought to be remedied by its work are indicated in its *Report* for 1905, by saying:—"Much legislation has been enacted which is futile and often harmful because directed either at the modification of great economic laws, which cannot be modified by statute; or at the treatment of sporadic and sensational facts. Estimates, guesses, prejudices, and limited individual experience have been the bases of action, rather than broad and final conclusions based upon accurate, properly arranged masses of facts."

III, VII, 3. have full play. The Courts have sometimes in effect read in the word "unreasonable" before "competition" in the Act. What is really condemned is *destructive* competition. One runner may outdo his rivals by greater energy as much as he can: but, if he puts his hand on another's shoulder to pull him back, while pulling himself forward, that is the unfair competition against which the Anti-trust Act is directed.

The purpose of the Federal Trade Act is to constitute an administrative and semi-judicial body of high standing, which shall continue with enlarged powers the work of the Bureau of Corporations; and collect such information in regard to the operations of giant businesses, as shall enable a good judgment to be formed on the character of the competition, which they wage against less wealthy rivals. It is to investigate any appropriate case; and, after hearing, issue an order directing compliance with the law. If this order is not obeyed, it may apply to the appropriate Federal circuit Court to enforce it; and that *must* take its findings, if supported by testimony, as conclusive (subject to certain conditions); though of course the findings may be set aside by the Court on a point of law[1].

This slowly matured and vigorous scheme has exceptional interest for Britain. For her attention has been much attracted by the events of the world-war, and by other causes, to the economies and facilities which giant capitals can obtain in production and in marketing. And since Britain's free trade, together with other causes, has in great measure safeguarded her against malign uses of any monopolistic power thus obtained, her people have been increasingly inclined to look with favour at the beneficial results of the massive organization; while taking little thought as to the dangers that might arise from it. In fact "combinations," when they are merely particular forms of *constructive cooperation*, often bring with them such great material

[1] It should be observed in passing that the Anti-trust Act applies to combinations of railways, as well as industrial trusts. But the chief gravamen of the charges under it against railways refers to the hurt which railway fusions may inflict on customers of railways; while industrial trusts are charged with depriving other businesses of reasonable access to markets, in the first instance; and thereby injuring the public ultimately.

advantages, as almost to hide from view any contraction of the field for the creative enterprise of young businesses that they may cause. That evil might probably be rather small, if Britain's financial and military position remained substantially as it was before the war. For, though history records few cases in which constructive cooperation has not after a while degenerated in some degree towards restrictive and even destructive uses of monopolistic power; yet the same brave and free spirit, which has kept British ports open to all products that compete with her own, might have continued to ward off monopolistic pressure.

But the war has enlarged the range of things of which the country is unwilling to be greatly dependent on external supplies: and it has necessitated so great an increase in the Revenue needed by the Exchequer, as to strengthen the hands of those who desire to levy import duties on many manufactures. Such proposals are sometimes associated with suggestions that combinations for the regulation of prices should be sanctioned and even encouraged by the State. The avowed aims of such a combination are no doubt constructive: it is to be militant only in regard to invasions of British territory by powerful foreign producers or traders, singly or in combination. But history shows that men engaged in any industry, which is faced by foreign competition, are inevitably and almost unconsciously impelled to exaggerate any indirect injury that may result to the public from such competition; and recent events suggest that human nature has not changed in this respect. Such men have special knowledge of the industry and trade under discussion: and complacent officials have always been inclined to take the path of least resistance, and accept expert estimates in these matters with but little consideration of the unconscious bias by which such estimates may have been warped. The dangers directly arising from this source are increased, when those, who speak thus with expert authority, are associated for the attainment of any common ends, however beneficial in themselves: for such conditions are specially likely to taint constructive cooperation with some touch of militant restrictive monopoly. The recent courses of German cartels will be found to point in this direction. For the present we are concerned with

III, VII, 4. American experience to the effect that, if the danger becomes considerable, it can be adequately met only by a special official organization; which differs from an administrative Department of Government in that it concentrates the greater part of its energies on progressive studies, resembling those of a great technical laboratory[1].

4. *Actions, which are harmless on a small scale, may become injurious when practised on a large scale, especially if their purpose is to obstruct the highway of business.*

Under ordinary circumstances, an individual tradesman, who has taken offence at a customer, may refuse to deal with him: but a conspiracy to drive a man from the neighbourhood, and render his property in it valueless, cannot be justified under ordinary circumstances. The law against malicious boycotting is akin to an anti-trust law: each aims at preserving the right of well-behaved persons to make free use of the common highways of business.

The law and commonsense alike sanction the meeting of any two people, or the standing of a cart for a time by the curbstone, even in a busy highway. But a large assembly of persons (or a collection of carts) sufficient to hinder the full use of the thoroughfare by others, is broken up by the police: and if the obstruction can be shown to have been deliberately planned with the purpose of injuring some person's business, or otherwise annoying him, it is an offence. Wrong-doing of this kind cannot be directly controlled by Courts of Law, nor can the initiative in complaint against it be left to private action. It must be controlled by the Executive, whose ordinary constable clears the highway by appropriate orders; the magistrate being ready in the back-ground to enforce judgment in any case in which the policeman's orders are resisted. The Federal Trade Commission has responsibilities, similar to those of the policeman, in regard to vast highways on which the traffic is immensely complex. Long-continued, organic and scientific study of great

[1] Some exceptional provisions in regard to American export trade are noticed below, in Chapter XII.

masses of detail takes the place of the policeman's simple view of the obstructing crowd; and its decisions are authoritative, subject to certain conditions. It is responsible for taking the initiative, and coming to a provisional conclusion as to whether any price discrimination, or exclusive dealing, is a *bonâ fide* constructive business transaction or is a destructive strategical manoeuvre aimed at preventing a rival from making use of the highway of business. The first place among unfair methods of competition, which are denounced by the Anti-trust Laws, is held by price discriminations; the chief variety of which is that of malign local price-cutting.

A dealer is *primâ facie* free to choose the prices at which he sells his goods. If, for instance, he has two shops, one in the East end of London and the other in the West, he will often ask higher prices in the West than in the East; partly because he cannot sell at high prices in the East, and he cannot pay the high rent of his shop in the West if he charges low prices there: his action rouses no suspicion of malign motive. But the Standard Oil Company habitually pursued the consignments of a rival to retailers; and told them that, if they persisted in buying from the rival, it would sell its oil close to them at a price which involved a temporary loss to itself: it thus rendered their trade impossible. It did this so systematically and with such large resources, that many independent refiners sold out to it at a loss; and others, who would have entered the business, refrained. "Size without any predatory power makes a corporation beneficent; but size with this evil endowment makes it a menace to freedom....The prospect that a trust will resort to predatory practices terrorizes the rival in advance, and prevents him from appearing[1]."

The duty of the State in this matter is not to hinder the action of the great forces of economic evolution; even when they involve the destruction of old businesses, which have no other fault than that of being unable to turn those forces to good account. Its protective intervention is not called for on behalf of incompetent competitors with the trust: but it is called for when the trust sets itself to destroy a rival, who is

[1] Clark, *The control of trusts*, p. 123. As to some discrimination in retail trade, see Appendix J, 3.

III, VII, 4. prepared to sell things of good quality at lower prices than the trust is charging for them elsewhere. The greater the immediate sacrifice which the trust is willing to make in order to drive such a rival off the highway, the greater is the *primâ facie* reason for thinking that the interests of the public require that the rival should have a fair chance of developing his business, and attaining economies of production on a large scale, with fresh enterprise. The case is only *primâ facie*: for instance, the purpose of the rival may be to blackmail the trust: and the task of investigation is therefore both difficult and delicate; but it is not impracticable[1].

Discriminating prices are commonly associated with the "dumping" of certain goods, especially by countries with high protective tarifs, in foreign markets. But, as will be seen later on, the chief purpose of such dumping is to maintain prices in the home market: the desire to destroy rivals in foreign countries plays a much smaller part in such dumping than is commonly supposed. On the other hand, the intimate financial association of some American railways with particular powerful trusts has caused price-discriminations, aided by discriminating railway charges, to attain a portentous power of destroying inconvenient rivals. Many are the devices, by which the laws against price-discrimination with a monopolistic purpose are evaded; but the Interstate Commerce Commission and the Federal Trade Commission, working in unison, seem likely to repress most of them ere long: and indeed monopolistic strategy of this kind is so definite that it can hardly evade the pursuit of painstaking, capable investigation, well supported by authority; though it has relatively little to fear from those milder and less penetrating forms of bureaucratic control, which have hitherto sufficed for most of Britain's needs[2].

[1] The nature of the task will be illustrated by the notes on individual trusts contained in the following chapter.

[2] It may be added that Canada is hostile towards monopolies: her plan for controlling them is less systematic than that of the United States, but more systematic than that of Britain. Subject to unimportant restrictions, any six full citizens may apply to a judge; state in writing that they believe a certain combine to exert an influence injurious to public interests, and ask for an investigation. The judge is then bound to give them a hearing; and if he thinks a *primâ facie* case has been made out, he writes to that effect to the

5. *Relations in which the prices charged by far-seeing trusts, when not engaged in campaigns against rivals, stand to the probable costs of "independents."* III, VII, 5.

Before passing to the consideration of particular trusts, it may be well to say a little in continuation of earlier discussions as to the relations between cost of production and the price which a far-seeing trust will place upon its goods, in the absence of any strong incitement to destructive strategy. It has already been observed that a conditional monopoly must take account of the cost of production which its competitors must meet: but the particular forms of conditional monopoly, which belong to a modern trust and its relations to "independents," are so definite that there may be an advantage in returning to the subject.

The reports of the Industrial Commission appointed in 1898 to inquire into the conditions of American labour were, till recently, the chief authority as to the conditions of American trusts. It reached the following important conclusion:—"The testimony of substantially all of the construction men is to the effect that, unless a combination has some monopoly of the raw material, or is protected by a patent, or possibly has succeeded in developing some very popular style or trade-mark or brand, any attempt to put prices at above competition rates will result eventually in failure, although it may be temporarily successful." It finds that a short-sighted policy looks at the proportion of the total output of a certain commodity which is controlled by a trust: if that be large (and there are many trusts which

Registrar of Boards of Investigation, who must appoint a Board for the purpose. It is to consist of three persons; one nominated on the recommendation of either side to the question; and a third nominated by those two. Their report is published in the *Canada Gazette*: if unfavourable, it may lead to the withdrawal of any tarif protection which the offenders have had, or to revocation of patents; together with a fine which is increased with each day (after a certain interval) during which the grievance is maintained.

Somewhat similar provisions are included in the Australian Industries Preservation Act 1906—10: and in 1912 an Australian Interstate Commission of three members was set up, whose extensive duties included various steps for dealing with combinations that tended to restrain trade or commerce by unfair competition, or to the detriment of the public. New Zealand has moved in the same direction: and South Africa has done the like in regard to the Meat and Shipping trades.

III, VII, 5. control about two-thirds of it), there is a temptation to argue that the trust can regulate prices without much attention to cost of production. The argument is valid for short periods, but only for those[1].

For a far-sighted trust's policy looks rather away from the ephemeral relations between the output under its control and that of the independents: its main business is with the potentialities of independent output in the future. If concerned with minerals, it cares little for minute calculations of outputs of mines already opened: it cares much for estimates of the cost of opening out new mines within striking range. It cares little to know what part of the plant owned by the independents is nearly obsolete: it cares much to know what are the difficulties in the way of starting rival works of equal efficiency with its own, not necessarily for all parts of its work, but for some of the more lucrative. It takes account of the fact that, now more than ever, a powerful capitalist often likes to push his way even into an industry with which he is not personally familiar, but in which he knows that high profits can be reaped. Such a man, in conjunction with associates who have the requisite technical knowledge and administrative faculty, and who have sought out him, or have been sought out by him, may be able to put up a plant that will be as well or better organized than that of the trust, because it will incorporate the most advanced ideas from the first. Accordingly a well-managed trust reflects that, if it puts its prices so high as to hold out the prospect of good profits to new rivals, after fighting through the campaign of underselling which it is prepared to arrange, the rivals will appear. That is to say, it adjusts its price rather closely to the cost of production *including profits*, on which a new-comer in an ordinary competitive market would base his calculations. But it adds to this something for the insurance against extra risk which a new-comer into its market would expect to face.

It may seem that this cost of production is of a different kind from that which the producer in a competitive market needs to watch. But that suggestion goes too far: the difference between the two cases is mainly one of degree. It is true that, in a competitive market a producer's connection has no firm

[1] *Report*, vol. XIII. pp. xvii, xviii, and xxi.

hold of a long life. He must give himself to holding his own against existing rivals; and it is not generally worth his while to spend much care on the effects which his action may have on the appearance of new rivals: for they are sure to appear in any case.

In this matter his position differs from that of even a conditional monopolist. But he also has his far-seeing strategy as well as his tactics for passing occasions: and his strategy has to do with the costs of whole processes of production. The prudent leader of a great trust will remember that, though there are very many men competent to manage a small business, there are not many who can manage a large one; and that only a small percentage of those, who are competent for the affairs of a large business, can rise to the high peak of the management of a huge trust. There is always "plenty of room at the top": and, if the highest post is very high, the difficulty of finding adequate successors to the few intellectual giants who have built the lofty edifice is almost insuperable. Youths of exceptional faculty are often found in lowly work of various kinds in large businesses as well as small. But, as soon as they become conscious of their strength, they are likely to be attracted by the chance of developing their own powers of initiative; and the lower posts in a vast business seldom offer as much scope for that, as do those of a small business, in which, on occasion, a subordinate may be called to do what he can at a task which has been supposed to be beyond his powers. It has been justly said that small businesses are the nurseries for the best brains in large businesses.

The trust must therefore reckon with the possibility that it will not continue for long to have as large a share of the best business genius of the country as it had, when it first achieved its semi-monopolistic power. Its capital may enable it to outbid all others when a new important patent is to be sold: but the weaker successors of the strong men who have created its success may fail to appreciate, and even to welcome, the genius of men who are stronger than themselves. It seems probable that the combative phase of monopoly, introduced by some industrial trusts, may pass away more quickly than earlier phases in times of less rapid evolution. Probability is a

III, VII, 5. chief guide in all matters: it is the only guide in regard to matters, as to which the present age can find no close precedent in the past, and cannot expect to yield close precedents to the future. Thus there are many reasons why a trust should not make use of its semi-monopolistic power to put its price much above the level at which an independent business could produce, if not hampered by the pressure of the great giant: the policy of destroying independent rivals in order that it may raise its price is not so much to its own interest, as appears at first sight.

But this consideration may have little weight with bold enterprising men, who value success for the proof of power which it gives, almost as much as for the wealth which it brings. And, since many monopolies owe much to the partial exclusion of foreign competitive products by a protective tarif, there seems much force in the suggestion that, when a commodity protected by a duty comes under the control of a combination, the duty on it should be revoked[1].

[1] Francis Walker, *Causes of trusts and some remedies for them*, p. 23, referring to the precedent set by Canada; see above, p. 523 fn.

CHAPTER VIII

TRUSTS AND CARTELS: AMERICAN EXPERIENCE, CONTINUED

1. ***The United States Steel Corporation is a unique aggregation of many giant businesses; but it leads, rather than controls, the steel industry.*** III, viii, 1.

We may next consider some illustrations of a general rule, which has already been partly indicated. It is that an aggregation so powerful, as to be a representative "trust" in the present use of the term, is likely to be under no great temptation to have recourse to those exceptionally cruel and malign forms of competition, which have frequently been used by a business on its way to obtaining the dominant position in an industry. Moreover, when such a dominance has been long set up, the leaders of the business are likely to be well advanced in years; to be sensitive to public opinion; and, above all, to have learnt that, though a triumphant pleasure attaches to the attainment of great riches, their possession does not insure the full fruition of life. A man may have used fierce, and possibly even somewhat unscrupulous, methods of combat, while still uncertain of success; and yet, when he has fully attained great wealth and power, may perhaps use these chiefly as means by which he can earn the respect of others and of himself. Instances of this, while not rare in old countries, are specially conspicuous in America: and they appear to be contributory causes of the tendency of some trusts, which have had troubled courses in early days, to take on a milder character, and to act with more careful regard to the interests of the public, when they have once attained almost irresistible power. But unfortunately the peaceful position thus attained depends in great measure on personal and other conditions, which are liable to change: and

III, VIII, 1. America is in no way relaxing her energetic and thorough studies: they are pioneering the way for the rest of the world by examining the responsibility of the State in regard to the powers for evil, as well as for good, which modern conditions have put into the hands of monopolistic aggregations and associations. The facts which follow in this chapter, are not in any sense consecutive or even fully representative history: they are selected merely as particular illustrations of broad tendencies.

It has already been observed (above, II, III) that an exceptional combination of causes has promoted consolidation in the heavy steel industries. For the metal can pass through many stages without ever getting cold: waste gases can be used to generate horse-power to be applied directly, or through electricity; and high chemical and other technical skill can find large scope in the supreme direction of many massive processes. Rolling mills, engine shops, etc., can often find occupation in slack times by enlarging and repairing their own plant, and that of the furnaces, and above all of the mines: and rails or plates, which happen to have been made unmarketable by slight flaws, can yet be turned to account in posts of no great responsibility about the mines, the furnaces, etc. Thus a business, which owns the necessary supplies of coal and iron ore, is in a very strong position: and one, that lacks these advantages, is likely, after falling into difficulties, to be willing to accept terms of purchase that will yield a profit to another business, which is fully equipped.

These conditions, as we shall see in the next chapter, have contributed towards the formation of the German Steel-works Union; which is the most far-reaching, though not the most firmly established of all cartels: and their tendency to create a giant consolidation in America has been strengthened by other causes. For, though it is true that a capital of some twenty million pounds suffices at present for the equipment of a single set of fully efficient steel works; yet a fusion of many works in different parts of the Continent of America is able to make considerable savings by sending each order to be filled at that works, which is best adapted for it by situation, special appliances, and freedom from other engagements, etc.

Already in 1900 considerable progress towards such expansion and fusion had been made by the Carnegie Company; which owned much of the best iron ore and coal for coking purposes in America. In 1900 disturbances were threatened by proposed extensions downwards of some of the higher stage steel businesses; and by plans of Carnegie for making a railway of his own to carry much of his traffic, and by other developments. This brought powerful financial interests into the field, and with them came the notion of monopolistic advantage: it had not previously appeared as a motive for expansion: but gradually rose to a level with the pursuit of technical efficiency.

Stress was laid on the inevitable rise in the value of the iron and coal properties owned by the companies, which were to be amalgamated; and, partly for this reason, the favourable terms, which Carnegie claimed, were conceded to him. Ultimately nearly all the principal steel businesses were fused into the United States Steel Corporation, with a total capitalization so much in excess of the market values of the constituent companies, that the promoters were able to take, as their own remuneration, cash and securities, which were worth at the time some sixty million dollars and soon rose much in value.

This amalgamation created an epoch, first by the methods of its capitalization; and secondly by the admission, practically involved, that the additional economies of administration to be obtained by an increase in the size of an individual establishment, gradually dwindle as the size increases.

The second point may be taken first. Several hundred separate properties were included in the great amalgamation: and in order to keep the subsidiary companies efficient, considerable autonomy was conceded to each of them. But, lest each should regard the others as competitors rather than allies, an elaborate profit-sharing plan was set up, purporting to interest the President and the other officers of each in the profits of all the others. And meanwhile the activity of each was stimulated by setting before it the ambition to show results as good as, or better than, those of any other doing like work under like conditions.

The market values of the various companies incorporated reached a total of eight hundred million dollars: which, ac-

III, VIII, 1. cording to the investigations of the Bureau of Corporations, exceeded the total value of their tangible properties by only one hundred million: but the total capitalization of the United States Steel Corporation in 1901 (including underlying bonds, etc.) was fourteen hundred million[1]. The greater part of this excess is apparently due to the valuation of the ore properties; which the constituent companies had reckoned at one hundred million, and the Corporation at seven hundred million: this may indeed fairly be regarded as an instance of the common practice of promoters of a fusion, under which Preferred stock is issued to the full amount of the visible properties of the several businesses. Equal amounts of Common stock, given to purchasers of Preferred, are understood to represent the good-will of the businesses fused; together with the value of the additional earning power, which the fusion is expected to derive from its new economies, and its monopolistic advantages. This practice of capitalizing good-will is not altogether unreasonable; but it has been the cause of many abuses[2].

The values of the ores owned by the Steel Corporation have risen greatly since 1901: its chief businesses have been excellently managed: and, even before the great war, its securities rose sufficiently to make this high capitalization appear not very unreasonable. But of course it owes much to the Protective tarif, which enables it to sell some of its goods at higher prices than those at which similar European products could otherwise have been obtained.

It has not attempted to regulate prices independently: but has taken counsel with its chief competitors as to the prices which the market will bear. Its lead has generally been willingly followed; and indeed there are some who think that its statesmanlike policy has been even more advantageous to some of its rivals than to itself: certainly its business has not grown as fast as some of theirs have. At least nine-tenths of the total steel output of the country appear to be now represented at the conferences, held under its lead, at which schedules of prices and other matters are arranged.

[1] See the *Report of the Bureau of Corporations on the Steel Industry*, vol. I. 1911, pp. 166—169 and 373—382.

[2] See above, pp. 335—6.

The position is however not free from anxiety from the national point of view. Ere long nearly the whole of the iron ores in the country may have been explored, and be owned by a few giant businesses, acting more or less steadily in concert. The great Trading Companies of yore worked for some time bravely and steadfastly for their own profit, and the prosperity of the country; but, as time went on, the places of active Venturers, strong in their self-restraint, were filled by weaker men, inert and greedy of gain. No such extreme deterioration is indeed likely under modern conditions: but there may be increasing need for vigilant study, on the lines set out for the Federal Trade Commission, of the action of what may become in effect a monopoly many times more powerful than any yet known. For it would have "its feet firmly planted on the ground": that is, it would in great measure control those resources, supplied by Nature, without which no rival to it could make headway. Even incomplete monopolies, thus planted, are likely to be more solid and durable than apparently stronger monopolies if based on superiority in manufacturing technique, or in business ability, or in financial strength; or even in all three together.

This class of consideration applies to several other American industries, in which there has as yet been either no monopoly or only a local monopoly. For instance, the Reports of the Bureau of Corporations on the Lumber industry, indicate growing tendencies to local concentration of ownership of timber. Timber lands are already becoming rather scarce; and a powerful financial movement to concentrate these concentrations might develop a dangerous monopoly of timber. Further, lands, that have been denuded of timber, are commonly sold at low prices; and, if bought up by strong capitalists, might introduce a hitherto unknown tendency to gigantic ownerships of agricultural land[1].

Again, the Bureau of Corporations has called attention to the danger that the chief sources of water power may be exploited

[1] On the other hand the Industrial Commission itself suggested "combination under proper supervision" as a remedy for the waste of national resources involved in the use of fine anthracite coal for purposes for which inferior coal would suffice. An individual coal owner cannot materially affect the price of coal in the winter; and he will suffer, if he has not kept his men together in the summer while others have done so. But a single corporation, owning the

III, VIII, 2. by a few strong capitalists. It is true that its price must in the long run be governed by the price of power generated by coal: but the great excess of the cost of such power over that of power obtained from water on a large scale, may yield a monopolistic revenue, which properly belongs to the State, and needs to be jealously controlled.

2. *The power of exceptional constructive ability, combined with astute destructive strategy, is illustrated by the history of the Standard Oil Company: its financial strength has gradually overshadowed a considerable part of American business.*

Attention has already been called (III, VII, 2) to the facts (1) that the Standard Oil Company was the first to constitute a "trust," in the original sense of the term; (it then represented an association of businesses, effective for strategic purposes, but yet evading the prohibitions of monopoly, which the law-courts had based on the Common Law); and (2) that its remorseless underselling of rivals, with less capital than its own, who were making good supplies at reasonable prices in particular localities, was a chief cause of the stringent legislation against local price discriminations. But the Company has never had any approach to a monopoly of the sources of supply of mineral oil: its monopolistic power has resembled that of a railway, whose network practically covers a great district; while it is able to evade any regulations that may require it to give facilities for the traffic of other companies to pass over its lines.

It began with a comparatively small group of lines of pipe, and could do little without the aid of railways. But it offered very large business to some of them: it played off one against another with great ability, not disdaining corrupt influences; and it was thus enabled to induce some of them to carry oil for it more cheaply than for its rivals. It hampered those opponents not merely by selling at specially low prices in their neighbourhood; but also by paying for a time very high

whole field, might do better for the country by refusing to work much in the summer; and allowing some scarcity of coal in the winter to raise its price sufficiently to cover the cost of attracting miners back in the late autumn; when the demand for labour in agriculture, building, etc. was slackening.

prices for crude oil from any wells, from which a rival had expected to derive his supplies. It worked on these plans, in so far as not estopped by the law-courts, with great ability and persistence, and in many fields of enterprise: insomuch that, though it had a capital of only a million dollars in 1870, it was paying forty million dollars in dividends in 1907[1].

Again it took a leading part in the use of bogus independent companies and fighting brands; which it used to destroy rivals in places where its monopoly was threatened: meanwhile it maintained high prices where it was exempt from competition. A bogus company, really owned by the Standard Oil Company, would offer good oil at a low price in the neighbourhood of an obnoxious rival: it would search out his customers, retaining a staff of spies for the purpose, and offer oil to them at exceptional rates. Even where there was no urgent fear of competition, a similar company, representing itself as an opponent of monopoly, would turn a prevalent anti-trust sentiment to the account of the great trust. "Fighting brands," which it seems to have been the first to use, are somewhat analogous to the fleet of "fighting ships," maintained by the Hamburg American Company to underbid obnoxious rivals[2]. These brands differed in no essential from those in ordinary use: but they could be offered for militant purposes at low prices, without affording ground for a charge of "local price cutting"; for they were not sold at higher prices anywhere.

The Company was indeed dissolved by a Federal Court in 1912; which ordered that the shares of all its constituent companies should be divided among its shareholders in proportion to their holdings in it. But nine strong men hold

[1] It showed great foresight, and was quick "to buy up lands along the route which a rival line was to follow, or to secure rights of way of its own access across such routes,...or to enlist the support of railroads in refusing to a rival rights of way across its tracks" (*Report of the Bureau of Corporations on the Petroleum Industry*, 1907, vol. I. pp. 21, 24, 25). The State of New Jersey has attracted undertakings desiring to evade the laws, which many other States have made for the protection of the public: and registration in that State has helped the Standard Oil Company in restricting facilities to others for use of the rights, which they might have demanded from its pipe lines, as "common carriers" (see the same *Report*, vol. I. chs. V, VI: and vol. II. chs. X—XII, summarized on p. 668).

[2] See above, p. 435 fn.

III, VIII, 3. between them most of these new shares; and, if they continue to work together, the policy of all the constituent companies may remain as before. Probably cautious counsels will prevail, at least for a time: and when those nine men pass away, the dissolution of the Company, which is at present merely nominal, may become real[1].

3. *Monopolistic control in the tobacco industry effects great economies in marketing: the huge profits of the Tobacco trust tempted it, and enabled it, to use strong measures for the suppression of interlopers.*

The tobacco industry has no high technique which calls for the ceaseless energies of a multitude of inventors: but each manufacturing business spends much on pressing its products on the notice of retailers and of the public. For these and other reasons, many statesmen have thought that a Governmental monopoly of tobacco could be more easily and successfully worked than any other: and that it could be made to yield a higher net revenue than could be got from customs and excise duties on it; at all events in countries with land frontiers over which petty smuggling of tobacco cannot be completely stopped. Such monopolies have not been very successful; because their task is really more difficult than it seems: and Government officials have not the energy, the alertness, and the special faculties of fine discernment, which have enabled the managers of the American Tobacco Company to amass vast wealth, from a partial monopoly of tobacco obtained by able management and strategic marketing[2].

Many giant businesses have owed their first successes to the possession of important patents; and, in spite of its simple technique, the tobacco industry has offered some scope for patents. In 1884, when cigarettes were coming into general

[1] W. H. Vanderbilt, a man of like mental structure with them, but of more purely constructive purpose, said of them:—"I never came in contact with any class of men as smart as they are....I don't believe that, by any legislative enactment or anything else, you can keep such men down. They will be on the top all the time." Quoted by Miss Tarbell, *History of the Standard Oil Company*, Appendix 59.

[2] An instructive study of the causes of the small measure of success attained by Government tobacco monopolies is given by Madsden, *The State as a manufacturer and trader*.

favour, a cigarette machine was produced which multiplied fifty-fold the output of an operative. Successive improvements on that machine set up strong competition among the leading American manufacturers for important patents; and by 1890 nearly the whole of the trade in cigarettes was in the hands of five firms; each of which spent lavishly on advertisements till 1900, when they amalgamated. The new trust extended its operations into other branches of the tobacco business: it adopted the ordinary evil devices of bogus independent companies and "fighting brands"; and by 1910 it had acquired four-fifths of the whole tobacco trade, cigars alone excepted. Its expenses were relatively low in buying, in advertising and in premiums to middlemen; and "its rates of profit were ordinarily more than double those of its competitors[1]."

It should be added that the Supreme Court dissolved the trust in 1911; and divided up its property and business among seven "successor" companies. The securities of these companies continued to be held chiefly by those who had held the securities of the trust; as had happened when the Oil trust was dissolved. But the sequel has been different. The successor tobacco companies compete with one another in considerable measure: and they spend more on advertising in various forms, and on other expenses of marketing than the trust needed to do. Therefore their net profits are less in the aggregate than

[1] *Report of the Bureau of Corporations on the tobacco industry*, Part III, 1915, p. 3. The leading firm in the amalgamation "was valued at $250,000 in 1885. Without other additions than surplus earnings...the par value of the securities to the end of 1908 amounted to nearly $39,000,000; or 156 times the capital value of the business in 1885....These enormous profits...rest upon the monopolistic advantages obtained in this industry through concentration of control" (*Ib.* Part II, 1911, p. 38). It is well known that the American Tobacco Company's invasion of the British market led to the amalgamation in 1901 of thirteen of the largest British tobacco businesses, under the name of "The Imperial Tobacco Company"; that the two trusts fought hard for a year; then came to a working agreement, and finally set up the British-American Tobacco Company to export to countries other than Britain and America. In 1902 the British Company had offered large bonuses to dealers who undertook not to sell American goods for a term of years. The American Company replied by an arrangement that all profits on American sales in Britain, together with £200,000 for each of four years would be distributed to their customers, without requiring a boycott of other manufacturers (*Ib.* Part I, pp. 169; and 469, 470). These figures suggest the need that may arise even in Britain for the authoritative defence of independent producers against monopolists.

III, VIII, 4. were those of the trust, and from their point of view there is great waste. From the public point of view there is some waste: but the diversion of profits from the owners of the trust to middlemen, is not so much to be regretted as it would be in the case of an industry, the leadership of which calls for inventive and constructive ability of the highest order in almost unlimited quantities: on the whole, the dissolution of this trust seems to have been a gain. We now pass to problems similar to those raised by Deferred rebates in the shipping industry.

4. *Insistence on exclusive dealing, and other tying contracts, are generally harmless on a small scale: but, when used as aids towards monopoly, they may be mischievous.*

The Tobacco Trust at one time refused to supply any dealer who handled competitive goods. Regular dealers seldom saw their way to abandon the whole of its products in favour of a relatively small producer; even though he offered a few things, which had great attractions to consumers and promised high rates of profit to dealers. Partly because rival tobacco could be retailed as an adjunct to various businesses, the trust did not push this expedient very far: but the International Harvester Company even insisted on the dealer's keeping in stock a "full line" of all the company's machines suitable to his business[1].

Similarly the Electric Supply Company refused to sell those of its products, on which patents still ran, to anyone who did not buy exclusively from it other products, the patents on which had expired. Complaints against similar action by patentees of machinery for use in the boot and shoe industries have been numerous in America; and more recently in Britain.

The conditions of British industries seldom call for strong authoritative intervention in such matters: but they have attracted much attention in Canada and Australia. Even in Britain an Act of 1907 prohibits conditions, which prevent any-

[1] See the *Report* on it by the Bureau of Corporations, 1913, pp. 304—10. *The Economist* of 7 September, 1918, reports that it has recently been dissolved by the Supreme Court, on the ground that it was so large as to make the restriction of competition direct and substantial. This decision, being independent of any proof of actual exercise of the power of restriction, may have far-reaching consequences.

one, who obtains or leases a patented thing, from using any article supplied by a third person. This law can be enforced easily; though the larger undertakings involved in the American laws of 1914 could not be thoroughly enforced without the aid of a strong permanent Bureau or Commission to search out the facts needed to decide whether any exclusive, or "tying," contract tends "substantially to lessen competition or to create a monopoly"; and thus to set out a case on which a law-court can pass judgment. For the question at issue is not whether the actions to be restrained are wrong in themselves; but whether they are "unfair" methods of competition when used by powerful capitalists for the destruction of weaker rivals[1].

Unfair competition in this technical sense is not to be classed with criminal practices. But the feverish pursuit of wealth may induce men, capable of great work, to drift into distinctly criminal courses[2].

5. *Difficulties in the way of forecasting the future of trusts; especially in regard to their influence on the stability of industry and trade.*

The future of an individual life can be in great measure predicted from an observation of its earlier stages; because human nature is relatively constant and our knowledge of it has been accumulated through many centuries. But the future of an economic tendency is more difficult of prediction; because it will be governed by conditions which have not yet

[1] Speaking generally any vessel may steam down a river at such a rate as is convenient to itself. But if big ships, in competition with small craft, are charged with raising a high wash on purpose to injure their rivals, questions are suggested, which cannot be decided without technical guidance.

Attention is called to the British Act of 1907 in an excellent compendium relating to *Trust laws and unfair competition*, published by the Bureau of Corporations, 1915.

[2] The National Cash Register Company, whose technical achievements are in the first rank, has been convicted for malicious libels in regard to competitors; and for causing its agents to injure internal parts of rival machines when in actual use, and similar practices. In such cases the Bureau of Corporations has rendered good service in obtaining evidence which could not be got without great expense by the relatively impecunious competitors of the trust. If the trust had believed that those machines were not worth the prices charged for them, it would not have cared to injure them secretly. More details on this subject will be found in Seager's *Principles of Economics*.

III, VIII, 5. come into sight: certain influences, which are likely to take part in governing the future of trusts, may however be observed.

Note has already been made of the dependence of trusts on a supply of business ability of so high and rare an order, that very few men of any one generation, even in America, have given evidence of possessing it. There may have been a considerable number, who have possessed it, but have not had access to positions in which it might be turned to account. The opportunities for such men are no doubt increasing in some directions: but in others they are being contracted; and the growth of trusts is likely to prove hostile to them. The momentum of a huge business, imparted to it by men of high creative genius, will carry it a considerable way: for routine, well set up, and supplemented by technical studies may give fairly good results under the guidance of men of high ability, even if lacking creative genius: and the supply of such men is not likely ever to run short. But the vaster a business, the greater is the danger that it will be dominated by routine when the men of energy and genius, who made it, have passed away[1].

It may indeed be urged that any tendency towards quiescence, that may be shown by an old trust, is not without compensating advantages from the public point of view; partly because it makes in some degree for the stability of industry. Again stress is laid on the facts that the recent advances of technique have gone so far as to insure to mankind a mighty command over the forces of Nature, even though technical progress should slacken a little: and that progress depends increasingly on professional students with eyes turned partly towards concrete results; as well as on those employed by great businesses to work on laboratory lines for the solution of definite practical problems. It is argued that enlightened heads of a great trust, even if somewhat inert themselves, are likely in the coming age to devote corporate funds without stint to such purposes: and thus constructive work will proceed. Meanwhile intimate

[1] When a great combination is effected "initial success is due to the ability and prestige of the leaders. As time goes on new leaders must be found. But nepotism is likely to appear in the established management" (Taussig, *Principles of Economics*, ch. 63, § 4). Several other authorities have laid stress on the dangers which old trusts are likely to run from nepotism.

comparisons of the work of similar establishments in the same trust will aid the departmental managers, as well as the central control, to turn to good account any zeal for progress that they may possess; and national and international congresses of technical experts will tend in the same direction. All this may be true: and yet it seems probable that the total constructive activities of the nation will be neither as vigorous nor as freely exercised, as they would have been if nearly every establishment, large enough to avail itself of the full economies of massive production, had been under independent control.

Again it is true that the economies in marketing, belonging to a trust with almost undisputed sway, make net contributions to aggregate national wealth; the importance of which is not to be entirely ignored, merely on the ground that they fall chiefly to the share of those who are already rich. Moreover a trust, whose dominion is not threatened, generally promotes steadiness both of output and prices, so far as it conveniently can. For it is inclined to that policy by the magnitude of its investments; by the broad interests, which its chief proprietors commonly have in the stability of general business; and by that relative immobility which attaches to its gigantic organization. Accordingly no small motive suffices to set it on sudden change: and for the same reasons, it is at once more inclined, and more able, to oppose any assault on its dominion by violent measures, which convulse its own industry and disturb many others: though of course, even when the dominion of a particular trust is not threatened, command of its securities may be abused in a stock-exchange campaign, in which some of its chief proprietors hope to gain more by the furtherance of great strategic schemes, than they can lose by a temporary depreciation in the value of their holdings of that trust[1].

[1] A striking instance is that of the Amalgamated Copper Company; which is commonly called a trust, though it had no monopoly. The guarded account of it given by the Industrial Commission (*Final Report*, 1902, pp. 230—5), contrasts with the vehement statements and suggestions collected from newspapers of an earlier date in Moody's *The truth about the trusts* (pp. 1—42): and with the still more penetrating and outspoken account in T. W. Lawson's *Frenzied Finance.* Even with the aid of the Federal Trade Commission, a long time must elapse before the history of such scandals is sufficiently certain to

III, VIII, 6. There is therefore no reason for surprise in the fact that several studies of the history of trusts claim to show that they make for increased stability in the general conditions of industry and trade. So great have been the changes in the structure of industry, and in the control of monopolistic power by State agencies, in the two decades over which the effective history of trusts extends, that the past gives but little guidance even as to the near future: but a little may be said about it[1].

6. *A great part of the railways and the chief manufacturing and mining businesses of America are largely under the control, for good and evil, of a comparatively small number of powerful financiers.*

The influences of interlocking directorates within the field of American railways were noted at the end of Chapter VI. Many

afford the basis for definite general conclusions. The Industrial Commission truly said that "when the great supplies of nature come under the operation of gigantic forces, in adapting them to the uses of man, the best good of all legitimate interests requires publicity of resources and methods, and such Governmental supervision as may tend to preserve an equilibrium, and prevent demoralization and disaster." It may be added that the famous French "Secretain" attempt to manipulate the price of copper, late in last century, belongs not to the history of trusts, but to that of giant speculation in organized markets: a good account of it is given by M. Jannet, *Le capital, le spéculation et la finance au XIX siècle*, pp. 320—331.

[1] The period investigated by the Industrial Commission, chiefly 1830—1900, included some changes of an almost convulsive character: they were connected chiefly with the suppression of pools, of trusts of the old kind, and of controlling companies; together with the general prominence of simple giant aggregations. An indirect effect of that prominence was a great increase in the quantity of stock-exchange securities that had a national, and even an international market: for where a small corporation was absorbed in a great trust, its property became at once part of a concern, whose affairs were recorded in central price lists. Many of the new trusts had not then "been tested by a period of depression with the consequent liquidation and reorganization": and "the methods of conducting the business of industrials are more secret than those in the management of railroads." This remark is taken from a special report on "securities of industrial combinations and railroads" under the able direction of Professors Jenks and Kemmerer (*Report of the Commission*, vol. XIII. p. 917). It sets out a number of statistical charts representing stock-exchange histories of many trusts and several railroads. The charts support the common opinion that up to 1900, at all events, trusts exercised a distinctly disturbing influence on the general courses of business. But subsequent history lends more support to the notion that, for good and for evil, the influence of trusts in the future will make for quiescence rather than for strenuous movement.

great organizers of railways have accumulated fortunes, which have overflowed into the general funds of the stock-exchange. The Standard Oil group controls several banks; and it has a dominating influence on many railways and industrial trusts. And the great financial houses, with that of Morgan at their head, hold a very large part of those securities, which carry effective voting power over leading railroads, trusts, and other large businesses. Insurance companies, and others, which hold securities giving voting power, are used by financial magnates to serve the purpose of financial campaigns. A committee of the House of Representatives, 1913, found by a majority that in effect there existed a "Money Trust"; not indeed consolidated, but held together by mutual understandings and communities of interest. Their conclusion has not met with general assent: but there is cause for thought in the fact that they reached it[1].

This predominance in American business of a few scores of wealthy men, themselves largely under the influence of a small number of powerful individuals or groups, has modified the attitude of trusts and other great businesses to one another; and has tended on the whole towards increased quiescence and serenity in the broad courses of industry and trade. For a disturbance in any part of the whole field is likely to injure interests in which some of the chief leaders are concerned; and such men are often disinclined by age and the multitude of their large concerns for entering on arduous campaigns. The irruption of an ambitious genius of the first order, such as Harriman, may disturb the quiet at any time: but the general tendency is towards broad pacific understandings; similar to those of narrower scope, which preceded the pools of earlier times, and have survived them. Thus the wastes of furious competition, and the strain of anxiety lest some unexpected move should largely falsify business expectations, have become less than formerly.

[1] A broad view of the alliances of the chief financial powers in America in 1904 is given by Moody, *The truth about the trusts*, pp. 490—493, and frontispiece. The failure of the great International Mercantile Marine Company, organized by Mr Pierpont Morgan, illustrates the risk that even a great genius runs, when he makes a large venture in a difficult field, of which he has no intimate knowledge.

III, VIII, 6. This gain has however been purchased at a heavy price. The defences of public interests in America against monopoly have rested, partly on the growing efficiency of authoritative regulation, but still more on the growing abundance of free capital. Advocates of the trusts were themselves prominent in the contention, that if a conditional monopoly put its prices above the levels at which a well equipped independent company could afford to produce, the capital required for such a company would be quickly provided. But the growing harmony among the dominating financial interests has raised a fear that the grip of monopoly will be tightened steadily, though quietly; and that the camaraderie among the great financial powers will put effective, but unobtrusive, obstacles in the way of any new enterprise that threatens an unwelcome intrusion into the dominion of any of the great financial groups. This fear has so impressed Congress that the 1914 (Clayton) Anti-trust Act includes several stringent provisions against interlocking directorates generally; with special reference to direct alliances among banks, and between railroads and other businesses. Experience only can show whether these regulations can be made effective without considerable hurt to legitimate interests; though it is true that initiation of proceedings under the Act will be reserved in the main for Boards, who will bring an exceptional expert knowledge to the matter. They will know what not to do, as well as what to do: and they will be able to furnish any Court, with which a decision may rest, with technical guidance of the highest order[1].

[1] Section 8 of the Clayton Act provides (with due notice) that no one shall be at the same time director in more than one company (other than financial or carrying) whose total capital exceeds a million dollars. It also makes a similar provision as regards banks; but the limit of capital is raised from one to five million dollars: "trust companies," which accept deposits of securities belonging to various concerns, and pool the dividends, so as to reduce the risks on particular holdings, are reckoned with banks. Section 10 prohibits a carrier company from interlocking directorates with any business whose annual dealings with it exceed fifty thousand dollars. And Section 7 provides that no corporation engaged in commerce shall hold or use stock of another such corporation in such a way as "to restrain commerce...or tend to create a monopoly." Their several *rôles* in regard to these regulations are assigned to the Federal Trade Commission, the Interstate Commerce Commission, and the Federal Reserve Board.

Britain has so far escaped the necessity of making provision of a like elaborate

It will be noted that these regulations, though contained in an Anti-trust law, are really directed against tendencies, which extend beyond the sphere of monopolistic aggregations and spread over a large part of the field of financial and other understandings and associations. We are thus brought to those problems in which the chief place belongs to Germany, as that of monopolistic aggregations belongs to America. It will be found that each of these two apparently diverse sets of problems is moving in the direction of the other.

The central fact emerging from American experience is that investigations in regard to antisocial policies of trusts and cartels can be efficiently made only by a strong staff of men who give their whole time to the work. In such work there is but little use for the special faculties of the lawyer. He has an important *rôle* to play; but it comes at a late stage, and consists in securing that legal rights and equities are duly observed. Of course the initiative might be taken by individuals who conceive themselves to be aggrieved; but they seldom have the time, the faculties or the knowledge required for the work. They are apt to lay undue stress on matters which specially concern them, and to pass by the larger issues which are of national concern: and they are often afraid to attack powerful interests, whose hostility might destroy them.

kind: but Canada has gone a little way in the same direction. As already observed (above, pp. 522, 523 fn.) she has arranged that, on the initiative of any six persons, suggesting the existence of a combination injurious to the public, there shall be appointed a Board of Investigation, consisting of one of the complainants, a representative of the combination and an independent chairman. This simple contrivance may be of good service in regard to elementary difficulties. But it aims mainly at finding a reasonable compromise in contentions between individuals: and would be of but little use in the defence of public interest against powerful assaults by obscure routes, such as those which occupy the attention of the Federal Commission. In this respect, Britain's industrial problems are more nearly akin to those of the United States than to those of Canada.

CHAPTER IX

TRUSTS AND CARTELS: GERMAN EXPERIENCE

III, IX, 1. 1. *Germany's leadership in the evolution of cartels.*

Mediaeval gilds devoted much of their energies to the regulation of production and prices: but for the greater part their origin was in social affinities rather than in the strategy of the market-place; and the same is true of many modern combinations. In all old countries, and especially in Germany, professional, trade, and industrial associations found much to do in making life more pleasant, and business transactions more simple and more genial, before they set themselves elaborately to bring competition under the yoke, to regulate it, and to diminish its wastes[1].

It was noted in Book I that, though the industrial civilization of Germany is of much earlier origin than that of England, yet several centuries of war and internal discord had stripped

[1] The various stages of this evolution are shown in the *Handbuch der Wirthschaftskunde Deutschlands*, edited by Dr Stegemann, 1904, vol. IV. pp. 474—730. The section on *Kartelle und Konventionen* is part of an exhaustive chapter on *Organisation und Einrichtungen der Industrie.*

Prof. Schmoller (*Volkswirtschaftslehre*, vol. I. p. 449) says that from 1750 to 1870 men saw only the bad side of associations, "which had their origin in older technical, social, and commercial conditions; and hindered rising talents from building new enterprises on a larger scale and with more complete technique." Men quickly learnt that businesses of modern type were bound to conquer: and "the last word of economic wisdom seemed to be that competition should be developed; and that every combination of traders and of producers should be restrained or prohibited." But in Germany since 1879 a movement set in for the promotion of gild-like combinations (*Innungsverbänden*) in provincial and national affairs: and similar combinations were set up in the great industries, with local and central organizations with their "general secretaries; chief offices; special newspapers, tending to influence the press, Chambers of Commerce, Parliaments and Governments; and great public meetings."

her bare of capital and enterprise: so that the impact of English methods in the middle of last century gave her a shock comparable to that of a new country, which is being suddenly developed by immigrants from a leading centre of industry. But in the first half of that century her universities had developed a supply of mental motor force, which enabled her to turn the lessons of her teacher to a new account, and thus fitted her people for a new type of leadership. Hardship had prepared them to work steadfastly for relatively low earnings: and discipline, both military and bureaucratic, had inclined them to rate the advantages of a secure salary very high, and to rate rather low those of opportunities for independent enterprise of a somewhat hazardous nature; while the tedium of long meetings for the discussion of other people's affairs is less burdensome to them than to the impatient Anglo-Saxon.

Above all, their business men of various grades work longer hours than are usual in Britain. Many of them take a long break in the middle of the day; and then work on till eight in the evening with more fully renewed vigour than is generally to be got by the short break, common in Britain. Their plan has many disadvantages especially in regard to the amenities of family life: but it contributes to the force of assiduity.

Endowed with these qualities, they have developed large organization with such a perfection of detail and so logical a consistency, that the record of German cartels will make a classical chapter in economic history; even though they may fail to attain their chief objects, and may give place to an ordered system of aggregations similar to that which is being evolved in America: a result which is perhaps not improbable.

In this, as in other matters, national character and national institutions have acted and reacted on each other. American impatience of routine (abetted indeed by the jealousy with which individual States regarded Federal intrusion in their affairs) had caused American Company Laws to be inefficient and chaotic: and some troubles which have led up to the stringent American action against the abuses of trusts, would have been stopped by the Company Law of Britain. The yet more stringent German Company Law gave some feeling of security amid the tumultuous movements of cartels and giant

III, IX, 1. businesses: it has not been fully justified by events; but it has promoted the evolution of German business on lines congenial to the temper of her people.

The steadfastness, patience, and amenity to discipline of the Germans inclined them to seek the sheltered haven of a cartel, in spite of the partial loss of freedom, and the troublesome negotiations involved in it: but they might not have rushed quickly to that haven, if the methods and circumstances of industry had continued to move with as slow and measured steps, as they had done during the first half, and even the third quarter of last century. The sudden uprising of German business from relative quiescence to the strenuous activity, which had belonged chiefly to English-speaking peoples, introduced a new sense of insecurity: and that in turn enhanced the charms of a promise of even partial shelter from the turmoil[1].

The scale of operations rapidly increased. But every new expansion of cartel activity opened out new difficulties and new troubles. Some interests were advanced, and some depressed, by every large development: and the stronger the cartels became, the louder and more eager were the complaints of those who were injured by them, or even feared that they might be injured. So, early in this century, the German Government took the matter in hand: and in 1903 an official debate was commenced, which is sometimes described as the Kartellen-Enquête. It was organized by the Ministry of the Interior; which sent to each debate representatives of its own: and invited some representatives of the cartel or cartels, whose conduct was chiefly under discussion, and of businesses that were specially affected by it. It invited also several leading economists, who addressed themselves, for the greater part, to questions connected with the interests of the working classes and the public generally.

[1] Consul-General Oppenheimer of Frankfort, subsequently British Commercial Attaché at Berlin, has sent a series of reports on German conditions which are specially instructive to the economist. He says (*Report* for 1904, p. 64) that it "has been officially recognized in the Prussian Diet that commercial combinations had become an economic necessity of self-defence, because industry was being ruined by its own exaggerated competition: for with the keenness of a comparatively young industry, orders, even if practically unprofitable, were accepted all over Germany to swell the figures of the turnover of the individual firm."

The debates seem to have been organized with remarkable ability, and they brought out a good deal of useful information: but they are not comparable in efficiency with the prolonged, systematic study by trained experts, armed with compulsory powers of interrogation and inspection of documents, which has brought to light many of the secret policies of American trusts. No one gave any information which he desired to withhold: not all, that was given in debate, was published: the debates were inconclusive; and they ceased abruptly[1].

2. *Cartels, whose scope is limited to the regulation of prices in regard to standardized products.*

Before passing to the more complex policies of cartels which aspire to regulate production as a means towards influencing prices, a little may be said of those understandings and combinations among traders, which are confined to the direct regulation of prices: the simplest instances of these are in retail trade. A giant business often enforces a fixed schedule of prices for its goods on wholesale dealers; and indirectly, if not directly, on retail dealers. Or the initiative against the retail sale of such goods at a low rate of profit may come from the retailers. They in effect form themselves into a cartel, and will buy only of such producers as will not allow their goods to be sold retail below the price fixed by the cartel. This practice if pursued in moderation is capable of defence; as has been indirectly suggested above: but when carried to excess it may overload a

[1] The official report of them is published under the title *Kontradiktorische Verhandlungen über Deutsche Kartelle.* A brief abstract of such parts of them as relate to export bounties by cartels is given in the so-called "Fiscal Blue Books" of 1903—4; [Cd. 1761] and [Cd. 2337].

When the debates opened, the chief expert representative of the Ministry of the Interior was Dr Völcker: a man of great ability and so much special knowledge, that the cartels seem to have regarded him as properly belonging to them. In the middle of the great debate on steel cartels, which forms the centre of the whole discussion, he changed sides. In the first half of that debate he appears as the representative of the Government; but in the second he appears as director of the mighty Steel-works-union (*Stahlwerksverband*); and a little later he gave a tart reply to Professor Wagner's suggestion that it might possibly be necessary to "apply a certain compulsion to speak out, as in England" (*Kontradiktorische Verhandlungen*, vol. IV. pp. 252—4).

III, IX, 2. retail trade with more retail stores than can earn good profits on each turnover, since that has been brought low[1].

It were useless to try to regulate permanently the prices of harvest products, such as wheat or cotton: for Nature will have her own way as to the chief movements of such prices. It is true that combined action by farmers in keeping back grain after harvest may affect prices a little; and such movements may conceivably become rather more important in the future. Again, a temporary artificial rise may be effected by powerful speculators: but, as we saw (above, II, v), they are almost sure to lose in the long run; unless the rise is based on exceptional information as to harvests, etc. and merely anticipates a rise which would have come to pass a little later without their efforts. Speaking generally, far-reaching regulative combinations are confined to things, the production of which is mainly in the hands of capitalist undertakers, and is not violently disturbed by the caprice of Nature.

And there is a further limitation of the scope of regulative associations. The things, of which the prices are to be regulated, must be defined. This is generally done by the use of technical trade terms: but at the back of these there is an implicit reference list to some standardization by mechanical, chemical, or other tests. The prices definitely agreed on from time to time may refer primarily to certain prominent varieties, leaving the prices of other varieties of the same kind to be deduced from these standard prices by adding or subtracting a given percentage[2].

[1] See above, pp. 280 and 300.

[2] As Prof. Brentano says: "Cartels can exist only in branches of production which supply great quantities of goods of fixed types; *res, quae pondere, numero, mensurâ consistunt*" (*Süddeutsche Monatshefte*, April, 1904, p. 259).

It may however be arranged that goods bearing certain brands in great repute shall be priced somewhat higher than others: or again that goods, which are nominally of the standard class, but are in fact less desirable, should be priced rather low. For instance, it is possible to agree as to the minimum first class cabin fares between two ports, for ships offering the average of personal comfort and speed of journey; and to allow specially slow lines to carry nominally first class passengers at lower fares. Again, complex price-lists can be fixed for different varieties of steel girders and iron pipes. The Westphalian Coal Syndicate publishes price-lists for several sorts and qualities of coal; and, in spite of this classification, purchasers show preferences for particular mines, in which they believe that the general rules as to uniformity of size and freedom from dirt are carefully observed.

It is almost impossible to arrange a uniform price-list for carpets or curtain stuffs into which wool of different qualities, cotton, jute, and other materials are worked in varying proportions and with incessant changes in fabric as well as in pattern. There is no room for cartellization of such things as biscuits, or ladies' hats, in which versatility is demanded as well as high quality.

Of course nearly all standardized commodities are raw materials or half-finished products, or implements, suitable for purchase by people who look to make a profit by turning them to account in their own business; and who therefore are likely to meet the danger of oppressive action on the part of a combination, in control of things which they need to buy, by a counter-federation of their own. That is apt in its turn to stimulate the growth of similar federations on the part of traders or producers who need to buy some of their products; and so on till the end of the chain that stretches upward to the ultimate consumer, and downward to the producer of raw material: the chain reaches far in the steel industries[1].

The conditions, which favour standardization, are nearly the same as those, which increase the violence of unregulated competition, and thus supply a strong motive force in favour of regulation: for they involve generally the use of elaborate and expensive plants and therefore heavy fixed expenses, and therefore a great divergence between total cost of production and prime cost. When these conditions are present, some self-willed producers and reckless weak producers are tempted to pour their goods on the market, even when it will absorb no more except at a very low price. This fact increases at once the difficulties of price regulation by cartels and the desire of many producers for it.

[1] According to an official return (see Riesser, *The great German Banks*, p. 169), there were in 1905 about 385 domestic cartels, distributed thus: coal 19; iron 62; other metals 11; chemicals 46; textiles 31; bricks 132; earth and stone 25; food 17; the rest being scattered: about 12,000 works participated directly in these concerns. It is obvious that the number of cartels in an industry is not a measure of the total strength of the cartel movement: the brick-making industry for instance owes its large number mainly to the fact that the interest of each of them extends only over a small area. The number of cartels seems to have increased in the following decade.

III, IX, 2. Some of the most important cartels have indeed been in mineral industries: for mineral products are, as a rule, easily standardized; and combination is generally easy, because large capital is needed for each mine, and the number of firms which must be brought together in order to make an effective combination is not very great[1].

Experience shows that whenever discipline has to be called to the aid of honourable understanding at all, it must be thorough. For its task is difficult. The more successful a cartel is in obtaining better prices for the producer than he could get without it, the stronger is the inducement to outsiders to force their way into its market; and the stronger is the temptation to its members to evade their agreement, and attract more than their share of the custom by indirect concessions[2].

[1] This rule is subject to some important exceptions. When a new mining industry grows up spontaneously and without the aid of imported capital, shallow veins alone are worked; shafts are inexpensive, and there is no great economy in large production. But, when the shafts become deep, only large mines can give a good return. Further, when it becomes clear to the capitalist mineowners of a great industrial district that new and more distant mines must be opened up, they take time by the forelock and buy large areas of mineral property while land is still to be had cheaply. Thus the approaching exhaustion of the coal in the Ruhr basin has set wealthy ironmasters to develop the basin of the Lippe: and this migration of coal mining has added another to the many causes that are putting the heavy iron industries of Germany under the control of a few great capitalists.

[2] The Outsiders get the benefit of high prices fixed by the cartel, making use perhaps of some of the workers whom members of the cartel have been forced to discharge: and therefore the cartel has seldom much chance of success unless it controls from sixty to ninety per cent. of the production in its district. The devices, by which a member of the association can evade a mere rule as to prices, are numerous. Perhaps he takes a receipt for the full official price, though in fact he has accepted a lower one. Or he bills the goods as being of a lower quality or less in quantity than they really are: or, which is much the same thing, he makes no charge at all for certain consignments; or he renders extra services without being paid for them: or he gives long credit, and that to customers whose position is dubious. Rumour is sure to assert that such things are done, whether they are or not: and the rumour often brings about its own accomplishment. A pushing buyer plays off one seller against another, hinting to each that others are not strictly true to the agreement. For instance a business, which had sent a great deal of freight by each of two American railroads, has been known suddenly to give all to one of them, in order to make the other believe that it has just secured secret rebates from the charges agreed upon between the two lines; though in fact it has received none. Thus it obtained rebates from the second line, which thought itself betrayed.

We may pass by simple agreements as to division of territory, for they presuppose considerable monopolistic power; and though they have had some success in transport industries and a few others, their problems are not germane to this chapter[1].

An effective lasting control of price at an unnatural level does not seem to have been ever obtained by a cartel or other federation, unless provision has been made for determining how much of the products, in which all are interested, shall be put on the market at any time; and how much of this total shall be allotted to each member of the combination as his quota.

This provision has been developed with many varieties of detail. In some cases each member is allowed to exceed his quota on paying a proportionate fine to the common fund. He is generally allowed to produce as much as he likes, in addition to his quota, for sale in foreign countries; and in some cases in such home markets as are beyond the range of the combination. Such an agreement is more difficult to make than one with regard to prices; but provided it embraces most of the convenient sources of supply, it is rather more stable; because it does not offer so large scope for evasions. Its advantages are so great, that it is becoming the dominant form of industrial federation in Germany: though time has revealed weak points in it; some of the most important of them being such as were not foreseen, and perhaps could not easily have been foreseen. It was brought far towards its present masterful position by the Westphalian coke cartel: but a good deal remained to be done by the great Westphalian coal cartel, which speedily adopted and improved it, thus becoming what is technically called a "Syndicate." We may trace the orderly evolution of the methods of German cartels by reference to this leading cartel, and some of its chief followers.

[1] Each producer is likely to consider his legitimate sphere of influence to be very extensive: and he can often trespass on his neighbours' spheres by indirect means. Again, external competition causes trouble: the interest, that each man has in meeting it, varies with the locality in which it chiefly appears; and there are heartburnings, whether the expense of the battle is left to those who are more immediately interested, or is borne by a common fund.

International agreements for the division of the markets of the world among the producers of different countries have had some success, especially in regard to steel rails; they presuppose the existence of strong national associations.

III, IX, 3. 3. *The Westphalian coal cartel, or Syndicate, affords the leading instance of an organized control of the output and marketing, as well as of the prices, of the products of a great industry. Its policy has contributed to the growth of "mixed" coal and steel companies at the expense of "pure" coal mines and steel works.*

The Westphalian coal cartel is the most powerful in the world: (the next in power to it is the Steel-works cartel; which is its chief ally and has an even larger range of influence, but is not so firmly knit, as we shall see). It has always been considered to be "good" in the special sense that it strives strenuously to avoid violent fluctuations of prices; and does not sacrifice this aim to that of raising them high above cost of production. Its organization is skilful. Supreme power rests with the general assembly of its members, with voting powers roughly proportional to their output. The general assembly keeps matters of principle in its own hands: but it delegates the arrangements of details to an Advisory Council and an Executive Committee: and it arranges that the majority of the members of the sub-committees, who decide thorny questions connected with the distribution of quotas, shall not be members of its own body. It may be well to describe its working in general terms, since its leadership has been followed so far as practicable by other cartels, which have set up Syndicates. It will be best to refer to them here as Syndicates.

Every purchaser must apply to the Bureau of the Syndicate. In some cases he may specify the producer, or "brand," which he prefers; and that producer is directed to forward the goods to him, payment being received by the Bureau. But, as a rule the source of supply is selected by the Bureau; which takes account of the suitability of each firm for an order, of the extent to which its quota is still not filled up, and of its geographical position relatively to the purchaser. This plan secures a little technical economy, and great economy in advertising and hunting for orders, and in transport. It enables the Syndicate to keep a control over the output and the marketing, so thorough as often to constitute a local monopoly: for it is able to inflict serious losses on any outsider that ventures into its domain.

The Bureau can sell cheaply where it thinks fit; for the firm which fills up any particular order has no more interest in the price than any other member: the whole receipts of the Syndicate, after deducting outlay for strategic and administrative purposes, are divided among the members in proportion to their authorized production. Thus each firm retains for itself the gains arising from the economy and efficiency of its management, except as regards marketing[1].

If the concentration of marketing could be attained by methods that are free from cumbrous negotiations and effort, it would be a great social gain: for marketing is not wholly constructive work; and, the less energy is devoted to it, the better for general well-being. But the machinery of a Syndicate is complex: and it is said that a producer, who desires to be relieved of the main burden of marketing, can often get it done more cheaply by dealers than by a Syndicate; at all events if account is taken of the indirect hindrances which Syndicate dealings involve. Also, those things, which a Syndicate can market, are necessarily such as are in large demand and to some extent standardized; and therefore they are rather easily marketed. But, after all deductions under these heads have been made, something must be set to the credit of cartels, on account of their elimination of wastes in the competition between goods of somewhat similar character, which the purchaser cannot judge at sight: the wastes in the marketing of coal for domestic use in England are deplorable. A much larger deduction must be made on account of the tendency, inherent in human nature, to apply to antisocial uses any power of control, whether monopolistic or not, that had been acquired mainly for worthy purposes[2].

[1] For details, see Walker, *Combinations in the German Coal Industry*, Part III. ch. I.

[2] Leaving larger matters for later discussion, instances may be given of small tyrannies. A site near coal mines (*A*) had been chosen for the erection of iron works (*B*): the supply of good coal at rather low price, on which reliance had been made, continued till *A* joined the coal Syndicate; after which *B* was supplied by the Syndicate with inferior coals at a higher price. Somewhat later the manager of *B* visited some Belgian works, and found that they were being supplied by the Syndicate with coals taken from *A*, and delivered at a price so much below the current German price, that the Belgian works gained

III, IX, 3. The coal cartel originally befriended steel works which had no coal of their own: for it compelled "mixed" steel works, as a condition of membership, to account to it for all the coal which they brought away from their mines: coal consumed in working the mines themselves is always exempt. This meant that such mixed works paid a full share of the expenses of the Syndicate on the coal used in their steel works: so that the steel works, which had no coal mines, obtained their coal about as cheaply as the mixed works did. But the mixed works rebelled: membership of the coal cartel was of little use to them because they seldom wanted to sell their coal: so they preferred to become, or remain, independent. After a time some of them began to sell coal in considerable quantities, especially when the steel trade was rather dull: and the technical advances, which enabled waste gases of blasting furnaces to be used for the whole of the operations of complex iron works, tended to increase the coal which mixed works could advantageously put on the market.

This result went so far towards defeating the chief purpose of the Syndicate, that it invited back the mixed works by allowing them the same privileges in regard to their own coal, when used in their steel works, as had always been allowed on that used in working the coal mines. This action of the Syndicate put the pure coal mines and the pure steel works at a disadvantage, in spite of their greater care in the management of details, relatively to the mixed works. So, instead of thwarting the cartel, the mixed works set themselves to dominate it and use it for their own purposes. They used the heat and power, derived from their waste gases, for making heavy products; some of which were sold ready for use. Others were sold to higher stage steel works at lower prices than those works could make them, after paying for the coal needed in making them; and a few were worked up on their own premises into fine finished products.

by selling to France the coal which it drew from its own coal mines and using only that from *A*. (Oppenheimer's *Report* for 1905, p. 33.)

Early in 1907 the Syndicate prepared itself to deliver brown coal briquettes: and then prohibited any of its customers from buying such briquettes from any other source under penalty of 50 pf. per ton on all supplies of coal, coke, and briquettes drawn from it. (Oppenheimer's *Report* for 1906, published in 1907, p. 51.)

It is true that similar changes were taking place on a vast scale in America, which was of about an equal age in this respect with Germany; and, on a smaller scale, in Britain. But the exceptional rapidity, with which the older and weaker firms were supplanted in Germany by giants, was in great measure due to the influence of the coal and other cartels. For the mixed businesses, growing fast, and aiming at yet faster growth, were prepared to pay relatively high prices in order to secure increased "participations," or "quotas," from each cartel, with which they were connected, when a new division was arranged; so they bought up coal mines wherever possible; especially such as were already members of the Syndicate, in order to annex their participations[1].

Thus an artificial stimulus was given to that flow of capital into the steel industry which would in any case have resulted from the notoriety of the power of its newly acquired technique. Ambitious men did not wait for the gradual expansion of demand that was to be expected from improved conditions; but enlarged their plant quickly in order to be able to claim larger quotas later on. Meanwhile the "pure" coal mines found that, though the market for coal was expanding fast, and the cartel was rapidly extending its sales, they were prevented from producing any more than before; because of the rapid increase in the quotas assigned to giant mixed works. That increase went so far, that the cartel was compelled to force largely increased sales abroad, at prices below those at which it entered the coal in its own accounts; thus causing a deficit in the accounts, which had to be covered by what was in effect a levy on all the works, including those whose output was thus forcibly restricted.

Henceforward the centre of interest passes from the coal cartel to steel cartels. But the coal cartel has a solid position; and it may possibly continue to have great power of a character similar to that which it has now, when the problems of steel

[1] Their right to do this was sustained by the law courts: though the cartel had denied it. Each member of the cartel used to be allowed to increase his participation by 1000 tons for each additional shaft sunk: but in 1904 that privilege was withdrawn: so recourse was had to buying mines that were weakly held.

III, IX, 4. cartels, which have been changing rapidly during recent years, may perhaps be very different from those of to-day: for its dominion over a large area is secured by the heavy cost of bringing coal from a distance. But an extreme use of its partial monopolistic power would lead to increased encroachments on its province by brown coal, the uses of which have made recent technical progress; by coal from other German sources; and, near the Rhine, Elbe and Weser, and the shores of the Baltic and North Sea, by British coal. Also the State owns the railways, whose services are essential to the Syndicate; and as they are also chief purchasers of its products, the State has exercised a considerable influence over its policy. Thus the cartel, in spite of its strength, has not had much opportunity for offence: and it has not desired to offend.

4. *Causes that specially favoured the advance of giant businesses in German steel industries: phases of their cartellization.*

Thirty years ago Germany's output of steel was not very great; but now it exceeds that of Britain in about the same ratio as her population does; though in a considerably less ratio than does her area, and consequently than the demand for it by her railways, bridges, etc. This advance has been sometimes attributed in large measure to the beneficial influences of her cartels and her trade policy. It is in fact less than it seems at first sight. For, speaking generally, her exports of steel products are of much lower value per ton than those of Britain; a notable exception being in her exports of electrical plant. Her exports of steel manufactures are much less per head of the population than are those of Britain: and Britain's imports of machinery come mainly not from her but from America[1]. But such as it is the advance seems to be amply explained by four well-known

[1] Ships, among the highest grade products, are not counted in such statistics. Britain is the chief producer and the chief exporter of them. Germany imports more than three times as much of them as she exports: though her exports of steel include some sent by her to Holland to build vessels for German use. Those who advocate the Germanization of Britain's economic policies, habitually omit Britain's sales of ships; they compare the exports of the two countries as aggregates, and not per head of the population; and measure steel exports by weight and not by value; and thus obtain three illusory advantages in argument.

causes. The first is that superiority of German educational methods over British as a preparation for the work of modern business, of which much has already been said. The second is the fact that, while British supplies of ore have been rapidly dwindling and becoming more difficult of access, Germany obtained ever easier access to rich stores of iron ore in Lorraine, Luxemburg, and the adjacent territory of France[1]. The third is that these ores, though not well adapted to older methods of steel production, are eminently adapted to methods invented by the Englishman, Thomas. The abundant phosphorus in these ores, is now turned to account in the production of heat, and of power which is available for the purposes not only of smelting works themselves, but of any rolling mills and other "higher stage" steel works that are associated with them.

The direct effect of this economy in promoting the expansion of German steel industries has been generally recognized: but insufficient attention has been given to its indirect effect in accelerating the suppression of obsolete plants: and this is the fourth cause. The proportion of up-to-date to antiquated plants is always greatest in an energetic and rich country, which has but recently found its way to utilize large natural resources. Many of the British steel plants which were at work before the German steel industry became prominent, were in the hands of men who had inherited the material, but not the intellectual resources of those who had set them up: and family traditions hindered the infusion of energetic new blood.

In Germany, on the other hand, the control of steel businesses, partly because they were new, was mainly in the hands of men, who had been nurtured in frugal habits, and expected to work for eight or ten hours a day, and for three hundred days in the year, very much as had those who created the British steel industry two generations earlier. And the direction of new supplies was in the hands of energetic financiers, some of whom were eminently endowed with the high Semitic faculty of going straight to the roots of large business problems.

[1] Of the iron ore production of the German Zollverein in 1911 nearly 18 million came from Alsace Lorraine, and 6 million from Luxemburg; but only 6 million from Old Germany.

III, IX, 4. The German banks have surpassed even those of America in the promptitude and energy with which they faced the risks of turning a large flow of capital into an enterprise, before men of less keen intellect had discovered that it is one of those to which the future belongs. The influence of the banks, acting partly in concert with cartels, has favoured giant businesses in the steel industry: and the supersession of small businesses by large has brought more economy and less indirect harm in the heavy steel industry than in any other, except that of transport.

We have seen how the coal cartel ultimately became the ally, or rather the servant of the strong; though its policy was always moderate and free from harshness: but the first great cartel in the steel industry, that for heavy "half finished" products—the *Halbzeug-Verband*—showed little mercy to pure rolling mills and other works that needed those products: and the "higher" cartels, which these mills formed among themselves, were even harsher in their treatment of makers of the still lighter steel goods who bought their products. In each stage of production men rejoiced that a cartel helped them to raise their prices against the home consumer, but each group craved a freer market in which to buy its material. The smelting furnaces could buy nearly everything that they needed, except coal, without any artificial rise in its price; and could sell at prices raised both by protective taxes and cartel manipulation. But other works, confined to a single stage or perhaps to two or three, had to strive on the one hand, to prevent tarif and cartel from pressing heavily against them when buying; and on the other, to get as much help as possible from tarif and cartel in their endeavour to sell at good prices in the home market. Complaints that the export prices of rails, girders etc. were lower than prices charged at home for the blocks from which they were made, were among the causes which prompted Professor Wagner in the official debate on cartels to suggest that "if the whole industry is gripped by cartels, trusts and giant businesses, then arises the final claim that the whole be nationalized[1]."

[1] *Kontradiktorische Verhandlungen*, vol. III. p. 425. Wagner implied that this condition was already reached in America: but, as has been noted above,

It is admitted that German financiers are prompt to support industries that have great capacity for profitable development; and that this enrichment of the wealthy enables them to offer better employment to industrial and domestic workers than they otherwise could: but the chief advantages of German methods can be obtained without losing those of British methods.

5. *The Steelworks Union is a "general" cartel, designed to harmonize the interests of the various stages of the steel industry, in regard to production and marketing, and to the bounty conferred by the Protective tarif.*

It is obvious that there are many secondary functions of cartels (such as the promotion of technical studies, the organization of appropriate information as to distant markets, the collecting of debts under certain conditions) which can be more economically, if not more efficiently performed by a single powerful cartel representing many branches of a great industry, than by several cartels, each working for only one branch. But at present we are concerned chiefly with the two dominant aims of a cartel—that of maintaining prices at fully remunerative levels; and that of mitigating the sharpness of price-fluctuations in regard to the particular products for which the cartel is responsible. We have now to consider the difficulties which arise in the relations between a cartel in a single stage of an industry, and cartels or individual producers in other stages. Suppose that the price of a finished product is falling rapidly

Congress is caring for the interests of small men: and practices making for monopoly, which are common in Germany, are forbidden in America. Two days were given to the Halbzeug-Verband; and one day was occupied by a bitter controversy between the manufacturers of wire nails and the cartel, which supplied the rods used in making them. Consul Oppenheimer (*Report* for 1902, pp. 26—7) says that the cartel of wire nail manufacturers made in six months a profit of £60,000 in the home market, and suffered a loss of £43,000 in the foreign market: and it was strengthened in this oppression of the home consumer by an agreement with the wire rod cartel to supply no material to a manufacturer of tacks who did not belong to his own cartel. Cartels fight cartels: but they can make common cause against the helpless home consumer.

As to the export prices of girders etc. in comparison with the home prices of the blocks from which they were made, see Heymann, *Die gemischten Werke im Deutschen Grosseisenindustrie*, 1904, p. 215.

III, IX, 5. through the action of general causes, over which local cartels have little control: then a cartel, which hinders the fall in prices of any raw or half-finished material needed for that product, increases thereby the loss, which the fall of the price of the finished product inflicts on its producers. Therefore this action of a cartel in any one stage of a large industry tends to be injurious to producers in later, or so-called "higher" stages: and the conflict between them commonly results in the formation of cartels in those higher stages. The stronger position in such a conflict is occasionally that of the higher stage cartel: but if, as often happens, the lower stage cartel controls some material whose sources of supply are limited, it is the master. Innumerable conflicts of this kind have been waged in Germany and elsewhere, without seeming to point to any general conclusion.

But in recent years Nature, in association with human counsels, has gone a long way towards two kindred and yet partially opposed solutions of the difficulty in those industries in which the trouble was greatest. The first remedy is a breaking away from cartel influence by powerful capitalists: they find their advantage in working through several stages of a great industry, so that each department of a large business gets its material from a lower stage department of the same business, without any external interference as to the price at which the material is entered: these huge "mixed" businesses tend to ignore and frustrate the efforts of single stage cartels.

A second remedy in the form of a "general" cartel, which should embrace all classes of steel works except the very finest, had long been discussed as the ideal solution. The difficulties in its way were very great. Perhaps no combination of patience and organizing genius less than that of Germany could have overcome them even partially: but the need was pressing in order to allay home discords: and Germany was characteristically eager to organize a military array that might speak in the gate on even terms with the United States Steel Corporation. So, a scheme was ultimately developed, which went far towards realizing this ideal aim. It was found impossible to control under a single rule the higher, finer and more various stages of the industry. But nearly all the "heavy" steel works of Western Germany came together in 1904 to form a "Steelworks

Union," which should completely control the output and marketing of their simplest ("A") heavy steel products; and should control the output of those next in order (the "B" products)[1].

Such a federation has advantages over a trust, in that it leaves freedom of internal administration to the individual works: but it is less efficient technically. For as Herr Jutzi says, a trust "can arrange division of labour in every detail: it can diminish or estop one establishment whose condition is unfavourable, and enlarge another to make up: and it can produce the goods in demand in those places which are most suitable for the purpose, account being taken of geographical, technical and business conditions." But if a Syndicate goes far in such directions, it rouses internal discord; and charges of favouritism and interested motives are brought against its management[2].

[1] The reasons for going so far, and no further, are thus set out in the answers given by the Union to interrogatories of the Ministry of the Interior, and published in the *Kontradiktorische Verhandlungen*, vol. IV. pp. 500—560. It is able to control marketing as well as output for "A" products (including not only blooms, blocks etc., but also rails, girders, sleepers etc.) because they come only from a small number of great mixed works "whose financial and technical conditions are much alike." It has also controlled the output of "B" goods, on which a little further work has been expended, such as sheets, railway axles, wheels etc., though its few attempts to conduct their marketing have not prospered, and therefore its direct influence over them does not reach very far. If it did not control their output, its mastery of A products would be weakened: for "as most of the associated works produce them also, they would have been able to devote themselves to making B products in case of a decline in the market for A products: and thus to invite over-production and increase depression of prices." It endeavours "so to arrange its prices that they will return suitable (*angemessene*) profits to its members (*seinen Werken*); but so that its customers shall not be injured and rendered incapable of continuing work." Having referred to the fact that the peculiar character of the iron ores, to which Westphalia had access, had caused a sudden and excessive influx of capital which had caused violent fluctuations, it stated that "it opposes a broadening of the range, or an increase in the size of the businesses during the period for which its contract runs...and it strives for the greatest possible simplification of the work done by the individual steel-works owner." It appears not to have succeeded in the first of these two aims. But its efforts towards the second constitute its chief claim to contribute to the technical economy and efficiency of the steel industry. They have not however reached very far: and the *Kartell-Rundschau*, 1910, p. 638, quoted by Dr Tosdal in the *Quarterly Journal of Economics*, Feb. 1917, says that the partial utilization of equipment remains as before.

[2] See *Die deutsche Montanindustrie auf dem Wege zum Trust* by W. Jutzi, leitender Handelsredakteur der *Kölnischen Zeitung*, 1905, p. 43.

III, IX, 5. It allows a customer to specify, as far as is practicable, any particular brand that he prefers; and the higher price, which is conceded to a brand that is in great demand, is said to act as a stimulus to improvement in quality. Of course the stimulus to economy and efficiency in administration is little impaired by the discipline of the Union; but a new trade-mark cannot easily attract attention, when overshadowed by it. Its own direct marketing costs are of course very low: the A products of every country are marketed cheaply, because they are standardized and sold in large quantities. But there are numerous minor cartels and dealers' unions below it, each of which has its own expenses and charges. The Union has a seat, without a vote, in each dealers' union with which it is associated; and it reserves the right to veto the wholesale prices set by such an association[1].

Meanwhile there has been a continued increase in the fusions among coal mines, among steel works, and among businesses that own both. It seems that in 1910 two-thirds of the whole Westphalian output of coal was controlled by ten fusions, which also controlled nearly one-half of the production of the Steel-Union[2].

The Union does not confine its action to mere regulation of output and prices. It has also some constructive cooperative functions: it takes part in organizing international exhibitions, and it obtains information as to foreign markets pertinent to the industry. It is also a convenient centre for arrangements, such as those, under which the many different shapes and sizes of plates required for ship-building are distributed among various firms; so that each can find fairly steady employment for a limited number of rolls.

But complaints are made that it is too heavy a body to move quickly. Its great weight increases the anxiety which is felt on each occasion when its contracts come for renewal; for doubts then arise as to the willingness of the great mixed businesses,

[1] "The wholesalers also assign to each retailer his definitely prescribed territory; so that from the Syndicate to the consumer competition has been practically eliminated." See *Report of the Federal Trade Commission on Cooperation in American Export Trade*, 1916, p. 13. It includes a number of instructive answers from American Consuls in various countries as to cartels, etc.

[2] Dawson, *Industrial Germany*, p. 95.

which are its masters, to be content with their already large privileges. If it fails, the structure of the German associated coal, iron and steel industries will probably approach very near to that of the American[1].

There seems to be no certainty as to its length of life. But during the war, in 1915, when there was considerable anxiety as to its renewal, a project was launched for a yet mightier *Stahlbund*, which was to extend its control to stages higher even than B goods.

Before leaving the Steelworks Union a little may be said about its efforts so to adjust prices for the various stages of production, that each branch of the steel industry may have a fair portion of the bounty, which the Protective tarif allots to steel producers at the cost of German steel consumers, and in a less degree of other German industries that produce largely for export. This practice is the chief instance of a policy that seems to be just in principle; and it is well executed.

It is clear that, if any steel manufacturer buys his material at a price, which the cartel controlling that material has set higher for home than for export, he is likely to have difficulty when competing in foreign markets with others who have bought similar material, whether of German origin or not, at lower prices. A great part of the time of the Kartell-Enquête was occupied with complaints that German manufacturers of tinplates and of wire were driven out of neutral markets by British manufacturers, who obtained their material from Germany for ten shillings a ton less than was charged to themselves. The steel cartels were specially harsh in such matters; for they

[1] The *Report of the Federal Commission* already quoted contains (Part II, p. 16) an observation from the American Consul at Berlin, which may perhaps contain a touch of irony:—"The introduction of reinforced concrete came at the time of increasing building activity: the cement trust took advantage of it...and practically captured the entire building construction market and bridge work by substituting concrete at a much lower figure than steel girders could be purchased from the Verband. About two years too late, the Verband opened an office for competition against the concrete firms and reduced prices. If this had been done sooner, the triumphant entry of concrete construction might have been retarded for some years." That is to say, its lethargy alone prevented it from inflicting a grievous injury on the public in the interest of the steel industry.

III, IX, 5. had long before obtained redress from the coal cartel, for the smaller hardship that they were compelled to pay more for (German) coal than foreign competitors, who also used German coal. The coal cartel faced this difficulty, recognizing that the export of products, in making which coal had been consumed, obtained a vent for German coal as surely as if it had been sold abroad by aid of a special export price. Steel works which bought their coal paid in the first instance the full home price for it: some of the steel was sold at home, some abroad. The coal cartel wished them to have the coal used for the exported steel cheaply: and so it returned them a "refund" on a percentage of their coal, equal to the percentage of their product which they exported[1].

But some steel cartels were slow in giving similar refunds to those who used their products in higher stage work for export: and even when that practice had become general, it was carried out with little system and much friction, till the Steelworks Union took the matter in hand. It made great improvements: but even as late as 1908, German manufacturers, tendering for a gasometer to be built at Copenhagen, were undersold by British competitors making use of German steel obtained at low export prices: so the Union changed its policy. It no longer made uniform reductions on the export of any one class of steel to all countries: but kept those reductions small for exports to Britain and Belgium; while keeping them large for countries which do not generally export steel goods[2].

[1] Herr C. Kirdorf on behalf of the Coal Syndicate protests against the common use of the term "bounty" to describe what is merely a drawback or rebate—*Ruckvergütung* or *Nachlass* (*Schriften des Social-Vereins*, No. 116, p. 282). The Protective duty gives a bounty to the German producer at the cost of all German users: when that share of the cost is returned to a German user for exportation, it only leaves him where he would have been, if no bounty had been given to the producer of coal from whom he bought.

[2] For this purpose the Union insisted that no export price should be quoted by any authority other than itself: thus greatly increasing at once its own labours, its own authority, and the difficulty of producers in conducting export trade. This worked so badly that in 1909 the Centre party in the Reichstag proposed a law, to the effect that pure rolling mills etc. which exported part of their produce, should be granted certificates for the duty-free import of such raw material as was represented in their exported goods. But this, like the rather earlier petition of pure rolling mills for a general remission of the

The steel industry has pioneered the cartel organization of numerous varieties of manufactured products, far in advance of other industries: and it is the main representative of that task. But it contains only a small part of the associations which pursue (under various names) policies more or less akin to that of the Steelworks Union and its subsidiary cartels. Many of them find great difficulty in arranging modifications of their standard prices to meet the variations in the qualities, sizes, or shapes of similar products coming from different sources: but perseverance and ingenuity have conquered in a notable manner. In the case of one set of goods produced by artistic specialists, an expert appraiser was called in to set the price on each article.

duties on raw iron, scrap iron, and half-finished goods, came to nought. (See Sir F. Oppenheimer's *Report*, 1909, pp. 119 and 117.)

The suggestion of the Centre party was on the same lines as the existing fiscal rule, under which the exporter of grain receives a permit to import a corresponding quantity of grain duty-free. That rule has indeed been much abused; partly in consequence of the permits being transferable, and available for grains at frontiers other than those at which the exports, that gave rise to them, left the country. But this does not seem to have been the ground on which the Centre party's suggestion was opposed.

CHAPTER X

TRUSTS AND CARTELS: GERMAN EXPERIENCE, CONTINUED

III, x, 1. 1. ***Monopolistic tendencies of some German giant businesses in association with cartels and banks.***

A partial solidification of the various branches of the American steel industry was initiated by the foundation of the United States Steel Corporation: but it has been broadened by the interpermeation of financial interests with those of the steel industry. The chief financial powers in America have indeed had their origin in industry and trade, but more especially in industry, during the memory of living men; and American industrialists for the present control finance, perhaps as much as they are controlled by it.

But Germany, though younger than Britain, is older than America in this respect: and the rise of some German industrialists to a high place in the ranks of finance has gone together with an ever closer interweaving of broad financial counsels in the control of particular industrial interests. In both countries the cooperation of financiers and industrialists of wide experience and far reaching faculty has led to the development of policies, each of which aims at making for the larger and more permanent interests of those on whose behalf it is contrived; and with no further hurt to the rest of the people than seems to be involved in a well-ordered pursuit of that particular aim. This limitation is indeed of considerable importance from the point of view of the student of social well-being: but it may stand over for the present.

Fortune is said to favour great legions. Perhaps the reason is that a strong army, well led, will recover from the effects of ill fortunes, and forget them; while good fortune is likely to bring its success to a climax, and thus become prominent. A weak army, weakly led, makes little use of good fortune: and ill fortune, which may probably have accompanied its final disaster, is not overlooked by the historian. Similarly the powers of finance everywhere help a strong business to rise to great undertakings; while they are shy of assistance to a weak business, when in distress. In Germany the connection between business success and financial aid is especially close, as we saw when discussing the financial basis of business organization (above, II, IX, 4): and banks are alert and forward in associating themselves with the strongest industrial enterprises. Thus it has come to pass naturally that a large majority of the great German banks have been interested in the Steelworks Union; while a few have sided with the pure rolling mills[1].

Each of the great banks has representatives on several other banks and on a vast number of industrial enterprises. For instance the main purpose of Georg von Siemens, the founder of the Deutscher Bank, was to "foster and facilitate commercial relations between Germany and other countries[2]." Accordingly it took a leading part in fusing industrial and banking interests: and in the hands of Herr von Gwinner, it developed the practice of inviting leading industrialists to its councils; though indeed they do not exercise much influence on banking policy. But representatives of banks have exercised, for two generations at least, a strong control on industrial businesses which they support: and they "have always taken special care...to provide for the disposal of the products of the industrial companies in question to suitable industrial enterprises on which the banks were able to exercise some influence[3]."

[1] This statement by Riesser, *l.c.* p. 179, is representative of the "connection of the German great banks and their concentration" with "the economic development of Germany"; to quote from his title page. For instance, when the management of the great Phoenix steel works hesitated to join the Union, the powerful Schaaffhausen'scher Bank, which had taken a great part in founding that and other important steel works, compelled it to enter the Union (*ib.* p. 516).

[2] Details of its plans are given by Riesser, *l.c.* pp. 420—440 and 472—481: similar statements in regard to other great banks are also given by him.

[3] Riesser, p. 375. He gives (pp. 897—920) details of some six or seven hundred representatives of important joint stock companies who have seats on

III, x, 1. These tendencies have very little kinship with cartellization: they correspond rather to a strain of character which is specially American; though they are developed with an intricacy of detail, which is appropriate to the German temper, with its faculty for quiet mental activity throughout long hours. And indeed we see here yet another reason for thinking that German tendencies towards cartellization are likely to yield place to those that are more distinctively American, as regards the larger affairs of industry and trade; though the activities of relatively small cartels in particular branches of industry and marketing show no signs of weakening[1].

The steel industries are a unique group; because practically the whole of the plant, as well as the material of every steel business, consists of steel products: and it is not probable that any other group of industries will exemplify as large and coherent an illustration of semi-monopolistic cartel organization as it has already done. Perhaps the woollen (and worsted) industry, and the cotton industry come next to it in width of range. In 1913 there were 55 textile cartels in Germany. Not much progress had been made by attempts to weld them into broad groups; but plans had been proposed for "the formation of a central national organization for the whole German textile industry, including trade associations as well as cartels...and for the organization of a special credit institution for the textile industry, similar to the German agricultural banks[2]."

one or other of the great German banks. And the Federal Commission, *l.c.* Part I, p. 62, presents in a great chart the direct and indirect connection of the Deutscher Bank with German and foreign concerns, many of which are dominating factors in important cartels.

[1] See Riesser's account of the influences of capitalistic concentration in the mining and metallurgical industries (*l.c.* pp. 725—749): he gives special attention to the widely ramified interests of the great iron and coal magnates, Herr Thyssen and Herr Stinnes.

The interpermeation of the interests of German banks is shown by his lists (pp. 642—6) of the banks which constitute the five great groups, each of which is led by one of the great Berlin banks; the Deutscher Bank being at the head. Their total capital (including surplus) was over a hundred million pounds in 1908. These tendencies seem to have been strengthened, temporarily at least, during the world-war; but it would be premature to express any opinion on the solidity of the new strength.

[2] *Report of the Federal Trade Commission on Cooperation in the American Export Trade*, Part I, p. 260, based on statements in the *Kartell-Rundschau* 1909, and 1915.

2. *The tendency of some of those industries, which embody the best results of German genius, to domination by a few giant businesses, with mutual understandings, while avoiding formal cartellization.* III, x, 2.

This tendency to domination by one or two giant firms is of course most clearly marked in those industries which embody the chief triumphs of the German creative genius; notably the electrical and the chemical industries. In 1900 the electrical industry was led by Siemens and Halske, and by the General Electrical Company (known now throughout the world as "A. E. G.," these being the initials of its German name): but beside these two there were twenty-six others of some importance. The twenty-eight companies were clustered in seven groups, supported by seventy banks. But fusions and communities of interests proceeded apace: and now the two leading concerns hold four-fifths of the electrical business of Germany in their own hands. Also they frequently obtain controlling interests in electric lighting and power works; which are their chief customers. The two act in concert on many occasions, especially in external trade: thus they have organized a special bank (Elektro-Treuband) for financing electrical undertakings. In 1912 the Siemens group gained financial control of the Bergmann Electrical Co.; but preserved its independent form, and claimed to allow it autonomy, on the ground that the health of the entire German electrical industry depends upon sharp competition among two or three large concerns, which encourages invention, and develops technical and commercial organization in the competing plants[1].

The German dyestuff industries again are too confident in

[1] This statement is derived from the *Report of the Federal Commission, l.c.* Part I, p. 278. It gives a chart representing many scores of connections of the A. E. G., through its leading officers and members of its Board. The Siemens group does not lag far behind.

These industries have the advantages of making standardized products that are required by the hundred thousand, or even million. Their plant is expensive; but it works for the greater part cheaply, when once set up. Thus only powerful capitalists can compete: and as failure by any product to work well might occasion much inconvenience, purchasers are apt to require well-known trademarks. These technical advantages enforce the suggestions made by representatives of the giant businesses on the direction of electricity-using companies street railways etc. in favour of those businesses.

III, x, 3. their magnificent technical mastery to care much for cartel organization. Every business has had its own patents and its own secrets; and the strongest have clustered together mainly in two groups, the Badische, and the Höchst-Casella[1].

Another great instance of the German tendency towards trusts is the growth of the German Metal Buying Combination. It had its origin in the London firm of Merton, in association with some members of the Cohen family. As it progressed, its headquarters were transferred to Frankfort: and its world-wide associations before the war constituted a most powerful community of interests[2].

3. *The increasing responsibilities of cartels to their several industries, and to labour.*

It would be unreasonable to lay much stress on the fact that the two great industries, in which German leadership is most conspicuous, owe little or nothing to the methods of cartellization. Those methods may possibly be beneficial to ordinary industries, and yet unsuitable to those that are exceptionally strong: systematic instruction is not shown to be misdirected by the fact that it is likely to hinder rather than help a pupil of genius: he goes best by his own way.

Nor should great importance be attached to the extravagant and even suicidal policies, that have been occasionally adopted by inexperienced cartels, which have generally worked on a

[1] *The Board of Trade Journal*, July 4, 1918, gave some details of this process. At that time nearly all the products of the chief businesses in the chemical industry were pooled: but a few specialities were reserved, temporarily at least, by individual firms. The dividends had recently averaged about 20 per cent.; and much capital had been written off. The Chairman of the Bradford Dyers' Association said early in the year that "the German colour and chemical works, and many auxiliary businesses are now embraced in one huge organization, with a working capital approaching £m.50"; while a good deal more is being obtained. The German Government assisted, of course with a view to military exigencies.

[2] The Imperial War Conference, in a *Report* [Cd. 9177] issued in October, 1918, gave an account of recent developments of the Frankfort Metallbank and Metallurgische Gesellschaft. It attributed their prodigious power partly to subtle financial intrigues; and partly to "the high development of scientific training and industrial research in Germany"; and recommended that certain measures, partly temporary, should be taken by which German control over the non-ferrous metallic reserves of the empire should be restrained.

small scale. An increase in the volume and the complexity of those affairs, for which a cartel is responsible, intensifies the gravity of the issues to be decided at meetings of the Council; and increases therefore the inclination of the larger capitalists to give time and thought to controlling the meetings. The Council of a mighty Syndicate generally bring to bear powerful minds, a fine sense of proportion and a wide purview: and they have access to inside information as to many branches of industry and trade. Their characters incline them to prefer large deferred gains to the smaller immediate advantages, at which weaker men grasp: and their large command over capital makes it easy to follow a waiting policy.

But yet it is doubtful whether the weight of the task to which they are committed will not increase faster than their strength, fast as that grows. The Westphalian Coal Syndicate and the Steelworks Syndicate have already taken powers to handle and convey coal and iron respectively, and thus they may probably soon be considerable employers of labour; while the Coal Syndicate, if it acts on its new power of purchasing coal mines, will have taken a long step towards becoming a trust. Again, the Steelworks Union, and some syndicates, which are responsible for marketing several kinds of products, have been compelled to prescribe the kind which individual firms must produce, whenever it happens that demands for the different kinds are moving unevenly. Again the assignment of their total contingents to the several members, when a fixed rule would give no good result, forces the leaders to take on themselves some of the responsibilities of collective ownership. Thus new difficulties grow at least as fast as old difficulties are overcome: and the tendency of some cartels to attain monopolistic power was becoming more prominent before the war. It is notable that much assent was given at the Enquête to Professor Brentano's exclamation: "if we are to have a monopoly, we should at all events prefer it to be a State-monopoly[1]."

[1] *Kontradiktorische Verhandlungen*, IV. 233 and 245. Another trouble is instanced by the complaint of some vigorous young members of the Cement cartel that, if they had been allowed to push their own brands, they would have obtained a strong hold on the market; but, under cartel management, consumers do not become familiar with their brands. Therefore any apportionment of contingents based on the special requests made for their brands is unfair: and

III, x, 3. Meanwhile there is some sort of an understanding that the weaker firms will not be entirely suppressed. The leaders state indeed, with unquestioned sincerity, that they do not make it their policy to put prices so high as to enable ill-managed firms to survive: but they are not altogether free agents in the matter.

During the war there has of course been no disposition to disturb existing arrangements: but not long ago there were many rumours of internal conflicts, which seemed to threaten the lives of the Coal and Steel Syndicates; their place being taken by "a vast trust, arranged by the few leading concerns of the mixed type; which would thus end by being Americanized, after a process of evolution through an essentially German system of syndication[1]."

"Labour" was not able to speak for itself at the official Inquiry into Cartels: but in 1905 two memorable meetings were held of the great German association for social studies (*Verein für Socialpolitik*). The first, opened by Professor Brentano, was on "the condition of labour in private giant businesses": the second, opened by Professor Schmoller, was on "the relation of the cartels to the State." Prof. Brentano contended that, as the law does not recognize collective agree-

if, on the other hand, the contingents are proportioned to the potential output of the firms, a premium is given to the creation of superfluous plant, followed by neglect in its management.

[1] Oppenheimer's *Report*, 1910, p. 157. In his last Report (1914, p. 11) he indicates clearly the inherent tendency of Syndication combined with a Protective tarif, to promote disastrous fluctuations of output and prices, in spite of a genuine endeavour to diminish them. Thus during a slump in an industry, a feeling grows that a Syndicate is needed to take charge: and that often causes reckless extensions, in order to justify high figures of participation. The same desire induced some makers of drawn wire, during a recent boom, "in their anxiety to be able to show a large *clientèle*, to sell their manufactured articles even below the cost of their raw material (rolled wire); as was expected, a syndicate of drawn wire is now (June, 1914) being actively negotiated. But even syndicates already in existence are often powerless to prevent their members from engaging upon such boom extensions, though everybody knows that no syndicate is started without demands for fantastic figures of participation: they can levy a fine upon over-production (and during a boom such a fine is gladly paid), but sometimes the industrial constellation forces their hands: they encourage extensions by taking an indemnified delivery of the over-production." He gives recent instances of such action by the Coal and the Raw Iron Syndicate: and explains in some detail its evil results.

ments by operatives, the giant business stands as a unit against an unorganized crowd of individuals; and "the conditions of work are settled by the one-sided decision of the employer." Another speaker enlarged this argument by referring to the informal increase of the autocratic power, which resulted when the giants acted as a unit in a cartel: the great coal cartel was already urged to put a stop to "that competition of employers of labour which results in the pushing up of wages" (In-die-Höhe-treiben der Löhne).

It was argued that, if a single business has a quarrel with its employees, it can generally arrange that the work, which would have been allotted to it, shall be taken over by another member of the cartel; while the contingent of the first is made up, in some measure at least, at a later date. It was also urged that the power of employers, thus concentrated by cartel organization, tends to render the ordinary strike ineffective: the workers are therefore forced to look more and more to political action, associated with "demonstration-strikes" for a mitigation of their evils.

Much stress had been laid during the official debate on the statement that cartels exercise no *direct* influence on rates of wages: but it is obvious that their meetings facilitate organized strategical policy in wage conflicts. And, when Herr Kirdorf, the head of the Coal Syndicate, repeated that statement during the Social-Verein's debate on Prof. Schmoller's motion, the answer of labour came promptly that a recent meeting of the Council of that Syndicate "was closely followed by a nearly uniform reduction of wages throughout its district[1]."

[1] See *Schriften des Vereins für Socialpolitik*, No. 116 (A.D. 1906), pp. 135—150, 169, 187, 411. A miners' representative (*ib.* p. 192) referred to a recent strike as partially successful: but later on, in the debate on Prof. Schmoller's initiative, he added (*ib.* p. 412) that the operatives had less chance of success in combat with a cartel than with a giant business. It is urged as a ground for confidence as to the future relations between cartels and labour, that the position of the operative has improved more on the average in those industries, in which cartels are prominent, than in others: but this is not a secure ground. For the most prominent cartels are naturally in industries, which the genius of the German people and their special advantages have enlarged and made prosperous. Making high profits, the employers can afford to pay high wages. As they use advanced labour-saving machinery, which

III, x, 4.

4. *Functions of the State in relation to cartels.*

The German Government has persistently upheld the right of businesses to combine with one another at their will, even though their tendencies be clearly monopolistic: but it has also held itself bound to intervene, when necessary, in order to prevent the power thus obtained from being used to the detriment of the public. It has twice made approaches to the coal industry with the purpose of influencing the policy of the Westphalian Coal Syndicate: and many writers advocate a vigorous extension of State ownership of coal mines. But mine-owners affirm that those, which it possesses, are badly managed; and miners declare that its mines are bad employers of labour[1].

In spite of recent geographical and scientific discoveries, Prussia's deposits of potash constitute an important partial monopoly. If they were owned by a single company, with sole regard to its own profit, the price would probably be set so much above cost of production as to yield a huge monopoly

often represents a value of several hundred pounds per employee, it is worth their while to pay wages high enough to attract the most highly skilled and resourceful artisans for the more responsible posts; and indeed for such work the most highly paid labour is generally the cheapest. Even their unskilled labour must often be well paid, though for another reason: for these growing industries demand more labour than the neighbourhood can supply, and recruits have to be attracted from great distances. But still they pay wages much below those prevailing in Britain.

[1] In 1904 the Prussian Government set the Dresdener Bank to buy secretly for it a controlling majority of the shares of the great Hibernia coal mine: but, suspicion having been aroused, other great banks manœuvred in various ways (which were upheld by the Supreme Court on appeal), to prevent this; and the Government was left with a large minority holding of the shares. It owns many mines in the Saar district: and later on it endeavoured in vain to use this as a lever for entering the Westphalian Coal Syndicate with a large voting power. Herr Gothein, an active member of the Kartellen-Enquête, a mine-owner, and a leading authority on the general conditions of Germany, argues (*Die Verstaatlichung des Kohlenbergbaues*, 1905) that State ownership is impracticable; though it would rescue the country from great dangers, if ideally managed. On another side, Dr Kollmann gives a brilliant picture of an ideal *Deutscher Stahlwerksverband* which might organize the whole of the industry, and become a national organ for research.

But employees are likely to pay more attention to such stories as that recorded by *The Economist* (21 May, 1910) of a lock-out in the German building trade; which lasted so long that some employers abandoned it: whereon the Stahlwerksverband was invoked to bring them to order by refusing to supply them with girders, etc. They were thus forced to continue the lock-out.

revenue, at the expense of stinting German agriculture's supply of a much needed fertilizer. Private owners tend to exercise their influence in the cartel in that direction: but, partly by legislation, and partly by means of its large holdings of the deposit, the Government compels the price for domestic sales to be kept rather low; while leaving the cartel free to put the price for exportation where it will. In this single case a cartel's export price is above its home price[1].

Again, shipping on the Rhine and other inland waters has been threatened with a general syndicalization; partly under the influence of coal and steel magnates, who already have large fleets: so the three Governments of Prussia, Baden and Bavaria have obtained controlling interests in such shipping.

Nowhere, and certainly not in Germany, is there any doubt as to the high public services which trade organizations can render to the moral and material well-being of their members and of the general public: and Schmoller, in his opening address, recently mentioned, said that Germans rejoice in their development of the principles of association (*Genossenschaft*); they are therefore proud of their cartels; and yet prouder of the great men who founded them:—men who "had the widest outlook, the highest persistence and invention; and also the greatest tact and commonsense....The best of them were not mere money-makers: but on a level with the best generals and statesmen in talent, in character, and in achievement." But nevertheless the conclusions, for which his long address prepared the way, are not altogether favourable to cartels. "The setting up of cartels implies a revolution of the constitution of German economy. The raising of prices in many directions injures all consumers, all not cartellized industries." For these and other reasons he developed a plan by which the whole affairs of the cartels would be within the knowledge of a department of the State. The State should intervene to prevent unfair prices, with special reference to export prices: and it should override decisions which excluded or which punished

[1] The cartel has done good work in explaining to agriculturalists the uses of potash: but it has difficulties with some of its weaker members. Its story is well told by Dr Tosdal in the *Quarterly Journal of Economics*, Nov. 1913. See also Dawson, *Industrial Germany*, pp. 124—7.

III, x, 4. members harshly. It should compel the adoption of "compromises between organized sellers and buyers. This holds especially for settlements of the rates of wages[1]."

German opinion seems inclined to advocate publicity as a hurt-less remedy for social hurts. But it is content with general profession: it lacks concentrated resolution and insistence. It seems to appreciate, even less than British public opinion does, the urgency of that class of questions which the American Bureau of Corporations, matured as the Federal Commission, has pursued with untiring energy. It has not yet learnt that though monopolistic powers in certain directions are necessary results of modern conditions, they are apt to cause grave evils unless controlled: while for obtaining effective control, even autocratic power is of little use, unless based on organized, long continued, authoritative studies.

The Kartellen-Enquête was a unique concession by the Government to a growing feeling of anxiety that giant businesses would master cartels, and thereby master the State, unless the State awoke to the dangers and difficulties of the situation. But, as we have seen, it was brought to an abrupt and unsatisfactory conclusion; which was thought to be partly caused by unwillingness on the part of the Syndicates to respond to questions which penetrated below the thin stratum of official inquiries. So long as the general opinion of a great people acquiesced quietly in such subordination of public to private interests, its example could not afford good guidance. There are strong reasons for thinking that the exploiting of the masses of the people by the dominant classes, through the agency of cartels, made an important contribution to the discontent which broke into violence after the war.

[1] *Schriften des Vereins für Socialpolitik*, No. 116, pp. 254, 270, 271, and 431.

CHAPTER XI

AGGREGATION, FEDERATION, AND COOPERATION IN BRITAIN'S INDUSTRY AND TRADE

1. *Introductory: a glance backwards.*

III, XI, 1.

Several excellent accounts have recently appeared of aggregations and federations in British industry and trade: and, partly for that reason, no details in regard to them will be given here, except by way of illustration[1]. The purpose of this and the following chapters is to apply the instruction, which seems to be afforded by recent experiences, especially in America and Germany, to problems of Britain's present and near future: and to suggest that the strong individuality of the British race may find its highest development under the guidance of the spirit of constructive cooperation. It is true that giant businesses alone are capable of some of the chief tasks of industry in the present age. But, where their presence is not demanded by technical considerations, the immediate increase of strength, which would

[1] It may suffice to name (1) Macgregor, *Industrial Combination*, 1906; (2) Macrosty, *The trust movement in British industries*, 1907; (most of the businesses described in it however have had no considerable monopolistic tendencies; and belong to the class which are described in the present work merely as "giant businesses"); (3) Levy, *Monopoly and Competition, a study in English industrial organization*: a careful piece of work published in Germany in 1909; English translation, 1911; (4) Carter, *The tendency towards industrial combination*, 1913, a reasoned record of facts reaching nearly up to the world-war. The American Industrial Commission had published in 1901 a good short account of "Industrial Combinations in England" in its Report, vol. XVIII. pp. 1—74.

The history of British giant businesses generally, as well as of distinctly monopolistic aggregations and federations (so far as they desire to take the public into their confidence) can be read from year to year in the spacious records of their proceedings, which they cause to be inserted at high charges in appropriate journals: files of *The Economist* are specially helpful in this matter.

An excellent terse survey of aggregations and federations in British Industry is given in the *Report on Cooperation in the American Export Trade* by the Federal Trade Commission, 1916, vol. I., especially p. 88.

III, XI, 1. result from a rapid enlargement of their sway, might be purchased at too great a price: the value of that free individuality, which has made Britain great, is apt to be underrated in a hasty view. All praise must be given to the constructive work of German cartels: but it can be dissociated from their restrictive and militant policies. "Cooperation" in the special use of the term, which is familiar to British workmen, is but one outcome of that fortitude in purpose, tempered by the spirit of good fellowship, which has spread the British race over a great part of the world: constructive cooperation in the larger affairs of industry and trade is both required and facilitated by the character of Britain's industries and her geographical configuration.

Before looking forward, let us take a glance backwards. We have seen that monopolies of early times were seldom without plausible motive, and often did excellent work in their youth: but they were apt to outlive the strength and high purpose of their founders, and to become obstructive as well as incompetent in their old age. Moreover the Tudors granted them recklessly to eager courtiers; and thus was set on foot that intense hatred of monopoly among England's people, which was destined to exercise a great influence on her later history. Hatred was mingled with contempt in the eighteenth century; when the great Joint Stock and Registered Companies, which had done good service in the past, became for the greater part inert, effete, and even corrupt. In the first quarter of the nineteenth century the very unwise and rather selfish use, which British landlords made of their monopolistic control of Parliament to raise their own rents at the expense of the food of the people, intensified this hatred of monopoly still further. And lastly the advantages, which a country may derive from perfect freedom of enterprise in industry and in trade were emphasized, and even exaggerated, by observation of the vast increase of the country's economic strength in the second and third quarters of the century, when Protective duties were gradually abolished.

During much of this time business was chiefly in the hands of self-sufficing, self-made men; who were often crude, but always vigorous. They worked harder than any other set of business men in the world; and their superiority in strength over competitors was continually increased by their growing command of the economies of production on a scale that was relatively large then, though small in comparison with that which prevails now. England's flocks of sheep had contributed to set up her woollen industries by aid of an automatic organization of industries and trades, more highly developed than any other that had been spread over an equally wide area: and had prepared the way for the automatic organization on an even larger basis of her cotton industries.

Thus many diverse influences, some of them partly accidental, combined to give British manufacturers and merchants the upper hand over those of other countries in the third quarter of last century: and this success engendered easy-going habits of life and work among many of the sons and grandsons of those whose strenuous, if sometimes uncouth, energy had revolutionized industry and trade. In the next two decades some signs of weakness became evident: but in the present generation there has appeared a firm resolve to reconsider British methods in relation to the problems of the new age; and to the solutions of those problems which were being worked out in America, Germany and other countries.

Of course suggestions, derived from the experiences of any one country, cannot safely be applied to the problems of another, until account has been taken of the degree in which each experience depends on circumstances that are not to be found in the other. Thus, on the one hand, attention needs to be directed to the opportunities for stringent monopolistic control of the machinery of industry, and of prices, which America derives from geographical causes, and—though to a much less extent—from her Protective tarif; and which Germany derives from her Protective tarif. And, on the other hand, it must not be forgotten that Germany's strong, though harsh, military-bureaucratic organization has enabled her Government to intervene with a firm strength and security, that are not to be found in the interventions of the Government of a democratic country: while America, conscious of this difficulty, has studied the problems of monopoly with unrivalled thoroughness. Her conditions have given to these problems a breadth and intensity far in excess of any that have appeared elsewhere: and her methods

III, XI, 2. are not suitable for adoption without reserve in other countries. But they have been developed with so much energy, and so much sincerity and openness, that they seem to offer guidance of high value to Britain in view of the recent revival of some broad monopolistic tendencies. For the two peoples are akin not only in race, but also in openness of character and directness of action; and the same principles of Common Law apply to the regulation of monopolies in both.

2. *The strong individuality, which created Britain's industrial leadership, is still her most important asset. But it needs increasingly to be supplemented by readiness to cooperate with others in large affairs; while the supersession of small businesses by large in many industries is inevitable.*

As we have seen, the industrial faculties of England developed tardily, and owed much to the guidance of Dutch teachers who had learnt much from City States: even the enterprise of her navigators lagged long behind that of the Portuguese. But gradually she became, first a rival, and then a leader of the strongest: partly because the ocean defended her from the military violence that crippled Holland; but mainly because her people had never been either inclined or compelled to look to authority for instructions. Each man settled his own affairs, subject to but little discipline save that of custom. And since the shackles of custom were not felt, they merely narrowed the range of action of individuality: they did not destroy it. So individuality accomplished great things, with ever-enlarging scope: and as the ages passed, a great part of the world came under British influence; Scotchmen joining with Englishmen, and often leading them.

He, who respects his own individuality, is unlikely to be a tyrant: he may be wanting in tact, and in quickness to assimilate that which is good and helpful in the temper and habits of others. But he is sure to be frank, and likely to respect the individuality of others: refusing to be regimented, he is unlikely to regiment others. Thus individuality and resolution, combined with toleration, have made the British Empire great and coherent.

But such toleration is not inconsistent with an excessive

respect for one's own judgment and faculty: and, though confidence in one's own resources may be an almost unmixed good in matters that are within their reach, it may be a source of some weakness in larger matters. That is to say the specially British qualities which made Britain great, when business was on a relatively small scale, may not suffice for her need now: for industry and trade are growing in breadth and depth at a rate unprecedented, even in the age which is sometimes described as that of the "Industrial Revolution."

As late as the middle of the last century the capital, required to enable a business to command the most efficient and economical methods of production then known, was relatively small: and specialization on a rather narrow range of work was facilitated by that quiet organization of industry which tends to grow up, almost inevitably, where the technique of production and the character of the goods produced do not change very rapidly. Thus, it was reasonable to attribute a great part of Britain's industrial strength to small growing businesses: any loss that might arise from slight imperfections in their plant fell mainly on themselves; while the energy and elasticity, which they contributed to industry, accrued in large measure to the whole country.

But when the energetic creator of a business of moderate size died, he often left it liable to payments to members of his family, who could not take part in developing it. Thus its resources were straitened; and its owners perhaps lacked the energy, the initiative, and the delight in hard work by which it had been created: but yet they had a just pride in the family name; and they were reluctant to turn it into a joint stock company, in order to attract new capital. It was therefore apt to lose creative force, even if the branch of industry, to which it belonged, retained nearly the same technique as had prevailed in the preceding generation: while, if its plant needed to be organically changed in order to maintain relative efficiency, its continued existence might even be a hindrance to progress. Instances of this kind have been so numerous, that a new tradition is in danger of growing up, to the effect that a small business must be out of place in the new age: for that belongs to large businesses.

This tradition in its exaggerated form is repeated parrot-

III, XI, 2. wise: and it is all the more mischievous, because there is much important truth at the back of it. If an old business is small, it is rather likely to be a stagnant business: but an enterprising man, who sees his way to fitting the work of a small business into the large frame of national industry, may render as high service to the country now as ever. The expansion of technique has taken many branches of industry beyond his reach: and it is likely to take more, with ever increasing speed. But, on the other hand, it is enlarging rapidly the whole area of industry; and it is developing new ways in which the deliberate cooperative standardization of products (especially such as are component parts of larger products) may outdo old-fashioned stagnant custom in the opportunities offered for narrowly specialized work.

The present group of chapters will be much occupied with this class of consideration; because there is reason for thinking that the advantages which some other countries, and especially Germany, have derived from a semi-military organization of industry are not in fact as great as may appear at first sight; and because immediate material gains, obtained at the expense of a diminution of the spirit of free enterprise, may prove to have been too dearly bought, even from a merely material point of view.

It is true that the new age, with its rapidly rising standard of education for the working classes, is greatly enlarging the field from which to recruit men fitted to originate new ideas, and to face the risks involved in putting them into execution. It is true that America owes a great part of her industrial prowess to men who began life in low station. And it is true that the Jewish race, especially in Germany, supplies an almost inexhaustible reservoir on which to draw for new methods of making profit, most of which inevitably make for the good of the nation. But yet a nation cannot fail to become poorer in character, and perhaps even in material wealth, if comparatively few of her people have larger opportunities for resource in new construction, and for courage in taking risks, than commonly fall to the lot of an official in a great Company or in the service of Government.

We ought therefore to cherish strong individuality as a

priceless national asset: but at the same time to recognize that, like other noble qualities, it is liable to be misapplied; and that it may even degenerate into a morbid desire for secrecy and isolation. It has indeed sometimes been charged—though apparently without adequate cause—with being responsible for an unreasoning disinclination, which is occasionally found among certain classes of British business men, to unite their efforts in tasks, that are needed for the proper development of industry but are too large for a single business.

The adage "an Englishman's home is his castle" represents a side of national character that was developed in centuries of successful struggle against the semi-military despotism, from which nations subject to the invasion of great Continental armies could not escape; and has been a chief foundation of the British Empire. But, in so far as it induces a manufacturer or trader to shun associated action, on the ground that it would enable his associates to penetrate into the secrets of his business, it may be a source of national weakness rather than strength. What each gains by his secrecy is less, in many cases, than what he might gain by a liberal policy of give and take with his associates. There is however some ground for doubting whether this secrecy is caused, as much as is sometimes suggested, by jealousy. Perhaps a more potent and general cause is a certain lack of imagination; which has long been noted as a characteristic of those whose minds have not been expanded by an adventurous life, or by some high intellectual ambition. This is indeed yet another penalty which the country must pay for having neglected so to broaden national education as to bring the student into direct touch with the large real problems of the modern world.

Those English manufacturers, who pioneered the methods of modern industry, had little education: but they went early to work, and were in direct touch with realities throughout their lives. In the modern age, they spend long years at school, and perhaps at College; and if ultimately they become officials in a giant business, they may never get very close to realities. But if they enter a business of moderate size, even after the freshness of early youth has passed, their real education is likely to reach far. If the heads of such businesses are eager to learn,

III, XI, 3. and willing that their experiences should be helpful to others; they will greatly increase their chance of holding their own, in spite of the fact that giant businesses can afford to make larger and more frequent experiments than they can. Strong individuality, resolution and directness of purpose may enable a multitude of British businesses of moderate size to hold their own against powerful aggregations in all those industries, in which no over-mastering technical advantage belongs to massive, continuous production: provided these qualities are united with frank willingness to learn from others; and to cooperate genially with others in matters in which unfettered association has large opportunities.

That combination of individual liberty with orderly cooperation, which is characteristic of the British people, is not indeed specially prominent in industries, in which technical influences make most strongly for integration, such as will be considered in the present chapter: but they will come to the front in Chapter XII. In Chapter XIII they will again fall partly into the back-ground under the influence of the ever increasing temptation, which modern conditions offer, to enter into sectional combinations for getting the upper hand in matters of bargaining. But at the end we shall reach new movements, which give scope for all that is best and most characteristic of the race.

3. *Movement towards aggregation in the British coal industry.*

Our first illustrations are naturally taken from the coal and iron industries: though these are no longer distinctively British[1].

Coal and iron are indissolubly connected: iron—or, as we rather say, now, steel—industries are rivalled only by transport industries in their use of coal: and coal mines are large consumers of iron products; insomuch that, especially under the rule of German cartels, steel works often find some outlet for their spare energies during a general depression of industry, in improving and developing the plant of their mines. In so far as this influence reaches, it tends to stabilize employment and prices; and

[1] See above, pp. 60, 61.

is a benefit to the nation as well as to individual businesses, that pursue a far-seeing policy in such matters.

The Westphalian Coal Syndicate pioneered the route by which the steel and other dominant cartels made their way to power: and it may be well to diverge from the main course of our argument to consider some curious episodes in the history of British coal, before passing to the steel industry, which in Britain as elsewhere shows the problems of aggregation, and federation in their fullest developments. Germans themselves admit that the fundamental ideas not only of their simple cartels, but also of their Syndicates, were anticipated by more than a century in the Newcastle Coal Vend. Its power was based on having good access to the sea for the products of exceptionally rich mines[1].

Later on, in 1897, Sir George Eliot suggested the formation of a giant company to purchase all the British coal mines, except those owned by iron-masters; and to work them as a unit. He laid stress on the undoubtedly inordinate wastes involved then, as now, in marketing coal competitively; and in necessarily

[1] See above, p. 509. The English coal trade has nearly always been full of episode. It was regulated now in the interests of the naval strength of the country, now of operatives, now of consumers; and monopolies were granted on condition of paying a tax and selling in London not above specified prices. Engrossing was prohibited. Meanwhile combinations among coalowners, traders, and shipowners were constantly starting into life. At last the concentration of the greater part of the then unprecedented demand of London for the coal, which could be brought cheaply by sea from Newcastle, bore fruit in the formation of the Vend in 1771 (even earlier, according to the H. of C. Committee of 1830). A central committee watched the market, and decided at the beginning of each month how much should be offered at Newcastle for sale in London. Exports to the Continent seem not to have been controlled. A start was made with 800,000 Newcastle chaldrons (about 2,000,000 tons) as a nominal basis; and there was assigned to each colliery a quota on this basis. Say the nominal quota of a colliery was 20,000 chaldrons: if then for any particular month the Vend was fixed at 60,000 chaldrons, it would be entitled to a fortieth of this, *i.e.* to 1500 for that month. Each colliery fixed its own prices in Newcastle for the year at whatever level it chose: but it might not change during the year. The shippers selected their own coal, and sold at what prices they chose. A series of commissions of inquiry pointed increasingly to the belief that the London consumers' best protection lay in the growing competition of other coal-fields; and this was justified by events. The pretence of the Vend to steady prices was not seriously regarded. It sold cheaply abroad: its coal could sometimes be had in Petrograd at half the London price. Its story has been told many times. Its close similarity to the modern cartel is emphasized in Cohn's *Geschichte des Verkehr-wesens*; while its picturesque side is best seen in Macpherson's *Annals*.

III, XI, 3. leaving coal unworked near the boundaries of adjacent mines. A high limit was to be assigned to the profits which the trust could divide without the sanction of the Board of Trade. The project received much favour: it was abandoned mainly on account of difficulties in detail. But amalgamations have long been in progress in South Wales; where the steam coal is of such excellence as to have a high monopoly value, especially for naval use[1].

Stress has sometimes been laid on the apparent paradox that, while many German cartels owe much of their strength to Protective duties on competitive imports, the strongest German cartel is concerned with coal, which has no such Protection. But in fact coal is defended by its bulk: and the prices of coal along the banks of the Rhine and the Elbe are governed, not by the fiat of the Westphalian Syndicate, but by the prices of British coal, including the low cost of bringing it by sea and river. Its case is in some measure representative of salt and cement—two other products of the earth, which contain but small value in considerable bulk[2].

[1] See *The British Coal Trade* by Prof. H. S. Jevons, pp. 317 to 334. A large and suggestive chart of the various fusions, and communities of interest of the Cambrian Coal Combine, before its recent extensions, is given in the *Federal Trade Commission's Report on Cooperation in American Export Trade*, vol. I. p. 344. Sir George Eliot's scheme was commended by Prof. Brentano at the *Kartellen-Enquête* (*Kontradiktorische Verhandlungen*, vol. I. p. 749). The difficulties that have opposed the formation of effective permanent associations in the British coal trade in recent years are set out by Carter, *l.c.* pp. 223—240.

[2] The Portland Cement Manufacturers' Association has something approaching a monopoly for the finer sort of cement. But its common sorts can be made so cheaply in so many districts, and its cost of carriage is so heavy, that many scattered works for producing them long maintained some partial local monopoly. The movement for amalgamation however continued and was nearly completed during the war. Its large resources are however used constructively rather than combatively. It educates the public in the uses of cement, and small producers in the technique of their work. Compare above, p. 571 fn.

Salt is the only important material, other than coal, of which Britain has a predominant supply. It has given rise to a good many semi-monopolistic ventures in heavy chemical industries, based on it; some of which have not prospered. The success of the great firm of Brunner and Mond appears to reflect high technical skill and business ability, combined with a moderate and steadfast policy.

4. *Plasticity of structure throughout the steel industry. Conflicts and harmonies of interest among its several stages.*

The steel industry is so manysided and various, and yet its several stages and branches are so closely associated, that their mutual relations afford, in Britain as elsewhere, an epitome of almost every kind of amicable association and combative combination. They call for strong faculties, careful study and alert action. No nation has undisputed preeminence in them.

If an engineering firm anywhere needs a cutting tool that will bear an extremely high temperature, he must buy it from Sheffield: and yet the tungsten used in it has come chiefly from Germany; though Germany owns little of the ore from which tungsten is made, and nearly half the known supplies of that ore are in the British Empire. Again, German cutlery made largely in standardized shapes, which are struck out in the rough by powerful machinery, can be sold for common uses in Sheffield itself; and this result is partly due to British adherence to old tradition: but yet Sheffield skill makes fine cutlery of such excellent quality that none can surpass it: perhaps none can equal it. Sheffield is the home of some of the most delicate of British steel industries; and also of those which are beyond the range of any but a mammoth business: and Sheffield is in all these respects an epitome of Britain[1].

It has already been observed that the steel industries are of exceptional interest, because they constitute a group, each member of which is a chief customer, and often the only customer of several other groups. If a cartel in any one stage pursues a restrictive policy, the hurt thence arising may spread far and wide: but its first, and often its chief, effects are likely to be felt in the stage of steel production immediately above it, and —in some cases—in the stage immediately below it. Partly, for these reasons, a steel business can extend vertically upwards or downwards without passing into a different "atmosphere" of technique: much of the additional plant, that it will require, is likely to differ only in detail from some which it has been already using, and perhaps even making. And, with exception for the first stages of the industry, nearly every class of employee that

[1] See above, p. 213.

III, XI, 4. is needed in the new extension is already on hand. These first stages have in effect become one in relation to some of the larger problems of the future: for the economy resulting from their fusion must gradually overbear all resistance. And yet a man, who has inherited a fairly good business in any one of them, cannot be blamed very severely if he is somewhat slow to realize fully how much it belongs to the past.

This is no doubt an extreme case: but other stages of the steel industries afford similar, though less striking instances of the increasing need which the present age creates not only for a broad view, but for a longsighted view of business problems. Courage is misapplied when it struggles against the inevitable; as happens sometimes when British iron-masters remodel old works, although they cannot be brought up to the level of modern technique without being recast by aid of additional capital, and on a larger scale. In this connection our attention is called to the fact that "the United States Steel Corporation, which alone controls an output of iron and steel greater than the whole production of the United Kingdom"; and the vast Thyssen Company of Germany, are abandoning the practice of reconstructing a works that has fallen behind. They allow it to plod on, while they set up new works of the most advanced model to take its place: when that is ready, the old is dismantled, and either reconstructed entirely, or abandoned[1].

Somewhat similar cases occur in other industries: the small miller long fought bravely but hopelessly against the giant flour mill; and the small dyer against the giant dye works: but their contests were as hopeless as that of the hand loom weaver in contest with the power loom. And yet their fate may have been in some measure better than his; for in many industries, when the small employer abandons his own works he may hope that he will be ere long "found as a high official of large limited concerns. ...He may not have the hope of large profits: but he undoubtedly has great uses, in his readiness to adopt and try new things —in the application of his inventive genius, and in the practical knowledge that he himself acquires, through actually working

[1] *Report of a Committee on the position of the iron and steel trades after the war* [Cd. 9071], 1918, p. 20. This is one of a series, as to which some general remarks will be found on pp. 601—2.

in his own shops and in daily contact with his own men. It is to be noted that many of the men at the head of great works to-day, in the capacity of directors, have only a theoretic knowledge of the works they direct, as compared with the practical knowledge which their fathers and grandfathers had before them[1]." This is one of several ways in which the individuality of the small business man remains an important asset. Moreover, there are good grounds for rejoicing in the fact that the progress of technique, while pushing him out of the main track of many industries, continually opens to him new opportunities, if he will apply energy and resource to developing some speciality[2].

5. *Illustrations drawn from the steel industry of the national interest in the standardization of products, the intensive specialization of businesses, and the maintenance of open markets.*

The advantages, which a business derives from vertical expansion, are chiefly in regard to the organization of its work, and to the economies of marketing. As a rule it obtains few additional economies on the technical side of production: for there results little or no increase in the resources of plant and skill which it commands for any particular task. But it can so adjust the output of its lower stages to the requirements for material of the upper stages, that scarcely anything needs to be bought except for the lowest stage; and scarcely anything needs to be marketed except from the highest stages: while in the special case of a steel business, as has already been observed, it is often possible to shift *temporarily* some labour and some plant from work for one stage to work for another. In any case the higher stages can rely on the quality of the material supplied from the lower, and on its adaptability to their wants; especially if "planning" and "routing" are organized scientifically[3]. A steel business may even transfer some plant and some skill *permanently* from working for one stage to working for another; when the adjustment between successive stages is upset by changes in the proportions of its various products.

If the business is sufficiently large to contain several sets

[1] *Report on the Engineering trades after the war*, 1918 [Cd. 9073].

[2] See above, pp. 244—9.

[3] See above, pp. 369—375.

III, XI, 5. of organizing brains of the highest quality, each stage may attain to the highest efficiency. But such conditions are very rare: and, on the whole, the elasticity of national energy seems likely to be better advanced when each stage occupies the whole attention of a strong enterprising business. When the total stock of brains of the highest originating and constructive faculty in a business is not very large, the interests of the business and the country are likely to be best served, if its whole energies are concentrated on a range of tasks not too large and diverse to be completely grasped by one set of minds.

Variations in process and in product can then be tried without stint, even though a successful issue will effect only a small percentage of economy: and new ideas, at first crude, may germinate and develop, till they become important additions to economic strength. So vital to Britain's prosperity is the maintenance of full freedom for horizontal, rather than vertical expansion, that the country has a deep interest in defending the home market for everything, that a manufacturer may desire to purchase, against an artificial manipulation of its prices by a cartel.

Britain's open markets supply the shipbuilder with reasonable security as to his purchases: and so important is that advantage that, as we have seen, Germany exempts steel for ship-building from import duties. Lord Furness tells us, indeed, that "the shipbuilding firms on the [British] coast buy many details in this country cheaper than they can themselves produce them, and yet the manufacturers of these details make very substantial profits. This they do of course by specialized production and concentrated management." Engines and boilers are built by each firm to the requirements of various classes of ships. "Each builder has some points of excellence, which in combination would...tend to place British construction on a higher plane in the markets of the world. Each has an expensive staff producing designs and patterns identical with those of its competitors[1]."

[1] From an address delivered in 1908, see Appendix II to Levy's *Monopoly and Competition*. Progressive standardization in the steel industries is described above, II, III, 4.

Standardization of parts can of course be carried very much further than can that of the whole of a great complex, such as a ship. But the extent, to which a shipbuilder can rely on a prompt supply at reasonable prices of various classes of material or component parts that he needs, depends in a measure on the standardization of the general type to which he is working. This standardization had been carried far in individual works, before the war, of course chiefly in regard to cargo vessels. The North-east Coast Institution of Engineers and Shipbuilders has been engaged on a genuine task of constructive cooperation while drawing up a "guidance specification": and, of course, in any type of engine, where the general design is similar, the habitual adoption of such a specification would greatly diminish costs[1].

The lack of cooperative standardization in British industry is conspicuous in regard to locomotives. Every considerable railway has its own models, though the materials are to some extent standardized; and it makes nearly all its own engines; partly because a railway is able to borrow money for extensions at exceptionally low rates[2].

Passing to another aspect of the problem it may be remarked that the electrical industry owes much of its progress to a few giant businesses; but there seems reason to think that constructive cooperation in regard to standard details and other matters might hasten the specialization of the numerous works engaged in it in Britain now[3]. Similar constructive cooperation

[1] This paragraph is reproduced in substance from *The Report of the Committee on shipping and shipbuilding industries*, p. 33; where it is urged that the Government should appoint a Standards Committee of Shipowners, Shipbuilders, and Marine Engineers to carry the work further. It is recognized that local and other variations in the work to be done will require the number of standard types to be considerable.

[2] See above, pp. 322—3. The Committee on the Engineering trades reports [Cd. 9073], p. 12, that it would be well that "the railway companies should themselves agree upon a limited number of types for their own use, and produce them to a limited quantity in their own workshops, giving to the manufacturers in this country a reasonable share, at competitive prices, of the types required: and thus obtaining a reliable check on their own cost of production." The unification of railway control, whether under Government or otherwise, would stay the wastes that are caused at present by the lack of standardization: but it would increase the need for large independent locomotive works, in order to provide some check on the wastes and ineptitude of a huge organization, which has nothing to gain by alert and economic methods of work.

[3] The Committee on the Electrical trades reports [Cd. 9072], p. 8, strongly

III, XI, 5. has done much, and may do very much more, in developing agreements as to standardization, which will enable firms of moderate size to specialize on the production in vast quantities of particular component parts of machines in large use by manufacturers, or in yet larger use by the public. A suggestion has indeed been made that some of the munition plants, set up by the Government during the war, should be sold on easy terms, subject to the condition that they should continue intensive, variously specialized work, similar to that for which they were set up. Such, for instance, might be "the manufacture of ball-bearings, piston rings and spinning spindles....A motor-car manufacturer can buy, cheaper than he can produce them himself, his yearly output of, say, 1000 engines of three or four sizes from a specialist producing ten or twenty thousand of the same sizes for ten or twenty car manufacturers. Or take a machine-tool manufacturer, producing a collection of 500 machines of various designs in a year, who has hitherto been in the habit of making all their levers, pulleys, gear, and hand wheels. He may have some automatic or semi-automatic machines for producing these goods, but a specialist producing such parts for the trade can supply a superior article at a lower price[1]."

Specialization of this kind is generally effected automatically: but we are told of a notable recent case in the machine-tool trade, in which it has been deliberately organized. Ten firms have agreed that, while setting up a common selling agency, they shall retain individual independence, on the understanding that each will limit its production to a single type of machines. This plan seems likely to prove of great national benefit, if generally adopted, with due provisions against excessive monopoly prices. Under a Protective tarif the economy resulting from the specialization would probably not suffice to prevent the plan from working against the general interest[2].

in favour of the "amalgamation..., or the development of the practice of association for common purposes" in order to obtain this end. It does not however seem necessary that this association should extend much beyond the organized study and development of standards.

[1] See the *Times Engineering Supplement*, January, 1917.

[2] The following details of the plan are given in the *Times Engineering Supplement* for June, 1917:—"the two Birmingham firms will concentrate on the production of light radial drilling machines, certain sizes of milling machines, and capstan lathes. The Manchester firms will provide grinding machines (the

The experience of the State in organized specialization of work during the world-war is helpful, in spite of the exceptional conditions under which it has been obtained. On the financial side indeed little can be inferred from it: for the State being sole producer and sole purchaser has had no expenses of marketing, and little reason to consider whether its products might be left on its hands. Necessity has ruled: and the future value of its factories has not needed to be estimated by skilled accountants in order to make up scientific cost valuations for its output. But its experiences on the technical side are suggestive.

Its new works have been scattered wide over the land, partly in order to tap new sources of supply of labour suitable for repetition work. The fact, that it did not find much need for gigantic individual establishments, tends to support the opinion that standardization, specialization and thorough organization, whether automatic or deliberately contrived, may enable a multitude of businesses of moderate size to attain nearly every important efficiency and economy that appear at first sight to belong exclusively to giant businesses. But that inference might carry too far, unless full account were taken of the concentrated power of study and experimentation on a vast scale, which lies at the back of orders given to the munition factories.

Thus again we are brought to the fact that thought, initiative and knowledge are the most powerful implements of production. In relatively small work, such as that of chemical dyes and optical glass, the main responsibility for them may well rest with a few giant firms: but in larger work they belong to the world as a whole. No one country can make great advances in it in secret: alert rivals are soon able to select the best points in any new departure, and perhaps to improve on some of them. And yet a country, that is content to wait upon the new knowledge acquired by others, will always lag somewhat behind; and her products will hardly obtain full credit, even when in fact they are made according to the most advanced technique. For this reason, among others, it seems that the

work of one firm), milling machines, and boring mills. The Halifax shops will produce heavy radial drilling machines and the lighter sizes of slotting and planing machines, while the Scottish firms will manufacture the lighter lathes and heavy slotting, planing, and other machines." See also above, II, IV, 4.

III, xi, 5. growth of a considerable number of great firms in all heavy industries, and especially in heavy steel industries, is to be welcomed: the present age offers ever increasing scope for large experiments, of vital importance to progress, which cannot easily be arranged cooperatively; while yet they involve outlay and financial risks too heavy to be borne by any but a giant business.

To conclude:—such a growth will of course tend to impair the supply of that individual initiative, which is by far the most important element of national wealth: but that tendency may be relatively slight, if an open field be kept for small businesses in appropriate industries. An important means to that end is constructive cooperation in every fitting matter, and especially in such standardization as will enable the small man to work for an open market. Of course the standardization must be on broad lines; partly because an exceptionally large part of British manufactures is designed to be sold to peoples of widely differing habits and requirements: and partly because some element of variety is an end in itself in regard to many things designed for personal use; while it dominates nearly all that aim at artistic distinction.

Moreover the causes, which have impelled American and German steel industries towards extreme aggregation, are at work in Britain. The recent Committees on the iron and steel trades, and on the engineering trades, recommend severally "that British iron and steel manufacturers should be urged to form combinations for the purpose of laying down large and well-designed new units"; and "that in the interests of the country the engineering manufacturers be encouraged to work together in larger units, either by amalgamation or by joint pooling of resources, by specialization of production, and by organization of export sales, and for the purchase of raw materials." There seem to be solid grounds for these recommendations, at all events in regard to some branches of the steel industry. It will be urged later on that many developments thus indicated, are measures of constructive cooperation, free from any suspicion of danger to public interests; though others are in some danger of being perverted to antisocial purposes. They are thus representative of British temper: which is not addicted to militant aggression, but yet sometimes drifts in that direction under the pressure of circumstances, and without that deliberate harsh purpose which has been prominent in some German cartels; for indeed self-analysis is not always congenial to the British business man.

6. ***A monopolistic tendency in a branch of a great industry, the highways of which are in general free to all comers.***

In the chief branches of the larger textile industries each considerable factory contains several similar groups of rooms; so that it might be split up into several factories with little loss of technical efficiency: though there would of course be relative losses in the costs of management, of building, of power (unless power were obtained from central electrical works) and in other ways. Three chief processes indeed—that of wool-combing for making worsteds, and those of dyeing and finishing—cannot be thus subdivided: so they are generally remitted to specialized businesses and these have some opportunities for semi-monopolistic policies; as to which something more will be said a little later.

The cotton industry generally offers no special allurements to monopolistic enterprise: but yet Coats' business, entirely British, has an exceptional claim to be regarded as having cosmopolitan dominion. Its strength is based in great measure on Lancashire's advantages, both on the physical and the human side, for the apparently very simple tasks of making fine cotton yarn and converting it into thread: she combines indeed an admirable climate for the purpose, and unique manual skill and organization[1].

The simple art of making cotton yarn into a thread strong enough to take the place of silk and linen threads seems to have been set up early in the eighteenth century near Paisley. It quickly spread among humble folk; and, early in last century, two considerable firms were set up there to carry on the business: they soon united their forces, and they gradually absorbed nearly all their competitors. The great combination thus formed seems to have been managed with ability and

[1] This subject will be further considered in the next chapter.

III, XI, 6. moderation. Its trade-marks have immense value; because as has already been noted, the mischief done by using inferior sewing thread would often be immeasurably greater than the price of good thread; and the ordinary purchaser cannot judge its quality by inspection. It has definite working alliances with the only other great British thread business,—the English Sewing Cotton Company,—with the Fine Cotton Spinners' and Doublers' Association; and with the powerful American Thread Company. The "Thread Combine" thus formed is the outcome of consolidations of several groups of firms of moderate size, dominated in great measure by the giant businesses of Coats. It makes no immoderate use of its monopolistic power: but yet some of the measures by which it fortifies its monopoly are perhaps more harmful than appears at first sight: and we may pause a little to consider them[1].

Its home trade is very much smaller than its foreign trade; and it can use either part to assist the other financially and otherwise. It has factories in several countries; and in others it sometimes puts a stop to troublesome competition by a threat to set up factories of its own. Its excellent organization of production and marketing enables it to make vast profits, while selling at prices that leave no very large margin above the costs of a rival. It might then be supposed to be above the temptation to resort to any expedient which is open to criticism[2].

[1] See p. 403. The two great firms of Coats and Clark were fused early in last century: and other firms were subsequently absorbed; though many of them continued to work in partial independence. The task of marketing is committed to a powerful Selling Agency. It even undertakes the marketing of the English Sewing Cotton Company, whose products are similar to its own, though not generally in direct competition with them. The products of Lister and Co., though different in kind, appeal to the same retailers; and are also marketed by it.

[2] It commonly divides thirty per cent. on its ordinary shares: nearly half of its capital is in preferred shares at the almost unprecedented rate of twenty per cent. In defence of this result of course it might plead, that some other businesses are in effect yielding dividends on their original capital at very high rates: but have avoided the appearance of doing it, by enlarging their nominal capital. Its practice of retaining, on various sorts of threads, the names of many firms which have been absorbed by it, causes some consumers to suppose that they have a choice among the products of many competitive firms; and are thus protected. The Committee on Trusts, early in 1920 criticised its methods severely. Its vigorous answer suggests that further investigation may be instructive.

But in fact it makes use of a modified form of that "tying clause," which has been a prominent and most evil weapon of monopolistic power in America; and has been vigorously combated in the interests of the public. Coats' well-earned reputation for thorough and honest work has caused consumers to prefer its goods to others at equal prices: and therefore a firm which has not yet convinced the public that its goods are thoroughly to be trusted, is compelled to offer them at a rather lower price; being of course content with a lower rate of profits than that which is earned by Coats' goods. If the young firm could prove to the public that its goods are, at all events, so nearly on a level with Coats' products, that they are worth having when sold at a rather lower rate of profit, then it could gradually obtain a place in the market. But Coats refuse to supply any dealer who gives such a firm the chance of doing that; and this action seems to infringe the spirit of the Common Law, which prohibits the entrance to the highway of business from being blocked by a giant aggregation[1].

The name of Coats has dominated this mighty growth: but its case is exceptional. Nearly all the great aggregations in the textile industries have grown out of understandings, passing into federations, and ending in fusion. This general tendency has already been noted as especially strong in such industries as those of combing wool, and bleaching, dyeing and finishing textile materials[2]. For each such operation requires generally but little time in the hands of a highly expert staff, equipped with large technical appliances: the market value of an expen-

[1] The Drapers' Chamber of Trade is said to insist on uniformity of retail prices. Perhaps they are right so far as their own interests are concerned; in spite of the fact that their profits on handling thread are naturally low relatively to those on most other branches of their trade. But the huge profits of the Coats' aggregation owe nothing to technical economies of massive production; and the Drapers' rule, which in effect obstructs the entrance to the industrial highway of firms, who might supply good thread made by the best appliances, being content with a lower rate of profits than that of Coats', is *primâ facie* opposed to the public interest.

[2] See above, p. 232. But mere fusion, without thorough organization and strong centralized control, may bring disaster: as is shown by the strange story of the early days of the Calico Printers' Association. A strong Committee investigated its affairs; and made recommendations for its re-organization, which form a classical document. See Macrosty, *l.c.* pp. 144—152 and 360—387. More recently its career has been fairly successful. Its Chairman,

III, XI, 6. sive material is much affected by the efficiency with which it is performed; and textile manufacturers gain by paying to a central Association a price that may yield it a high profit, while being less than their own cost for doing the work themselves less efficiently. The tasks are too various to be easily brought under a standard price list by a federation: so they afford exceptionally favourable fields for giant amalgamations.

speaking on 15 September 1920, claimed that its powerful organization had obtained good results, especially in marketing at great distances. But he added that "the recent merging of the two principal firms of English colour makers into one highly capitalized corporation...was to the advantage of neither the colour-making nor the colour-consuming trades....Our objection has from the first been that any scheme aiming finally at the concentration of the dye-making works of the country into one monopolistic enterprise would, in practice, disorganize the working mechanism and *esprit de corps* of the firms amalgamated—it would increase the overhead working costs, stifle that healthy rivalry which is one of the main inducements to economical, efficient, and progressive working, and furnish the opportunity for price inflation irrespective of manufacturing costs. We are glad to note that our view is gaining a wider public recognition that the foundations of dye manufacture must be broadened if the maximum of efficiency in production is to be secured."

CHAPTER XII

AGGREGATION, FEDERATION, AND COOPERATION IN BRITISH INDUSTRY AND TRADE, CONTINUED

1. *Some British textile industries have developed efficient standardization and specialization almost automatically.* III, XII, 1.

The broadest, and in some respects most efficient forms of constructive cooperation are seen in a great industrial district where numerous specialized branches of industry have been welded almost automatically into an organic whole.

The preceding chapter was mainly occupied with the sources of the strength of some giant British businesses. The present chapter and the next will be chiefly devoted to various forms of cooperation, in which there is some constructive purpose; though the desire to get the better of others in buying or selling plays a considerable part in many of them, and develops a strong and even antisocial temper in a few of them. Associations for the purpose of marketing are known to be specially prone to such morbid development: and it is important to insist that they nearly always do some important constructive work; and often do no other. The last chapter will indicate the general bearings of the present work as a whole on the methods by which existing institutions may best be modified and applied for the harmonious development of the faculties of the people, and of their material advantages.

It will be well now to call to mind the facts that (1) the partial standardization effected by custom has effected much automatic organization of industry: (2) this organization included specialization, which in large measure dispensed with

III, XII, 1. the necessity of any complex arrangements in each individual business, since the *external* economies, which even a small business thus obtained, were generally far more important to it than those which the largest business in the world could obtain by its own efforts: (3) recent developments of standardization have greatly increased the security with which a business can rely on getting whatever partly finished materials it needs, provided the market for them is open: (4) German experience shows that the organization of a cartel is possible only in industries whose products are in great measure standardized; and that the fear that the prices of materials, which a business needs, may be artificially raised by cartels inclines it to extend its operations vertically, even when that course would not otherwise appear desirable[1].

Britain was indeed the chief home of the automatic cooperation of many industries; as it was also of the reasoned analysis of the "natural" tendency to such division and organization of labour as is needed to make it collectively efficient. "Observe the accommodation" says Adam Smith "of the most common artificer or day labourer; and you will find that the number of workers, who have contributed to it, amounts to many thousands[2]." In the present age industry is so complex and products are so subtle, that "hundreds of thousands" may be substituted for "thousands." And it may be added that almost every branch of industry in a western country depends directly or indirectly on hundreds, if not thousands of other branches, at home or abroad, for various parts of its plant and material. In one sense the whole world, in so far as it is in touch with western trade, is a single workshop: in a much fuller sense every compact industrial district is one.

The modern methods of massive manufacture were pioneered by the textile industries, chiefly using wool as their material: and their advances in automatic organization in England, especially during the seventeenth and eighteenth centuries, have already been studied[3]. We may now turn to Lancashire,

Lancs: automatic Specialisation

[1] References in connection with these four points are:—(1) pp. 196—200; (2) p. 167; (3) pp. 221—234; (4) pp. 547—549; and 557, 558.

[2] *Wealth of Nations*, Book I. ch. I.

[3] Above, I, III, 5 and Appendix C, 4.

where may be seen perhaps the best present instance of concentrated organization mainly automatic. Nature had favoured Lancashire with good access to the sea, to coal and to iron; and also with a climate remarkably suited to the great cotton industry. Moreover the character of the population fitted them to develop the engineering industries. Thus makers and users of textile, and especially cotton, machinery have had nearly all the advantages of concentrated effort that could belong to a population of more than a million persons in a single composite business; while avoiding the cumbrous network of organization that would be required by it. Therefore dealers of various kinds flock to Manchester from all quarters of the globe; and they are able, by aid of motor cars, to enter into direct contact with makers of innumerable specialities spread over an area of some two hundred square miles[1].

It is generally recognized that the chief economy in production, as distinguished from marketing, that can be effected by a cartel or other association of producers, is that of so parcelling out the demand for various sorts of the same class of product that each business can specialize its plant on a narrow range of work, and yet keep it running with but little interruption. This specialization is however thoroughly effected without conscious effort in the Lancashire cotton industry; and especially in those branches of it, which are mainly in the hands of a multitude of independent businesses of moderate size. As is well known, fine spinning, coarse spinning, and weaving are localized separately. Individual firms frequently specialize on a narrow range of counts for spinning. Blackburn, Preston, Nelson and Oldham are centres of four different classes of staple cotton cloths, and so on[2].

[1] As is set out more fully above, p. 286; see also p. 50.

[2] Fuller details are given by Chapman, *Lancashire Cotton Industry.* See also the *Report of a Departmental Committee, appointed by the Board of Trade, to consider the position of the textile industries after the war* [Cd. 9070], 1918; pp. 49, 50.

That Committee is one of several appointed during the pressure of the war, which cover between them the greater part of the chief industries of the country. They are of the very highest authority on the technical matters, with which they are severally concerned: and of exceptional value to economists. But, when regarded from the broader point of view of the collective interests of the nation, they necessarily lack the safeguards which would have been supplied if

III, XII, 1. It has often been remarked that, when any branch of an industry is greatly in advance of foreign competitors, it has nearly as full opportunity to organize itself deliberately, and ultimately to pursue a monopolistic policy, as if it were privileged by a Protective tarif: the case of high-class wall papers is in point. But automatic organization has predominated in the British textiles, and especially in the cotton industry which "by reason of its magnitude and the extent to which specialization has been carried, is probably the most efficient distributing organization in the world": though it is admitted that the alertness, assiduity and knowledge of foreign languages possessed by Germans have given them a large place in this British task. It is admitted also that the minor textile industries often adopt wasteful methods of marketing: and would gain by the adoption of "some form of combined representation, or cooperative selling[1]."

Trusting almost exclusively to automatic organization the British cotton industry has surpassed all its rivals in size and

the ordinary practice in times of peace had been possible during the war. For then the doors would have been open to duly qualified witnesses, who might desire to offer supplementary or rebutting evidence to some that had already been given (see above, p. 443). That practice seems to be the only thorough safeguard against such developments of bureaucratic control, sometimes under the influence of particular sectional interests, as are specially dangerous in a democratic country, such as Britain is rapidly becoming. A partial safeguard—the best perhaps that was possible during the war—was provided by a strong "Committee on industrial and commercial policy after the war," on which the several special committees were represented; thus providing for the harmonious treatment of their several interests. But those interests in the aggregate are but a part of the interests of the nation as a whole. It often happens that national interests receive more careful attention in Minority Reports (or Reservations) than in Majority Reports: for the Majority of a Commission or a Committee are generally chosen for their special knowledge of the matter in question: and they are therefore not always in a position to be wholly impartial.

[1] The marketing of cotton goods generally is highly specialized. The "shipper" concerns himself with external trade: "he not only forms connections in various parts of the world for distributing his yarns or goods; but he finances and conducts these goods through their various processes." That is, he buys goods, has them inspected, and sends them out to be dyed and finished on commission. The majority of shippers specialize on markets: as for instance the Eastern, the South American, or the Levant. Yarn and grey cloth are now increasingly intrusted to special agents; who represent a number of mills and thus "enable the producer to devote his time almost entirely to works management and purely industrial questions." (See the *Report on Textiles after the War*, pp. 117 and 50.)

in efficiency. In fact, in those finer goods, which owe most to skill and admit of the highest rates of remuneration to labour, it is without a rival. Nor are the woollen and worsted industries of Yorkshire very much behind the cotton of Lancashire: they have indeed many strong rivals in the coarser qualities, and they often follow the lead of Paris in fashion goods; but the most highly valued cloths for men's attire can be made only in Britain. The high automatic organization of these industries, as of the cotton industries, is in great measure due to the fact that their plant is made in their own districts, with constant intercommunication of ideas between machine makers and machine users. Nearly the whole of it is of British invention, and sought for by rival industries in other countries. On the other hand the silk industry, for which the damp British climate is not well suited, is on too small a scale, to be well organized automatically. Its machinery is said to lag rather behind the best practice of some other countries; and it is inclined therefore to look for artificial aid. Nearly the same may be said of several other minor textile industries[1].

2. *Constructive cooperation among kindred businesses, whether independent, or in single ownership and under central control.*

We have seen several reasons for thinking that a giant business in strong hands may do more for the advancement of technique, than is usually done by a number of small businesses with an equal aggregate output; but that on the other hand the giant business does, as a rule, comparatively little to educate high creative faculty: and that, though it has exceptional facilities for marketing, much of the most highly organized and effective marketing in the world is an almost automatic result of the work of a multitude of producers, with only moderate capitals, but aided by merchants and other dealers of various sorts. In the present Section, we are to consider some kinds of associated action, which claim, in effect, to unite some of the advantages of these two tendencies of industry: after-

[1] The relations between standardization and specialization in textile and in boot and shoe industries have been discussed from another point of view above, pp. 229—234.

III, XII, 2. wards we shall pass to methods of associated marketing by businesses which preserve complete independence as regards production; but unite their forces in various degrees for various purposes of marketing, some of which are militant and restrictive.

We may begin with an instance of pure constructive cooperation, without any apparent drift to use it as a means of maintaining prices at higher levels, than would otherwise prevail. The British Pottery Manufacturers' Association has among its purposes "to deal with the quality, supply, purchase, and control of raw materials and stores, where desirable, in the interests of the members; to deal with all questions relative to cost and conditions of transport; to consider means of facilitating the extension of export trade; to bring about closer cooperation with the technical arts, and designs sections of the pottery schools; to promote general propaganda, and to undertake advertising in connexion with the industry; to consider the best means of encouraging and utilizing improvements, inventions, and patents for the general good and advancement of the industry; to deal with all matters connected with more economical production, including costing; to watch national and local legislation affecting the industry....Experts are to be appointed, and assistance given to members in overcoming the technical difficulties which constantly arise in so complex an industry; and the Federation has power to purchase, work, and exploit any patents, secret processes, or other improvements in the general interests of the members[1]."

Cooperative action in this instance does not seem to involve centralized control: but it must be admitted that the greater part of such action derives its chief coherent force from a cash nexus; in the form either of association for the regulation of prices, or of consolidated ownership. And yet mere associations for the regulation of prices seldom have much constructive influence: their main energies are given to preventing sales of

[1] "To give effect to this extensive scheme, the following Committees, besides General Purposes and Advisory Committees, are being set up:—Wages and Conciliation; Supply and Purchasing; Oven, Kiln, and Saggar; Transportation; Advertising and Propaganda; Machinery and Milling; Arts and Designs; General Research; Patents, Inventions, and Improvements; and Commercial Intelligence and Statistical." From the *Trade Supplement to the Times*, December, 1918.

certain classes of goods at prices which they regard as unsatisfactory; and they work, not so much for an increase of national wealth as for a distribution of it specially favourable to themselves.

When the importance of "the personal element" on business organization was under discussion, attention was called to the far-reaching influence of a single masterful mind, making itself felt through well-chosen chiefs of departments[1]. But industry, in passing from the nineteenth to the twentieth century, entered on a phase, in which its aggregations became too massive to be easily mastered by a single man, even in a country as open to new developments as is the United States: and Mr Carnegie, a dominant example of such a mastery, handed over his heavy burden to the United States Steel Corporation. There is less cohesion in the British steel industry; and other industries will afford illustrations better suited to our purpose[2].

The Bradford Dyers' Association is fairly representative. Its business is that of dyeing on commission the products of those textile industries of which Bradford is the centre: so its policy is not troubled by problems of marketing. It cannot indeed claim very much of one economy, which is important in the work of some similar associations—that of saving cross freights by directing each customer to the factory most suitable for his purpose: but this is a small point. It gives each of its members freedom and responsibility in the management of details; while it collects into its own body a strong force of high business faculty for organizing the whole and for directing the broad policy of each branch. In regard to technical matters, it delegates all difficult questions to a capable scientific staff. It provides a uniform system of costing for all the branches; and it buys in large quantities well and cheaply by means of a strong special staff. This may be taken as a fair representative of the methods of industrial associations, whose main purpose is constructive[3].

[1] See above, pp. 362—364, especially the footnote on p. 364.

[2] Notable fusions in the British steel industry are associated with the names of Armstrong; Vickers; John Brown; Dorman and Long; Palmer and others.

[3] Constructive cooperation in the improvement of methods takes many

III, xii, 2. But all such Associations have to face a dilemma: on the one hand, if the staff of each business, or department owned by it, are paid fixed salaries, they may be found lacking in energetic enterprise; and the case is not much better if their remuneration varies a little with the net profits of the Association. If on the other hand, accounts are kept of the profits made on their own work, and their salaries are varied in accordance with those profits; no direct incentive is given to energetic cooperation for the efficiency and prosperity of the whole. A solution of this difficulty seems to have been found in the plan of the Calico Printers' Association; under which the "commission," or other bonus, allotted to each business, is made to depend not simply on the net profit shown by its own working during the year; but on that in conjunction with the net profit of the Association as a whole. This plan claims to encourage alert enterprise, while discouraging any policy of a branch, which might be detrimental to other branches. Uniform costing accounts can be made a means of indicating relative inefficiency, and stimulating enterprise; especially when several businesses in the Association are engaged on the same kind of work. For a statement of either the minimum, or the average, cost of each process, circulated by the Central Control among the members will stimulate any, whose costs are rather high, to amend their ways.

Closely akin to this device is the cooperative dissemination throughout all members of an Association, by the Central Control or otherwise, of information as to improved methods, and even distinct inventions, that have been worked out by any of its members. In so far as this community of property in progress merely brings to the more backward members a practical

forms. Thus skilled technical staffs are kept for this purpose by The British Portland Cement Manufacturers; by The United Alkali Company; by Lever Brothers, and by many others, in whose work science plays an important rôle. And similar provision is made, where the work is mainly mechanical. Thus the Fine Cotton Spinners' and Doublers' Association keeps special experts for dealing with every part of a cotton spinning mill, who are too expensive to be employed by a single firm; but are in effect available for all. The Bedstead Makers' Federation induces its members to assist one another's works by communications for the purposes of comparing, criticizing and improving: and so on. This constructive work must be recognized as socially beneficial, even in those cases in which it is combined with an antisocial price policy.

acquaintance with the best technique that prevails in the industry concerned, its effects are wholly good. But though the heads of an independent business may be willing to spend toilsome days and anxious nights in developing an idea, which holds out some promise of greatly raising its status: yet the same men may be rather supine in such matters, if they know that the honour and reward, which may result from their exertions, will belong to the Association as a whole. In short, an Association is an admirable agent for the dissemination of knowledge of technique, and even for its advancement, in so far as that can be done by "team-work": but the spread of Associations over a country might dry up many of the sources of truly original invention. This danger is partly avoided by arrangements which seem to be adopted by the Cable Makers' Association: any member, who makes a distinct advance in technique, is allowed to have the sole benefit of it for a time; or, as an alternative, other members (but no businesses outside the Association) are permitted to use it on terms advantageous to the inventor. It is possible that German competition, as well as German suggestion, is in some small measure responsible for some developments such as that of "The Sheffield Cutlery Trades' Technical Society." Electrical manufacturers in their private capacity, and through their Association, are furthering the development of the sciences, in which they are specially interested, by educational endowments and otherwise; and so on.

As time goes on, such Associations may probably develop many-sided constructive functions in regard to technique; especially in connection with the applications of "Scientific Method" to broad problems of standardization, and costing. Here American guidance comes to the front; and indicates that no correct measure of costs can be got by mere inspection of a particular operation performed under given conditions, taken in connection with the rate of payment of the operatives concerned. That measure is well enough for the short run; but, in the long run, the cost of the operation to the employer will be in great measure governed by its cost to the employee; that is, by the fatigue caused by it. To make such studies much time and thought on the part of able men are needed; and the results are a valuable property to the whole industry concerned. Therefore they may best be undertaken by an Association; and the broader the scope of that Association the better[1].

Similar considerations emphasize the importance of a great design to set up a single vast "Association for scientific research in relation to cotton and the cotton industry"; which may be the forerunner of far-reaching changes in Britain's industrial structure. For it aims directly and exclusively at enabling the country to do a large part of her work better and less wastefully than she otherwise would do: it has no design of enabling one section of the nation to get the better of others in bargaining[2].

Throughout this volume reference has frequently been made to the need of associated action in regard to the applications of science to industry. The dye industries stand at the head of this account: glass and metal industries come not far behind. There are a few occasions on which the State may properly intervene directly; and the aid which it has given to the formation of the colossal "British Dyestuffs Corporation" seems a strong instance of this: but in more leisured times careful study will need to be paid to some questions connected with such a policy. For if public assistance is given to a private corporation in acquiring special knowledge, which has a high pecuniary

[1] Here reference may be made to *Efficiency Methods* by McKillop, recently published, which gives, in compressed form, an account of scientific management suitable to English conditions.

[2] Although it is not yet fully set up, a little may be said about its scheme. Stress is laid on the facts that England's lead in the industry resulted from concentrated original thought, making use of what little aid could be got from the science of the time: but that latterly scarcely any great creative idea has appeared in the industry; though the progress of science has suggested many questions, the solution of which might render great service. A thorough study of such questions would involve very great expense: and, without neglecting the aid that can be got from Universities and other national resources, a fitting scope is offered for large scientific enterprise on the part of the British Cotton industry, including "growers, spinners, manufacturers, dyers, bleachers, printers, finishers and merchants." It is to collect reports of appropriate scientific work throughout the world; and to set out the results in forms adapted for use by the industry. It is gradually to develop its own Research Institute: and it is to foster solid methods of education in the cotton districts. It is to be strictly "cooperative," in that all will contribute for the general good. None will seek any exclusive advantage for himself; and its purview is so broad, that it may probably develop (with whatever aid can be got from academic laboratories) a full study of the mechanical, physiological, and psychological elements of strain in every important operation of the industry. See also p. 597 n.

value, some provision must be made for securing that all, who desire it, shall obtain access to that knowledge on reasonable conditions. This matter is difficult, because competitive industries in other countries might endeavour by various means to obtain it for their own use, without giving anything in return: and yet no sufficient provision for the avoidance of undue discrimination would be afforded by the rule that the corporation should be prepared to absorb any considerable business that desired to have access to its results.

This is indeed but one side of a difficulty, which the world has in part outgrown, and may outgrow altogether. Even now science is so far cosmopolitan, that progress, made anywhere, quickly becomes the basis of new advances everywhere. And it is possible that scientific industries might advance all the more rapidly, if an international agreement were reached to the effect that every State should endow research for the purposes of industry, in proportion to its industrial strength: and provide that all knowledge to which its aid contributes, shall become public at once. A league of all nations for such purposes might aid in the building up of a wide international comity[1].

3. *Some minor functions of producers' associations.*

Automatic organization is still the chief origin of standardization of product, specialization of task, and the advancement of knowledge in relation to industry; and indeed its action becomes ever stronger and more rapid. But yet its influence is being increasingly overshadowed by those of far-reaching forethought and carefully planned organization. A good instance for our present purpose is that of cost-accounts.

Truly scientific cost-accounts are indeed not yet in sight: no near approach to them can be made by any slight effort; and they are not likely to be attained save by several generations of hard work. But the rate of progress has been much increased

[1] In regard to public institutions for this purpose in Britain reference may be made (partly on the basis of Benn's *Trade as a Science*, p. 132) to the National Physical Laboratory, the Leather Sellers' College, the Imperial College at Kensington, and the proposed Institute of Technical Optics at Clerkenwell. Staffordshire has her Design and Industries Association, and Manchester her School of Technology; Leeds and Bradford make special provision for the Woollen Industries; and so on. This incomplete list may probably be more than doubled in a few years. See also above, pp. 99—102, and 131—135.

III, XII, 3. by the prominence, which the financial unity of many semi-independent businesses under a central control has given to flagrant diversities among the methods of cost-reckoning, that are to be found even in similar businesses[1].

Another direction in which producers' associations are likely to work for the public good is that of reducing unreasonable additions by traders to the prices which producers receive. Many of the services rendered by middlemen are of vital importance, and are fully worth the costs incurred for them: but in some cases, the number of middlemen is in excess of the real requirements of their work: and they earn goodly incomes by large additions to the prices of comparatively small quantities of goods that pass through their hands. Then there is need for a remedy; and none can apply it so well or so thoroughly as an association of producers: but this power gives large opportunities for action, which benefits particular sections of the nation at the expense of others; and thus is often the more dangerous to public welfare, the more attractive it is to those who wield it: to this matter we now pass[2].

[1] This is an instance of the rule that the progress of knowledge must generally wait on an extension of conscious ignorance. (See above, II, XI, 1; also Appendix A, 1.) The Ministry of Munitions has had unusual opportunities for comparing, contrasting, and improving the methods of cost-accounts.

It is well known that no method of cost-accounts can be perfectly adapted to all industries nor even to all businesses in the same industry. But the advantages of uniformity in this matter are so great that it might be well to set up officially several standard methods, indicated perhaps by the letters A, B, C, etc. Each such method might have several minor variations, properly numbered in regard to specific points: the chief of these might be the methods of distribution of particular items of general, or overhead, costs among particular products. Such an order having been set up by Government or by other means, investigations for the purpose of assessing income tax etc. would be facilitated by a statement of the particular standard method employed, and of any minor variations as to specific points. The Industrial Reconstruction Council has already issued an able and helpful paper by Mr M. Webster Jenkinson on *The Workers' Interest in Costing*: and the Federation of British Industries is rendering excellent service to the country by its work towards a consistent system of cost-accounts for general use.

[2] It is known for instance that the prices, which makers of wall-papers receive from merchants, have sometimes been doubled before they reach the decorators; and doubled again when sold to the public. Of course wall-papers come in varying degrees under the class of fashion and fancy goods, in regard to which the profit on the turnover must be very high (see above, pp. 281—2). The enormous additions, which are made to the prices of fish received by the fishermen, are sometimes attributed to effective combinations among a larger

4. *Associations of producers for constructive work in marketing; especially in connection with export trade.* III, XII, 4.

The business of marketing in the present age differs from that of earlier times chiefly in matters of detail: though the business of production has been for the greater part so revolutionized as to be almost unintelligible to an able industrialist, even of the eighteenth century, if he could come to life again. But the slowness of progress of marketing has increased its apparent relative "importance," when that is measured by the amount of occupation which it affords to the population. The new age has set mechanical power to do most of the hard work of production. But the burden of marketing must still be borne mainly by men: and the present tendency of associated effort to become broader, and to reach further, in marketing, than in making, is in great measure the result of natural causes[1].

So compelling are the present developments of technique, and the intensity of international competition, that prudence, as well as courage, calls for freedom for all kinds of association that can render important services, even though they are liable to be turned to evil account. But the larger that freedom, the more urgent are the duties of students to examine, and of Authority to control probable abuses of the opportunities offered by it: and these abuses are more closely connected generally with the operations of marketing, than of production. This need for caution seems to be recognized in the guarded statement of the Committee on commercial and industrial policy after the war, that "It is very desirable that in all important British

number of intermediaries than the trade really requires. The time is not ripe for agreements among fishermen to sell only to traders, who would undertake to keep prices to retailers and to the public at reasonable amounts: but such tasks may not prove too heavy for a later age. Reference may again be made to some details of marketing discussed in Appendix J.

[1] The chief influences of modern technique on the methods of marketing have come through the printing press, through rapid transport, and through long distance communications by telegraph and telephone.

It is true that in earlier times a large part of the population spent some time in marketing; but nearly every small trader made most of the things which he sold; and was in fact a producer rather than a trader. That habit has few survivals now: few traders produce any considerable part of what they sell. A generation ago the baker differed from most other shopkeepers in selling chiefly his own products: but even he is now often merely a trader, selling wares made in a huge factory.

III, XII, 4. industries there should exist strong, comprehensive, and well organized associations, which should be clearing-houses of information of common interest, and should be competent to voice the opinions and the needs of their respective trades as a whole[1]."

Some of these purposes are served fairly well by Chambers of Commerce, especially such as represent the homes of definitely localized industries: and larger problems of industry find their place among the manifold affairs of Chambers, when meeting in Association. But there yet remain great gaps in the work to be done: and accordingly the "Federation of British industries" has set itself to promote the formation of representative Associations for particular industries; "to collect them and their leading members into a central federation for dealing with matters of common interest to all industries, and for mutual support"; to allot to each industry or trade a duly proportionate "voice in the discussion and decision of questions of common interest"; and thus to give effective "assistance in the promotion and development of British trade." The groups, which it represents, include the greater part of the adult population, but they do not include all. Nearly every group and sub-group, included in it, has direct interests in promoting the importation of some products, and is apt to be more or less jealous of the importation of others: but that considerable part of the adult population, which is not included, has seldom any direct reason for such jealousy: and yet the chief burden of the wastes caused by jealousies among the various groups of producers and traders falls ultimately on that large non-vocal group[2].

Britain's industries have a larger concern than those of any other country in external trade: and a special interest attaches to the work of Associations of her producers for organizing the direct sale of their goods through their own agents. The work is primarily constructive; though it may develop militant tendencies to meet the competition of rival exporters from other industrial countries.

[1] [Cd. 9035], 1918, p. 35.

[2] The Federation aims at developing the efficiency of each group; at smoothing away any frictions that may arise among groups, or perhaps sub-groups; at supplying to Government wise and well-balanced advice in regard to its choice of representatives of particular groups; and in other ways of national importance.

Not long ago Britain's exports, like those of other countries, were in the main sold at chief ports, or other cities, to local traders, who marketed them in detail: and her imports were bought chiefly at similar centres. But now improvements in the internal communications of even backward countries enable an enterprising British or German merchant, or an agent of a manufacturing business, to penetrate far into the interior. So energetic are the tentacles of trade which each great industrial country is throwing out, that no one can long hold his own if he neglects opportunities that are thus open to all: and therefore the importer must seek to sell his goods ever nearer to the ultimate consumer; and the importer must seek to buy his raw products ever nearer to the original producer. Meanwhile international competition develops in backward countries, as well as in those where competition has always been active; and the trader must be increasingly alert to meet rivals who bring to bear in the competition a more thoroughly organized energy and a larger capitalistic force than were often met in earlier times. He must even be on his guard against oblique strategy[1].

Accordingly America's Federal Trade Commission suggests that cooperation in her export trade is needed to meet the competition organized by the six hundred German cartels; and by associations of manufacturers in various British industries designed "to handle their business in certain important markets, and to carry on an aggressive campaign for its extension....It is against such organizations as these, uniting powerful groups of foreign concerns, backed by great banks and aided by railway and ship lines, and assisted by foreign Governments, that hundreds of comparatively small manufacturers and producers must compete if they engage in export trade[2]." Therefore the

[1] This may be illustrated by an extreme instance. When the great war broke out, a German advertising agency had bought the sole control of the advertising space in eighty-one principal Italian newspapers; together with the right to veto, without reason given, any announcement in the news columns which might be disagreeable to it. Such warfare cannot be met by an individual producer or trader: but it may be in great measure met ultimately by organized efforts on the part of all industrial countries; and then all of them will be a little poorer than if the warfare had never begun. (See *Times, Trade Supplement*, September, 1918, p. 136.)

[2] *Report on cooperation in American Export Trade*, Part I, pp. 5, 6. See also an article on "Export problems and American foreign trade policy," by William Notz, in *The Journal of Political Economy*, February, 1918.

III, XII, 4. Commission, while repressing all competition within the United States, which "restrains trade, substantially lessens competition, or tends to create a monopoly"; yet recognizes that a strict enforcement of this principle on American traders might be oppressive, when they meet the assaults of German and other competitors, whose methods are unrestrained. It therefore proposes "to allow American firms to cooperate for export and to permit the use of certain methods abroad, which are legal in foreign countries, but are not permitted in the United States." It urges that the tasks required in the export trade are often too heavy to be borne by individual producers; while merchants may lack the technical knowledge and special interest needed for making the most of goods that lie outside of the ordinary course of trade. Cooperative organizations "can afford to advertise, to study foreign demands and customs, to make demonstrations,—to collect credit information, and to extend credit[1]."

These considerations tend to show that, if a business desires to extend its export trade, and is for any reason not content with the services rendered to it by merchants, it has a strong claim to be allowed to unite with others in like position in a Federation for the purpose; and that a relatively free hand may be allowed to the Federation.

An agent appointed to control the export trade of a giant business in a large market has some exceptional advantages. He can have a thorough technical knowledge both of the goods which he handles, and of the requirements and tastes of local traders and consumers in regard to them. He can recommend that certain goods be offered, temporarily at least, at prices that

[1] Accordingly Congress passed in 1918 an Act ordaining that existing laws "shall not be construed as declaring to be illegal an association entered into for the sole purpose of engaging in export trade,"...provided its effect "is not in restraint of trade within the United States, and is not in restraint of the export trade of any domestic competitor of such association...and does not intentionally enhance or depress prices within the United States of commodities of the class exported by it, or substantially lessen competition." It orders that when the Commission "has reason to believe that any association violates the Act, it shall require its officers to appear before the Commission; and, after investigation, to issue appropriate recommendations." If they are not adopted, the matter is to be referred to the Attorney-General for "such action thereon as he may think proper." These details are given, because they suggest lines on which Britain may find it advisable to move in the near future.

do little more than cover costs; on the ground that, though they have not yet attracted the attention of his market, they are likely to obtain a strong position there, when their use has become familiar: and so on. But even a giant business cannot afford to have a strong representative in every overseas market.

A great association of producers may however maintain a number of competent agents; though they indeed will not always have an intimate knowledge of each of the various products committed to them. But, much friction is caused when an agent of an association is found to have sold a larger proportion of goods supplied by one member of it, than of similar goods supplied by another. Even the tireless assiduity of German cartels has not fully overcome this difficulty, except in regard to simple half-products, so completely standardized, that a Syndicate can become the owner of the whole output of its members; and, after selling that in different markets at such prices as seem best to it, can divide out the net proceeds *pro ratâ*.

But several partial solutions of the difficulty are now on trial. For instance, in the Engineering industry, some small companies have been set up by particular groups of manufacturers, for the purpose of pushing some of their wares in particular countries; the selection being so made that none of the goods handled by any one are competitive: each manufacturer can give his own instructions as to the prices to be asked for the goods. The home manufacturer has to give credit: the companies "have not adopted the system of merchant houses of paying for the goods[1]."

A bold extension of this plan appears in the setting up of a vast central Association, which is to appoint an "Agent-in-Charge" of each important overseas district: he is to assign to particular agents under his control the care for certain products of particular members of the Association; subject to the condition that no one agent is responsible for two products which compete with one another. On that plan each manufacturer can issue what instructions he likes as to his own goods[2].

[1] *Report on the engineering trades* [Cd. 9073], p. 19.

[2] This is the plan of the "British Manufacturers' Corporation," recently founded by Sir Charles Mandleberg. "The Agent-in-Charge in each country must necessarily be British, and possessed of commercial experience and

III, XII, 5. Meanwhile trade between Britain and her overseas kindred is being fostered by "Trade Commissioners," each of whom has the duty of keeping British producers and exporters in touch with the conditions of that part of the Empire, to which he is assigned. This important work has a broader, but perhaps less penetrating and thorough influence, than the intensive methods which we have been considering[1].

5. *The strength of the semi-automatic organization of export trade by independent merchants: functions of banks in relation to the trade.*

Large as are the tasks which may be accomplished by Associations of manufacturers, or other producers in developing export trade, room will probably continue to be found for the services of the merchant in organizing and financing it: the merchant may have done in the past much that should have been done by the producer; but there seems some danger that the pendulum, which has swung too far in one direction, may swing too far in the opposite.

knowledge of the language and trading customs acquired by previous residence. Of high commercial standing, his position and prestige would give him influence in checking chicanery, securing the best selling agents for exclusively British goods, commanding the best legal services for members of the Corporation, and obtaining advanced news of likely trade openings." He would have a considerable staff: and he "would recommend and appoint selling agents for members when desired, either for single firms, groups, or combinations, so arranging that competing firms would not be represented by the same agent. After appointment, selling agents and manufacturers would conduct their business direct, the Agent-in-Charge only intervening in emergencies, power of attorney being given to him to act in disputes." Thus every manufacturer "would be put into a position for getting into direct touch with his foreign customers. He would get to know their precise needs on the one hand, and, on the other, he would be able to put before them his entire range of products." While these remarks were passing through the press, it was announced that this Corporation had been fused with the Federation of British Industries; see above, p. 612.

[1] "A Trade Commissioner stationed in any Dominion or Colony, and responsible for a particular area, has to make himself fully conversant with:—(1) The Business Houses trading in his area, as well as the local manufacturers and public bodies. (2) The quantity and value that the country purchases of articles which the British manufacturer and merchant can supply. (3) The tariff and customs regulations for goods entering the country. (4) The foreign goods competing with British, their method of sale, their character and price. (5) Freights and charges and the comparative rates between British ports and foreign ports serving his area." (*The Board of Trade Journal*, April, 1918.)

A great merchant is likely to be a man of larger capacity than is generally to be found among salaried officers of a corporation. The variety of his operations gives opportunity for a broad study of character and conditions, and is of especial use in the difficult and important task of deciding where credit may safely be given: while the knowledge, obtained in each class of his many-sided dealings, serves him in others. He works for gain: but he generally benefits his country. His personal connections, as well as his patriotism, incline him to give preference to home goods, other things being nearly equal. If British producers fall in any respect behind their competitors, it is in their own interest, and that of the country, that they should be warned to bestir themselves. There are nearly always some producers who are capable: the merchant is specially able to select them; and, by so doing, he advances the industry to which they belong: an alert and wise use of his discretion may in the long run be of even greater benefit to his country than to himself. No doubt he sometimes selects products of some country other than his own, as the best suited for his purpose: but he is not very likely to do that, unless the corresponding industry in his own country is either not yet fully developed, or somewhat somnolent, and in need of a hint to amend its ways. It is however true that a special agent may be expected to send home some account of the reasons for any preference shown to rival goods; and a merchant seldom does as much.

It is to be remembered that the modern age calls increasingly for the concentration of thought, as well as of plant, on relatively narrow ranges of thorough specialized work: and there is therefore a certain presumption in favour of the relegation by the producer to the merchant of as much of the work of marketing as possible. Any reverse movement at the present time needs to be supported by very strong arguments; and it is to be noted that both German cartels and American giant businesses delegate as much of the work of detailed marketing as is practicable to semi-independent corporations or dealers: also that the merchants that act for German cartels are often themselves cartellized. Also the multiplication of Associations of business men must increase the time which they divert from action to talking and hearing others talk: it often happens that

III, XII, 5. the least progressive of them find most leisure for talk, and exercise an undue influence thereby. The British habit of concentrating the day's work into a few hours of high strain increases the evil, that arises everywhere from frequent attendance at meetings, which must necessarily be long[1].

It is to be noted also that the merchant supplies a part of the capital, needed to "carry" produce on its way to the ultimate purchaser: and that he has special facilities for supplementing his own resources. It is true that the producers as well as the merchants can draw command over capital from Lombard Street for the purpose of financing some classes of their export trade: but that course is not always available in regard to goods sent to a producer's agents in distant lands for sale there[2].

On the whole we may perhaps conclude that there are many cases, in which agents of a producers' association may market abroad particular classes of goods with more intimate technical knowledge, and perhaps with more assiduity than are generally to be found in the independent merchant: but that yet the advancement of a country's export trade must in the main depend on his judgment and enterprise.

British banks serve the common interest by drawing command over capital from branches in residentiary districts, and

[1] In one important case this delegation has led to an increase of concentration. For the United States Steel Corporation, having set up a huge corporation, "Steel Products," to market its products, went further, to invite independent steel works to use its services. They have generally adopted this suggestion; and nearly the whole of America's steel output is sold through a single channel. The immediate economy and efficiency of the plan are obvious; but time alone can show whether it is free from latent disadvantage.

As to German practice, the *Report on Cooperation in the American export trade* (Part I, pp. 98—114 and Part II, pp. 3—89) is exceptionally full of suggestive information. In many cases the merchants, or associations of merchants, through whom the sales are effected, are so tied down by regulations as to the additions made by them to the prices at which the cartels hand over goods to them that they may almost be regarded as agents of the cartels.

[2] Of course a merchant, who stocks goods on a large scale, may sometimes set his own brand on them: but producers admit that he tends to steady the market by absorbing goods, when other demands are slack; while he can deliver more quickly than the manufacturers can do unless they keep large stocks themselves. Again he sends them larger and more regular orders than they might otherwise obtain, and saves them a vast amount of detailed work, which might hinder the application of their energies to that work which specially belongs to them.

lending it out in manufacturing districts; and the requirements of the export trade reinforce suggestions already made (see above, II, IX), in regard to the interests which the public has in the extension of the scope of work of British banks. While those services, to which they devote most of their strength, are of unapproached excellence, they make little attempt to rival German, or even American banks in the direct furtherance of the larger ventures of industry. By limiting their operations to a multitude of relatively small risks, they are enabled to base their advances chiefly on capital deposited with them; and therefore to return extremely high dividends on relatively small paid-up capitals. There are therefore some strong arguments, both of equity and of national advantage, in favour of the exertion of a slight pressure on them, by legislation or otherwise, tending to increase the ratio which their paid-up capitals bear to their total liabilities. They could then, with safety to themselves and their depositors, undertake a rather greater share than they do now of the larger responsibilities of the country's business abroad, as well as at home, while they would still cover so great a part of their liabilities by fluid assets, as to be certain of the ability to meet promptly further larger demands that might be made on them.

Like many German and other great banks, they might thus be inclined to hold on their directorates, or in their employment, a considerable number of men in the early prime of life. Each would select such as had direct knowledge of those matters of industry or trade, to which it was devoting special attention; and would require them to give at all events the greater part of their time to the work, in return for commensurate remuneration by salary or otherwise[1].

[1] Sir Charles Addis, in a notable article in the *Edinburgh Review*, July, 1918, points out that a mere technical expert would not be in place on the Board: but should advise financiers on the technical side of a project. He indicates that some German banks are burdened by undigested securities through having neglected this caution.

He remarks that the London floating loan market averages £m.300 of bills under discount, together with £m.100 lodged by bill brokers with banks as security against loans: and that the variety, extent and elasticity of its resources are without a parallel elsewhere. And yet it is over-susceptible: because too large a part of those resources belong to its customers, and too little to its owners.

CHAPTER XIII

AGGREGATION, FEDERATION, AND COOPERATION IN BRITISH INDUSTRY AND TRADE, CONTINUED

III, XIII, 1.

1. *The regulation of prices by associations of producers.*

It has already been argued (above, II, II, 4) that there is little fundamental difference between sellers' monopolies, and buyers' monopolies: that in many cases a mere change of wording will enable what is commonly regarded as a sellers' monopoly to appear as a buyers' monopoly; and that, even where this cannot be done, there is no general principle by which it can be decided whether a sellers' or a buyers' monopoly is likely to be the stronger. A federation of producing businesses is often a monopolistic seller of products; and, though more rarely, a monopolistic buyer of materials or of plant[1].

These considerations suggest that many of the most important applications of the principles, to be discussed in this chapter, relate to the "marketing" of labour and of employment, rather than of material goods: but their study must be postponed to another occasion; because the various elements, and especially the "human" elements, which enter into them, are large and various. It may however be well to note at once that the class-selfishness to which some capitalist-producers are tempted when they see the way to raising prices by associated

[1] It may appear as a monopolistic buyer of skilled labour of a certain sort: but when the labour required in an industry is of a highly specialized kind, while the plant available is more than adequate for the existing stock of that labour, an association of workers may have the upper hand as a monopoly of sellers. If the bargain be regarded as one for the purchase of employment, instead of for the sale of labour, the workers become the buyers; but the essential features of their monopoly are unchanged.

action against other producers, and ultimately against the general public, sometimes does more harm through its indirect than through its direct results. For trades unionists often understand the matter better than the public does; and in consequence are less willing than they otherwise might be to forego a strategic advantage in response to a plea that it would cause more hurt to the nation than benefit to themselves. Conversely, employers' associations for the regulation of wages have sometimes been turned to account for antisocial regulation of prices. Concerted action, on the lines of the *Whitley Report*, as to which a little will be said soon, will probably work for good in these matters, though it is not without its dangers.

III, XIII, 1.

The main principles of cartel-like associations have been discussed in Chapters IX and X; and what has to be said now, turns chiefly on differences between the German and the British peoples in character and in methods of organization. British associations, or cartels, are less under the influence of military discipline, and generally less harsh in their methods than German: but, as we shall see, their task is increased by the presence of many old firms with inherited plant and traditions.

The relatively mild policy of British steel Associations gave great freedom to each business to choose its own lines of development. While such powerful and enterprising businesses as those of Armstrong and Vickers were content to buy the steel on which they worked, there was no over-mastering advantage in deep vertical expansion similar to that, which threw the dominion of the German steel industry into the hands of a relatively small group of giant capitalists; since none others could reach out to such expansion: so that cartel policy inevitably strengthened the strong relatively to the weak. But, human nature being what it is, association which is knitted tightly together in constructive work, often develops common militant action; and in this case it is liable to be turned towards restrictive combination of the harsh German type.

Britain's control of the tin-plate industry is no doubt the result of several causes: but the chief of these has been that those engaged in it could make sure of obtaining the steel bars needed by them at reasonable prices. Associations to regulate these

III, XIII, 1. prices were not indeed absent: but they were not tyrannical; and indeed they could not raise prices much above those in the world market, as importation was free. So the German tin-plate industry which probably might have kept on at about even pace with the British, if the price of steel bars had not been raised against it by a cartel, was left far behind[1].

Larger questions are opened up when we come to the relations between the steel industries and the shipbuilding industries. The steel industries are reasonably jealous of any appearance of monopolistic discrimination in the freight charges by railways or shipping companies, which seem to favour foreign customers; who might divert traffic from them; they complain sorely when rather higher charges are maintained for home producers, who have no alternative course by which to escape[2]. Reciprocally, shipbuilders complain that "the Steel market is largely controlled by the Steelmakers' Associations, which regulate both prices and area of supply": they say that though "the Combines have not hitherto been able to exercise any very great influence in raising prices, owing to the existence or imminence of foreign competition," yet "in certain specific cases combines have taken full advantage of their position, when foreign competition was excluded": the last five words are noteworthy[3].

In fact though numerous verdicts in favour of facilities for regulating prices by combination can be obtained from particular industries, so long as each is thinking chiefly of the prices which it receives; such verdicts cover only a part of the ground. What one branch of industry gains by such regulation is apt to be more than lost by another branch which buys from it, except in so far as the loss can be shifted on ultimate consumers: and they are indeed often the main losers.

[1] See Jones, *The tinplate industry*, chs. VII and IX: also Levy, *Monopoly and Competition*, p. 205. Experiments in the vertical fusion of steel-bar and tin-plate making have not prospered; partly perhaps because German steel-bar makers were selling cheaply abroad bars for which German tin-plate makers had to pay high prices.

[2] See *Report on iron and steel trades*, pp. 34—6; and *Report on engineering trades*, p. 31.

[3] *Report on shipping and shipbuilding industries*, p. 26; and *Report on engineering trades*, p. 31.

2. *When markets are perfectly open, the interests of the general public are defended in great measure by the alert watching of producers in each stage of industry against undue raising of the prices of their plant or material: but this defence is impaired when the price in each stage is arranged by a combination of producers in it.*

Associations of producers are liable to develop price policies, of which the chief purpose is to stay dissensions in the group affected, and to introduce harmony and good-will where sharp competition formerly prevailed. Concord is indeed obtained within a section of the nation: but generally at the expense of injuries to the nation at large, and particularly to other sections of it, which far outweigh the good achieved by concord within that section. But these evil results are less conspicuous, and much less prominently advertised than are its immediate benefits: and so the public is apt to be misled. It may be admitted that, if the businesses, according to whose needs the prices are set, are alert and equipped with the best plant, skill, and organization, the public interests are not likely to be much hurt; and they may even be advanced. But it often happens that the costs of production, including normal profits, which are to be covered are those of businesses which lag somewhat behind: and, here Britain appears at a disadvantage relatively to some other countries. For the great age of her industries puts difficulties in the way of their rapid reorganization.

In America and Germany many industries are controlled by relatively small numbers of powerful capitalists; most of whom are intent on large ambitions, and have little interest in inherited plant or traditions. They desire to make great gains by great transactions; and the cost of production, which they have in mind, is nearly always that of an alert business, equipped with modern appliances, and making for great aggregate gains by large output at rather low costs per unit: thus a complaint by a quiescent business that it cannot work at such costs may receive but scant attention. Those who are weak, through fault or misfortune, are left to go to the wall; or they are bought out, and their works are recast, or abandoned. In Germany the alert and all-pervading influences of the great banks make for good in these directions.

III, XIII, 2. But in Britain an association of producers often depends in great measure on the adherence of worthy firms, that reckon costs of production on the basis of good solid work or well-tried methods and with well-tried plant. They are content to sell generally at, or near, old high prices to those with whom they have an established connection; and in case of pressure they sell at forced prices, subject to no rule: but their support is desired by a projected association: partly because they may be a source of trouble if left outside. The path of least resistance is to take their costs as normal costs: with the result that alert members of the association claim credit for not pushing prices above normal costs, while inly rejoicing at the great excess of those prices over their own costs. No doubt an association, working on these lines, has little defence against strong attack: but it is likely to be vocal, and to show some ingenuity in proving that it is threatened by unfair competition, especially if that comes from overseas; and can be convicted of selling occasionally at very low prices[1].

The manufacturer or trader is indeed strongly interested in obtaining materials, plant or product on terms, at least as low as those paid by competitors who sell in the same market: for, as a general rule, he loses the whole of any extra prices which he pays above those paid by most of his competitors; and he gains the whole of any lowering of prices which accrues to him alone. Hence it may be inferred that, so long as enterprise is entirely unshackled, the nation need not actively exert itself in regard to the prices of such materials and plant; since those, who have the most knowledge of such matters, are also those most deeply interested in obtaining

[1] The fact that provision must be made for the needs of businesses whose plant and energy are not of the best is well known, and it seems never to be denied; though frank, open statements on the subject are rare.

The National Association of British and Irish Millers was however told publicly in 1901 that "in arranging for fixed prices, it will be seen that the worst equipped and most unfavourably situated mills must be considered, and must of course make a profit: therefore the larger mills must of course work at such a margin of profit as shall, and indeed does, invite outside competition." To meet this some millers have "invoiced and charged flour at the price of the grade below" that to which it really belonged. (Quoted by Macrosty, *l.c.* p. 220.) If it had been possible to absorb the new competition, this clear avowal might not have been made: and the Association would have been able still to plunder the public.

them on favourable terms; and most alert to oppose any unfavourable change.

But this inference is not valid when the price of the material or plant in question is controlled by a cartel, that covers the market in which any set of producers are interested. Of course an artificial rise in that price might go so far, that the consequent rise in the cost of finished products of the industry would materially curtail their sale; and, in such a case, nearly all those in the industry would be alert to oppose the rise. But the increase by, say, a tenth in the cost of a particular material or implement needed by the industry will often cause only a very minute increase in the total costs of its output, and therefore will not greatly affect the volume of its sales: and, in that case, the public may derive scarcely any defence from the opposition of producers in a late stage of the industry to an artificial rise of price in an earlier stage. In fact such producers have often argued publicly in this manner: "What each of us wants, is to know that his competitors will not get anything needed for their work at a lower price than he does: for, in that case, we can all safely pass on any moderate increase in costs, with profits, to the consumer: let us then make no trouble about a moderate uniform increase of price in regard to this or that secondary plant or material that we need." For instance, makers of galvanized sheets for roofing, care very little what price they pay for their steel, so long as they know that all other makers pay the same; and that they have nothing much to fear from the competition of slates, tiles, felt or other roofing materials. In fact they watch changes in the prices of such materials with more attention than they do the price of steel, when that is fixed by general agreement: that is to say, their own interests do not lead them to be active in protecting the ultimate purchasers of finished steel products against an artificial increase in the price charged by a cartel of heavy steel producers. Thus one small cause of increase in the cost of the finished product passes without resistance; and, if it stood by itself, it might do but little harm. But similar causes bring about other small increases in the cost of the finished product: and ultimately the public is liable to suffer much from an accumulation of small burdens, no one of which by itself would be a matter of serious concern to it[1].

3. *Cartel policies of exclusive dealing are often fortified by deferred rebates.*

Attention has already been called to the severity of the device for developing the monopolistic power of Coats' business, which consisted in refusing to sell to any trader, who handled similar goods at prices somewhat less in excess of costs of production than those fixed by Coats: in effect that apparently mild rule closed the entrance of the highway of business to any firm, which desired to establish a connection in the trade. Several British cartels have adopted the same device, with considerable success. But others have had recourse to that uncompromising policy of exclusive dealing, fortified by deferred rebates, which we have seen evoking drastic repression in America. It no doubt closely resembles in form the scheme by which the South African and other shipping trades have been partially monopolized: but, when applied to manufactures, it lacks generally the extenuating circumstances, which are found in fast-liner traffic. It aims of course at securing the control of a trader's custom by allowing a high Rebate or discount on the normal high charges of an association: and by deferring payment for some years; with the intimation that it will be forfeited, if the recipient meanwhile buys from anyone who is not a member of the association[2].

[1] In the export trade, where British producers compete chiefly with those of other industrial countries, an artificial rise in freights for exportation is of relatively small concern to the merchants, who pay it in the first instance. The producers and consumers are more nearly concerned: but they are seldom in a position to take action in the matter. Some similar maladjustments have been noted, above, pp. 443, 444.

[2] This practice has been adopted by several associations, whose products are needed for building houses and cottages, including several sorts of steel products. Its fiercest application in Britain has been made by an offshoot of the notorious American Shoe Machinery Company (see above, pp. 233—4; and 536—7): and the British Court of Chancery decided in 1907 that the leaser of machinery under this clause, binding him to use it to its "full capacity," may not cease to use it, when it ceases to be efficient for his purpose: he must go on working

An alert, well equipped producer may be able to earn good profits by sales at prices lower than those, which the association is thus induced to fix; and traders, if free, would welcome his supply. But they are not free; save in the very rare case in which this producer is able to supply all their wants: for, if they buy one class of thing from him, they lose their rebates on all their purchases. Therefore such producers cannot sell unless they submit to the edict of an association: and that is liable to be managed partly in the interests of its less energetic members, and to allot to others quotas of production too small to keep their advanced plant in full work. Thus, the public pay more than is necessary for their goods; though independent energy and enterprise meet but a scanty reward. A sectional association may gain by such means: but there is a net loss: and if every section adopted them, every section would be poorer. That is to say such policy is antisocial[1].

4. *A combination in a British manufacturing industry, even when not protected by a tarif, may yet be able to raise prices artificially by the equivalent of double costs of transport between Britain and other countries.*

We have now to consider the extent of the defence, which the British people derive from the free importation of manufactures, against the raising of prices unduly by associations at home. Of course, freedom of entry into Britain does not imply free carriage for the goods that come to her: nor free carriage for the goods, by which she effects payments for such parts of them as are not covered by obligations of other countries to her. In this matter large allowances must be made for the services of her shipping industry; for interest on her exported capital;

it even though it has been superseded by better machinery and has become incapable of being worked at a profit. This may be good law; but, if so, law provides inadequate protection to public interests.

[1] Cases are known in which an association makes itself responsible for paying profits on twice the plant, which would suffice to produce all the goods that it can market at the artificially high prices, which are required to enable its less alert members to work at a profit. This evil is often a little reduced in fact, though it is made more obvious, when badly equipped firms are allowed to lie idle; and yet receive, at the expense of the public, profits on the full quota which have been assigned to them.

III, XIII, 5. and for some other matters that are independent of the particular imports concerned: but, that being done, any increase in her imports must be covered by a corresponding increase of her exports in order to pay for them. All her exports of any importance, except coal, are manufactures in the production of which she has no advantage, other than the abundance of her capital and the energies of her people: and, for various reasons, she does not pay, and she ought not to pay, for a great part of her imports by the exportation of coal[1].

Therefore almost every increase in Britain's importation of manufactures has to be covered by an increase in her exportation of other manufactures; and every such change involves double costs of transport; those of her own increased exports, and those of the imports which come in return for them. Thus there is a *primâ facie* case for thinking that British manufacture A, which fears the importation of rival products, paid for (together with double costs of transport) by the exports of another manufacture B, is somewhat lacking in alertness and energy.

This *primâ facie* case is indeed subject to various exceptions, arising out of particular conditions of industry, and with one that is common to most branches of industry. We need concern ourselves here with this alone. It arises from the facts that B products may probably be offered for sale abroad at lower net prices (after allowing, that is, for cost of carriage) than are exacted at home: and that A products may similarly be offered in Britain at lower net prices than are charged for them in the country of their origin: we pass to consider this point.

5. *The policy of dumping. The claim of combinations to stabilize home industry.*

It is customary to sell abroad at lower *net* prices (that is, at lower prices after deducting all costs) than at home: and it

[1] Coal is not "produced" by man: he merely takes it out of nature's limited store houses. The position which Britain will hold in the world some centuries hence will depend largely on the care with which she has husbanded her stores of it: any generation which exports it, in order to pay for those manufactures, in the production of which Britain should hold her own, will inflict an injury on coming generations.

is suggested that this tendency implies attitudes of producers and traders towards foreign competitors, somewhat different from their attitudes towards their own countrymen. There is no doubt a good deal of truth in this suggestion. But indeed the tendency has broad roots in the fact that almost every one is inclined to allay conflict in a market, which he regards as belonging to him in "particular"; while he is often inclined, and sometimes compelled to adopt a different policy, when pushing his way into a market on which he has no special hold[1]. III, XIII, 5.

In a sense the home market of any national industry is its "particular": and an association of businesses in it is likely to arrange prices in it somewhat on the plan of a cartel, even though it has no very firm cohesion. Its members are likely to agree not to press sales in the home market; when it is so unreceptive that it will not take more of their produce at prices, that cover or nearly cover full costs of production: with the understanding that those producers, who cannot conveniently hold their hands for a while, shall sell abroad at whatever prices they can get. From these small beginnings there are sometimes developed large policies of systematic "dumping" of a considerable part of the output of an industry in foreign markets, and especially in any that are regarded with jealousy. Early in last century, as has already been noted[2], Britain was the chief offender in this direction: and the lapse of several generations was needed to undo the hurt, which she thereby caused to her own reputation. In recent times Germany has been the chief offender; and the present inquiry may be continued with reference to her policy in this matter. We need not concern ourselves with the suggestions, that the exceptional energy, with which she has developed this commercial policy, is a necessary part of her

[1] See above, pp. 182; and 400—402. The case was put by a witness before the Industrial Commission (*Report* XIII. p. 493) thus:—"Business that is at my door I think belongs to me, but I am willing to make a sacrifice to get a foreign market, because by that very process I reduce my cost at home. By a foreign market I mean a market outside of my natural territory. I would say the Chicago merchants sold for less money in Omaha than they did in Peoria, because they are either competing with St Paul on one side or St Louis on the other; and I would say that they sold for less money in Denver than in Omaha, and for even less in San Francisco than in Denver."

[2] Above, p. 157; and below, pp. 781—2.

III, XIII, 5. militant policy: and that she "dumps" in order to prevent the rise of rival industries in other countries. For in fact very little of the cheap selling abroad by cartels in the steel industry, and others of which Germany has no monopoly, has this excuse—whatever it may be worth.

Of course a policy of dumping can always be stopped by special import duties on dumped wares, if it is worth while: and there seem to be a few cases in which it may be worth while. But some caution is needed in this matter: for that remedy is likely to be advocated with energy, and with the advantages derived from intimate knowledge of details, by individuals, and by associations, who desire to keep prices in the home market high enough to yield profits to businesses that are not very alert, and still use plant that is not up to date. Moreover it appears that some of those, who are prominent in emphasizing the case against artificially cheapened imports into Britain, are themselves inclined to sell abroad at very low prices, in order to maintain very high prices at home. There is indeed something to be said for declining to protect a British industry even against artificially cheap imports, if it carries far the practice of lowering its own export prices relatively to its home prices: and in any case care must be taken lest provisions made for the purpose of repressing malignant forms of underselling be so worded, as to condemn methods of trading which are practised on occasion by honourable British firms. This danger is likely, if ignored, to lower the reputation of the country for fair dealing.

The Report of the Engineering Committee already quoted has that danger clearly in view: and recommends the adoption of legislation similar to that of America, which orders that selling at low prices—that is, at prices less than those prevailing elsewhere—be prohibited, not absolutely, but only "Provided that such act or acts be done with the intent of destroying or injuring an industry in the United States, or of preventing the establishment of an industry in the United States, or of restraining or monopolizing any part of trade or commerce in the United States[1]."

[1] [Cd. 9073], pp. 27, 28. Some claims for Protection against the dumping of foreign goods in Britain imply a moral indignation against the practice. It is,

We may now pass to consider the claim that the effect of cartel policy in general, and especially the policy of selling at very low prices abroad, tends to stabilize industry. It may be admitted to have some force in regard to any depressions of credit, industry and trade that happen to be localized in a particular country. For then sales at home may be almost impossible save at extremely low prices; and an extension of sales abroad will tend to turn the Foreign Exchanges in the favour of the distressed country; at the same time that they facilitate the maintenance of some moderate degree of employment at home. On such an occasion, however, every one has always been eager to sell abroad cheaply; and there has been little need for organized action in the matter.

But in the last few generations there have been very few cases, and none of very serious importance, in which a single country has been struck by a severe dislocation of credit, industry and trade; while the rest of the western world remained almost undisturbed. Almost every recent wave of high or low commercial activity has spread, not very unevenly, over all countries in which large scale capitalistic production has prevailed. When the Steelworks Union for instance has the greatest need for disposing of surplus steel, the British market is not likely to absorb much except at very low prices.

Also the policy of maintaining rather high home prices for steel products when general credit is bad, obstructs the recovery of credit. For when the deepest depression has passed, businesses of all kinds begin to consider repairs and extensions of plant, for which opportunity was lacking in the preceding period of expanding credit and of work at high pressure; and there is, in consequence, a new demand for steel products: this in its turn sets retail and other businesses on increased work. The policy of the Steel Union tends to delay this revival: and thereby it has probably done more to increase the evils of industrial fluctuations than all its other efforts have done to diminish them. Its constructive efforts have been excellently seconded by the

therefore, of interest to note that "The Chairman of an important Metal Association stated" to the Commission on Trusts (see its Report, § 8) "that he would not agree that British firms dumped in the aggregate much more than foreign firms."

III, XIII, 5. close association of Germany's great banks with industry: and, if the policy of selling abroad at much lower prices than at home worked effectively for the stabilization of industry and trade, she would have suffered less from commercial depressions, when under the influence of her cartel policy than Britain has done during the same time. But in fact the opposite seems to have been the case.

The matter has not been fully examined. But we know that Germany has been struck by every recent storm of bad credit that has struck other countries; and that in 1901 she suffered very much more than others did. Also we know that industries, which are under the control of an ambitious cartel, are frequently disturbed, even while the sky generally is clear, by rumours that some of its leading members are threatening to desert it. The firmly-based coal cartel has itself been shaken by such rumours: the Steel Union has seldom been free from them; and an investigation of the prices of heavy steel products by Dr Vogelstein for the nine years ending in 1903, showed that every one of them had fluctuated in Germany as much as, or more than, in England[1].

Thus, while large acknowledgment is due to the ability, with which the Steel Union strives to distribute the benefit of Protective duties among the various sections of the Steel industry; all that can with certainty be said in its favour is that its breadth of view has lessened the evils, which would otherwise have been caused by the tendency of cartels to press the interests of particular sections of the nation against those of the nation as a whole. In that respect British associations have something to learn from it[2].

[1] *Schriften des Social-Vereins*, No. 106, p. 128. This statement seems to be supported by a comparison of Sauerbeck's records of price movements in Britain, with those shown in *Die Bewegung der Waarenpreise in Deutschland von* 1815 *bis* 1902. See also above, p. 572 fn. It has already been noted (p. 572 fn.) that the rumours of a coming syndicate set up violent expansions of plant in order to justify high figures of participation. Some observations on the influences exerted by German and British policies in regard to steel on the well-being of the operatives concerned will be found in Appendix O.

[2] Thus *The Report of the Engineering Trades*, already quoted, says (pp. 9, 10) "Whereas the manufacturers are in the habit of quoting a reduced price for steel for direct export (the margin has been as much as 20*s*. per ton), such steel manufacturers refuse to make any rebate to English engineering manufacturers, even when it is proved to their satisfaction that the goods to be manufactured from that steel were, in fact, for export purposes."

On the whole it may be concluded that the restrictive methods of German cartels have no claim for imitation on the ground that they make for the stability of industry. But this does not imply that it is beyond the power of associated action to work in that direction. For instance, many a ship has earned *net* more than its full cost in a single year; while in some other years its earnings have not covered its expenses: and the consequent violent variation in the values of ships and in the demand for new ships is a chief cause of instability in the steel industry. Consequently a suggestion has been made that ship-owners, shipbuilders, marine engineers, and all combined should endeavour to promote shipbuilding *on falling markets*. Such action by an association would be in a high degree constructive[1].

Policies which are appropriate to a military and partially autocratic Government, such as was that of Germany before the war, are likely to be unsuitable for a democratic Anglo-Saxon country. A strong democracy has a great respect for law: and therefore, although its Government is often somewhat inefficient in business administration, it can rely on full justice being done by Courts of Law in a suit, in which the interests of both parties to a contest are set out clearly by able and well-instructed advocates. That is likely to be the case when the issue is between the claims of two powerful private interests. But when a large public interest is at variance with the interest of the nation as a whole, Counsel for the nation find generally that their clients are not able to supply them with information as full, as penetrating, and as technically thorough, as that which comes easily to the hand of a private interest whose concerns are in question. In fact a democratic Government is at a distinct disadvantage in this and

[1] See *Report on the shipping and shipbuilding industries* [Cd. 9902], p. 30. Mr E. J. Benn, *Trade as a Science*, ch. IX., suggests a good model constitution of a Trade Association, and its District Committees with special reference to the export trade, to scientific research, to educating labour in the objects of its industry, and to educating employers to a proper understanding of the labour point of view. It should receive recognition, and perhaps financial aid from Government, subject to certain conditions; one of which is that it does not attempt to regulate prices within the home market. This scheme is developed in his *The trade of tomorrow*.

III, XIII, 5. other respects relatively to a capable autocratic Government, well served by a congenial bureaucracy. (See below, pp. 850—1.)

Bureaucratic methods are alien from the genius of democracy: and, though the British Government has been compelled by the emergency of war to make large uses of them, it is to be hoped that it will return to the wholesome method of taking the nation into its counsels by full publicity as soon as possible. It can turn the balance in its favour by organizing the knowledge, that is necessary to enable it to present the case of the nation on fairly even terms with the case of a private interest: and, by making public the knowledge it thus acquires, it can bring public opinion along with it. By Commissions of inquiry, sitting with open doors, and similar means, it can enable the people to appreciate its actions and its motives: it can thus gain more strength for itself and for the nation than is possible by intervening in industrial procedure in any other way[1].

The *Report of the Committee on Trusts* recommends that means be provided for the investigation of businesses or combinations of businesses, "which have for their purpose or effect the regulation of the prices or output of commodities or services, produced or rendered in the United Kingdom, or imported into the United Kingdom, or the delimitation of markets in respect thereof, or the regulation of transport rates and services, in so far as they tend to the creation of monopolies or to the restraint of trade." Annual reports by the Board of Trade, which is to have direction of the matter, are to be provided "whereby the fullest information as to the activities of Trade Associations may be made available to the public, and complaints may be promptly and thoroughly investigated, so that doubts and suspicions may be dispelled, or, on the other hand, the true facts ascertained as to evils for which a remedy is required." The Committee express the opinion "that it will

[1] Some peril seems to be threatened by suggestions such as the following, made in the generally excellent *Report on the Engineering trades* (p. 26) in regard to trade combinations:—"No secrecy should be allowed. All trade combinations should register their terms at some Government Department such as the Board of Trade....The terms should not become public property: but their registration would...enable the Board of Trade to take any steps that might be necessary in the event of such combinations being harmful to trade or prejudicial to the consumer."

be found necessary ultimately to establish further machinery for promptly and effectively dealing with such abuses as the Tribunal of Investigation may discover[1]." III, xiii, 5.

[1] Such a Tribunal is to be set up in cases in which a preliminary inquiry made by the Board of Trade gives inadequate results. It is to have "a person of legal qualifications as permanent chairman, and from two to seven other members selected by him from time to time from a panel appointed for the purpose by the President of the Board of Trade after considering nominations made by representative trade organizations, including the Cooperative Movement and Trade Unions, which Tribunal shall have power, on the application of the Board of Trade, to make orders for further information on the matters in hand."

This plan seems excellent in many respects, provided the branch of the Board of Trade which is responsible for the work is as strong a body as the Federal Commission. If so, the able men, who give their whole lives to the task will be in a good position for ascertaining what information should be required: and then it would be sufficient perhaps to provide for an appeal to an ordinary Court of Law. For when the case of the nation is presented to such a Court, by counsel instructed by such a body as the Federal Commission, there seems to be a gain on the balance in obtaining a judgment on the purely legal aspects of any matter of contention, from a Court, which approaches the matter with an open mind. In so far as the problem is one of business rather than law, a lawyer, as such, has no special authority.

The Report is brief: but much information is added in important papers by Mr Percy Ashley; and by the Secretary, Mr Hilton. Sir John Macdonell adds an authoritative and much needed statement as to the law relating to combinations.

CHAPTER XIV

THE DECLINE OF EXCLUSIVE CLASS ADVANTAGES IN INDUSTRY

III, XIV, 1. 1. ***The spread of education, and technical changes which lessen the strain of physical work, are mitigating many of the disadvantages under which the manual labour classes lie.***

The industrial sectionalism, with which we have so far been concerned, is based on varieties of occupation: and so rapidly do capital and labour—whether mental or mainly manual—migrate from one occupation to another, that time itself brings some remedy and some retribution for any harsh or unwise action on the part of those engaged in a particular occupation. But the case is different with the semi-monopolistic advantages which the upper strata of industry have always possessed over the lower. These advantages have indeed changed their form considerably: for at one time they were in great measure incidental to the superior political position of freemen over serfs and others of lower degree; while now, in Britain at all events, there are scarcely any exclusive political privileges. But meanwhile the scopes of industrial technique and business relations widened so much, that the superior education and larger outlook of the well-to-do classes became of increasing importance in all but the simplest forms of business; and on the whole the division between the "upper" and "lower" classes in industries seemed to grow broader during the second and third quarters of last century.

More recently however an opposite tendency has set in. The movement towards the better education of the people at large, which had been gradually growing, received a great impetus from the Education Act of 1870; and it has proceeded so fast and steadily that the more alert of the working classes now stand on nearly as high an intellectual level as do the great majority of the middle classes.

Meanwhile the hours of manual labour have been shortened, and excessive strain on muscles has been lessened by the increased use of steam power, and its distribution by electricity. Perhaps the percentage of artisans who are so tired at the end of the day's work as to be disinclined to use their minds actively, is not a tenth as great as it was a century ago; and meanwhile the abundance and cheapness of periodical and other literature, adapted to their requirements, and even specially devoted to their interests, have increased very fast. In the result some leaders of the working classes are able to hold their own in discussions of grave problems of politics, as well as of industry, with the foremost men of the time[1].

The influences of school education may be developed or impaired by those of the home; and the full effects of improved schools cannot show themselves till they have been at work for at least two generations. Partly for this reason, occupational status still goes much by inheritance. A large majority of the sons of unskilled labourers, of artisans, of men in the upper grades of office work, of employers, and of professional men are in occupations which have about the same social prestige, and yield similar incomes to those of which they heard most in their childhood[2].

This result may be partly due to the fact, that even now an average middle class family with an income of two or three

[1] Working class leaders have an advantage in this matter over many men of at least equal capacity in other ranks of life, in the fact that they have attained leadership mainly by their power of expressing clearly and forcibly their views on matters of large general interest. Moreover they are the selected representatives of classes much larger numerically than are those of the well-to-do: and are therefore likely to have at least as large an average of high natural ability. It appears that they put the cases of their clients before Commissions of Inquiry at least as effectively as do the representatives of employers (I feel justified in saying that this was the general impression of the members of the Royal Commission on Labour, 1891—4, who had exceptional opportunities of forming a judgment).

[2] No doubt a lad who has true business genius has at least as good opportunities for developing it in the actual work of production or trade as elsewhere; but such a lad rises quickly to wealth: and he is apt to be regarded ultimately as evidence of social inequalities, whereas in fact his history points the other way (see above, pp. 358—361).

III, XIV, 1. hundred pounds is likely to spend more of it on the dignities and amenities of life, and less on food and drink and other direct sources of enjoyment, than does an average working class family whose aggregate incomes reach to about the same amount. The minor amenities and conveniences, thus acquired, serve as a passport to the consideration of an employer who is filling a position in his clerical staff, from which a rise to important duties may come rapidly to anyone who proves himself capable. Meanwhile the universality of education has deprived the lower order of office work of a claim to be held superior to that of the skilled artisan; and yet tradition has caused the word of command in the counting house to be expressed in gentler form than in the works themselves. Though a very small thing in itself, the irritation, which has been expressed increasingly during recent years by manual operatives against this distinction is a striking sign of the times[1].

The preferential advantages, possessed by those born of well-to-do parents in regard to the higher posts of industry, have in effect something of the nature of monopoly: but they are not based on any exclusive compact. They are thus in contrast with such trade-union regulations as restrict particular classes of work to those, who have acquired their skill in it under the auspices of the appropriate craft. Some of these exclusive regulations appear to be justified by special conditions: but speaking generally, they are not on the same footing, as is often alleged, with those which prohibit anyone to give medical advice in return for payment, unless he is duly authorized to do so. For the patient cannot, as a rule, form a good opinion as to the quality of the advice given him; while the employer, or manager of a

[1] Of course the serfdom of Mediaeval England was a survival of times when the ruling classes were in effect officers of a nation in arms: and the terse military words of command extended into domestic life. So long as "manufacturer" was really a man who "works-with-his-own-hands," there was no broad line of division between him and those who worked alongside him; though on occasion they might be subject to furious physical violence. But machinery made the ordinary manufacturing unit so large, that the employer did best for his output, by working at it only with his mind: and the separation which thus arose between him and his "hands" was imperceptibly increased by the noise of machinery. The noise of battle demands short sharp words of command: and noise has been a contributory cause to similar methods in the factory itself: while the quiet of the counting house is conducive to quiet and easy speech.

cooperative business, can form a good opinion as to the quality of the work done for him by an artisan. Therefore the cases for partial monopolies by trade unions and by the medical profession are not on like footing; though it is true that trade-union discipline works for good in some respects, and that the discipline of the medical profession might be pushed to antisocial extremes.

2. *Real and apparent divergencies of interest among the manual labour classes; for some of which a remedy is sought in collective bargaining for particular tasks.*

Trade unions have in some cases systematized a practice which has prevailed in many workshops, without any formal organization: it is to censure, and in some cases penalize, anyone who appears to them to injure the collective interests of the workers by doing more than his share of the work: the work in sight is regarded as a "work-fund" to be distributed as equally as may be. The practice is of older date than the introduction of mechanical processes: but it has been inevitably fostered by them.

When hand work was dominant, an artisan could gain distinction and reward by work that approached in character to that of an artist. For that reason he seldom worked fast: and his comrades could not complain that he absorbed more than his share of the work that was to be had.

But in the modern machine work, and especially in repetition work, output is apt to be judged by quantity; subject to the condition that its accuracy and finish be sufficient for the purpose in view: and the capable mechanic earns distinction and money by giving his machine every opportunity to do its utmost. He is alert to tend its wants, to keep everything in the right place; and thus to secure that it is seldom idle, and never makes bad work. He makes the machine diligent: and the reward of its diligence goes partly to the operative, and partly to the employer who has secured his services. But his comrades look askance. Excellence of handicraft does not reduce the stock of work to be done: but large quantity of output may be obnoxious, because it invites a reduction of piece-work price; and because it uses up more than they regard as one man's share of the work on hand.

No doubt there are exceptional conditions under which slackness of employment in a narrow range of work may be percept-

III, XIV, 2. ibly increased by exceptional activity on the part of particular workers. But the notion that the condition of the working classes generally can be improved, if each group of them refrains as much as it can from using up the "work-fund" at its disposal, is the chief cause of the most bitterly antisocial policies into which the working classes have ever strayed. No doubt the chief immediate sufferers are as a rule particular employers or groups of employers: but, such stinting of production is most common in industries that make goods for general consumption, or else machinery (including ships and locomotives) to be used in increasing the supply of such goods: and therefore in the long run the working classes, as a body, are themselves the chief sufferers from it. Any section of industry that adopts the practice is likely to lower considerably the purchasing power of the wages of other workers[1].

The exceptional degree in which British artisans lent themselves during the later part of the century to antisocial practices in regard to stinting of work generally, and refusing to manage more than one semi-automatic machine at a time, stands out in strange contrast to the general nobility and generosity of their character: for that appears not to be surpassed, even if it is equalled, among the corresponding classes of any other

[1] Misconceptions on this subject are still prevalent. But Mill well observed: "What constitutes the means of payment for commodities is simply commodities. Each person's means of paying for the productions of other people consist of those which he himself possesses. All sellers are inevitably, and by the meaning of the word, buyers. Could we suddenly double the productive powers of the country, we should double the supply of commodities in every market; but we should, by the same stroke, double the purchasing power. Everybody would bring a double demand as well as supply; everybody would be able to buy twice as much, because everyone would have twice as much to offer in exchange." This matter is considered in my *Principles of Economics*, VI, XIII.

It would be wrong to suggest that so astute a writer as Mr G. H. D. Cole supposes that there is any sort of work-fund: or that so public-spirited an enthusiast, as he has shown himself, would purposely mislead his less skilled followers. But it is to be feared that some of them may be encouraged in defence of antisocial practices by his observation that "a big hourly or daily output (in a general shop) does produce unemployment, because it prevents 'the nursing of work.'...The adoption of 'scientific' systems of payment, which give the worker an inducement to 'go all out' irrespective of the volume of work available, undoubtedly tends to increase the amount of temporary unemployment, and this is one of the most serious criticisms that can be levelled against it." (*The payment of wages*, pp. 75—6.)

country. The explanation of the paradox seems to be that this evil side of trade-union policy was developed at a time when Britain's machine industries were so far ahead of those of any other country that they had little to fear from external competition; while in other countries the necessity of making the most of the relatively imperfect appliances, in order to make way against British competition, was so urgent and so prominent that vested interests in the sectional control of machinery had little chance of being developed. But the fathers have eaten sour grapes and the children's teeth are set on edge; there is now scarcely any industrial plant in Britain, which has not its equal in America or some other country; and such remnants, as still exist, of unreasonable refusals on the part of her artisans to get the most that is possible out of her plant, tend to make her position as a leader of industry lower than it otherwise would be: and, since Britain's working classes are the chief consumers of the products of her machine industries, each group of her artisans is likely to lose by antisocial practices on the part of other groups more than it can gain by its own[1].

The latent good in many men was brought out by the nation's great emergency in the recent war: what success Government munition and other works had, seems to have been in large

[1] Reference to this matter has already been made; above, pp. 103, 136—7. The extremist case of this sectional selfishness which has come under my notice is that of a glass worker in the Midlands, who boasted that his local union had mastered the wage problem. No member might apprentice more than one son to the industry: no one else might enter at all. Consequently the supply of labour decreased absolutely, and not merely in reference to the population; and wages had been forced up to £1 a day—a rate much more exceptional then than now. It was objected that the industry must necessarily migrate: he answered:—"Scarcely in my time; the fixed plant cannot be lightly abandoned. If it migrates, I will follow it: two or three weeks' wages will cover the expenses of moving." This "Achilles' heel" of Britain's industries attracts as much attention abroad as it does at home. For instance, an American writer, quoted in *The Economist* of April 26, 1919, remarks: "In England men are thoroughly wedded to the system of restricted output. In New York one man will run three gear-cutting machines, but an English working man will run only one." During the war cases are recorded of boys, straight from a Board School, put on to a simple operation, who averaged £4. 15*s*. in a normal week, and without strain, earned at the same prices at which men had refused to earn more than £2. 10*s*.: and women earned £6—£10 where men had loitered down to £4—£5. Those instances are given in an instructive article by Sir Lynden Macassey in the *Edinburgh Review*, April, 1919, p. 333.

 measure due to its power of compelling antisocial practices to be set aside in work for it; and to the hearty willingness of the workers to make sacrifices less exacting than those of their comrades in the trenches. The Government's control of work, in regard to munitions and some other things, rode on the top of this wave of patriotic unselfishness, with results, which are notable; though inferences from them are not directly applicable to ordinary conditions[1].

Since the appeal to a strong worker not to work so hard as to cast reflections on others who are less able, or even less industrious, is a chief cause, so far as the employees are concerned, of the vastly inferior *per capita* output of British industries to those of America: welcome may be given to a movement in the direction of "collective" piece-work; under which a job is taken on contract by a group of workers, not necessarily of the same craft; and often including unskilled workers, and even boys. If it is done quickly, the payment for it will exceed the aggregate of the time-wages of all; and the surplus is then divided out, generally in proportion to the time-wages due to each: this causes each member of the group to benefit by the energy and ability of every other. The scope of the responsibilities of the manual workers is not materially increased so far: but a second step is under discussion, which may have that effect; and, if successful, will go a long way towards lowering the monopoly of high responsibility which still generally belongs to the employing class. It is suggested that, *in alliance with organized office workers*, a Shop Committee should arrange with the owners of the works that they should be free to take a contract from a customer. This suggestion, though without practical weight at present, is significant of a broad tendency which manual workers are showing to endeavour to bring over brain-workers to their side. Unfortunately the faculties needed for the higher work of business can be judged only by those who have those faculties. Under election from below several incompetent managers are likely to work havoc before one is found, who is capable of taking rightly those risks which are needed for progress.

[1] A little has been said on this matter above, pp. 224—5; 491—2.

3. *Some further observations on the movement, voiced by the Whitley Report, for enlarging the influence of employees over those affairs, connected with their employment, in which they are most nearly concerned.* III, XIV, 3.

We now return to changes in the conditions of employment. The world-war brought together men of all social ranks in the trenches, and thus helped them to know one another. It also enforced rapid changes in organization within industries and between industries: and it increased the need for explaining to all the urgency of new developments, and for enlisting their co-operation in overcoming the difficulties in the way. Thus all were inclined to consider suggestions, such as were made in the Whitley Report, for setting up Joint Works Committees, leading up to Joint Industrial Councils for each district, and then to Joint Industrial Councils for the nation[1].

One of the main purposes of the Whitley Report is indeed to raise the status and develop the self-respect of the workman, by enabling him to form and express well considered judgments on all those aspects of the business in which he is employed, which specially affect him; and in a less degree on the general policy of the business, in so far as there is no need for keeping them private. In all these matters "frank talk heals"; and, as the workman's knowledge and faculty expand, growing self-respect will give firmness and moderation to his policy.

[1] See above, pp. 393—4. The urgency of this movement was increased by the hurried, and sometimes ill-considered action of Government, which was over-strained by the immense burden of the task imposed on it: for though the ablest men in the country put their services at its command, often to their own great inconvenience and pecuniary loss, many important secondary tasks had to be entrusted to people who lacked experience, perseverance, sound judgment, and knowledge of their own limitations. "Industrial Unrest" was the subject of a series of Commissions of Inquiry which reported shortly afterwards. All of them assigned chief places to nerve-strain caused by the events of the war; fatigue due to overlong hours of work; to frequent disturbances of arrangements through changes in Government orders, by which the serenity of employers and employed was disturbed: to the setting aside of trade union rules: and to the disproportionately high wages sometimes obtained by unskilled labour, and even by boys. For instance, in reference to the *West Midlands Area* [Cd. 8665], pp. 7, 8, it is reported that work was being done at piece rates "fixed in peace time when not only were conditions more leisurely, but orders were received in dozens and grosses, where now they are received in thousands and tens of thousands"; and

III, XIV, 3. The Report suggests that the Joint Industrial Councils and Workmen's Committees, already described, shall include in their aims the better utilization of the knowledge and experience of the workers: settlement of general principles for fixing, paying, and readjusting wages with a view of securing to the workers a share in the increased prosperity of the industry: arrangements for fixing wages, piece-work prices etc. both generally, and in regard to particular jobs: technical training and industrial research: the development of inventions made by the workers, with the cooperation of the employers; and legislation affecting the industry[1].

That is to say, it is proposed that everyone shall contribute, both as an individual and in association with his comrades, to the solution of such business problems as are of most direct interest to him and to them. This cooperation may be expected directly to promote correct understandings, by every individual and group, of the desires, grievances and capabilities of all: and indirectly to enable the more able and enterprising minds in each several rank to approach gradually towards a full comprehension of the supreme difficulties and strains involved in the piloting of a progressive business in a progressive branch of industry. The remainder of this chapter will be much occupied with the contrast between these two kinds of business work—one of which is more or less within the grasp of every thoughtful and responsible person: while the other requires somewhat rare faculties; and in many cases, a longer special training than is needed for navigating a ship on the ocean, if not for making a correct diagnosis of a subtle disease.

"in many cases the wage reaches six, eight, and ten pounds a week, or even more, by workers with no previous experience. At the same time the Tool-maker and the Gauge-maker, both skilled men whose skill is the basis on which the machine operates...are receiving considerably less than the piece worker....The injury to his self-respect is as great as that to his pocket....The Leaving Certificate System prevents him from taking up repetition work himself."

[1] It may probably promote, among other things: "Suggestions as to improved methods of manufacture, tools, jigs, gauges: new methods of production: class of labour to be used on new types or reconstructed machines: criticism and adjustment in existing piece-work prices...due regard being had to custom etc.: cooperation with the management in supervision: shop troubles and grievances: suspensions and dismissals consequent upon slackness in trade: shop rules—timekeeping, meal hours, cleaning-time etc.: changes...between payment by

4. The control of a great part of business organization may be diffused: but decisions as to the taking of risks generally, and of new departures in particular, should remain, for the present at least, in the hands of those who will bear the burden of the risks. III, XIV, 4.

Judicious, orderly and vigorous management of routine will often suffice to enable a business to prosper in an industry, the methods of which are for the time practically stereotyped. But such management, while useful in its generation, has contributed very little towards progress: and, if routine had been universal, a country of the size of Britain would have afforded support for only a few million people, barely supplied with the necessaries of life. Progress has been effected on the scientific side by students and by business men: on the practical side by those business men, who have been alert to invent or adopt new ideas; to put them into practice, bearing the risks of loss; to improve on them, and again to improve on them. At each step these men have weighed many complex considerations, one against another: and finally they have acted boldly and freely, because that which they risked was their own.

No doubt in many industries the capital, required for efficient work, has become so large as to exceed the resources which are commonly to be found in the hands of a single owner, or even of a private partnership. And it is true that the directors of a joint stock company must sometimes take decisions, which are in effect final, as to large risks to be borne by capital of which they themselves are relatively small holders: but those directors are nearly always men of wide business experience; who have been in effect selected and are still in

time and according to results: matters relating to welfare: demarcation between trades, with the free sanction of the Trade Unions concerned: advice on workshop conditions and other matters affecting labour." See a paper by an engineer in *Labour and Capital after the War*, edited by S. J. Chapman, C.B.E., pp. 151—2.

At the moment of writing there appears to be some differences of opinion as to the relations of the Whitley Councils to the great National Industrial Conference, which is to collect, digest, and disseminate information and suggestions that make for industrial progress; and probably to develop some other functions. It may perhaps be more directly representative of crafts, as distinguished from industries, than the Whitley Councils are.

III, xiv, 4. a measure supervised by strong stock-holders, who themselves have been trained in the fierce arena of great transactions[1].

Now, though the employees of a business may often contribute advice and aid in the general management of a business; they are seldom in a position to form good judgments as to new developments of the business, nor even as to the selection of the risks to be taken in its ordinary course. Were it otherwise, businesses owned by the workers themselves would certainly have had a great past: and the general spread of enlightenment would have insured for them an ever increasing rapidity of growth in the future. For so thorough is the organization of capital supply now, that the past successes of businesses owned by working-men would have enabled such of them as were in good repute to obtain from bankers and others large supplies of capital at low rates. It may therefore be inferred that the chief hindrance to the advance of working-men to the control of business lies in a lack, not of capital, but of the training and habits of mind needed for dealing with the larger problems of business policy; and especially deciding on doubtful ventures in regard to technique and plant, to marketing; and last, but not least, on the selection of the right men to fill the higher and more responsible posts. In these matters only those working-men who are of exceptional ability can form fairly good judgment: and, even if no jealousy intervenes, they are in great danger of being outvoted. These difficulties are greatest in those industries in which technique is changing most rapidly: that is, those on whose enterprise and resource the general progress of the world and the industrial leadership of a nation most closely depend[2]. This observation is consistent with the fact that a great part of the supply of business genius of the highest order, especially in America, has come from the working classes: for such genius is in great measure innate; and an alert youth in a factory or counting house has great opportunities for sharpening his wits in relation to realities[3].

[1] See above, pp. 316—328.

[2] The experiences of cooperation and copartnership are of interest in this connection: see below, Appendix P.

[3] See above, p. 359. The supply has indeed not been in full proportion to the large numbers of the working classes: but this may be due partly to the

5. *Britain can obtain her necessary supplies of food and material only by continued leadership in those industries, which make large use of the most expensive mechanical appliances: that is in those industries which have the greatest need of the bold, judicious, unfettered undertaking of grave risks under difficult and ever-changing conditions.*

No thoughtful person regards with satisfaction the extreme inequalities of fortune, which are conspicuous in the present age; and, in great measure, have taken the place of the inequalities in military and political power, which have prevailed in earlier ages. As the herdsman and the gardener are more careful to protect from hurtful disturbance such cattle and plants as are of exceptional value, so an enlightened communistic régime would take care that those, whose thought and work were of high value to the State, were able to give all their strength under favourable conditions to the discharge of their special functions. But that ideal Golden Age, which almost every people has thought to discern in the past, permitted no sumptuous expenditure save on public account—*Privatus illis census erat brevis; commune magnum.*

The imagination, which endowed the individual with heroic virtue, endowed the State with an equally heroic wisdom and activity in the service of all: and imagination, though vain, was logically consistent; for the State at any time and place is the chief emanation of the character of mankind then and there. Of course a despotic State may represent the aims of a military minority, but we are now concerned with a self-governing people. The State, which they evolve, will reflect whatever purity of aim and nobility of purpose are to be found in their lives, but no more: it is likely to be much less efficient for its purposes than they are for theirs, because its tasks are much heavier than theirs. Nevertheless the State is the most precious of human possessions; and no care can be too great to be spent on enabling it to do its special work in the best way: a chief condition to that end is that it should not be set

fact that natural faculty is in some degree inherited: and therefore a man who has the genius needed for brilliant business success is more likely to be the son of a parent who has made some considerable advance himself, than of one who has not.

III, XIV, 5. to work, for which it is not specially qualified, under the conditions of time and place.

In the early military ages, the despotic ruler—whether a monarch or a dominant section (such as the Roman *Populus*, which called itself the "Republic")—could accumulate capital; by means of a large command of forced labour of slaves or serfs: such labour was capitalized in the great Roman Aqueducts. Modern appliances for manufacture, and for transport by land and sea of imported food, materials and other things, in exchange for manufactured and other products, have enabled nearly the whole population of every western country to enjoy a greater amount of comfort than was to be had by any but the very rich a few centuries ago. They have so diminished the strain on human muscles that education is now a real force; whereas without such aid the strain of severe manual labour would have left most operatives at the end of the day's work, so tired that the brain would have been unable to make good use of any faculties that it had acquired. *But yet a modern Government seldom accumulates capital*: it is a brave borrower.

In some countries a good deal is accumulated in driblets by peasant proprietors and other "small-folk": but in the progressive western world the task is for the greater part in the hands of the middle and upper classes: and they consequently receive nearly all the direct money income derived from it. But that direct net income is small in comparison with the indirect benefits derived from the increased efficiency that the aid of capital bestows on man's productive work: these benefits belong to the whole nation; and much the larger part of them in the aggregate goes to the working classes. More machine power goes to the production, and more shipping goes to the carriage, of each pound's worth of a labourer's purchases than to each pound's worth of an artisan's purchases; and several times as much goes to each pound's worth of his purchases as to each of those of the very rich man. And yet, it must be repeated that the artisan, even when earning as good an income as many of those who are regarded as middle-class brain-workers, seldom saves as much as they do[1].

[1] The chief causes of this difference are no doubt to be found in traditionary custom and inherited qualities. But a minor cause may be found in the fact

It is to be remembered that the income derived from capital did not increase as fast as the savings from which it was derived, until the time came for the State to borrow a great part of it at a high rate for the purposes of the world-war: and that, if the private capital at the disposal of Britain and America had not been available, German troops would have treated Britain as they did treat Belgium. Moreover, it seems probable that, if the motives and opportunities for the accumulation of private capital in Britain were considerably reduced, while average human nature and conduct remained much as it is now, her total supply of the material appliances needed for high grade manufacture and trade would be so much reduced by wear and tear, obsolescence, and exportation, that ere long her people would become relatively poor. In fact it might soon become so small, that an even distribution of the whole income of the country among all her inhabitants would bring down the incomes of all below that of the artisans and other well-paid manual workers now. Even as things are, such a division would give more meagre results than is generally supposed[1].

that the widow of a working man and his daughter can earn their livings and accept aid in ways, for which derelict members of the middle classes have not been prepared by previous experience.

[1] Professor Bowley's *The division of the product of industry*, 1919, shows the total income of Britain, derived from home sources, to have been in 1913—14 £m.2,000 or £m.2,100: which "would not have yielded more than £230 per family of five; or £170 net after all rates and taxes were paid, and an adequate sum invested in home industries. The income brought home from abroad amounted to about £m.90, or £10 a family. The average family is not however five as is frequently assumed, but about 4½ persons....The average net income of a family...would have been £153 from home-product, or £162 if income from abroad is included....There are on an average nearly two earners to a family."

Suggestions in this direction had been occasioned by anxieties, less than those of the present troubled time. Thus in my *Principles of Economics* (first edition, 1890, pp. 47—8) it is observed that since the repeal of the Corn-laws "the average money income of the people has more than doubled; while the price of almost all important commodities, except animal food and houseroom, has fallen by one half or even further. It is true that even now, if wealth were distributed equally, the total production of the country would only suffice to provide necessaries and the more urgent comforts for the people....The average income per head in the United Kingdom, which was about £15 in 1820, is about £33 now; *i.e.* it has risen from about £75 to £165 per family of five. There are not a few artisans' families, the total earnings of which exceed £165, so that they would lose by an equal distribution of wealth: but even they have not more than is required to support a healthy and many-sided life." In the third edition, 1895, this estimate

III, XIV, 5. If Britain is to hold her place in the world, her growing population, ever more dependent on external supplies of food and materials, must be provided with enlarged and improved mechanical appliances for production; and therefore ever greater net annual additions to her accumulated capital must be made in order that her total real income (or National Dividend) may be as large relatively to her population as was that of an artisan's family before the war: and a new spirit, in harmony with the patriotic emotions of the war, must rid her of her Achilles' heel[1]. If everyone will get as much work as possible out of his plant while in charge of it; and, in those industries in which the plant is very expensive, will agree to work in shifts, so as to keep the plant at work for twice as long as the normal working day, then wages will be raised automatically far above their present level: and yet there will be an increase in the inducements so to develop plant as to greatly increase the National Dividend. Then all workers may receive as good pay as the artisan does now: and the artisan, together with those office workers who are on about equal level with him in the faculties required for their work, may speedily rise much above it[2].

Thus the future may be made brighter than the past by greater community of thought, action and sympathy; by a fuller recognition of the dignity of man, and cordial cooperation

of £33 per head was raised to £40: and in the seventh edition, p. 713, the guess is hazarded (on much slighter foundations than those of Prof. Bowley's study) that the income of the 49,000,000 inhabitants of Britain may be taken at £2000,000,000 or £40 a head; which was less than that of many artisan families even before the war, when the purchasing power of money was still high.

[1] See above, p. 641 n.

[2] The economy to be obtained by compelling a single outfit of untiring mechanical plant to work twice the number of hours which can reasonably be required of human beings, who are easily tired, and whose life needs to be developed outside of their work as well as in it, is urged by Lord Leverhulme in *The Six-hour day.* He insists, as many others have done, on the wastefulness of the British method of keeping the supply of plant and horse-power per thousand operatives somewhat below the American standard. It is suggested in my *Principles* (pp. 695—6 n.) that two sets might work alternately. With a seven-hour day one might work from 6 a.m. to 9 a.m. and from 12.30 to 4.30 p.m.: the other from 9.15 a.m. to 12.15 p.m.; and from 4.45 p.m. to 8.45 p.m.: they might change places at the end of each week or month. With a six-hour day no one need work more than three hours continuously.

among all the various ranks of industry, and by a continued development of the fundamental principles of the Whitley Report. When man has been raised to a level far higher than he has yet attained, he will have raised the State also to far higher possibilities than it has yet reached: and then industry is likely to be recast on some plan not yet in sight. For human nature has developed new possibilities in almost every generation under quiet and orderly conditions; and it has progressed very fast in this country during the last fifty years.

One indication of this progress is the increasing solidity and breadth of socialistic schemes: for instance "labour" is no longer regarded as exclusively manual; and the Guilds now suggested are to make use of the best scientific, technical and administrative ability that they can attract. But it seems that these new schemes, like those of earlier times, look only at the surface difficulties of business; and do not attempt with patient care to track out the effects of effects, and the causes of causes. In particular they appear to regard economic progress as a thing that goes almost of itself: they take little thought for its dependence on deep insight, on farseeing fore-sight, on sound judgment in selecting new developments of technique and organization, and on the courage of leaders of industry in taking selected risks on their own shoulders. Even the most advanced schemes for National Guilds seem to ignore the fact that the State has been a borrower rather than an accumulator of capital; and to take little or no account of the superhuman ability required on the part of those persons in whom the chief functions of "the State" are to be concentrated, when called on by a Guild to advance more capital in order to replace some that has been lost in an ill-fated venture, or to enable some new venture to be put through. No doubt the State, like man himself, is to be born anew in the new age; but no definite provision is made for this re-birth; and meanwhile the intimate dependence of progress on the right taking of risks, seems to be ignored[1].

[1] But such schemes may point the way to solid progress in a later age, when some oversights have been corrected by experience. And bold imaginations, though unbalanced and dangerous as guides, often contain a solid kernel, from which are evolved in a later age important results, far removed from the aims with which they were originally associated. So a short account is given in

III, XIV, 6. 6. *Some general conclusions. Sectional, national, and international interests. Anglo-Saxons have generally eschewed the more antisocial forms both of competition and combination. Collective control of industry would be unfavourable to the best selection of men for its most responsible work.*

In this Book and in Book II we have been occupied chiefly with the relations of sectional to national interests. But it will be well to revert for a while to the point of view of Book I, from which national progress was seen as in great measure dependent on world progress; and to consider the partial likeness, which the relation of national to cosmopolitan interests bears to that between sectional and national interests.

Many sectional interests within a country are concentrated in particular places, in consequence partly of unequal distribution of mineral and other natural resources, partly of more or less accidental localization of special industrial aptitudes. But special local interests are generally recognized as definitely subordinate, on moral and on political grounds, to those represented by the central Government: while devotion to national interests, to the almost complete exclusion of those of the rest of the world, is implicit in much ordinary conversation, and is proudly asserted even by some thoughtful people.

The recent growth of a strong sentiment in favour of a League of Nations, may ultimately have some power to foster cosmopolitan interests. It is an evidence of under-currents of thought and feeling, which were felt at the Universities and elsewhere half a century ago, and are now becoming prominent. Science is already almost completely international: nearly every change of political thought and sentiment in any one western country soon spreads some waves over others; and the same is true of progress in industrial technique. Capital is also in great measure international; facilities for travel and the transmission of news by wire and by air are enabling the new education of the masses of all western peoples to become increasingly international. Recent discussions, arising out of the emergencies of the great war, have quenched many jealousies,

pp. 657—660 of some proposals for setting up National Guilds in the place of the present mechanism of industry and trade.

and have effected friendly compromises in regard to conflicting interests: but yet the time seems far off at which each country will deliberately abstain from any action, which would bring benefit to her, on the ground that it would cause somewhat greater detriment to others. If that end is ever reached, the way to it may perhaps be led by the increasingly independent, but also increasingly cordial, relations between Britain and her Dependencies. In all international trade policies, her great Dominions are able to take full care of their own interests: but her Crown Colonies and India are not in equally strong positions; and therefore Britain is morally bound to attach to each of their interests at least as great a weight as if it were her own[1].

In Books II and III we have been increasingly occupied with the observations that the term "competition" has many different interpretations in common usage; that the same is true of the term "combination"; and that consequently indiscriminate praise or blame of either is futile. Varieties of competition seem to fall in the main under one of the following three heads: (*a*) friendly emulation, implying cooperation in case of any need, as when two friends rival one another in the ascent of a difficult mountain: (*b*) ordinary business competition, in which each of several neighbourly producers or traders endeavours to get ahead of the others; but neither makes, nor tolerates the making by others, harsh judgment of their actions: (*c*) competition with destructive aims, in which each would go to some trouble and expense in order so to hurt others, as to clear the field for his own advance. The largest and the most savage developments of destructive competition on record have been incidents in campaigns for crushing inconvenient competitors by a Juggernaut car of combination striving for monopoly. And it is noteworthy

[1] In particular no plea should be entertained for Protective taxes on imports into Britain competitive with some of her own industries, however strong the national need for developing them may be; unless a similar principle is applied to selected Indian manufactures, whose youthful strength is insufficient for competition on nearly even terms with rival imports from Britain and other western countries. These considerations are developed a little further in pp. 26—9 of a Memorandum by the present writer on the *Fiscal Policy of International Trade*, printed by order of the House of Commons, C. 321 of 1908.

III, XIV, 6. that some vehement strategic denunciations of competition as essentially malign and rancorous, have been uttered by advocates of combination for the purpose of raising prices to artificially high, if not to monopolistic levels.

Again, the term "combination" has three similar connotations. It is often applied to constructive association[1]. Sometimes it refers to joint action for the regulation of prices; as for instance by cartels or trade unions, which keep the door open to all *suitable* applicants for admission, but nevertheless set themselves to push up the prices of what they have to sell: sometimes it suggests deliberate destructive competition by a group of businesses aiming at monopoly. So long as the term "suitable" in the second of these connotations is interpreted with reference to the interests of the community in obtaining good service, and without any design to stint supply in the interests of a section, it does not offend against the fundamental ethico-political rule that everyone should have free access to the highest orders of work of which he is capable—*carrières ouvertes aux talents.*

In this matter manufacturers and other employers are more directly—though not more deeply—interested than the nation generally: and they seem to fail in their duty to themselves and to the nation, when they unconsciously countenance evil developments of trade-union policy, by setting up associations of the combative order of German cartels. An urgent obligation lies on the State to search out and correct such malign practices by methods of the same thorough and uncompromising character as those of the American Federal Commission: for by such means only is it possible to allow unfettered liberty of association for constructive purposes, while curbing antisocial devices.

There is indeed but one moral rule and there should be but one aim of authoritative control, for the operations of trade, for the attitude of employers towards employees, and for the attitude of employees to their work. Every sort of association that enriches life by giving to the individual broader, and therefore presumably higher, interests than those which directly concern his own well-being, is to be cherished: but any tendency to curtail important activities unduly (*i.e.* before they have reached the point at which

[1] Such as that described above, pp. 603—616.

fatigue becomes a serious evil) in order to obtain an artificial advantage in bargaining, is to be condemned as antisocial.

The predominance of constructive over destructive forms both of competition and of combination is even more important to Britain than to other countries: for her responsibilities in the world are far greater relatively to her natural resources than are those of any other land. Because she has achieved so much relatively to her resources, she is bound to foster her acquired sources of strength with exceptional vigilance and energy.

She needs to obtain vast quantities of food and material from countries, that have relatively large natural wealth, by exporting to them commodities made by such excellent appliances that her working classes will be able to obtain the larger necessaries and comforts of life—even after allowance for expenses of transport—at the cost of no great amount of labour of her own. If her industries follow America's lead in largeness of supply of plant to each worker: and if the short-sighted selfishness which has developed the evil practice of stinting output (whether by trade unions or by employers' associations on the cartel model) be abandoned, then she may prosper: but she may rapidly fall from her high place, if she becomes slack in any respect.

A characteristic of the last few decades has been the increasing affinity between industrial evolution, and progress towards government of the people by the people: and therefore it is worth while to reflect that the special qualities, which made England an industrial leader, were shown in her political evolution during many centuries, in which her industries lagged behind those of other lands[1]. They had indeed deeper roots and acquired much larger scope, than those that were needed by the earlier forms of merely industrial organization; and their first great achievement was to enable her gradually to develop true popular self-government on a large scale. A bold guess may be hazarded that a thousand years hence, when all economic institutions,

[1] See above, pp. 35—39, and 179: also below, pp. 700—718.

A tribute should also be paid to somewhat similar national characteristics which have preserved the independence of Switzerland; though the geographical conditions, which have helped her to maintain it, have also confined its influence within narrow bounds.

III, XIV, 6. and nearly all economic rights have been remoulded several times, a chief outstanding fact in the history of the past will be the spread of the Anglo-Saxon language over a great part of the world, regarded as the result of the early faculty of the Anglo-Saxon temperament for ordered freedom.

Self-restraint in the statement of claims, and resolute persistence in those which have been finally approved, have generally enabled Anglo-Saxon peoples to move forwards steadily: retrogressions have occurred, but they have been rare. And, as an indirect, but perhaps necessary, consequence of this character, both competition and combination in Anglo-Saxon countries generally have been more inclined to construction than to destruction. It is indeed true that some violent ebullitions of competition, chiefly in pursuit of monopolistic combination, have occurred in America: but they do not appear to have been numerous relatively to the rapidity of growth and change in her industrial structure, to which no near approach has been seen elsewhere. America has attracted the most eager and excitable strains of the Anglo-Saxon, the Celtic, and Slavonic races: and yet Anglo-Saxon moderation and stability have enabled competitive and monopolistic abuses to be kept within relatively narrow limits, with but little direct intervention of authority. The chief weapon of the Bureau of Corporations has been publicity.

So far we have been concerned chiefly with movements, which have passed, with more or less success, through the ordeals of sustained working and many-sided experience. But we may now allow ourselves to venture a little on untried ground, and speculate as to the future; not being deterred by the reflection that the fond fancies of one age as to noble possibilities of social development have not very often evoked as much approval as mirth in later generations.

We may begin by reference to National Guilds: for they claim with some partial justice to be developments of movements, which may be traced in nearly all phases of civilization during more than two thousand years; and to have earned some sort of certificate from the past. In fact however those parts of their policy, which are at once most novel and most alluring at first sight, seem on consideration to involve grave hazards to social stability and progress.

7. *National Guilds.*

It has already been noted that the (Whitley) Works Committees and Joint Industrial Councils embody something of a movement in the direction of loyalty to others engaged in the same *industry*, by the side of, and occasionally in preference to, loyalty to the same *craft*. The claims of industrial Guilds have drawn support from this movement; which belongs especially to the last few decades, and is in the reverse direction from that which set in a century earlier. For, as the eighteenth century passed into the nineteenth, the dominant industrial unit ceased to be a workshop, owned by the leading craftsman in it: and after two more generations had passed the employer, even if he had been a working man himself, was chiefly concerned with the organization and the finance of a large establishment; though, especially if engaged in engineering, or allied work, he would of course supplement technical studies by some manual experience[1].

Towards the end of the nineteenth century, the number of tasks handled in the same factory became so great that the various craftsmen engaged in them had scarcely any common bond: each craftsman in the factory looked to his own Union for guidance and aid in regard to pay and other matters. Loyalty to craft gave scope to some of his higher emotions: but the general interests of the business in which he was engaged did not appeal strongly to him. So the suggestion that the State should own all capital and directly control all industry appealed to his idealism, as well as to his desire for greater material comfort: and he was inclined to approve the mystic reasoning with which Marx "coquetted," and which claimed to prove that though a worker has a right to his own earnings, yet any part of them which he or any one else uses in facilitating production, encroaches on the rights of the State. He often regarded the Marxian doctrine, that all profit derived from private capital is "theft," as an overstatement of an important

[1] Some employers are skilled craftsmen. One, whose engineering works were large and various, told me that he had mastered his whole plant: he could step into the place of any operative, and show him how to do his job easily and neatly.

III, XIV, 7. truth. So far socialistic tendencies went very much on the same lines in most Western lands.

But the attitude of Anglo-Saxon workers differed from that of Germans and others, who rejoiced in the apparent vigour of autocratic Government, and cared little about freedom for its own sake. Fabians made something of a compromise with pure Marxian doctrine. But in recent years their influence has declined in Britain relatively to that of a school, which insists that though collectivism might increase the material comforts of the workman, it would not develop his self-respect: the postman is not made free by escaping from the control of an employer, who may be sympathetic; and coming under that of officials, who must obey orders, and have no power to indulge their sympathies.

The new movement therefore puts into the forefront the dignity of the worker, whether with hand or head, as a man: it claims thus to evoke his full energies and give them free play: and finally so to increase production that material well-being would be raised generally, even though the State, while annexing private capital, give in return bonds of its own which will yield an income equivalent to normal interest on the capital for a period of say forty or fifty years. Business men may continue their activities in the service of their respective industries: but the whole of the operations of each industry will be controlled by those engaged in it, who in their collective capacity, *as a Guild*, will pay rent to the State for the means of production.

On this plan control is to be guided by the highest available technical knowledge and business experience. For, though the State takes over all business plant, with some sort of compensation to its owners, the Guild is to avail itself of every suitable faculty that will participate in its task. While all its members vote on its main problems, the policy thus directed will be carried out by those whom the Guild may consider most capable: whether they are compensated ex-capitalists, experienced managers; or manual workers, who have shown high faculty under the new conditions. Thus the plan is on a different intellectual level from those which regard the whole product of industry as belonging to the operatives; and think but lightly of any work that is not manual. It leaves trade-unions, or their successors, in full control of the internal management of particular crafts, but the main organization of industry is to be based on "function"; and there are many industrial functions beyond the scope of any one craft, and therefore of any trade-union.

III, XIV, 7.

In order to avoid arousing strong opposition, while the movement towards the goal is still rather weak, caution is recommended. "The keynote is to be Encroaching Control": but, when the goal has been reached, "economic sovereignty is to be shared between the Guilds (with whom will lie the initiative in the economic no less than in the purely industrial sphere) and the State (which stands by as guardian of communal interests that might otherwise be lost sight of)[1]." As a means to this end, the shop committees are to begin by making impossible the position of any foreman, whom they do not approve, "such passive approval to be transformed at the earliest possible moment into active election by the workers themselves, so that the shop steward becomes the officer not of the Union only, but of the industry." "Collective Contracts" arranged by the Union, which itself distributes the money received, are to be increasingly substituted for individual contracts. "As the functions of the employer pass from him one by one, his fundamental character as a profiteer will become more obvious...and this will fatally impair what is even more essential to his power—his prestige[2]."

The scheme is thus elaborated by Mr G. H. D. Cole: There is to be set up in each works, subcommittees elected by all the workers in the several shops; and a Works Committee elected, directly or indirectly, by all the shops. A District Committee is to consist of members elected by the several Works Committees, together with craft representatives elected by the local crafts. These are to lead up to a National Guild Executive and a National Delegate meeting of representatives of each craft in each district. Foremen and Managers are to be elected by those manual and clerical workers respectively who would serve under

[1] Bechhofer and Reckitt, *The meaning of National Guilds*, 1918, pp. 284, 5.

[2] *Ib.* pp. 286, 7. A writer is quoted with approval by them (p. 335) who says:—"A corrective for judicial arrogance will need to be discovered: perhaps...by rendering the Judiciary elective...by Guild and Civic Congresses."

III, xiv, 8. them, for each works and for the whole Guild. Similar provision is to be made for experts, for each works, for each district, and for the whole country[1].

The Central national control of all industries is to be in the hands of (*a*) a Guild Congress representing producers; (*b*) Parliament representing "the people as consumers"; and (*c*) a somewhat mysterious body, on which "not merely all the citizens, but all the citizens in their various social activities are represented"; which is on occasion to settle controversies between the Guild Congress and Parliament[2]. He insists that "the Collectivist Utopia would be a world of public trusts: the Guild Utopia will be a world of producers' cartels, worked in the interest of the whole community. If the Guild is not to fall into mediocrity it must preserve the distinctness of works from works, of locality from locality and of nation from nation. It is the organization of human differences on the basis of human identity[3]."

In the present economic system, discipline is enforced in great measure automatically "by an unseen hand." It is often rather harsh; and its severity calls for frequent mitigation by human effort. But if automatic discipline is removed, an all-pervading authority must be invoked to check abuse in small matters as well as in large. Unless Guild organization develops some notion, of which it at present seems to have made no forecast, it may probably drift into chaos, from which relief can be found only in a military despotism[4].

8. *Possibilities of the future.*

Let us now imagine some possibilities of the future, which may be attained without casting the experiences of the ages to the winds; and without supposing that methods of organization,

[1] *Self-government in industry*, 1918, pp. 257—268.
[2] *Ib.* pp. 86—88.
[3] *Ib.* p. 154. Marx might have envied this phrase.
[4] In this matter, as in some others, Mr Cole (*Self-government in industry*, pp. 234—9) seems to follow closely in the paths of St Simon, Fourier, and other early socialists of noble character and vivid poetic imagination. The last new version of the Golden Age is to bring out latent powers of goodness in human nature: the task of regulation is to be as simple as it would be if all men were as unselfish and earnest as the writer himself: the vast difficulties of modern business organization are so completely left out of account as to imply that they have never been seriously studied.

which have never attained lasting success on a considerable scale, will prove permanently efficient under the wand of a socialistic prophet.

Stress must be laid on the extent to which industrial strength is being increased by the broadening of the basis, from which can be drawn men endowed with the high faculties needed for the more responsible posts in industry. Until recently the supply came almost exclusively from a rather thin upper stratum of the population. It alone had a great surplus of material resource over what was needed to supply the necessaries of life; and sufficient freedom from oppressive manual toil to be able to devote much mental energy, save in exceptional cases, to the larger problems of thought and work.

But it has now a larger sense of social responsibility; and, aided by the application of natural forces to much of the heavy work that wearied the manual worker, it has contrived larger opportunities for the masses of the people to develop the high faculties born in them: and the State can now look to the main body of workers as the source of much of that higher administrative work, which used to belong almost exclusively to the well-to-do. This change was emphasized by the Whitley Report, and it will be promoted by Joint Industrial Councils; though their efforts may not reach far towards a wide dissemination of the supreme tasks of conceiving new ventures, weighing their promises and their risks, and making a wise selection. There is a rapid increase in the number of those who have the strength and the elasticity of mind and character needed for the larger responsibilities of industry: but unfortunately the probability that the best men will be brought to the front is being diminished by several causes.

Records of a man's work in one grade of industry throw but little light upon his fitness for a higher grade, in which different faculties are required. Everything, that is within a man, does indeed come out in close intercourse with those whose qualities are at least as high as his: but in a large business those, whose own qualities are high, are seldom brought into much direct contact with the main body of workers. The foremen and other officials of medium grades are not always quick to appreciate fully any higher qualities that may be latent in

III, XIV, 8. a young artisan: they judge him probably by his output; but that, though a good measure of his value as an operative, is a very poor measure of his higher capabilities. The small employer, who knew all his men, could draw a broad distinction between the value to the business of a particular operative, and the value of his work: and would go out of his way to retain anyone who, though not specially expert and quick with his hands, would be likely to develop such faculties of judgment and resource, that considerable responsibilities might be thrown upon him later on; and thus the man who had latent high qualities would be drawn upwards. But such a man might not be much liked by a foreman or other minor official of a large business, whose horizon is more limited than his own: and his value is likely to be reckoned merely by his output[1].

This likelihood, that in a very large business the latent capabilities of a man will fail of recognition by his immediate superiors, is to some extent both a cause and a justification of a tendency to promote according to seniority: especially if the work to be done is such that the output of any one man is not easily to be distinguished from that of others. As is well known, this tendency becomes an almost absolute rule in many kinds of employment under Government: for officials, who have made their way by seniority, are naturally inclined to promote by the same rule[2]. National Guilds propose at starting to annex the services of men who have been trained in independent businesses: and that device may serve for a time. But when those men have gone, and the Guilds have to train their own leaders, they are likely to find unexpected difficulties in the causes just indicated.

To sum up this group of considerations:—Moral and economic advances depend increasingly on the extent to which

[1] This is a different thing from saying that his value would be reckoned in proportion to his output. For it is obvious that the work of a man in charge of very expensive plant, who gets out of it a quarter as much again as another, may be worth twice as much as the other one, if neither has any latent capacity for higher work than that on which he is engaged. The phrase "equal pay for equal output" has its uses, but is liable to be grievously misapplied.

[2] Reference may be made in this connection to the first and fourth Sections of Book II, Chapter x, see also pp. 580—4.

the most strength-giving influences can be brought to bear on character: and among these a chief place must be assigned to the selection of men for responsible posts in accordance with indications that they are likely to develop in those posts faculties, for which they have had relatively small need in the past. Only independent heads of business are in a position to make such a selection with free hands; and only they have full incitement to exercise their best energies in the selection.

But yet there is room for large hopes. Leaving wars out of account, we may perhaps reasonably hope for a gradual extension to nearly the whole population of those resources and opportunities, which are needed for comfort and for the full and harmonious development of the higher human faculties, on the following conditions: (i) that mankind set themselves greatly to increase the supply of mechanical appliances, which are to raise the condition even of the humbler classes of mankind by acting as slaves for them: (ii) that they make these slaves so numerous and powerful; and manage to keep them at work for so long hours by alternating shifts of attendants, that even the lowliest of human operatives need work only during short hours; though with energy while at work: (iii) that they raise the level of general education till there are scarcely any adults, who can only do such simple work, as is within the capacity of a properly guided mechanical slave: (iv) that they develop assiduously the channels by which those who are endowed with high faculties of thought and invention, of enterprise and administration, may rise rapidly to posts of responsibility commensurate with their qualities: (v) that they keep constantly in view the broad distinction between tasks of orderly business management, which conscientious officials perform adequately; and tasks of constructive enterprise, on the bold and enlightened discharge of which economic progress mainly depends, though they are often beyond the power of the official, and even uncongenial to his temperament: (vi) that they recognize (*a*) that the most progressive business men value the freedom to take risks on their own account, and to earn a reputation for able leadership, by success in leadership which cannot always easily be proved otherwise than by its pecuniary results: but (*b*) that an adverse

III, XIV, 8. tide which retards all rowers does not materially diminish the zest of emulation in a race; and therefore (*c*) that enterprise may be maintained, even though those who are rich are required to make large contributions for national purposes: (vii) that they remember that all taxes on resources, which might probably have been used for the increase of the material slaves of man, are prejudicial to the whole people; and in some respects especially prejudicial to the poorer members of it: and that therefore the produce of exceptionally heavy taxes on capital, or on income derived from it, ought not to be used to defray *current* expenditure: (viii) that at junctures such as the present, when the national burden of debt is an enormous heritage of evil for coming generations, they insist that the produce of all taxes, which tend considerably to check the accumulation of private capital, be devoted to the reduction of that debt: (ix) that they take account of the tendency of capital to emigrate from a place in which it is unjustly handled; though a country, which nourishes and stimulates capable business enterprise, will continue to attract capital, in spite of its being subject to somewhat heavy taxes there: (x) last, but not least, that employers, as well as other capitalists; employees; and in short all classes and groups, eschew all practices which tend to raise the market values of their services or products by making them relatively scarce.

The problem of social aims takes on new forms in every age: but underlying all there is the one fundamental principle:—viz. that progress mainly depends on the extent to which the strongest, and not merely the highest, forces of human nature can be utilized for the increase of social good. There are some doubts as to what social good really is; but they do not reach far enough to impair the foundations of this fundamental principle. For there has always been a substratum of agreement that social good lies mainly in that healthful exercise and development of faculties which yields happiness without pall, because it sustains self-respect and is sustained by hope. No utilization of waste gases in the blast furnace can compare with the triumph of making work for the public good pleasurable in itself, and of stimulating men of all classes to great endeavours by other means than that evidence of power which manifests itself by lavish expenditure. We need to foster fine work and fresh initiative by the warming breath of the sympathy and appreciation of those who truly understand it; we need to turn consumption into paths, that strengthen the consumer and call forth the best qualities of those who provide for consumption. Recognizing that some work must be done that is not ennobling, we must seek to apply the growing knowledge and material resources of the world to reduce such work within narrow limits, and to extirpate all conditions of life which are in themselves debasing. There cannot be a great sudden improvement in man's conditions of life; for he forms them as much as they form him, and he himself cannot change fast: but he must press on steadfastly towards the distant goal where the opportunities of a noble life may be accessible to all[1].

Organic life on this little planet, which has been inhabitable for only a few thousand years, may indeed perhaps claim to have made fair progress, morally as well as physically, in a minute fraction of the period during which the stellar universe is known to have been nearly in its present form. Other planets, which have been suitable for the maintenance of organic life during much longer periods, may have gone a long way towards solving socio-economic problems, of which we are only able to touch timidly the outskirts. In particular they may have probed many of those responsibilities of the individual to the State and of the State to the individual, as to which we have learnt so much in the last few generations, that we appear to have made some considerable way towards fathoming the depths of our ignorance. But it seems that, the longer we ponder, the greater must be our diffidence in prediction, and the more profound the awe with which we regard the Divine Governance of the Universe.

[1] This paragraph is substantially reproduced from an article on "The old generation of economists and the new," published in the Harvard *Quarterly Journal of Economics* in 1897: and something more is said on similar subjects in the last chapter of my *Principles of Economics*.

III, XIV, 9.

9. *Nature and limitations of the constructive work of a democratic Government in regard to industry.*

To return to the hard realities of actual life:—It has been indicated[1] that, although the semi-military organization of Imperial Germany was well adapted for the methods of bureaucratic control, other methods are needed by a nation which governs its own Government: but a little more must be said on this subject.

Each of the numerous Government offices in Westminster is in some measure bureaucratic. Its officials have for the greater part been trained from early manhood onward in its work; and promotion has been governed by seniority, with some little reference to the claims of exceptional ability. In broad matters however the ultimate decision depends on a Minister, whose knowledge of the technique of his Department is seldom great. He is likely to bring a fresh and alert mind to its problems, but he has many other things to think about: and he has done his duty well, if he listens carefully to the suggestions of his chief subordinates; and endeavours to bring the Cabinet, and afterwards Parliament, to adopt such of them, as seem to him well conceived and likely to prove beneficial. His competence to decide on its business problems is therefore likely to be inferior to that of a man of equal natural ability and energy, who has given his whole time and strength to the thoughts and the actions that relate to the same business problems; and who has tested his judgment by applying it to many various risks which appertain to them, and which he has borne on his own shoulders. A Minister must continue to devote much of his energy to the great tasks of political statesmanship; and must apply those faculties of persuasive oratory, to which his high position is largely owing, in advocating the chief measures of general public policy, on the success of which the Ministry depends for the maintenance of its position. That is work of the highest importance: but in regard to his responsibilities as head of a vast business it is a grievous, if not a disastrous hindrance.

[1] Below, pp. 850, 1.

Consequently, for good and for evil, the main effective responsibility for the conduct of the higher business of a Department rests with its chief permanent officials. They have perhaps entered on their work with eager enthusiasm: but enthusiasm is seldom in high favour with their seniors. For, though Ministers are likely to select as private secretaries men of alert and enterprising minds, they often acquiesce in the common rule of promotion by seniority, save in exceptional cases: and this rule perpetuates itself, because those, who have prospered under it, appreciate its convenience more fully than its shortcomings.

Therefore a new technical advance is apt to be regarded coldly by a Government Department; for regulations which have been worked out with much care for the control of old established methods, may not be applicable to the new method: so it is likely to be treated as an enemy not exactly of the public, but of the public as represented by the Department[1].

But when private enterprise has toiled and invented and experimented and failed; and again invented, and experimented, and perhaps succeeded a little; and then has further invented and experimented and quite succeeded, the public official enters on the scene. He endeavours to absorb the latest ideas: he brings the might of a bottomless public purse to bear on their finance; and he annexes some leaders of the new industry to carry the chief burden of the technical side of the work. If the enterprise needs the use of public rights of way—as for instance tramways and electric light do—he has so great an advantage of position, that his victory is almost inevitable: and indeed in

[1] For instance "the officials responsible for drafting the London Building Act of 1894, had in view nothing more advanced than the time-honoured method of brick and stone construction, and were apparently unaware of the fact that steel-frame construction and reinforced concrete construction had already been applied with satisfactory results as regards safety, durability and economy both on the Continent and in America. As neither of these methods could be employed with economy under the requirements of the Act, steel-frame construction remained under a ban until 1909, and reinforced concrete construction was similarly handicapped until 1915." *Engineering Supplement of the Times*, March, 1918.

The following is a representative case. An intelligent Borough Engineer had his attention called to a dangerous place on the road. Reference being made to an inexpensive remedy, by which he held that most of the danger would be removed, he added:—"I dare not do it. An accident might still happen: and then I should be held responsible for it: a thorough remedy would be very expensive. As things are, an accident there would not hurt me: for I should merely have left the case as I found it."

III, xiv, 9. such cases private enterprise may be patriotic enough to regard its own despoilment with satisfaction. Even in the railway industry, in which Government control has some exceptional advantages, it seems to have borrowed almost every new idea from independent work[1].

The industries in which Government Departments and Local Authorities have succeeded are few in number, but important. They are mainly concerned with "things that sell themselves"; that is, things which are in large demand, and more or less standardized by natural causes. The chief of them are connected with facilities for transport, and the distribution (by aid of way-leaves) of water, light and power: they all meet elementary needs; call for little or no adaptation to changing habits, or varying tastes; and make use of plant, the central ideas of which have been worked out by private enterprise and gradually become common property.

State Management possesses advantages, where many routine operations are "performed under the public eye, or for the service of individuals, who will immediately detect and expose any failure or laxity"; especially if "there is but little capital expenditure, so that each year's revenue and expense shall represent with sufficient accuracy the real commercial conditions of the department." These conditions, indicated long ago by Jevons[2], are fulfilled in an eminent degree by the postal business: and the first, though not the second, is fulfilled by all other important businesses in which State Management has had much success.

It may be noted in passing that mining does not seem to belong to this class. For, though the miner merely transports a product from one place to another, and does not make it; yet the selection and organization of underground routes require

[1] "The telegraph, the telephone, the electric light, the railroad track, the locomotive, the air brake, the block signal system were all introduced by private companies. In most cases it took Government experts from ten to twenty-five years to discover them after they had been in use on private lines": said President Hadley writing in the *Yale Review*, Feb. 1896, p. 406. Many Municipal tramway schemes have failed: but private enterprise, which initiated them, has brought their technique on so far, that the predominant advantage, derived by local authorities from their ownership of the roads, has set them now in the saddle: and the victory, thus almost forced upon them, has been exploited by eager politicians as affording a strong argument in favour of Government businesses in general.

[2] See *Methods of Social Reform*, p. 338.

decisions to be taken on important details, that are presented in manifold combinations and are not easily to be reduced to rule. There is therefore no cause for surprise in the fact that even the strong German bureaucracy (before the war) was found to get but small profits from its coal mines, while yet it was not generous to its employees[1].

But the relations among the various Departments of a modern Government are numerous: and when a much vaunted public enterprise has turned out badly, the resulting losses can be so distributed and buried under a mass of Departmental detail, that their true history cannot be unravelled without the aid of a semi-judicial inquiry: in fact, it generally remains obscure; and those, who are responsible, escape their just censure[2].

Thus Governmental administration is apt to suffer from lack of concentration of authority and lack of elasticity in methods of procedure. Very few large practical problems lie wholly within the competency of any one Department: and a decision on some trifling issue may not be reached, till the correspondence about it among various offices in Whitehall has cost the nation many times as much as the whole value of the matter in hand. If that matter is of private, as well as public concern, the delay and waste of time to individuals lend support to the belief that it is better to suffer some hurt from official control or charges, than to strive for a remedy. Of course, such

[1] See above p. 574 fn. At the time of going to press, evidence before the Coal Commission is making prominent many of the evils that have arisen or might arise from local coal monopolies; and from cheap railway charges for long distance coal transport, by which such monopolies are to some extent curbed. Something has also been established as to the good and evil of concentrated private ownership under State control; and as to evil that might probably have been caused by nationalization of the mines. Much enthusiasm, but very little solid argument, has been prominent in pleas for nationalization.

[2] Difficulties of this kind have obstructed the formation of a good judgment on many of the ventures of the Coalition Government during the war: the unwieldy majority, which was awarded to it under the supreme necessity of presenting a united front to the foe, has quenched inconvenient inquiries. Transferences of control (often no doubt made for sound reasons) from one Department to another have obscured accounts; as for instance when the Shipyards at Chepstow and Beachley passed from the Ministry of Shipping to the Office of Works. And during the war, when the Government was spending two or three thousand millions a year; wasteful duplication of work was rampant: and "the accretion of Departments, their clashing and overlapping," became the subject of general comment.

III, XIV, 9. troubles are great in a democratic country, where permission to alter established practice may require the sanction of a Minister, who has no technical knowledge of the matter; and who may be about to move to another Ministry, or to go out of office. These and similar difficulties led to the appointment in 1917 of the Machinery of Government Committee; whose Report is much to our present purpose. It lays stress on the fact that the centre of each Department's work ought to be an organized study of some one of the broad functions of Government; and not of the activities of Government in regard to the interests of particular classes of persons[1].

This fundamental unity in regard to the matters entrusted to a Department being secured, it may reasonably be required to have recourse to "the advice and assistance of advisory bodies so constituted as to make available the knowledge and experience of all sections of the community affected by its activities": but "there should be no omission in the case of any particular service of those safeguards which ministerial responsibility to Parliament alone provides." This last suggestion is enforced by the weighty observation that "a more efficient public service may expose the State to the evils of bureaucracy, unless the reality of Parliamentary control is so enforced as to keep pace with any improvement in departmental methods[2]."

If the applied science of administration is mastered by Departments; and members of Parliament generally lack the leisure, the inclination, or the ability to form independent judgments as to recommendations made by Departments in regard to broad problems of public policy; then Parliament will in effect often do little more than register the decisions of a Bureaucracy: and democratic rule will be stultified by the absence of an adequate response to the question: *Quis custodiet ipsos custodes?* Government Departments are chief custodians of the interests of the nation: Parliament cannot do that work; but its duty is to control that work: *i.e.* to make it efficient, to prevent its being obstructed by internal friction, and to resist unnecessary expenditure of public money. To do this Parliament needs to take its own arduous functions as seriously as Bureaus need to take theirs.

[1] [Cd. 9230], 1918, § 18. [2] *Ib.* pp. 11 and 16.

We pass to scientific studies in the narrow sense of the term. The National Physical Laboratory and the Committee of the Privy Council on Scientific and Industrial Research are recognized as doing work of the highest value. But there is danger that, when relying on private advice, a Department or the Cabinet may be influenced by biased opinion in deciding what industries should be aided on account of their exceptional importance as "key" or "pivotal" industries. And yet the State has clearly some duties in the matter; especially when supporting independent organized effort[1]. III, XIV, 9.

In so far as State assistance is given to such developments by direct money grants, Parliament is likely to be vigilant. For this, among other reasons, such grants are to be preferred from the national point of view to the taxation of imports that compete with the products of essential industries: though in a few cases a combination of the two plans may be necessary. The exclusion of particular imports often tends to divert employment from the energetic industries, that make for export, to those which are favoured by the exclusion: it does not effect any net increase of employment, and its indirect costs to the nation are frequently underestimated, because they are not conspicuous. On the other hand, the whole costs to the nation of direct subsidies are definite and conspicuous: those who are favoured by them are brought immediately under the eye of the people, and their accounts are liable to public audit. The danger that a subsidized business may abuse monopolistic power is so obvious

[1] See above pp. 179, 180. Among the industries now prominent in this connection are those connected with tungsten, magnetos, optical and chemical glass, hosiery needles, thorium nitrate, certain gauges, and many drugs. But it is recognized that technical, military and even political developments may cause rapid changes in such a list: and therefore it is proposed that a Special Industries Board, consisting of commercial and industrial experts, in association with a Department of State, shall be set up to work in close relation with the Department of Scientific and Industrial Research, and with others interested in the development of industry. It should recommend on occasion that financial assistance should be given to vigorous firms, which are pioneering the way in such industries, by studies, experiments, and production, that may be amply remunerative to the country as a whole, though not to the pioneers. The functions of the State in this matter have been made urgent by a sudden increase in the dependence of military operations by land, by sea, and lastly in the air, on scientific and technical developments; some of which were not in sight even a few years ago. In case of urgent need only, "the Government should itself undertake the manufacture of such articles as may be essential for national safety." *Report on Commercial and Industrial policy after the war* [Cd. 9035], 1918, pp. 31, 32.

III, XIV, 9. as to be unlikely to escape the notice of the official investigations, to which it must be in any case submitted[1].

It is perhaps true that the power of Government to control the administration of a great Departmental business is on the increase: that the power of the nation to govern its Government is on the increase; and that the number of giant undertakings which have the apparent (though perhaps not the real) maturity of standardized routine method, needed to make them in some measure suitable for Governmental ownership, is on the increase. But it seems to remain almost as true now, as in former times, that the heavy hand of Government tends to slacken progress in whatever matter it touches; and finally that "business influences are apt to corrupt politics; and political influences are apt to corrupt business."

Increasingly during the last hundred years national well-being has depended on the progress and dissemination of sound education. It is clear that a great part of the funds for this purpose must be supplied by the State, though public officials are not generally well fitted to control the methods of higher education: and in regard to them the State may be well advised to trust as far as possible to the guidance of the Royal Society and other bodies of advanced students, in association with the Universities. In regard to popular education it is to be remembered that drinking troughs are in vain supplied for horses, if their bearing-reins are kept so tight that they cannot reach the water. Therefore, if education in any broad meaning of the word is to become a reality, reasonable conditions of life are necessary[2].

[1] See the Memorandum of the Board of Trade on *State assistance to the dye industry* [Cd. 9194], 1918. Grants in aid may be made up to 40 per cent. of costs of (1) general plant and buildings, (2) laboratory buildings and equipment, and (3) laboratory maintenance for certain periods. In return restrictions are to be imposed as to prices that may be charged, and as to the profits that may be divided. Thus the great power which has been obtained by the combined firms of British Dyes and Messrs Levinstein seems (in the present state of the industry) almost an essential for rapid progress: and it is to be strongly controlled in the general interest.

[2] This is the main drift of the *Report of a Committee on Social Conditions in relation to Adult Education* [Cd. 9107], 1918. The Master of Balliol was in the chair.

APPENDIX A[1]

A NOTE ON METHOD IN ECONOMIC STUDY

1. *The progress of science, while increasing the stock of knowledge, increases also the area of conscious ignorance. Relations between economic analysis and ethical aspirations.* APP. A, 1.

Absolute certainty is possible only in regard to (1) particular individual facts; and (2) deductions by strict reasoning from axiomatic premisses, such as those of pure mathematics. Even sciences, which deal with concrete facts and conditions as definite and immutable as those of physics appear to be, cannot claim certainty over the whole of their area. In biological sciences the area over which certainty extends is relatively very small; and in the social sciences it is less than in those which deal with the lower forms of life.

Even the physical sciences made but little progress in their youth; partly because they had no adequate apprehension of the vastness of the area, which lay beyond their knowledge. But by patience and perseverance each generation of workers has corrected, and brought certainty into, doctrines which had previously been faulty and uncertain; and at the same time it has opened out new ground in which uncertainties abound and certainties are rare: the certainties of physics increase in number, but its uncertainties increase much faster.

The experience of economics during the six or seven generations, in which it has been studied seriously, has been similar, though cast in a smaller mould. Adam Smith cleared up many obscurities and uncertainties: but the area of his

[1] See above, p. 7.

APP. A, 1. conscious uncertainty was far greater than that of his predecessors. Ricardo's bias was towards making his ground certain, so far as he went, rather than towards broadening his outlook: and his vigorous narrow certainties had such sway that men rested on them, with the result that little truly constructive work was done for a long while; though in consequence of that very stagnation, the science appeared to increase in certainty. But the combined constructive efforts of students in the chief countries of the western world have made the area of economic certainties perhaps fully twice as large as it was in, say, 1860: and at the same time they have increased in even larger proportions the area of conscious economic uncertainties. Those matters as to which there is no longer uncertainty are but little discussed; while conflicts of opinion are prominent over the widening area of uncertainties. The quiet agreements do not attract the attention of hasty critics; the turmoil of conflicts does.

A chief cause of the great recent extension of the area of uncertainty in economic discussions is to be found in that growing volume of responsible doubt as to the general sufficiency of the existing social order for the requirements of man's nature, to which reference has already been made. In an age of violence prudent men strive rather to strengthen those elements of social order which are already the strongest, than to inquire whether it might not be possible, in more fortunate times, to improve them away, and substitute better elements in their place. The rigid outlines of the doctrines of Ricardo and the earlier Mill were partly caused by the temporary return of Europe, between 1790 and 1820, to a reign of violence: and John Stuart Mill was so much under their influence when young, that he laid down canons as to the province of the economist, which seemed to exclude the use of all faculties except the intellectual. But these rigid limits were unsuitable to the latent warmth of his nature: and, as he indicated on the title page of his *Principles of Political Economy*, he softened the hard outlines of economic science by an admixture of "social philosophy." This movement was carried further, at first chiefly under German influence: and it has now gone so far in England and America and other countries, that it may be regarded as cosmopolitan; social studies of a general character are now largely mingled with others that are more strictly scientific[1].

To the scientific group belong retrospective statements in the indicative mood, as to the causes which have been (certainly or probably) operative in bringing about past events; and prospective statements, also in the indicative mood, as to the results which may be expected (certainly or probably) to follow from the action of specified causes. All opinion is liable to be tainted by unconscious bias; but that taint can be kept low in matters in which every serious student can equip himself with the knowledge and the implements for investigation and reasoning, that have been accumulated by the progressive labours of many generations of strong workers in the same field. And, though confusion may for a time be caused by the intrusion of partisan or interested disputants, yet patient study prevails progressively in all issues that are within its grasp.

On the other hand, expressions of sentiment or desire in the optative mood, as to the relative claims of different social aims, must necessarily rest in the main on the personal authority of individuals. For instance the social benefits, which would result from an increase in the supply of material comforts and luxuries, are of a different order from those which would result from improved health, increased leisure, better musical opportunities and so on: and when a difference of opinion arises as to the preference which people ought to show for any of these, the issue cannot be decided by scientific method.

Again, it may be suggested that, though the rigid rights of private property, which prevail under the present social order, may justly claim to have done a great and necessary work; yet human nature has now so far developed, that social benefit would result from some softening of these rights in such ways as would promote the more equal distribution of wealth. Now such a proposal offers scope for turning to account the stores of knowledge and scientific apparatus, that have been accumulated by economic science; and therefore there is a certain obvious

[1] Mill's term "philosophy" is perhaps not wholly appropriate. A better term appears to be "policy" (not current "politics"); which corresponds to the full title of the great German Association, commonly known as the *Social-Verein*; but of which the official title is *Verein für Social-Politik.*

APP. A, 2. convenience and appropriateness in its being discussed from the special point of view of the economist. But some of the questions involved in it, and especially those which relate to the development of human nature, have not yet been brought within the scope of scientific treatment, at all events by the methods of economics[1].

To conclude:—economic studies are not to be limited to matters, which are amenable to strictly scientific treatment. But those conclusions, whether in detail or in general, which are based on individual judgments as to the relative desirability of different social aims, or as to matters of fact which lie beyond the scope of any individual's special studies, should be clearly distinguished from those which claim to have been reached by scientific method.

2. *Similarity amid diversity of the methods of physical and social sciences. The need for elasticity in the uses of economic terms.*

A few words may be added as to the guidance which the experiences of the physical sciences suggest to their younger sisters, the social sciences.

The path to be followed was pioneered by the sciences of mechanics and astronomy and by other studies of inorganic matter; because they meet less obstacles to exact observation and reasoning than are encountered in a study of organic development. They discovered at a comparatively early stage that complex problems must be broken up into elementary parts; for there is indeed but little chance of finding a class of complex problems which resemble one another so closely that

[1] An illustration will perhaps make more clear the way in which exact but limited knowledge may be combined with broader estimates that rest on uncertain foundations. A navigator who has for some time been unable to take good observations, and is in waters where the currents are uncertain, must be content with probability: he can do no more than make sure that his conclusion as to the distance and direction which his ship has travelled since his last good observation contains no error that is not inherent in his guess at movements of the currents, or in the figures shown by his log; but he may not rest content with less. The function of economic analysis is to render a service within its sphere similar to, though less thorough than, that which the science of navigation renders within its sphere: the value of such services is seldom very much diminished by a little uncertainty as to some of the data.

the same sort of systematic reasoning can be applied to all of them, and thus each be made to throw light on the others.

But the opposite is true of the elementary parts into which complex problems can be broken up. Each such part of any one of them is likely to belong to the same class as a number of elementary parts of other complex problems; and by systematic study, general rules can often be discovered which apply, more or less nearly in the same way, to each member of the class. Similarities and dissimilarities between different members are fruitful of suggestions. Gradually a general rule appropriate to them is developed; and the rule becomes more definite and also more elastic, as the fundamental laws of Nature which underlie it are more distinctly apprehended. Meanwhile provisional conclusions in regard to various elementary parts of complex problems are brought together, and worked up into broader partial truths: and thus by the cumulative work of successive generations, intellectual machinery is built up which can work its way through even very refractory material. The most prominent change in method which has resulted from this experience is an increase in the stress which is set upon the study of *tendencies*; as distinguished from the comparison of the same or similar events under very different conditions or at widely different stages in their evolution.

It was not till the seventeenth century that the physical sciences appreciated the full importance of the fact that when several causes act together and mutually affect one another, then each cause produces two classes of effects; those which are direct, and those which result indirectly from the influences exerted by it on other causes: for indeed these direct and indirect effects are apt to become so intricately interwoven that they can by no means be disentangled. So far the results were negative: they seemed to indicate that the task of following out and understanding the combined action of several causes, which are in various degrees mutually interdependent, is beyond the power of human faculty. But a way out of the difficulty was found, chiefly under the guidance of Leibnitz and Newton. An epoch-making process of reasoning showed that, though the indirect effects might grow cumulatively, and ere long become considerable, yet at first they would be very small indeed

APP. A, 2. relatively to the direct effects. Hence it was concluded that a study of the tendency to change, resulting from each several disturbing cause, might be made the starting point for a broad study of the influences of several causes acting together. This principle is the foundation of the victory of analytical methods in many fields of science. Its best known triumph is that of the Nautical Almanack which takes account of the disturbing influences exerted by any two planets on one another directly; and also indirectly as the result of their disturbances of other planets[1].

Social sciences have profited slowly at first, but with ever increasing rapidity, from such experiences of their elder sisters, the physical sciences. Facts are closely studied in well selected groups: tendencies which are observed as provisionally suggested by each of several similar groups, are first subjected to critical analysis, and then set up as provisionally established. But they remain ever on their trial. New experiences, apparently inconsistent with the old, may threaten their credit: but if a closer study shows that differences in conditions account for the differences in observed results, the credit is improved. Each such well established tendency is a real asset of knowledge: but it is seldom of much practical service, till its manner of working in combination with other tendencies has been studied. The task is long, but each of several generations has already contributed to its achievement: and now the number of those who work at economic science in Western Europe, the United States and some other new countries, is so great, that the progress made in a single decade can be clearly marked. The result is not to set up economic doctrines: they are left for

[1] This method is not easily grasped without the aid of mathematical symbols; but its central idea can be indicated vaguely without their aid. If A is a state of things influenced by conditions B and C; while B and C are so connected that a change in B sets up simultaneous tendencies to change in both A and C; then the changes produced in A and in C will at first be very small, though they may increase continually and cumulatively. Now since the immediate effect which a considerable change in B exerts on C would be very small; the immediate effect which the change B exerts on A *indirectly* through a very small change made by it in C, must be a very small part of a very small thing (in mathematical language it must be "a quantity of the second order of smalls") and be negligible provisionally. But yet its accumulated effects may need consideration in special cases, among which those considered by the Nautical Almanack hold a place.

political partisans, and elementary preceptors. It is to set up principles of record and analysis, so carefully applied that those who seek knowledge for its own sake, increasingly agree as to the general character of the tendencies to be expected from any set of conditions; and even, in some small measure, agree as to the course of action most appropriate to those conditions. There is however a special difficulty in social studies. No one can have first-hand knowledge of any considerable part of the conditions and other facts relevant to any issue. Therefore the first duty of every student is to be diffident: and his second is to shun controversy.

A business man is generally the best and often the only authority on those transactions for which he is directly responsible; but he must depend largely on second-hand information in regard to movements of production and trade in places and under circumstances remote from his own: and conclusions which are valid in regard to a single business, or even a single industrial group, are often not true in regard to larger units.

For instance, artificial restrictions on the number of workers, or on the output in any one skilled industry, influence the wages and profits immediately concerned in a different manner, and often in the opposite direction, to those of similar restrictions when applied generally. This fact is analogous to the fact that, though a shipwrecked man will increase his chance of reaching the shore, if he is able to rest one hand on the shoulder of another of the crew, yet the general adoption of this practice would greatly increase the chance that they would all be drowned.

Therefore an economic doctrine cannot be tested, as has frequently been suggested, by such questions as:—"Consider your own case: would the doctrine be true in regard to it?" The answer to that question may probably be in the negative; and yet the doctrine may be true in regard to the general case to which it claims to apply. If so, its practical importance will be increased by the fact that its truth would not be likely to be suggested by the ordinary experience of life, and could be grasped only by considerable observation and thought. In short, though direct practical experience of particular events is the basis of all economic knowledge, and is the exclusive source of

APP. A, 2. supply of the material used in the construction of economic science; yet by itself it reaches but a very little way towards the great task of deducing general guidance for the future from the instruction of the past.

Those studies, which are of little interest to any but experts, can escape ambiguity by the adoption of a great number of technical terms; each of which is defined sharply, and has no variations of meaning. But technical terms must be kept within very narrow limits in studies which relate to the affairs of the market-place: and unfortunately there are not enough terms in ordinary use in any language to enable each one of them to be allotted permanently in one particular sense with sharply defined boundaries. This difficulty is not very troublesome in ordinary conversation; where, as a rule, each one is concerned only to know that a word, which he uses, will be taken by his hearers in the sense intended. It is of little concern to him that elsewhere, and in other conditions, the same word may be commonly taken with rather different breadth or shade of meaning: for differences as to interpretation can be cleared up easily by question and answer. But the written word must carry with it all necessary explanation: and therefore a writer is bound to consider whether the particular use, which he is attaching to an important word in any inquiry, has been made clear by the context; and if not, to state explicitly what he means by it there. In another inquiry, he may desire to use it in a rather different signification, as is common in ordinary conversation: but, if so, he must be alert to indicate the change in the service to which he is putting the word. This is no doubt a counsel of perfection, to which few, if any, have attained. But the more nearly it is reached, the better will be the prospects of cooperative progress by men of affairs and by professional students in the discussion of matters of general interest, without the aid of an elaborate technical terminology[1].

[1] Bagehot, a master of literary form, and a leader in affairs, urged economists "to write more as we do in common life where the context is a sort of unexpressed interpretation clause"; and warned them against attempts to "express various meanings on complex things with a scanty vocabulary of fastened senses" (*Postulates of English Political Economy*, pp. 7, 8, 9): and an attempt is made here, as in my *Principles of Economics*, to conform to this precept.

APPENDIX B

SOME EARLY PHASES OF INDUSTRY AND TRADE[1]

1. *Beginnings of specialized industry and long distance trade.*

APP. B, 1.

The spirit of economic nationality has had many phases and many degrees in every phase. Sometimes it has been broad and genial; sometimes it has been intense and narrow. It has rarely been a universal good. But its evil results have seldom lasted long after their immediate cause has passed away; while its good results have borne fruit many fold.

In early times it was generally very narrow: because the whole range of man's moral vision was short; and even at a small distance other people appeared to him as strangers and aliens. The stranger or enemy—for one word often sufficed for both—could seldom reckon on more than the good faith and courtesy that belonged to the herald's tabard or the flag of truce. Except in this last respect, the instinctive habits of mutual aid among neighbours, and of common hostility to strangers, in the earlier stages of civilization seem not to have differed very widely from those which prevail among lower animals[2].

Within the family, or village, or clan there was little or no buying and selling, and not much even of formal and explicit barter: but the hard clear cut lines of that definite bargaining, which has so largely fashioned human life for good or for evil, came to the front when strangers sought strangers for the satisfaction of their own wants and the disposal of their own superfluities. Trade proper, and especially trade organized by a distinct class of traders and merchants, arose first out of the relations between groups of men, clans, or other rudimentary

[1] See above, p. 33. [2] See Kropotkin's brilliant *Mutual Aid*.

APP. B, 1. economic nations. It was international trade rather than domestic trade: Hermes was the God of money, trade and theft; of hospitalities and embassies.

Gradually there arose division of labour, and specialization of skill. It did not extend to nearly all industries. But it was occasionally carried a long way by sporadic groups of artisans, who gradually attained a subtle hereditary skill in choice metal or textile work: their light goods travelled far, with but little protection from physical force, though often under some sort of religious sanction. Thus trade at Delphi and Olympia was protected by the truce of religious festivals before the time of Zeus and Apollo; as was that of Mecca before the time of Mahomet. And wherever the sway of an organized church extended over a wider area than the sway of political rulers, commercial intercourse owed much to the religious security of fairs and pilgrimages, of national games and church festivals, of monasteries and sanctuaries[1].

For indeed, as Heeren seems to have been the first to show, the course of history has been largely shaped by the need of commerce in its earliest stages for easy land routes: because traffic by river has many limitations, and traffic by sea requires great resources. Traffic over moist land, or through jungles and forests, is difficult or impossible without expensive roads: and the earliest long trade routes were over the vast dry plains of Asia and Northern Africa. The desert generally afforded an easy path, wherever there was water enough to support life[2].

The cessation of agricultural work, as soon as the green of spring passed into the brown death of early summer, forced men to exert themselves to manufacture light and refined wares for

[1] The influence of war and brigandage in affecting fellowship and solidarity among traders, honest and dishonest, peaceful and warlike, has been often discussed. See *e.g.* the earlier chapters of Roscher's *Handel und Gewerbfleiss*, Walford's *Fairs past and present*, and Robertson Smith's brilliant article on "Mecca" in the tenth edition of the *Encyclopædia Britannica*.

[2] It gave some little scope to the Law of Squares in transport and trade, even on land. But the work was slow. A camel spends the whole of a favourable season in carrying eight chests of tea, about half a ton, in two journeys from Kalgan to Urga (600 miles), at a cost of about £6 (*Journey in Mongolia*, 1902, by C. W. Campbell, British Consul [Cd. 1874, pp. 8, 9]). A caravan carrying a hundred tons would be nearly a mile long; and a single modern fast ten thousand ton ship can do about as much carrying in a year in spite of some delays in ports, as two thousand such caravans.

sale, and to serve as carriers and merchants between neighbouring lands for those goods that would bear the expense. Caravans carried spices and flavours, of which a small quantity satisfies a strongly felt need. And, what was much more important, they carried the best products of the subtle hereditary skill, which had grown up here and there among the more advanced peoples. These products, slight as their bulk was, served as an educating influence wherever they went: they stimulated the mind in the same way as the aroma and splendour of the choice natural products which they accompanied did the senses. All routes, however long and difficult, were open to delicate and refined textile goods and embroideries, to trusty steel and well-wrought weapons; and to various forms of work even in common metals, which contained more poetry than metal[1].

Great highways were made chiefly for political and military purposes: they connected seats of provincial Governments, camps, and depots with one another, and with the central authority; or they ran out to frontiers liable to attack. But though they were seldom laid out with any great regard to the needs of commerce, they effected a good deal for it; and they are noteworthy as the first large embodiment of public resources. Strong rulers have generally been impatient of the trade particularism of the several groups of their subjects; they have tried to break it down, and to spread freedom of trade and intercourse among the various provinces under their rule. For

[1] The chief long distance trade of early times was that between Southern Europe and Western Asia; all of which was forced to go part of the way by land. But most of it made much the larger half of its journey by sea. For a long while the route by the Persian Gulf was the easiest and most secure; and its advantages contributed much to the trade of ancient Phoenicia and Greece. The foundation of Alexandria contributed to the supremacy of the Red Sea route; in which water carriage prevailed even more strongly. The Persian Gulf route was however partly revived in Venetian times: and the trade between Europe and the East remained very light in proportion to its value even after the Ocean route had come into use. Mr Chisholm's address to Section F of the British Association in 1907 gives a list of the cargo of a Portuguese ship coming from India about 1590 which consisted almost wholly of spices, precious stones and similar things; while the outward cargoes were also very light. So great were the risks and so heavy the duties of the Mesopotamian route, that the silver value of spices was 60 or 100 times as high in Venice as that which had been paid for them in India; though both silver and spices are exceptionally portable.

APP. B, 2. all artificial barriers within the limits of their own territory have hindered the growth of that political unity and strength, which has been their chief aim. But, as Heeren insisted, the very extension of empire often leads to an increase of local autonomy; the most despotic rulers have tolerated semi-independent kings, and even republics, within their rule. Partly for this reason, commerce has seldom been injured as much by revolutions which have substituted one dominant race for another at the centre of power, as by the anarchy which has followed the total decay of despotic power[1].

2. *Even small towns carried on a sort of international trade with other towns, and a sort of colonial trade with neighbouring country-folk. Town patriotism, and town selfishness. The City States.*

Sacred festivals, and the markets associated with them, received protection from religious sentiment and authority in very early times. A certain immunity was afforded to traders proceeding to them, before civil order had been established over large areas by organized central rule; and the *Pax Romana* established a wonderful viability in the lands bordering on the Mediterranean, and in some others. In every age each considerable, civilized nation has possessed many trade centres, connected with one another by more or less easy and frequent intercourse: and each centre had as a rule some sort of sense of collective interests, partly political, partly economic. But there appears to be no record either in early or mediaeval times of a warm and strong common sentiment holding together the industries and the trade of a large area: there was no national trade in the full sense of the word. The individual might have his share in the commercial and other relations between the village or small town in which he lived and its immediate

[1] For the early history of roads see Lardner's *Railway Economy* and Huber's *Entwickelung des modernen Verkehrs.* A river may consolidate military rule almost as well as a system of roads. And Schmoller suggests (*Grundriss der allgemeinen Volkswirthschaftslehre*, § 102) that the compactness and stability, which the Nile gave to Egypt, helped it to maintain a well organized system of finance, such as was characteristic of the City States. The Nile Delta was a luxuriant garden, interspersed with canals, almost an earlier Holland.

neighbourhood: but he had scarcely any interest in the affairs of the empire as a whole. APP. B, 2.

When a group of people in daily intercourse with one another had to earn their living under difficulties, and to rely on one another's aid in contending with those difficulties, a feeling of brotherhood almost invariably grew up. If the difficulties were partly of man's creation, and had in them any savour of injustice or oppression; then to contend with them was more than mere enterprise. It became a religion, and a source of inspiration; and by its aid the community was knit together in living bonds, which grew with its growth. But with the strength came germs of weakness. Exclusive rights and privileges rose in prominence over duties and fellow-services: the bonds, that held the community together, might still increase in strength, but they lost vitality and elasticity.

In order to secure its position the better against the stranger, the town would form, if allowed to do so, a "gild merchant," or special "department of town administration whose duty was to maintain and regulate the trade monopoly[1]." From maintaining the monopoly for the town, the gildsmen soon got to maintaining it for themselves. The "simple merchant," not a member of the gild, was often put on the same footing as the stranger, and was estopped from trading as he wished. He might not buy some things at all, or he might not buy anything in order to resell it, nor till it was clear that the gildsmen did not care to have it. The Gild often bought from a common purse; and, if an individual gildsman bought anything from a stranger, he would often loyally fulfil the obligation to let the other gildsmen have a share in his bargain[2].

And the neighbouring country-folk fared as badly as did the colonies of a selfish mother country in later times. The craftsman was indeed willing to submit to a little loss when purchasing the goods of other crafts; provided he and they could agree on town regulations which secured a high priced, if limited, market for all their goods among the surrounding

[1] Gross, *Gild Merchant*, ch. III.

[2] The Dublin Gild of the Art of Merchants is an early instance of special racial aptitude for stringent regulation. Gross (*Gild Merchant*, ch. VIII).

APP. B, 2. country-folk: as Adam Smith observes, these often gave a greater share "of the annual produce of society...to the inhabitants of the town than would otherwise have fallen to them; and less to those of the country[1]."

The town frequently made and enforced a rule that no grain should be sold away from the land except by the landsfolk themselves in the market-place. Sometimes no one might buy more than enough till every citizen had supplied his present need. Sometimes no buyer might overbid another. Sometimes the public authorities kept large stores or magazines of grain; and sometimes bakers were ordered to keep a good stock in hand. But gradually the trade in grain became so massive, that stronger forces than those of governmental authority were needed to deal with it. And one of the first manifestations of a spread of economic nationality over large areas was the granting of a more or less complete freedom of traffic in grain within the boundaries of a province or a whole country, but not beyond[2].

As Schmoller says:—"The omnipotence of the council ruled the economic life of the town, when in its prime, with scarcely any limit; it was supported in all its action by the most hard-hearted town selfishness and the keenest town patriotism—whether it were to crush a competing neighbour, or a competing suburb, or to levy heavier fetters on the country around, to encourage local trade or to stimulate local industries." And the trade of even neighbouring towns was "international" in some respects. For "a complicated system of differential tolls was everywhere devised by which some towns were favoured and others were put at a disadvantage, in each case either in return for corresponding concessions or in accordance with the varying hopes and fears to which trade gave rise." And Southampton made separate treaties with seventy other towns[3].

[1] *Wealth of Nations,* Book I. ch. x. See also his discussion (Book III. ch. IV) as to "How the Commerce of the Towns contributed to the Improvement of the Country."

[2] The successive stages of this development, and their relations to the size and other conditions of the town populations to be served are well set forth in Schmoller's *Epochen der Getreidehandelsverfassung* in his *Jahrbuch* for 1896. A short similar study following geographical lines is given by Lexis in the *Handwörterbuch für Staatswissenschaften,* s.v. *Getreidehandel.*

[3] See his Essay on *The Mercantile System* edited by Ashley, and Mrs Green's

But economic nationality could not reach its full development except in a city which, whether formally subject to a Suzerain or not, had practically full control of its own affairs. In such a city public spirit gradually acquired the largeness of view, and sometimes—not always—the stability of purpose, that befit the large responsibilities of a powerful State. Inland towns often became rulers of provinces. Maritime towns sometimes acquired an imperial sway, being drawn to it almost unconsciously and without any other original purpose than that of securing their own trade against violence. On the seas their ships could seldom trust to any other protection than their own; and they were all equipped for fight. But when they had arrived safely at a foreign port, their difficulties had only begun. They still needed protection for themselves and their goods against the rude violence of the mob, and against the more orderly violence of its rulers.

For this purpose "Factories" or forts were established along the shore of the Mediterranean from the beginning of history; and they grew in importance and costliness as the effective area of the world's trade increased. And the empires acquired by several Italian cities, and especially by Venice, anticipated that, which an English joint stock company some centuries later developed on the basis of a few forts on the sea-coast of India.

Venice was Latin, and was never quite young. She soon came under the charm of Byzantine power and magnificence. Reversing the old Roman rule, she for some time confined to the aristocracy the rights of distant commerce; except in so far as she, like Marseilles and some other ports, kept them in her own hands. She built her own ships; but she often hired them out to private merchants, keeping however a controlling hand over many trades.

Gradually she got to love empire for its own sake: and,

Town life of the fifteenth century, vol. II. p. 53. Sometimes a charter would give a town "as much liberty as the citizens of London have" in certain trade matters. *Ib.* p. 51.

Even as late as 1575 the Mayor and Corporation of London forbade the bringing of Norwich wares into London without their being first taken to Blackwell Hall; there to be packed away, sold at stated times, and charged with heavy tolls. But such anarchic action could no longer be endured by the central government, and it was cancelled.

APP. B, 2. though she was never cruel without occasion; though she enforced her will with a comity that soothed and even attracted foreign customers, yet she was a stern ruler. She placed armed ships at the entrance of their rivers, for fear any foreign merchant should give them better terms than Venice would do: for indeed they had often to deal with Venice rather than Venetians. She was jealous of any competition; but she could cooperate heartily with those whose work supplemented hers; and the love between her and Cadore of the mountains, with her forests of pines ready to make the tallest and straightest of masts, was deep and strong.

She excluded the products of foreign skill and forbad her own artisans to emigrate; and at last she ceased even to learn. Her industries lived on the reputation and skill they had inherited from the days of freedom and growth. But the heat of the day continues to increase for some little time after the sun has begun its downward course: and the impetus which Venice had obtained from enterprise, fostered by freedom and only tempered by regulation, carried her onwards for a while, even after excessive regulation and the want of stimulating competition had begun to lower her vitality. Her fall was hastened by external events; especially the spread of the Ottoman empire and the diversion of the route to India from the Mediterranean to the Ocean. But List's verdict stands:—"If we inquire of history what were the causes of the downfall of the Republic of Venice and of its commerce, she replies that they principally consisted in the folly, neglect and cowardice of a worn-out aristocracy, and in the apathy of a people who had sunk into slavery." The further development of that verdict however contains the kernel of a doctrine about which controversy has raged increasingly during three generations.

List admits indeed that "...Unrestricted freedom of trade was beneficial to the Republic in the first years of her existence; for how otherwise could she have raised herself from a mere fishing village to a commercial power?" But he continues, "a protective policy was also beneficial to her when she had arrived at a certain stage of power and wealth, for by means of it she attained to manufacturing and commercial supremacy. Protection first became injurious to her when her manufacturing and commercial power had reached that supremacy, because by it all competition with other nations became absolutely excluded, and thus indolence was encouraged. Therefore not the introduction of a protective policy, but perseverance in maintaining it after the reasons for its introduction had passed away, was really injurious to Venice[1]." In fact however her supremacy never reached to that height. Therefore if indolence was encouraged by supremacy, it must surely have been encouraged also by her near approach to it: and the history of Venice would seem to lend some support to the opinion that external competition tends to stimulate and to maintain the resource and energy of a nation's industries.

Again, List does not deny that ruin came over Spain shortly after she had adopted the Venetian system of Protection, though he holds that "at the time of Charles V (first half of the sixteenth century) the Spaniards were more advanced than the English and French in every respect"; and he admits that Colbert's Protective regulations were followed by poverty. But he avoids the suggestion that the enfeeblement of competition tended quickly to quench the energy; which had been started by the sudden opening of profitable careers to manufacturing initiative[2].

3. *The industries of shipbuilding and trade were so developed by Holland, as partially to anticipate much that is characteristic of modern capitalistic predominance, and industrial technique. Industry and trade led up to finance.*

Sir W. Temple, writing of the early signs that the commercial supremacy of Holland would lead to that of larger nations, implicitly classes Holland with the Free States and Cities, and England with the greater nations. His survey may be quoted:—"Not many Ages past, Venice and Florence possessed all the trade of Europe; the last by their Manufactures; but the first by their Shipping: and the whole trade of Persia and the Indies, whose commodities were brought (those by land and these by the Arabian Sea) to Egypt, from whence they were fetched by the Venetian fleets, and

[1] *National System of Political Economy*, ch. I.
[2] *Ib.* chs. V, VI, XXVII.

APP. B, 3. dispersed into most of the parts of Europe: and in those times we find the whole Trade of England was driven by Venetians, Florentines, and Lombards. The Easterlings, who were the inhabitants of the Hanse Towns, as Dantzick, Lubeck, Hamburgh, and others upon that Coast, fell next into trade, and managed all that of these Northern parts for many years, and brought it first down to Bruges, and from thence to Antwerp. The first navigations of the Portuguese to the East Indies broke the greatness of the Venetian Trade, and drew it to Lisbon: and the revolt of the Netherlands, that of Antwerp to Holland. But in all this time, the other and greater nations of Europe concerned themselves little in it; their trade was war. The kingdoms and principalities were in the world like the noblemen and gentlemen in a country; the free states and cities, like the merchants and traders. These at first despised by the others; the others served and revered by them; till, by the various course of events in the world, some of these came to grow rich and powerful by industry and parsimony; and some of the others poor by war and by luxury: which made the traders begin to take upon them, and carry it like gentlemen; and the gentlemen begin to take a fancy of falling to trade[1]."

Holland was large enough to serve as a basis for the largest trade that was then possible; and while not neglecting either agriculture or manufacture, she gave her main strength to the industry of commerce. At a time at which manufactures, however concentrated, could obtain only the minor economies of production on a large scale, she showed that its major economies were already within the grasp of concentrated commerce. She thus pioneered and prepared the way for England, who two centuries later was to develop the major economies of massive production in manufactures also: but in the earlier age the power of concentrated capital could

[1] *Observations upon the United Provinces*, A.D. 1672, ch. VI. Temple was a large-minded man: but the evil side of the statesmanship of that age is shown in the conclusion of his survey of the state of Europe in 1671 where he sums up evenly the merits of three courses open to England: (1) to preserve our present alliances and thereby the peace of Christendom or (2) to encourage France to an invasion of Holland or (3) to join with France upon the advantages they can offer us for the ruin of the Dutch.

make itself felt only by command of shipping and merchants' stocks.

APP. B, 3.

By far the most important form of movable capital, until quite recent times, consisted of live stock, to which indeed the kindred origin of the words "capital" and "cattle" bears testimony: but agriculture offered little scope for the concentrated and highly organized employment of capital. Thus the opportunity for pioneering new and larger methods which lay in the hands of landowners was much less than that of the merchants, and especially of maritime merchants. For they generally owned their own ships; and, till well on in the eighteenth century, ships were much the most costly implements of industry in the world. Manufactures are commonly regarded as the industries which are most closely concerned with progress in mechanics. But in this and in every preceding century the ship has been the embodiment of more sustained thought and more organized experience than any other machine.

It was no accident that the origin of the vast modern system of joint stock undertakings can be traced to the necessity, which was felt even in the ancient world, for combining the resources of many people, in order to bear the expenses and distribute the risks of the shipping trade. But, though the ancient Romans made military roads at least as well as we can now, the arts of navigation are of relatively recent growth. In the early Middle Ages ships were small and heavily built, and they carried but little freight in proportion to their bulk. They were unable to progress at all except with a favourable wind: they did not venture out of sight of land in uncertain weather; and they carried but small cargoes.

But from the thirteenth century, when the compass came from the far East to the West, the arts and the appliances of navigation progressed fast. Ships became large and yet lighter of build and more easily handled: their net tonnage increased relatively to their gross tonnage, and even more relatively to the crews needed to work them. The art of tacking was discovered; and, as ships improved in structure, they were able to sail nearer to the wind and to dispense more and more with harbours and anchorages. Voyages went with larger freights and lower charges; with more security and less loss of

APP. B, 3. time, and therefore with less loss of capital: and there was of course a vast increase in the volume of trade and extent of trade: *i.e.* in the number of tons that were carried a mile; or, to speak more shortly, in the number of "ton miles."

But meanwhile the importance of the Mediterranean was being lowered by the spread of the Ottoman power, by the weakening of the police of trade, by the growth of piracy, and by the diversion of the traffic between Asia and Europe to the Cape route: and the more vigorous races of the North were gaining in knowledge, in wealth, and in opportunity. The scattered forces of the Hanseatic Federation could not however develop the latent economies of concentrated trade to their full extent; and, although Antwerp showed some signs of rivalling the trade of Venice, her career was cut short when the Scheldt was closed against her. No other single town was strong enough to fill her place: so the task fell to Holland, whose position and waterways combined every physical advantage for it, and whose people had every aptitude for it.

The Southern half of the low lands formed by the deltas of the Rhine and the Meuse was the earlier in economic development: the Dutch, like their pupils the English, were slow of invention[1]. But the toughness of their fibre was unsurpassed. They possessed singular self-control: and they remained frugal and persistent for more generations than any other rich people had done before them. The sons and grandsons and great-grandsons of a wealthy merchant were seldom above work; and some special form of refined trade-knowledge was often the best part of their rich inheritance[2].

Holland seemed poor in physical resources: but her poverty was a part of her strength: for it led her to give her whole energies to developing those resources which she possessed. The chief of them lay in the fact that she contained in a small

[1] Huet, *Memoirs of the Dutch trade*, A.D. 1700, ch. I, tells how Bruges had the first great trade in herrings; and how even the art of fish curing, to which the Dutch owed the first great spring of their shipping industries, was borrowed from the South. Many years elapsed before they carried the lessons, which they had learnt from the Flemish textile industries, to a sufficient excellence for export trade.

[2] The evil arising from a lack of this steadfastness is well shown in Ehrenberg's study of the rise and decay of the brilliant Augsburg.

compass the mouths of great rivers which bring to a focus many courses of rich and easy trade. Amsterdam was popularly said to be built upon herring bones: for her wealth rose out of the earnings of fishermen who fished first for their own markets, and then for sale as fast-day food for other peoples. Thus her domestic industries paved the way for her export industry of the services of carriage to other countries: for, as Petty said, "The Labour of Seamen and Freight of ships is always of the nature of an exported commodity[1]." And he and others maintained that Nature had been as kind in giving to the Dutch but a poor home on the land, as in giving them rich provinces of water by sea and river. If they could have grown corn and wood easily themselves, their early call to life on the waters would have been less distinct. But having little vent for their capital in agriculture, they kept it long in commerce; and their excellent system of banking and commercial credit made their rapidly growing wealth in a fluid form available for all uses. Thus the rate of interest was low with them. Their shipowners and merchants could always obtain the loan of capital on easy terms; and it was used freely to join their natural watercourses by canals, thus making much of their land into a greater Venice. They spread out their industry upon the waters, so that their several towns were in constant, close, and cheap communication with one another; and for heavy traffic as well as for light.

They could meet the needs and hit off the fancy of customers in each place with choice of things drawn from many sources. They could select from many markets the fittest and the most opportune for the sale of any particular ware. Further, they could buy quickly and sell quickly: and therefore with but little loss for spoilt goods relatively to the turn-over, and but little capital locked up in idleness—a consideration of great importance at an early stage of economic progress, when movable capital was scarce: the rates of interest and profit were still high even in Holland in comparison with those of the present age.

And, just as an organized post can deliver letters more cheaply than could be done by private messengers; so, by

[1] *Political Arithmetic*, p. 19.

APP. B, 3. sending out ships in quick succession on circular tours, they could deliver and fetch goods, and especially small parcels of goods, from and to a great number of ports very cheaply. The knowledge which they got of one class of customers or producers in one trade helped them to know of other customers and producers in that trade and in allied trades: in matters of this kind almost every piece of knowledge is on the way to others, as is almost every house on a postman's beat. And the economy of this unity and concentration was still further increased by the arrangement that each town should give special attention to some particular branch of trade; the detailed knowledge of which became the collective hereditary property of her merchants. Thus Holland's trade was the cooperative work of many units, each of which was organized cooperatively; though indeed jealousy among neighbours was not rare[1].

Turning the power of specialization that comes from effective unity in another direction, they adapted their vessels to particular tasks. Petty remarks that, as the cloth manufacture employs many classes of artisans, each trained for a special work, so Dutch commerce employs different classes of ships for precious or coarse freights, for long voyages, for coasting and for minor traffic, "for ports where they need never lie aground, for ports where they must jump upon the sand twice every twelve hours"; and so on. And a tract on "Trade and Commerce with the Hollanders," which used to be attributed to Raleigh, says that a Dutch ship of two hundred tons needs "but nine or ten mariners where we need thirty."

Nor did their high organization of energy end with their commerce. They anticipated, a little later than Venice had done, but much more thoroughly, the great nineteenth century principle of interchangeable parts in the manufacture of their ships. Dutch shipwrights could specialize themselves on

[1] Temple mentions as one of "the chief Advancers and Encouragers of trade in Holland, the custom of every town's affecting some particular commerce or staple, valuing itself thereupon, and so improving it to the greatest height: as Flussinque by that of the West Indies; Middleburgh, of French wines; Terveer by the Scotch Staple; Dort by the English Staple and Rhenish wines; Rotterdam by the English and Scotch trade at large and by French wines; ...Friesland by the Greenland trade; and Amsterdam by that of the East Indies, Spain and the Straits." *Observations on the Trade of the United Netherlands*, 1672, ch. VI. See also Huet, *l.c.* ch. III.

different classes of work so that one man shall be always and only employed in the manufacture of keels of one and the same dimensions; another of ribs, another of beams, another of rudders, and so on. They adhered to one pattern mainly for ships of one hundred tons, and again for ships of five hundred tons; and, carriage being easy, the different parts of a ship could be ordered from different makers and put together easily. By this means "the labour must be less, and consequently the prices must be less, though wages should continue as high as ever[1]."

Further, Holland led the way in banking and financial organization on a large scale, and, in this matter also, she handed on the torch from the City States of North and South Europe to England and other western countries. In early times financial enterprise drew its resources, and obtained its opportunities from trade rather than from industry. For industry offered few economies to production on a great scale; it belonged to artisan rather than to capitalist organizers: but trade, and especially long distance trade, when conducted with ability and good fortune, yielded high returns on relatively large investments. A chief field for the operations of financiers was always found in the demand for loans to needy rulers and other magnates. But, as industry grew, an ever larger field was provided by the growth of industrial cities; where the products of innumerable workshops yielded in the aggregate rich opportunities for financial enterprise: and those merchants, whose powers of insight and imagination fitted them for handling large commercial risks, rose quickly to be leaders of finance. Some of them tripped, fell, and disappeared: but the survivors built up a great edifice of high finance that lasted long. So it was in the great cities of Northern Italy:—Genoa, Milan, Florence and Venice: in Augsburg, Frankfurt, Hamburg and other Northern cities: and so it was above all in Holland, leading the way

[1] *Considerations on the East India Trade*, 1701, ch. XII. The discussion by the unknown author of this pamphlet, of the efficacy of labour as applied in the manufacture of cloth and watches, is one of his many claims for rank almost on a level with Adam Smith. He goes on to this discussion of Dutch shipbuilding as out-topping all other things "performed by the labour of man." For some similar facts relating to Venice see H. Brown, *Venetian Republic*, ch. XI.

APP. B, 3. in this also for England. Thus financial faculty was evoked by the large handling of material goods; and, as Professor Sombart's study of *The Jews and Modern Capitalism* has shown, the presence of an adequate material basis for finance attracted the faculty by which high gains might be reared on that basis.

He claims indeed that the rise of almost every important centre of financial activity can be traced to the advent of Jews; who generally came from afar, and not even from lands with similar customs, language or climate: and this accentuated their original tendency to regard as strangers those, who were not of their own race, and to be regarded by them with distrust. And he accumulates evidence that religious persecution moulded the international distribution of economic strength as much through the forced migrations of the Jews, as through the forced migrations of skilled artisans. Whether his position be fully established by further investigation or not, it seems certain that the superior mobility of financial ability and resource must be allowed credit for a larger share in governing the mobility of industry in the middle stages of its development, than has been generally given to it[1].

[1] He seems indeed to have underrated the difficulty of deciding which of two contemporary and allied movements exerted the greater influence in promoting the other. He shows convincingly that places which expelled the Jews became poor; and that places which attracted them became rich. But it is to be remembered that, if a town was failing in economic strength its merchants might probably regard the competition of Jewish rivals as a chief cause of its impoverishment and clamour for their expulsion; and thus accelerate a decline which had deeper causes. Again, the expelled Jews (whose knowledge of the economic conditions of various places was even more exceptional then than it is now) would be likely to move to those places which had high and large financial capabilities: and, of course, those places derived part of their strength from that very liberality of spirit of which their hospitality to the Jews was an evidence. The strong brains of the Jews fitted them for many tasks; they took good part in several industries and in colonization. No other race has maintained vigour of intellect and character during so many centuries. And Roscher, *Die Juden im Mittelalter, betrachtet vom Standpunkte der allgemeinen Handelspolitik*, 1875 (reprinted in his *Ansichten*), makes an instructive survey of the many "old" peoples, who have rendered similar services (during shorter periods indeed) for successive growths of new peoples.

4. *It is true that economic development passes generally through three stages, in the last of which manufacture predominates: but List's assumption that manufacture is necessarily superior to other industries seems to mistake accidentals for essentials.*

When this stage in the industrial evolution of the world had been almost perfected, a seer arose to tell its story with epic force. List was not altogether a kindly historian, especially as regards England. But his story was full of suggestion and dramatic interest. It told how the world passed from its mediaeval to its modern phase in economics, and to a large extent in politics, by the expansion of ideas, sentiments and methods of action, which had previously been unable to expand beyond the limits of towns. He showed how the "Mercantile" (or, as he preferred to call it, the "Industrial") system, by which the transition from economic mediaevalism to modernism had been effected, had had for its aim to carry over these ideas, sentiments and methods from the life of towns to that of whole nations; and thus to create "an agricultural-commercial-manufacturing state like a city which spreads itself over a whole kingdom, or a country district raised up to be a city." He was a broad-minded man, full of knowledge and insight; and economic history will for ever owe him a great debt. Many of his most important teachings are associated with his well-known doctrine that economic development in the past has generally shown three clearly marked stages. That doctrine, taken broadly, appears to be securely established; but its full interpretation presents several difficulties.

In List's first stage the people are not ready for the "higher" forms of industry; they buy manufactured goods with raw products, and are strengthened and educated by their purchases. In the second they are ready for the simpler forms of manufacturing industry: and, by resolutely practising these, they can educate themselves for more difficult work. If they do this, they reach the third stage in which manufacture predominates; and they have some share of industrial leadership.

On this basis he founded his great practical precept that in the first stage commercial intercourse with more advanced nations should be welcomed without stint, for the sake of its educative

APP. B, 4. influence; and because it supplies the machinery etc. needed for further advance: in the second stage the nascent manufacturing industries of the country should be fostered by import duties on things, which they are beginning to be able to make; and in the third stage Protection, having done its work, should disappear. It is well known that the wisdom of each clause of this precept has been questioned from several different points of view: and that there is no general agreement as to the point at which he designed to draw the line between the second and the third stage. But these matters, though important, are not to our immediate purpose. Our special concern now is with List's suggestion that the second stage of a country's industries is *higher* than the first, and the third *higher* than the second, in proportion as manufactures take an increasingly prominent place among them.

To begin with, Knies (1853) pointed out that List's account needed to be supplemented by the observation that the successive industrial stages of different nations show an increasing tendency to "synchronize": for backward nations can, by aid of modern developments of the means of intercourse, absorb advanced industrial ideas and methods with a rapidity that was impossible in the ages to which List had specially directed his attention. But when Knies wrote, the time had not yet come for discerning that the character and conditions of industrial leadership are liable to great modifications, in consequence of changes in the relative ranks of different sorts of industrial work.

In the middle of last century it was still reasonable to think of agriculture and mining as necessarily characteristic of the lower stages of industry, and of manufactures as completely possessed of the higher. But developments which had their roots in mechanical inventions of the eighteenth century, have grown at an ever increasing rate throughout the nineteenth. Semi-automatic machines have taken on themselves some of the responsibilities which used to weigh heavily on artisans in the larger staple manufactures; and they have lessened many others. Thus not a few of those manufactures which most impressed men's imaginations when List wrote, have now lost their right to be ranked among the higher industries; while other economic activities, some connected with manufacture and some not, have risen to the high places thus vacated. These changes call for a halt in our general study of industrial evolution. It is no longer reasonable to assume, as a matter of course, that an increase in a country's manufactures must be welcomed more heartily than other developments of her economic activity. No doubt England's chief strength, when List wrote, lay in manufacture. But as we have just seen, Holland's chief strength always lay outside of it; and yet she pioneered some of those paths of thought and action, in which many of the chief triumphs of industry have been won, both before and after List's time. And, as we have seen, not all of those characteristics of manufacture, to which its importance is owing, are of high quality. The substitution of repetition work in massive standardized production, even though it be true to a thousandth part of an inch, is not an advance, from the human point of view, over skilled handicraft: it increases man's power over matter; but it may diminish his power over himself.

APPENDIX C[1]

ENGLAND'S EARLY INDUSTRY AND TRADE

APP. C, 1.

1. ***Origins of the energies, which were ultimately turned to account in England's industry and trade.***

Even in the present age, when travelling is easy and safe, and strangers are hospitably received almost everywhere, those who seek their fortunes in a far country are generally sturdier, bolder, and more energetic than the comrades and relatives, whom they leave behind: and this rule was almost universal in the early ages of violence, when the sword, the spear, and the arrow were the only passports to new lands. England was peopled by successive hordes of immigrant warriors; and, whatever may be the rule in the modern age of machine guns, the bravest were the most likely to survive in the days of hand to hand conflict. Her people therefore had an exceptionally large share of the solid qualities by which men have won their chief victories in difficult industries.

The energy thus imported was sustained by their predilection for open air rural life. England's climate is moist and even sometimes melancholy: but it is almost free alike from oppressive heats and long continued frosts, when outdoor occupations are scanty and difficult: and the relatively rich growths of winter grass, which were offered in farm land and forest, enabled the people to indulge their liking for animal food in a degree which was rare in fairly well populated countries: roots and other crops for winter consumption were still unknown.

Conditions were favourable also to a good supply of strong cereal food, much of which was indeed taken in the form of

[1] This Appendix is associated with pp. 33—41.

a drink which was midway between mild ale and grain steeped in water. Also an exceptionally large part of the population lived sufficiently near to the open country to have opportunity for work on land, generally in their own occupation, so long at least as population was scarce: and the rule, that every artisan is an agriculturist at times, while every agriculturist does some rough work in or about the house, was even more general in England than in countries where life in cities and large villages was more in favour.

Another influence which food-supply exerted in early times on the vigour of the population, was seen when food had been made scarce by failures of harvest or by the ferocity of contending armies. Maitland's great dictum, that "Agrarian history becomes more catastrophic the further we trace it backwards," has been supported by investigations into the evil alliance between famines and disease. During severe famine, rotten poisonous food, both animal and vegetable, was eagerly devoured. Famine induced disease, and disease militated against the strenuous cultivation of the land: in fact famines and plagues worked more evil through the general weakness which followed them, than through the deaths which accompanied them. It seems however to be established that pestilence was seldom followed in England, as it was abroad, by ergotism, which caused an enduring lack of nervous as well as physical strength; and that this immunity was largely due to the generous food of Englishmen in ordinary times[1].

Lastly it is to be observed that England's position lent but little support to any pretension, which the king might advance, that a strong army was necessary to defend the country against invasion. Some of her kings were strong rulers, but their strength belonged to themselves rather than to their position: it did not often descend like an heirloom to weak successors.

[1] The process by which food-supply has been steadied in recent times will be discussed in Appendix I; when some further light will be thrown on Maitland's great dictum (*Domesday Book*, p. 345). He gives strong reasons for thinking that the amount of land needed to supply cereal food for a given population was much greater than has been generally supposed: he suggests that "no more than one third of the arable land was sown in any one year," and that it was necessary to "face the possibility of garnering but six bushels an acre...of which two must be retained for seed" (*ib*. pp. 438 and 517—9).

APP. C 1. No doubt the limitation of royal power was of interest to the nobles in the first instance, rather than to the common people: but indirectly it helped to maintain the sturdy independence, at all events of the middle classes—*i.e.* the smaller gentry and the well-to-do yeomen and craftsmen. And further the whole of the people gained something, amid their manifold distresses, from the outdoor exercises and sports, which it was the policy of the magnates to foster among their followers.

Norman rule established formal political unity throughout England: but while conquerors and conquered were becoming a single people, the very toughness of their character was causing obstinate local interests to grow up everywhere; partly indeed because commercial intercourse, except along the rivers and the sea-coast, was hindered by the lack of good roads. England long remained backward in this respect: for the great roads of early times were chiefly built for strategic purposes and by forced labour; and the English King had no great occasion for them, and no great power of making them. So this vital factor of national economic unity was neglected[1].

Thus England lacked concentration: her people always made use of the estuary of the Thames, of the marshy network of rivers of the East coast, and of the small harbours of the South coast. But they left nearly all the larger affairs of their own seas to Italians and to Easterlings. They received from foreigners high-class goods and services; and in return they gave crude wool and skins and minerals, which they had received from the bounty of Nature. The foreigners, who carried the trade, brought revenue to the king, but were not loved by his subjects. Further to increase his revenue, and to educate his people, he favoured the settlement of foreign artisans among them: they were not much better loved than the foreign traders, but this educative policy was truly constructive.

The royal power could protect foreign artisans in England fairly well: but it was not ready for the larger and costlier task of protecting English traders in distant lands. Some

[1] Rogers held that during the Middle Ages, though the local roads were bad, the old Roman roads were kept in good repair. But this is doubtful. See Denton, *England in the Fifteenth Century*, pp. 171—182: and Cunningham, *Growth of English Industry and Commerce*, II. § 130.

start indeed was made with the Company of the Staple, trading under direct royal authority. But the chief extensions of national trade were intrusted to private companies; who received more or less of a monopoly, direct or indirect, to recompense their private outlay on behalf of the order and security of trade, at first with England's near neighbours, and afterwards with all the four Continents. The privileged companies provided a fairly thorough substitute for a national trade policy; and they fostered the growing rush of the strong Norse blood into maritime adventures, which were ultimately to plant the English race firmly in a great number of the richest districts and the best ports of North America and Asia.

While English merchants were slowly feeling their way to liberating the trade of their country from dependence on foreign capital and enterprise, internal trade was in process of being developed in spite of the lack of adequate roads. As now-a-days good roads are the feeders of railways; so rough roads and packhorse tracks fed innumerable waterways, small and large. Only a small part of the total area of the country was very far removed from water that would carry a boat or shallow barge, and that small part of the country was thinly populated: nearly all considerable towns, and even important villages, monasteries etc. were situated near deep water[1].

Crude metals, and mill stones, and other heavy things, for which the demand was urgent, would go round almost any distance by water, in order to avoid a long land journey: and even at a relatively late date, the monstrous bulk of the crop of hops grown in the South-east of England came partly by water to the international Stourbridge Fair near Cambridge, whence they went by water in all directions. Wheat and other grains would seldom bear the expense of a long journey by land; though a few other rather bulky things, such as salt-fish, would on occasion force their way nearly everywhere[2].

Wool was the only thing of first commercial importance that

[1] Towns now remote from the coast are described as ports by the chroniclers; and such towns as York and Doncaster "exercised the right of sharing in wrecks at sea, as though they stood on the sea-board" (Denton, *l.c.* p. 183).

[2] An interesting contemporary map of Stourbridge Fair is reproduced by Selfridge, *The Romance of Commerce.*

APP. C, 1. went in every direction, taking no refusal: and the head-waters of nearly every stream that flowed to an Eastern port, however small, received from land-carriers wool that was on its way to the Continent. Thus it pioneered the way to highly organized internal transport, just as later on it was to pioneer the way to highly organized industry. Coarse woollen cloth shared with leather the chief services that portable commodities rendered to substantial comfort. Raw wool in the early time, and manufactured wool in a later time, were the principal means of bringing into the country imports of all things, and especially of the much coveted precious metals: and it was regarded, for various reasons, sound and unsound, as the main buttress of national power in early times; while its manufactures were a main embodiment of industrial prowess in the beginnings of England's industrial leadership. The prominent place which wool holds in English history is not a mere episode, interesting to the chronicler. It is the dominant outward manifestation of that deep-set firm resolve to concentrate energy on things which make for solid and enduring results, which is the chief foundation of the place that England has won for herself in the world.

It is perhaps a relatively small matter that weavers shared with bakers the position as leaders in the formation of craft-gilds. Bread and clothing were chief representatives of the domestic commodities. Bread could not stray beyond its local market: but division of labour in the woollen trade went early in union with production for general markets, and thus worked towards the development of a class of dealers as distinguished from the actual makers[1].

Towards the end of the twelfth century "two and a half stones of wool," says a writer in 1805, when the woollen manufacturers were still predominant over all others, "would purchase an ox, whereas a labourer will now earn the value of a stone of wool in a week. At that time it would require sixty days, so that poor sheep walks were as valuable as the best land[2]." During the following century England had become fairly prosperous, in spite of civil troubles; but her cloth seldom tempted

[1] Ashley, *Economic History*, I. p. 192.

[2] Whitaker, *History of Craven*, quoted by James, *History of the worsted manufacture in England*, 1857, p. 47.

a foreign buyer, and she exported raw produce only. Early in the fourteenth the strong hand of Edward III set on foot such large schools of skilled foreign artisans, that she began to be able to sell coarse stuffs abroad, though still dependent on importation for all fine stuffs. This was the turning point: but several more centuries passed before the best handling of her own wool was in her own workshops.

The foreign artisans thus imported, as well as those who in later times sought England as a refuge from persecution, were drawn from many parts of Europe; and each group tended to set up that particular sort of woollen or worsted fabric for which its own home was noted. There soon appeared an astonishing variety of manufacturing processes, each of which belonged to one or two localities: and thus the great fairs were—like modern Exhibitions—schools in which people learned that the habits and resources of their own villages, and even their own counties, represented but a small part of what went on in the world.

2. *The desuetude of mediaeval institutions and habits of life and action; and the growth of a labouring population, detached from specific obligations and rights, prepared the way for conditions of which the present dominant relations between employer and employed are the result.*

During the thirteenth century and the first half of the fourteenth, a certain impatience of the customary conditions of tenure and service had been spreading among the people[1]. It would have prevailed ere long without any external aid; but in fact it received a mighty impetus from the destruction of a third part of the population by the Black Death in 1348—9. Such an event would have caused a great dislocation of social and economic relations at any time: but, coming when it did, its force was increased greatly in fact, and even more in appearance. For, just as the rise of prices about 1870 set the agricultural labourers on improving their position by migrating to the

[1] The great variety, complexity, ambiguity and changefulness of these conditions, and the narrow limitations of present knowledge with regard to them, have been set out by Maitland and Professor Vinogradoff; see *e.g.* the summaries in *Domesday Book*, pp. 60—61; and *Villainage in England*, pp. 220 and 312.

APP. C, 2. towns; so the feeling of power which the villeins derived from the new scarcity of labour set them to surrender their holdings and purchase licences to live within the walls of the city[1].

The immediate effect of the Black Death was of course to create a scarcity of labour relatively to land, and of both labour and produce relatively to the stock of money: that is to raise the price of produce, and therefore the money wages needed to yield the accustomed food etc. to labour, at the same time that it raised the amount of produce which it was worth the while of the superior holders of land to give for labour. But they could not realize the situation, or perhaps they refused to realize it: they endeavoured violently to force back labour to a position worse than that which it had held before the Black Death; and their shortsighted selfish cruelty accelerated that break up of the structure of society, which they were anxious to sustain. It was ordered that everyone, who could not show a satisfactory occupation in the country, and had not already found footing in an urban industry, should be compelled to work at the money wages which were "accustomed to be taken" in the neighbourhood in which he used to serve two years before the Black Death--a rule that could not be enforced strictly, but yet was a potent aid to oppression: and that in turn strengthened the spirit of revolt.

If a labourer migrated in search of other employment he was liable to be arrested, to be put in the stocks, and ultimately to be branded with a hot iron: and the enforcement of this rule

[1] R. E. Prothero, *English Farming*, ch. II. "The break up of the Manor"; and ch. III. "Farming for profit," sets out the whole position very clearly.

The disarrangement of social relations caused by the Black Death was so violent as to arrest general attention; just as when a great river in India or China changes its course, the destruction of all land marks, over which its torrents have swept on the way to their final bed, completely destroys for a time all traditional customs. New customary rights grow up in a few short generations, and in a few more they are thought to have descended from time immemorial: the great deluge remains as an epoch in the history of the learned, while the incessant minor calamities, which have made plasticity and mobility the only enduring features of custom, are but little considered. "Just before the outbreak of the Black Death, the wages of agricultural labour were exceptionally high:...the rise was due to earlier pestilence": and in the following century "twenty outbreaks of plague have been recorded" (Denton, pp. 218 and 105). In fact the Black Death "fell in the middle of a period of social convulsion, and only gave a more radical character to its later half" (Steffen, *Geschichte der englischen Lohnarbeiter*, p. 310).

was entirely in the hands of those in whose interests it was ordained. Such discipline tended to drive the rural labourers, now défiant with a nascent consciousness of power, away from agriculture. Authority, urged on by the landowners, decreed in vain that every boy and girl who had served up to the age of twelve at the plough or cart should abide ever at the same labour: and later on it added that no country man other than a freeholder of 20*s.* might apprentice his son to an industry. The latter rule was more easily enforced than the former; and, in consequence, the woollen and other industries sought rural districts where formal apprenticeships could be avoided. A little later the towns felt symptoms of decay, for which their own narrow regulations had prepared the way: and they had to petition for leave to draw apprentices from outside[1].

The reconstruction of social and economic order moved forward without any reversal, though not without some checks. The ebullitions of 1381 and 1450 (the Peasants' Revolt and Jack Cade's rebellion) indicated much, but effected little. Meanwhile however a steadily expanding freedom of thought was reinforcing freedom of action: the Lollards protested against the manner in which the monasteries discharged their stewardships for the poor; and their criticisms cut deep into the foundations of all authority that seemed in conflict with reason.

[1] This was nearly the last phase of the many changes which the Craft Gilds had undergone since they had superseded the earlier Merchant Gilds. It seems doubtful whether there ever was a time at which all those who assisted in the work of a craft had a reasonable prospect of attaining full membership; and it is known that great distinctions of wealth gradually showed themselves within a gild, and between gilds; and that members of "yeomen gilds," set up by journeymen, were of lower status than those of full craft gilds. The decay of many towns in the fifteenth and sixteenth centuries is attributable to the selfishness of the gilds, their inability to adapt themselves to changing conditions, and their general mismanagement. See Unwin, *Industrial organization in the sixteenth and seventeenth centuries*, Introduction and chs. I, II; Ashley, *l.c.* ch. II; Cunningham, *l.c.* pp. 236—353, 441—447; and 145—525; and Webb, *History of Trade Unionism*, ch. I, especially pp. 35—38: also the chapter on "the control of industry" in Salzmann's *English Industries of the Middle Ages.* There is some interest in a comparison of this history with that, which Dr Clapham shows (*Economics Journal*, June, 1910) to be the true explanation of the decay of the Norfolk worsted industry from about 1830. He proves that the lack of water power and that of cheap coal were by no means the only factors. A third commensurate with them was the violence and corruption which marked the resistance of the old highly-concentrated forces both of employers and employed to the technical changes demanded by the new era.

APP. C. 2. The extravagance, made fashionable by Edward IV, hastened the sale of landed properties to men, who regarded land as a source of revenue to the neglect of its amenities. The strong hand and parsimonious habits of Henry VII made for quiet steady work: but his frugality was rendered odious by the methods which his ministers adopted for filling his coffers. And the dashing extravagance of Henry VIII, being backed by an unprecedented accumulation of treasure, set going a display of wealth, which inevitably made for poverty; even though industry and trade were flourishing, and knowledge was being increased by leaps and bounds through the Revival of Learning.

Thus "rogues and vagabonds" did not wait for the Reformation and the dissolution of the monasteries, but plagued Henry VIII while he was still a faithful follower of the old religion. In Elizabeth's reign, the most skilful, thrifty and energetic artisans from many parts of the Continent crowded into England. Some of them brought a good deal of capital, or rather command over capital in the form of various documents which the age was getting to use freely. But even more important additions to the real wealth of the country were artisans, who could teach something that Englishmen did not know, and had good cause for wishing to know: one of these might easily be of more commercial value to the country than a draft on a foreign banker for money equivalent to several hundred pounds. And yet so grievous were the "growing pains" of the social body in transition, in spite of the vehement remedies prescribed by the unskilled political practitioners of the age, that vagabondage was still rampant; and all wages continued to fall, if we can trust the doubtful indications of statistical records[1].

[1] Steffen, *Geschichte der englischen Lohnarbeiter*, has analysed the history of wages in England, making careful use of the data compiled by Rogers and others; and his chief results, so far as relevant to our present purpose, may be summarized thus:—He takes as representatives the amounts of wheat that a carpenter's and an agricultural labourer's day's wages would severally buy; and he further shows that no great difference in the results (so far as the period under view is concerned) would have been made if the standard ration had been taken to consist of wheat and meat in proportions by weight of about five to one. Wages thus reckoned appear to have been rising considerably just before the Black Death: they made a great jump upwards in the next half century, in spite of a rapid increase in the population: they continued their

APP. C, 3.

3. *Further preparation for modern relations between capital and the various orders of the industrial population. The constructive work of early trading monopolies.*

The total quantity of movable wealth required to sustain the new methods of industry was not very great: it attracted

upward movement during the fifteenth century, though at a slower rate, the growth of population being relatively slow; they fell generally during the sixteenth century, rising indeed a little during the early years of Elizabeth's reign, but falling rapidly towards its end; the increase of population meanwhile becoming a little more rapid. They seem to have reached their lowest point early in the seventeenth century (in the reign of James I); and thence to have risen slightly in the case of agricultural labour, but fast in the case of carpenter's labour, till the middle of the eighteenth century; beyond which we need not go at present.

But in all this there is a large element of conjecture. No near approach to accurate estimates in regard to the purchasing power of wages even in our own time is attainable: and of the numerous questions, which arise in regard to early entries relating to wages, only a very few can be answered even approximately. For instance the representative wages quoted above are necessarily those of men who work by the day; because the allowance in kind to those permanently employed varied much, and cannot be traced. The high wages during the fifteenth century, shown in Rogers' tables, have contributed to the erroneous notion that it was the golden age of English labour. But Denton (*l.c.* p. 214) seems to have established—though the matter is not wholly free from controversy—that the day labourers could not look for employment for more than three days on the average. They may indeed in some cases have occupied land on which they could use their free time; but the evidence on this matter, as well as in regard to the benefits which they could get from common land, is so vague as to be almost without statistical value. Modern experience of large common land in some parts of the Continent suggests that its chief benefit accrues practically to those who are well to do, and can supply some hay (or other fodder) to eke out the scanty winter growth.

Again the price of English wheat is governed now by that of imported wheat: and therefore it is generally low after a wet summer, in spite of modern facilities for curing damaged grain; but much of that wheat for which the labourer had then to pay the highest price after incessant rains, was such as would not be marketed at all to-day. We do not know how far this evil extended; nor do we know how much allowance must be made for the fact that the coins in common use were habitually clipped and sweated: the coin was counted out to the labourer; but it was generally weighed to the wholesale seller of grain. Again the silver, even in new coins, was always being lessened to the detriment of the working-man: it had been about halved in the four and a half centuries which followed the Norman Conquest; and Henry VIII and his children took quickly a third of what remained.

If the comparison between present and earlier times is carried further, account must be taken of the prices of meat and other things which were cheap then, but are relatively dear now: and allowance must be made for manufactured and oriental products and for a multitude of services and other things which were very dear or even inaccessible in early times.

APP. C, 3. attention chiefly because England had been so singularly ill provided with it during the Middle Ages. For then nearly every product that was adapted for the larger commerce came directly from the land, and belonged to men who had no inclination to use their resources for any other purpose than the promotion of their own pleasure, power and prestige. They were, however, perforce responsible for England's first capitalistic industry, that of mining; and, shortly after the monasteries had ceased to pioneer the intensive capitalistic cultivation of land, the landed gentry began to take up their task. The shipping industry was far more greedy of free capital than any other till quite recent times it absorbed a good part of the little that was to be had in the fourteenth and fifteenth centuries. Ere long the great merchants became the chief financiers of England, in an even more marked manner than they had of other countries; partly perhaps because Edward I had expelled the Jews, just when England's commerce was beginning to lead its own life.

When an able financier, whether Jew or Gentile, had once found a footing, his resources were likely to grow by leaps and bounds, so long as he and his heirs maintained their ability and their liking for financial pursuits; unless indeed their careers were cut short by violence, or powerful debtors repudiated some large debts. For the habitual rates of interest corresponded to the impatience and lack of arithmetical faculty of rich men and monarchs, who were not accustomed to be thwarted, and had no turn for accounts[1].

[1] It has been suggested that the sudden growth of great fortunes in early times is hard to be explained in view of the small amount of capital employed in industry and trade, except on the supposition that the ordinary rate of profits in business was extravagantly high. But perhaps insufficient account has been taken of the frugality of early merchants and financiers until they had become wealthy; and again of the marvels of rapid accumulation at a high rate of net profits. Suppose that merchants, father and son, conducted a business with such unbroken frugality, ability and good fortune as to net ten per cent. of annual profits, in excess of all their personal and domestic expenses, on the average in each of sixty years: their capital would then have been increased three hundred fold. And interest on loans has even greater marvels; because the hasty and sanguine borrower often accepts a loan for a short period, say three months, at say five per cent. This would accumulate at compound interest to three times its original value in six years if no payment were made meanwhile; and would be multiplied eighty fold in twenty-four years: at five per cent.

The situation was a little changed by great mortality among the nobility and higher gentry in the final struggles of the Roses. The Tudors and the Stuarts filled the vacancies in a great measure from the ranks of rich traders: thus we read that trade is not "practised by the nobility of the Kingdom as it is in other states from the father to the son throughout their generations...the son being left rich scorneth the profession of his father, conceiving more honour to be a gentleman[1]." And again those who draw income from land are apt to "consider trade as no otherwise necessary in a nation than to support younger brothers, and are ready to thrust all public taxes upon trade that they may ease the land[2]." In all this the cultivation of the land gained a little; but industries and the common people lost much. There was however some compensation in the tardy growth of powerful companies for commercial and industrial enterprise: for these enabled rich men, who did not desire to take an active part in business, to supply it with some of their capital and draw good returns from it[3].

The most prominent English trading company in the Middle Ages was not a Joint Stock Company but a *Regulated* Company: that of the Merchant Adventurers. It was in their support that Bacon wrote to James I: "Trading in companies is most agreeable to the English nature, which wanteth that same

a month, a rate at which some people borrow now, a debt of £1 would become £100 if allowed to accumulate for eight years. Few people reflect on such arithmetical results; but the professional lender has always known them.

[1] Mun, *Treasure of Traffícke* published in 1664 (but written a good deal earlier), p. 5 of McCulloch's edition.

[2] *Britannia Languens*, 1680, p. 3 of McCulloch's edition. The observations on "the new nobility" in Sombart's *Luxus und Kapitalismus*, pp. 10—24, contain much similar matter in regard to England and France.

[3] Professor W. R. Scott has written the history of *Joint Stock Companies to 1720* with notable thoroughness. It may be observed that a few Joint Stock companies connected with the water supply, the draining of land, and fishing appeared rather early; and a few manufacturing companies in Scotland were founded between 1660 and 1690. But 1690 may be taken as the beginning of the modern Joint Stock era for most purposes. Rogers' study of *The first nine years of the Bank of England* has made clear the peculiar conditions of credit at the end of the seventeenth century: and the diagram, in which Prof. Scott (*l.c.* vol. III) sets out the daily variations in price from May to September 1720 for the South Sea Company, the East India Company and the Bank of England, makes a vivid presentation of marvellous events.

APP. C, 3. general view of a republic which runneth in the Dutch and serveth them instead of a company[1]."

A Regulated company was an association of merchants, each of whom managed his business in his own fashion, subject to the general regulations of the company and to his payment of a certain contribution to a common purse. From this purse were paid the expenses of defence, of "factories" (*i.e.* fortified trading stations), ambassadors; and such other expenses as belonged to the trade as a whole, rather than to the business of any individual.

The Merchant Adventurers earned the gratitude of the country by the courage and ability with which they handled a great part of her trade with the Continent during several centuries: but, when the larger problems of trade with Asia and America called for bold expenditure, they were hampered by lack of coherence and by that tenuity of common purse, which were inherent in their constitution. They suffered, as all other institutions did, from the drowsiness of old age, from which there was no alert public criticism to awaken them. Regulated companies thus gradually yielded place to those on Joint Stock: they were in fact the product of transitional circumstances.

The general principle of Joint Stock association, especially in maritime enterprise, belongs to the Ancient World; and it has remained without great change to the present time. But the early English Joint Stock Trading Companies, like the Regulated, required and obtained exclusive privileges, in order to recompense them for their great outlays: and they became the chief guardians of the country's trade with other continents; until the time was ripe for Governments so to take over the care for security on land and sea, that even small men and small companies might trade at their ease. Their discharge of this trust was not without reproach. But their worst faults were not developed till the Mercantilist policy, of which they had

[1] Quoted by Craik *à propos* of the small part which trading by individuals played in English commerce even later, as seen *e.g.* in Roberts, *Map of Commerce*, 1638: but in fact even wealthy Holland instituted companies, whose common purse might defray the outlay needed by distant trade for defence and other common ends. Of course strong merchants may have exercised individuality as members of a Joint Stock, and still more as members of a Regulated Company.

been chief ornaments, sank into a corrupt and inept old age; as will be noted later on.

In short, such exclusive trading was in its origin "constructive"; since it enabled the great companies to perform such large work for the nation, as would in turn enable the nation as a whole to achieve yet larger work. The task set them called for courage and prudence, for large power of organization, and administrative skill. It called into activity qualities that are to be found only in great nations; it developed them, and made the nation greater.

It is true that the monopolies caused England's commerce to be divided up into distinct compartments; but the partitions gradually disappeared: and there was left a world trade so broad in its scope, so unified in its central relations, and so large in its volume, when judged by the standards of that age, that it would have made an epoch in history, even if it had not incidentally founded the British Empire.

Meanwhile there were other industries, much smaller in the aggregate than agriculture, and giving much less scope for large individual capitals than maritime trade, which were in some sense capitalistic even at an early stage. The miller, whether he used wind or water power, needed an expensive plant: his position helped him to mercantile transactions of considerable scope; and he did not always rise above the temptation to usurious dealings with producers of grain and consumers of flour. Reference has already been made to the early sinking of capital in the search for minerals. But, except for copper and other valuable ores, mines could not be carried far down; for there existed no adequate appliances for pumping out the water: and therefore, though the English coal industry became important in the sixteenth century, it offered no special attractions to very large capitals. And in the seventeenth century several imported minor industries were set up on more or less capitalistic bases. But the evolution of capitalistic production is of course best seen in the textile industries, especially that of wool: for it was the basis of a great part of the movable wealth of the people[1].

[1] The introductory chapter of Levy's *Monopoly and Competition* gives some details as to alum, salt and glass. The fiduciary element, which exists in all large cooperative and joint stock undertakings, has been always latent in the

APP. C, 4.

4. ***Work done in the household for the use of the household gave way to production, mainly in cottages and small workshops, of goods, the ultimate marketing of which was organized by professional traders.***

In the early Middle Ages, the food, clothing, houses and utensils were made almost exclusively of local materials by local labour. And—partly because English roads remained exceptionally bad till the middle of the eighteenth century,—this old rule held in regard to a large part of the consumption of the rural population, long after specialized industries with high technique had established themselves firmly in places that were in early touch with the greater world. According to the old rule "women spun and wove wool into coarse cloth, and hemp or nettles into linen; men tanned their own leather": in the winter evenings nearly every man took a hand at making rough tools and household utensils, with the aid of the village smith for iron work; while "travelling carpenters, smiths and tinkers visited detached farm-houses and smaller villages at rare intervals[1]."

businesses of monasteries, among which for this purpose the colleges of Oxford and Cambridge may be reckoned.

The various causes which enabled joint stock companies to flourish in particular trades and industries, though generally only for short periods, are set out in Schmoller's *Geschichtliche Entwickelung des Unternehmens*. He shows how the difficulties of getting one set of people to confide their capitals to the permanent control of others, with whom they were not in contact, were evaded rather than overcome. For many companies were only family groups; some, as those of the Publicans, were also held together by common professional interests. Others were in effect short-lived associations for carrying out some task which involved greater capitalistic risks than were convenient, perhaps possible, to the individual: the permanent companies of modern times owe their strength in great part to moral qualities of recent growth.

[1] See R. E. Prothero, *English Farming*, p. 29, for details. Similar conditions of life and work may be observed to-day in Tyrolese villages. Even in summer, in the interval between hay and grain harvests, the advent of a shoemaker will collect all the members of a family who are not on the high "alps" to do the less skilled work of making into shoes for the family the leather, that has come from their own cattle and been cured in the village tan-pit.

In rural districts remnants of household industry were common up to the eighteenth century. Thus in 1727 Laurence, *Duty and Office of a House Steward*, says:—"'Tis supposed that all materials are found, and laid at hand for the workmen, (except glazier's) which is much the best way, for workmen, sometimes are apt to impose, and use bad materials." Quoted by Rogers, *History*, VII. 620.

Unwin, *Industrial organization in the sixteenth and seventeenth centuries,*

In this stage there was a good deal of work for wages; but for a long while most of it was performed as service due by serfs or by semi-free labour; or by free, but inferior, holders of land to their superiors. The greater part of it may be classed as *household industry*, because it was rendered in the *homes* (or other premises) *of the consumers* of the products. It is thus contrasted with *domestic industry* in that broad sense of the term in which it includes all the various arrangements under which things were made, either for sale or under contract, in the *homes of the producers*.

Domestic industry in this broad use of the term, began to get the upper hand of household industries, except in purely rural districts, about the thirteenth century: and its dominance was maintained till the eighteenth. In all its forms it offered scope for a single independent artisan; with or without assistance from his family: but for the greater part it made use of hired labour on a small scale; and therefore should not be contrasted, as it has been by some writers, with the wage system. It includes all handicraft, whether organized in Gilds or not; and it may be regarded as consisting of three broad classes; which, like nearly all other groups of adjacent economic classes, shade into one another by imperceptible degrees.

In the first class are those industries, which worked up local material to meet a steady local demand for goods of customary quality. The producer was thus in personal contact with those who supplied his requirements and those who bought his products: and he had scarcely any occasion for the services of capitalist traders. For his implements were inexpensive: he needed not to hold any great stock of materials or finished goods at any one time: and, though his outlook was narrow, it reached to all the persons and places with whom his business was directly concerned. All his work was within the range of *homely* associations and habits of mind.

The second class of domestic industries made staple products from familiar materials. Some of the materials had generally to be obtained from afar by aid of traders; and the greater part of the products had to be sold by aid of traders; that

pp. 53—4, suggests that the class of masters was largely developed in the latter part of the fourteenth and the earlier part of the fifteenth centuries.

APP. C, 4. is, by men who had larger resources and a wider connection, than belonged to homely producers. But yet the breadth and steadiness of these industries enabled homely producers, congregated in the same neighbourhood, to make almost automatically a market of their own to which traders steadily resorted to supply the materials and other things needed, and purchase the things ready for sale; and each producer carried the risks of his own share of the process of production, in the trust that, so long as the conditions of outside markets were favourable, traders would do his marketing for him, under the influence of mutual competition, on terms advantageous to him. Speaking generally this trust was justified by the event: though the exceptions fill a large and gloomy page in economic history[1].

The third class of domestic industries was that conducted by small master producers, who supplied factories or workshops with their plants, and were independent of external control in all matters of detail; but yet manufactured to the order of capitalist "undertakers," who bore all the risk of marketing, and often even supplied the material to be worked up. This arrangement has already been described (above, I, III, 5) as belonging to the third stage of domestic work.

To sum up the position:—when the material used was costly; and especially when the homely producer would have difficulty in getting the most appropriate sorts, and perhaps be tempted to mix in some inferior sorts; then the merchant, who contracted to buy the product, generally supplied the material, thus carrying his financial aid a good deal further.

[1] The two following pictures make a pair. The first is from a Devonshire account of 1630 (quoted by Cunningham, *l.c.* II. 499):—"The gentleman farmer or husbandman sends his wool to the market, which is bought either by the comber or the spinster, and they, the next week bring it thither again in yarn, which the weaver buys; and the market following brings it thither again in cloth, where it is sold either to the clothier (who sends it to London) or to the merchant who (after it has passed the fuller's mill and sometimes the dyer's vat) transports it." The second is a statement by Gaskell (*Artisans and Machinery*, 1836, p. 13) referring to the time when water power was beginning to be applied to spinning:—"The domestic manufacturers were scattered over the entire surface of the country. Themselves cultivators, and of simple habits and few wants, they seldom left their own homesteads. The yarn which they spun, and which was wanted by the weaver, was received or delivered, as the case might be, by agents who travelled for the wholesale houses: or depôts were established in particular neighbourhoods, to which they could apply at weekly periods."

One step further was taken, when the plant required was beginning to grow expensive; for then it also was supplied by the merchant. The cutlery and several other industries, which spend much labour on small products made of cheap metal, have always been among those in which the homely producer could supply his own material most easily and with the least risk to the merchant who bought his wares: but the needs of the smith for the water driven triphammer and of the grinder for the water driven wheel, started the plan under which a capitalist let out space and power in a large building to individual artisans and other homely producers; "homely" because their resources and outlook were narrow, though they no longer worked in their own homes, and were not literally "domestic" workers[1]. And there were yet two other motives which sometimes induced the capitalist to collect a number of workers into a single large building, supply them with plant and material, and pay them either by wage or on small contracts. One was the advantage of keeping the whole of some valuable materials under his own eye, so as to secure that nothing was pilfered or badly handled: the other motive operated in the case of new industries, especially such as were imported from Italy or elsewhere, and needed the supervision of foreign skilled workers[2].

The transition from each of these phases to the next was seldom made at a bound: it went generally by many little steps; and these steps were not always on the same lines. Throughout all of them the production was, for the greater

[1] This plan is still in work, steam power taking the place of water power: but possibly the cheap supply of electricity in cottages as a source of power may send some of these homely producers back to their own homes; a matter which will appear later on to be of some social importance.

[2] Thus it has been observed that in Tudor times capitalism was especially appropriate to exotic trades:—"The planting of new trades was a capitalist undertaking, organized by moneyed men, who were prepared to wait some years for the full return on their outlay"; especially when, as often happened then, they obtained, gratis or for payment, a monopoly for a considerable time. And a similar tendency showed itself in a rather different form from early in the eighteenth century; "any trade which had been constituted under the control of large employers in its older habitat, was likely to be introduced in the same form; and, as capital was an important factor in the transferring of a trade to a new area, there was a tendency for the industry, as transplanted, to conform to the capitalist type." Cunningham, *l.c.* pp. 78 and 518.

APP. C, 4. part, "domestic," in that broad use of the term, in which it implies merely that the making—as distinguished from the marketing—can be conveniently conducted in the house or out-buildings of a single independent worker or small master.

As has been indicated above (I, III, 5 and 6) the term "domestic industries" has been used by various authorities in narrow technical senses, which are inconsistent with one another: some for instance confining it to cases in which the small producer works up material belonging to traders, while others confine it to cases in which the material is his own: these ambiguities have suggested the use here of the term "homely producer" to include all those whose resources are so small and whose outlook is so narrow, that they cannot obtain good direct access to general markets[1].

[1] Prof. Bücher gives in the *H. W. der Staatswissenschaften*, s.v. *Gewerbe*, a careful analysis of five main groups. The first is what has been called above "household industry" (he calls it "*Hauswerk* or *Hausfleiss*"); the second wage-work; the third handicraft ("*Handwerk* or *Preiswerk*"); and the fourth "financed work" ("*Verlag* or *Hausindustrie*"); the fifth is factory industry. (*Verlag* is rendered by the translator of his *Industrial Evolution* as "commission work": but that term seems too narrow.)

The famous 1806 *Report on the Woollen Manufacture* (quoted by Ashley, *l.c.* II. pp. 252—3) classes the Yorkshire woollen system, in which the small masters bought their own wool and sold the cloth to merchants, as "Domestic." But Prof. Bücher and Held (whose *Zwei Bücher zur Socialen Geschichte Englands*, 1881, exercised a great influence in England) class it as handicraft; and confine the term "domestic" to cases in which the merchant supplies the wool to the manufacturer. That was done in some cases in the West of England; and the 1806 *Report* regards this as akin to the Factory System, in contrast with the "Domestic." Hence it may be concluded that "Domestic" cannot be safely used as a technical term; though it may perhaps be used to include all work done in their own premises by small producers, who do not attempt to market their goods themselves. Dr Cunningham uses it broadly (*l.c.* II. 497), and shows cause against Prof. Schmoller's proposal to exclude gild industry from it.

The word "manufacturer" originally meant a man who makes with his own hands: but in the nineteenth century it meant a factory owner. Ure (*Philosophy of Manufactures*, 1861, p. 1) says that "manufacture is a word which has come to signify the reverse of its intrinsic meaning...the most perfect manufacture is that which dispenses entirely with manual labour." He however ignores all manufactures except the textile. See also Held, *l.c.* p. 549.

APPENDIX D

THE ENGLISH MERCANTILISTS AND ADAM SMITH

1. *Mercantilism differed from policies of earlier times, not so much in general tendency, as in the ability and energy with which it was enforced and in the largeness of its scope*[1].

The purpose of this Appendix is to develop suggestions made in the third chapter of Book I, especially at its end, to the effect that Mercantilist policy contained a few principles applicable to all stages of economic evolution; together with many that were appropriate to the stage in which it had its origin. It is here argued that the conduct of public affairs in England in the middle of the eighteenth century was bad, and that the potential virtues of Governmental intervention in business were overshadowed by its actual vices: but that Adam Smith's doctrine, carefully interpreted, supports its active intervention in many affairs in an age in which it has acquired the power and the will to govern the people wisely; and the people have acquired the power and the will to govern their Government with knowledge, discretion and restraint.

Adam Smith is less open than many other economists to the charge of formulating sharp, short statements as to things which appeared to be fixed and primary elements, but were really variable compounds. And yet he is perhaps more responsible than anyone else for the belief, which long prevailed, that Mercantilism was a definite, unified body of doctrine; and that it worked mischief by inventing diverse shackles which hampered the natural freedom of trade. We now know that it was not a body of definite doctrines which

[1] This Appendix is associated with I, III, 4.

APP. D, 1. arose suddenly, quickly overcame all minds, and after a time was wholly discarded: it was rather a tendency of thought and sentiment which had its roots in the far past; which never, even at the height of its power, completely dominated all minds, and which has not yet completely disappeared.

And that which was characteristic of Mercantile practice, as distinguished from the practice of still earlier times, was almost wholly to its credit. The narrowness and confusion of thought, by which it was marred, were not new: but the consistency, system, and energy with which it was pushed, and the largeness of the affairs with which it was concerned, brought these defects into prominence. So far as it differed from the corresponding practices of earlier times, it was seldom less liberal than they, and often more liberal.

Trade in the precious metals has attracted more attention than it merits: because human nature, and especially primitive human nature, has a deep-seated tendency to idolatry; that is to the cult of symbols in preference to that of the things which they symbolize: and money is the symbol of wealth. But more: the precious metals are the most durable and generally acceptable forms of wealth. A store of them serves as the "fly-wheel" to growing wealth generally. And money promotes the circulation of things towards those who can turn them to best account, and can thus increase wealth.

As Schmoller says:—"The limitation of the exportation of the currency and of the precious metals frequently occurs in the case of the towns as early as the thirteenth century. It was not because money payments or industry or trade suddenly played an altogether new *rôle* in the days of Cromwell and Colbert, that it occurred to people to guide the course of exportation and importation and colonial trade, and to subject them to governmental control. On the contrary, it was because just then, out of the earlier small communities great national communities had grown up, whose power and significance rested on their psychological and social concert, that they began to imitate, not merely what Charles V had done in Spain, but what all towns and territories of earlier times had done, from Tyre and Sidon, from Athens and Carthage onward; to carry over what Pisa and Genoa, Florence and Venice, and the

German Hanse Towns had done in their time to the broad basis of states and nations[1]."

Again, "Mercantilism and bureaucracy (*Cameralistik*) overrated the possibility of ordering and arranging anew everything by the State, by law and by the will of Princes: even morality and justice appeared to the first thinkers from Hobbes to Frederick the Great as products of State regulation. Institutions appeared to them to be everything, the free play of individuals to be but little...It is the business of the rulers to prevent there being too many producers or too few, to resist *Polypoly* and *Monopoly*[2]."

2. ***The discovery of the New World altered the form rather than the substance of trade policy with regard to the precious metals.***

Large war-chests have been held by the great military nations Germany, France and Russia. Thus warlike rulers in old times used to put a stock of silver or gold on the same footing with a stock of bowstaves at one time, and of gunpowder at another: for instance the importation of various luxuries into England was ordered to be accompanied by certain quantities sometimes of bullion, and sometimes of bowstaves[3]. And when the new era of territorial expansion came together with the influx of larger stores of the precious metals, desires which had always been present became active and prominent. For during the Middle Ages the stock of gold and silver in Europe was dwindling, and any nation that could maintain its stock unimpaired was gaining ground relatively to its neighbours: but afterwards, when the West was procuring larger supplies than the East was taking away, any nation which had not rapidly increased its stock would have lost ground relatively to others. There is no fundamental difference between the defensive policy

[1] *Mercantile System*, pp. 10, 60, 61.

[2] Schmoller, *Grundriss der allgemeinen Volkswirthschaftslehre*, pp. 63 and 85. For early regulations of industry in England see Riley's *Memorials of London Life*; and Schanz, *Englische Handelspolitik*, IV. ii, especially pp. 478—480. The old regulations throw some light on the strategical side of the science of modern government, but not on its tactical side.

[3] In 1397 an ounce of gold was substituted for the two marks of silver which the law of 1339 had ordered to be brought back for each sack of wool exported.

APP. D, 2. of trying to keep the national stock of precious metals in the country from diminishing rapidly, before the discovery of the New World, and the offensive policy of trying to augment the stock afterwards. The influx of silver from the New World may have set a score of tongues talking about the trade in the precious metals, where only one had been talking before: but it did not narrow trade policy[1].

The Mercantilists knew that, "although treasure is said to be the sinews of war, yet this is so because it doth provide, unite and move the power of men victuals and munition, when and where the cause doth require. But if these things be wanting in due time, what then shall we do with our money[2]?"

Even Adam Smith admits that countries which have not many fine manufactured or other goods containing great value in small bulk, cannot well supply the sovereign with the means of maintaining an army abroad during a great war: "it is in such countries therefore that he generally endeavours to accumulate a treasure as the only resource against such emergencies." As Sir Dudley North said (1691), Stocks of money are no better

[1] There has been a tendency in England, though not apparently in Germany, to follow Prof. Ochenkowski (*England's wirtschaftliche Entwickelung*, pp. 10—11) in drawing a sharp contrast between the eager quest for the precious metals of the Mercantilists, and the "childlike" and "naive" contentment of their predecessors. In the Middle Ages, he says, "the end directly sought was the complete development of sound human faculties, which should be the basis of the economic well-being of the individual and at the same time the support of social order" (pp. 248—9; compare also pp. 256—261). No doubt much authority can be found for this in the phrases of canonical writers, of royal ordinances, and of gild statutes. But it is to men's conduct, and not to their phrases on set occasions, that we must look for a true knowledge of their habits of thought: this holds as to all phases of life, and to none more than to the mediaeval.

[2] Mun, *Treasure by Foreign Trade*, ch. XVIII. *Britannia Languens*, 1680, maintained that while "anciently the event of war" turned on "personal strength and roughness," wars had come to be "managed by *much Treasure and little Fighting*, and therefore with little hazard to the richer nation": and Defoe a little later said, "'tis the longest purse that conquers now, not the longest sword." The doctrines "money is the sinew of war," and "he who has iron can take gold," have supplemented one another since early times. Macchiavelli in the Italian turmoil of iron and gold (and silver) at the beginning of the sixteenth century, maintained that gold will not always buy good soldiers, but that good soldiers will always conquer gold: but, as his friend Guicciardini says, this is practically false, though true theoretically. In fact it is easier to buy soldiers with money, than to get money by soldiers. See Ehrenberg, *Zeitalter der Fugger*, I. p. 7.

than stocks of logs, only that "Money is much better for transportation[1]."

The Mercantile policy of maintaining a favourable balance of trade in the precious metals was from the first more liberal than that "balance of bargain" system which some meddlesome rulers had previously tried to enforce; for that ordained that each single venture of each single merchant should bring back at least as much gold and silver as he took out[2]. The later and specially English developments of Mercantilism rose above the notion that the trade with any one foreign country was to be condemned on the ground that that trade showed on the balance an export of the precious metals: bullion sent to India, as Mun argues, brought back to England goods which could be sold on the Continent at such high prices, that even a small part of them could bring back more bullion than was sent out for the whole of them.

When a Mercantilist policy prohibited, or taxed, or otherwise narrowed the purchasing of certain classes of things from foreigners, it might have claimed to resemble the shutter which is drawn partly across a fire, with the effect of lessening for the time its total supply of air; but which by concentrating the remainder on some burning coals hurries their dull red heat into a white glow, which spreads through the furnace and ultimately evokes a greater heat and a larger feed of air than if there had been no restriction. Mercantile writers often seem to go close to this modern doctrine, but yet they miss it[3].

[1] *Wealth of Nations*, IV, 1, and p. 17 of McCulloch's edition of North's Essay. Hume, whose opinions on money were very enlightened, argued to the same effect. And the American colonists justified their adoption of paper and other fancy currencies in the eighteenth century, on the ground that having but few portable commodities that were in much demand abroad, and being compelled to buy even their ruder manufactures from England, they were in constant danger of being denuded of their gold and silver coin.

[2] Described with fine humour by Richard Jones, whose great services to English economics have been insufficiently recognized.

[3] Thus Hales' *Discourse of the Commonwealth*, 1549, argues that foreign paper should be taxed up to a price which would enable it to be made in England; because "they do not best provide for his grace's profit that procure only a present commodity, but rather that commodity that may long endure without the grief of his subjects." But his explanation is disappointing. He does not state or imply that the country has latent natural advantages for the industry, which would enable it to thrive unaided if once it could outgrow its infant difficulties; for indeed the industry had already had a trial. His reason is that

APP. D, 2.

Mun's intelligence was no doubt sharpened by his zeal for the interests of the East India trade. And later on the intelligence of Tory writers was sharpened in the same way. For France sold much to us, and bought little from us; and France supported the Stuarts and opposed the Dutch. So at the end of the seventeenth and beginning of the eighteenth centuries the Tories were inclined to make little of our adverse balance with any particular country; while the Whigs wrote with nearly equal ability, but less insight, on the other side. They ignored Mun's doctrine; and argued:—"We purchase great part of our linen from Hamburg, Germany, and Holland, for which we pay them in manufactures: the rest we make ourselves; and if the value of £600,000 in linen should be imported from France, must not so many of our people be deprived of their employment[1]?" They took no account of the fact that French goods could be paid for indirectly by means of England's exports to other countries.

Political bias then, as always, had a great power of enabling people to see just those parts of economic truth which fitted in with their policy, and to remain honestly blind to those which did not. But yet the economic wrestling of the politicians of the eighteenth century did good service. They overhauled trade statistics, searched out their inaccuracies and misleading suggestions; and, as the eighteenth century passed on, their successors continued the work and laid the foundation on which inductive studies of the course of international trade have been built up[2].

"it were better for us to pay more to our own people for those wares, than less to strangers: for how little gain so-ever goes over, it is to us clear. But how much so-ever the gains be that go from one of us to another, it is all saved within the Realm" (ff. 38, 38 *b*). Thus gold and silver are regarded as the ultimate gains of work.

[1] *The British Merchant* (vol. I. p. 304 of second edition):—a celebrated collection of papers edited by Charles King, and collected and published in 1721. The general Maxims of Trade, with which the collection opens, are good instances of a sophistical use of half truths, which is not infrequent even now. For instance: "The exportation of manufactures is in the highest degree beneficial to a nation." And "the importation of such goods as hinder the consumption of our own...necessarily tends to the ruin of multitudes of people."

[2] A brilliant and entertaining sketch of "Tory Free Trade 1673—1713" is given in Ashley's *Surveys*. Compare also Cunningham's *Growth of English Industry and Commerce*, vol. II. § 220. Davenant gives the impression of having

3. *The decline of the monopolist trading companies. The misuse of industrial monopolies.*

APP. D, 3.

The expenses of trade with distant Continents were too heavy for the small common purses of Regulated Trading Companies: and trade with England's neighbours gradually ceased to need any special organization for defence. Therefore in the seventeenth and eighteenth centuries, the chief controversies in regard to monopolies related to those of the great Joint Stock Trading Companies. Fortrey (1673) says of them: "The whole commodity being in their hands, they will make the most that can be made of it, none having the like commodities to undersell them. And the like advantage they have again in what they buy; whereby in truth our own commodities are sold the dearer to strangers, and foreign commodities bought much the cheaper: when both would happen contrary in a free trade, where each will undersell the other to vent most, and also purchase at any rates to prevent the risk." They had a strong organization, unity of purpose, a rich purse and a long life; and they could afford to invest much capital and effort in building up a political and commercial fabric, which would give good return at a distant date. Fortrey says that it is urged that such companies "keeping the trade to themselves only, will have what commodities are to be vented abroad at their own price, whereby the workmen are many times discouraged and sometimes undone. And on the contrary what commodities are brought home in exchange they sell at what unreasonable rates they please, the whole commodity remaining in their hands; whereby the people in general are very much damnified, and the companies only enriched." And yet though it is "something difficult to determine," he concludes that "the prejudice that may happen by them to the workmen or home chapmen...is fully recompensed by the clear profit they return to the public of which they are members as well as others":—a characteristically hazardous conclusion from arguments which appear to be fair representatives of his time[1].

half perceived certain truths at one time; and, at another, of having fallen back into old errors: as indeed Adam Smith himself did.

[1] *England's Interest and Improvement*, pp. 34—5 of McCulloch's edition. It is notable that the Merchant Adventurers though only a Regulated Company were accused of "stinting" the trade in cloth; and denied that they would or

APP. D, 3. The companies adopted elaborate checks and counter checks, the expense and the delay of which caused their trade to be not very profitable to themselves, even when they were stinting at both ends: that is when they were both offering to the home producer a poor vent for his goods, and making foreign goods artificially scarce to the nation. They were compelled to go much by rule, and rules framed at a distance were often inappropriate to a sudden emergency or changed conditions: their instructions were prevented from doing frequent harm only by the continually recurring clause that the agents must after all use their own discretion. In spite of their being often well supplied with capital, they had not those resources derived from division of labour, and that aid of subsidiary industries which a free commerce finds in a large centre of trade.

Again there were complaints that the agents looked after their private interests; and as years went on, the Dutch and English East India Companies suffered much from the private trading of their own agents. At first the English Company had often made very high profits: its voyages in 1607 yielded profits of 234 per cent. But towards the end of its career, when suffering much from the vigorous competition of free traders and the faults of its own servants, it only gained £850,000 yearly from its trade in tea; though it charged the English people £1,500,000 more for the tea than they would have paid for it in Hamburg or New York if allowed to purchase it there[1].

could do so. But their Secretary Wheeler in 1601, can give no better evidence of this than the special pleading that "any matter of setting price was never once mentioned in any Court of Assembly of the said Company....Every one studies to keep his feat (*sic*) and trade as secret to himself as he can, for fear of his fellow, lest being copied it might be taken from him." Macpherson, *Annals*, II. pp. 499—502.

[1] *The first letter book of the East India Company*, 1600—1619, edited by Sir George Birdwood, is full of prohibitions against private trading by its factors, which were often defied. Complaint is made (p. 317) that "The private trade of our factors has been carefully carried for their own lucre with the great neglect of ours, converting all the rich and precious things to their own use, and nothing for the Company but pepper and gross commodities."

The Company took no mean view of the probable profits of the trade It bargained in 1610 to fit out and finance a ship for the use of two Dutch merchants with the proviso, that if the net profits per cent. are under a hundred, they shall receive no "factorage": but they are to have six per cent. if the net profit is two hundred per cent.: rising gradually till "if four hundred be made net profit upon the hundred, as £60,000 for £12,000, then they are to have 10 per cent." (*ib.* pp. 365—6).

The histories of some privileged companies might be written—"Charter, prosperous trade, keen competition, encroachments, decline, debt, difficulties, disappearance[1]." But there were exceptions. Thus the Hudson's Bay Company was governed by a succession of able men, few in number, resolute and moderate, who looked far ahead, undertook expenses that were beyond the reach of "the particular," and fell not very far short of the ideal which had been pictured by their advocates. And there long remained much to be said for a strong company that could hold its own in war and diplomacy with the highly developed States of Asia: and there was much force in the plea, that while the trade to the West Indies could take care of itself, the trade to the "East Indies" (that is to the Pacific generally) was not ready to stand alone even at the beginning of the nineteenth century[2].

Adam Smith held that the resources at the command of the public for controlling the directors of Joint Stock companies, *at the time at which he wrote* (1775), gave no good reason for thinking that the directors would exert themselves sufficiently to succeed (without an exclusive privilege) in businesses, other than those "of which all the operations could be reduced to such a uniformity of method as admits of little or no variation." He had an advantage over the present generation in his personal

[1] Cawston and Keane, *The early chartered companies*, p. 85.

[2] Macpherson's *History of European Commerce*, 1812 (pp. 315—410), contains a detailed and forcible answer to Adam Smith's attacks on the East India Company. The Company lost its monopoly of trade to India in 1813: but it retained that to China till 1833; when it ceased to trade altogether. It discharged purely political functions till 1858; and then it ceased to exist, after the full strength of the nation had been needed to grapple with the difficulties that had grown up under its management—vigorous and upright as that had unquestionably been.

The Dutch East India Company was much better managed than the Dutch West India Company. The Dutch Greenland trade increased fifteen fold on being released from the dominion of an exclusive company, to the great delight of De la Court, the real author of the book commonly known as De Witt's *Political Maxims*.

Powerful attacks on monopolies are made in (Decker's?) *The Causes of the decline of foreign trade*, 1744, and in Tucker's *Tract on trade*, 1750. Much is said in Lecky's *History of England in the Eighteenth Century*, of the share which the East India Company had in the direct corruption of politics; and of the injurious influence exerted on the tone of society by the crude extravagance of East and West Indian Nabobs.

APP. D, 3. knowledge of the class of men who were directors in his time, and the way in which they did their work. He was therefore on strong ground when he suggested that a director, whose holding in the stock of a company was but a small part of the whole, might be inclined to pretermit a task that would increase his work, and add perhaps £1000 to the income of the company; but that he might probably have risen to the occasion, if his holding had been so large a part of the whole that a very considerable share of the £1000 would have accrued to himself. And it is to be remembered that the tone of morality, to say nothing of public spirit, was very low in England at the time; perhaps lower than even in the time of Charles II[1].

It has long been known that some of the evidence on which Adam Smith relied against the companies was biassed. Professor Scott has developed this objection; and shown instructively that the companies sought for the greater part undertakings, which at the time were new in kind, and needed resource. This was of course partly because undertakings, which required larger capitals than were easily to be got under a single hand, had to wait for the joint stock movement to become strong before they could be begun. And further Joint Stock companies, though often fraudulent from the beginning, are seldom started by men lacking in initiative. The intrusion of routine into businesses, for which routine is inappropriate, comes at a late stage: and it is doubtful whether there was in Adam

[1] This seems to be Adam Smith's meaning. But Prof. Scott, *l.c.* I. 452, holds that he makes the mistake of "regarding the aggregate holding of the management in relation to the total capital of the company as the measure of efficiency." (This point has been noted above, p. 313 fn.) Prof. Scott has made important contributions to our knowledge by accounts of many Joint Stock companies which succeeded, although engaged in new and hazardous enterprises. In ancient as well as recent times it has been generally recognized that a chief function of joint stock association was to divide risks, of which few or no individuals have been able and willing to bear the whole. But many of the more frail joint stock undertakings of that time were not registered: and, if they failed, their memory seldom survived their decease very long. The strong companies, who survived, are at the service of the historian of our own time; while the others are not: and it seems probable that the misadventures of companies which were known to Adam Smith, and other responsible writers in the eighteenth century, justified his conclusions in great measure. The scope of his work prevented him from making explicit use of more than a very small fraction of the facts by which his opinions had been fashioned.

Smith's time a single very old company in existence which had escaped such an intrusion.

There is moreover great force in Prof. Scott's argument that the companies gained by associating men of different aptitudes in a common enterprise, and combining "the specific and detailed knowledge of the trader with the broad outlook of the man of affairs." And of course they enabled much capital, that would otherwise have lain idle, to bring forth good fruit; though in this matter there is a danger, which cannot be examined here, of a confusion between leaving money idle and leaving capital idle. The two things are closely akin from the point of view of the individual, but not from that of the whole community.

The whole position seems to be well put in the *Considerations on the East India Trade,* published in 1701, when the South Sea Bubble was not yet in sight. It says, that "in the time of Sir Thomas Gresham, wonderful things are storeyed...For every hundred pounds at the end of the year, besides principal returned again, two or three hundred pounds are said to have been divided between the customs of the King and the merchants gain." The writer adds that in his time the stock in trade (largely in the hands of companies) was a hundred fold as great as then; and, though the rate of profits was but a tenth as great, the aggregate contribution to wealth was ten times as great as then.

Though the monopolies granted to the great trading companies were originally part of a constructive, rather than a restrictive policy; yet no similar defence can be maintained on behalf of the great majority of industrial monopolies. A very few of them were granted on the plan of modern patents, to encourage and reward those who had devoted trouble and expense to victory over some difficulty in manufacture; and they were constructive in tendency. But such invention was of the rarest occurrence in England during the time when monopolies were granted most freely: in fact most of them were given to favourites, or sold for sums not comparable in value to the injury inflicted on the people[1].

[1] As Hume shows (*History of England,* ch. XLIV and Appendix to it)

APP. D, 3. Restrictive regulations, which have an indirect constructive result in promoting national power and dignity, are rightly judged with exceptional favour. But this fine feeling is not without its perils; for it is apt to be turned to account by persons who stand to gain by the restrictions. Such persons are most dangerous when they are honestly convinced, as they often are, that they are striving for the public good as well as their own. Among the monopolies which did most to maintain sectional jealousies and to delay the growth of national unity were those granted to particular towns to enable them to put down inconvenient rivals[1].

The Navigation Laws, though of most doubtful wisdom when regarded from the point of view of peace, had strong claims in view of the need for maritime defence. The exclusive or preferential privileges, which they gave to all English ships, could be defended on similar grounds to those that were granted to a particular company on condition that it provided for its own protection. The most famous of them were directed by England against the Dutch in the middle of the seventeenth century.

As is well known, Adam Smith held that they had contributed to national defence at no very great cost; and had been therefore wise, though "not favourable to commerce, or to that opulence which can arise from it." There is no sufficient evidence that the increase of England's naval power, which came about the same time, was largely due to them. But it

Elizabeth was one of the most wantonly mischievous traders in Monopolies. It is characteristic of her that when Lee brought to her notice an epoch-making invention for knitting stockings by a machine—almost the only invention of any considerable genius and practical force which is known to have been made by an Englishman before the eighteenth century—she said, "I have too much regard for my poor people who obtain their bread by knitting." So he took his invention to France. The practical problem to be solved was not easy: but Elizabeth's solution was clearly a wrong one. See also Levy, *Economic Liberalism*, ch. III. It is shown by W. H. Price, *English Patents of Monopoly*, that, though the few patents which were given to real inventions, were generally granted with honest purpose, they did not yield the same good results as such patents do now.

[1] As *e.g.* to Bridport for rope making, to Worcestershire towns for woollen cloths, to York for coverlets, etc. In some cases plausible reasons were suggested: and indeed the Tudors were masters of the fine art of writing preambles.

is to be remembered that merchant ships were still convertible into ships of war, and merchant crews into fighting crews, at a moment's notice; and that Englishmen endorsed Bacon's dictum:—"The dominion of the sea is an epitome of monarchy...The treasures of both Indies seem but an accessory to the dominion of the seas[1]."

4. *England's colonial policy in the eighteenth century.* Though the opening up of the mines of the New World did not alter the keynote of trade policy as regards the precious metals, it undoubtedly made that policy more prominent. Many bold spirits crossed the ocean for the love of adventure: but there was no touch of that desire for more elbow room, and for the escape of a growing population from the pressure of the law of Diminishing Return, which prompted the cities of ancient Greece to send out colonies, and which has grown up recently in Western Europe.

On the contrary, the most ardent advocates of colonial expansion across the oceans were foremost in their eulogies of the force that Holland and the City States had derived from their compactness, and made light of those which Spain and France derived from their large lands. They set themselves to prove that the colonies either, as in the case of Virginia and Barbados, attracted "loose vagrant people,...such as could never have lived at home to do service to their country"; or as in the case of New England were mainly a refuge for "the sort of people called Puritans," of whom many, "wearied with church censures and persecutions," sought a refuge in Germany and

[1] *Advancement of Learning* (1605), VIII. Evelyn takes as the motto of *Navigations and Commerce*, 1674, a doctrine, supposed by Cicero to have been learnt by Pompey from Themistocles: *Qui mare teneat, eum necesse est rerum potiri.*

Full accounts of early English Navigation Laws are given by Macpherson, and Craik. See also Schanz, *Englische Handelspolitik*, II. ii; and an article on "Schiffart" by Lexis in Conrad's *Handwörterbuch.*

During a part of the eighteenth century the chief benefit of the laws went to New England shipbuilders; and helped to build up a naval power which was for a time stronger in proportion to its size than any other. Child's partial anticipation of List's notion, that navigation laws, which would be useless to the Dutch, were necessary for England, is maintained boldly in spite of some awkward facts (*Discourse on Trade*, 1688, ch. IV). A vehement attack on them is made in Section IV of *Britannia Languens*, 1680.

APP. D, 4. Holland; and, "had there not been a New England found for some of them, Germany and Holland had probably received the rest: but Old England, to be sure, had lost them all[1]."

The Mercantilists were not the first to claim the right of Sole, or Exclusive Markets for the mother country in the trade of her colonies. For the right is an old one, inherited by the mediaeval from the ancient world: the Romans, for instance, could not as a rule purchase products of the colonies of Carthage, except through Carthage. But while Englishmen at home were becoming ever more impatient of the shackles imposed on their trade by the selfishness and inertness of privileged companies, the monopoly of the colonial trade by the mother country was exciting at least as much discontent among Englishmen beyond the seas. They were beginning to put forward the claim either to remain as part of the nation in all senses and share in its rule, or to be allowed full economic independence.

The rule of the Sole Market was not applied quite rigidly. Certain exceptions were made as to the markets in which the colonists might buy and sell; but on the other hand numerous rules were made, prohibiting them from making things or carrying things for themselves, which the mother country preferred to make for them or to carry in her own ships. The story of these various devices is not without interest. For almost every one of them some plausible excuse could be made; and in partial recompense for almost every hardship inflicted on the colony, there was some sort of set-off in the shape of a special privilege granted to the colony in its trade with the mother country. Of course the threads of naval and commercial policy were intertwined; and one reason for favouring trade with a country's own colonies was that the sailors engaged in it were likely to retain a strong spirit of patriotism, and could be enlisted in the Navy at need.

[1] Child, *Discourse of Trade,* chapter x. pp. 137—8 of 1751 edition. Adam Smith did not fall into the error, which became prominent in the nineteenth century, of supposing that mere increase of territory must needs be an economic gain. But his mistake in supposing that the thirst for gold and silver was the almost exclusive motive for exploring the New World was specially inexcusable as regards England; as is shown by Roscher (*Geschichte der Englischen Volkswirtschaftslehre,* ch. II) on the authority of Hakluyt's *Collection of Voyages*:—a collection so full of marvellous geographical discoveries that this planet cannot afford material for another like it.

England was on the whole more generous to her colonies than was any other country. They did indeed complain justly that "negro slaves were the only considerable object of foreign commerce, which England does not compel to be first landed on her shores" before it may be imported into the colonies: and that rigorous rules were made with the avowed purpose of crushing in the bud colonial industries which, had they once got a fair start, might have entered into effective rivalry with the English. But it was open to England to threaten that if the colonists were unreasonable "the Government would be forced, contrary to their practice, to do what other nations do of choice; viz. place standing forces among them to keep them in order and oblige them to raise money to pay them[1]."

It is true that England could boast to her colonists that the money proposed to be raised for them by taxation was to be spent not for English purposes, but exclusively for the protection and defence of the colonies[2]. And yet it is also true that Englishmen at home were to have the monopoly of those manufacturing industries without which no modern country can be in the first rank of civilization; and which Mercantile exaggeration treated as the essential conditions of political power and of intellectual progress. This selfishness, perhaps, did more to lower the moral character of Englishmen than to retard the higher development of the colonies: for the colonists found unexpected ways of using their minds. But in England's treatment of Ireland it was carried to its logical extreme and "sapped the industrial instincts of the people[3]."

[1] Gee, *Trade and Navigation*, ed. of 1750, p. 78 (first ed. 1730). He is willing to "encourage them in the raising of silk, hemp, flax, iron" (we were then largely dependent on foreign supplies of iron on account of the lack of charcoal to smelt it), "potash etc., by giving them competent bounties in the beginning, and sending over judicious and skilful persons at the public charge to assist and instruct them in the most proper methods of management"; and he is opposed to "the heat that some people have shown (without reason) for destroying the iron works in the Plantations and pulling down all their forges, taking away in a violent manner their estates and properties, preventing the husbandmen from getting their ploughshares, carts, and other utensils mended": and so on. He would allow them to have their own hemp, flax, etc. worked up by licensed weavers for their own use. But if they want any of it worked up for sale, even to their neighbours, that must be done at home; and similarly as to iron. Of course all such policy pressed more heavily on the Northern colonies, than on those which could raise sugar, tobacco, etc.

[2] Lecky, *England in the Eighteenth Century*, ed. I. vol. III. pp. 313, 323.

[3] This is the keynote of Sir H. Plunkett's striking *Ireland in the New*

APP. D, 4. Adam Smith's criticism of the Mercantilist Colonial System of the various countries of Western Europe and his picture of the general relations between the Old World and the New are of fascinating interest even now: though perhaps his lights are a little too high and his shadows a little too deep. In particular he was certainly wrong, as Ricardo pointed out in his masterly chapter on the Colonial Trade, in supposing that the mother country could get no benefit by compelling a colony to deal exclusively with her. It is important to bear in mind that the Colonial system was abolished before Ricardo's exposure of his error was generally accepted. It was abolished not because it *could* not conceivably confer any gain on the mother country, but because it *did* not.

England's difficulties with her colonies came to a sudden head partly because, though she was liberal, they were specially inclined to resent interference; and partly for the paradoxical reason that she was becoming able to hold her own on the seas against all comers. Walpole, with masterly inactivity, had shut his eyes to the enterprise of smugglers; and thus prevented the monopolies from irritating the American Colonies. But the defeat of the French removed from the colonies all fear of being left to defend themselves against a powerful enemy: the narrow quasi-Mercantile love of authority induced a pedantic King and his ministers to override the wise tolerance of Chatham; and the bond of union was quickly snapped.

The successful rebellion of American Colonists, and the great increase in the trade between England and America which came after the change of flag, brought home to the minds of the mass of the people the force of much that Adam Smith had spoken to deaf ears a short time before. But they had not realized then, and perhaps men do not realize even yet, the grandeur and the moral strength of Adam Smith's large Imperialism, when he proposed that England's chief Colony should become the kernel of a great empire, in which she herself should

Century. He continues, p. 13: "When the legislative restrictions upon industry had been removed, the Irish, not being trained in industrial habits, were unable to adapt themselves to the altered conditions produced by the Industrial Revolution, as did the people in England. And as for commerce, the restrictions which had as little moral sanction as the penal laws, and which invested smuggling with a halo of patriotism, had prevented the development of commercial morality, without which there can be no commercial success."

play a leading, but not a dominating part. So the Mercantile element was gradually extruded from the relations between England and her colonies[1].

But there was nothing to take its place: perhaps there was no room for a consistent policy. The chaos which followed may even have possibly been the best thing under the circumstances. For the economic and political conditions of the colonies, and the means of communication between them and the mother country changed so rapidly, that any complete system adapted to one generation might have caused friction in the next. And indeed the problems of colonial policy in the seventeenth and eighteenth centuries, had but little real resemblance to those of the twentieth. Interferences with liberty of trade, which once were thought reasonable, would not now be tolerated by any "Dominion"; though they might be endured by such a settlement as that of Algeria, in which the bulk of the inhabitants are not of white race. Dominions take the position of younger sisters, rather than that of daughters. Further, by aid of the telegraph, many things can now be talked out, which could not bear the delays of a postal return service lasting several months; and which were then most advantageously treated by the almost autocratic ruling of a kindly mother country.

Again, the only markets for loans at that time were local or at best national. The international loan market belongs to a later stage, and is indeed largely the product of the electric telegraph and international civil law. The people of the mother

[1] Dean Tucker, in 1774, boldly proposed to give the colonists freedom, and to "guarantee it against all foreign invaders whatever": and two of his arguments for that course, coming as they do from a mind of the finest quality, show how very recent is the growth of our present sentiments of economic nationality. It is urged, he says, "that if we separate from the colonies we shall lose their trade. But why so? The colonies we know by experience will trade with any people, even with their bitterest enemies, during the hottest of a war, and a war undertaken at their own earnest request and for their own sakes." (*Four tracts*, pp. 195—6.) He is proud of that "bold, free Constitution, which is the prerogative and boast of us all" that set them for independence "the moment in which Canada came into the possession of the English, and...they had nothing to fear from a foreign enemy" (pp 153—4). But business is business. He would like to regulate them out of opportunities for developing rival industries; the law, making it "a capital offence to inveigle artisans and mechanics to leave the kingdom,...is unhappily superseded so far as the colonies are concerned: and a disjunction from the northern colonies would effectually put a stop to our present emigrations" (p. 206).

APP. D, 5. country were always ready to send out capital to their own branch houses in the colony; or to lend it direct to colonists with whose personal character they were acquainted. For in case of default they could appeal to courts where their own law was administered under the ultimate control of their own courts of appeal: but very few people would take the risk of lending to a colony of any other country than their own. An agreement for almost exclusive trade in goods with the mother country might therefore cause the colony a little direct loss; and yet be on the whole to her interest, because it multiplied and strengthened the threads by which she held on to the capital market of the mother country. And even now the exceptional ease with which loans of all kinds can be raised in the mother country is an important asset to a young colony.

5. *Some broad conclusions as to English Mercantile legislation and administration.*

There is no general economic principle which supports the notion that industry will necessarily flourish best, or that life will be the happiest and healthiest, when each man is allowed to manage his own concerns as he thinks best. No considerable thinker has ever denied that *if* the rulers of a people are immeasurably superior to their subjects in knowledge and insight, there are many directions in which the people may be forced against their will for their good: and such conditions undoubtedly did exist under the Norman and Angevin Kings. But the gap in intelligence and resource between rulers and the great body of the ruled had been narrowed by habits of independent action that had been evoked when money payments took the place of services, more or less regulated by custom, in regard to all varieties of tenure: and again by the failure of the regulations by craft gild and town authority to accommodate themselves to the changing methods of industry: and again by the partial movement of industries into the country: and again by the partial re-aggregation of industries in large villages or towns, not always of ancient date: as well as by the Lollard movement, and other precursors of the Reformation.

Mercantilist statesmen might have been expected to see

APP. D, 5.

that the change in the structure of industry, which was already established, must inevitably go further: they might have made provision for further growth, and devoted careful thought to guiding it. But as a rule they seem to have adopted the more easy course of crude prohibitions and restraints. They prohibited changes of occupation, especially by agricultural labourers; and again the ownership of more than two looms by anyone in a rural district, and again the intervention of a middleman for the sale of goods which the resistless march of specialized industry was producing for general consumption. Also their Act of Settlement (1662), "the most false, mischievous and pernicious system that ever barbarism devised... disenabled the poor from settling where they please[1]"; and their prohibition of all new cottages with less than four acres, was a crude careless act, because it was not accompanied by any provision of such land. They seem often to have sought the easier path out of a difficulty, in preference to that which would have worked the most good in the long run; and in particular to have lent too ready an ear to the representations of vocal, organized groups of producers and traders. They seldom ranged themselves on the side of movements which, though still weak, were yet destined to render great services to the country. They regulated wages, using sympathetic phrases, but in fact siding in the main with the employer against the workman, and especially the farm labourer[2].

[1] Arthur Young, *Political Arithmetic*, 1774, pp. 90, 4.

[2] Thus the famous Statute of Artificers, 1562, which continued substantially unchanged, though not generally enforced, proposed to adjust wages to the rising prices of provisions. No doubt it benefited some operatives. But its penalties against paying wages higher than those ordained were more conspicuous than those against paying less. It lowered more rates than it raised. It left money wages lower relatively to the price of provisions than they had been: and their relative fall continued fast after it had been enacted. Money wages indeed rose only 50 per cent. while prices rose 150 per cent. during the sixteenth century (see Rogers' *Work and Wages*, ch. XII, especially p. 349; Unwin, *l.c.* p. 120, but also p. 143, tending slightly in the opposite direction, and compare the figures quoted from Steffen above, p. 708 fn.).

Hewins, *English trade and finance*, p. 113, holds that the Statute of Artificers "gave the working classes into the hands of landlords and employers": though an amendment passed in the first year of the reign of James I "forbad Justices of the Peace, who were clothiers, to fix the wages of weavers." But no such protection was thought necessary for the agricultural labourer: he was left entirely in the hands of men who had an interest in buying his labour cheap.

APP. D, 5.

Mercantilism in its later phases was often almost consciously obsolete; and, partly for that reason, weak and corrupt. And there is a certain satisfaction in turning back to Tudor times, when its policy had not yet fallen under suspicion. The upright, incorruptible, capable Burghley is commonly taken as a typical representative of English Mercantilism in its best days: and its strength and weakness is well illustrated by the resolute despotism with which he enforced his own irresolute opinions. He was by nature neither a Catholic nor a Protestant. He half inclined to Elizabeth before Mary's succession to the throne was nearly certain. Then as a jealous Catholic he became intimate with Pole: but before Mary's death he was intriguing with Elizabeth. Finally he based his policy on the principle that the "State would never be in safety where there was a toleration of two religions." The Achilles' heel of Mercantilism lay in the eagerness with which its leaders enforced conclusions, which they themselves had adopted without any strong sense of intellectual responsibility[1].

It is manifest that the term Mercantilism is not altogether a satisfactory description of the economic characteristics of that period intermediate between the Middle Ages and the modern age; which may be taken to have begun with American Independence, the French Revolution and a number of concurrent mechanical inventions. List's suggestion, that Industrialism

This evil effect of the Statute lingered on well into the eighteenth century. Thus Vanderlint (*Money answers all things*, 1734, p. 148) says: "At length, as is notoriously known, the dearness of labour hath been found so burdensome to our farmers that the gentry and Justices of the Peace, in their open quarter sessions, have lately in several places attempted to redress this evil by regulating the servants' wages." This confidence of landowners in their own equity explains a good deal of English economic history. It is probably true that no other class has possessed for so long so unrestrained a power over the fortunes of others and has abused that power so little; but yet they have abused it grievously.

Fortunately well-to-do artisans were often able to do better for themselves than the Justices did for them. Thus in 1771, the wages of London tailors had been settled at 2*s.* 6*d.*: but "many master tailors gave some of their men 3*s.* a day"; they paid the 15*s.* at the end of the week openly; and then put 3*s.* more for a man "in some place where he knows where to find it: and if this money is not laid for him on the Saturday night, the master may be certain not to see his face on the Monday morning"; quoted by Galton, *The tailoring trade*, p. xlvi.

[1] Professor Pollard, s.v. "Burghley" in the *Encyclopædia Britannica.*

would be a better name, points to the fact that Mercantilism—for we must continue to use the name—had two sides, one concerned with the regulation of trade and the other with the regulation of the industrial and social order of the population at large. On both sides, the commercial and the social, its general tendency was to relax and soften restrictions and other regulations of earlier times; but yet to give to such of them, as were retained, more power and cogency: for they were supported by the whole force of centralized Government, which became in each successive century, though not in each successive generation, stronger and more fully imbued with the spirit of economic nationality.

During her centuries of apprenticeship England developed her own version of Mercantilism. It was English in that it stood in a middle position between the versions adopted by the great countries, and those adopted by most of the City States, and by Holland. For it was more under the influence of merchants and of the people generally than in the Latin countries; and it was more under the influence of kings, statesmen and landowners, with no special trading experiences, than in the City States and in Holland.

In the latter half of the eighteenth century England had outgrown the stage at which Mercantile regulations were capable of doing much good; and those of them, which had not been repealed or fallen into disuse, were almost without exception working harm and causing irritation. For they were old and detailed; and old details are nearly always inappropriate. And they were used as bulwarks for monopolistic privileges, which, whatever their original merits, were sure to be turned to ill account by those who had inherited wealth from energetic ancestors; and who for that very reason had less energy than the average trader, and had more care to defend vested interests than to overcome new difficulties.

6. *Colbert's genius gave a great impetus to French industries. But his Mercantile policy, crystallized in the hands of weak successors, was an important contributory cause of the cult of "Natural" freedom, which occupied the minds of the French people a little later.*

APP. D, 6. We must now turn aside to France. For, though the English reaction against Mercantilism began earlier than the French, the French moved much more quickly than the English, which it influenced greatly.

So responsive were the French to authority and leadership even in details, that in France perhaps more than anywhere else, certainly more than in England, the success of a paternal economic policy depended on the genius and wisdom with which it was carried out, rather than on the soundness of its scientific basis. Sully's Stoic preference for agriculture over trade and manufacture had worked great good for France, because of his fearless, energetic uprightness. And Colbert's more moderate preference for trade and manufactures over agriculture had wrought even greater good; because, while as upright and strong as Sully, he had more knowledge of his business and a greater mastery of details. In prescribing uniform sizes for certain goods he misapplied, or applied prematurely, the principles which underlie the modern movement towards standardization. Other statesmen in England and elsewhere had endeavoured to develop mediaeval traditions on similar lines: but he went beyond all in resolution and even in extravagance.

His rules turned to bureaucratic folly in the hands of feeble successors: but he himself was ceaseless in his endeavours to find out where his rules worked mischief, and to modify them; or, on occasion, to wink at their evasion. Like all protectionists of genius, he never lost sight of the fact that there is a *primâ facie* case against all obstacles to free trade; and that, to justify their existence, it must be proved that they develop industry and trade in some directions more than they check it in others. But, even more than most other protectionists of equal genius, he exaggerated the constructive force of his expedients. He dwelt fondly on each little favourable sign; and he instinctively looked away from its evils[1].

But while strengthening the custom-houses at the frontier and sharpening the outlines of international trade, he abolished

[1] It may be noted that the extravagance of French Mercantile regulations was prominent in the minds of English economists in comparatively recent times. See for instance Mill, *Political Economy*, v. xi. 7.

as many local customs barriers as he could; and he blurred out those features of interprovincial trade which till then had had much of the real character, and something of the form, of international trade. He aimed at welding France into a united industrial country, which should export highly finished and high priced goods in return for cheap raw materials and the precious metals, the sinews of war, for his extravagant master: and he aimed at creating the strongest navy in Europe. His resolution and the despotic power, which he wielded, enabled him in a decade to effect changes that seemed to belong to a century. Nowhere else did Mercantilism develop so quickly its beneficial influences: and its evil influences were kept well in check in France, so long as his hand was at the helm. But it depended for its success on one master mind; it did not enlist the critical and constructive faculty of a nation in its service, and it lacked versatility. The centralized administration of France, while admirably adapted for turning existing knowledge to a speedy account, proved itself inferior to England's enterprise in the power of adapting itself to new wants and of devising new methods for overcoming new difficulties: therefore its mistakes led to a sudden and fleeting reaction towards free trade[1].

During the first half of the eighteenth century France was learning more from England than England from France. But French influence is clearly seen in the tone of the Scotch Hume in the middle of that century: and, though his thought reacted much upon that of France, yet that debt was far more than repaid by the influence which France in her turn exerted on Adam Smith; who was the pupil of the Physiocrats and of Turgot in their pursuit of economic freedom, as well as of Petty and Locke and Hume[2].

[1] The paternal policies of the French rulers, of which Colbert's is the most conspicuous, were much misunderstood, and unfairly judged in England until recently; and this fact partly excuses the exaggerations of List's vehement eulogy of Colbert. The whole movement is well described in Levasseur's *Histoire des Classes Ouvrières en France avant* 1789. See also Neymarck's *Colbert et son Temps*, especially Part II.

[2] Hume's hatred of monopolies and artificial privileges, to which reference has already been made, seems to have been derived from his study of contemporary and past facts at least as much as from the general principles of liberty. In fact, though he was fond of Turgot, he was impatient of the confident dogmas of the French "Economists."

 The new French system was the work of greater thinkers and more interesting men than that which went before it. But though it was in harmony with the words that were on men's lips, it was alien to their latent habits and instincts: it never became an effective part of the principles of action of the ordinary Frenchman in common life. Economic liberalism has been assimilated by many leaders of thought in France, but not by the great body of the people; and, partly for that reason, its doctrines have been stated there with more confident precision than anywhere else.

The suffering of the French people under the pressure of the extravagance and privilege of the ruling classes, had moved the hearts of Sully and Colbert, of Vauban and Boisguilbert: and it became so grievous in the middle of the eighteenth century as to dominate all French economic thought. Under the influence of Rousseau, and afterwards of the American Revolution, the demand for the abolition of monopolies and privileges ceased to be content with partial reform of details. The same spirit that levelled all social distinctions without compromise, and without consideration for special cases or for indirect effects, bore fruit in the absolute wording of the economic dogma, "Let people make whatever they like and move wherever they like":—for this is the true meaning of *Laissez faire* and *Laissez passer*: phrases which have come to be used by politicians in a sense entirely different from that which properly belongs to them; with results most detrimental alike to clear thinking and fair controversy. *Laissez faire* did not imply that Government should abstain inertly from constructive work: it meant simply that anyone who thought that he could make anything with advantage, whether on old lines or by a new method, should be at liberty to do so. *Laissez passer* had its chief application to difficulties that did not exist in England. It meant that all the various obstacles to the free passage of goods between the various Provinces of France should be removed. England had realized her Zollverein many centuries before. France got hers at the Revolution: Germany had still to wait for another half century. *Laissez passer* was however sometimes interpreted that all frontier duties, even those between different countries, should be abolished: and for that the world is not ready yet[1].

The American Revolution, which impelled England towards broader views of her national economy and of the duties which she owed to her colonists, set France for the time even further on the path towards freedom of trade. Pitt welcomed the proposal made by her that the two countries should trade almost as though they were one. But the English people held back; and shortly afterwards war obliterated all traces of the great endeavour[2].

The Physiocrats, and in a less degree Turgot, believed that an absolute government instructed by the philosophers was the best adapted for enabling the people to thrive in the practice of the new principles. But here Adam Smith, following the tradition of his chief English predecessors, parted from them[3].

7. Adam Smith frequently showed that the interests of individuals may lead them to action which is not the most conducive to the well-being of the community, themselves reckoned in. But he held that Government intervention was likely to be exploited by intriguing traders.

[1] Turgot wrote to Hume in 1766, "Our economic philosophers, followers of Quesnay, will maintain vigorously their master's system. It is a system from which English writers are at present very far; nor can we hope to see them adopt it for a long time to come, so difficult is it to conciliate its principles with the condition of monopolising the commerce of the universe." See Leon Say, *Turgot*, ch. III.

[2] Lecky, *Eighteenth Century*, V. pp. 37—46 (ed. I), gives an instructive account of the debate in the House of Commons on the proposal.

[3] No doubt the Physiocrats were somewhat influenced by the fact that a democratic nation is often harder than an autocratic ruler would be, to a nation subject to it. For instance, the economic and the general interests of African slaves and American Indians were cared for better by the French, and even the Spanish, Governments than by English colonists, who were masters of their own destiny. But the true cause of this fact is that no one is so good a judge of his own case as are onlookers, who have no personal interest in it. The Slave Trade indeed shows to a greater disadvantage than any other incident the English "concrete" method of judging each case by itself and with reference to its own special incidents. For the best knowledge of those special incidents lies with those who are most nearly affected by them; and these are the very people whose judgments are likely to be unconsciously warped by their interests. It should be noted, however, that the laws relating to slaves in some of the aristocratic colonies of the South were "of extreme ferocity"; but those in the bourgeois Pennsylvania were mild. See Lecky, *England in the Eighteenth Century*, ed. I. VI. p. 282.

APP. D, 7. The Mercantilists have no doubt suffered injustice by being taken too literally. But to do more than justice to them, is to hide away the real causes of the intense opposition to their doctrines, which was aroused in the minds of Adam Smith and other far-sighted men; who, being nearer to them than we are, knew what sort of men the bureaucratic officials were, and what sort of advice they would get from self-confident amateurs such as Sir James Steuart and Gee[1].

Adam Smith himself frequently stated or implied that it would be possible for an omniscient and omnipotent Government to direct the actions of merchants, and other people, in a course more conducive to public well-being than that in which they would be led by their own interests. But he did not believe that Governments, such as he knew them, would have any considerable share of the knowledge of detail, the ceaseless forethought, the untiring invention and resource, the constant attention to the relative proportion of various elements and the sound judgment of them, which would enable an omniscient Government to have an advantage over the automatic action of private interest. He held that, even if a statesman is the ablest man in his country, he cannot divide out his mind among a great number of trades and businesses; and give to each of them a better judgment, than will be worked out by the combined mental activities of hundreds of more or less able merchants, who give much of their time and strength to that one thing. And as to the moral integrity of statesmen, he was less sanguine than the simple-minded Quesnay and many of his followers; for they anticipated some modern socialists in the faith that, so soon as a wise and righteous

[1] Adam Smith never mentioned his contemporary Steuart; but probably had him in mind all the more. Steuart was a Jacobite who lived much in France, and whose political sentiments were much impressed by French associations: his economic thought is mainly a mixture of fresh, shrewd individual observations with crude remains of old Mercantile fallacies.

Gee, finding that many of our fishing galleys went straight from Newfoundland to the South of Europe, would discourage that practice; and even prohibit it, unless they cleared from a British port on their way back. He would thus make it "their interest to stick to their fishing and coasting, which I am persuaded would be more to their advantage than their voyage to the Straits [of Gibraltar]; for where people have business enough in a very few employments, it is the surest way to get riches." The fishing folk may think otherwise: but the Statesman instructed by Gee will know better.

system should have been established, the upright motives, by which they themselves are led, would be found in the ordinary man, frail as they knew his virtue still to be.

Adam Smith concedes that "by such [Mercantile] regulations a particular manufacture may sometimes be acquired sooner than it could have been otherwise, and after a certain time may be made at home as cheap or cheaper than in the foreign country[1]." But he insists that the immediate loss is certain, and the future gain problematical. Here and elsewhere he contrasts on the one hand the abstract chance that such a policy might be carried through with benefit to the nation by statesmen of superhuman knowledge, intelligence, activity, and probity; and, on the other hand, the concrete realities of the world in which he lived. Schmoller, the ablest apologist of Mercantilism, sums up the situation by saying:—"It is easy to understand how disgusted an honourable man like Adam Smith must have been by the filthy (*schmutzig*) hunting after their private gains by the business men, whom he was able to observe day by day in London[2]."

Another characteristic of Adam Smith's attitude to freedom of trade, which had been but partially anticipated by the Physiocrats, was the prominence which he gave to the interests of the great body of the people; or, as is sometimes inaccurately said, of the "consumers" as distinguished from the "producers." The earlier free traders, Dutch and English, had not indeed neglected that point; but they had urged the benefits of freedom chiefly as a means of promoting the commercial activity of the nation and augmenting the sources of public revenue: and their opposition to the exclusive privilege of a group of traders or producers was based chiefly upon the injuries which it inflicted on others who were engaged, or might wish to engage, in that particular trade or industry; or in some other that was directly dependent upon it[3]. But Adam Smith went beyond them in laying stress on the losses which the people suffered from an artificial constriction of a channel by which their needs might be supplied.

[1] Book IV. ch. II (p. 422 of vol. I of Cannan's edition).

[2] *Die Englische Handels-politik des* 17 *und* 18 *Jahrhunderts*, p. 23.

[3] Compare Laspeyres, *Volkswirthschaftliche Anschauungen der Niederländer*, pp. 164—5.

APP. D, 7. It has been supposed by List and by other writers, especially in Germany, that when Adam Smith urged that it would be wise to allow the individual greater freedom in trading with foreigners, he desired to substitute cosmopolitan sympathies for a national spirit in trade. But in fact he had a strong national spirit himself; and the arguments, by which he and his followers advocated their policy, would certainly have fallen on deaf ears, if they had called on the ordinary Englishman to count a benefit to his fellow-countrymen as of no greater importance than an equal benefit to foreigners.

Adam Smith protests that "the modern [Mercantile] maxims of foreign commerce by aiming at the impoverishment of all our neighbours...tend to render that very commerce insignificant," and that if England and France "were to consider their real interest without either mercantile jealousy, or national animosity, the commerce of France might be more advantageous to Great Britain than that of any other country, and for the same reason that of Great Britain to France." But he goes on, "Being neighbours, they are necessarily enemies, and the wealth and power of each become on that account more formidable to the other[1]."

Again, "If any particular manufacture was necessary for the defence of the society, it might not always be prudent to depend on our neighbours for the supply; and if such manufacture could not otherwise be supported at home, it might not be unreasonable that all other branches of industry should be taxed in order to support it. The bounties on the exportation of British-made sail-cloth and British-made gunpowder may perhaps both be vindicated upon this principle." And similarly he admits the scientific plausibility of arguments in favour of bounties to herring fisheries on the ground that "though they do not contribute to the opulence of the nation...they contribute to its defence by augmenting the numbers of its sailors and shipping...at a much smaller expense than by keeping a great standing navy[2]." These suggestions foreshadowed the impulse which the recent world-war has given to Britain's inclination to incur considerable present sacrifice, in order to increase her

[1] Vol. I. pp. 459, 460 of Cannan's edition.
[2] *Ib.* vol. II. pp. 23, 19.

self-sufficiency at times, when hostile submarines might lower her command of imports, in spite of her powerful navy. APP. D, 7.

Again in matters of purely trade policy, though he urges that we should not injure ourselves merely for the sake of injuring other nations, he admits that when there is a prospect that, by injuring them we may cause them to cease injuring us, it may be wise to do so even at some cost to ourselves. He admits that the policy of retaliatory duties is not only defensible theoretically, but may occasionally be prudent, even when account is taken of all the complications which it involves.

He discovered numerous and important exceptions to the "natural law of liberty," and these discoveries were seldom *à priori*; they were nearly all supported by inductive studies of the world around him. Further, his views of Nature and of life were very broad. It may be true that he unconsciously assumed that there was "something of a Scotchman" inside of every body: but he was fond of watching varieties in national character. He was the last person in the world to think that wealth was the aim of life; the last person to suppose that the ideals of a noble life should be subordinated to the growth of riches by any wise and self-respecting individual or nation.

And yet, as a shrewd observer of human nature in the eighteenth century, he concluded that a strict logical separation of the business element from the emotional elements of private and public policy was the best, and indeed the only possible, safeguard against the weaknesses of ambitious statesmen and the wiles of fraudulent traders. His position was:—let us first ascertain how the nation may best do its business, regarded as business. That being done, let us bring into the problem higher considerations: let us take account of the fact that the life of a nation is something more than the aggregate of the lives of its members; and let us face material loss bravely, if it must be encountered on the way towards a higher end. But let us count the cost; and let us move with special caution if the cost to the State will bring with it any political advancement, or any material gain to the individuals or the "interest" by whom it is urged[1].

[1] Some misunderstandings of Adam Smith's position have been imported into this country from Germany; but unfortunately the corrections of those

APP. D, 7. mistakes, which have been made in Germany, have not been noted here. Thus Adam Smith says:—"By pursuing his own interest he [the individual seeking an employment for his capital] frequently promotes that of the society more effectually than when he really intends to promote it" (Book IV. ch. II. vol. I. p. 421 in Cannan's edition), and Knies, in a spirited effort to induce his countrymen to substitute a real broad-minded Adam Smith for that doctrinaire whom many of their writings portray and label "Adam Smith," says that this critical passage is commonly quoted from a German translation by Stirner, which omits the word "frequently"; and thus makes Adam Smith express a doctrine, as fundamentally opposed to the whole trend of his thought, as it is to that of List himself. See Knies, *Die politische Oekonomie vom geschichtlichen Standpuncte*, ed. of 1883, p. 226. In the preceding pages Knies had given many instances of strong expressions of Adam Smith as to the failure of the private interests of landowners, traders and others to direct their actions into that channel which would be most to the aggregate wealth, their own of course being reckoned in; and reckoning therefore being made only in terms of money value, not of true social value. And Held (*Sociale Geschichte Englands*, p. 160) is wroth against those who take Adam Smith's "doctrine of the natural and necessary harmony of all interests as a general and fundamental principle," ignoring his constant arguments to the contrary; and laying excessive stress on occasional passages in which he speaks of "the unseen hand which leads a man to this end, though he has not intended it himself." Such men he concludes "can be excused only on the ground that they neither see nor hear anything beyond a few phrases, which dominate their minds."

APPENDIX E[1]

THE BRITISH MOVEMENT TOWARDS FREE TRADE

1. ***The policy of Protective duties was discredited in Britain by the mismanagement of the Corn Laws: Sliding Scales of duties, designed to keep prices steady at a high level, made them very unsteady.*** APP. E, 1.

It has already been indicated that the British movement towards free trade in the second quarter of the nineteenth century was strengthened by the mismanagement of Protective duties on wheat. This Section and the next are occupied with details, which may not be of general interest; though they bear directly on a great controversy.

Adam Smith's anger was roused by the inconsistency of statesmen who compelled the farmer to sell his produce retail, and forbad the manufacturer to do the same thing. English statesmen, like others, had begun by prohibiting the exportation of grain; then they allowed it subject to taxes and other conditions; and later still they encouraged it by bounties when the price was below a certain level. These bounties aimed at steadying the national market for grain: in an ordinary year enough was to be grown to allow for exportation, in a bad year all was to be retained at home, and thus scarcity was to be avoided. But the bounty tended to send abroad the surplus of a good year, so that in a bad year as much importation became necessary as if there had been no bounty. Thus the double cost of carriage was wasted, and English people had to pay for their food in good and bad seasons alike at rates which would naturally arise only in bad seasons. During the years 1773 to 1792 the English corn trade was left practically

[1] This Appendix is associated with I, IV, 5, 6.

APP. E, 1. free to follow its own course; and Adam Smith's judgment as to the evil influence of the bounties on exportation received some support from the fact that during these years the price of wheat fluctuated less than during the preceding period; in which costly bounties had been given with the avowed purpose of steadying prices, and with a side view at their effect in raising rents.

The course of prices during the war was irregular. War risks and high freights, blockades, and currency troubles were origins of disturbance in which effects came at irregular intervals after their causes: and to these were added an abnormal number of very bad harvests[1].

On the whole the war brought prosperity to landlords and farmers: they learnt to take a lofty view of their stations and the mode of expenditure appropriate thereto. They had been shaken by a fall in the price of wheat from 155*s*. in August, 1812, to 73*s*. 6*d*. in December, 1813; and Committees of the two Houses in 1813—14 investigated the price which was necessary to give the farmer a fair profit, with just about that amount of bias which is commonly found, when persons representing any one interest meet to appraise its claims relatively to others. They thus prepared the way for the law which was to prevent the peace from bringing its natural blessings to the English people. In 1815 the importation of wheat was prohibited except when its market price was above 80*s*.: although when it was at that price, the wages of the ordinary labourer and his family would barely purchase enough bread to satisfy their hunger, if spent exclusively on bread.

The rents of land had been made very high by the war and bad harvests, which raised the limited home supplies to extravagant prices: the rate of interest had also been raised high by the destruction of capital, as was shown by the low price of consols. The landlords, like many people even now in such cases, argued unconsciously in a circle: they thought that

[1] In eleven years out of twenty-two, viz. 1794, 5, 9, 1800, 4, 7—12, the harvests of corn and especially of wheat were deficient: in some the scarcity was "of a desolating character extending over the greater part of Europe." (Tooke, *History of prices*, II. 347.) When crops were rather poor in England, but not abroad, freights with insurance sometimes reached from 40*s*. to 50*s*. a quarter for voyages of no very great length.

rents ought to be sustained so as to continue to pay about this high rate of interest on the inflated prices; and in such reckonings, though not when setting a price on their land for sale, they were likely to leave out of account the income of social amenity and political influence to be derived from it. They believed that the stability of Government and the safety of the country depended greatly on the maintenance of the dignity of their order[1].

In 1828 recourse was had to a vigorous application of the plan of taxing the imports of corn on a sliding scale, that is, so that the tax was high when the market price was low, and low when the market price was high. Great benefits to the farmers were anticipated from this plan; but it turned out to be injurious to all concerned: and, since its failure contributed greatly to the downfall of the system of Protection, the motives which led up to it, and the causes of its failure deserve some detailed notice.

Its advocates seem to have somewhat overrated the advantages of steadiness of price; to have greatly underrated the cost which the various schemes proposed by them for obtaining it would inflict on the nation; and to have made no approach to a solution of the scientific problem:—what are the conditions under which an import duty, whether simple or on a sliding scale, will make for stability? Conditions can indeed be imagined under which a sliding scale might form part of a policy that would make for stability. But under the conditions of wheat supply and demand in their time, it necessarily made for instability. Let us look into this.

European wheat trade in the first half of the nineteenth century was conducted under very difficult conditions. Wheat is too heavy to be carried long distances, even on good roads: and the roads in Central and Eastern Europe were very bad. Some parts of North-Western Europe had good roads, and some had excellent water communications: but, as most of them

[1] The more old fashioned among them would have endorsed Arthur Young's dictum: "None but a fool can imagine that the landlords of a great Empire are to yield to the transitory sons of trade and manufacture." (Quoted by Buxton, *Finance and Politics*, I. 74.)

APP. E, 1. bore a relatively dense population, they needed their own crops for themselves; and, indeed, wheat is not partial to moist lowlands. The main trouble however arose from the facts that (1) large organized production and trade need confidence on the part of producers and exporters that they will find a steady market for any goods which they may offer; and (2) the only means by which the price of an uncertain crop, such as wheat, can be steadied to the home producer, are just those which make the country's demand for imported wheat uncertain and unpredictable. The two chief means that might be adopted for that purpose are (*a*) to give an export bounty on wheat when its market price is below a certain level; and (*b*) to tax highly or even prohibit its importation when the price is below a certain other limit, not much higher than the first. Several responsible writers have urged that, if it were thought worth while to incur the expense of artificially steadying the price of wheat, a two-sided arrangement on these lines would have been the best.

Such a scheme might effectively maintain a steady price, in a case similar to that of Greece to-day, though of course at a great cost to the country: for her total demand on the world market for wheat is very small relatively to the aggregate supply, which will in any case pass through the Mediterranean from the east and the west, the north and the south. But even in such a case as hers, no arrangement of import duties could steady prices unless accompanied by export bounties, so contrived as to carry off any surplus of home production over consumption which might be caused by several excellent harvests in succession.

But England's position in the first half of last century was very different. She was the only large importer of wheat: and therefore it was to her interest to let the foreign producer know what tax he would have to pay on selling it to her. A moderate fixed duty would have discouraged him only a little: he was almost wholly discouraged by being told that unless England had a bad harvest his wheat would be admitted only after paying an exorbitant tax. Tooke, after making a special study of the subject concluded that, when wheat was scarce in England, it was a good deal more likely than not to be scarce also in North-Western Europe generally: and, so far as this was the case, the foreigner could expect to sell under a low tax only when he had not much to sell. Consequently he grew little or nothing definitely for the English market; and England's imports were made up of the surplus of wheat crops of districts, in many of which rye was the staple food; and the supply which she got from any one port would often vary tenfold from one year to the next[1].

Thus the sliding scale made the foreign growing of wheat for the English market to be an act of gambling rather than of sober business: and it also induced, if it did not compel, the importer to arrange his sales so as to intensify the fluctuations of prices; and so that his wheat greatly injured the English farmer without greatly benefiting the English consumer. The farmer did not sell at very high prices, and the English consumer often paid very high prices; while the English Exchequer reaped scarce any profit. For the importer took care not to sell till the English stocks were nearly exhausted; and the consequent rise in price let his wheat in at a low duty. Of course speculators are always inclined to hold back for an expected rise in price: but, when a small rise in price will bring a large reduction in duty, it is worth while to wait for that rise, even at a great risk of failing to sell at all[2].

[1] This can be traced for the years 1800—30 in J. Marshall's great *Digest* of official statistics published in 1833, vol. II. p. 104; and for 1828—30 in Tooke's *History*, vol. VI. pp. 451—3. The irregularity of the figures there given is in great contrast to the regularity of the corresponding tables in recent numbers of the *Statistical Abstract for the United Kingdom*.

The total prohibition of the importation of wheat when the price was below 80*s*., which ran from 1815 to 1828, caused the highest price of a year to be often nearly 50*s*. above the lowest. The expectation of a price approaching to 80*s*. induced farmers to sow wheat even on damp, cold hillsides, hiring labour, in tacit combination with one another, at wages that often needed to be eked out by allowances from the parish.

The sliding scale was in operation from 1828 to 1843. The following average prices (in shillings and pence) for these 26 years are eloquent:—83, 8; 72, 3; 65, 10; 54, 5; 43, 3; 51, 9; 62, 0; 66, 6; 56, 11; 56, 9; 60, 5; 66, 3; 64,3; 66, 4; 58, 8; 52, 11; 46, 2; 39, 4; 48, 6; 55, 10; 64, 7; 70, 8; 66, 4; 64, 4; 57, 3; 50, 1.

[2] A few more details may be added. The duty was practically prohibitory when the price was low. It fell to 16*s*. 8*d*., when the price was 69*s*.; and then the merchants received 52*s*. 4*d*. net. But if they held back till the price was 73*s*., they paid only 1*s*.; and received 72*s*. net. *Consequently they*

APP. E, 2. In the result prices were very irregular. In 1819—1822 great numbers of farmers failed, because grain was abundant: a group of indifferent medium harvests kept them fairly prosperous till 1831, when they were again brought into straits by good harvests[1].

2. ***The repeal of the Corn Laws could not produce its full effect at once. It did not cause a great fall in the price of wheat: but it kept the price almost stationary in Britain while it was rising in neighbouring countries.***

Some authoritative writers have claimed that the history of British wheat prices before and after 1850 proves that the Corn Laws did not raise prices very much, and therefore did not inflict great injury on the people. As much stress has been laid on this argument, it calls for examination.

The difficulty of obtaining grain from abroad in the second quarter of last century did not lie in scarcity of land for growing it, or of people willing to work on the land for low remuneration. If England had offered a fairly steady demand for ten million quarters of imported wheat, many rich areas would have improved their communications with great European rivers and have been able to send her large supplies at a low cost. But as things were they lacked the incentive for such developments:

manœuvred to get the price towards 73*s.*; and then they imported (or took out of bond) suddenly large quantities: and thus lowered the price a little. That brought the tax up somewhat; and therefore other merchants were warned off from intruding on their market. Many English farmers could not wait, and sold at relatively low prices. Therefore they did not gain much by the tax: while the Exchequer gained very little: but the poor consumer paid terribly. The foreigner who happened to have a surplus gained on it. But, as in another year he might probably be unable to sell for exportation to England at all, he grew little or nothing specially for exportation. A full study of the problem is made by Tooke and Newmarch, *l.c.* vol. III. ch. I. In vol. V. p. 168, it is observed that many farmers being in arrear for rent, or pressed for payment of a debt, force the whole or nearly the whole of their stock for sale immediately after the harvest: and of course relics of this tendency remain now.

[1] They weathered that misfortune better than the last, for by the preceding experience "they had been taught prudence," and had become "a different class of men to what they were" (*H. of L. Committee on Agriculture*, 1836, Q. 3163, 4).

for they could not expect to sell their wheat in any country except England, at a price very much higher than that of their own homes. So, when at last England's market was thrown open, she had to rely largely upon those sources of supply which were already in fairly close touch with the sea[1].

APP. E, 2.

Therefore the full effect, which the opening of England's ports to wheat exerted on the available supply of wheat, would not be likely to show itself for many years; and meanwhile prices in the world's market for wheat were disturbed by the new gold supplies beginning about 1850, by a series of wars and by some exceptional harvests. In many years indeed these disturbances exerted a much greater influence on the price of wheat than had been exerted by the rather low import duties levied in England after 1843.

To go into particulars:—Bad harvests had been exceptionally frequent during the great war; but they were exceptionally rare during the next twenty years. In each of the six years 1832—7 the home crops were sufficient for the people's consumption: the import duty was practically inoperative; and prices were relatively low in spite of it[2].

[1] Accordingly, when Jacob, the best authority on the question, was sent to investigate the Baltic and Black Sea sources of supply in 1826—27, he reported that, "if the quantity of corn grown in this country were diminished one-tenth... we should have to pay the foreigners double as much as we now pay the English farmer. There is corn enough...but it must be drawn from such a distance with land carriage." He adds that some of the mariners did not understand the use of the compass: and that Russian grain seldom passed out of the Mediterranean.

It is true that the coast line from Hamburg to Riga was the chief source of England's supplies of wheat then and for some little time afterwards; that the five great river basins which these ports served were so far distinct that variations in the price of wheat between different parts of Prussia were much greater than between different parts of England: and that prices were habitually rather high in Westphalia, where population was relatively dense. See a study of this problem for the years 1816—41 by Rawson in the *Statistical Journal*, vol. v. He makes out his case both by exclusive reference to wheat, and —which is fairer—by comparing wheat in England with rye in Prussia. His analysis of the causes of such variations seems superior to that in the better known study by Cliffe Leslie of "Prices in Germany in 1872." Marshall's *Digest*, 1833, Part II. pp. 98—100, contains the chief results of a Foreign Office inquiry in 1826 as to the prices of wheat in various places from 1700 to 1825: towards the end, the inquiry ranged over 32 European and 4 American markets.

[2] See Tooke and Newmarch, *l.c.* vol. v. pp. 53—66 and p. 223. France in

APP. E, 2. After two bad and several moderate harvests, the rains of 1845 together with the potato disease caused such distress that Peel committed himself in 1846 to complete repeal (save for the Registration duty) in 1849. The harvest of 1849 was good: but, except in that year, the price of wheat was kept low in the years 1847—52 by abundant, almost untaxed, supplies from parts of the Continent in which the harvests had been good, though those in England had been bad: it has been estimated that under the old régime English prices would have been 20*s.* higher than they actually were. In 1853 harvests were bad throughout Northern Europe, and prices ruled high: but they were not higher in England than on the Continent, though they always had been under similar circumstances before.

During all these years the main roads were being improved everywhere: and railways were helping to keep the "Gazette" prices of English wheat down nearer to those of foreign wheat at English ports than before. But the railways of the Continent were of relatively little service. They had indeed made an appearance in Central Europe before 1846; but, of course, they went first to thickly peopled districts, which had little grain to spare. And it was not till the Crimean War had shown the supreme military importance of railways running to the frontiers, that many of them were driven through the large wheat-fields of Central and Eastern Europe.

The Crimean War was accompanied by general bad harvests; freights were for a time very high, and the Russian trade was of course interrupted. To these powerful causes of high prices another was added. For before the repeal of the Corn Laws the world's stock of gold had been shrinking relatively to the work it had to do; and, in consequence, general prices had been falling: but the new supplies of gold, coming suddenly from California and Australia, upset men's cool judgment and forced general prices up to a temporarily inflated level.

It was just when all these exceptional causes were working together that that rise of wheat to a little over 70*s.* occurred,

particular was a large exporter: her high import duty was therefore inoperative; and her wheat prices of course fell very low. The significance of this fall has sometimes been mistaken, and used amiss in controversy.

which has been urged as a chief reason for doubting the influence of free importation in lowering the price of wheat. And a second rise in 1867 to a price a little above 60*s*. had been forced to the same service; though it is amply accounted for by simultaneous exceptionally bad harvests in America and Europe in 1867, following after the indifferent harvest of 1866.

This brings us to the time when the conditions, which govern the trade in wheat, began to assume their present form: and the price of wheat in England ceased to be materially higher than in neighbouring countries, in spite of her rapidly increasing and unique dependence on foreign supplies. She was favoured by her geographical position relatively to America: and later on prices in Germany were influenced by the increasing stringency of her Agrarian policy. Thus prices in England have fallen increasingly below the prices in Germany and France: it is true that they did not fall much between 1849 and 1875: but in the same time they rose greatly in those countries. This contrast embodies the chief result of the repeal of the Corn Laws: it did not cause a great fall in the gold value of wheat in England; but it did prevent a great rise in that value[1].

[1] The following table is taken from the article by Conrad in the *Handwörterbuch der Staatswissenschaften* on "Getreidepreise." It represents prices per metric ton in marks.

Year	England	France	Prussia	Province of Prussia	Westphalia
1816—20	364,0	265,5	206,2	181,8	240,8
1821—30	266,0	192,4	121,4	109,2	132,6
1831—40	254,0	199,2	138,4	133,8	147,8
1841—50	240,0	206,6	167,8	160,4	182,0
1851—60	250,0	231,4	211,4	199,6	223,6
1861—70	248,0	224,6	204,6	195,0	218,6
1871—75	246,4	248,8	235,2	225,0	246,0
1876—80	206,8	229,4	211,2	202,2	222,4
1881—85	180,4	205,6	189,0	182,6	197,6
1886—90	142,8	193,2	173,9	165,6	183,6
1891—95	128,2	178,5	165,5	163,2	173,4
1896—1900	134,3	178,6	160,9	157,9	168,4
1901—05	140,3	178,1	163,9	181,9	165,8
1906	142,5	—	173,4	170,5	178,0
1907	143,5	—	200,3	202,0	202,0

During the whole period France has produced nearly all the wheat she requires; but she has long ceased to export it in considerable quantities. The

APP. E, 3.

3. *Although economic science was much advanced by Adam Smith's successors, their views were generally less broad than his: and their doctrines were sometimes converted by weak or partisan adherents into absolute dogmas*[1].

Adam Smith's successors had less of that breadth and moderation which come from a long training in philosophic and scientific thought. Most of them had a great experience of affairs, and had accustomed themselves to speak with that force and directness, which give special value to the utterances of a business man when he is speaking on matters within his personal knowledge; but which, when he strays beyond them, often tempt him to make simple sweeping statements of broad scope without the necessary limitations and conditions. And unfortunately two strong but exceptionally abstract thinkers, Bentham and James Mill, threw their influence on the side of large generalizations. As a rule however the dogmatism which seemed to pervade the chief English economic writings of the first half of the nineteenth century was apparent, rather than

Province of Prussia has always produced wheat largely in excess of her own requirements. Westphalia has needed increasingly to import supplies from other parts of Germany, or from abroad. Prussia, though formerly an exporter on the balance, now imports more than any other country except England: though of course ordinary statistics do not distinguish her trade from that of Germany. A comparison between Westphalian and English prices is specially instructive, because both Westphalia and England import wheat largely.

The prices in London are about as low as anywhere in England. The prices in Berlin for the more recent of the years here shown are rather above those in Westphalia; though Berlin is on the border of the chief wheat lands of Germany.

Germans have paid special attention to relative variations of prices of rye in Germany and Russia: and have rightly laid great stress on the fact that, there being no true world market for rye, these variations are more erratic than those in the price of wheat. A few paradoxes which have disturbed some English writers seem to be explained by the fact that a country may import rye on the balance from another, where the average price is higher, if her own has been harvested in bad condition, and that of the other in good.

[1] This Section and the next are, in part, reproduced from my Presidential Address to the Economic Section of the British Association in 1890, which is accessible in *The Statistical Journal* for that year. Professor Nicholson well remarks that "as Adam Smith had influenced Pitt, so Ricardo influenced Peel": and in view of the relative lack of independence of Ricardo's chief followers "fortunately it was Peel who translated his ideas into practice." *Cambridge Modern History*, vol. x. pp. 773—4.

real. It represented a dry businesslike mode of speaking, in which much is left to be filled in by the common sense of the listener; it was not a premature attempt at a systematization of knowledge. But it misled adherents as well as opponents; and the efforts of English economists during the subsequent half-century have scarcely sufficed to liberate their science from this tradition of dogmatism.

The change may, perhaps, best be regarded as a passing onward from that early stage in the development of scientific method, in which the operations of Nature are represented as conventionally simplified for the purpose of enabling them to be described shortly; and entering on a higher stage, in which they are studied more carefully, and represented more nearly as they are, even at the expense of some loss of simplicity, definiteness, lucidity and consequent popularity. The English economists of fifty years ago were gratified, rather than otherwise, when some faithful henchman, or henchwoman, undertook to set forth their doctrines in the form of a catechism or creed; whereas now they recognize that every short clear statement of economic doctrine must be a truism, unless it be false.

It has, indeed, been an unfortunate thing for the reputation of the older economists, that many of the conditions of England at the beginning of this century were exceptional, some being transitional, and others, even at the time, peculiar to England. Their knowledge of facts was, on the average, probably quite as thorough as that of the leading economists of England or Germany to-day, though their range was narrow. Their thoroughness was their own, the narrowness of their range belonged to their age; and though each of them knew a great deal, their aggregate knowledge was not much greater than that of any one of them; because there were so few of them, and they were so very well agreed.

Their agreement with one another made them confident; the want of a strong opposition made them dogmatic; the necessity of making themselves intelligible to the multitude made them suppress even such conditioning and qualifying clauses as they had in their own minds. Therefore, although their doctrines contained a vast deal that was true, and new, and very important; yet the wording of these doctrines was often so narrow and inelastic that, when applied under conditions of time and place different from those in which they had their origin, their faults became obvious and provoked reaction.

It was clearly to the interests of England that her manufactures should be admitted free by other countries: therefore any Englishman who attempted to point out that there was some force in some of the arguments which were adduced in favour of Protection in other countries, was denounced as unpatriotic. Public opinion in England acted like the savage monarch who puts to death the messenger, that comes running in haste to tell him how his foes are advancing on him; and when John Stuart Mill ventured to tell the English people that some arguments for Protection in new countries were scientifically valid, his friends spoke of it in anger—but more in sorrow than in anger—as his one sad departure from the sound principles of economic rectitude. But killing the messengers did not kill the hostile troops of which the messengers brought record; and the arguments which Englishmen refused to hear, and therefore never properly refuted, were for that very reason those on which Protectionists relied for raising a doubt in the minds of intelligent and public-spirited Americans as to the scientific soundness and even the moral honesty of English economics. It is however to be remembered that, in that age as in the present, exaggerated notions of the scope and cogency of economic doctrines have been less frequent in calm academic discussions, than in heated political controversies: and especially in those in which business men, however capable and upright, have sought to find in economic doctrine a support for practical conclusions in harmony with their own experiences, opinions and sentiments:—and, in some cases, their own business interests.

4. *Overstatements of arguments in favour of Free Trade have retarded the general acceptance of that part of it which may justly claim to be of universal validity.*

The first great difficulty which English economists had, in addressing themselves to the problems of cosmopolitan economics, arose from the fact that England was an old country—older than America in every sense; and older than the other countries of

Europe in this sense, that she had accepted the ideas of the new and coming industrial age more fully and earlier than they had. In speaking of England, therefore, they drifted into the habit of using, as convertible, the two phrases—"the commodities which a country can now produce most easily," and "the commodities which a country has the greatest potential advantages for producing"; that is, will always be able to produce most easily. But these two phrases were not approximately convertible when applied to other countries; and when List and Carey tried to call attention to this fact, Englishmen did little more than repeat old arguments, which implicitly assumed that New England's inability to manufacture complex products had the same foundation in natural laws as her inability to produce oranges. They refused fairly to meet the objection that arguments, which prove that nothing but good can come from a constant interchange of product between temperate and tropical regions, do not prove that it is for the interest of the world that the artisans who are fed on American grain and meat should continue always to work up American cotton for American use three thousand miles away. Finding that their case was not fairly met, the Protectionists naturally thought it stronger than it was, and honestly exaggerated it in every way.

Looking back then, it is easy for us to see that English economists made a grave error of judgment as to the proportions of one leading problem of their own age, though not of their own country. They misjudged the needs no less than the potentialities of backward countries, and especially of new countries. They took too little account of the fact that, though any one county of England, which had latent resources and faculties for an advanced industry, would attract that industry to itself from other counties; yet what is true of counties is not true of countries.

If the neighbourhood of coal and other causes concentrate those English industries in which man's command over Nature is rapidly increasing, chiefly in the middle-west, the benefits arising from this new power are in great measure spread over the whole country. Those born in Devonshire and Sussex who have a turn for the rising industries, can generally remove to them

APP. E, 4. without snapping their main ties as human beings. But a new country may be dominantly rural; may lack the stimulus and culture of a nervous town life, and have no access to the economies of manufacture on a large scale: she will then derive comparatively little consolation from knowing that there are busy hives of industry and thought in remote lands.

The failure of English economists to allow for the special circumstances of new countries did not end here. They saw that Protective taxes in England had raised the price of wheat by their full amount; because increased supplies of it could be raised in England only at a more than proportionately increased cost of labour. They saw that the high price of bread had kept a large part of the population on insufficient rations, and had enriched the rich at the expense of a much greater loss to the rest of the nation. They saw that this loss had fallen upon those, who were unable to lose material wealth without also losing physical, and even mental and moral strength; and that even those miseries of the overworked factory women and children, which some recent writers have ascribed exclusively to recklessness of manufacturing competition in its ignorant youth, were really caused chiefly by the want of freedom for the entry of food. They were convinced that the benefits claimed for Protection in England were based, without exception, on false reasoning; and they fought against it with the honest, but also rather blind, energy of a religious zeal.

Thus they overlooked the fact that many of those indirect effects of Protection which aggravated then, and would aggravate now, its direct evils in England, worked in the opposite direction in America. For, firstly, the more America exported her raw produce in return for manufacture, the less the benefit she got from the Law of Increasing Return (*i.e.* the law that manufacture on a large scale is more economical than on a small). Thus her case was contrasted with England, who could manufacture more cheaply for her own use the more of her manufactures she sent abroad; and for this and other reasons, a Protective tax did not nearly always raise the cost of goods to the American consumer by its full amount.

5. *It does not appear that any eminent economist maintained a position of hostility to the Factory Acts; though they were bitterly opposed by some writers who had a superficial knowledge of economics.*

A reproach is sometimes brought against the British movement towards free trade, to the effect that the economic principles on which it was based, led to a condemnation of the Factory Acts.

It is to be observed that neither Ricardo, nor any other member of the great coterie by which he was surrounded, seems to have been quoted as opposing the early Factory Acts. It is however true that Lord Lauderdale, a brilliant free lance, keen withal and suggestive but erratic and unstable, opposed the Bill of 1818 in the name of "the great principle of Political Economy that labour ought to be left free." The Bill was chiefly concerned with the conditions of work of young children: and J. S. Mill may have had this contention in mind when he remarked, that however undesirable it might be to interfere with the freedom of labour without due cause, it was clear that "freedom of contract in the case of young children is but another word for freedom of coercion[1]."

The most eminent economists in the period intervening between Ricardo's age and J. S. Mill's great work on economics, were perhaps Tooke, McCulloch, Newmarch, and Senior. The first three, though they wrote mainly on business affairs and said little on the human side of economics, were supporters of the acts. Tooke was the author of the celebrated *Merchants' Petition of* 1820, which initiated the movement for free trade, and the founder of the Political Economy Club: he superintended during many years the official investigations of the conditions of work in mines and factories, which resulted in reform. Newmarch, his coadjutor in the later volumes of the *History of Prices*, wrote (vol. v. p. 421) that it was "difficult to overestimate the importance of the factory acts." McCulloch, at whose bourgeois attitude Carlyle gibed with more eloquence than knowledge, endorsed their policy (*Dictionary*, p. 43).

[1] See Mill's *Principles*, v. xi. 8. Lauderdale's remark is quoted by Smart. *Economic Annals*, 1801—1820, p. 668.

APP. E, 5. Senior had perhaps a stronger intellect than any of these: and he was made Professor of Political Economy at Oxford, on the ground of his reputation as a very able man, with great knowledge of the world. He accepted the office, holding that though in other sciences a man must travel far before he was in a position to form a good opinion of his own, in political economy he could speak with confidence, when he had merely walked "to the end of his garden." After a five years' tenure of office, he passed to other work; and, when reappointed after an interval, he had learnt that economic problems were not simple; and he made brilliant contributions to the science. In his earlier phase he had opposed the Factory Acts: in his later phase he was one of their heartiest supporters[1].

These facts raise suspicion that the term "economists" must have been used in a sense in which it referred, not to the leading students of economics, but to politicians and others who affected to speak with economic knowledge, though with but a slight foundation for their claim. It is to such men that Greville refers in a passage which has been frequently repeated, and has even been used by economic authority of the first rank as sole and sufficient evidence for the statement, that English economists generally had eagerly opposed factory legislation: that is to say, it is taken to refer to the chief students of economics at the time, whereas in fact it refers exclusively to

[1] There seems to be some reason for thinking that, in his earlier phase, Senior fell into a rather common mistake as to the effects of such a change as a compulsory reduction of the hours during which manufacturers kept their machinery at work. He seems to have ascertained "by observation" that the total net profits earned by many mills did not exceed the loss which they would incur if compelled to reduce by an hour the time during which the machinery was running; and to have converted this result into the conclusion that those mills would make no net earnings if their hours were thus reduced. And yet it was well known that Robert Owen's brilliant experiment at the Lanark Mills claimed to have proved that the increased energy and care with which operatives, and especially children, worked for shorter hours, increased the output per hour greatly. And it was known that, even if a somewhat reduced output had resulted from the change, the manufacturers would have received some compensation; because the prices of their products would certainly have risen somewhat, both in the home market, and in those numerous foreign markets of which England had a firm hold. It was not possible indeed to be certain how far these palliatives would reach. But to ignore them altogether was unreasonable. And, in any case, it was wrong to claim for his conclusion, as Senior appears to have done, that it was based on direct observation.

members of Parliament. Speaking of the 1844 debate on the "Ten hours' bill," he says: "Some voted, not knowing how they ought to vote. Melbourne is all against the bill; all the political economists of course: Lord Spencer is strong against him[1]."

This use of the term "economist" is not unknown in our day. It was adopted by those who, desirous of "keeping down the rates," organized themselves to oppose liberal public expenditure on the education of children; ignoring the fact that those who were giving their main energies to the study of economics, much as they might differ on other matters, were to a man convinced that parsimony in popular education is uneconomical and even wasteful. The following extract from a leading organ of public opinion when the case "Regina *v.* Cockerton" had made prominent the question whether rates might be levied to defray the expense of continuation schools is in point: "the judgment will not result in justifying either the elation of the economist or the despair of the educationist."

And a similar misuse of the term had found vogue in the discussions on the Factory Acts. Thus "Alfred" writes: "There had arisen in this country a school of political economists who professedly pointed to *The Wealth of Nations* as the text book of their practical philosophy, though they as a rule omitted to state that that celebrated book contained contradictory doctrines; they preferred popularizing the portions of Adam Smith's great work, which supported what they believed to be their own interests, failing to take any notice of portions of the same book fundamentally opposed to their favourite dogmas. These political economists were 'on principle' opposed to all state interference between labourers and capitalists[2]." There can be little doubt that "Alfred" has Miss Martineau in mind. W. Cooke Taylor refers to her "The Factory Controversy" as to be studied with great advantage for a knowledge of "the doctrine of the orthodox economists[3]." She wrote a

[1] Greville, *Memoirs*, vol. v. p. 241.

[2] *History of the Factory Act*, p. 115. This, the standard work on the subject, is attributed to Samuel Kydd. Miss Martineau's aid was acknowledged by a considerable present from manufacturers. Her simple diction, her honesty of purpose, and her lack of scientific capacity, combined to make her a good instrument for their purpose.

[3] *Modern Factory System*, p. 397.

APP. E, 5. series of tales designed to enforce what she thought were economic doctrines: and, describing her preparation for the work she says: "In order to save my nerves from being overwhelmed by the thought of what I had undertaken, I resolved not to look beyond the department on which I was engaged[1]." Now everyone who has endeavoured patiently and thoroughly to work to the roots of economic problems, has learnt that so many lines of communication run from every one of them to others, that no sound opinion on any of them, which is not exceptionally simple, can be formed, without a considerable knowledge of economics as a whole[2].

[1] *Autobiography*, I. 194.

[2] A short statement to the effect of this Section has been already made in my *Principles*, Appendix B.

APPENDIX F[1]

THE ZOLLVEREIN

1. ***Though the first fruit of Germany's consciousness of her unity was a desire for commercial federation, yet particular interests ruled many of the devious steps by which the goal was ultimately reached.***

Stein's liberation of the peasant from the yoke of customary service, and List's striving to hinder the merchant from importing English and other wares which might enter into competition with the weak manufactures of Germany, were in outer appearance movements in opposite directions: the one increased economic freedom, while the immediate tendency of the other was to check it. But they sprang from the same roots and their ultimate tendencies were in harmony.

The only part of Germany in which manufactures flourished vigorously early in the nineteenth century was Saxony; and perhaps partly as cause, partly as effect, she alone adopted the policy of free trade. By aid of the splendid system of education which she pioneered, she was able to hold her own in competition with British hosiery and other manufactures, in spite of her scarcity of capital, and her partial adherence to old fashioned methods[2]. Prussia and several other states, which had much

[1] This Appendix is associated with I, VII, 1, 2.

[2] In 1812 more than a quarter of her spindles were worked by horses and other cattle; more than an eighth by hand; the remainder only being driven by water. Pohle, *Entwickelung des deutschen Wirtschaftslebens im 19 Jahrhundert*, p. 12. In 1845, when Saxon hosiery had almost driven English out of American and many Continental markets (partly indeed because of cheapness attained by a very large use of cotton as a material), an English hosiery manufacturer reported (evidence as to Frame-Worker Knitters collected by Commissioner Muggeridge, Q. 2819, 2820) Saxon operatives to be "much better clad and have a much more reputable appearance than the same class of operatives here, being much better educated," though their average wages were from 3*s.* 6*d.* to 4*s.* 6*d.* weekly.

APP. F, 1. through traffic, were inclined to facilitate the internal trade of Germany; but nearly all desired to levy taxes on imports of foreign manufactures, especially from the rich and highly equipped factories of Britain. They were able to make strong points of the "slaughter sales" of British goods in their markets, in times of commercial distress: and to insist that the British sliding scale tax on imported wheat, caused violent fluctuations in the price of wheat in many parts of Germany. Without attributing malignity to these actions, they were willing to give ear to such declamations as that of List, when he declared that between 1820 and 1840 the Germans had been to no good purpose "debased to be carriers of water and hewers of wood for the Britons: they were treated even worse than the down-trodden Hindu[1]." Therefore it was inevitable that internal free-trade should be combined with a broad moderate system of duties on imported manufactures[2].

In one sense List was a free-trader: for he believed that the restrictions of the Zollverein as regards external trade would ultimately prepare the way for a perfect freedom of trade on the part of Germany, when she had grown to full strength, and could speak in the gate on even terms with England. And another South German, the economist Nebenius, a chief advocate—Roscher says the chief advocate—of the Zollverein, was an adherent of the English classical school, and regarded the astringent element in the Zollverein as a medicine, needed by a temporary malaise[3].

[1] See Roscher, *Geschichte der Nationalökonomik in Deutschland*, pp. 965 and 973.

[2] The belief that German customs officials could not be trusted to form a good opinion as to the value of imported goods pushed simplicity to absurdity. Some things were not taxed at all: of the remainder all but 43 were charged 1*s*. 6*d*. per cwt., without any reference to their value. Each of those 43 had its own rate of taxation per cwt., with the promise that the charge should never be more than a tenth of the value. But that value was taken from fine qualities of the goods: so the coarse qualities destined for the poorer consumers sometimes paid taxes equal to their values. Bowring, Evidence before the Committee on Import Duties, 1840, Q. 793, 834.

[3] Roscher says (*l.c.* p. 960): "If List rendered the service of making so-called public opinion receptive of the thoughts of the Zollverein, though indeed only on large vague lines, and in a way that must have been more deterrent than attractive to statesmen; yet his contemporary Nebenius was the first to give vitality (*Lebensfähigkeit*) to the same thoughts by a practical formulation of them that claims our admiration." He is jealous lest any suspicion should

Although the tendencies which were working all over Germany towards unity were largely idealist and even spiritual, yet the main driving force came from the needs and the ambitions of Prussia. Her position was exceptional: for her territory consisted of some seventy fragments; and her frontier lines were, in the aggregate, about eight times as long as those of a fairly compact country of equal area. She therefore eagerly desired a fusion, at least so far as trade was concerned, of her territory with that of the adjacent states. The patriotism and the broad ambition of the rulers of Prussia combined in "the first step towards what is called the *Germanization* of the people[1]."

2. *The general drifts of the German tarif subsequent to the full establishment of the Zollverein.*

Up to 1865 the taxes levied on imports by the Zollverein were generally high, though seldom extravagant. But there then set in a movement towards free trade, stimulated by the continued prosperity of England under her free-trade régime, and the sudden prosperity of France under the relatively liberal tarif which she had adopted in 1860. We have already noted that England's prosperity was partly due to exceptional and transitional causes: and the splendour of France under Napoleon III was partly the result of lavish borrowing. But neither of these facts was noted at the time; and the valid arguments in favour of free trade were exaggerated by Prince-Smith, and the other members of the so-called "English"

fall on his hero of being a follower of Adam Smith, or a friend of England. He says Nebenius even rejoiced at the advances of Russia in Asia, because they were injurious to England, *ib.* p. 965: but he is revolted by List's reckless misrepresentations of Adam Smith and England.

A good account of the Zollverein is given in P. Ashley's *Modern Tariff History.* See also Miss Hirst's *Life of List*; and Eckert, *Zur Vorgeschichte des deutschen Zollvereins* in Schmoller's *Jahrbuch* XXVI., especially p. 101.

[1] Bowring's *Report on the Prussian Commercial League,* 1840. Prussia yielded at every point good bargains to those, who joined her Union; and she put some pressure on those, which remained outside, by charging high transit duties on goods passing through the Union to the sea and elsewhere.

Of course Saxony was very unwilling to come in. But her manufacturers even then wanted a good vent for their hosiery; and the King could not resist the money, which would make him independent of his Parliament (Macgregor in evidence before Committee on Import Duties, 1840, Q. 368).

APP. F, 2. financial school in Germany. Bismarck also favoured the movement on political grounds; because it would oppose an additional obstacle to the entry of Austria into the Zollverein. The movement was sustained for twelve years: and 1865—1877 may be regarded as a time of relative free trade.

The reaction which began in 1877 was the result of many causes. The crisis of 1873—4 had affected France but slightly; because the inflation, which preceded it, had found her in a chastened spirit: and it struck Germany very hard because her military successes, and the rush of fresh capital, obtained through the war indemnity, had thrown her people off their balance. Business men formed extravagant expectations, discounted them; and then launched into large enterprises and speculations, for which the resources of the country were as yet insufficient. The subsequent depression lasted long: and its burden was exaggerated in appearance by a fall in prices; which was caused partly by the adoption of a gold standard by Germany and some other countries, partly by a check to the yield of the new gold-mines. Thus there was a great "over-production," in the sense that many industries had increased their productive plant to such an extent that their products, while in full work, exceeded the amount which the public would buy, when credit had been shaken, except at prices much below those which had been expected when the plant was set up. Consequently people were willing to listen to suggestions that the home market should be protected in the interests of producers against the incursion of foreign goods. The depression of prices was general: English and other manufacturers were forcing some of their goods at abnormally low prices on the German market: and this intensified the demand for Protective tarifs.

Further, the Imperial revenue was inadequate to the demands on it. To levy increased contributions from the separate States would cause friction; diminish the freedom of the Imperial Government; and be open to the objection that, being assessed in proportion to population, they pressed unfairly on the poorer States. Bismarck was never a convinced free-trader; and he used the discontent of the manufacturing classes as a lever for raising the tarif to as high a level, as was consistent with his dominant aim of obtaining increased revenue. It was not an extreme, or so-called "prohibitive" tarif: and it was in part "educative"; that is, designed to carry weak industries through their early difficulties in competition with older rivals in England and elsewhere. But it was also largely governed by parliamentary exigencies even at the outset: and, as time went on, these became very powerful. In particular, the leaders of the heavy iron and steel industries made common cause with the leaders of agricultural industries in support of high import duties on metals, and on those kinds of agricultural produce in which large landowners were most interested.

This drift continued long and brought a general increase in nearly all import duties, the chief exceptions being for raw materials. Germany's neighbours followed suit and raised their tarifs also; partly because they were influenced by her example; and partly because, if their trade with her was to be restricted by taxes, they thought it well to secure as large a part as possible of the revenue from those taxes. Thus the policy of commercial agreements, both general and special, became increasingly prominent. The chief of the general agreements was the "most favoured nation clause," whereby each party to a treaty bound itself to give to the other at least as favourable treatment as to any third country: while special clauses were continually abating the severity of certain items of the general tarif. But on the whole its pressure increased till 1891; when Count Caprivi arranged treaties, mostly for ten years, by which great reciprocal concessions were made between Germany and some other European countries. Though there was a bitter tarif war between her and Russia in 1893, her foreign trade in those ten years was rather more free than between 1879 and 1891; but much less free than between 1865 and 1877.

Meanwhile, however, various causes had increased the dependence of the Imperial Government on the political support of the landowners of North-East Prussia: they urged that Germany's food should be grown under the protection of German cannon; and that the population of the agricultural districts, and especially of the military provinces in the north-east, should be induced to stay on the land. In concert with the leaders of the iron and other staple trades, they induced

APP. F, 2. the Reichstag to pass in 1902 a bill providing for an extremely high tarif. Its details were however so arranged that it enriched the great landed proprietors, who raised broad crops of grain largely by aid of Slavonic migrant labourers; but at the same time injured on the balance the small cultivators, who raised very little grain as a rule.

APPENDIX G[1]

EARLY INDUSTRIAL CONDITIONS AND FISCAL POLICIES OF THE UNITED STATES

1. *The course of internal and external trade was for long governed mainly by difficulties of communication and by scarcity of capital. But steam traffic opened European markets for wheat, and the people moved to western prairies.* APP. G, 1.

The Plantations in America were at first little more than patches on the coast, and in the neighbourhood of a few rivers. Their industries were nominally restricted by the stringent prohibitions of Mercantile statesmen at home to manufacture anything which English manufacturers wished to sell to them. But these prohibitions could not always be enforced: indeed many of them were probably not expected to be. America was not ready for the finer branches of manufacture: but the simpler clothes and utensils used on farms and in the villages could be, and were, made largely in the winter months from native material by local labour. For indeed, when machinery was still simple, nearly everybody even in English villages was an agriculturist during three months in the summer: and in the depth of winter nearly everybody helped to make or repair the rude predecessors of things which the modern farmer buys of the ironmonger, the clothier, or the dealer in boots, harness, or furniture[2].

[1] This Appendix is associated with I, VIII.

[2] In 1800 there were in the States but six cities, each containing more than 8000 inhabitants: together they had about 200,000 inhabitants, or a twentieth of the population. In 1900 there were 545 such cities with an aggregate population of about 25,000,000, about a third of the whole population.

The crudity of the economic life of the poorer agriculturists is the starting point of Dr Quintance's *Influence of farm machinery on production and labor*, 1904. He says (p. 2) on the authority of Mr McMaster: "The poor whites of Virginia in 1790 lived in log huts with the chinks stuffed with clay: the

APP. G, 1. The soil and climate of the Atlantic border were not very favourable to the production of grain, and its transport to Europe was costly; while meat of course could not be exported except in salt. But the forests of New England still supplied the materials for ships, which could more than hold their own against any other of equal size: and it was not by accident that America built the first effective steam-boat. That boat was clear notice that the New World was about to become a teacher of Europe in industry: but in fact preparation for that task had been long in progress.

In the old world a man, who happened to be a little raised above his neighbours, could get them to work for him at low wages: but in America he could not; so he turned his shrewdness to labour-saving inventions. His affairs were generally on a small scale; and his inventions penetrated down to petty domestic difficulties. It is therefore easy to see the humorous side of many "Yankee notions": but the spirit which lay at the back of them was pregnant with great things. It was the spirit of protest against the servitude of free man to dull, heavy work.

Here may be noted a strong contrast between America and Europe which was prophetic of the future. England continued well into the nineteenth century the old practice by which industrial centres had endeavoured to maintain a monopoly of their skill and knowledge; and she prohibited the exportation of machinery and the emigration of skilled artisans: so Europe smuggled in the machinery, and copied it with the aid of imported artisans. America did not disdain to do the same on occasion. But she preferred to find out what was the human task which an English machine had taken over, and to re-invent other machinery for herself; and this in some cases turned out to be better than the English.

walls had no plaster; the windows had no glass; the furniture was such as they had themselves made. Their grain was thrashed by driving horses over it in the open field. When they ground it, they used a rude pestle and mortar: or, placed in the hollow of one stone, they beat it with another." See also Weeden, *Economic and social history of New England*.

Marshall's *Digest*, A.D. 1833, points out that the exports of grain and other agricultural produce from the United States for the twenty years 1806 to 1826 were less than those of Ireland: much went to the West Indies, and was paid for by sugar-bills drawn on London.

Early in last century Jefferson prophesied that the West would not be settled for a thousand years. Few people were as capable of forming as good a judgment on the matter as he was; and that he was so wrong, shows only that he did not anticipate the nature of the forces which were to weld together the East and the West. It is difficult for us to think ourselves back into his world, where those forces were as yet not dreamt of.

In 1800 there was very little population west of the Alleghanies: but in 1830 the populated area to the west of them was larger than that of the east. People crossed them by rough roads; and, as soon as possible, betook themselves to rude barges on the Ohio and its branches. They came upon fertile land, but their produce could not go back by the way by which they themselves had come: so it was marketed southwards; and for some years the Middle West was bound to the Southern rather than the Eastern States[1].

In 1825 the Erie Canal brought traffic from the great lakes to New York, and other canals were contemplated for uniting the Mississippi valley with the Atlantic. But at that very time the "application of steam to the navigation of the land," as Cobden said, was bringing to bear that great economic force which was to make Jefferson's prophecy appear foolish: there were 3000 miles of railways in 1840, and 30,000 in 1860.

Meanwhile the Irish famine, the European ferment of 1846—8, and the fame of the abundant rich land and the high wages to be had in the United States, had swollen the tide of immigration; and the repeal of the English corn-laws had opened the prospects of a large foreign market for wheat. The more enterprising agriculturists moved westwards, leaving farms in the east to be had by immigrants almost for nothing: they themselves sought the richer land of the Mississippi valley, where the soil would yield almost continuous wheat crops, when indulged by occasional fallows. This was the first of those great movements of the more adventurous part of the population, which

[1] As Prof. Emery points out, the Middle West might perhaps have sided with the South in the great Civil War, if that had taken place before 1850 (*Cambridge Modern History*, vol. VII. p. 695). In early times the American's sense of patriotism was mainly directed towards his own State.

APP. G, 2. caused them to multiply more rapidly than their fellows; and in this and other ways endowed the nation with enduring vigour and growth. The ranchman indeed has marched ahead of the wheat farmer; but the large areas, over which his cattle roam, have found occupation for only a few men, and very few of these have had homes of their own. To the wheat farmer, on the other hand, "the acquisition of the home, not the market, has been the primary impelling force[1]."

The mere wheat farmer does not require, nor even find much use for that technical knowledge which is almost essential to mixed farming[2]. The experience of his immediate neighbours, who know the ways of the soil and the climate, is generally a better guide than traditions brought from the old world. He is called on only to be brave, alert, and willing to work hard for a deferred reward. Without these qualities he is not fit to be a pioneer: with them, he has a fairly secure prospect of leaving behind him a well-to-do family strong in mind and body.

2. *Protective tarifs in favour of American manufactures were originally advocated as an investment of national capital in national education, which would bring rich returns in the future.*

The early fiscal policy of the country was intimately connected with her early industrial structure: the present brief account of it was originally intended to accompany a study of present fiscal policies: but it is kept in this place for reasons explained above (p. 12).

The keynote of the claim of early American protectionists was set definitely in 1789 by Hamilton's often quoted argument:—"Though it were true that the immediate and certain effect of regulations controlling the competition of foreign with domestic fabrics was an increase of price, it is universally true that the contrary is the ultimate effect of every successful manufacture.

[1] See Mr Powers' weighty testimony in the *Report of the Industrial Commission*, vol. x. p. 180.

[2] Nearly the same may be said of "corn" (*i.e.* maize); which is the pioneer crop for some soils and climates. It is favoured by the negro population: and is now the heaviest grain crop in the States, but its influence on economic development has been much less than that of wheat.

When a domestic manufacture has attained to perfection, and has engaged in the prosecution of it a competent number of persons, it invariably becomes cheaper. Being free from the heavy charges which attend the importation of foreign commodities, it can be afforded cheaper, in process of time, than was the foreign article for which it is the substitute. The internal competition which takes place soon does away with everything like monopoly, and by degrees reduces the price of the article to the minimum of a reasonable profit on the capital employed."

Here, as in *The Wealth of Nations*, stress is laid on the force of acquired skill and high organization, rather than on that of large capitals. And it is to be remembered that that lack of acquired skill, for which Hamilton demanded an artificial remedy, was itself in large measure an artificial product of selfish Mercantilist Protectionism by the English Government in the days of its power. But yet his argument was not to bear much fruit till a new quarrel had arisen between England and her old colonies[1].

For up to about 1807 America's rapidly growing mercantile marine was earning very high freights in the carrying trade; and she had eager markets at high prices for food in the West Indies, and for food and timber and other requisites of war in Europe. This gave her merchants a great command over European goods, in which English textiles took a large place. English cloth was indeed not able to pursue triumphantly rough cloth woven from home-made yarn into its crevices in the industrial system: but it met American factory-made cloth on nearly equal terms in open market, and could beat it there. During all this time the maritime provinces were more interested in trade than in manufactures, and their political influence went mainly, with that of the South, in favour of free trade.

But in 1807 commercial quarrels in Europe had begun to stretch across the Atlantic; and in 1812 there was again war between England and her old colony. From 1807 to 1815 English goods were excluded from American markets more

[1] Considerable progress had however already been achieved by simple industries even under that hard rule: and the list of the industries described by Prof. Dewey, *Financial History of the United States*, pp. 77—8 as existing in 1789 is large and various.

APP. G, 2. thoroughly than they would have been by a very high Protective tarif. Capital and enterprise, driven from the sea, turned to home industries, and expensive plant increased apace. New England, whose industries had been overshadowed by her commercial and shipping interests, swung round through a neutral attitude to one of gradually increasing eagerness for fiscal legislation on Hamilton's lines. In 1816 the first systematically Protective tarif in favour of manufactures was adopted[1].

The tarif was raised in 1820 and in 1824: while in 1828 a strange political combination led to one so extreme and so ill devised as to cause a reaction. In particular the South was offended by it: and in 1833 it was displaced by a tarif, which went very far in the direction of free trade. That was followed by remarkable prosperity, which however led to over-confidence and a severe crisis in 1837[2].

On the whole the evidence seems to show that until about 1825 there was much public spirit, and comparatively little sordid self-interest, in the forces that sustained Protection to native industry. The reason for this was that the people engaged in manufacturing industries, of such a nature as to benefit from Protective duties, were as yet not very numerous; and they had not great weight at the polls: so that politicians, as well as others, were able to regard tarif questions from the point of view of public well-being rather than of particular private interests[3].

[1] There voted for it 17 Representatives from New England, and 23 from the South and South-west: while 10 from New England and 34 from the South and South-west voted against it. The middle and western States gave 48 votes for it, and 10 votes against it. See Dewey, *l.c.* p. 163.

[2] The clumsy "tarif of abominations" of 1828, was suspected of being partly the work of people who wanted to make Protection odious. The "compromise tarif" of 1833 was suggested by Henry Clay, who was to become the leading parliamentary advocate of Protection, but thought it was necessary to appease the spirit shown in South Carolina's "nullification ordinance" by which she declared the tarif of 1828 to be "null and void." See Dewey, *l.c.* ch. VIII.

[3] Some exceptions to this general statement will be found in Sumner's *Protection in the U.S.* Many interesting details as to the conditions of industry from contemporary Americans are given in Taussig's *Tariff History*; and others by American witnesses are to be found in the British Official Reports of the time. It is clear that in textile work the Americans were hampered mainly by the high price of machinery, and the high rate of interest which they had to pay on loans: they economized machinery and labour by using rather better cotton, than was

The half century, of which 1833 is the middle point, is the chief battle-ground for advocates and opponents of "educative" tarifs designed to protect nascent industries: such Protection being claimed on the ground that they are required, (*a*) in the interests of military and political security, or (*b*) in the interests of variety of social life and industrial opportunities, or (*c*) because they have so great undeveloped economies of production on a large scale, that sacrifices incurred for their education will be returned with abundant surplus to future generations. Both sides appeal to the evidence of facts, and especially statistical facts. But the facts are too complex, and the interweaving of the results of different causes is too intricate for such a treatment; and therefore each side has been able to find in the facts that conclusion which it desired.

Looking away from details to broad considerations, we can see that Protective tarifs increased the manufacturing population relatively to the agricultural; and thus developed centres of complex and various social life and high culture, and provided an ever-widening choice of occupations for people of varying temperaments and capacities: but at the same time they hindered the development of the agricultural resources of the country. This involved some retardation of the growth of commercial centres; which are nearly, though not quite, as important from the social point of view as the industrial centres. So far there appeared a valid, but not a strong, ground for intervention by the State in favour of nascent manufactures, under the particular circumstances of time and place. And, of course, another *primâ facie* valid ground lay in the fact that

used in England even for those rough goods, which alone they attempted to make. The labour in the New England mills was intellectually of the highest class that has ever given itself on a large scale to such routine work; it appears to have been more efficient than the English in all matters needing merely promptitude, energy, and general intelligence; though inferior in manual training: it was paid well, but not very highly paid in proportion to its efficiency. The English Committee on Manufactures of 1833 was told that self-acting mules were avoided because "labour is cheap and machinery dear" (Q. 2651); also that the Americans chiefly used home-made machinery, especially for the coarser kinds of goods. Large use was made of wood, because iron was dear; and American contrivance had already enabled each operative to control several looms for the simpler kinds of work. A Connecticut manufacturer said to them, "In making fine yarn we lay aside all our advantages, and have to take up all our disadvantages" (see Q. 640, 2649—50, 2678—9).

APP. G, 2. many, though not nearly all, manufactures had great latent powers of economy through production on a large scale; and that those who pioneered the way had a *primâ facie* claim to public aid in the public interest. But unfortunately such aid, when given in the form of Protective duties, is seldom free from serious indirect evils, economic, political and moral, which cannot be discussed here. A little may however be said as to some peculiar features of the American controversy in the middle of the nineteenth century.

The advocates of Protection to manufactures were able to argue that the main source of America's wealth lies in her great expanse of rich agricultural land very much more even than in her mineral resources: that the farmers had been allowed to appropriate that land; and that therefore there was no injustice in compelling them to contribute to the building up of progressive industries, which would enrich them, or at all events those who inherited their properties. This end, if desirable, might perhaps have been better attained by other means than those which were advocated by the manufacturing interests: but their argument was not without force. The agriculturists could however reply that they, or their predecessors in title, had only availed themselves of opportunities for hard, if not hazardous, ventures, which were open to every one: that no exclusive favour had been granted to them after they had once committed themselves to their tasks; and that therefore they were not in a similar position to manufacturers who asked for favours, which their predecessors in title had protested were not to be expected after the first difficulties had been overcome. "No one," said Clay in 1840, "in the commencement of the protective policy ever supposed that it was to be perpetual. We hoped and believed that temporary protection extended to our import manufactures would bring them up and enable them to withstand competition with those of Europe." And in 1860, when the tarif was again raised after some fluctuations, very little was heard about the need of educating young industries.

APP. G, 3.

3. *Subsequently more stress was laid on instances of malign underselling by British manufacturers. Statistical evidence as to the influence of high tarifs on national prosperity is necessarily inconclusive.*

By 1860 the most prominent manufactures had emerged from their infancy; and obtained increased voting power at the polls by that very increase in their strength which lessened their moral claims to the support of the patriotic citizen. Politicians therefore had a strong motive for attracting the votes of those interested in manufactures, and especially those which could not claim the protection due to the weakness of infancy without provoking the amusement and the anger of the general public. Consequently they were compelled to fall back on arguments, which had no special connection with the peculiar conditions of the rapid development of a Continent by an alert western nation: and these they found in exaggerations of the harm caused by the occasional descent of some British manufacturers to the hateful practice of selling below full cost in America in order to crush rivals less amply provided with capital.

Adam Smith protested against those Mercantilist practices, by which each nation strove to flourish through the misfortunes of others: and his chief successors held high the banner of international comity which he had raised. The common man is indeed apt to justify modes of conduct by his own country to others, which he would condemn as mean or oppressive in the relations of private life; and English manufacturers and statesmen have been ready to boast of the commercial injury which their policy would inflict upon other nations. But this temper brings its own penalty in the life of nations, even more surely than in the life of individuals. And amidst the new commercial problems which England is required to face at the present time, attention may be called to the fact that the high Protectionist policy of America, from which England has been a chief sufferer, was largely due to the sedulous spreading among the American people of stories as to her own ungenerous dealings, which had unfortunately some solid foundation.

For instance great stress was laid by protectionist writers on the alleged fact that "upon the adoption of the first tariff law in the United States in 1792, the merchants of Manchester

APP. G, 3. contributed $250,000 to be invested in goods, to be sold in the markets of the United States at low prices, or to be given away if necessary, in order to discourage the investment of capital in manufacturing."

Again List quotes from an American official Report Brougham's saying in 1815 that "it is worth while to incur a loss on the exportation of English manufactures in order to stifle in the cradle foreign manufactures." And an American witness told an English Committee in 1833, that the English cotton manufacturers sent goods, that were a little out of fashion, to America to be sold for what they would fetch; "preferring to do it where it would do the most mischief to their competitors" and "with a view to breaking up the system of manufacturing in America[1]."

Perhaps the most frequently quoted statement is one taken from the Report of the Committee on the state of industry in the mining districts in 1854. In England it never attracted much notice and was speedily forgotten: but in earlier decades almost every American had it brought to his notice. It begins: "The labouring classes generally in the manufacturing districts of this country, and especially in the iron and coal districts, are very little aware of the extent, to which they are often indebted for being employed at all, to the immense losses which their employers voluntarily incur in bad times in order to destroy foreign competition, and to gain and keep possession of foreign markets. The great capitals of this country are the great instruments of warfare against the competing capital of foreign countries, and are the most essential instruments now remaining by which our manufacturing supremacy can be maintained."

It is probable that the injury done to American manufactures by all these paltry processes of international warfare was small; and certainly less than that which has been worked in America and elsewhere by manufacturers and traders who sell below cost price in their own country, not under the goad of necessity, but with the deliberate intention of supplanting a

[1] List, *National System*, p. 87; and *Report of Committee on Manufactures of* 1833, Q. 845—854. See also Carey, *Social Science*, I. pp. 289—291; and Curtiss, *Protection and prosperity*, p. 408.

neighbour. Such as it was, however, the injury roused a patriotic indignation, and was systematically exploited for the furtherance of their own ends, alike by interested manufacturers and by disinterested advocates of a Protective policy[1].

Statistical evidence relating to our own times is apt to be distorted by personal bias, of which neither party to current controversy is willing to acquit the other. There may be therefore some advantage in attempting to gauge the difficulties of interpreting such evidence by reference to a notable controversy of past times. Now as then statements as to sales of imports below cost, with the malign purpose of ruining home manufactures, were commonly based on particular cases: but statistical evidence was brought to show that Protection raised national prosperity in general.

A chief difficulty arose from lack of agreement as to the length of time which elapsed between a tarif change and the full development of any of its good or evil results. For the time to be allowed would vary with the nature of the product, and also with the character of the good or evil result under discussion; and each case needed to be treated on its own merits: but on this point no agreement was reached, or even systematically sought. And since tarif changes followed one another at intervals shorter than might reasonably be claimed for the full development of their results, advocates of free trade were apt to think that advocates of Protection attributed a benefit to a high tarif, which should more properly be put to the credit of a low tarif which preceded or which followed it: and *vice versâ*.

[1] Much stress was laid on this class of facts in Thomson's *National Economy* (see especially p. 285). It was based on Carey's work, and was the chief text-book of American Protectionists several decades ago.

Inquiries made in America in 1875 convinced me that the relatively few cases of such practices as had occurred in an earlier generation, had had some considerable influence in checking new industrial experiments, through the effect which they exercised on the imagination. For those who were contemplating a bold venture often knew their own stocks of capital to be small, and had formed exaggerated notions of the amount of English capital ready to be devoted to underselling them. In Ontario at that time the rising manufactures were still weak technically and were poorly supplied with capital: so it seemed clear that there was real cause to dread the hostile selling of American goods at special export prices. But there was no evidence that the well-established and rich industries of the United States had then any great cause for fear in this matter.

APP. G, 3. Again the tarif did not affect directly more than a small fraction of the industry of the country; and, while its results for good or evil were being developed, other changes often occurred, which modified the bases of national prosperity. Such changes were the growth of the European demand for American produce; which was in some measure dependent on changes in European tarifs, and even more on the development of improved means of transport by land and water, at home and abroad. Again changes in currency and credit altered temporarily or permanently the real value of the money unit in which prosperity was measured; and so on. Disputants on either side were apt sometimes partially to ignore these disturbing causes, and sometimes to attach to them vast importance. How could the questions thus at issue be decided? The most refined and elaborate analysis, the most patient and intimate study of details were needed as a preparation for the task: and though it may be over bold to say that the task can never be performed, it is certain that no one has claimed to perform it, who has realized any considerable part of its difficulty. For the present, though probably not for ever, it is true that in this matter "the inductive or historical method absolutely fails us[1]."

[1] This is the conclusion of Prof. Taussig's profound study (*Tariff History of the United States,* p. 122) in regard to the period in view. He continues the argument on similar lines down to recent times: but the issues raised then are not appropriate to the present volume.

It may be noted that Carey's *Social Science* and Grosvenor's *Does Protection Protect?*, basing themselves on almost identical statements of fact, applied them, the one to prove that nothing but good had ever resulted from a high tarif and nothing but evil from a low tarif; and the other to prove the exact opposites. I endeavoured on my return from America in 1875 to form an independent opinion by tracing in a book (each page of which contained a hundred horizontal lines, one for each year of the nineteenth century) curves showing all the available and relevant statistics for the United States and other countries; grouping each class on a separate page, and writing across the page brief statements of relevant events which were not in statistical form. That plan led me to the conclusion that each party to the controversy unconsciously stretched or compressed, so as to suit his case, the length of time which he supposed to elapse between a particular tarif charge and its chief results. But in this matter, as well as in the neglect of important causes relevant to the issues under discussion, the laxity seemed greater on the Protectionist than on the Free-trade side.

APPENDIX H

TECHNICAL INFLUENCES ON AGGREGATION IN PARTICULAR INDUSTRIES[1]

1. *Influences of way-leaves: railways; petroleum wells; water and gas supply and postal industries. The mining industry.*

APP. H, 1.

High roads have often been broken up into short divisions, each under a separate management; and bridges, which are vital links in them, have been private property. But in every case public authority has regulated the tolls which might be levied: for otherwise tolls at any one link might be so heavy as to choke through traffic, and thus in effect to be taxes on all the neighbouring links.

Railways were originally designed as high roads: anyone was to be free to run a train in return for fixed tolls. But as the trains became faster and more numerous, and long distance traffic became more common, each company needed to have exclusive control of its own traffic; and ere long consecutive links were welded into a compact unit, with through trains and an organized time table for them. Such fusions increased the services which the railways could render to the public, and were generally welcomed. They were not open to the objections, raised against a combination between parallel lines, that they created powerful monopolies: and indeed, by supplying new alternative routes between distant industrial centres, they often introduced effective competition as regards services, if not as regards charges, where it was much needed in the public interests. So the main lines have gone from strength to strength: they have increased in length, and their feeders have

[1] This Appendix is associated with the second and third chapters of Book II. Its introductory remarks as to railways refer briefly to matters discussed more fully in Book III.

APP. H, 1. multiplied. The consolidation of railways has proceeded almost without interruption in nearly every country of the world, in which they are not all in the hands of Government; and the power of a great railway to starve out small independent railways within its domain has often proved irresistible, in spite of legislative efforts against it.

The plant of great railways may of course become obsolete, and need to be changed. But (it being assumed that the aerial traffic will not supersede that on the surface of the earth) their position as landowners will ever increase in strength; and will, as a rule, be the stronger the longer their strips of land, and the more numerous the industrial centres which they connect. Improvements in the construction of ordinary roads may indeed enable nearly all detailed trade, and personal traffic over moderate distances, to pass in motor cars on public highways; but the hold of railways on long distance heavy, but rapid, carriage of goods and passengers seems not to be threatened.

A petroleum well has much in common with the shaft of a mine: but when access to the surface is once provided, the oil generally rises to the surface automatically under the pressure of its own beds: and in many places the industry of crude petroleum is a transport industry, dependent in great part on long pipe lines. These need large way-leaves; and thus resemble in many respects the pipes and wires along which water, gas and electricity travel in that large group of undertakings which are often described as practically "indivisible"; because a breach in continuity of transport would be very wasteful.

The way-rights of this group of industries are essential to them, and make large use of public property. Therefore they have attracted the attention of Local Authorities; and are beginning to claim that of Central Governments. For instance, the bringing of water supply from Wales or the English Lake District to large cities in remote counties is apt to raise conflicts of interest among the various localities affected; and thus to give rise to large national problems. Similar conflicts have arisen in regard to municipal tramways, when they shoot out feeders into districts under the control of several Local Authorities. But the ever enlarging enterprise of motor traffic on public roads is throwing such controversies into the shade: for it has concentrated the searchlights of public inquiry on the suggestion that the provision of a system of main roads, open freely to all, and extending over the whole country, must be regarded as a single transport business, so immense that the nation as a whole is alone fully qualified to undertake it.

Somewhat similar remarks are applicable to the great transport and communication industries of the Post Office, Telegraph and Telephone. The most costly business of all, that of national defence, is of necessity unified, so far at least, that its strategy can be treated as a whole: and it is to be noted that strategy involves mobilization, that is transport and communication: and railways themselves, if not owned by Government, are necessarily taken under its control in war time.

The command of all convenient routes of access to the shore, where it offers sites for deep-water berths, might be a source of great monopolistic power, were not the charges of docks controlled by public authority. Again owners of land surrounding a rich mine might charge way-leaves, which would absorb nearly the whole net profits of the mine, if the law had not provided against it.

Although mining is commonly classed as a "productive" industry, yet, since the plant of a large mine is little more than a long series of narrow railways through long tunnels, with a few shafts for vertical traffic, it is in fact very much of a transport industry; and unbroken continuity from the face of the working to the top of the shaft is essential to it. This may be a small matter if the rich veins lie near to the surface; and in such a case, a small mine can hold its own against a large one, provided it works for local consumption, and can be well financed locally. The main causes of the general increase in the size of mining concerns in old countries are, that the veins near the surface are becoming exhausted: and that improved and cheaper apparatus for hoisting, together with increased value of the product, causes shafts to be sunk very deep; and deep shafts cannot pay their way without long lines of railway underground.

APP. H, 2.

2. *Electricity in the service of man.*

It is well known that the business of the military strategist is to bring fighting power to bear promptly and decisively on each critical issue as it arises: electricity enables energy to be brought to bear instantly where and when needed, not indeed without some limitations, but in general much more easily and efficiently than can be done by any other means; and this over both large distances and small. The expense of a copper cable of sufficient diameter to carry a large volume of electricity without much waste over long distances is indeed heavy. But there are already many cases in which electricity generated by water power, by the waste gases of furnaces, and by burning inferior coal at the pit's mouth, is used to light far off cities and to work railways, factories, etc. at a distance. Rand mines receive power brought from several rather distant waterfalls: and it has even been suggested that Alpine streams in summer, and Rhine-Westphalian coal in winter (when most of the Alpine streams are frozen) will supply electricity for a good deal of western Germany. The economic value of great waterfalls is indeed apt to be exaggerated, especially when little account is taken of the seasonal variations in their volume: but there is reason to believe that small streams, descending from great heights, may ultimately be an important source of energy available for domestic and industrial uses. Something may also be expected from the co-ordinated use of multitudes of small inexpensive windmills; and perhaps even from the rise and fall of the sea, provided that good and cheap means of storing electricity can be discovered[1].

The economy of powerful generating engines is of course within the range of the large manufacturer; and at first it seemed probable that the small manufacturer would have to pay a good deal more for the energy, which he bought from a central supply company, than it cost to his more powerful rival.

[1] The rise and fall of the tides cannot be utilized without disproportionate expense, save under very exceptional conditions. On the other hand (as has been observed above, p. 162) the sun's heat may conceivably be turned to account so effectively as greatly to raise the economic strength of the tropical zones relatively to the temperate zones; provided a supply of water, or some other cooling agent, is accessible.

But in fact a municipality or private company, which supplies a considerable district with electricity, can produce it more cheaply than almost any other undertaking can (the chief exceptions being found where electricity can be obtained by turning to account the heat of waste gases); and it can supply energy with greater steadfastness and uniformity than anyone else can. It can produce cheaply because its numerous customers are likely to spread their aggregate demand for *power* not very unevenly over nearly twelve hours of the day: and therefore the maximum load for which the central supply has to make provision is much less than the aggregate of the maximum loads for which provision would need to be made by the individual consumers independently. Also it can supply a steady driving force; because the draft, made on its strength by the sudden starting of one of the heavy machines driven by it, is practically negligible in proportion to the total energy which it is producing; while the same cannot be said of the private electrical supply even of a very large factory. This steadiness of work is especially important in regard to looms and other machines which need to be started smoothly at the same pace as that of their normal working: and the small textile manufacturer, who buys his electricity, can use a separate motor for each machine more safely than can almost any rival who makes his own electricity.

It has recently been proposed by responsible persons to link up the whole country through central power stations placed at the most economical points and near coal. By this means it is claimed that fifty million tons of coal annually would be saved; and also a great part of the present immense cost of transporting coal large distances. There seems good reason to hope that some tentative steps will soon be taken in this direction.

On the whole then it may be concluded that the advance of the electrical industries will help the small factory in competition with the large factory, and the workshop in competition with the factory, etc. The cheapness, handiness, and versatility of the implements, to which electricity can be supplied, may sometimes aid the poor man to make experiments at his own risk; and it may thus contribute to the maintenance of strong, independent, individual character. In this it will cooperate with or perhaps supersede oil and gas engines, which are now its rivals in many uses. The importance of electricity in connection with past and probable future developments of the technique and ownership of transport agencies and other businesses belongs to other parts of our study.

3. *The expansion of the carrying capacity of ships, and of the business unit in the shipping industry.*

The services which water has rendered to industry and trade always have been so general as to be inconspicuous; and therefore apt to be underrated. But water power was the first to raise hopes that mankind might be eased from severe toil by the benignant help of Nature[1]. Water power inaugurated the modern era; in which man directs while Nature does nearly all the hard work, and in consequence massive production has marched from victory to victory. No heavy commerce could be carried over long distances even a hundred years ago, except by water; and in some parts of the world wells are, even now, the most important forms of fixed plant. Water has ever been an absolute necessary to all, and has opened out large opportunities for the wealthy.

Ships have always been the largest things that have moved under man's control, for the same reason that the largest animals find their home in the seas. Nature's forces were first harnessed to the work when a boat was set to run before the wind, while man sat in the stern to steer with a pole. Sails were developed, and set to tack against the wind: ships increased in size and speed; and man no longer used his own muscles, even when aided by a windlass, to control the massive rudder. He

[1] As to the hopes raised by water power, Karl Marx quotes Antiparos, a Greek poet, whose elegiacs may be rendered thus:

"Spare now your weary limbs, ye women that work at the hand-mill;
Spare them, and sleep while the cock crows to awake you in vain.
For the good water-nymphs have undertaken your labour,
And they hop lightly along over the spokes of the wheel:
So that the great thing turns on its axle, ceaselessly groaning,
Making the vast mill-stones grind out the nourishing corn.
Let us then live the light lives of our fathers, and resting from labour,
Gladly enjoy the rich gifts granted by bounteous Gods."

harnessed steam power in that work also, calling electricity to his aid for its easy transmission; and now he merely moves an easy handle, which directs the power to direct the rudder, to direct the course of a ship that carries the population of a good sized town with all their effects across the Atlantic in five or six days. For, when once a ship has become so large that almost every part of its equipment is too heavy to be moved by hand, every further increase of size must bring economies with it. A navigating officer can direct the course of a big ship as easily as of a small one. An increase in the size of winches and cranes driven by steam and electricity adds nothing to the difficulty, and not very much to the responsibility, of turning the handles which set them in motion.

Meanwhile the improved organization of appliances for lifting heavy masses, and sucking up grain in bulk from the hold of the ship to warehouses or railway trucks, enables the largest ship to discharge its old cargo, take a new one and depart in less than a quarter of the time that was required by a small ship fifty years ago. Therefore large ports which accommodate very big ships, and can supply a continuous large stream of passengers, or goods, or both, have an ever increasing advantage over smaller ports: and so on.

This tendency is of course most marked in regard to long distance traffic. Coasting vessels and those which trade in the narrow seas will long continue to frequent small and shallow harbours: coal is still carried most cheaply to some English villages by vessels which "jump upon the sands," very much as their Dutch prototypes did many centuries ago: and the long threatened extinction of "tramp" traders by the competition of the subsidiary cargo ships of the large lines, is constantly being deferred by the opening out of new trades for the cheaply built, versatile tramp of moderate size. But, while the average size of the vessels that enter the Eastern ports of England and Scotland is likely to continue to be rather small, it seems probable that the chief trade across the Atlantic, and between it and the Pacific will be carried in very large ships. A few passenger ships will be very fast; but, as coal and oil become dearer, very large cargo ships will make long voyages with a consumption of fuel for each thousand tons of cargo very

APP. H, 3. much below that which is customary now. So long as coal remains cheap, a slight economy in its use per ton of freight carried at a given pace seems to be practically of less importance than the numerous advantages which a ship of moderate size has over a large one in making up its cargo. Nevertheless the expansion of the shipping unit has had an important influence on the size of the business unit in the shipping industry, as is indicated in Book III, Chapter III.

However great had been the commercial demand for very large ships, it could not have been satisfied until not only the scientific construction of the girder bridge, of which the large ship is a noble example, had made great progress; but also the methods and plant of the steel industries had reached a very high development: larger still are the demands which the great navies make on that industry[1].

[1] The manufacture of a huge armour plate needs the concurrent efforts of several of the most powerful fixed machines; and all independent movements must be intrusted to locomotives. A chief task of the most costly cranes, is to handle naval cannon; and the armour of a big ship weighs several times as much as all its cannon, though it carries twelve of the largest size: the ship, in which Columbus discovered America, could not bear a cargo whose total weight equalled that of one of them, together with its mountings, etc.

APPENDIX I

NOTES ON THE DEVELOPMENT OF BROAD MARKETS FOR GRAIN AND OTHER CRUDE PRODUCTS[1]

1. *The catastrophic condition of food supply in early times and its gradual improvement.*

APP. I, 1.

This Appendix supplements the account of wheat exchanges in II, v, first by developing Maitland's great dictum that "agrarian history becomes the more catastrophic, the further we trace it backwards"; and secondly by a few remarks on recent movements towards the organization of markets for cotton and some other crude products.

There have been vast improvements, mechanical, chemical, and biological in the arts of agriculture: but grain is raised, and its flour is prepared for food and consumed on essentially the same plans now as in the time of the Pharaohs; though the processes of milling, and the methods of the marketing of grain, belong in the main to the age of steam and electricity. In fact a modern wheat market is as representative of modern ideas, as the wheat field and the loaf of bread are of the unchanging elements in human life. Further, so closely has man's progress depended on the supply of his "daily bread," that the history of the economic well-being of the great bulk of mankind has been commonly taken to be almost convertible with the history of the ordinary family income, expressed in terms of the staple grain of the country. No other economic records are so continuous and definite as those connected with the prices of staple grains; and the history of countries with a fairly dense population shows no instance, until recent times, in which the incomes of the great mass of the people exceeded very greatly the price of the grain needed for their sustenance.

[1] This Appendix is associated with the fifth chapter of Book II.

APP. I, 1. For this reason, records of the price of grain, in normal and in abnormal years, afford the best simple measure for comparisons of the real purchasing power of money over many centuries; as is to be argued in a complementary Volume to the present. But, while the average value of grain in terms of human life has been fairly stationary over the centuries, its price has often varied greatly between neighbouring districts at the same time: and it has fluctuated violently from one year to another, in all those ages and places in which the marketing of grain over long distances was impracticable.

These exceptional features of the value of grain were probably always recognized more or less by thoughtful people. But they were first clearly set out about a hundred years ago, when Tooke convinced the Commission on the Depression of Agriculture, 1821, that an exceptional "principle" applies to staple grain; because a fall in its price cannot generally increase its consumption as human food; and, when it becomes dear, people will still buy enough of it to keep them alive so long as they have any means of purchase: in modern phraseology the demand for it is exceptionally inelastic[1].

Under the rule of Rome the ports of the Mediterranean were united into a coherent market of wheat, and were connected with a network of good roads. But during the greater part of history, few places, that were not near to great waters, could draw any considerable supply from distant lands, to meet their urgent demand when faced by a continued deficiency of their harvests.

Gradually traffic by land and sea became easier and less perilous, while local monopolies were weakened by a growth of movable capital; and consequently the irregularities in prices from place to place gradually diminished. England has been less severely and less frequently devastated by wars than other

[1] The Report, drafted by Huskisson, quoted Tooke's statement (see Tooke and Newmarch, *History of Prices*, vol. v. p. 69). It is of course true that when wheat is scarce, inferior grains, potatoes, etc., may be taken from livestock and used as human food: but Tooke had collected evidence, which has been enlarged recently, that an exceptional cheapness of wheat does not cause the well-to-do working classes to eat more bread; though some wheat is lost through negligent treatment on the farm and in the kitchen and some is fed to cattle, and some stands over for future consumption. It appears that the present large consumption of wheat in the United States is due to similar causes.

European countries: almost all of her territory has been reached by imported grain, without the need of any long land journey; and the central authority has been able to overrule the desires of Provincial Governments to set up barriers against their neighbours. It might therefore be expected that her history of grain prices would be less catastrophic than that of other European countries: and this appears to have been the case. But strange variations are occasionally recorded even as regards English prices. Thus Macpherson tells us that in 1288 the price of wheat was five times as high in London as in the North and West of England: and in nearly all the years, in the period 1259—1400 for which Rogers has more than a few entries of wheat prices, his highest is at least twice as great as his lowest; while in many it is three times as great. The intensity of these local variations diminished irregularly on the way through the centuries: and so did the fluctuations from year to year; at all events when exceptions are made for times of civil war and unrule, and for currency disturbances[1].

Similar results have been collected for France by d'Avenel from a very broad and fairly homogeneous basis. Her movement towards steady conditions was broken by internal wars, religious and other; and by foreign wars, especially those of Louis XIV, and the exhaustion which followed them: but in the main it was on the same lines as those of the English movement[2].

[1] Rogers' results are smoothened, perhaps unduly, by his rule to omit, as possibly erroneous, all extreme quotations; and by his obtaining the greater part of his data from Monasteries, Colleges and other great corporations, which bought generally wholesale, and often from great distances: some of them even brought their wheat habitually by sea and river from remote parts of the country (*History*, IV. p. 213). His practice of assuming that all payments were measured in weight may have overrated some local variations and underrated others: and wages, when paid in silver at all, were sure to be reckoned by tale; and therefore he seems likely to have overrated the purchasing power of wages generally. Internal trade in grain was permitted only to licensed dealers during the greater part of English history. In 1663 it was permitted to everyone so long as the price of corn did not exceed 48*s*. The main outlines of these movements of law and opinion are shown clearly in the chronological tables inserted in Walford's *Famines of the World*.

[2] France lacked the advantage possessed by England of being able to draw grain by water carriage from distant places nearly up to distressed districts: and her records often show the highest local price to be ten times as great as the lowest for the same year. But d'Avenel, *Histoire économique de la propriété...et des prix* 1200—1800, boldly undertakes to reduce the silver content of coins, and

APP. I, 1. Let us turn from the West to the East. Indian records extending back into the eighteenth century show violent fluctuations of prices even in great central markets, such as Delhi: they show much more violent changes in secondary markets; while, in places remote from any metalled road, their movement upwards was limited only by the price of a man's life, after a series of bad harvests; and by the value of the grain as fuel, after a series of good harvests. Gradually the local unevennesses were smoothed out by the making of metalled roads and railways. Thus Sir Theodore Morison tells us that in the eighteenth century, and even later, a village of Northern India, which did not lie on its one great metalled road, and had no share in its scanty water communication, was in effect isolated: there was but slender accommodation in shallow grain pits for the surplusses of successive good harvests: and after bad harvests when those pits were exhausted, there was practically no further reserve on which to draw: so the price of the village went its own way, with but little reference to the prices even of the neighbouring country. But now "the whole of Northern India is practically one market for food grains, and the price of wheat in a district in which the crops have failed is the same, with but a very small addition for the cost of carriage, as the price in a district which had a bumper harvest." In regard to India generally he concludes that before 1850 prices fluctuated violently, and fluctuated in different localities independently. After 1860 they were comparatively stable, and fluctuated simultaneously[1].

the varying measures of grain, to modern units. His diagram, representing mean prices for the years 1200—1890, is a document of surpassing instruction. All that can be done here is to select almost at random a few groups of the prices, which he records (reduced to francs, or their equivalents in silver, per hectolitre) for different places. In 1180 they varied from 0·87 to 16·60; in 1250 from 2·60 to 31·00; in 1313 from 8·37 to 36·00; in 1315 from 2·47 to 28·63; in 1464 from 0·56 to 7·85. The years about 1420 were exceptionally disturbed by local famines and shiftings of currency: and (neglecting entries marked as doubtful), we find 2·82 and 61·80 in 1419; 12·07 and 79·03, both for Paris, in 1421, a year in which Strasburg shows 3·68: while Albi shows 152·22 in 1422 and 14·64 in 1423, a year in which Strasburg shows 2·72.

[1] *Indian Industrial Organisation,* pp. 172, 216, 305. He quotes the following inverted prices into the rupee for a chief grain (Gram) in Lower Bengal: 1714, 130; 1774, 16; 1751, 70; 1752, 20; 1756, 59; 1769, 15; 1790, 90; 1792, 36; 1794, 82. (*Ib.* p. 293.) Variations of inverted prices are of course

We are thus brought to consider, from a different point of view, those characteristics of custom, which have already (II, II, 1) been noted in relation to the development of technique. There is a sense in which it is true that custom dominates early forms of civilization; for in them status and methods of work, utensils and implements are all ruled by custom: and, though even in such matters, custom is found on investigation to be much more plastic than it appears to those who live under its sway; yet conscious, deliberate, direct breaches of custom were undoubtedly very rare. Wages also were in large measure governed by custom; though they varied greatly between neighbouring localities under influences, which cannot now be traced. Of course they often consisted largely of board or allowances: these, not being rigidly defined, had large scope for fluctuation in times of scarcity: and, then as now, harvest wages varied more than others in accordance with passing circumstances.

Thus, even in these relations of life in which custom appeared to hold sway, its authority was temporarily overthrown by the near approach of famine: and it was undermined, when the population of any locality had so far outgrown the means of subsistence that some emigration was almost compulsory; or, on the other hand, had been decimated by plague or flood or any other calamity. There seems to be no evidence that it ever had any sway at all over the market prices of harvest products or of cattle: and dealings in these were far more important than any other among primitive agricultural peoples[1].

variations in the amount of a thing that can be bought for a rupee, or other uniform payment.

The following peaks and depressions of inverted prices for the period 1763—1800 for wheat at Delhi, are taken from a paper by the Chaplain to the East India Company in the *Statistical Journal*, 1843, p. 248: 1763, 20; 1768, 47; 1773, 10; 1777, 60; 1783, 6; 1787, 45; 1792, 12; 1798, 120. Reference may also be made to a paper by Colonel Sykes in the *Statistical Journal*, 1847, pp. 289—316; and to diagrams relating to Indian prices in the last century, prepared by the present writer and published in the *Report of the Committee on the Indian Currency*, 1899.

[1] Conversations held some years ago with experienced Indian administrators, in which the practice of Indian village dealings in agricultural products, and the minor commodities of the Hat (or village market), was compared with the deal ings of the villagers in remote English rural districts, led me to the conclusion that custom had less to do, and keen bargaining had more to do, with the purchases of Indian Raiyats than with those of the English village. It may be

APP. I, 1. The revolution effected by modern methods of transport is conspicuous, when the conditions of mediaeval Europe or of India a hundred years ago are compared with those, under which the populations of Western Europe draw large supplies of wheat from new countries. But many new countries would still be poorly provided with railways, if they were dependent on their own stocks of capital: technical advance is the chief source of their prosperity; but it would not have availed them very much, had not the capital needed for marketing their crops been mostly provided from external sources. It is true that they are dependent on their own resources for making roads: but that difficulty is partly overcome by trusting to railways, made by external capital, to do most of their transport; while they themselves make but few roads, and those of poor quality. For in the West of America "the average cost of transportation on wagon roads has been estimated at about 25 cents per ton per mile, and on the best improved roads in this country [America] between 10 and 15 cents, as compared with 8 cents on some European roads, one half of one cent by railroad, and one mill by steamship on the Great Lakes[1]."

Railway and other companies build elevators to store and grade this grain; and these aided by "loan companies, banks, implement companies, and general dealers" all help to make it

hoped that suggestions derived from studies of India and other countries in like conditions, conducted in the spirit of Maitland and Professor Vinogradoff, may explain many of the apparent paradoxes of English mediaeval history: and show that custom is often the gradual result of economic conditions; even where it appears at first sight to be their governing cause, rather than their effect. Contemporary facts, statistical and other, can be cross-examined freely: fragmentary records of past times cannot. Something more is said on this subject in my *Principles*, VI, x, 3; and in my *Present position of Economics*, 1885.

[1] *Report of the Industrial Commission*, about 1900 A.D., vol. I. p. lv.

Some reasons, independent of the lack of capital, militate against the making of good roads in districts whose atmospheric and geological conditions are those of the chief wheat regions of Canada and the United States, and in parts of Russia. Stone is not easy to be had in vast stretches of prairie land: a cart can make its way over the prairie in dry summer, and a sledge moves easily over the snow in winter. And when the country was being opened up, the first connections between considerable towns were often effected by broad gauge railways, which cost less to make than good roads: in 1875 I travelled between two considerable towns whose only connection was, for this reason, by railway.

"possible to bring a vast area under cultivation by means of a relatively small amount of agricultural capital[1]." The economies of the world market for wheat are mainly due to improvements in transport, and the communication of news; combined with modern facilities for bringing command over capital from rich districts to those which hunger for it. And as we have seen above (pp. 258—262) they owe much to subdivision and specialization of the risks of constructive speculation, such as would have been impossible without the aid of an organized market. The farmer can now either sell his wheat, and set all his capital in it free at once: or he can store it, if he expects its price to rise, and meanwhile borrow money on it.

2. *Cotton Exchanges. Partially organized markets for wool and some other crude products.*

While the most important markets for products in the world are those that deal in staple grains, and especially wheat; the next most important are those connected with cotton. The cotton markets of New York, New Orleans, and Liverpool are intimately associated; and may for some purposes be regarded almost as a single market. Together they practically control the price movements of the chief sorts of cotton for the whole world.

The grading of cotton is a more delicate and difficult affair than that of grain. For the manufacturer of cotton stuffs is generally very nice in regard to the quality of the yarn on which he works: and therefore the spinners must be equally nice as to the quality of their raw material. Further, as payments for work in cotton mills are chiefly by the piece, the introduction of inappropriate material is apt to breed friction; and it often leads to disputes, that are more costly than the direct losses occasioned by slight faults in the product. Partly for this reason, a heavy strain is placed on those, whose duty it is to adjust the differences that must be paid when cotton is tendered, which is not exactly of a standard grade, but yet is so near to it as to be good tender. It might appear that the

[1] See Professor Mavor's illuminating article on "The economic results of specialist production and marketing of wheat," *Pol. Sc. Quarterly*, Dec. 1911.

APP. I, 2. difficulty should be solved by still further curtailing the range of sorts which may be offered as legal tender in lieu of the exact standard grade. But that course would much increase the chance that a powerful clique might succeed in engineering a "corner": for it might buy cotton (or wheat) of a specified grade for delivery at a certain date to a greater amount than the total stock available; and thus be able to demand ruinous terms from those who could not deliver[1].

The cotton market is more complex than the wheat market: for yarn itself is a raw material for cotton cloths which are themselves raw materials for many industries: and both yarn and cotton cloth are apt to be sold forward in great volume, for long periods and at prices run very fine. The spinner, who contracts to deliver yarn at a price, generally secures himself by buying futures of raw cotton: and the manufacturer undertakes engagements for the delivery of piece goods a long while in advance; because spinners or brokers are willing to undertake to deliver to him, at prices and times specified beforehand, such qualities and quantities of yarns as he may desire. Even the broker dealing in raw cotton often buys "futures" to match each of his sales; for his sales are apt to be in some narrowly specified sort of cotton, and his dealings on the general market must be in a standard grade: he thus bears himself only the risk that the sort of cotton which he has contracted to deliver

[1] There has consequently been some tendency to enlarge the range of sorts that may be offered on payment of a difference, in spite of the fact that a miller or spinner may be much inconvenienced by failing to get almost exactly what he wants: for it has been observed that such success as has been reached by attempts at corners on wheat and cotton exchanges, has been largely caused by the narrowness of the range allowed. And indeed it has been suggested that the authorities of an exchange should be empowered to relax the rigidity of the rules (several methods have been suggested), when divergence of the prices at the time of settlement for the contract quality differs widely from those for other qualities at the time, and from prices for that quality in the past, and in terms of rather distant futures.

The Report of the U.S.A. Commissioner of Corporations on *Cotton Exchanges*, 1908—1909, devotes the greater part of three considerable volumes to a study of the advantages and difficulties of the various methods adopted in various Cotton Exchanges, notably those of New York and New Orleans: the general upshot apparently is that the Committee of the Exchange should adjust those differences from time to time to existing commercial conditions; in spite of the possibility that their decisions may on rare occasions be biassed by their own interests, or by the manœuvres of powerful speculators.

will rise relatively to that which he has bought. But as in the parallel case of a wheat market, this is a small affair. Dealings in yarn futures have never been common except in England; and it appears that they are declining, in consequence of the tendency to an increase of the differences in value between yarns of different makers, which would be classed together in an official grading.

Futures in cotton are quoted many months ahead and may therefore exercise some direct influence on the sowings of the coming crop: but at present cotton growers are less alert than the greater part of those who grow wheat for export. The influence of organized marketing has gone together with a very great diminution in the addition, which is made to the price received by the grower for raw cotton, by the time the cotton reaches the manufacturer: and there seems good reason to believe that it has contributed to this result; though the development of railways, telegraphs and telephones has no doubt been the dominant cause of it. Until recently it appeared that the same causes had combined to diminish the fluctuations in the price of cotton. But between 1900 and 1909 these fluctuations increased; and for this retrogression the reckless use of the future system must be held in part responsible[1].

Wool cannot be graded as easily as cotton. Not merely does each fleece present widely different qualities, which must be "sorted" before they can be used: but, further, each district has its own varieties; and, even if the breeds were all the same, differences of soil and climate would soon differentiate them. Consequently a bale of English wool is apt to be of uncertain

[1] The Commissioner of Corporations, *l.c.* vol. III. p. 304, seems to prove this. The movements of cotton prices during the world-war are yielding matter for an instructive study at a later date.

A good deal has been written as to causes and results of the absence of organized markets for cotton in Germany. The chief causes seem to be the lack of concentration of German cotton industries; and the great distance of Bremen, the chief port of importation of cotton, from any of them. It is however to be noted that Bremen traders could speculate freely on the Liverpool exchange; and, what is more important, they were able to insure constructive ventures by "hedging" operations there. See also the papers on "Anticipation in the cotton market," and "Dealings in futures in the cotton market" by Chapman and Knoop, *Economic Journal*, 1904, and *Statistical Journal*, 1906.

APP. I, 2. quality, and to trouble the manufacturer by not being throughout perfectly adapted to exactly the same methods of handling. This difficulty is less in the case of wool from new countries. New Zealand sheep for instance are descended from similar ancestors, imported not long ago; and raised on large runs, where there is much uniformity of average circumstance and great freedom of interbreeding. Thus certain standards of imported wools give a definiteness to the great markets of London, and other large centres: while the local wools are perhaps less under international influences than are local wheat crops. Also, fashion is constantly displacing one kind of wool from a high place, and putting another in its stead; whereas what little fashion is seen in cotton goods, lies in the pattern rather than in the texture. Changes in relative values of different fibres are therefore much greater in wool than in cotton.

But still the total market for wool is so great, and the demand of the western world for woollen goods is so much less easily satiated than for cotton, that the wool market of the world is very highly organized on a pattern, which resembles that of the cotton market as closely as the difficulties of the case will allow. The Bradford Conditioning House takes samples carefully, and weighs them, before and after they have been desiccated, on machines accurate to within a twenty thousandth part of the weight tested: and it appears that markets for wool "futures" have existed at Roubaix-Turcoing and Antwerp.

There are more or less highly organized markets, in which "futures" are bought and sold, for maize, rice and other grains; for jute and other textile materials; for petroleum and for vegetable oils; for cotton seed, quinine and for many other goods. And at the centres of certain industries a large speculative business is done in some of their special products; as for instance in beef and pork products at Chicago.

We may pass to the markets for iron and metals. Some of the chief products of ore and coal can be graded fairly well: the demand for them is liable to extreme fluctuations under the influence of changes in commercial credit generally, and especially in the credit which the public accords to new joint stock companies, and to extensions of old companies. Consequently highly organized markets exist only for certain definite iron and steel bars, etc.: "futures" are sometimes sold so recklessly as to invite a corner; and the price of Scotch or Cleveland bars may rise for a time to an unreasonable level, relatively not only to the general prospects of trade, but even to the prices of other descriptions of iron and steel of substantially the same quality.

Nearly every important branch of modern industry, except agriculture, is apt to be thrown out of gear at once by a check to the supply of coal: while a check to the supply of iron, however widespread its indirect effects may be in the long run, does not strike sharply on more than a few industries. But these few are important; and their business is in general quick and urgent; partly because prompt delivery of the machinery and other plant which they produce is often essential to their customers, and is likely to be enforced by contract under rigid penalties. The largest users of iron are getting more and more into the habit of owning iron mines, with results that are studied in Book III[1].

The markets for copper and tin are highly organized and are liable to great fluctuations, and that for two reasons. One is that the old and narrow sources of supply are giving way to new and richer sources: these are largely in places remote from the chief seats of industry, and are apt to move almost as fitfully as the sources of supply of gold and silver themselves. Another reason is that these two metals are imperiously needed for certain specific purposes, and a scarcity of either may arrest, or throw out of gear, large industries. Electrical developments have indeed increased the demand for copper at an almost unparalleled rate: though some authorities hold that the demand for it, as well as for some other metals, will be largely modified by aluminium; for its abundance, lightness, electrical conductivity and strength in certain alloys seem to promise a new era when the already great progress in the methods of its production and treatment has gone a little further[2].

[1] The peculiarities of the English speculative market in iron, its relations to the world iron market, and the curious episodes of 1904—5 are described by Mr Macrosty in the *Economic Journal*, September, 1905.

[2] The control which German financiers obtained over the chief sources of some metals before the world-war, may ultimately be found to have been a contributory cause to these fluctuations.

APPENDIX J

SOME MINOR PROBLEMS OF MARKETING[1]

APP. J, 1.

1. *The costs of marketing perishable products, when demand is imperious and supply is uncertain, are always high.*

No modern has carried his demand for choice food to as extravagant lengths as Lucullus did: but all well-to-do people consume many things which would not have borne the journey to the table of Lucullus, pay what he would for them; and opportunity has developed a habit of consuming things out of season and out of place. The habit has spread downwards. It has passed over those of the middle classes, who are forced to keep up on slender means a certain dignity of house, dress and education: but it reached the better paid artisans of Anglo-Saxon countries some time ago; and it is making its way throughout the western world.

Even a century ago and even in the richest countries, only a few persons could afford to pay prices for ordinary comforts and luxuries sufficient to defray the expense of bringing them from far: the systematic massive trade over large distances for various sorts of food, to be consumed by the people at large, waited for cheap and rapid transport by railway. The leadership which England obtained in the service of railways was a chief contributory cause to the relatively luxurious life of the artisans of her cities and industrial districts in the middle of the last century[2].

[1] This Appendix is associated with the sixth and seventh chapters of Book II.

[2] In *The food of London*, "which discusses the sources of supply..., and machinery of distribution of the food for a community of two millions and a half," by George Dodd, 1856, will be found a full and suggestive account, which may be compared with present conditions. The tonnage of British steamships at that time was only a twelfth part of the whole: but they were of course

The more perishable a product is, the greater of course are the losses of the trader who handles it; and the higher the charges he must make for those parts of it, which he sells in good condition, in order that his business may be fairly profitable. But his losses may be small if the demand for the product is steady, and its supply is under perfect control. For instance, the hot morning rolls which nearly every well-to-do family before the war consumed in Continental towns could be supplied cheaply, because the demand could be anticipated before the baking began. But a Café, dependent on excursionist traffic which varies with uncertainties of weather, cannot afford to keep a supply of perishable food at low prices. And yet fruit and vegetables in rural markets are cheap: because everyone is contented to buy the things that are on hand, and little goes to waste.

Speaking generally, extreme influences of perishableness on costs of supply are exerted only when it is associated with imperiousness of demand, and with uncertainties both of demand and supply; as in the case of an imperious wealthy demand for choice fruits, flowers and fish, which pays relatively little attention to seasonal variation and temporary changes of supply. It is well known that retailers who are able to meet almost any sudden demand for things, which must on occasion be supplied from afar at great expense, and with much loss on the way, are to be found only in fashionable districts. They must devote care and expense to a certain dignity of appearance: there is seldom any effective competition to compel them to sell even

pressed into the service of perishable food. There were a good many large dairies in the outer ring (now regarded as one of the inner rings) of that "district covered with houses" called London; but in 1853 the "Eastern Counties" and other railways brought 3,000,000 quarts of milk annually from the country. It has been said, partly in earnest, both in New York and London, that a family returning from a summer holiday at a farm house had some consolation in being able henceforward to rely on a constant supply of fresh garden and dairy produce.

When passing in 1875 through boundless fields covered with cattle on either side of the Union Pacific Railway, I asked the wife of a local farmer what was the price of butter. She replied that no one took the trouble to make it, except one farmer two hundred miles down the line; he sold it for half-a-dollar a pound and sent it along the line to anyone who might want it. Similarly the early great ranch holders in California—a splendid fruit and vegetable country—when they wanted to provide delicacies for a visitor, opened a tin of Eastern peaches or pears.

APP. J, 1. common things cheaply; and their prices all round are very high[1].

The influences exerted on the price of fish by the difficulty of preserving it are notable. It can be had at low prices in East London and other places, where the popular demand for fried fish is very large and constant, and it can be obtained direct from wholesale markets. But well-to-do customers pay generally prices, that exceed those received by the fishermen, by larger percentages for the inferior than for the better kinds of fish[2].

Some apparent irregularities are seen in the retail prices of things which are joint products coming from a single source. For instance the relative prices of the better and the inferior joints of beef vary very greatly from place to place, and in some cases from season to season; because the demands for the two kinds vary irregularly. Thus in some country districts on the Continent, where beef is nearly always boiled or stewed, the prices of the best parts are not much above those of others, and are very much below those of all large cities, and of England generally: but a concourse of rich summer visitors in a place, where but few of the people eat fresh meat, will often raise the price of the best joints much above those current in England. The vast and almost exclusive demand for those joints in the fashionable quarters of London, exercises but a moderate influence on their price, because the inferior joints of the same animals are sent to the poorer districts from the central markets which supply all London[3].

[1] Universal Providers are however making some exceptions to this general rule.

[2] The prices received by the fishermen for inferior fish are generally low: but the costs of conveying them, duly preserved, through wholesale and retail dealers to customers are not much below those for the better sorts. Though the excess of retail prices for fish over those paid to the fishermen is very high; the inherent difficulties of the trade, aided perhaps by strategical movements on the part of professional dealers, have proved very fatal to attempts at its direct cooperative retail distribution.

[3] Except in very hot weather meat can be kept a long time by modern appliances: and the influence of weather on its price is most noticeable in working class districts, where such appliances are rare. On a Saturday night in summer before the war the prudent housewife could buy good meat for fourpence a pound.

2. *Influences on the costs of marketing exerted by varieties of individual requirements and tastes. Illustrations as to furniture and as to fashion goods.*

Furniture is a representative of goods, which the retailer must select with reference to the general requirements and tastes of those by whom he is surrounded. If he is situated in a working class quarter, a comparatively small stock, calling for but little thought, will satisfy nearly all demands: it can be turned over rather quickly: and, if cash payments are in vogue, it can be profitably marketed at prices not much in excess of the very low costs of the steady, massive, mechanical production of such things. It can be sold cheaply and therefore it must be sold cheaply; for his customers, especially those who buy for cash, are alert: many of them can judge fairly well the strength and durability of the things shown to them, and they are likely to have made comparisons of various stocks before purchasing.

But a wealthy district offers scarcely any scope for a shop which presents only a few varieties of each sort of furniture for inspection. It is not enough to make provision for the different scales of expenditure of the several sub-classes of the well-to-do class: for each customer will have his own preferences among similar things of about equal costs. In fact a person may easily prefer one piece of furniture to another, which serves a similar purpose but is more costly: and, in that case, he may make a better bargain at a shop where a large choice is offered at high prices than at another, where prices are kept low in order to force a rapid sale on a relatively small stock scantily displayed[1].

It has been generally assumed until recently that no retailer is likely, even in a good thoroughfare, to attract as much custom as would enable him to turn over rapidly a stock containing a great variety of similar goods for the choice of

[1] This may perhaps be made clearer by a numerical illustration. Let us suppose that the wholesale prices of three pieces of furniture serving the same purpose are £10, £11 and £12 respectively. The purchaser would at equal prices have preferred the first to the second, and the second to the third. Going to a shop which shows all three, but adds 5*s*. in the £ to wholesale prices, he gets the first for £12. 10*s*. If he had gone to a shop which added only 3*s*. in the £, but happened to show only the second, he would have paid £12. 13*s*. for what he liked less than what he did buy for £12. 10*s*.: and if it happened to show only the third, he would have paid £13. 16*s*. for what he liked much less.

APP. J, 2. the fastidious. But modern abundance of capital, modern developments of the arts of advertising, and modern facilities for attracting customers from a territory containing several hundred thousand well-to-do inhabitants, have changed the situation. It has been proved that a vast and well appointed establishment, well placed and under fine management, may earn so good a reputation, and attract so large a custom, as to secure rapid turn-overs of a vast and varied stock at remunerative prices. Everything then goes on a great scale; and lavish, though careful, expenditure on every side is good economy.

The new-born desire, even among people whose taste is not very highly cultivated, for furniture that shows individuality, and does not bear the mark of massive production by machinery, has done much to revive the artistic energy that distinguished the furniture trades of England and France in the seventeenth and eighteenth centuries. But the machine is found to be capable of imitating much of that fine individual work, with a delicacy and appearance of wayward fancy, which deceive all but experts[1].

Nearly all the conditions just discussed are intensified in the case of fashion goods. Those who create them must have

[1] A piece of noble old furniture can be taken to pieces; and the carving on each part of it imitated by an inexpensive machine, which guides a cutting tool on a fresh piece of wood to follow the movements of a fine metal finger that moves along the model. If the copies are to be sold as originals; care is taken not to send two of them to the same neighbourhood.

True and subtle originality is most frequently found in work, the full design of which is gradually evolved in the mind of the worker as he proceeds. But it seems that there is very little truth in the opinion that all furniture, which has been made by hand, has shown traces of the individuality of the craftsman. Some of it did: and because it was good, it was defended from rough wear, and has come down to us almost unharmed. But in places where nearly all furniture is made by hand, there is much monotonous weary work, without interest or initiative. Thus a visitor to the Grödener Tal, in Tyrol, may find a nest of artists whose wooden statuary is sought for the adornment of cathedrals far and wide: and he may come across a peasant, with hard hands, who loves haymaking more than his winter work at wood carving, though that is of high artistic excellence. But he may also find in the same neighbourhood people who carve toys by the cartload, many of which are crude, ill-shaped reproductions of a pattern that has been set to them. An inquiry as to such a load evoked the answer:—"Before our father died, he taught us to make horses like this, and we cannot venture on anything new." The horses' necks were all bent in the same impossible and ugly curve.

high faculty, reaching up towards a real, if rather slender, sort of genius: and those who handle them must be intensely alert. It is true that, in this as in other industries that are rapidly changing, disproportionately large gains are reaped by men, whose ability resembles that of the bird that is specially quick to run in and pick up some of the grain that another has unearthed: but his customers get what they want, and have no cause to complain. He is a representative of a class that is becoming increasingly prominent: for the rule of fashion is spreading, till it will soon have little ground left to conquer. Neighbours are becoming strangers to one another as persons: but in matters of etiquette, even country-folk look to the arbitrament of the larger world, and in matters of costume they now learn quickly what passes there[1].

Changes in fashion are not now products of a wayward fancy, which is its own reward. They are, in large part at all events, deliberately planned several months before they obtain vogue. They are planned with a view to successful effect: for if they fail in that, they reap only a short-lived commercial success. But those who control them have always a general interest in causing anyone, who wishes not to be out of fashion, to discard the costumes of last season: and they are able to secure for themselves some of the gain which arises out of the ownership, or early preparation, of large stocks of material adapted for fashions which they have foreseen further ahead than other people. In every such movement there is much exercise of skill and taste of a high order: but since everything is done hastily, the effects are generally cruder than those which people of a lower mental quality would have evolved by the patient method of ancient custom: and this would be so, even if the commercial value of their schemes did not depend in part

[1] Even so long ago as 1893 it was said by one who spoke with knowledge on "Nottingham lace trade and fashion" (*Economic Journal*, vol. III. p. 714), "A peculiar hat is seen in M. Worth's rooms, and in a week women readers of weekly papers in the remote country districts of England are fully acquainted with all its peculiarities: though the richest and best creations of Paris are never exposed in shops, partly for fear they may be copied. It is no uncommon thing for the retail dealer to be told what is the fashion by his customers. Twenty years ago the customer came into the shop with the question on her lips." (Bray, *A about dress*, p. 233.) Newspaper dealers in working-class districts, find that a very large portion of their business is in cheap fashions journals.

APP. J, 3. on the extravagance of the changes introduced, and on the large opportunities for display of wealth and of alertness by those who discard the declining fashion most promptly and completely.

3. *Some variations in the additions made by the retailer to wholesale prices, which are due to causes other than variations in direct costs of marketing.*

The retailer's hold on his customers is largely dependent on their general belief that he is acting well by them: he is not compelled to adjust the price of each particular thing to its cost together with a proportionate share of the general expenses of his establishment. Of course in any case he would need to add a large percentage to the wholesale price of things that are likely to spoil, or go out of fashion; that need much care and technical knowledge in selection and handling; and of which the stock must be large relatively to the sales: while in any case he would not need to add a large percentage to the wholesale prices of such things as sugar, or plain calico, or simple stationery. But in fact he goes far beyond this natural inequality in the rate of gross profits which he requires from different classes of goods. He sells at a very low profit everything which is bought so habitually, and of the quality of which the customer is so good a judge, that the market would not bear his charging a price appreciably higher than that at which a pushing rival can afford to sell it. But on the other hand, the traffic will often bear an extravagant rate of profit on things of which the customer is no good judge, especially if they are such as appeal mainly to wealthy people who do not trouble themselves much in order to save a little money.

At one time the retailer used to discriminate between different individuals by bargaining with each, in order to get as much as possible out of each. But this petty form of discrimination was early discarded in England, and even broader discriminations between different classes of purchasers are on the whole less prominent than they were. It was in fact England's early recognition of the high value of time, that led her to pioneer the way in having only a single price in the same shop for all customers who bought under like conditions[1].

[1] If a greengrocer charged the same price for vegetables which a customer

An instance of broad differentiation between different classes of customers which is not opposed to modern usage, is that of a shopkeeper with one establishment near the terminus of a suburban line chiefly frequented by season-ticket holders; and another near some large hotel, which is chiefly frequented by foreigners. Unless his prices at the former shop are about the lowest in the town, he will hardly earn his rent: even if he offers a new class of goods with which his customers are not familiar, he must price them low, or otherwise his repute will suffer: and, for the same reason—unless he deals in works of art or other goods of which no two are just alike—he must charge the same prices to all. In the second shop he is tempted to charge much higher prices: because he will in any case never see again the greater part of his customers, and they will not compare notes about him.

4. ***The standardization of raw food products for marketing purposes.***

As the standardization of engineering plant promotes the standardization of other engineering products, so the standardization of seeds tends towards the standardization of vegetable products. Grains and fruits raised from the same stocks under similar conditions will always vary in some degree: but the task of standardizing raw food products, sufficiently to enable them to be marketed fairly well by description and quantity, is likely to become easier. At present however it is often a large and laborious task.

The growing imperiousness of demand, combined with the growing subtlety of the brewing trade, makes the brewer increasingly willing to pay a little premium to middlemen for supplying him with hops carefully graded: he would often

carries away, as for those which he sends out in a cart, he would give unequal services for equal prices, even if he gave no credit in the latter case. Placards announcing "Fixed prices," or "English prices" (the two phrases being convertible) were commonly exhibited in many of the best shops in the larger towns of the Continent a generation ago: but in most places they have done their work, and there is no longer any need for them. In some Oriental bazaars several thousand words often go to every pennyworth of dealing. Dealers in the South of Europe have been known to ask six times the lowest price which they were prepared to accept.

APP. J, 4. lose more than he gained by buying at first hand from the farmer.

Again experience shows that a retailer does not succeed as well with butter of varying qualities, as with a steady supply of a uniform quality, even though that be rather below the average. The consumers get accustomed to that kind; whereas where the quality varies, they resent any sorts that fall markedly below their best experience. Therefore various devices by wholesale marketing, or large scale production for the steady supply of particular qualities of butter are found to render services for which the retailer is ready to pay, because the consumer increasingly demands them.

But the middleman is being ousted from remunerative functions in regard to dairy produce by the spread of cooperative association among farmers. This movement has been pioneered by the highly educated Danish farmers: a creamery using the most advanced plant, and uniting in the same process the milk from perhaps a thousand cows, attains automatically a steady level of uniformity. The level is high, because the demand for a high standardization of product leads to high standardization of plant—in this case the cows; and this has been effected by cooperative cow-testing associations. Finally, the trade-marks, used by the various export associations, which conduct practically the whole of the Danish external trade, have been merged in a national compulsory trade-mark, applied with due tests by a Government official to all[1].

[1] A similar movement on a smaller scale has been applied to eggs: they are collected at short intervals, and each collection is kept together; for youth is the chief merit of an egg. There are however few agricultural products, whose merits are as simple and as much under human control as these. Even as regards butter, an instructive, if biassed, argument that grading is best accomplished by a powerful merchant after the butter has been made, was recorded in the *Report of the Royal Commission on Agriculture*, vol. IV. 1896 (Q. 62,333—62,393). It is suggested (Q. 62,349) that a rise in the minimum standard demanded in London for butter, so great that sorts which were sold twenty years previously for a shilling a pound had become unsaleable, was connected with the arrival of cheap, wholesome margarine. The 800 Minnesota creameries which make butter for New York, do not sell direct to wholesale dealers. They find it advantageous to employ "a receiver" (a special sort of commission agent). His operations, as described by Professor Weld to the American Economic Association in December, 1914 (*Report*, pp. 128—9), illustrate the view that a stratum of middlemen, which appears at first sight superfluous, often does work which would need about an equal number of men if the stratum were eliminated.

This lead has been followed in France, Ireland and other countries; and even in America. But American mobility goes, as a rule, better with forms of association responsive to quick changes of condition, and readily influenced by strong individuals[1].

5. *The hold which small shops retain on poor districts.*

Mere otiose habit plays some part in the persistency with which many of those, who can least afford it, indulge in the luxury of buying in small quantities from small shops near at hand. But the hold of the small shopkeeper on poor districts rests for the greater part on solid economic foundations: some of these foundations are themselves the product of evil and unnecessary conditions: but others are likely to endure so long as a considerable part of the population live on small incomes and are inadequately housed.

To begin with, the cost of service in one of these shops is often so small as to be almost negligible. It may be attended by the wife of an artisan: he and she may want to increase their small incomes; or perhaps to accumulate a little capital

It is to be noted that butter and eggs, though perishable, are marketed on a relatively small margin between prices paid by consumer and received by producer: though fruit and vegetables, as to which supply and demand in any one market are uncertain, require large margins (*ib.* p. 131).

[1] It has been very successful in the cooperative organization of the great trade in citrus fruit from the Pacific Coast to the Eastern States. Local associations guarantee honest packing, etc.: and send their fruit to officers of a broad based federation, to be forwarded to wholesale dealers; who alone have as yet been successful in marketing these products, that are uncertain in supply as well as in demand; and they are apt to perish through gluts in particular markets, even while other markets are relatively bare. The Federation itself can however organize broad telegraphic information, which enables it to start the fruit in directions, in which it is not very likely to fall from the first grade to a low one, or even beyond, by being kept waiting too long.

Cooperative marketing is discussed in two instructive studies:—*Co-operation at home and abroad,* in regard to Europe, by C. R. Fay: and *Co-operation in agriculture,* in regard to America, by G. H. Powell. The general conclusion that cooperation in marketing among producers, must serve an apprenticeship to the work of professional dealers, before it can undertake the task of selling fickle products to distant consumers generally, was reached by the Industrial Commission (*Report,* vol. VI. pp. 430—2). In many cases, "there must intervene brokers or commission men of some sort, capable of handling receipts in bulk, and breaking them up among the representatives of the wholesale and retail trade."

APP. J, 5. which may enable the man to set up as a small employer in his own craft. The wife wastes no time in the shop; but is busy with household affairs till she is summoned by the shop bell. This source of supply of small shops seems likely to endure long.

And there is perhaps an equally permanent demand for them. When an unexpected need suddenly arises, it is convenient to send out a child to shop close by. But the chief sources of the demand for numerous very small shops are the improvidence of many, and the want of storage of all who have no adequate houseroom. There are indeed some people not habitual drunkards, who cannot keep away from any alcohol they may have in the house: so they pay the retailer a very high wage for taking charge of their stock of it, and serving it out to them a little at a time; and under the circumstances they make a good bargain. In many districts no one buys coal by the ton, except to sell it again; and even a hundredweight in a box may tempt to extravagance, and attract greedy neighbours asking for a loan. So it is often bought by the pennyworth[1].

Further the small shopkeeper may often indulge in the honest boast, that he is the banker of his poorest neighbours in their time of distress. He in effect lends to them on far lower terms than anyone else could, except as a matter of charity: for his ordinary business automatically gives him an insight into their character and their needs. The occasions, on which this aid from him is really necessary and on the whole beneficial, are indeed happily diminishing under the influence of improvements in education, sobriety, insurance by various

[1] Miss Octavia Hill, on taking a room in a poor district, found no coal-box; and for that and other reasons, she thought it best to fall in with this practice. And, when Prof. Conrad started a cooperative store in the country and tried to sell coffee by the pound, the men told him that their wives consumed it so much faster, when bought by the pound than by the quarter ounce, that they spent more on it than before, even though he was selling it at a cheaper rate. (See his *Report on Retail prices*, p. 122.) Similar habits seem to prevail even more strongly in southern and eastern countries; and it has been well said that the size of the smallest coin in common use is an inverse measure of the stage of civilization. In some Indian villages a whole rupee is an unknown coin: while See maintained that an American workman must be so lacking in stamina as to be of little use, if he "buys his groceries by the quarter dollar."

agencies; among which cooperative stores are to be held in exceptional honour, on account of their courageous endeavours to induce the people at large to make expenditure run a little behind income: and the time is not in sight at which there will be no need for such aid.

On the other hand the plea that has been urged with some vehemence especially in France, that the small shopkeeper has a right to live, cannot be accepted without qualification: though a sudden economic change like that which deprived hand-loom weavers of a livelihood may indeed call for emergency measures[1].

6. *Marketing and industrial peculiarities of various capital cities.*

The remarks made above (II, VI, 6) as to the industrial conditions of large cities generally, apply in the main to capital cities: but yet they stand in a class by themselves. For they offer the best opportunities to those traders, who aim at earning very high rates of profit on relatively small sales of choice goods, made in part by artisans with whom they are in immediate touch. Also they are the largest general markets for common goods; and they have always been chief centres of government and finance, of wealth and fashion and luxurious expenditure. Again, while many of the functions of Government tend increasingly to be delegated to Local Authorities, modern means of communication have increasingly concentrated the supreme control of the financial enterprise of each country in her capital. London, Paris, and especially Berlin, have greatly increased their dominion over the industry of finance during the present generation: and this change is representative of a general tendency for industries, that need little space and horse-power, but much wealth and much alertness, to seek

[1] Some opponents of Grands Magasins have maintained that no one has the right to follow more than one occupation. "If you allow a Grand Magasin to sell everything, draperies, hats, boots, umbrellas, books and perfumes you rob me, who am a specialist of my livelihood." Many proposals, some of which have been partially accepted by the legislature, for retarding the growth of these intruders by taxes increasing progressively with the variety or the magnitude of the sales of a retail dealer, are set out in full by Ef. Martin Saint Léon (*Le petit commerce français, sa lutte pour sa vie*, ch. v.).

APP. J, 6. capital cities. They do so partly for reasons of industrial economy, but chiefly for the sake of the special advantages in marketing which they find there.

The high grade industries of London are of several kinds. Some of them work up the choicest materials, by labour of the highest and most varied qualities. London's import trade brings to them rare materials, the best of which are chosen in docks and warehouses for London industries; and the rich residents of London offer a critical but generous demand for their products. Similar customers from elsewhere go to London for their finest purchases; because the local demand has called into existence employers, who will pay the highest price for the best of materials. The most capable and critical of workers in nearly all the smaller industries, and in some of the larger, seek London; where the highest wages are to be earned by working on the most costly materials for the most exacting customers. Thus, though printing is the only very large industry which looks to London as its head quarters, there are many important industries of which the highest excellence is found only in London[1].

On the other hand, the low grade industries which congregate in London owe comparatively little to the marketing advantages which are to be found there: and indeed many of their products are among the lowest of England's exports. They are developed in London by a peculiar class of workers who are fairly alert,

[1] "In certain trades, even though the dominant influences are against her, there are special kinds of work which tend to be retained by London. In some cases this is explained by the necessity for prompt execution of work; or when, from its artistic or complicated character, the direct and constant supervision of the buyer or his agent is desirable. It happens also sometimes when great excellence is demanded. Thus we find that, while Birmingham makes much jewellery from well-known patterns, London is the centre of the finer work that is marked by originality of design; that the best carriages are still made, and made throughout, in London; that the best surgical instruments and the best cutlery are secured by the combination of London workmanship and Sheffield steel; that the best scientific instruments, the best work in stained-glass windows; and, in spite of the number of provincial factories, the best organs continue to be made in London." Booth and Aves in *Life and Labour of the People*, A.D. 1903, IX. p. 184. The London market attracts and educates tailors, who earn nearly the best wages of their trade in the world, and make quite the best coats: on the other hand, London rookeries shelter men and women from Eastern Europe, who make nearly the lowest grade of coat for nearly the lowest wages.

and keen; and, though not very strong in body or character, can do light monotonous work quickly and well. Also they are keenly appreciative of the excitements of London life: they buy fish and other food to suit them at prices far below those, which are commonly entered in official price lists: house-room is dear; but they are content with little of it.

Since French genius generally excels in fine work, for which great mechanical power is not needed, it is only natural that Paris should be unrivalled in the attractions which she offers to delicate and artistic manual skill; and be herself the factory and the mart for nearly all the finest French products: but she is without a great specialized industrial entourage, such as those of which Lille and Lyons are centres.

Berlin, Vienna, and other capital cities resemble London and Paris in having the largest populations and the largest aggregate of manufactures of any cities in their several lands. But no one of them is the central mart of a very widely spread specialized industry; though it is true that a group of men of rare genius and energy have made Berlin the chief seat of the German electrical industries, which are at present the most important in the world. New York, though not a centre of Government, may yet be classed for the present purpose among capital cities. For instance she has almost a monopoly of the finest American jewelry; though common jewelry is seldom made there. She has special difficulties, because many of the poorest and weakest immigrants are dropped within her borders by the stream that passes through her to the West.

Speaking generally, however, the wealth and knowledge and sense of social responsibility of the Governments; and of the wealthy populations of capital cities, are lessening the causes which have specially adapted many of their industries to decadent populations. New facilities for traffic are enabling large numbers of those, who work in them, to have their homes in suburbs, where the children can play in fresh air: and the same facilities are giving to the residents in such suburbs advantages that are beyond the reach of country folk. *Rus in urbe, urbs in rure,* the cherished ideal of the philosopher, may ere long be realized in old countries, and even more fully in alert new countries, in a degree that seemed beyond hope

APP. J, 6. even a short time ago: and the economies of making and marketing may no longer promote unwholesome overcrowding[1].

[1] It is true that the rate of mortality is not exceptionally high in London and several other great cities: but that does not prove that the general conditions of life in them are healthy, any more than the high mortality in hospitals proves that their conditions are less healthy than those of ordinary houses. People, who are strong and vigorous, flock to a great city in quest of the high earnings to be obtained there by energy and ability in all the various ranks of life: and those who fall into ill-health are apt to retire to places where rents are lower: not infrequently indeed to the homes of their childhood. A country district that yielded specially high earnings and attracted specially good lives, while shaking itself free from lives that show signs of weakness, would probably show a far lower rate of mortality than is to be found in any great city. In an article entitled "Where to House the London Poor," published in the *Contemporary Review*, February, 1884, the present writer advocated tendencies, of which Mr Ebenezer Howard was already a leader; and subsequently bore fruit in his crusade for "Garden Cities."

APPENDIX K

ON EDUCATION, WITH SPECIAL REFERENCE TO A BUSINESS CAREER

1. *The development of faculties at school*[1].

APP. K, 1.

Studies cannot be arranged in order of merit absolutely. Those studies are best for a child in any phase of its development, which call into the fullest play the highest activities of which it is capable in that phase. For instance, kindergarten methods of assorting flowers may probably be more educative to the very young child than formal lessons in language. That phase being outgrown, a boy is likely to get more true education for a time from the study of words than from almost any other: for he is still too young to apply scientific method in spontaneous study of things. His mind is now ripe for a little, but only a little, of the strong discipline of mathematics; and some training in music and drawing seems to be enjoined by Nature as well as by Greek precept. But he has more to gain from handling words than from any other exercise: for the materials for his work come to him gratis and in abundance; and in building with them, he is called on to exert the highest spontaneity of which he is as yet capable. Demands are made on his general intelligence, his judgment, his sense of proportion, his logical acumen, his perceptive sensibility and his taste; and in a greater or less degree he can rise to these demands. He is architect, engineer, and skilled artisan all at once. There seems also no doubt that Latin is the best language for some parts of this work.

The boy passes gradually out of this phase and becomes fit for the next. In that he may begin to make a scientific study

[1] This Section is associated with II, x; especially pp. 356—7. Much of it is reproduced from a letter published in the *Times*, 5 March, 1905.

APP. K, 1. of things, whether they be material, or the ideas which are the truest realities. This work cannot be pushed far at first without a strain. But the study of the relation between cause and effect should be begun early: large use being made of verifications by experiment, such as are afforded by elementary hydrostatics, even without the aid of mathematics. History should also be treated in some degree as a study of cause and effect: though here verification is seldom possible, and the bias of a historian or a teacher may make the worse appear the better reason.

Studies of the laws of nature of chemical products and of mechanical agencies, with reference to successive increases in their efficiency, are of primary importance in the education of youths who are likely to hold responsible positions in industry, or in almost any branch of trade. They tend in high degree to stimulate alert intelligence in general; and in particular that kind of intelligence in which British manufacturers led the world in the first half of last century; though now they are outpaced often by Americans, and sometimes by other peoples. For these and similar reasons, it seems desirable that the study of languages should retreat gradually into the background after the age of about fifteen; though it should retain a considerable place for several more years. And, as a corollary, it seems to be required that the headmasters of some, at least, of the chief schools should be thoroughly imbued with the spirit of science in its relations to things, as well as to events and human actions. But while language falls into the background, the spirit of literature should come into the foreground. Appreciative study of English classics should be encouraged: and, above all, the difficult task of teaching boys to write their own language well should have precedence over the easy task of correcting relatively crude faults in Latin and Greek composition[1].

[1] The practice of compelling boys to learn Greek accents, which they are told to neglect in pronunciation, and which were unknown to the Greeks themselves, occupies precious time and energy. It injures character, by suggesting a low appreciation of the value of time; while the study of constructive science has the opposite effect, for its ever-growing ambitions are greedy of time.

No doubt many of the ablest business men and statesmen have received an almost exclusively classical education. But that result is fully accounted for by the facts that nearly every boy, who has had first-rate educational advantages in childhood, has gone to a classical school; and that nearly all the ablest pupils

2. *University training for the responsibilities of business*[1].

APP. K, 2.

The higher education of professional men has always been arranged with reference to the services which they may render to the State: but little care has been taken, till recently, to make similar provision for business men. Britain is now setting herself to that task; though as yet with less energy than America and even Germany are doing.

It is indeed true that a man is likely to be more efficient in business who has braced his mind to hard work in subjects that have no connection with it, than if he had occupied himself with an enervating form of technical instruction, however directly that might bear on his after work. But, provided the studies be themselves of a truly liberal character, the closer their relation to his after work, the more active is his interest in them likely to be. To a colliery manager, who has made a thorough study of geology, the shafts and galleries of a mine are a scientific museum and laboratory: his mind grows with his work, and he may increase the world's wealth of knowledge. As geology is related to mining, so is economics to general business. As the miner needs to make more intensively, but with a narrower range, the same studies as the geologist makes; so the business man needs the same kind of studies as the economist does: but

from such schools have gone to Universities, at which a knowledge of Greek and Latin is required, and classical studies have had a chief place.

Some measure of the disturbing influence thus caused may be obtained by reflecting on the large preponderance of artistic ability at Florence in her prime: art was the chief route to public esteem, and therefore able, high-spirited youths became artists. To take another illustration: let us suppose that in England the headmasters of the chief schools had been selected for their musical attainments; and that music had dominated her University curricula. Then the ablest boys would have been regarded as the *peculium* of a musical headmaster: and, if he had happened to be colour-blind, and a lad with the genius of a Rembrandt had unfortunately shown some musical ability, he might have grown up to be a moderately good musician. One of the ablest and most enterprising headmasters in England not long ago objected to mathematical studies, on the ground that Euclid calls for no mental faculty except memory. Being himself "science-blind," he had no notion that a boy with a mathematical bias quickly grasps Euclid's method, and afterwards merely glances at the general line of one of Euclid's arguments, filling in the details for himself.

[1] Much of this Section is taken from papers printed in connection with the foundation, in 1903, of the Cambridge Curriculum in Economics and some allied branches of Political Science.

APP. K, 2. his range is more circumscribed, and his penetration reaches further into particular details.

Every study exercises, in various degrees, perception, imagination and reason. Perception may be trained in childhood. The springs of imagination belong to early youth: it is the greatest of all faculties; and in its full development it makes the great soldier, the great artist, the student who extends the boundaries of science, and the great business man. Reasoning cannot be carried far in complex problems, till youth passes into manhood. The business man needs all three: especially he needs imagination to put him on the track of remote and invisible effects of causes which are obvious, and of the hidden causes of visible effects. General intelligence and common sense will, of course, go some way towards the solution of his problems: they are, in fact, better guides than mere academic training unaided by them; and in simple matters they almost suffice. But in others a greater effort, a larger range of view, and a more powerful exercise of the imagination are needed. For instance, to get at the real effects of plausible schemes for increasing steadiness of employment he must have learned how closely connected are changes in credit, in domestic trade, in foreign trade competition, in harvests, and in prices; and how all of these affect steadiness of employment for good and for evil. He must watch how almost every considerable economic change in any part of the Western world affects employment, in some trades at least, in almost every other part. If he is to look for those causes which are far off and weigh them in the balance, then the work before him is a high discipline for the mind. In such problems as this it is the purely intellectual, and sometimes even the critical faculties, which are most in demand.

In addition to a strong and alert mental faculty, the business man needs to have acquired a knowledge of human nature, together with the power of managing men, and to this end the social training afforded by life in a residentiary university of the Anglo-Saxon type is specially serviceable. For such a life draws out the faculties which are needed in the social relations of those who have to deal with large bodies of men and large public interests. On the river and in the football field the student learns to bear and to forbear; to obey and to command.

And, what is even more important, the comradeship of generous youth, unless marred by extravagance or vice, tends to develop the sympathies, which separate man by an impassable gulf from the most powerful machine which modern skill has taught "almost to think." Indeed an employer, whose sympathies are dull, often falls short even as a profit-winner; unless he has thought much, and cared much, about those sides of his work-people's life and characters, which are not directly reflected in the wages bargain. To learn this from personal contact is ever more difficult: for he is now often separated from the mass of his employees by several strata of subordinates. He lives among his own class; and this association is apt to make him look at labour questions from the employer's point of view. But undergraduate sympathy tends always towards what is, or appears to be, the weaker side: any bias, which an undergraduate may bring to these questions, is apt to be on the side of the employees. And such a bias does him no harm: for he will not take long to learn the full force of the employers' side of the case. Thus trained, he is often able, as both English and American experiences show, to read the minds of the employees more readily than can be done by an employer, even if much older than himself, who has not had that training. He interprets between the two sides: and thus that broad sympathy grows, which enables different social classes to put themselves in one another's points of view and welds the nation into one.

APPENDIX L

CONDITIONAL MONOPOLIES IN MULTIPLE OWNERSHIP[1]

APP. L, 1.

1. ***Problems relating to an industry, which would constitute a powerful monopoly if in a single ownership. Illustration from the incidences of taxes on agriculture in a densely peopled country.***

There are two chief cases of multiple ownership of properties each of which would constitute a monopoly, if in a single hand: they illustrate important, but widely different principles. The ownership of the agricultural land of a country would confer a hard monopoly of the supply of food; if it were in a single hand, and food could not easily be imported from abroad. The monopoly of all the land and buildings of a great city, if in a single hand would appear as a latent menace to all its inhabitants: but the power given by it could seldom be abused without lasting injury to its owner; and, in fact, the multitude of owners of land and buildings in an ordinary town have an exceptional interest in developing its prosperity. These contrasted cases are now to be discussed.

It is a common belief, at all events in a country which has no foreign trade in agricultural produce, that land has a monopoly-value; because its total area is fixed by Nature. The belief would be fully justified if the cultivators of the land acted in concert, and so adjusted the supply of produce, that its aggregate price yielded the maximum excess over the costs (all included) of cultivating it and marketing the produce.

But the problem is more complex in a country where there is no such combination; whether the cultivators are tenant farmers or independent owners. It is indeed true that, even in such

[1] This Appendix is associated with III, II, 4, p. 421.

a country, a fixed tax on the land itself, taking no account of the manner in which it is cultivated, would act on the owners of land in the same way as would a similar tax in a country in which all the land was in a single ownership, thus constituting a vast monopoly. For such a tax would not affect the action of the cultivator (whether owner or not), nor the pressure which an owner could put on his tenant farmers: and, since it would not affect the amount of produce raised, therefore it would not affect the consumer. A landlord might stipulate that the tax should be paid by the farmer; and that would affect the incidence of an unexpected change in the tax. But, in so far as the future of the tax could be anticipated, the amount of the rent which the farmer could be induced to promise to pay would be diminished by the tax: therefore in effect the tax would be paid by the landlord[1].

In fact, however, nearly all taxes on agricultural land are assessed on its market value: and their incidence is much affected by the varying degrees of viscosity of the several elements of the problem. For the market value is partly due to recent investments of capital in the land; and the expectation that a tax will be paid on further investments tends to check a generous investment in improvements; and therefore to diminish production. The extent to which it will do so within a few years cannot be set out in any definite formula: but its effects have some affinity to those of a tax on agricultural produce in general, to which we may now pass, it being remembered that the country is supposed to have no external trade in such produce.

Agricultural produce is consumed by everyone: it absorbs a great part of the incomes of the working classes, a considerable part of those of the middle classes; but only a small part of those of the rich, even when the consumption of their domestics is reckoned in. All industries are interested in it about equally from the point of view of consumption: but the makers of agricultural implements and artificial manures and

[1] The tithe rent charge on each piece of land is fixed without reference to its yield (except as regards hops): and, though it varies with the official prices of staple grains in recent years, it does not materially affect the inducements to apply labour and capital to any particular piece of land. Therefore it acts almost as a fixed tax on land regarded as a monopoly in single ownership.

APP. L, 1. the transport industries alone look to it for any exceptional market for their products or services.

The greater part of the burden of this tax would therefore be distributed among the people generally as consumers, the pressure diminishing almost regularly with every step upwards in normal income. Farmers and agricultural labourers, besides bearing their shares of the burden in about equal proportion with others in the same ranks of the social scale, would further suffer from any shrinkage in their employment which resulted from a shrinkage of consumption caused by the tax: but no other very large class of producers would be affected by the tax in an exceptional degree. The consumption of most kinds of agricultural produce is however seldom very elastic: and therefore the reduction in their output caused by the tax would probably not be very great. Thus the chief influence of the tax would be a rise in their values on the market after paying the tax; and that would enable the landlords in the long run to make bargains with tenant farmers on more favourable terms to themselves.

It is an old remark that if a tax of one-tenth were imposed on agricultural produce; and yet (the demand for it being inelastic) its consumption were not diminished, nine-tenths as much as before would serve to remunerate the labour and capital employed in raising it; while one-tenth of the share, that used to be retained by the farmer for himself and his men, would go in taxation. Therefore the share left for the landlord to retain and to pay his tax with would be the same in amount as before: one-tenth would go to the taxgatherer; and the remaining nine-tenths would have the same value as his old rent had, except of course in so far as the landlord himself was a consumer of agricultural produce. That is to say a tax on raw produce, the demand for it being very inelastic, would not injure the landowners; because the produce of their lands is sold at competitive prices. But if land were a monopoly, and its produce were sold at prices fixed on monopoly principles, the price might have already been put so high, that an increase in it would compel some diminution of consumption at whatever cost of well-being: and in that case a part of the burden (in addition to the tax on their own consumption) would fall on the landlords.

Even as things are, the tax might possibly exert a small influence in this direction. For, if the increased expenditure of the poorer part of the population on their food crippled their consumption of other requisites of efficiency and vigour, it might in the long run so restrict the growth of the population in energy, if not numbers, as to hinder the rise in the real value of rents which would otherwise have occurred. Whether it did so or not, would depend mainly on the way in which the proceeds of the tax were spent; in other words, whether it was onerous to the population generally, or not.

It should be noted that the peculiar position, which land holds in the economic system of densely peopled countries, arises from the two facts (1) that the area of land is absolutely fixed by Nature; and (2) that the other requisites of economic development are capable of increase. In Russia the wealth of a landed proprietor has been measured by the number of "souls" which he could command to work on his land: and in some parts of Australia, where the soil is favourable to pasture and corn cultivation, but water is scarce, the effective value of land is governed mainly by its water supply. It is possible to conceive a planet in which the total available water is insufficient for nearly as large a population as the land would support with an adequate supply of it: and in that case, though water is mobile and land is not, water might hold as dominant a position in the economics of the population, as land does in a densely peopled country of this world.

Allowing yet more free play to fancy, it may be observed that if the stock of some important machines, say printing presses, could be supposed to be permanent and fixed in the same way as is that of land, a tax on them (independent of the work done by them) would be paid entirely by the owners of the existing printing presses, provided it did not drive any of them out of use; just as would a similar tax on all land. For they would all sell their services for what could be got (without any reference to the cost of production of printing presses). So the tax would not affect the output of printing, nor therefore its price: it would simply intercept some of the earnings of the presses on their way to the owners.

APP. L, 2.

2. *Interests which owners of land, and of good business connections, have in the semi-monopolistic advantages, that a city may develop by large local expenditure, well administered.*

Local taxation is commonly divided into that which is "onerous," and that which is "beneficial" or "remuneratory." Onerous local taxes, or "rates," are said to be those which are levied for purposes in which the locality has but a partial interest. Remuneratory rates are said to be those which supply the means of obtaining local benefits, in such wise that—under good management—they render services to the locality which outweigh their costs. These descriptions are adequate for some purposes: but they ignore the fact that, as a locality has some special interests which are not shared by the rest of the country; so the permanent residents in a locality, and especially the owners of land and buildings in it, have some interests which do not extend in full measure to other residents. Let us go into some details.

A national tax levied evenly on a whole people and spent on education, sanitation, etc., in such a way as to confer on them benefits in the form of health and energy and earning power, which are more than equivalent to the charges levied on them, is remunerative. In so far as it is levied mainly on the well-to-do, and spent mainly in the service of the working classes, it is *primâ facie* onerous to the well-to-do: but the purposes, for which it is levied, tend to make the country rich in material wealth and in the amenities of life; and therefore the tax is in some degree remunerative even to them.

Exceptionally heavy local rates levied in a town for the purposes of education, are said to be in some measure onerous; because those, who have benefited by the education, may leave the locality. But, if local industry and trade are developed by the facilities to which good education has given increased strength, the expenditure may lead to net immigration; and thus greatly benefit local owners of land, buildings, and established businesses.

On the other hand, if mismanagement caused the rates of a town to rise greatly, while there was no corresponding increase in the attractions which the town offered to industries in general (that is if there were a great increase in those rates which were in the main onerous), its population would grow slowly and might even shrink. Those who for any reason could not leave the town would tend to avoid industries on which the rates pressed with exceptionally heavy weight, and to drift into those on which the rates pressed lightly. Conversely taxes, so spent as to add to the advantages of living in a town more than the equivalent of their cost, would develop its industries generally: though, if devoted to a purpose, which was of great importance to some industries and of but little to others, its influence would act unevenly. Thus, if there were a scarcity of available building ground in the town, those industries, which gained very little on the balance from the expenditure of the new taxes, might actually decline to make way for those which stood to gain greatly by the change. An increase of onerous national taxes will no doubt tend to drive the industrial population out of a country: and good finance will tend to attract industries to it: but the rates of growth of population of neighbouring countries do not differ nearly as widely as do those of neighbouring towns or cities in the same country: and such differences as exist, are due, save in a very few cases, to broader and deeper causes than differences in the pressure of taxation.

Much of the collective property, which the inhabitants of a well-managed town have built up, is at the disposal of any who choose to come to it, provided they can obtain suitable premises on moderate terms: but a considerable part of it is the exclusive property of those who own the soil, the buildings and the businesses established there. The firmer their hold on the town, and the firmer the hold which the town has on them, the more nearly do their interests approach to those of a town, such as Eastbourne, which was planned by a single owner on his own land, and remains largely under his control. Its permanent residents, if well advised, and able to override those residents who have no permanent interest in the development of the town, may sacrifice present income to relatively large deferred gains, in a constructive policy resembling that of a far-seeing monopolist. They seldom attain to so high a level; but they yet rise much above that of monopolistic ownership in weak or tyrannous hands.

APPENDIX M[1]

NOTES ON RAILWAYS AND THEIR PROBLEMS

APP. M, 1.

1. *Early phases of English railway traffic and finance. Causes of the rise and decline of canals.*

"Railroads" were originally roads on which rails of wood or metal were laid down to facilitate the passage of ordinary vehicles. They were introduced generally in some colliery districts during the first half of the seventeenth century: they enabled a horse to draw rather more than two tons, whereas, on an ordinary good road (of the kind then usual) his load was under one ton. Thin plates of iron were soon put on the wood; and in 1738 cast iron rails were used, and cast iron wheels followed. In 1804 Trevithick's locomotive drew ten tons of iron on a railroad: but stationary steam engines remained for a long while in effective competition with it. Stephenson's engine ran on the Stockton and Darlington Railway in 1825: but no railroad was licensed for passengers till 1830[2].

The early locomotive could move fast; and it had no difficulty in routing the mail coach. But it had very little power; and it was so extravagant of coal, that it could not draw heavy and bulky goods of low values at rates comparable with those charged by canals. If therefore the canals could have adapted themselves quickly to the increasing demands of

[1] This Appendix is associated with III, IV, V, VI. See also I, IV, 4.

[2] *The Companion to the British Almanack*, 1841, contains an account of the 135 Railway Acts passed from 1800 to 1839. Horses are the "power used" almost exclusively till 1826: soon afterwards locomotives predominate. *A treatise on railroads...and the comparative value of canals and railroads*, by Nicholas Wood, 1825, contains a thoroughly scientific study of the mechanical problems concerned. But he sees many advantages on the side of canals, provided they be administered vigorously. The history of artificial waterways in England from 1761 to recent years is sketched in the *Final Report of the Royal Commission on Canals and Waterways*, 1909 [Cd. 4979].

England's economic development, they might have even now carried a great deal of the internal trade of England: and the somewhat hazardous movement of her heavy industries towards the sea might have been kept within more moderate limits.

But unfortunately large capital, enterprise and organizing faculty were needed for developing chains of small canals into a great system. It was not an easy task to enlarge a canal, so that it could carry and pass through its locks, barges much larger than those for which it had been constructed: and there were but few canals which were so far self-contained as to be able to derive much benefit from such an enlargement, unless similar improvements were made by its neighbours. No doubt exceptional outlay is sometimes made by a particular locality for the improvement of an inland water-way, as in the case of the Manchester Canal: but the financial aid, which the shipping industry has derived from public outlays on the improvement of harbours and of the channels which connect them with the sea, was not forthcoming to English canals in the time of their distress. So some of them were speedily choked up; and this further narrowed the scope for the profitable investment of capital in improving canals that had made connection with them. Lastly steamships completely outbid those canals (of which the Avon and Kennet canal connecting Bristol with Reading may be taken as a type), whose province it had been to enable goods received on one coast of England to be delivered near the other, without the uncertain delays of a long coasting voyage.

Even if railway locomotives had long remained unable to haul heavy loads economically, these causes would have ruined nearly all English canals, unless public funds had come to their aid. The time had not yet arrived for the general recognition of the fact that canals, being in effect public highways, need to be organized by Government, and perhaps financed by it. Nor is that surprising: for, till recently, roads were partly financed by private enterprise in return for tolls; and it was not easy to foresee how great an injury to the country might be caused by the lack of adequate depth and breadth of any link in the chain of canals[1].

[1] The Avon and Kennet canal adds much to the beauty of a branch of the

APP. M, 1. As things were, technical advance in the laying of railway tracks and the construction of locomotives proceeded steadily; and the load of a goods train soon surpassed that of a string of barges of moderate length. Two uniform gauges, one "broad" and the other "narrow," were adopted: and intercommunication between railways became easy. The coach from London to Oxford had occupied two long days in 1742: and its time had not been reduced below six hours, when it was supplanted by a train which took but one and a half hours. Before 1850 Lardner had sometimes found himself travelling at seventy miles an hour; and the 193 miles between London and Exeter were traversed in four and a half hours. These conditions had been partly cause, and partly effect, of the growing eagerness of Government and the public to welcome the fusion of railways which fed one another, the prohibition of fusions between parallel lines seemed an adequate safeguard against the development of railway monopolies. In the "thirties" railways served their apprenticeship: in the "forties" they learnt much of what they could do, and what they could not do. In 1844 a wave of confident expectation set in: it reached its climax in the violent speculation of 1845—6; and it broke down in the panic of 1847—8, of which it was a chief contributory cause. When it had passed away, England's economic policy had entered on a new career, and passed out of the special conditions to which this Section relates[1].

Great Western Railway, which faithfully preserves it in good order: and its lack of traffic has been claimed as a proof that canals are unable to render important services to England now. But some railways, even in England, were abandoned as being in unsuitable places. And, as is argued above (pp. 497—506), the last word has not yet been said in defence of English canals. As late as 1836, the first year in which speculation in railway securities ran wild, the canals attracted more new capital than any other class of investment, except railways, banks, insurance companies and mines (Levi, *History of British Commerce*, p. 220).

[1] A map of all the English railways sanctioned in 1844 (reproduced in the Jubilee number of *The Railway News*, 1914) shows the lines so scattered, and with so few common points, that there could not have been much effective competition among them; while their combination would not have much increased their monopolistic power. But the map (reproduced in Mr Cleveland-Stevens' excellent study of the development of *English Railways*) shows that by 1848 the foundations had been laid for the existing system of main lines with all their possibilities of far reaching competition, and eventually of their combined action. There is some interest in the comparison of the meteoric career of Hudson, the English railway king of the forties, with that of the American

It may however be added here, as belonging to early rather than recent history, that in 1844 an Act was passed, on Gladstone's motion, providing that every new licence granted for the construction of a railway, should embody a provision that the State might purchase it after twenty-one years at a very high price. He suggested two and a half times the railway's capital as the *maximum* purchase price: but eventually that was made the *minimum* price; and this was in face of the fact that a Parliamentary Committee had reported in 1840 that "as far as regards heavy merchandise, it appears probable that the canals will always secure the public against any unreasonable demands on the part of the railway companies." The net profits earned by a company were commonly assumed, in discussions on the Bill, to be likely to exceed ten per cent.: but they soon settled down to less than half that amount. In 1846 the securities of several lines had been selling at more than double their nominal amounts.

The next two years were full of trouble, but their lessons were well learnt; and the outlook for such railways, as were soberly financed and ably administered, remained without any considerable cloud; for the steam power, to which they had owed everything, had not yet moved towards its almost equally rich harvest on the ocean. For a long time all went well with England's railways; their expansion was not hindered by the narrowness of her territory; and they had no effective rival. Nearly all the existing main lines were well developed in the third quarter of last century. Railway outlay increased fast; but net receipts increased a little faster, till in 1872 they averaged 4·74 per cent. on the total "paid up" capital. Since that time the progress of railways has been less satisfactory, at all events from the financial point of view. Their capital has been doubled: and the proportion of net receipts to it has almost steadily diminished; though the gross receipts have increased faster than the capital, and the total amount of work done by the railways has increased much faster still[1].

Harriman in recent years. Each had daring and powerful constructive genius: each thought himself above the counsels of prudence, and perhaps even those of morality, of ordinary men.

[1] The number of passengers exclusive of season ticket holders increased

APP. M, 2.

2. *Curious contrasts in passenger traffic.*

Before 1844 English railways were of little use to the working classes. But a law was then passed that compelled every railway to run at least one train a day, in which people could be conveyed at a rate of not less than 12 miles an hour; at a charge not exceeding a penny a mile; and in carriages provided with seats and protected from the weather[1]. The railway companies resisted the change as far as they could; and, even twenty years later, there were few third-class carriages, except on Parliamentary trains; and these were often run (the Railway Commissioners not exercising their legal powers) at inconvenient hours, and kept in a dirty condition. For it was even then thought that the *ordinary* travelling of the working classes could not be worth encouraging: though they were tempted to make excursions by extremely low rates, three and sixpence being a common return fare from London to the southern watering places. But the notion that it would be good business to make third-class travel comfortable and rapid, gradually made its way; and finally triumphed in 1875 when the Midland put fairly good third-class carriages on all its trains[2].

It must however be admitted that there is some hardship in the rule that the ordinary charge for the poor man is adjusted to a comfortable method of travelling; so that he has not the choice of a rather less expensive method of travelling at a much lower cost, as he has on the Continent. It is true that the

about seven-fold in the fifty years ending 1912; but part of this increase in numbers was due to the rapid growths of urban and suburban traffic, and does not indicate a corresponding increase in volume. The number of tons of goods carried increased rather more than five-fold; the number of mineral tons which was rather more than twice that of general merchandise at the beginning of the period, had become three and a half times as great at the end.

[1] Lardner (*Railway Economy*, ch. x.) gives statistics showing how the total number of miles travelled by third-class passengers was less than that travelled by first-class passengers in 1844, but more than twice as great in 1848. The average distances travelled were about 26 miles by first-class, and 13 by third-class passengers. The extreme measures, by which railway companies used to make travelling in third-class carriages uncomfortable, and even intolerable to well-to-do persons, are humorously described in Acworth's *Railways of England.*

[2] Gladstone warmly supported the movement. Its principles are well set out in an article on "Railways in their Social Relations" in the *British Almanack* for 1865.

artisan, when seeking work, can often get his railway fares paid by his Trade Union; but a minimum charge of half a crown for the equivalent of a day's walk is too high. This evil might be removed by adding fourth-class carriages to a few passenger trains, and to some goods trains. The official English contention that the latter practice is unsafe, is inconsistent with the experience of other countries. Special workmen's tickets, adapted to those who live some distance from their work, are palliatives of these hardships; but inadequate[1].

APP. M, 2.

The excess of ordinary fares above the direct costs of transport is so great, that railways are apt to meet specially elastic traffic by very low fares, even when much of it must be carried at somewhat more than the average direct cost. Thus British railways, which carry comparatively few first or second-class passengers in the greater part of their work, sell first and second-class season tickets at charges below those of ordinary third-class tickets for an equal aggregate mileage: and yet the carriages used by them have to travel for the greater part empty one way in the morning and the other way in the evening; unless indeed they are put to sleep on a siding for the greater part of the day.

The principle of adapting passenger fares to what the traffic will bear, rather than to cost, is further illustrated by the practice of charging specially low rates for return tickets available only for a fortnight and lower rates still for week-end tickets. Those who can take but a short holiday are specially likely to be influenced by a low charge; and a reduction of a few shillings on the total expense of a week-end holiday, is more likely to influence conduct, than when it is but a minute fraction of the total expense to be incurred[2].

[1] On the Continent generally the working classes travel for about a halfpenny a mile; while in Prussia they travel fourth class for a farthing a mile. Where however the railways are sparse and circuitous, and especially in the mountainous regions of Central Europe, a journey on foot may be not very much longer in time than one by railway; and, partly through poverty, those who migrate in search of work, commonly go on foot. In France many express trains are only first class. But generally one can travel on the Continent in express trains second class for the English third-class fare; or for less, if one has a return ticket; but this saving is sometimes lost by charges for luggage.

[2] Further applications of this principle are when tickets for Family, School, Religious Society, Pilgrimage and other groups are issued at a low rate especially

APP. M, 3.

3. *The development of American railway regional and blanket rates.*

When the centre of the population of the United States had receded a considerable distance from the Atlantic, but had not yet reached the watershed of the Ohio, much goods traffic had about equally good access to the ocean by railway to Atlantic ports on the one side; and on the other by railway to the Ohio or the Mississippi itself, and the Gulf of Mexico. Difficult, rapid and ever-shifting as are those river courses, the ton-mile charges by steamers on them were much lower than those at which the railways could afford to carry ordinary traffic. But, in order to compete with the steamers, the railways made specially low rates between the Atlantic and the whole of the area, which had fairly good access to the Mississippi: and the rule, that railways might lower their rates in competition with water-routes, was generally adopted.

When the Pacific coast was developed, railways running west offered extremely low rates to San Francisco, in order to divert traffic from the naturally less costly route to Atlantic ports, and thence round Cape Horn to the Pacific coast: (the details of this conflict are being modified by the Panama Canal, but its main features are unchanged). Farmers and others in the Middle States, who saw goods carried past their doors to San Francisco at charges much lower than those which they were forced to pay for a "short haul" over a part of the same route, made complaints: and these evoked a clause in the Interstate Commerce Law of 1887 prohibiting a higher charge for a part of any route than for a longer part of the same route. This "Long and short haul clause" has however been found somewhat difficult of interpretation under ever-changing conditions[1].

in France, Switzerland and Italy, countries much frequented by rich foreigners. For the plan of a general reduction of fares, which works well enough in such a country as Hungary, would let off this foreign traffic at much lower charges than it can bear. These special facilities are not generally accessible to the foreigner; and they enable the poorer classes and others to make many pleasure excursions at a low cost. Compare the account of "Tarifs Spéciaux pour voyageurs" in Colson's *Transports et Tarifs.*

If anyone wants to go to London and back on a Saturday, he is not allowed to use a cheap week-end ticket; because such journeys imply urgent cause, and they are not likely to increase much in response to a lowering of fares.

[1] An article by Prof. H. G. Brown in *The American Economic Review,*

Meanwhile the economy of sending large trainloads, with little break of bulk, to Chicago and other great centres, together with the intense railway competition at those centres, had caused them to be adopted as "basing-points": that is, the charge for distant traffic to any point in the neighbourhood of a base was made up of a low rate per mile to the basing-point, together with the ordinary rate from the base to the station of delivery. If that station was nearer the place of origin than the basing-point, the charge became less for a long journey than for a shorter one. If this was prohibited, as it originally was, then the charges to all such stations were put at the same amount as those to the basing-point. That introduced some simplicity of arrangements, together with the inequalities and complexities that result from forced simplicity: and these results were extended much further when, instead of a single basing-point in a district, there were several. In this way in fact there was set up a single rate from St Louis to all stations south of the Texan border. For "as railroads were built and extended, one line would reach station *A* by passing through station *B*; and another line would reach station *B* by passing through station *A*; and so on through a ramifying network[1]." And when this process had gone some considerable way, no great further change was made by adopting a single "blanket" rate between the whole region and St Louis. Such arrangements may claim to strike out paths of least resistance: but they do not seem capable of general application; and they are open to grave objections.

A strict interpretation of the "Long and short haul clause" was perhaps advisable in early days when struggles for the mastery of particular railways, as well as conflicts between railways, were often waged with unscrupulous ferocity. For, when rates between competitive points were liable to be put down to very low levels for strategical purposes, such a purpose might well be hindered by the fear that the railway would lose on its intermediate traffic. There were some cases in which

December 1914, shows in entertaining fashion cases in which it may be in the general interest that traffic should be diverted from a short to a long haul.

[1] See p. 94 of an instructive chapter on "Regional rate structures" in McPherson's *Railroad Freight Rates.*

APP. M, 4. the rigid application of the clause worked harm: but latterly the Interstate Commerce Commission, having obtained increased powers, has seen its way to relax rules, which pressed hardly in special cases. Thus was afforded additional evidence that the function of a Legislature is to give powers to authoritative Commissions; and in case of need to recast a Commission, or modify its powers: but not to attempt to govern by law[1].

4. *The importance of railway statistics, and their difficulties.*

The operations of railways are apparently much more homogeneous than those of most other industries; and international railway statistics relate to exceptionally large volumes of similar facts. But much of this apparent uniformity is illusive. The conditions of railway work vary greatly between different countries and sometimes even between different districts served by the same railway; and therefore things represented by the same name, and necessarily classed together in statistical returns, differ widely.

For instance, the work done on the average by a passenger or goods train in going a mile—a "passenger train mile," or a "goods train mile,"—means very different things on the main line, and on a minor branch of a great English railway. An American train-mile often represents thousands of "ton-miles"; that is, tons of freight moved a mile: on English railways it seldom represents many hundreds and often not many tens of ton-miles. If "wagon-miles" be substituted for train-miles we get units that are more similar in some respects, but less in others: for though the service rendered by a train with

[1] For instance, the Commission still allows a railway to lower its rates to any seaport far enough to meet, though not to extinguish, water competition. And (see its *Report* for 1913, p. 25) after referring to such a case, in which the railway's long-haul rate was not reduced below what was necessary to prevent its being "obliged to retire from competition at the water-competition point," declined to compel it to reduce all charges to intermediate points to the same level, when that was below those rates that were "reasonable *per se*" for those points. It goes on to indicate concessions, mostly temporary, which it makes in cases in which the new rules appear to press heavily.

The Hepburn Act strengthened the Commission by making its authority valid, unless and until over-ruled by the Supreme Court on a question of law. The causes that led up to this change are set out by Ripley, *Railroads,* Vol. I, chs. XIII.—XX. See also an account of "Public sentiment and the Hepburn Bill," McPherson, *l.c.* ch. XIX.

thirty wagons is three times as great as that of another with ten similar loaded wagons, the costs of the two services do not differ nearly so much. Ton-miles, wagon-miles and train-miles are all needed as the basis of statistical comparisons. APP. M, 4.

A million ton-miles on a "heavy" English railway such as the Midland or the North Eastern represent much less work than a million ton-miles on a "light" railway in the South of England. Train-mile and wagon-mile statistics make the services of English trains appear greater relatively to those of American than they really are; while ton-mile and passenger-mile statistics mislead in the opposite direction. And, as has been argued, small wagons, many of them not nearly full, are in some degree necessary conditions for the prompt delivery of small consignments starting from any of several thousand stations to be delivered at any other[1].

Sharp tools cut inexpert fingers: and railway statistics, like most others that relate to complex matters, are open to the charge that they often mislead the ill-informed. It is also sometimes objected that they are of less service in administration than the careful observations and reports of the loading, working, etc. of individual trains; while these are regularly made on well-managed lines, to serve as a basis for the policy adopted by the central authorities. Statistics supplement, but make no claim to supersede, that essential work. The Committee on Railway Accounts and Statistical Returns, 1909, reported that without statistics it is not possible, but with them it is possible, to ascertain train load, or wagon load and length of haul: as well as the transport effected per engine hour in passenger traffic and in goods traffic: also the average receipts per passenger-mile and per ton-mile; and the average density of traffic per mile of road and per mile of track[2].

[1] See above, pp. 452—3.

[2] See [Cd. 4697], § 45. Conferences of British railway men, and their professional journals, do much for the cooperative advance of knowledge. But there seems to be some grounds for the severe judgment of a competent critic that "the defect in the prevalent British statistical system is that the manager actually never knows what his neighbour is doing: he has no opportunity as the American manager has to whet his curiosity on the good performances, which somebody else is making. Consequently, improvements in British practice spread but slowly, whereas in America every efficiency-producing device is studied and imitated as soon as it makes itself apparent in the ton-mileage

APP. M, 4. It is now universally recognized that cost of service can be no more than one among several considerations, to be weighed together "by the exercise of a wise discretion" before reaching a conclusion as to the reasonableness and justice of any particular railway rate: but yet American railways have already "made limited application of the principles of cost-accounting to more than one-half" of their vast mileage for "internal corporate administrative purposes[1]." And "an order was issued [by the Interstate Commerce Commission] effective as of July 1915, requiring all carriers, having operating revenues in excess of $1,000,000, to classify each of the various items of disbursement relating to operating accounts, according to the relation which such item bears to the freight service or to the passenger and allied services of the carrier; rules being given for apportioning items of expense common to both classes of service, excepting as to certain items under maintenance of way and structures, which are for the present to be left undivided....It is expected that this class of information will be of assistance, not only in rate cases, but also in making comparisons of changes in operating costs from year to year, and among various railroads in a given year[2]."

It may be noted that an assumption that the cost of each service is known, underlies every suggestion that the charge for it is put at that point which is most advantageous to a railway from a purely business point of view. For, if the gross receipts of a railway from a certain traffic are only a little greater than its direct and immediate costs, a reduction of the charges for it might be unwise (except for combative purposes),

figures" (*Railroad Administration*, 1910, p. 229, by R. Morris, Managing Editor of the *Railway Age Gazette*, N.Y.). A good short account of uses of the ton-mileage statistics was read by Mr Wedgwood of the North Eastern Railway before the British Association in 1906 and printed in the *Economic Journal*, March, 1909. The English North Eastern Railway made rapid progress under the guidance of Sir George Gibb, who paid special attention to railway statistics: he is known to have owed much to the stimulation of Mr J. J. Hill, whose devotion to them is regarded by many as an important contributory to the success with which he overcame the obstacles that a mountainous, sparsely inhabited country opposed to direct railway communication between the upper Mississippi Valley and the Pacific Coast.

[1] B. H. Meyer, at the meeting of the American Economic Association, 1912.

[2] *Report* of the Commission, 1915, p. 46.

unless it greatly increased the traffic: while an expectation of even a moderate increase of the traffic would have made the reduction of charges remunerative, if the direct costs of working had been much below the present charges. Suppose, for instance, that a certain traffic yields £10,000 of gross revenue; of which £8000 are reckoned as direct or prime costs of moving, and £2000 are allotted for general costs and profits. Suppose that a reduction of charges by one-fifth would double the traffic: then the whole of the receipts, £16,000, would be swallowed up by prime costs, leaving nothing for general costs and profits beyond the economies on the mere direct costs of operation from an increase of the traffic. If however the prime costs, accurately estimated, were only £6000; then after the same change, under like conditions, there would remain £4000 for general costs and profits, in addition to these economies of work on a larger scale: and the reduction would be excellent business. These figures illustrate the dictum that "railway business must be unbusinesslike so long as prime costs are reached by mere guesswork and are liable to wide error."

5. *The small and indirect, but yet valuable, aid which a study of the capitalization of railways may afford in regard to the regulation of the general level of their charges.*

Thus we are brought back to the suggestion, made in Book II (p. 336), that the correct capitalization of a railway or other semi-monopolistic business is matter of larger public concern than that of an ordinary company. The State must in any case take all reasonable measures to protect investors against the fraudulent infusion of "water"; that is additions to the nominal capital of a company, which are not justified by corresponding *bonâ fide* payments into its exchequer: though, as a rule, excessive capitalization of a company injures only those who buy its securities. For, if it has no monopoly, those who buy its products are protected against excessive charges by the competition of similar products in open market.

The nation has, however, an interest in the capitalization of any important public service, which is required to possess stability, solidity, and power of expansion. If a railway issues securities

APP. M, 5. much in excess of its actual outlay, it is unlikely to earn enough to pay good dividends. This will tempt it to issue more securities, and pay its expenses partly out of capital: but such action will soon bring it into disrepute, and it will be unable to borrow more on good terms. It will perhaps stint outlay on repairs and renewals. It may probably wish to raise its charges, but be unable to do so directly; and, if so, it is likely to let its services deteriorate, and in other ways to make the public pay the penalty of its inflation.

British business generally is renowned for the soundness of its financial methods: but British railways are sometimes tempted to charge to capital account, expenditure that is required for keeping their plant abreast of advancing technique: though, since such expenditure only places them on a level with new railway enterprise, and makes no extension of their business, it is of a kind which would be generally charged to income by a "conservative" American railway. Every such charge to capital increases the difficulty of maintaining dividends at a high level in the future[1].

Some strong American railways, desiring to evade popular demands for lower charges, have kept their dividends down by charging many organic improvements and extensions to income. But, if they continue to prosper, and to act on this plan, their net incomes will rise to so high levels relatively to their capitalization that the public will at last demand concessions in their interest. On the whole, even strong American railways tend to increase their nominal capitals; and their weaker neighbours are tempted to do the same, because they are weak.

In view of these difficulties a law was passed by Congress in 1913 directing the Interstate Commerce Commission to report in detail as to each piece of railway property "the original cost to date; the cost of reproduction new; the cost of reproduction less depreciation; and an analysis of the methods by which these several costs are obtained, and the reasons for their

[1] Parliament has sanctioned nominal additions, without any real change, to the capitalization of British railways, amounting in the aggregate to £198,000,000. In consequence the average net earnings in 1912 were 3·51 per cent. on the capitalization, instead of 4·51 as they would have been on the actual investments. These additions were made publicly: and a few people recollect some that are of recent date; but nearly all are forgotten.

differences, if any." This direction is in harmony with the Supreme Court's definition of "reasonable rates," which had been accepted by the Commission, viz. that they are "such rates as will, on the whole, make a reasonable return on the property fairly and honestly dedicated to the public service." The Commission has accordingly thrown itself with energy into this inquiry; which is perhaps destined to be exceptionally arduous and instructive to economists. [It may also be of supreme importance to British statesmen, in case measures for some sort of unified control of railways, which have come into view since this was in print, should be developed.]

APP. M, 5.

"Physical valuation" has been adopted as the name for the subject of the inquiry: and it conveniently gives warning that some elements of the whole problem to be solved lie outside its scope, and must be treated separately. For instance a new railway is not wholly exempt from the general rule that almost every business is likely to make some mistakes, before it attains the best adjustment of its resources to its work[1].

When the studies of the Commission have made considerable progress, it will probably be possible to arrive at an approximate judgment as to the relations between the total costs and the total charges of any particular railway that may fall under suspicion. Its original cost can be estimated roughly from the statistical history of the railway, and can be compared with similar estimates as to other railways: and its methods of administration can be noted; with special reference to the question whether fresh capital was raised to carry out simple improvements, the cost of which should have been defrayed out of income. Also, a direct comparison can be made of its charges

[1] This value due to a "trying out of the plant," or its adjustment of parts, called by engineers "adaptation or solidification" is one of the "intangible values," noted by Professor Ripley (*l.c.* II, p. 238) as lying outside Physical Valuation, which he describes at length. The general procedure of the Commission is indicated in its own Reports. Mr H. N. Hayes in the Harvard *Quarterly Journal of Economics*, argues that, though it is often impossible to get directly at the "original cost" of a public utility, yet an indirect route to it is available. For the ages of the units of expense being known, units of the same kind and age can be grouped together, and the prices paid for each unit in each year can be obtained from the books of the concern, or from other sources: but he admits that this method would not generally be available in regard to the cost of railway land (pp. 621 and 628).

APP. M, 5. as a whole, with those of other railways which have about equal facilities for obtaining a dense and regular traffic, equal costs for materials, etc. Some of these railways are sure to be managed efficiently and honestly: and they will serve as a touchstone for the rest.

In all such valuations it is difficult to decide what value to assign to railways' land, and especially such of it as is situated in the centres of great cities. It is said that the land needed for Paddington Station and its approaches cost only two million pounds; but that fifteen millions had to be paid fifty years later for the neighbouring Marylebone Station and its approaches: and the rise in value of the sites of some American termini has been much greater.

It may be added that, though the studies by the Interstate Commerce Commission in regard to railway capitalization have as yet made but little advance, it has seen its way in 1914 to allow an increase of five per cent. on the charges levied by the railroads between New York and Chicago; on the ground that, existing rates did not enable the weaker of those lines to obtain reasonable remuneration on their presumed capital; and "railways must live." In 1908 it had called attention to the fact that, the numerous holdings by railways of each other's securities, have caused the capital, on which the power of earning income might reasonably be claimed, to appear to amount to sixty-eight thousand dollars per mile; whereas only fifty-eight thousand dollars per mile of securities were in the hands of the public. It had pointed out also that, though these intercorporate holdings are not sufficient to give absolute control; yet, individual holders seldom vote, and the proxies given by them are not based on investigation: so that the intercorporate holdings being "in concentrated form, virtually dictate the policy of the corporations, whose securities are thus held"; with the result that vast systems of railways have come under the domination of the same group of financiers[1].

[1] This Report on *Intercorporate relations of railways* is a very instructive document. It starts from the position that "a single carrier in making a return of capital 'in the hands of the public' regards another carrier as one of the public....If however the problem be to state the amount of securities which are an actual or contingent claim upon the revenues of the country considered as a whole, the phrase 'in the hands of the public' must exclude all railway

Financial complications of this kind do not materially affect the relations between competition and monopoly in the British railway systems. British railway directors have the virtues, together with the defects, of their partial detachment from the speculative, as well as the technical, excitements of railway affairs. Most of them are well advanced in life: they have won the esteem of others by capable and upright control of large affairs; their pecuniary interests in the general prosperity of the country often exceed their personal interests in the finances of the railway, for which they are responsible. In short they are at least as incapable both of underhand intrigues and of indifference to the common good, as any body of men that can be found. It may be true that they have hitherto been inclined to adhere to well-trodden paths rather than venture boldly on new courses that hold out promise of advantage. But the importance and the resource of modern railway science are becoming recognized steadily, though slowly: and there is reason to hope that the general broadening of the scope of British education will ere long raise the alertness and resourcefulness of the supreme control of British railways to as high a level as that which has long marked its probity and public spirit.

holdings." Until 1908, no allowance had been made for this. The incident illustrates the extreme difficulty of rightly reading company statistics, even in cases where nearly all affairs are conducted in public.

The strategy of great railroads, 1905, by F. H. Spearman, contains a fascinating account of great campaigns in which Vanderbilt, Cassatt, Harriman, Hill, Gould and other men of Napoleonic genius for construction, and in some cases for destruction, won dominion and occasionally lost it. Illustrated by maps, it presents in short compass a general view of the more sensational episodes in American railway history, not easily to be obtained elsewhere.

In Vol. II of Ripley's *Railroads* will be found analytical accounts of various forms of pooling and combination, with their relations to Anti-trust Laws.

APPENDIX N

SOME AMERICAN INDUSTRIAL STATISTICS

The recent increase in the size of the representative industrial establishment in America[1].

The American Censuses from 1850 to 1880 relate to industrial establishments of all sorts, including those in "hand and neighbourhood industries" (or as we may say shortly, though not quite accurately, "workshops industries"), as well as in manufactures properly so called. The Census of 1890 gives returns on the old plan; and also in regard to factories only—the plan which has been followed since then. Consequently the most important comparisons for our purposes are between the years 1900 and 1910: though earlier figures have some useful suggestions.

The unit throughout is an "establishment": which is generally "a separated plant or mill": its size suggests the command possessed by it of the economies of *production* on a large scale. Economies of *marketing* are often better represented by statistics of "businesses": but on the whole, the establishment is doubtless the best unit[2].

The table given below[3] shows that the 208,000 establish-

[1] This Appendix is attached to p. 511.

[2] Further the boundaries of an establishment are more definite and ascertainable by Census officers than those of a business: and, as one important concern of a Census is with the local distribution of industries, confusion would have been introduced by grouping together plants in different places. But "two or more plants operated under a common ownership, or for which one set of books of account is kept," are sometimes regarded as a single establishment. (*Abstract of the Census* of 1910, p. 435.)

[3] The following is part of a table in the *Abstract of the Census* of 1910, p. 439:

ments engaged in manufacture in 1900 had increased to 268,000 in 1910: but meanwhile the total value of their output had increased from $m.4,831 to $m.8,529: that is their average output had increased from 232,000 dollars to 318,000: if we go back to 1850, when workshops etc. were reckoned in, we find the average output of an establishment to have been less than 4,000 dollars.

The wages bill of factories etc. increased between 1900 and 1910 considerably faster than the number of workers; but not nearly so fast as the value of the total output of products (which of course includes the cost of the material used); or of the net product (which is the value added to the material by the process of manufacture). This difference is mainly to be accounted for by the increased use of expensive plant, which is indicated by the fact that the horse power used had increased meanwhile from 10 to nearly 19 million units; that is, at almost the same rate as the capital employed. But prices were rising fast during this period and therefore the increases in total and net real output were less than is shown by these figures. The years 1900 and 1910 were years of climax: the Census figures in regard to manufactures belong to the years 1899, and 1909, preceding the nominal Census years[1].

Census year	Establishments (thousands)	Capital (million dollars)	Wage earners (thousands)	Wages (million dollars)	Value of products (million dollars)	Value added by manufacture (million dollars)
1850	123	533	957	237	1,019	463
1880	254	2,790	2,732	948	5,370	1,973
(1900)	(512)	(9,814)	(5,306)	(2,320)	(13,000)	(5,657)
1900	208	8,975	4,712	2,008	11,407	4,831
1905	216	12,676	5,468	2,610	14,794	6,294
1910	268	18,428	6,615	3,427	20,672	8,529

The figures in brackets for 1900 in the upper line relate to manufactures in the old broad sense of the term, and are therefore comparable with those for 1850 and 1880: those in the lower line relate to manufactures in the narrow sense, and are comparable with those for 1905 and 1910.

[1] The returns as to capital have always been untrustworthy: and indeed General F. A. Walker, who put the Census of 1880 at a single bound near to the very high level since attained by it, thought that they should not be

These statistics have an interesting bearing on the influence, which the growth of giant businesses exerts on the relative demands for capital and for labour, and on the character of the work required of labour. The two sets of figures from the Census of 1900, given in the table of figures on p. 847, indicate that the cost of materials bears about the same ratio to the total value of the product in workshops as it does in factories. This suggests that the stages through which material passes in very small establishments are so small, that they can be worked by manual labour with but slight assistance from plant, as easily as the larger stages worked by factories with more elaborate plant.

But a comparison of factories and other considerable establishments of various sizes shows that the cost of material is less than half the value of the finished product in rather small establishments; about equal to it in medium factories, with an annual output of $20,000 to $100,000; and about two-thirds of the whole value in plants with output of a million dollars and over. One reason seems to be that very large factories are chiefly concerned with work which can be done by expensive machinery, aided by a comparatively small amount of human effort: much of it does not require to be highly skilled; and the total cost of each process of manufacture is therefore rather small.

Industrial establishments having a less output than a $100,000 accounted for 20·7 per cent. of the whole in 1904;

published at all. They are perhaps a little less inaccurate in some directions now, than they were then: but their ambiguities have increased with the great increase in the number of establishments in the same ownership.

The following index numbers for the wholesale prices of commodities, are taken from *Bulletin* 200 (A.D. 1916) of the Bureau of Labor Statistics, p. 17: they show, of course, a less rapid rise in the prices of manufactured than of raw commodities.

	1898	1899	1900	1901	1908	1909	1910	1911	1915
Raw commodities	60	65	71	71	82	90	94	86	100
Manufactured commodities	70	75	80	78	89	93	96	90	100
All commodities...	65	70	75	74	85	91	95	88	100

but only for 17·8 in 1909. In the same few years the share of establishments with output between $100,000 and $1,000,000 fell from 46·0 to 43·8 per cent.; while that of giant businesses with not less than $1,000,000 output rose from 38 per cent. to 43[1].

Of course some large establishments had many more than 500 wage earners; and several such establishments had been set up as part of the same business unit. Business units so large were inclined to compete fiercely; then to enter into parley, and agree on terms of peace in regard to one another, supplemented perhaps by arrangements for the discomfiture of competitors who could not be brought into the agreement. Next, the alliances were strengthened and fortified: and, if they thus came into conflict with the law against combination in restraint of trade, a way out was found by amalgamation. But that did not lessen the dangers which they threatened to the public interest: it merely altered their form and thus called for new investigation and regulation.

[1] *Abstract of the Census* of 1910, p. 464. The corresponding figures for 1900 are not comparable, for they follow the old plan of including workshops etc.: indeed nearly half of the 512,254 establishments to which they relate, represent hand trades; and "in 68,523 of these all the work was done by the proprietor without hired assistance." (*Report of Census* of 1900, Vol. VII. p. lxxiii.) The neglect of this fact seems to have been the cause of some important statistical errors.

APPENDIX O

NOTES ON EMPLOYMENT IN BRITISH AND GERMAN STEEL INDUSTRIES

APP. O. *A comparison of the steel industries of Britain and Germany, with special reference to the pleas that Germany's cartel and fiscal policies in association have benefited the people.*

[The greater part of this Appendix was in print before the World-war: and the present tense, used in it, refers to the decade preceding the war. It takes no account of a suggestion, which has recently been made, that some sacrifice of general interests to the advancement of the heavy steel industry was deliberately made by the German Government, in view of the strength which predominance in that industry would afford in the great war, which it was preparing.]

Reference may be made at starting to the summary account given above (III, IX, 4) of the numerous causes, which united to give the German heavy steel industry a more rapid development than the British towards the end of last century. The chief of them were sudden access to abundant iron ores, suitable for making good steel by a new method: technical skill and alert energy on the part of Germans in using this method: ill-informed opposition to the method by the British Government, and indifference on the part of British iron-masters: and the great advantage which a young industry, not encumbered by obsolete plant, has over an old industry, when the time has come for recasting old methods. Nevertheless German policy has resulted in causing those, who make her steel, to receive low wages; and those Germans, who buy her steel, to pay dearly for it.

The tasks involved in cartellization are appropriate to the temper of the German people. The long hours of more or less intensive work, to which they are accustomed, enable them to attend numerous discussions without difficulty: the discipline, to which they have been seasoned in military service, inclines them to submit easily to cartel regulation; and, what is perhaps equally important, the semi-military organization of cartels is well adapted to the purposes of an autocratic rule, which regards peace as the time of preparation for war. Moreover an autocratic Government can exert certain kinds of discipline, which are not congenial to the temper of a self-governing people; and would, partly for that reason, involve lengthy discussions, and obstruct the proceedings of Parliament, if attempted in Britain. For instance, a cartel, which offends the German Government, may find that the charges for the railway traffic, in which it is specially interested, are quietly raised: or those on important rival products may be lowered, or the Protective tarif may be modified to its disadvantage: no such discipline would be tolerable in Britain[1].

There is another reason for the bias in favour of cartels that is shown by a Government that is largely under the control of a wealthy minority. It is, that cartel policy is greatly dependent on the aid of a Protective tarif, which tends to enrich many of those who are already rich; though it lowers the purchasing power of incomes generally, and especially those of the poorer classes. This again is an advantage from the point of view of German military autocracy: for the wealth of the rich is more accessible to the tax collector, than are the wages of the working classes, when once the taxes on ordinary necessaries have been pressed as far as they can well go: and the relatively low standard of comfort enjoyed by the German working classes in time of peace has lessened the expenditure needed for maintaining a large army in peace and in war. These injurious influences are apt to be obscured by invalid arguments, one of which calls for attention here. It is to the effect that Germany's system must be advantageous to her working classes, since it enlarges the funds which cartellized industries have at their disposal for the employment of labour: and it is suggested that Britain might therefore advantageously follow her example.

This suggestion seems based on exclusive attention to the interests of some industry that is being overridden in its own

[1] These remarks may be considered in connection with pp. 633—4 above.

APP. O. market by the foreigner; and to ignore the interests of other British industries, whose alertness enables them to get the better of rivals abroad. No doubt increased employment in the former industry can be given by shutting out its rivals: but, for every million pounds worth of increased employment so given by it, about a million pounds less employment is likely to be given by those industries whose exports have provided Britain with her power of purchasing imports. Capital will gradually shift from those industries, which are doing most to make the country strong; and will pass to those, to which she has so far owed less. Of course they may be "nascent" industries: or they may be such as can properly receive financial aid (direct or indirect) from the State for military, or other exceptional reasons. The easiest, though not the best, way of doing this may be to enable them to sell their products at higher prices and give increased employment, in consequence of the partial exclusion of rival imports: but such action will, as a general rule, only alter the distribution of good employment, and will not increase its total amount. Therefore, unless this shifting of employment is required for some exceptional reason of high policy, its net effect is likely to be an injury to employees as a body.

Protective tarifs and cartel-organization enable the German steel industries to obtain higher gains from their outputs of hardware, textile machinery etc., *when destined for use by Germans*, than they otherwise could; and the German people may perhaps derive a minute indirect gain from this. But that gain is generally only a small part of what has been artificially taken from them. The Steelworks Union is indeed able to boast that it divides out the benefits of the Protective tarif equitably among all steel "users": but, as has just been argued, that is true only with regard to those capitalist users, who apply steel material in business. Those who use the steel products as utensils in their houses, or buy products made by steel plant, have no place in this arithmetic.

The German people have indeed some relief in regard to the transport industries. For the Government has a special interest in the supply of steel for railways and ships. It buys steel for railways on advantageous terms. And, it allows steel for making ships to be imported freely; by which excellent provision it has conferred great benefits on the people. If that provision were extended generally, Germany would obtain the necessaries of life on the same advantageous terms as Britain does; and the purchasing power of wages would be at least as high relatively to their money value as in Britain. Not long ago it was higher: but now it is much lower in consequence of that Protective system, of which German cartel policy is a part[1].

[1] An American onlooker says:—"The English workingman gets higher wages than the German workingman. All the salaried men in English factories get higher wages, and work shorter hours, than the salaried men in German factories. The English agents in foreign parts not only get higher salaries, but insist on week-end holidays and on having several afternoons off during the week in order to play golf and tennis; whereas the German agent works every day and Sunday." Professor Carver, *Principles of Political Economy*, 1918, p. 347. The President of the North German Steamship Company, referring in Hong Kong to the question how it was that Germans had already (in 1910) obtained nearly half the trade of the port, though the port belonged to Britain, called attention to the early desertion of the English offices; and added, "But in some of the German offices those lights will be burning up to nine o'clock. That is the answer. We Germans are winning the trade of the world because of our capacity for, our willingness to *work, work, work*" (*The Times*, 21 March, 1919).

The Report of the Board of Trade on *The cost of living in German towns*, 1908, p. lii, sums up its results as to the comparative purchasing power of wages in Germany and England in the building, engineering and printing trades, by saying that "the German rate of money wages per hour is about three-quarters of the English rate: and the cost of rent, food, and fuel nearly one-fifth greater than in England": that is, English real wages are more than half as much again as German. The second half of this statement "is based on the English standard of consumption": the difference would have been rather less, if based on the German standard.

This result is confirmed by the evidence published in several Reports of the Tariff Commission. For instance, in that on *The engineering industries*, 1909, many witnesses referred to the rates of money wages in England and Germany: every one of them said that the rates per week were higher in England, and the hours of work shorter; and twelve gave numerical estimates of the difference. Three of these put it low: an equal number put the money wages per hour in England twice as high as in Germany. The average of all the estimates seems to coincide with the Board of Trade estimate, quoted above, that before the World-war the English money rate per hour was one-third greater than the German. *The Report on the shipping and shipbuilding industries* [Cd. 9092] 1918, p. 27 lays stress on the fact that in the steel industry "competition with Germany was, in the view of the steel makers, rendered difficult by the low wages prevailing there." Of course uniformly high wages throughout all industries in a country do not materially affect the *relative* values of her imports and exports of manufactured products: and therefore they have less influence on the course of trade than is suggested by the consideration of one industry alone. But this does not affect the authority of the Committee on the matter of fact.

APPENDIX P

COOPERATIVE AND COLLECTIVE ORGANIZATION OF INDUSTRY: METHODS PROVED AND UNPROVED

APP. P.

The great services to progress rendered by cooperation and copartnership; and their limitations[1].

Experience has partly moderated and partly confirmed the bright hopes that were entertained in this and other countries, about half a century ago, to the effect that cooperative production and copartnership together would gradually develop a set of working class leaders with wide business experience, and well able to judge what business risks can advantageously be carried by working men, either separately or in "copartnership" with experienced business men: and what must remain over for management by business men alone, or by the State. In the last two generations much has been learnt as to what can be done even under present conditions, and what could be done under a nearer approach to ideal perfection of human nature.

To begin with, the provinces of cooperative production and of production under some copartnership arrangement have been in a measure marked out. "Cooperative" undertakings in the technical sense of the term, that is those which are entirely in the hands of the manual labour classes and other people of small means, are seldom able to engage successfully in industries other than those of marketing staple goods for general consumption, especially by the working classes: and in the production of some kinds of these goods[2].

Copartnership has a wider scope. For it leaves the chief risks of the business concerned to men who have had experience in selecting risks, and abiding by the results of their selection: and

[1] This Appendix is associated with III, XIV.
[2] See above, pp. 293—5.

yet it gives to employees a substantial direct interest in the prosperity of the business; and a share in its direction, which places them in some respects almost on a level with their employers.

But the plan has some disadvantages. A business which has special methods of production, or special knowledge as to favourable markets, may fear that working men directors will be drawn on, without evil purpose, to communicate to comrades information, apparently unimportant, but yet likely to help any rival business that it may reach by indirect routes. And if the working man director is reticent, his comrades may suspect him of want of loyalty to the collective interests of his class. In vain do advocates of copartnership urge that the interests of employers and employed are closely allied; and that an exclusive loyalty to one side is antisocial: the fact remains that many trade-unionists, including nearly all who are of militant temper, look with some suspicion on copartnership[1].

Thus it has resulted that those copartnership schemes which have attained a lasting success have generally owed much to men who have anticipated by a generation or more that attitude to socio-industrial problems, which has become prominent in the last few years and has found a partial expression in the Whitley Report. They seem to have all been endowed in exceptional degree with the master faculties—sympathy, imagination, strength and tact[2].

[1] An extreme instance may be quoted from a manifesto issued on behalf of National Guilds, as to which something will be said a little later on: "Is there any objection to profit sharing and collective partnership with the men, not collectively as a Union, but individually?" "Yes: for every man so singled out is spiritually transferred from the side of labour to the side of capital. His concern is no longer to abolish the wage-system for himself, his fellows, and the nation at large, but to obtain all the profit he can extract from it." (Quoted by Bechhofer and Reckitt, *The meaning of National Guilds*, p. 295.)

Lord Leverhulme, writing with exceptional knowledge from the opposite point of view, throws part of the blame for the slow progress of the movement on suggestions that the adoption of copartnership by an employer is "generous" or "philanthropic." (*The Six-hour day*, p. 105.) Its true claim to be welcomed by employees, and therefore to succeed, is that it invites them to contribute to its efficiency such elements as lie within their power as comrades. There may be an element of benevolence in comradeship; but it must be unconscious: if it is obtruded, the verdict to be passed on it is *felo de se*.

[2] The Labour Commission of 1891—4 was much occupied with the aims and difficulties of copartnership. One of its members, Mr Livesey, was working out

APP. P. There seems to be but little force in an objection, sometimes raised against profit-sharing, to the effect that it gives an advantage to some classes of employees, relatively to others: for as a rule that advantage has been earned. Nevertheless there is something to be said for the proposal that, where practicable, the profits made in an industry in each year (or half year) should be ascertained; and some definite percentage of the whole be paid into a common fund, to be divided among all the workers in the industry in proportion to the wages earned by them in that period[1].

The fact that cooperation and profit-sharing have done much excellent work is evidence that human nature is ready for considerable advances towards an organization of industry on a plan more generous and under a less rigid cash-nexus than at present. But the fact that progress on these lines has been less rapid and continuous than had been hoped by many, suggests that further movements in this direction must be cautious as well as resolute: that each advance must be well established and consolidated before making new calls on the chivalrous spirit that lies deep down in human nature; and that the greatest error which reforms can make is to move so fast as to induce reaction. These considerations seem to have been insufficiently considered by advocates of speedy movement towards the setting up of "National Guilds."

an excellent example at the South Metropolitan Gas Company's works, which reckons two artisans and one clerk among its directors: see C. R. Fay, *Copartnership in Industry*, 1913, p. 105. In 1917, 64 English Copartnership Productive Societies made a profit of over twenty per cent. on a capital of £800,000, and paid about a sixth of that as Dividend on wages. In Scotland the United Baking Society made a profit of £80,000 on a capital of about £600,000 and paid a Dividend on wages of over £7000. In connection with these matters, see above, pp. 289—295 and 319, 320.

[1] This suggestion was made by Professor Cannan to the Coal Industry Commission in the course of a powerful argument against nationalization of the mines (see *The Times*, 25 April, 1919). Some of the opportunities, which profit-sharing plans afford for suggestions from employees to employers, can now be obtained through Works Committees. Joint Industrial Councils may not only consider broader questions of organization than those that lie within the scope of a single business: they may also tend to promote effective cooperation among businesses in such cases as that of several adjacent mines, which could economize shafts, internal transport, etc. by agreement or fusion.

INDEX

[*References under each heading are arranged generally in numerical order: but when the chief discussion of a subject is concentrated in a single place, that place is mentioned first.*]

CAMBRIDGE: PRINTED BY J. B. PEACE, M.A., AT THE UNIVERSITY PRESS